INSIDERS' GUIDE®

INSIDERS' GUIDE® SERIES

INSIDERS' GUIDE®
NORTH CAROLINA'S
CENTRAL COAST
AND NEW BERN 18TH EDITION

MARTHA L. HALL & STEFANI L. SYNDER

insider**info**.us

Published and Marketed by:
By The Sea Publications, Inc.
P.O. Box 4368
Wilmington, NC 28406

Insiders' Guide®
Is an imprint of
The Globe Pequot Press

Eighteenth Edition
1st Printing

Publications from The Insiders'
Guide® series are available at
special discounts for bulk
purchases for sales
promotions, premiums or
fundraisings. Special editions,
including personalized
covers, can be created in large
quantities for special needs. For
more information, please write to:

By The Sea Publications
P.O. Box 4368
Wilmington, NC 28406
www.insiderinfo.us
Or call (910) 763-8464

Cover Photo: Carolyn Temple

North Carolina Seafood Festival
October 2-4, 2009
www.ncseafoodfestival.org

"Cobalt Calm" by Emmett Westbrook
2009 Photo Competition Winner

The **Best Selection** on the Crystal Coast

Escape to the warm waters of the Crystal Coast. With over 800 vacation homes, Bluewater's experienced team can find the perfect beach rental carefully chosen to match what you and your family want to experience. Call now for the best times to vacation at the beautiful beaches of the Crystal Coast.

Book Now for Best Selection. Call Today!

Check Our Website for Internet Specials

866-595-1395 | bluewaterguide1.com

Bluewater
GMAC
Real Estate

TABLE OF CONTENTS

Thank you to our Advertisers...

*...for another great year
on the Crystal Coast!*

Light and shadow create art at the coast.

photo: Peter Doran

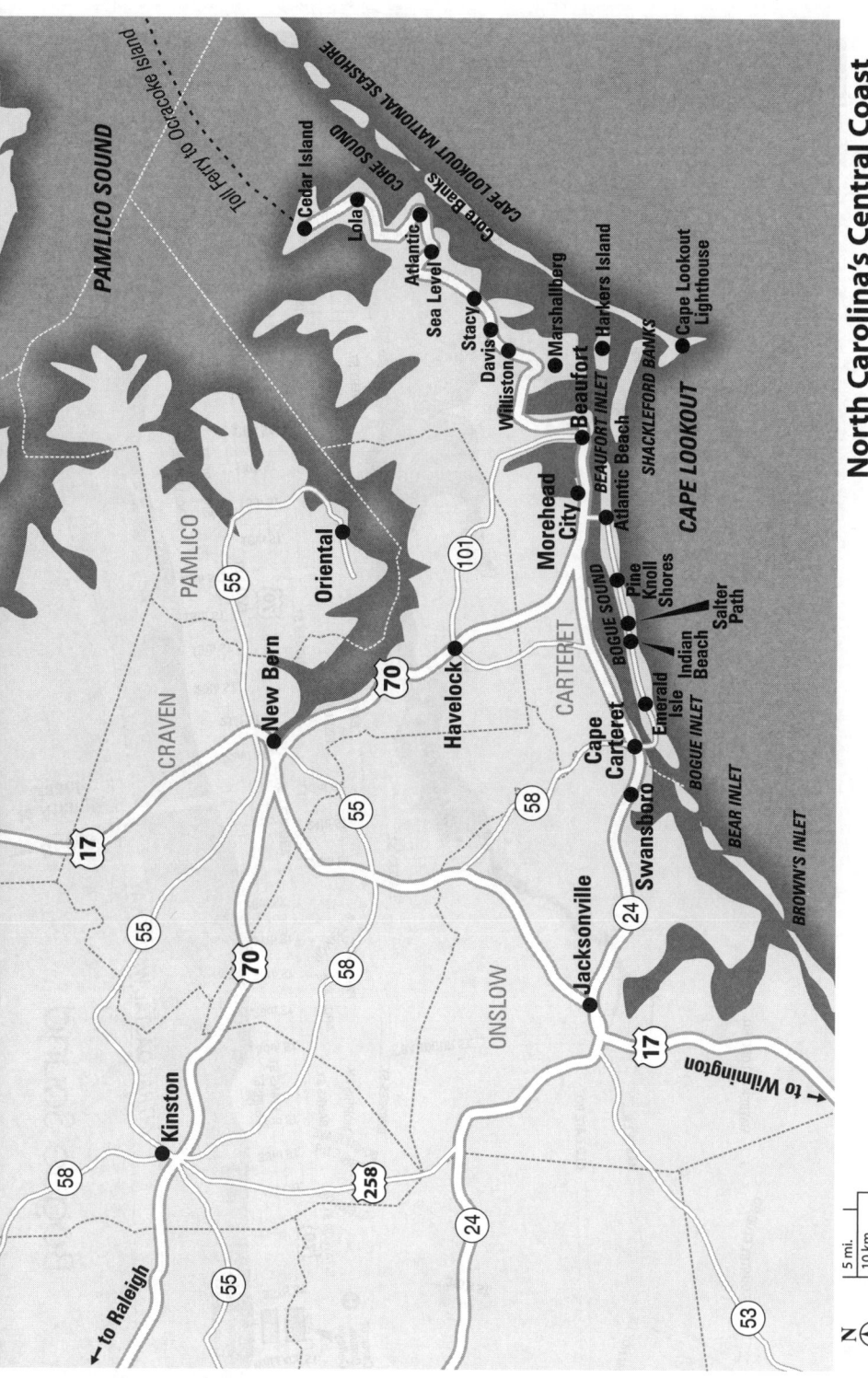

North Carolina's Central Coast

PAMLICO SOUND

Toll Ferry to Ocracoke Island

CORE SOUND

Core Banks

CAPE LOOKOUT NATIONAL SEASHORE

Cedar Island

Lola

Atlantic

Sea Level

Stacy

Davis

Williston

Marshallberg

Harkers Island

SHACKLEFORD BANKS

Cape Lookout Lighthouse

Beaufort

BEAUFORT INLET

CAPE LOOKOUT

PAMLICO

Oriental

(55)

Morehead City

Atlantic Beach

BOGUE SOUND

Pine Knoll Shores

Salter Path

New Bern

(70)

(101)

Havelock

CARTERET

Indian Beach

Emerald Isle

BOGUE INLET

CRAVEN

(55)

(55)

(58)

Cape Carteret

Swansboro

(24)

BEAR INLET

BROWN'S INLET

(17)

Jacksonville

ONSLOW

(17)

to Wilmington

Kinston

(258)

(24)

to Raleigh

(55)

(70)

(58)

(55)

(58)

(53)

N

5 mi.
10 km

Morehead City

N

2000 ft.
500 m

CALICO BAY

To Beaufort

Sugarloaf Island

CALICO CREEK

20th ST.

MAYBERRY LOOP RD.

20th ST.

COUNTRY CLUB RD.

MAYBERRY LOOP RD.

MANDY LN.

OLD GATE RD.

MANDY LN.

BARBOUR ST.

35H ST.

S. TAYLOR ST.

GLENN DR.

BRIDGES ST.

BONNER AVE.
MORRIS LN.
BANKS ST.
GUTHRIE DR.

PINEY PARK CIR.
HOMES DR.
ARON AVE.

SUNSET DR.

EVANS ST.

30th ST.
29th ST.
28th ST.
27th ST.
26th ST.
25th ST.
24th ST.
23rd ST.
22nd ST.
21st ST.
20th ST.
19th ST.
18th ST.
17th ST.
16th ST.
15th ST.
14th ST.
13th ST.
12th ST.
11th ST.
10th ST.
9th ST.
8th ST.
7th ST.
6th ST.
5th ST.
4th ST.
3rd ST.

34th ST.
33rd ST.

35TH ST.

WALLACE ST.

AVERY ST.
BAY ST.
FISHER ST.
BRIDGES ST.
ARENDELL ST.
EVANS ST.

AVERY ST.
BAY ST.
FISHER ST.

FISHER ST.
BRIDGES ST.
SHEPARD ST.
SHACKLEFORD ST.
ARENDELL ST.

70

70

H

Carteret Comm. College

Crystal Coast Civic Center

Bridge to Atlantic Beach

INTRACOASTAL WATERWAY

Bogue Sound

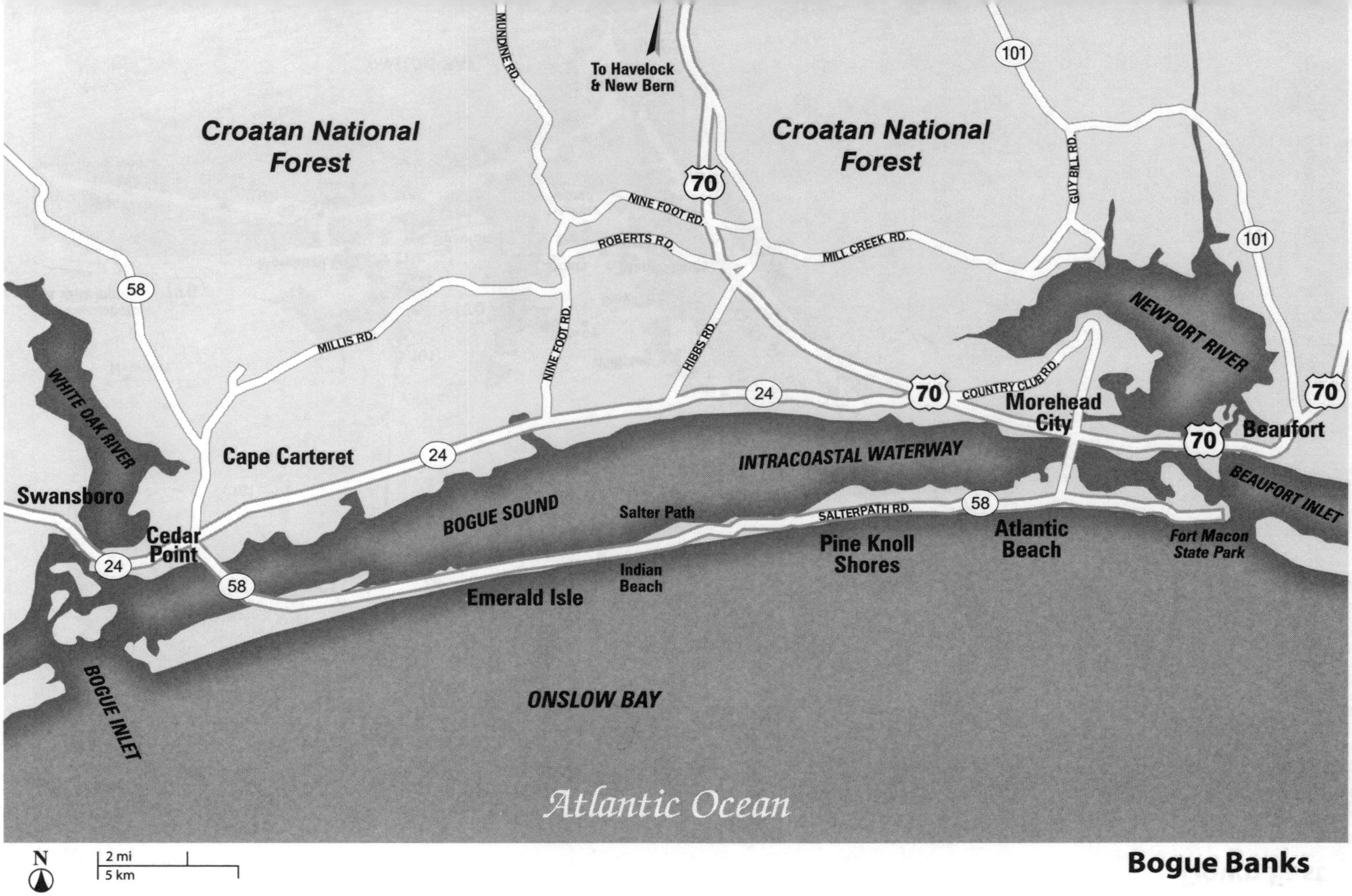

Bogue Banks

Atlantic Ocean

ONSLOW BAY

BOGUE INLET

BOGUE SOUND

INTRACOASTAL WATERWAY

Emerald Isle

Indian Beach

Salter Path

Pine Knoll Shores

Atlantic Beach

Fort Macon State Park

BEAUFORT INLET

Beaufort

Morehead City

NEWPORT RIVER

Croatan National Forest

Croatan National Forest

WHITE OAK RIVER

Swansboro

Cape Carteret

Cedar Point

To Havelock & New Bern

MUNDINE RD.

MILLIS RD.

NINE FOOT RD.

ROBERTS RD.

NINE FOOT RD.

HIBBS RD.

MILL CREEK RD.

GUY BALL RD.

COUNTRY CLUB RD.

SALTER PATH RD.

101

101

101

70

70

70

70

70

58

58

58

24

24

24

N

2 mi
5 km

Down East

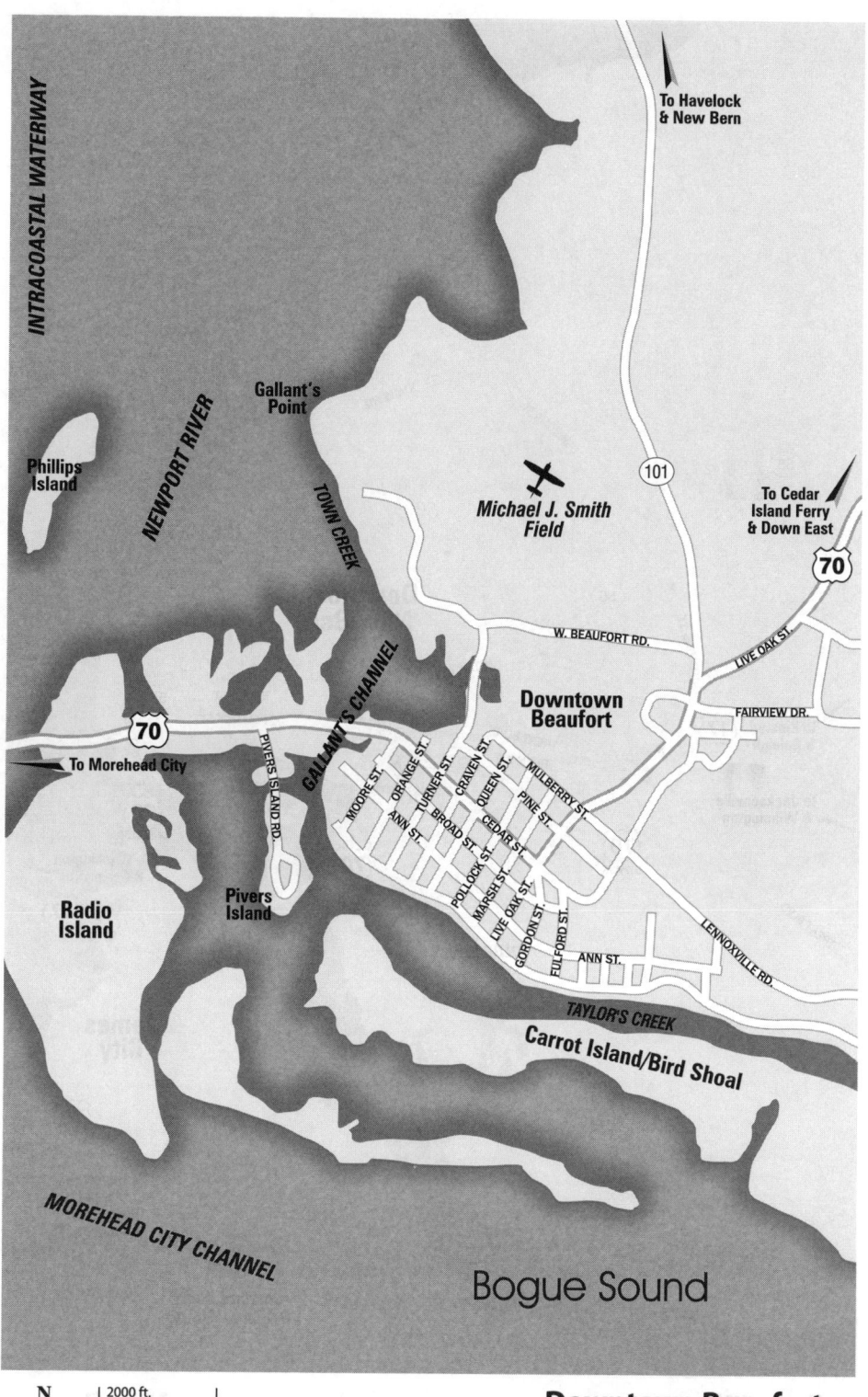

Downtown Beaufort

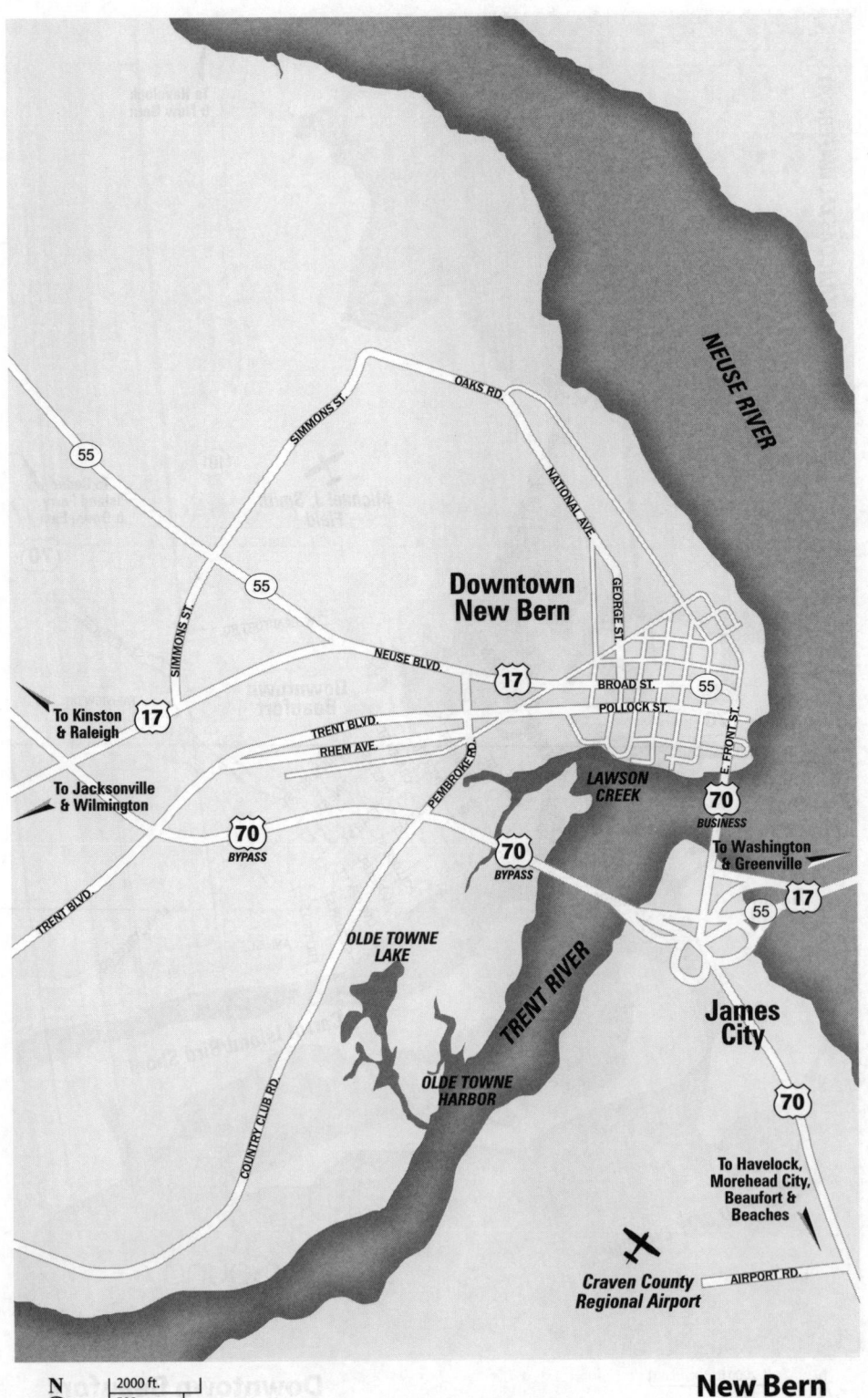

New Bern

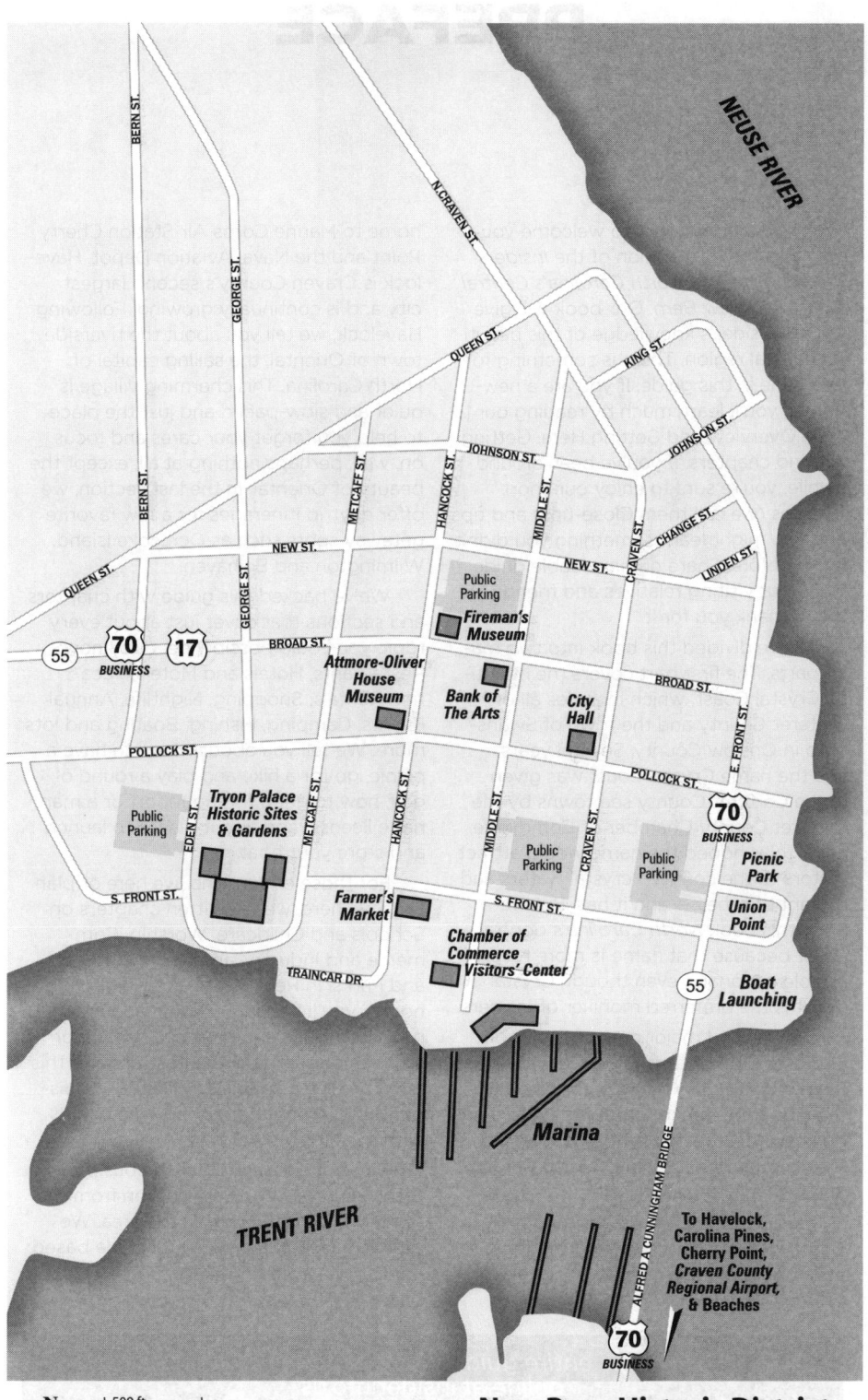

NEUSE RIVER

BERN ST.

GEORGE ST.

N CRAVEN ST.

QUEEN ST.

KING ST.

JOHNSON ST.

JOHNSON ST.

METCAFF ST.

HANCOCK ST.

MIDDLE ST.

CHANGE ST.

CRAVEN ST.

LINDEN ST.

NEW ST.

NEW ST.

BERN ST.

GEORGE ST.

QUEEN ST.

Public Parking

Fireman's Museum

55   70 BUSINESS   17

BROAD ST.

BROAD ST.

Attmore-Oliver House Museum

Bank of The Arts

City Hall

E. FRONT ST.

POLLOCK ST.

POLLOCK ST.

Public Parking

Tryon Palace Historic Sites & Gardens

METCAFF ST.

HANCOCK ST.

MIDDLE ST.

CRAVEN ST.

70 BUSINESS

Public Parking

Public Parking

Picnic Park

Union Point

S. FRONT ST.

Farmer's Market

S. FRONT ST.

EDEN ST.

Chamber of Commerce Visitors' Center

55

Boat Launching

TRAINCAR DR.

Marina

TRENT RIVER

ALFRED A CUNNINGHAM BRIDGE

To Havelock, Carolina Pines, Cherry Point, Craven County Regional Airport, & Beaches

70 BUSINESS

N

500 ft.
100 m

New Bern Historic District

PREFACE

It is our pleasure to welcome you to the 18th edition of the *Insiders' Guide® to North Carolina's Central Coast and New Bern*. Our book will give you an Insider's knowledge of this beautiful coastal region. There is something for everyone in this guide. If you are a newcomer, you'll learn much by reading our Area Overview and Getting Here, Getting Around chapters. If you've been around awhile, you're sure to enjoy our short features (we call them Close-ups) and tips, and you might learn something you didn't know before. Share our invaluable guide with your visiting relatives and friends — they'll thank you for it.

We've divided this book into two major parts. The first part covers the beautiful Crystal Coast, which includes all of Carteret County and the town of Swansboro in Onslow County. Several years ago the name Crystal Coast was given to the Carteret County sea towns by the Carteret County Chamber of Commerce. Local folks hoped the name would attract visitors to the county's crystal waters and brilliant beaches — and it has. But we titled this book *North Carolina's Central Coast* because that name is more recognizable nationally, even though Crystal Coast is the preferred moniker of Insiders.

The second major part of this book addresses the historic city of New Bern. Best known as the home of Tryon Palace, the city offers much to delight visitors and guests. It is Craven County's largest city, the second-oldest town in North Carolina and is rich with history.

Besides the Crystal Coast and New Bern, you'll also discover information about our neighboring city of Havelock,

home to Marine Corps Air Station Cherry Point and the Naval Aviation Depot. Havelock is Craven County's second largest city and is continually growing. Following Havelock, we tell you about the riverside town of Oriental, the sailing capital of North Carolina. This charming village is quiet and slow-paced and just the place to help you forget your cares and focus on, well, perhaps nothing at all, except the beauty of Oriental. In the last section, we offer daytrip itineraries for a few favorite getaway spots such as Ocracoke Island, Wilmington and Belhaven.

We've packed this guide with chapters and sections that cover just about every topic you could possibly need to know: Restaurants, Hotels and Motels, Vacation Rentals, Shopping, Nightlife, Annual Events, Camping, Fishing, Boating and lots more. We tell you about where to have a picnic, go for a hike and play a round of golf, how to get a fishing report or a marriage license, and about places to launch and store your boat.

For those of you who live here or plan to move here, we've written chapters on Schools and Childcare, Worship, Commerce and Industry, and Sports, Fitness and Parks. In Real Estate and Neighborhoods, you'll find information about our neighborhoods and buying a home. For some of our readers, the best parts of this book are the sections on Kidstuff – indispensable information for parents of kids with bundles of energy.

Please be assured that the businesses featured in this book are chosen from the many as being the best in the area. We decide which businesses to include based

See this entire guide plus additional content online at insiderinfo.us

on their quality, their uniqueness or their popularity.

Our general maps will help you see the overall picture. These should be used in conjunction with your regular road map. We also offer the following invaluable hints for getting around by car. For example, U.S. Highway 70 takes on a different name in each town it passes through: Main Street in Havelock; Arendell Street in Morehead City; and Cedar and Live Oak streets in Beaufort. N.C. Highway 58 also takes on a new name in each of the beach towns it passes through: Fort Macon Road East or West in Atlantic Beach; Salter Path Road between Atlantic Beach and Indian Beach; and Emerald Drive in Emerald Isle. Mile marker (MM) numbers are given to help you locate places along N.C. 58 on Bogue Banks.

If you are visiting, don't expect to see everything in one trip. If you have relocated to the area, we urge you to spend occasional weekends exploring the many treasures that surround you. We've writ-

ten about many of the wonderful sights, sounds and tastes of the Crystal Coast and its environs.

We've done our best to ensure that all the information is accurate. We are always eager to hear what our readers think so that future editions can accommodate your ideas and suggestions. Write to us in care of By The Sea Publications Inc., 3941-B Market Street, Wilmington, NC 28403, or visit us online and make your comments there: www.insiderinfo.us. You can see this and our sister publication the *Insiders' Guide® to North Carolina's Southern Coast and Wilmington* online — in their entirety, along with Internet-only bonus material, including our online Pets chapter.

Our hope is that the coast's lure and its varied pleasures will satisfy you as much as they do us and other Insiders. We trust this book will guide you well and that you will enjoy exploring, revisiting or living along North Carolina's Crystal Coast and in New Bern.

ABOUT THE AUTHORS

Martha L. Hall

Martha L. Hall is a freelance writer who found herself in a newsroom because she was a good speller. Her journalist husband and his editor constantly called from work, asking how to spell various words. One day they decided to offer her a job and save on the phone bill. She has been a features writer, a columnist and a lifestyles editor as well as a writer of advertorial copy for medical catalogs and an editor of novels. Like nearly every writer, she is working on a novel. Hers is about one of her favorite places — Beaufort. She also works as a substitute teacher in the Craven County school system, does publicity for RiverTowne Repertory Players in New Bern and is the editor of the *New Bern Herald*, covering the historic neighborhoods and downtown New Bern. Martha's favorite things are her husband, her three children, her grandchildren, her cat, singing, acting, reading any good book and collecting "see no evil, hear no evil, speak no evil" monkeys. (Please do not send her any monkeys. She has at least 1,500 of them and they have taken over her house and her life.) Martha likes to think of herself as a "Renaissance Woman," if that could be construed as someone who has done a lot of different things, never made much money but has enjoyed every minute of the time involved. She would list these things but it would be shorter to list what she hasn't done — she has never been an astronaut, a cowboy or a fireman.

Stefani L. Snyder

Stefani Snyder received her undergraduate degree in education with a concentration in English from Kutztown University and her master's degree in education from Wilkes University, both in her home state of Pennsylvania. As a first-grade teacher for the previous seven years, she decided to relocate to North Carolina in the summer of 2003 for the chance to be closer to her boyfriend (and, unfortunately, farther from her family). Along with a change in location came a change in vocation. During her time here, she had the opportunity to work for a local printing and publishing company where she learned even more about the area she was living in through the company's many area guide publications. Her time there culminated with her working as editor for two of their nine publications and editorial assistant for the remaining seven. She enjoys continuing to learn about and appreciate all the Central Coast has to offer. A true sun worshiper at heart, Stefani's favorite times are spent on the local beaches. She loves being outdoors, which includes camping, playing tennis and being on the water. Her hobbies include reading, walking on the beach or waterfront, gardening, cooking and drinking wine.

ACKNOWLEDGEMENTS

Martha L. Hall

It is always fun to cover the coast — my favorite place. Since 1946, which I shouldn't say because then everyone knows how old I am, Swansboro, Morehead City, Beaufort and New Bern have been places most important in my life and my heart. After all this time, it is amazing to watch these areas I have loved and lived in, grow and (hopefully) improve with the passing years. I would like to thank Molly Harrison, my editor, whose patience and expertise have been greatly appreciated this year. I would also like to thank the Insiders' Guide crew in Wilmington who are always ready to answer a question or e-mail a joke. Thanks to Susan, Matt and Melissa who always answer my questions — dumb or not. You guys are an amazing team. Thank you for letting me be a part.

Stefani L. Snyder

There's a lot to see, explore, experience and discover here on the coast of North Carolina. I hope that visitors can get better acquainted with the area and that residents can learn a little something they may not have known before. I am continually learning something new about the area, and I hope that you, the readers, are too. I would like to give a big thank you to Molly Harrison whose unending kindness, patience and knowledge have been very appreciated. To the rest of the Insiders' team, my thanks to you for welcoming me and being patient as I learned the ropes. Matt, Melissa and Susan — thanks for all of your hard work. I would also like to thank the businesses in the communities all throughout the area who took the time out of their busy schedules to answer my many questions. To Jeremy and my family, you are a constant source of support in my life and I thank you deeply.

GETTING HERE, GETTING AROUND

At the southern end of the great barrier island chain known as the Outer Banks lies the beautiful Crystal Coast, a narrow strip of land with 81 miles of coastline, beaches, dunes and waterways. The Bogue Banks portion of the Crystal Coast is geographically unique. It sits on an east-west axis, allowing a sunrise and sunset view over the ocean and sunbathers to lie on the beach facing the ocean due south.

The Crystal Coast is about many things, especially water and water activities. In this area you'll see thousands of boats — pleasure craft, sailboats in safe harbors, kayaks, the last of the menhaden fishing fleet, ocean-going research vessels, huge luxury yachts, tankers and container ships, and more than 6,000 commercial fishing boats, big and small, hauling in the catch.

About 95 percent of the visitors to the Crystal Coast arrive by car, although getting here by sea or air provides a beautiful journey as well.

In this chapter you'll find information for getting to the Crystal Coast and for getting around once you are here.

LAND

The Crystal Coast is less than a three-hour drive from the state capital of Raleigh, a straight shot on U.S. Highway 70, and only a couple of hours from Greenville, home of East Carolina University.

Travelers from the north or south will find that Interstate 95 or U.S. Highway 17 takes them to either U.S. Highway 70 and on to Morehead City or to N.C. Highway 58, which leads straight to Emerald Isle.

From the west, Interstate 40 will also take you to U.S. 70, which leads directly to Morehead City. From the east, the most picturesque journey into Carteret County, travelers must reserve space for the

Clean, uncrowded beaches are the hallmark of the Crystal Coast.

photo: Carolyn Temple

2-hour ferry ride from Ocracoke Island to Cedar Island (see the ferry schedule in this chapter). At the ferry landing, N.C. Highway 12 continues a short distance to intersect with U.S. 70 W. near the community of Sea Level, the highway's point of origin. (Interestingly enough, U.S. 70's other terminus is in Los Angeles.) From here, it's an unforgettable ride through lowland fields of junkus and Spartina marsh grasses and Down East fishing villages to historic Beaufort and the Crystal Coast or on to Havelock and New Bern.

Between Morehead City and Emerald Isle or Swansboro, the main thoroughfare is N.C. Highway 24, which offers views of Bogue Sound as you cross its bridges at Broad Creek and Gales Creek. Make the sightseeing brief, because this is always a busy highway with commuter traffic, schools and neighborhood developments along the 25-mile stretch between U.S. 70 and N.C. 58.

On the island of Bogue Banks, N.C. 58 runs parallel to the beach for more than 22 miles, from Atlantic Beach west to Emerald Isle. Mile markers along the way make it easy to find things. Mile 1 (MM 1) begins at Fort Macon State Park on the east end of the island and the markers continue west, ending at the high-rise bridge in Emerald Isle.

Bus and Taxi Service

Currently, there is no bus service to Carteret county. Bus service is offered in Havelock and New Bern. See our New Bern Getting Here, Getting Around chapter. Several cab and limousine companies service the area.

A-1 Yellow Cab
(252) 240-2700

A-1 takes passengers to Atlantic Beach, Beaufort, Morehead City, Down East and local marinas. They take passengers to to the airport in New Bern as well.

Atlantic Beach Taxi
(252) 240-3555

Atlantic Beach Taxi serves all the towns between Atlantic Beach and Emerald Isle as well as Morehead City and

will take passengers to the airport in New Bern.

Crystal Coast Yellow Cab
(252) 728-3483, (252) 726-3125

Crystal Coast Yellow Cab offers service to Atlantic Beach, Beaufort, Morehead City, Newport and Down East and will take and pick up clients at area airports.

Diamond Limousine Service
603 Bridges St., Morehead City
(252) 240-1680

Diamond Limousine offers service for local and long-distance trips, including airport transfers.

Sinclair Limousine
1703 Live Oak St., Beaufort
(252) 728-6853, (252) 241-6519

Sinclair Limousine offers several luxurious limousine options, including a Lincoln Town Car sedan, a Lincoln Town Car stretch that seats up to eight passengers and a Lincoln Navigator Super Stretch that seats up to 14. The limousines are clean, smoke-free, well-equipped and always driven by a professional chauffeur. Sinclair's services are offered all around the Crystal Coast and the surrounding area, and they offer airport service to New Bern, Greenville, Jacksonville and Raleigh-Durham International. Cold bottled water and ice are available in the limousines for passengers at all times. Rates are always

affordable, and you can find even more savings with their weekday specials. See our Wedding Planning chapter for information about their Red-Carpet Wedding Package.

Twilight Limousine Company
New Bern
(252) 633-0027

Twilight, based in New Bern, offers local and long-distance trips in a variety of vehicles, including a 20-passenger Hummer.

Car Rentals

This area has very few car rental establishments. More rental options exist in New Bern at Craven County Regional Airport.

Enterprise Rent-A-Car, 5317-B U.S. Hwy. 70 W, Morehead City (252) 240-0218

Gulls always follow the ferries looking for handouts. While it might be fun to feed gulls following the ferry, your fellow passengers might not appreciate the droppings on their vehicles — or on their heads. If you must feed them, ferry officials ask that you feed them only from the back of the ferry.

Ford Rent-A-Car, 5557 U.S. Hwy. 70 W., Morehead City, (252) 247-2132

AIR

Passenger airline service is available at several airports convenient to the Crystal Coast. You can reach New Bern by commercial carrier, or you can fly into New Bern or Beaufort by private plane. Flights directly to Carteret County are accommodated at the area's only airport in Beaufort.

Albert J. Ellis Airport
264 Albert J. Ellis Airport Rd., Richlands
(910) 324-1100

Commercial air service to the Crystal Coast is available from the Albert J. Ellis Airport, 20 miles northwest of Jacksonville off U.S. Highway 111 toward Richlands. It is the closest airport to Marine Corps Base Camp Lejeune in Jacksonville. The airport offers flights each day to Charlotte and Atlanta. Car rental and taxi services are available at the airport. Jacksonville Flying Services offers a full-service flight school.

Coastal Carolina Regional Airport
200 Terminal Dr., New Bern
(252) 638-8591

Craven County Regional Airport in New Bern is the nearest commercial service airport to Morehead City, Atlantic Beach, Beaufort and points Down East. This airport offers daily flights to Charlotte and Atlanta on USAirways Express and on Delta Connection carrier Atlantic Southeast Airlines. The general aviation side of the airport has a fixed-base operation, (252) 633-1400, offering full aviation services. The airport is equipped with GPS, ILS, pilot-controlled runway lights and a tower. Car rental agencies are based at the airport, and taxi services to Havelock and the Crystal Coast are wise to the arrival schedule for passengers' convenience.

Michael J. Smith Field - Airport
180 Airport Rd., Beaufort
(252) 728-2323

The Crystal Coast's sole airport, located in Beaufort, offers only chartered or private aircraft service. A modern facility, it is one of the busiest municipal airports in

North Carolina. The fixed-base operator is Seagrave Aviation, which handles all fueling, rentals, flight instruction, charters and sightseeing flights. The airport has pilot-controlled runway night lights, a localizer for 2.6, six different GPS approaches and a non-directional beacon (NDB) on runway 14. The airport is named for Capt. Michael J. Smith, a Beaufort native and pilot of the space shuttle *Challenger*, who perished with eight others when the shuttle exploded on takeoff.

Raleigh-Durham International Airport
Exits 284B-285, Morrisville
(919) 840-2123

Raleigh-Durham (RDU) is the major international airport serving North Carolina. RDU is a three-hour drive from the Crystal Coast. The airport is a major hub for domestic and international travelers and is served by numerous carriers and regional carriers. Car rentals, shuttle buses and a variety of parking options are available at the airport.

SEA

Visitors arriving by sea most often come via the Intracoastal Waterway (ICW), which provides access by water to the Crystal Coast and passes by Morehead City, Beaufort, Swansboro and along Bogue Banks. To reach New Bern by water, slip into Pamlico Sound and head up the Neuse River. Beaufort is a favorite stop for boaters on the north-south ICW run in the spring and fall. Transient dockage at either the Beaufort Town Docks or Town Creek Marina is hospitable, and anchorage and docking points are available in several areas for both overnight or long-term stays. See our chapter on Marinas for details.

Ferries

A variety of state-owned ferries and private ferries serve the Crystal Coast, offering visitors and residents an enjoyable transportation alternative via inland sounds and rivers.

STATE FERRIES

State ferries operate under the administration of the North Carolina Department of Transportation (NCDOT) and are large, seaworthy vessels. Three ferries connect Ocracoke Island with other parts of North Carolina. The Cedar Island-Ocracoke Toll Ferry is the state's most popular ferry and carries passengers and vehicles between the Crystal Coast and Ocracoke Island. This ferry is used by residents, visitors and workers traveling to the Crystal Coast from the north and by those leaving the mainland to travel up the Outer Banks. The Ocracoke-Hatteras Inlet Ferry connects Ocracoke with Hatteras Island and the northern Outer Banks. The Ocracoke-Swan Quarter Toll Ferry crosses the Pamlico Sound to connect Ocracoke Island with Swan Quarter in Hyde County.

The **Cherry Branch-Minnesott Ferry** carries passengers and vehicles and is a good connection between the Crystal Coast and Oriental. This is a free trip and a great way to get a quick ride on one of North Carolina's ferries. The Hammocks Beach State Park Ferry transports passengers, but no cars, to Bear Island.

Ferries do not operate in extreme weather, and all ferry schedules and tolls are subject to change without notice. For more information about state-owned ferry crossings, contact the N.C. Department of Transportation Ferry Division, (800) BY-FERRY. Reservations are always strongly suggested on those ferries that take reservations. No reservations are required if you are traveling as a pedestrian or with a bicycle. Following is a list of state-operated ferry schedules and fares.

Cedar Island—Ocracoke Toll Ferry

The Cedar Island-Ocracoke Ferry Service carries passengers and vehicles between the Crystal Coast and Ocracoke Island. The Cedar Island ferry terminal is about 45 miles east of Beaufort, but allow at least an hour and a half for the car trip.

Ferry reservations must be claimed 30 minutes before departure time or they will be canceled. For reservations and to verify times call (800) BY-FERRY (293-3779). Call the ferry terminals at Cedar Island, (252) 225-7411, or Ocracoke, (252) 928-1665, for information specific to that terminal.

2 hours crossing

Reservations recommended at least one month in advance

Year-Round Schedule

Depart Cedar Island	Depart Ocracoke
7:30 AM	7:30 AM
10:30 AM	10:30 AM
2 PM	2 PM
5 PM	5 PM

Fares (One Way):

Pedestrian, $1

Bicycle & Rider, $3

Motorcycle, $10

Vehicle and/or combination less than 20 feet, $15

Vehicle and/or combination 20 feet to 40 feet, $30

Vehicle and/or combination over 40 feet and up to 65 feet, $45

Maximum length 65 feet; up to five axles

Ocracoke–Swan Quarter Toll Ferry

For reservations and to verify times call (800) BY-FERRY (293-3779).

For other questions on departures from Ocracoke, call (252) 928-1665; from Swan Quarter, call (252) 926-6021.

2 hours crossing

Reservations Recommended

Year-Round Schedule

Depart Ocracoke	Depart Swan Quarter
7 AM	10 AM
1 PM	5 PM

 Tourism is big business on the Crystal Coast. It represents an estimated 20 percent of Carteret County's jobs and a $230 million annual income.

Fares are the same as those for the Cedar Island–Ocracoke Toll Ferry.

Hatteras–Ocracoke Inlet Free Ferry
40-minute crossing

No Reservations Accepted - Free Ferry

Summer Schedule

May 12 - Sept. 28, 2009	
Depart Ocracoke	Depart Hatteras
5 AM	5 AM
6 AM	6 AM
7 AM	7 AM
Every 30 minutes: 8 AM - 7 PM	Every 30 minutes: 7:30 AM - 7 PM
8 PM	8 PM
9 PM	9 PM
10 PM	10 PM
11 PM	11 PM
Midnight	Midnight

Jan. 1 - May 11, 2009 and Sept. 29 - Dec. 31, 2009

Departs Ocracoke and Hatteras every hour from 5 AM through midnight

Cherry Branch – Minnesott Beach Free Ferry

The Cherry Branch–Minnesott Beach Ferry is essential for commuters from Oriental who must travel across the Neuse River to work in Havelock, at Cherry Point Marine Air Station and surrounding areas. On the Crystal Coast side, the Cherry Branch terminal is off N.C. Highway 101, about 5 miles south of Havelock. This is a short ride for anyone interested in just experiencing a ferry ride while on the Crystal Coast. This 20-minute free ride allows for great views of the impressive Neuse River as well as a chance to sit back and relax for a bit and watch the water and the sky.

20-minute crossing

No Reservations Accepted – Free Ferry

Year-Round Schedule

Depart Cherry Branch	Depart Minnesott Beach
5:05 AM	5:25 AM
5:55 AM	6:15 AM
6:35 AM	6:55 AM
7:15 AM	7:35 AM
7:55 AM	8:15 AM
8:45 AM	9:15 AM
9:45 AM	10:15 AM
11:45 AM	12:15 PM
12:15 PM	12:45 PM

1:15 PM	1:45 PM
1:45 PM	2:15 PM
2:45 PM	3:15 PM
3:15 PM	3:45 PM
3:45 PM	4:05 PM
4:05 PM	4:25 PM
4:25 PM	4:45 PM
4:45 PM	5:05 PM
5:05 PM	5:25 PM
5:25 PM	5:45 PM
6:05 PM	6:25 PM
6:45 PM	7:15 PM
7:45 PM	8:15 PM
8:45 PM	9:15 PM
9:45 PM	10:15 PM
11:00 PM	11:30 PM

All ferry dates and times are subject to change, call (800) BY-FERRY (293-3779) to verify times prior to travel.

Hammocks Beach State Park Ferry

The seasonal passenger ferry (no cars) at Hammocks Beach State Park provides transportation from the park headquarters terminal to Bear Island. The ferry terminal is off N.C. 24, 2 miles west of Swansboro at the end of State Road 1511. If you are visiting Bear Island between Memorial Day and Labor Day, get to the ferry landing early to avoid long lines. Pets are not allowed on the ferry, and alcoholic beverages are prohibited in the park (see our Attractions chapter for more about Bear Island and Hammocks Beach State Park). Call Hammocks Beach, (910) 326-4881, to verify ferry times.

25-minute crossing – No vehicles

No Reservations Accepted

Memorial Day through Labor Day

The ferry runs daily. On Mondays and Tuesdays from the mainland, the ferry departs every hour on the half-hour from 9:30 AM to 5:30 PM. From Bear Island, the ferry departs every hour on the hour from 10 AM to 6 PM. On Wednesday through Sunday from the mainland, the ferry departs every half-hour from 9:30 AM to 5:30 PM. From Bear Island, the ferry departs every half-hour from 10 AM to 6 PM.

May and September

The ferry runs Wednesday through Sunday.

October through April

The ferry runs Friday through Sunday. A private water taxi service operates the ferry November through March. Call the park for details.

The Central Coast is truly termed "the place where the sky meets the sea."

photo: Peter Doran

Fares (round trip):

Adult, $5

Senior Citizens, 62 and older, $3

Children ages 6 to 12, $3

Children younger than 6, Free

PRIVATE FERRIES

Privately owned vessels also stand ready to carry passengers to popular destinations along the Crystal Coast. And you always have the option of hiring other private vessels complete with crew and catered meals or renting a sailboat, motorboat, houseboat or kayak to do your own navigating. Whatever your choice, there is a lot to explore by water on the Crystal Coast.

Along with state-owned ferries and private charters, the National Park Service (NPS) offers contracts to what it refers to as "concessionaires." These folks, operating under NPS guidelines, carry passengers and/or vehicles to the uninhabited Cape Lookout National Seashore (see our Attractions chapter). The Seashore is a 56-mile stretch of barrier islands made up of North Core Banks, home of Portsmouth Village; South Core Banks, home of Cape Lookout Lighthouse; and Shackleford Banks, home to wild horses.

The NPS allows privately owned ferries to carry passengers and vehicles to North and South Core Banks and Portsmouth Village, where there is also a landing strip for small planes (see descriptions below). These small ferries operate out of the Down East communities of Davis and Atlantic and don't have all the extras you will find on the state ferries because of the depth of the water in which they operate. They do have medium-size, seaworthy vessels equipped to carry a handful of vehicles, a few passengers and some equipment. They normally operate from April to December, although schedules and fees vary. Most concessionaires require reservations, so it is best to call ahead for schedule information, to check current fares and to see if there is room aboard for you, and also to check weather conditions. Each concessionaire can provide information on cabins and camping (see our Camping chapter). Pets in pet carriers are allowed by most concessionaire ferry services, and pets must be maintained with a 6-foot leash at all times on the islands.

Barrier Island Transportation
**Harkers Island Fishing Center,
Harkers Island
(252) 728-3907**

Barrier Island Transportation provides passenger ferry and water-taxi service to Shackleford Banks and the Cape Lookout Lighthouse area. No vehicles are accommodated. Fares are $15 round-trip per person, $10 for children 9 and younger, and $25 for overnight campers with gear. There is a parking fee on the mainland. Group rates are offered. The ferry leaves at 45 minutes after the hour starting at 8:45 AM, weather permitting through the summer. The ferry picks up on the hour until 5 PM. Service begins around Easter and continues through November or early December, depending on the weather. Reservations are not required but are recommended for large groups.

Calico Jack's & Cape Lookout Ferry Service
**Calico Jack's Inn & Marina, Harkers Island
(252) 728-3575**

Passenger-only ferry service to the Cape Lookout Lighthouse is a 10-minute boat ride from Calico Jack's Marina. The ferry departs for Cape Lookout or Shackleford Banks on demand for $10 per adult round trip, $6 per child. Campers with gear are ferried for $15 per adult and $12 per child. There is a $30 trip minimum, and there is a fee to park your vehicle in the departure area. Service begins in early March and ends in early December or later if the weather permits.

Davis Shore Ferry Service
(252) 225-4261

This ferry business serves South Core Banks and carries passengers, vehicles and all-terrain vehicles five times a day from late March through mid-December on a reservation basis. Fares are about $15 round-trip for adults, $7 for children ages 5 to 10 years, and free for children younger than 4 years of age. The cost for a round-trip standard-size vehicle is $75, and prices increase depending on the size and length of your rig. The service is generally closed January through mid-March. For information about the fishing camps in this area, see our Crystal Coast Hotels and Motels chapter or call (252) 241-6783. The cabins are rustic and can be a great alternative when seeking a little bit of respite from the hectic pace of today's world.

Island Ferry Adventures
618 Front St., Beaufort
(252) 728-7555
Barbour's Marina, Harkers Island
(252) 728-6181

Island Ferry Adventures offers ferry service from two locations — one in Beaufort and one on Harkers Island. They can provide transportation to all the surrounding islands as well as water tours, dolphin-watch tours and horse-watch tours. The prices vary depending on the destination. Weather permitting, the ferry begins leaving on demand at the top of each hour at 9 AM and continues through late afternoon or early evening, depending on the season.

Local Yokel Ferry and Tours
516 Island Rd., Harkers Island
(252) 728-2759

Local Yokel Ferry and Tours is operated by the Yeomans family and is the only ferry service that offers passengers a full view of Shackleford on the way to the Cape — complete with the horses, dolphin and waterfowl. The ferry begins operating at 9 AM and runs every hour in the summer, weather permitting. Call ahead for the schedule from November through March. Early trips and other special needs can be arranged. After a 15-minute ride, travelers find themselves on Cape Lookout National Seashore; five minutes and they're at Shackleford Banks. Rates are $15 for adults and $10 for children, and there is minimum number of passengers. Group rates are available and there is free parking on Harkers Island. Stay an hour, a day or bring a tent and stay the night.

Morris Marina Kabin Kamps
and Ferry Service, Inc.
1000 Morris Marina Rd., Atlantic
(252) 225-4261

From the Down East community of Atlantic, which is off N.C. 12, this ferry and cabin rental service transports passengers, vehicles and all-terrain vehicles to Portsmouth or to the south end of North Core Banks at Drum Inlet from March through early December. Trips are run by reservation only, and the time varies. Trips can also be run by request. Morris Marina's transportation cost is about $15 round-trip for adults with children younger than 6 years old traveling for free. Round-trip vehicle fees start at $75 for a standard-sized vehicle and increase based on size and length. Island transportation and delivery of supplies (ice, groceries, etc.) may be arranged. See our Crystal Coast Hotels and Motels chapter for cabin rental information.

Outer Banks Ferry Service
328 Front St., Beaufort
(252) 728-4129

Outer Banks Ferry Service operates year round seven days a week, weather permitting, and offers transportation to the Rachel Carson Reserve and to Shackleford Banks. The service runs on demand starting at 8:30 AM, depending on the season. Reservations should be made in advance. Costs range between $10 and $15 for adults, depending on the destination. Rates for children and groups are also offered. For those wanting other water adventures, this service rents house boats from April through October and also offers fishing-guide services.

ONCE YOU'RE HERE

Once you arrive, you'll find that a car is essential to see the Crystal Coast. There is very little public transportation service in the area, and one look at the map will show you that most communities are far enough apart to make a car the best way to get around.

There are some marked bike routes, but remember you're in a tourist area, and vehicle traffic is often heavy during the summer. Beaufort has a 6-mile marked bike route — a route guide is available at the Safrit Historical Center, 138 Turner Street in Beaufort. Biking in residential developments on Bogue Banks and in Morehead City neighborhoods is safe and pleasant. Morehead City continually adds

In some areas of the Central Coast, boats outnumber residents nearly three to one.

photo: Carolyn Temple

new walking and biking paths throughout town. The Atlantic Beach Causeway has biking and walking paths that link Atlantic Beach with Morehead City in relative safety. The wide shoulders of N.C. 58 from Fort Macon State Park through Emerald Isle offer bikers an opportunity for riding with traffic-watching care. Also, the Town of Atlantic Beach and the Town of Emerald Isle continue to add more sidewalks for walkers, runners and bikers. A 26-mile bicycle touring route is marked in and around Swansboro.

U.S. Highway 70 is generally very easy to drive from New Bern through Havelock and on to Morehead City, Beaufort and Down East. From Beaufort east, U.S. 70 is a two-lane highway that winds through communities, marshes and between canals. An important detail to remember about U.S. 70 is that it has many names as it traverses Carteret County. In Morehead City, it's Arendell Street, the main street through town. It's also the Morehead-Beaufort Causeway. In Beaufort, it's called Cedar Street until it takes a left turn and becomes Live Oak Street. And by any name, it's always heavily trafficked in the Morehead City and Beaufort areas.

Beach Wheels Bike Rentals
607 Atlantic Beach Cswy., Ste. 103,
Atlantic Beach
(252) 240-2453
www.beachwheelsbikerentals.com

Offering "different spokes for different folks," Beach Wheels Bike Rentals provides one of the best and largest selections of bikes on the island. Beach Wheels offers beach cruisers, adult bikes, children's bikes, tag-a-longs, adult trikes, tandems and more. In its seventh year of business, this company provides friendly and convenient service with free delivery and pick-up service anywhere on the Crystal Coast. Call ahead to reserve your wheels and when you arrive your bikes will be waiting.

Visitors Centers

A stop at the Crystal Coast Tourism Authority in Morehead City, 3409 Arendell Street, (252) 726-8148 or (800) SUNNY-NC (786-6962), next to the North Carolina Institute of Marine Sciences, can be very helpful. In Cape Carteret the Tourism Office is on U.S. Highway 58 at the Cameron Langston Bridge to Emerald Isle, (252) 393-3100. These centers are full of informational brochures and local maps, including street maps. Friendly staff will answer your questions and help you find your way. The North Carolina Ferry Division welcomes Crystal Coast visitors at its center at the Cedar Island Ferry terminal.

AREA OVERVIEW

The Crystal Coast is known for its sparkling, crystalline waters and miles of beaches and island sanctuaries. Salt water, white sandy beaches, breezes off the water and a casual atmosphere draw travelers by the thousands to the the Crystal Coast shoreline, and many people decide to stay and make the area their home.

Everything you want from a seaside vacation is here — dramatic sunrises on the ocean, egrets, gulls or white ibises lacing through blue skies, dolphins playfully break from inlet waters. As you stroll through towns in Carteret County, you hear songbirds call from surrounding live oaks. As you stroll the beaches, you can curl your toes in smooth beach sand and ease into evening as the sun sets in a copper disc. Away from the glare of bright city lights, you can gaze at a scatter of stars on a cloudless night.

A day can be as quiet or active as you desire. Each of the geographic areas — Bogue Banks, Beaufort, Morehead City, Swansboro, the Down East communities and western Carteret County — is different in its own special way and offers as much or as little activity as you want.

The Crystal Coast is located in Carteret County, a place that is off the beaten path, and many say that fact alone is exactly what makes it so desirable. By car you must travel approximately 100 miles from Interstate 95 before you reach the county. The nearest major city is Raleigh, a three-hour car trip away. Historic New Bern is just 40 miles away. U.S. Highway 70, the main artery running through the county, is a direct corridor to Raleigh, so the drive is easy.

Although not fast-paced, Carteret County is one of the fastest growing counties in the state. Its year-round population is just 60,232. It contains 526 square miles

and an ocean coastline of 81 miles, not to mention the miles of waterfront that stretch along Bogue and Core sounds and on the area's rivers and numerous bays, inlets and creeks.

The county is centrally situated on the North Carolina coast, perhaps the reason it was one of the first areas of the state explored and the third settled, giving it a rich history to blend with its natural beauty. To the north are the Pamlico Sound and the Outer Banks; to the south are the southern barrier islands, the city of Wilmington and the Cape Fear River.

Carteret County is at the confluence of the warm Gulf Stream waters from the south and cooler Labrador Current from the north. It provides a habitat for a widely varied mix of plants, a sanctuary for migrating birds and the northernmost point in the migration of exotic marine life such as the manatee. It is a place for visitors young and old to explore the wonder of a coast that on its brightest days is truly crystal.

Bogue Banks

Bogue Banks is the narrow barrier island that stretches below Morehead City, with its main highway N.C. Highway 58 nearly parallel to N.C. Highway 24. At the east end of the island is Fort Macon and the town of Atlantic Beach and at the west end of the island is Emerald Isle. The body of water called Bogue Sound separates Bogue Banks from the mainland. The 30-mile-long island is connected to the mainland by two high-rise bridges, one at each end — one bridge from Morehead City to Atlantic Beach on the east end and the other bridge from Cape Carteret to Emerald Isle on the west end. Because the ocean and sound beaches attract visitors and summer residents, you will find many

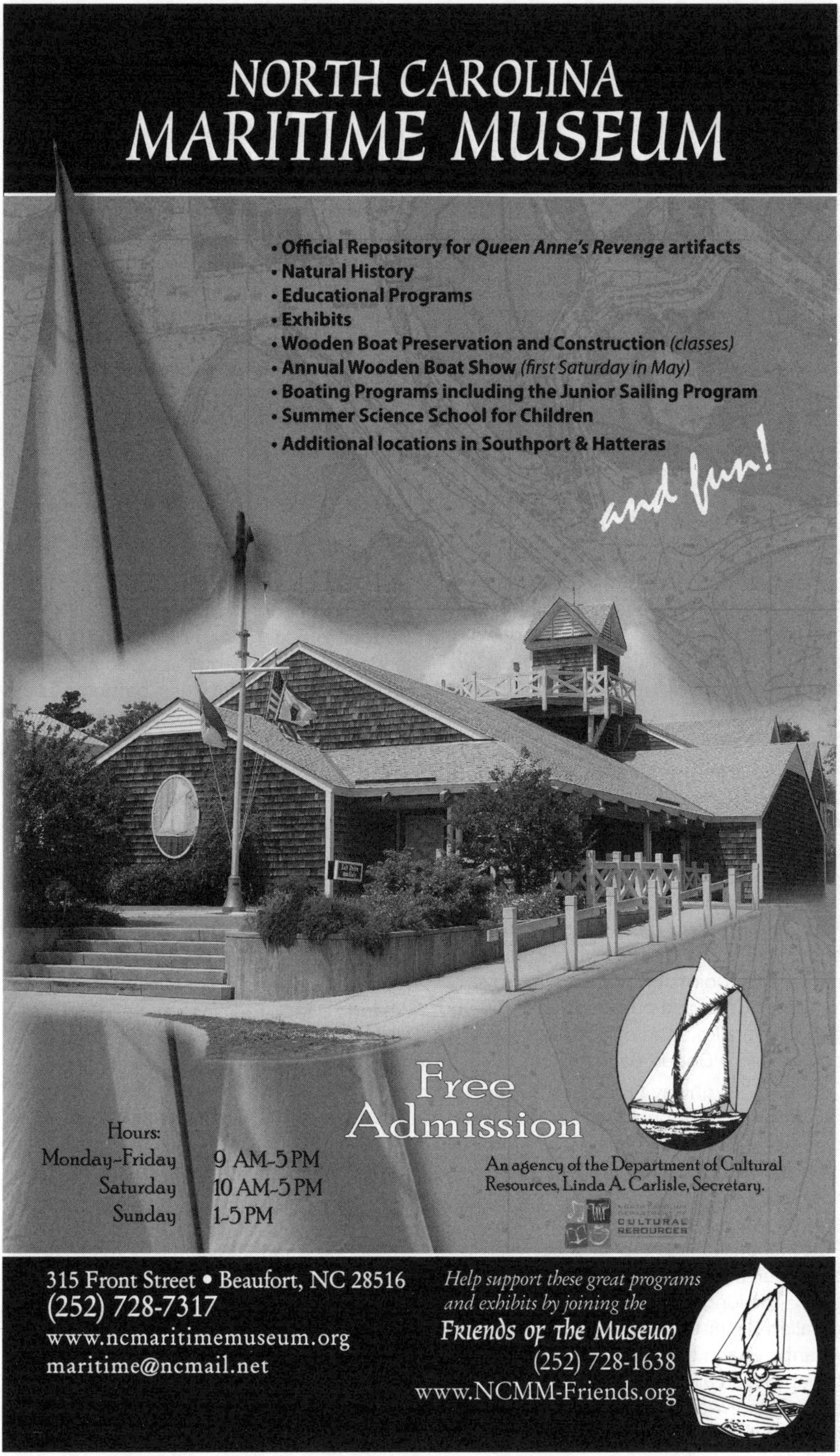
NORTH CAROLINA
MARITIME MUSEUM
• Official Repository for Queen Anne's Revenge artifacts
• Natural History
• Educational Programs
• Exhibits
• Wooden Boat Preservation and Construction (classes)
• Annual Wooden Boat Show (first Saturday in May)
• Boating Programs including the Junior Sailing Program
• Summer Science School for Children
• Additional locations in Southport & Hatteras
and fun!
Free Admission
Hours:
Monday–Friday 9 AM–5 PM
Saturday 10 AM–5 PM
Sunday 1–5 PM
An agency of the Department of Cultural Resources, Linda A. Carlisle, Secretary.
CULTURAL RESOURCES
315 Front Street • Beaufort, NC 28516
(252) 728-7317
www.ncmaritimemuseum.org
maritime@ncmail.net
Help support these great programs and exhibits by joining the
Friends of the Museum
(252) 728-1638
www.NCMM-Friends.org

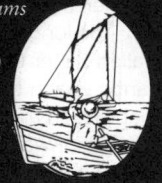

second homes, condominiums, hotels and summer rental cottages on the island.

Bogue Banks offers residents and visitors a special treat. The island runs east to west and its Atlantic Ocean side faces due south, so you can watch the sun rise in the east over the ocean, travel across the sky, and set in the west over the ocean. This barrier island changes with each storm or hurricane as sand is shifted or eroded away.

N.C. Highway 58 extends the entire length of Bogue Banks. Along the way it is marked with green mile markers (MM). The MM series begins with mile 1 at the east end and continues along N.C. 58 to mile 21 on the west end. In this book we give the MM number as part of the address for businesses on Bogue Banks.

The majority of Bogue Banks' development, both commercial and residential, is along N.C. 58, and in the Coast Guard Road area of Emerald Isle. A ride from one end to the other gives you an overview of the island communities. To illustrate how narrow the island is, in several places you can see both the sound and the ocean from the road.

Bogue Banks embraces five townships that often seem to blend together. Atlantic Beach is at the far east end of the island and borders the town of Pine Knoll Shores. Indian Beach surrounds the small unincorporated community of Salter Path, and Emerald Isle is at the far west end of the island. Each town has its own personality, points of interest and governing body. Checking our maps will help you get an overall picture of how these towns combine into Bogue Banks.

As N.C. Highway 58 passes through the different communities, it often takes on a new name. In Atlantic Beach, the road is called Fort Macon Road. East Fort Macon Road is the strip between the old fort and the main intersection in town. West Fort Macon Road is the strip between that intersection and the western edge of town. The longest stretch of the highway is called Salter Path Road, and it runs from Atlantic Beach through Pine Knoll Shores, Indian Beach and Salter Path. In Emerald Isle, the highway is called Emerald Drive. It really isn't as confusing as it sounds — N.C.

58 is just one road with several names that all spell scenery and coastline comforts.

ATLANTIC BEACH

Atlantic Beach is the oldest of the five towns on Bogue Banks. It was originally the site of a small pavilion built on the beach in 1887. The one-story building had a refreshment stand and stalls in the back for changing clothes. The popularity of surf-bathing was growing, and guests at the old Atlantic Hotel in Morehead City and other areas were transported to the sound side of Atlantic Beach by sailboat. The guests then trekked across the island to the pavilion, which faced the ocean. Supplies were dragged over the sand dunes by ox cart.

In 1916 the original pavilion and 100 acres were bought by Von Bedsworth, and the 100-room Atlantic View Beach Hotel was built, a lone sentry on the strip of island. The hotel later burned, but by 1928 a group of county citizens had built a toll bridge from Morehead City to today's Atlantic Beach and had developed a beach resort with dining facilities, bathhouses and another pavilion. This complex would also perish to fire just a year later. A New York bank took possession of the property and built a new hotel, and Atlantic Beach slowly began to grow into the town it is today.

In 1936 the toll bridge was sold to the state, and toll charges were dropped. In 1953 a drawbridge replaced the old bridge, and in the late 1980s, the drawbridge was replaced by the current Morehead City-Atlantic Beach four-lane, high-rise bridge. High-rise bridges play an important role along the Crystal Coast, allowing large vessels to easily maneuver the coastal waters. Past the North Carolina Port at Morehead City you will see tugs with barges, pleasure boats, long-line fishing boats and an occasional passenger cruise liner on the Intracoastal Waterway.

Today Atlantic Beach is home to about 3,600 year-round residents, although the population swells to a whopping 35,000 during the summer months. Atlantic Beach is a mixture of old-fashioned beach cottages, moderate vacation homes and modern condominiums.

The center of Atlantic Beach, known to old timers and locals as The Circle, is found at the southernmost end of the Atlantic Beach Causeway and offers oceanfront day parking and souvenir shops. Major changes are in the works for The Circle. A developer plans to construct high-rise condos, retail shops, restaurants, lodging and many other upscale improvements. New homes are going up in undeveloped areas throughout Atlantic Beach.

PINE KNOLL SHORES

Pine Knoll Shores is immediately west of Atlantic Beach and was incorporated in 1973. In 1918 Alice Hoffman bought substantial acreage on Bogue Banks (known then as "Isle of the Pines"). She made her home here, off and on, until her death in 1953. The property was then inherited by her niece, wife of President Theodore Roosevelt Jr., and her four children. These Roosevelts envisioned Pine Knoll Shores as a planned community, sensitive to the delicate ecology of the maritime forest that surrounds it. Today, town policies still strive to protect the environment. As it was being built, early town planners worked to ensure that Pine Knoll Shores would be a residential community, and it has remained so.

The town's 1,700 year-round residents share their community with the North Carolina Aquarium at Pine Knoll Shores, one of the state's three aquariums. This newly renovated aquarium is a must-visit for everyone regardless of their age.

Surrounding the aquarium is the Theodore Roosevelt Natural Area, a 265-acre maritime forest owned, maintained and protected by the state. It is one of the few remaining maritime forests on North Carolina's barrier islands. (See our Crystal Coast Attractions chapter for more about these sites.)

A historic marker stands at the corner of N.C. 58 and Roosevelt Boulevard (MM 7), noting the spot of the first landing of Europeans on the North Carolina coast. Giovanni da Verrazano, a Florentine navigator in the service of France, explored the state's coast from Cape Fear to Kitty Hawk in 1524. His voyage along the coast marked the first recorded European contact with what is now North Carolina.

INDIAN BEACH

As you leave Pine Knoll Shores and travel west on N.C. 58, you enter the resort and residential town of Indian Beach. It was incorporated in 1973, and offers residents and visitors beautiful beaches for sunbathing, surf fishing and watersports. The community is home to condominiums, mobile home communities and restaurants, which you'll find profiled in various chapters within the Crystal Coast section of this book. This town of about 100 residents surrounds the unincorporated community of Salter Path, creating an East Indian Beach and a West Indian Beach. So don't be surprised when you drive through Indian Beach, Salter Path and then Indian Beach again.

SALTER PATH

The first families to settle in Salter Path arrived in the late 1890s from Diamond City, which at the time was a whaling community on Shackleford Banks. Shackleford Banks is a 9-mile-long island that is now part of Cape Lookout National Seashore.

By 1897 approximately 500 people were living in Diamond City, a town with several stores, a school, a post office and church buildings. Hard storms in the late 1890s convinced many Diamond City residents that it was time to leave the island. Many cut their homes into sections, tied them to skiffs and floated or sailed their dwellings across the water. Once at the new home site, the houses were reconstructed. Many residents of Diamond City settled on Harkers Island, in the Shackleford Street area of Morehead City or in Salter Path on Bogue Banks.

Legend has it that the name Salter Path originated with Joshua Salter, a Broad Creek resident who often traveled by boat from the mainland to fish and hunt on Bogue Banks. Stories say he made a path from the sound side of the island, where he anchored his boat, to the oceanfront. Folks called the walkway Salter's Path, and like many things in Carteret County, the name just stuck.

Many locals credit the early residents of Salter Path with bringing shrimp into the culinary limelight. Early fishermen considered these delectable creatures a menace, and enjoyed instead such community fishing catches as the jumpin' mullet. But after local residents began to eat them, shrimp soon became a marketable and profitable commodity. Shrimping is now a lucrative industry along the Crystal Coast, much to the joy of residents and visitors alike.

EMERALD ISLE

It is said that this west end of Bogue Banks was originally home to nomadic Native Americans and whalers. The area was also home to about 15 families, who arrived in 1893 and settled at Middletown, a

small section of the island that is now part of Emerald Isle.

Other than those small groups, Emerald Isle was largely unsettled until the 1950s. Several years after Atlantic Beach was developed as a seashore resort, Henry K. Fort of Philadelphia bought the land that now makes up most of Emerald Isle along with 500 acres on the mainland, in what is now the town of Cape Carteret. Fort planned to link the island and his mainland property with a bridge and develop a large resort. When support for constructing the bridge could not be raised, he abandoned the project. Years later a ferry was created, and it carried motorists and pedestrians over to the Bogue Inlet beaches of modern-day Emerald Isle. The ferry landed near Bogue Inlet Pier, the first recreational spot at the island's west end.

Today, the Cameron Langston Bridge provides access from the mainland to Emerald Isle and the western end of Bogue Banks. It spans the Intracoastal Waterway, and from the top offers a great view of the waterway and Bogue Banks.

Emerald Isle has a year-round population of more than 3,500 and a seasonal population of more than 16,000. It is a thriving beach-vacation spot, with plenty to do for the entire family. The town's municipal complex and community center has large meeting rooms, a full basketball court and a gym (see our Sports, Fitness

and Parks chapter). The town also offers many public beach access areas for residents and visitors alike. Several new housing sections have been developed west of the high-rise bridge, in the area surrounding the Coast Guard Station, and a few choice spots have become fairly exclusive gated communities.

Beaufort

The seaport town of Beaufort affords residents and visitors a slice of early American life in a fishing and port town, with plenty of tourist attractions too. Not to be confused with the somewhat larger Beaufort, South Carolina, (pronounced BU-fort), Beaufort (pronounced BO-fort) is still a town of only about 5,000 full-time residents, and fishing and water trades still figure into its economy. With tree-lined streets and restored Victorian homes, Beaufort's historical diversity and Southern charm is everywhere. Front Street faces Taylor's Creek. Just past the creek is the Rachel Carson Estuarine Reserve, then Shackleford Banks, then the Atlantic Ocean.

Beaufort is the third-oldest town in North Carolina and was named for Englishman Henry Somerset, the Duke of Beaufort. The town was surveyed in 1713, nearly 20 years before George Washington's birth, and was incorporated in 1722. Beaufort is the geographic center of Carteret County and its county seat. The English influence is apparent in the architecture and, more noticeably, in the street names: Ann and Queen, for Queen Anne; Craven, for the Earl of Craven; Orange, for William, the Prince of Orange; Moore, for Col. Maurice Moore; and Pollock, for the Colonial governor at the time of the 1713 survey.

Beaufort offers a glimpse at a part of North Carolina's coastal history with restored older structures and landmarks. The Beaufort Historical Association (BHA) was organized in 1960 to celebrate the town's 250th anniversary. The association commemorates Beaufort's historic homes with special plaques, noting the original homeowner and the date in which the structure was built. To earn a plaque, a home must be at least 80 years old and have retained its historic and architectural integrity. The first home to be "plaqued" was the Duncan House, c. 1790, at 105 Front Street. Through the years the Beaufort Historical Association has moved several old structures — including an early American courthouse, jail and apothecary that were threatened with demolition — to an area on Turner Street, which is now open to the public daily. For more information about the Beaufort Historic Site, see our Crystal Coast Attractions chapter.

Beaufort has a designated historic district that includes residential homes, cemeteries, businesses, a restoration site, the county courthouse and several structures listed on the National Register of Historic Places. Each historic house and site has its own story to tell. The Old Burying Ground on Ann Street is one of Beaufort's most fascinating sites. Deeded to the town in 1731, the Old Burying Ground was declared full in 1825, and the N.C. General Assembly said no more burials would be allowed there. The town was ordered to lay out a new graveyard, but the townspeople didn't support the act and continued to bury their loved ones in the Old Burying Ground until the early 1900s. The north corner of the graveyard is the oldest section of the cemetery, although many of the oldest graves don't carry a marker. For a great self-guided tour, stop by the Beaufort Historical Association, 138 Turner Street, (252) 728-5225. A few of the notables buried here are Capt. Josiah Pender, whose men took Fort Macon in 1861; James W. Hunt, who had the distinction of marrying, making his will and dying the same day; Esther Cooke, mother of Capt. James W. Cooke, who once commanded the ironclad Albemarle; the Dill child, buried in a glass-topped casket; the common grave of the *Crissie Wright* crew, who froze to death when the ship wrecked on Shackleford Banks in 1886; and the child who died aboard a ship and was brought to Beaufort in a keg of rum for burial — in the keg. People leave trinkets on the child's grave, along with money, jewelry and small toys — although no one seems to remember how the practice got started.

With the town's waterfront revitalization project in the late 1970s, Beaufort took a new direction. The renovation involved tearing down many old waterfront structures not considered salvageable and building the wooden boardwalk, docks and facilities that bring more sailboats and pleasure craft than the shad boats that once lined the creek. Some businesses were encouraged to stay while others opted to move into the downtown area. Soon word of the new old town spread, and it hasn't been the same since. What was once a coastal hideaway is now a favorite spot for visitors traveling by car or boat.

Entering Beaufort from the west will take you across a drawbridge, which are quickly becoming relics along the coast. Because of increased traffic, plans have been in the works for years to replace the drawbridge. Where to locate the bridge has been a sticking point, and people in Beaufort are divided between maintaining the drawbridge or building a new bridge to ease traffic snarls.

Even with all the town's history, there is still much new development here. New structures continue to spring up, and new developments are under construction around town and in the town's surrounding areas. Development plans are underway for the old fish factory at the east end of Front Street and the land across the street.

Beaufort is home to a number of attractions, not the least of which are the wonderful North Carolina Maritime Museum and Watercraft Center, the Beaufort Historic Site, and the Rachel Carson Reserve, part of the North Carolina National Estuarine Research Reserve (see our Crystal Coast Attractions chapter for more information about these).

BEAUFORT'S NEARBY COMMUNITIES

Lennoxville is the community closest to Beaufort. It begins at the east end of Front Street in Beaufort and continues to the east end of Lennoxville Road, where it cul-de-sacs beneath an awning of huge live oaks. This is primarily an unincorporated residential area, with the exception of Atlantic Veneer (see our Commerce and

19

AREA OVERVIEW

 CLOSE UP

The History Place

One of the most popular places in Carteret County is The History Place, located at 1008 Arendell Street in downtown Morehead City. The History Place houses a museum, the Jack Spencer Goodwin Research Library, the Museum Store, the Les Ewen Auditorium, a banquet room and the Tea Clipper, which is a tea shop and cafe.

The History Place helps guests from around the globe understand what makes Carteret County so special, sharing the story of the area's past as well as its most important features. One wall of the exhibit space highlights the varied economic areas in Carteret County. From commercial fishing and tourism to farming and boat building, the county's livelihoods are discussed in separate displays. The remainder of the space is used to re-create the era from circa 1880 to 1920. There is a parlor, medical office, authentic schoolroom and more, each creatively using the varied artifacts the museum has gathered through the years.

Some of the museum's historical artifacts are one of a kind, like the original carriage that Confederate spy Emeline Pigott was riding in the day she was arrested and a trunk with her personal belongings. A group of researchers has judged The History Place to have "the best collection of Civil War and East Coast genealogies from Massachusetts on down."

The museum's auditorium/banquet room is the site of a variety of public gatherings — from weddings and dinners to business gatherings and receptions to concerts and parties. In addition, there is a conference room for smaller groups of 25 people or less.

The History Place was truly a labor of love, not only for the society and its members, but also for all of Carteret County. The clock tower in the entry of the museum is filled with bricks purchased by individuals and groups for $100 each to help fund the project. And it illustrates exactly what the society has done — they've built a world-class museum "one brick at a time."

The Tea Clipper has more than 120 varieties of teas and offers a variety of gourmet foods. It is one of the most elegant dining places in Carteret County. The History Place and the Tea Clipper are open from 10 AM to 4 PM Tuesday through Saturday. Both are closed on Sunday and Monday.

For more information on The History Place/Carteret County Historical Society, Inc. call (252) 247-7533 or visit the website at www.thehistoryplace.org

Industry chapter). Lennoxville is surrounded by water: Taylor's Creek on the south and North River on the north with Core Sound and a perfect view of Cape Lookout Lighthouse. The lure of waterfront living has stimulated the development of a few small but very upscale subdivisions along Lennoxville's forested waterfronts.

North River is a small community north of Beaufort on Merrimon Road. This community includes houses on both sides of the road and backs up to the body of water known as North River.

Here's an oddity — the **South River** community actually lies to the north of the North River community. Named for the body of water at its banks, South River is a small traditional fishing and hunting community. Some of the surrounding land is owned by recreational hunters and businesses, and several private airstrips are in the area. Many Native American artifacts and pottery pieces have been found in the South River area. Open Grounds Farm lies in the South River area and extends east to the Down East community of Stacy. This 50,000-acre corporate farm includes crops — namely corn, soybeans, cotton — and timber.

To the west of South River lies the community of **Merrimon**. This rural area borders the Neuse River and Adams Creek, which is a stretch of the scenic Intracoastal Waterway.

In recent years a few neighborhood developments have sprung up around South River, Merrimon and the Intracoastal Waterway. **Merrimon Bay**, **Ellinwood Estates**, **Sportsman's Village**, **Sandy Point**, **Jonaquin's Landing** and **Indian Summer Estates** offer waterfront and mainland lots, and most feature such amenities as community docks and boat ramps.

Morehead City

Morehead City is Carteret County's largest town with a population of about 14,000. The town began with an early land prospector from Virginia named John Shackleford. In 1714 Shackleford purchased approximately 1,400 acres throughout Carteret County and Morehead City. The second land owner in the Morehead City area was David Shepard, who in 1723 purchased the land now known as Shepard's Point. Other notable early settlers include William Fisher, Silas Webb, Bridges Arendell and past N.C. Governor John Motley Morehead. All of these names can still be seen around town.

In 1852 the state decided to extend a railroad line to connect Raleigh with the coast, and several towns vied to be the end location, hoping to bring growth to their communities. For a while it was considered inevitable that the line would end in Beaufort. In 1857 William H. Arendell, John Motley Morehead and others formed the Shepard's Point Land Company, purchasing 1,000 acres at the western end of the Shepard's Point. Sixty home lots were created, the first of which were sold during a public auction on November 11, 1857.

In 1858 John Motley Morehead sang the praises of the infant town: "The City of Morehead is situated on a beautiful neck of land or dry plain, almost entirely surrounded by salt water; its climate salubrious; its sea breezes and sea bathing delightful; its drinking water good and its fine chalybeate spring, strongly impregnated with sulfur, will make it a pleasant watering place . . ."

The sale of the land was successful, and more importantly Gov. Morehead was successful in his bid for the railroad's destination and ultimately one of two state deep-water ports. Morehead City was incorporated in 1861. When the N.C. Legislature authorized the incorporation of the town, surveyors laid out the streets and named the primary ones after men who had been influential in the area's settlement — Fisher, Arendell, Bridges, Evans, Shackleford and Shepard.

The town was started just in time to be taken over by the Union forces when they attacked Fort Macon on April 26, 1862, thus ending for a time any significant development. Even after the end of the War Between the States, Morehead City struggled to regain its commercial life until the 1880s, when the shipping industry began to bring business to town, once again turning the area into a hub of activity. In the early 1880s a new Atlantic Hotel was built in Morehead City, replacing the old Atlantic Hotel that had been destroyed by a hurricane. The Atlantic Hotel had 233 rooms and claimed to have the largest ballroom in the South. It drew the cream of the state's society to the coast until it was destroyed by fire in 1933.

The city began a road improvement program in 1911 to keep up with the town's steady growth. Better roads stimulated the growth of Crab Point, a part of the city east of Country Club Road and north of the 20th Street Bridge over Calico Creek. Morehead residents dubbed the area Crab Point because when tides came in crabs got trapped on the shoreline, making them an easy catch. In the early years Crab Point served as a port and had windmills for grinding grain and generating power

See this entire guide plus additional content online at insiderinfo.us

WTKF 107.1 FM
WJNC 1240 AM

THE TALK STATION

The Weekday Line Up

6 a.m.-9 a.m. - Coastal Daybreak with Ben Ball -
Call In Number **1-800-818-2255**
Eastern North Carolina's only radio morning news magazine, with special features, sports, entertainment and local and national guests.

9 a.m.-12 noon - Laura Ingraham -
Call In Number **1-800-876-4123**
Talk radio just got very interesting. Laura Ingraham is a political pundit with sassy spice and everything nice.

12 noon-3 p.m. - Rush Limbaugh -
Call In Number **1-800-282-2882**
The Nation's #1 Radio Talk Show. Rush is the Godfather of talk radio and you can hear him on The Talk Station.

3 p.m.-5 p.m. Dave Ramsey -
Call In Number **1-888-825-5225**
Dave offers life-changing financial advice.

5 p.m.-7 p.m. - VIEWPOINTS with Lockwood Phillips
Call In Number **1-800-818-2255**
Across the street, across the state, across the nation, Viewpoints is where you can express your point of view.

7 p.m.-10 p.m. Sean Hannity
Call In Number - **1-800-941-7326**
The Legacy lives on.

10 p.m.-1 a.m. - Jim Bohannon -
Call In Number **1-866-505-4626**
Jim goes into in-depth conversations with today's news makers, leading authors and the latest entertainers.

1 a.m.-6 a.m. Coast to Coast AM, with George Noory -
Call In Number **1-800-825-5033**
America's Most fascinating overnight radio program.

Saturday and Sunday starting at **1 p.m.**
SPORTING NEWS RADIO

www.wtkf107.com

for lumber companies. A private cemetery in the area has graves dating back to the early 1700s.

Today Morehead City is home to several large events, including the North Carolina Seafood Festival (the state's second largest annual festival) and the Big Rock Marlin Tournament (see our Crystal Coast Annual Events chapter for more about both of these events). The city continues to grow and strives to preserve its heritage as a fishing and port city. The most obvious recent improvements have occurred along the waterfront. Morehead City's leaders have provided a major face-lift to this charming section of town, resulting in wide sidewalks, new docks, bathroom facilities, public artwork, parks and a gazebo in City Park on Arendell Street. Waterfront restaurants, both new and old, and shops continue to bring visitors, and deep-sea charter fishing boats line the dock to give them a day at sea.

Some of the best places in Morehead City, however, are off the beaten path. You must cross Arendell Street, away from the waterfront, and walk down the side streets to Bridges Street, which parallels Arendell, to enjoy many fine old residences that have been refurbished. Some of these buildings have been turned into shops, bed and breakfast inns, art galleries and businesses. On the other side, a stroll along Evans Street will take you past charming older homes.

Swansboro

Swansboro is a historic, water-oriented town sitting on the Intracoastal Waterway along the mouth of the White Oak River. It is the only geographic area of those described here that is not in Carteret County. It is in Onslow County, on the west side of the Crystal Coast. Many fishing boats call Swansboro home, and residents keep

When you're in doubt about directions, stop and ask a local. Chances are you'll meet a friendly person and learn a lot about the area.

 **CLOSE UP**

Emeline Pigott:
Carteret County's Confederate Spy

It's no secret that North Carolina has a rich Civil War history, but what does that have to do with a young country girl from Carteret County and her petticoat? It's a true Civil War spy story containing secrets, love, duty, danger — and a really big skirt.

Emeline Pigott was born on December 15, 1836, in Harlowe Township located in Carteret County. When she was 25 years old, she moved with her family to a farm at Crab Point in what is now Morehead City. Located on Calico Creek, the farm placed Pigott and her family near to where the Confederate soldiers were placed to defend coastal North Carolina in the Civil War. When the soldiers of the 26th North Carolina Division were stationed, the Pigott family became involved in the Confederate's cause, pro-

The carriage Emeline Pigott was riding in at the time of her arrest is on display at The History Place.

photo: The History Place

viding help and aid whenever and however they could. A compassionate young woman, Pigott herself nursed the sick and tended to wounded soldiers, even bringing some of them back to the family farm to recover. Her family opened its home to the Confederate soldiers that were camped nearby, offering them a respite from the war.

These beginnings are seemingly what developed Pigott's passion and duty for the Confederacy and her role in trying to protect it, but it seems that one soldier, Stokes McRae, may have instilled a deeper motivation. He and Pigott fell in love, and, once engaged, they decided to wait to be married until after the war. McRae survived the Battle of New Bern but did not return from the Battle at Gettysburg in July of 1863. This devastating news refueled the fire within Pigott to fight for the Confederate cause, doing what was in her power to help in any way that she could.

Pigott worked throughout three counties, following Confederate soldiers throughout New Bern and Kinston continuing to care for the injured soldiers. She also collected mail in addition to food, clothing, medicine and other necessary items, hiding them in designated hollow trees and logs for the Confederates to collect. When she returned to Carteret County, the Union army had occupied the area. As her family entertained the Union officers, Pigott joined in the socializing and bravely used this opportune time to glean information from the Union and gather intelligence for the Confederates. Local fishermen worked with her by gathering information about Union boats' cargoes and destinations and then reporting the information right to Pigott.

Pigott also took on the more dangerous task of personally carrying valuable information and supplies, knowing that Union officials could search her at any time during her travels. With mail and other items combined, Pigott sometimes carried as much as 30 pounds of contraband, yes you guessed it, under her heavily pocketed hoop skirt.

In 1864 Pigott came under suspicion as she was out on her rounds with her brother-in-law, Rufus Bell. On their way to Beaufort they were stopped, arrested and sent to jail. While officials were finding a woman to perform a search on Pigott, she managed to eat some incriminating evidence and shred some mail before they discovered a very full skirt containing combs, pins, two pairs of men's pants, a shirt, five pounds of sugar and some army boots.

Pigott was imprisoned in the basement of a local house in New Bern (which can be seen today at the Jones House — it's a gift shop at Tryon Palace Historic Sites and Gardens). Stories differ on what happened next but she was released from prison and ended up returning to her family's farm where she remained until her death on May 26, 1919. Today, the family cemetery can be found at 20th Street and Emeline Place in Morehead City.

The History Place in Morehead City has an exhibit on Emeline Pigott that includes a trunk of her personal belongings and the carriage she was riding in at the time of her arrest. The Jack Spencer Goodwin Library is located within the museum and contains publications and an extensive picture file documenting the history of Carteret County, including genealogy materials and Civil War history collections. Information for this article was based on The History Place's Tarheel Junior Historian 48:1 (fall 2008).

sport-fishing boats at marinas in Swansboro. You can reach Swansboro by taking either N.C. 58 (from Bogue Banks) or N.C. 24 (from Morehead City).

From its origins as the site of an Algonquian Indian village to its current status as the "Friendly City by the Sea," Swansboro is a lovely place to visit because of its mild climate and friendly citizens.

The town began about 1730, when Jonathan and Grace Green moved to the area from Falmouth, Massachusetts. With them, and owning half of their property, was Jonathan Green's brother, Isaac. They lived there about five years until Jonathan Green died at the early age of 35. His widow, Grace, married Theophilus Weeks, who had moved with his family from Falmouth to settle on Hadnot Creek a few miles up the White Oak River.

After their marriage, the Weeks moved into the Green family home on the Onslow County side of the White Oak River. Theophilus soon purchased all of Isaac Green's interest and became sole owner of the large plantation. Weeks first farmed, then opened a tavern and was appointed inspector of exports at the thriving port. In 1771 he started a town on that portion of his plantation called Weeks Wharf, selling 48 numbered lots recorded as being "in the plan of a town laid out by Theophilus Weeks," thus earning him the title of founder of the town.

Originally called Weeks Point, the New-Town-upon-Bogue was established by law in 1783. The General Assembly named the town Swannsborough, in honor of Samuel Swann, former speaker of the N.C. House of Representatives and longtime Onslow County representative.

Swansboro (the later spelling of the town's name) was home to the famous Otway Burns. During the War of 1812, this native son became a privateer with his schooner, the *Snapdragon*. His participation during this "Second War of Independence" was acclaimed as an act of bravery and patriotism. After the war, he returned to the trade of shipbuilding and was later appointed keeper of the lighthouse at Portsmouth, where he died in 1850. He is buried in Beaufort's Old Burying Ground.

Swansboro's port continued to prosper, mainly because nearby pine forests produced the lumber, tar, pitch and other naval items shipped through the port. Prosperity continued until the end of the Civil War. Then, gradually, the town came to support itself with farming and fishing.

Swansboro features an historic downtown section built along the water's edge. Here you will find old structures, specialty and antiques shops, restaurants and plenty of space to stroll and gaze at the water and boats. The town's historic commission supervises the restoration of many of the town's oldest structures.

Down East

Down East is the local name for the land that stretches from the North River on the east side of Beaufort to Cedar Island, which marks Carteret County's northeastern boundary. Here you'll find picturesque scenery — marshes, canals and undisturbed places filled with wildlife, particularly as you get closer to Cedar Island. The portion of U.S. 70 that runs through Down East is a N.C. Scenic Byway, so designated by the N.C. Department of Transportation because it offers incomparable scenery and a chance to observe something different from the fast traffic and commercial areas along major interstates.

In the past, the livelihood of almost all Down East people depended on the water. Whether they made a living at commercial fishing, crabbing or boat building, people in this part of the county have a heritage tied to the water. Many still rely on the water to make a living, though more and more residents are finding employment in Beaufort or Morehead City or at the Marine Corps Air Station Cherry Point in Havelock. The love for the water remains obvious, however, by the number of boats, docks and fishing families found in Down East villages.

Currently no Down East community is incorporated, so the area is governed by Carteret County.

After leaving Beaufort on U.S. 70, **Bettie** is the first Down East community you reach. It lies between the North River Bridge and Ward's Creek Bridge. The next community is **Otway**, named for famous Swansboro privateer Otway Burns.

As you turn off U.S. 70 onto Harkers Island Road, **Straits** is the community you see flanking the road to **Harkers Island**. The Straits is also the name of the body of water that lies between the community and the island. The spelling of Straits is shown on early maps as "Straights." Later cartographers probably noticed the name was not applicable to a water course and changed the spelling to Straits, mean-

ing narrows. Years ago Straits was a farm community and a substantial amount of cotton was grown here. Straits United Methodist Church, c. 1778, was the first Methodist Church built east of Beaufort.

Originally called Craney Island, **Harkers Island** once was the home of a thriving tribe of Tuscarora Indians. By the turn of the twentieth century, all that remained of the Native American settlement was a huge mound of sea shells on the island's east end, now called **Shell Point**. Historians say the Native Americans were attempting to build a shell walkway through the waters of Core Sound to Core Banks. Standing at Shell Point today, you can see the Cape Lookout Lighthouse and nearby islands.

In 1730 George Pollock sold the island to Ebenezer Harker of Boston. Harker moved to the island and later divided it among his three sons, using the divisions "eastard," "westard" and "center." These have remained unofficial dividers, at least for the natives of the island. The Harker heirs did not part with their land for years, so the island population remained sparse for some time. In 1895 fewer than 30 families lived there. The population grew when folks from the Shackleford Banks community of Diamond City abandoned their town due to the devastation of hurricanes. Some loaded homes on boats and brought them to the safer ground of Harkers Island. With this new surge in population, schools, churches and businesses sprang up. Still, the island remained isolated until ferry operations began in 1926, with the ferry leaving from the island's west end and docking in the Down East community of Gloucester. A bridge to the island was built in 1941. Today, Harkers Island is home to the Core Sound Waterfowl Museum, the famous Core Sound Decoy Festival and the Cape Lookout National Park Visitor Center. See our Crystal Coast Attractions and Annual Events chapters for more information on these fascinating places and events.

As you leave Harkers Island and re-enter U.S. 70 headed east, **Smyrna** is the next Down East town. It was named in 1785 from a deed that conveyed 100 acres from Joseph Davis to Seth Williston. The land was on Smunar Creek, and the spelling was later changed to Smyrna.

Marshallberg is just off U.S. 70. Originally named Deep Hole Point, Marshallberg is built on a peninsula formed by Jarrett Bay and Core Sound. Folks say that clay was dug from the area and used to fill ramparts and cover easements at Fort Macon on Bogue Banks, leaving a large hole, thus the original name. It was later renamed for Matt Marshall, who ran the mailboat from Beaufort.

In 1880 W. Q. A. Graham established Graham Academy at the head of Sleepy Creek in Marshallberg. The school prepared its students for college, and students who didn't live in town stayed in the school's dormitories. Monthly board was about $5.50 per student, and the school's attendance in 1892 was 126. The academy was destroyed by fire in 1910.

Between Marshallberg and Straits is the small community of **Gloucester**, so named in the early 1900s by Capt. Joseph

Pigott for the Massachusetts town he loved. Back on U.S. 70 and a little way past Smyrna, you will find **Williston**, named for John Williston who was one of the area's first settlers. Williston has long been nicknamed "Beantown," though why is still a point of confusion. Some say it was because of the large quantities of beans grown in the community, and others say it was because residents had a reputation for loving to eat beans. The Williston United Methodist Church was built in 1883.

The village of **Davis** was settled by William T. Davis in the 1700s. People worked the water and the land to make a living. Farm crops, such as cotton and sweet potatoes, were taken by sailboat to Virginia to be sold or traded for flour, sugar and cloth. Davis residents were known as "Onion Eaters," either because of the number of green onions grown there or because Davis people simply liked onions. An Army camp was opened in Davis during World

Eastern North Carolina is defined by the water that surrounds it.

photo: Peter Doran

War II, and some of the old camp buildings remain along the water's edge.

Stacy is made up of two even smaller communities: Masontown and Piney Point. The post office was opened in 1885. Stacy Freewill Baptist Church is more than 100 years old.

Originally called Wit, **Sea Level** is still the fishing community it has always been. In 1706 the King of England granted Capt. John Nelson about 650 acres, with Nelson's Bay on the west and Core Sound on the east. That land is today's Sea Level. Sailors' Snug Harbor, the oldest charitable trust in America, opened a facility for retired Merchant Marines there in 1976. (The original facility of its type opened in 1833 on Staten Island.) The Snug Harbor center is now open to men and women from all walks of life. Taylor Extended Care Facility is a nursing home on Nelson's Bay. A satellite clinic of Carteret General Hospital operates alongside the nursing home.

U.S. 70 ends, or begins depending on how you look at it, in the township of **Atlantic**. This community was settled in the 1740s and was originally called Hunting Quarters. The first post office opened in 1880, and the name was changed to Atlantic. The community's nickname is Per, and old-timers refer to their home as Per Atlantic. In the 1930s progress arrived in the form of paved roads. Today, Atlantic is home to two of the East Coast's largest seafood dealers, Luther Smith & Son Seafood Company and Clayton Fulcher Seafood Company, as well as a 1,500-acre Marine Corps Outlying Landing Field.

From Atlantic, N.C. 12 takes travelers to **Cedar Island**, seemingly the end of the earth, where you'll find the North Carolina State ferry landing to Ocracoke Island and North Carolina's Outer Banks. Cedar Island was known by that name until two post

offices were established in the early 1900s. Then the east end of the island became known as Lola and the west end as Roe, each with its own post office and school. In the 1960s, the two post offices closed and a new one was opened. The whole island became known as Cedar Island again, but locals still use the old names. Some homes on the island date back to the 1880s.

Newport and Western Carteret County

Newport is known as "the town with old-fashioned courtesy." When traveling from Carteret County to New Bern on U.S. 70, it is the first incorporated town through which you pass. The town continues to grow as Morehead City gets larger and as Marine Corps Air Station Cherry Point in Havelock expands.

Chartered in 1866, Newport was first supported by logging, farming and fishing. Today, its nearly 4,000 residents work throughout the county and region. Newport is home to a development park on U.S. 70 and the National Oceanic Atmospheric Administration and National Weather Service's Weather Forecast Office that offers state-of-the-art weather tracking and forecasting. The town is situated beside Cherry Point Marine Corps Air Station.

Newport has many residential sections, an elementary school and a middle school, stores, a town hall and a public library. It is home to the popular Newport Pig Cooking Contest each April (see our Crystal Coast Annual Events chapter) and it boasts a strong volunteer fire department and rescue squad.

Northeast of Newport is the community of Mill Creek. This area continues to rely heavily on farming although many new homes are being built in the rural waterfront areas. Mill Creek can reached by driving through Newport or by approaching from N.C. 101 out of Beaufort.

Traveling west from Morehead City, N.C. 24 parallels Bogue Sound. The highway passes through several communities that dot this part of the county. **Broad**

> **i** *Out of the eight species of sea turtles found in the Indian, Pacific and Atlantic oceans, the coast of North Carolina sees five of these incredible marine reptiles: Leatherback, Atlantic Ridley, Green Turtle, Hawksbill and Loggerhead.*

Creek is an old community, once made up almost exclusively of commercial fishermen and their families. Some of these fishermen came to the area as long ago as 100 years; others came from Diamond City on Shackleford Banks after the devastating hurricanes forced them to vacate. Today, there is a middle school and much new residential development in the unincorporated town.

Ocean was once a thriving village with one of the county's first post offices. Now it is the home of the North Carolina Coastal Federation (a nonprofit conservation group that offers exciting excursions into the county's marsh and forest habitats) as well as an elementary school, a high school and many new developments. As you leave the unincorporated town of Ocean, the next little town is **Bogue**. With almost 600 residents, it was incorporated in a special election in September 1995 and now has a commissioner-mayor form of local government. The U.S. Marine Corps Auxiliary Landing Field is in Bogue.

At the junction of N.C. Highways 24 and 58 lie two communities: **Cedar Point** and **Cape Carteret**. Cedar Point (not to be confused with the Down East community of Cedar Island) is the westernmost incorporated town in Carteret County and the westernmost point of the county. The town was established in 1713 but not incorporated until 1988.

Chartered in 1959, Cape Carteret is one of the few planned communities in the county. The late W. B. McLean, one of the developers of Emerald Isle, initiated the town's development. In laying out "Cape C," McLean donated land for a Presbyterian church, a Baptist church and White Oak Elementary School. The first homes were built on the Bogue Sound waterfront near the foot of what is now the B. Cameron Langston Bridge, the high-rise bridge built in 1971 to replace the ferry. The town features stores, a town hall, fire and rescue departments, a school, a new library and community college annex.

If you turn right at the traffic light at the intersection of N.C. highways 24 and 58, you will go northwest on N.C. 58 through the Croatan National Forest and through several old settlements including **Peletier**, incorporated in 1997 and home to about 500 residents, the **Hadnot Creek** community and **Kuhn's Corner**. Kuhn's Corner marks the intersection that leads to **Stella**, a once-thriving village with stores, mills, a good many farmhouses and even a couple of large plantation houses. Traveling east on N.C. 58, you will cross the high-rise bridge that takes you to the beach town of Emerald Isle.

⌘ RESTAURANTS

The Crystal Coast proudly boasts of its boat-to-table seafood and why shouldn't it? This area is home to a blessed bounty of seafood year round. The fishing and seafood industries have been part of this area's history, heritage and economy for more than 400 years. Fresh from the sea, the local restaurants each have their own take on what happens next. Tasting the local delicacies — and how they're prepared — is a journey all its own here on the coast.

Getting to know a little bit about the area's culinary history gives more insight into the classic dishes (and the contemporary creations reminiscent of those classics) that may still be seen on menus today. Clam chowder, Down East light rolls, stewed hard crabs, collards and dumplings are the tastes and smells that speak of home in this area.

In the traditional waterfront restaurants, fried hush puppies are always served first and are a local cuisine tradition as well as a standard of quality. They are made with cornmeal, flour, eggs and sugar. Once blended, the mixture is dropped by the spoonful into hot fat and fried to a golden brown. Old-timers say the name derived from cooks who, while preparing meals, tossed bits of fried batter to quiet the dogs waiting for kitchen scraps.

Most natives were raised on conch and clam chowders, and even the newest eateries include these among their soups and appetizers. Local conch chowder is made with whelk, while traditional chowder is made with chopped seafood, water, butter, salt, pepper and diced potatoes. For a different flavor, some chefs might also add squash, onions and spices.

Peelers, pickers, jimmies, white bellies, hens, steamers, paper shells or softshells — no matter what you call them, they're still crabs. Learning the difference between the names and the stages of a crab's life is the hard part. Knowing when crabs are ready to shed and are marketable as soft-shells is important to the livelihood of many Crystal Coast crabbers. A peeler is a crab that will, if all goes well, become a soft crab within 72 hours. They are carefully handled and put in vats where they can go through this molting process. Jimmies are the large male crabs that measure 6 inches from upper shell tip to tip, and steamers or pickers are just regular crabs. The sure way to tell if a crab is a peeler is by the pinkish-red ring on the outer tip of the flipper or back fin. Those that complete the molting process are sold live or dressed. Many are packed with damp sea grass, refrigerated and shipped live to restaurants or seafood markets as far away as New York. Most are sold dressed, because live soft-shells are delicate to handle and have a life of only about three days. Insiders consider softshell crabs a delicacy, and favorite ways to prepare them include lightly frying them in batter or sautéing them in butter and wine.

Shrimp burgers, another popular local seafood treat, are little more than fried shrimp on a hamburger bun with slaw and special sauce. Each restaurant has its own sauce, which is the secret to a great shrimp burger. Some places have come up with variations (oyster burgers, clam burgers), but it's all basically put together the same way.

Collards are a traditional mainstay in the diet of most locals. A "mess" of collards cooking in the kitchen creates an unforgettable aroma that you either love or hate. These leafy green vegetables grow almost year round in this area.

Beyond seafood and traditional Southern local fare, rest assured that many area restaurants offer a nice selection of quality beef, poultry and vegetarian fare

Two Locations

2500 West Fort Macon Road	4560 Arendell Street
Atlantic Beach, NC 28512	Morehead City, NC 28557
252.726.9607	252.247.3119

The White Swan now has two locations, on Atlantic Beach they do catering services and take out orders with limited seating for dining in. With a more limited menu it is a great place to stop and feed the family and friends that want to get back to the sun and fun of the beach.

Morehead City White Swan offers take out orders as well as seating for about 100 guests. The menu offers a very popular seafood selection, fried or broiled. They also offer family style dining. They bring heaping bowls of your selection, allowing you and your friends to serve yourselves. It's all you can eat!

The White Swan has a long tradition of great food, friendly atmosphere at reasonable prices. Time after time The White Swan has been voted number one in food, and friendly staff. At the White Swan Restaurant you will find the prices very moderate and a good value for your dollar. The White Swan is a great place to bring you family and friends.

The White Swan menu features:
- North Carolina chopped pork barbeque
- Wet or dry pork ribs
- Barbequed chicken
- Fresh fried or broiled seafood
- A choice of country vegetables
- For the kids; hot dogs, hamburgers or chicken tenders

The award winning White Swan Catering Services can cater your next event for 50 guest or 1000 guests. They offer a very broad menu selection from the favorite pig picking to an elegant fare, White Swan can fit your needs and wants to your budget.

as well as contemporary cuisine denoting European, Caribbean and Latin influences. Area chefs are masters of their culinary art, presenting a wide array of delicious dishes, many of which are complemented by the fresh produce available from local farms.

This area is fortunate to have a wide variety of restaurants — from basic seafood to upscale gourmet. There are options for every taste and budget. Additionally, increasing numbers of fast-food and chain restaurants are springing up across the area. This guide does not review chain restaurants, under the assumption that you are already familiar with their fare. However, we do have a section at the end of this chapter on fast food — where we list some of the local eateries offering good, quick food.

Planning and Pricing

The Crystal Coast is a great dining destination that welcomes visitors and residents all year long but still retains seasonal peaks and valleys. When planning your dining experience, we recommend you call ahead to verify the information offered in these restaurant profiles and to check the hours or seating availability. While we intend to reflect each restaurant as accurately as possible, menu modifications do occur. Some area restaurants close during slow winter months or reduce their days and hours of operation. Those that remain open during the off season may limit their menu items to ensure freshness.

The serving of mixed drinks in North Carolina is regulated by the Alcohol Beverage Control Board. Restaurants designated as having "all ABC permits" can sell mixed drinks in addition to wine and beer. So it is best to ask what is offered when you call.

Dining out doesn't have to be expensive. Ask about any nightly specials the restaurant may be running. Many area restaurants also offer special discounts to early diners (particularly in the winter), and many have discounts for senior citizens and specially priced children's dinner menus.

Because of the large number of restaurants on the Crystal Coast and the limited space in this chapter, we refer you only to restaurants that continue to be favorites. There certainly are many more restaurants to choose from — check the local phone book, newspaper advertisements or ask around for other suggestions.

Restaurants are arranged alphabetically according to their location. We have given the mile marker (MM) number for those on N.C. Highway 58 on Bogue Banks to help you find them more easily. Most of the dinner establishments listed honor all major credit cards.

PRICE CODE

This price code will give you a general idea of the cost of dinner for two. Because entrees come in a wide range of prices, the code we use reflects an average cost of entrees, not the most expensive item or the least expensive item. For restaurants that do not serve dinner, the price code reflects the cost of lunch fare. Price code averages do not include appetizers, drinks, desserts, gratuity or the state's sales tax.

$	Less than $20
$$	$20 to $30
$$$	$31 to $40
$$$$	More than $40

Bogue Banks

ATLANTIC BEACH

Amos Mosquito's $$-$$$
Restaurant and Bar
MM 2, 703 N.C. Hwy. 58, Atlantic Beach
(252) 247-6222

Amos Mosquito's, known as Skeeter's to the locals, is designed to feel like nighttime on Shackleford Banks, with a "swampy" theme. Owners Hallock Howard, executive chef, and Sandy Howard, general manager, offer patrons reasonably priced dinners, simply presented and a treat to the palate. The kitchen strives for consistency in taste and the use of fresh, in-season vegetables and seafood. A typical dinner special is roasted whole red snapper for two accompanied by a trio of Thai dipping sauces. Other favorites include brown sugar–glazed meatloaf served with homemade smashed potatoes, slow-cooked pork ribs with sweet potato fries and the chef's incomparable crab cakes. Children are welcome at Amos Mosquito's. A special treat for them is s'mores: those old-fashioned chocolate, marshmallow and graham cracker concoctions. They are served in braziers so the kids can roast their own marshmallows while sitting at the table. (The staff cleans up the marshmallow mess.) Grown-ups generally prefer the melt-in-your-mouth homemade cheesecake and crème brûlée. The restaurant is open seven days a week during the season. Winter hours are shorter, so call first. Amos Mosquito's has a spacious patio for al fresco dining with a water view. The restaurant is a half-mile east of the Atlantic Beach stoplight.

Channel Marker Restaurant $$$
718 Atlantic Beach Cswy., Atlantic Beach
(252) 247-2344

Great food combined with great scenery makes this restaurant a local favorite. Channel Marker specializes in grilled fish and Black Angus beef. Overlooking Bogue Sound, the restaurant offers waterfront dining during dinner hours and has all ABC permits. House specialties include prime rib, grilled fish, land and sea combinations, seafood platters, steak-and-shrimp

kebabs and broiled lobster tails. The chef features unique specials each night and also prepares cold-plate entrees, grilled chicken breasts and stuffed flounder. Desserts include a large variety of homemade cheesecakes, crème brûlée and an award-winning double-fudge espresso cake. The dock in front of the restaurant is available for those arriving by boat, and the adjoining lounge (see our Nightlife chapter) has all permits and a large selection of liquor, wines and beers. The restaurant can accommodate banquets of up to 100. The restaurant and lounge are open every day, year round, for dinner. Lunch is served Saturday and Sunday during the summer. Channel Marker can also cater your event, everything from weddings to business functions, on site or off site.

Clam Digger Restaurant $$
511 Salter Path Rd., Atlantic Beach
(252) 247-4155

Open for breakfast, lunch and dinner, Clam Digger is a favorite of locals as well as visitors. You'll find fluffy omelets for breakfast along with French toast and other creative items. For lunch, enjoy a roast beef sandwich or cheeseburger or try a seafood creation. Dinner entrees include steaks and a variety of seafood, as well as pastas, chicken and pork. There is a special every evening — oysters on Monday, rib eye steak on Tuesday, three-

Private ferry services take passengers to South Core Banks and the Cape Lookout Lighthouse area.

photo: Peter Doran

McCurdy's
Restaurant & Deck
on Moonlight Bay

Great Food - Great View

505 Atlantic Beach Causeway
Atlantic Beach, NC
252-808-3663

www.mccurdysrestaurant.com

in season, so you can see the spectacular view, listen to the sound of waves and smell the aroma of salty ocean air. Crab's Claw offers catering for beach weddings, family reunions and other occasions. Call for off-season hours.

McCurdy's on Moonlight Bay $$$
505-A Atlantic Beach Cswy., Atlantic Beach
(252) 808-3663
www.mccurdysrestaurant.com

McCurdy's Restaurant & Deck, located on beautiful Moonlight Bay, offers an enticing dinner setting inside and out. Have a seat inside at the beautiful oak and tigerwood bar as you sip one (or more) of the 10 beers on tap, or choose a beer from their extensive list — it's huge. Can't decide? Try the beer sampler. You can dine inside, but we think a better choice is to enjoy your meal out on the covered deck while looking out on Moonlight Bay and taking in spectacular Atlantic Beach sunsets. McCurdy's uses fresh local fish prepared in a variety of ways, such as fresh-caught mahi mahi grilled over a live charcoal fire. Crab legs are also a favorite. Not a seafood fan? Not to worry. The dinner entrees also include in-house aged beef, pasta dishes, ribs and daily specials. Save room for the famous homemade desserts. McCurdy's offers a family-friendly atmosphere with a children's menu that is sure to please all of the kids. Often there is live entertainment during the season, and for you more nautical folks, feel free to come by boat — just call ahead to reserve one of their slips. McCurdy's has all ABC permits and a large variety of wines by the glass or by the bottle.

way seafood combination on Wednesday, shrimp on Thursday, flounder on Friday, chicken Parmesan on Saturday, and steak and shrimp on Sunday. Locals have the schedule memorized, and many enjoy the advantage of the take-out service. Clam Digger has all ABC permits and a large selection of wines and beers. The restaurant opens year round at 6:30 AM and closes at 9 PM.

Crab's Claw Restaurant $$
201 W. Atlantic Blvd., Atlantic Beach
(252) 726-8222

Crab's Claw is an oceanfront fine dining experience located in the heart of Atlantic Beach on the Boardwalk. The restaurant was established in 1997 and was recently featured in *Southern Living* magazine. The owners are both chefs and have a passion for the palate-pleasing experience. The chef prepares dishes with tender, loving care. Appetizers include such creations as Harkers Island little-neck clams, Caribbean curried shrimp, bacon-wrapped scallops and crab dip. Entrees include such treats as blackened tuna, grilled salmon, Cajun shrimp and chicken, crab cakes, steak, baby back ribs and seafood steamer pots. Patrons can enjoy a panoramic view of the Atlantic Ocean from the oceanfront deck and full-service steam bar. Crab's Claw has Atlantic Beach's only full-service oyster bar in season. Outside dining is available

Milazzo Italian Restaurant $$$
2710 W. Fort Macon Rd., Atlantic Beach
(252) 240-1155

Overlooking the ocean in Atlantic Beach, Milazzo Italian Restaurant features the area's most authentic Italian cuisine in a fun, family-oriented atmosphere. Milazzo Italian Restaurant specializes in Italian seafood and family-style dining and is open daily for breakfast, lunch and dinner. The lounge is cozy and offers a fantastic ocean view, an all-day dining menu, all ABC permits and an extensive wine list. Milazzo Italian Restaurant is located inside the

Sheraton Atlantic Beach Oceanfront Hotel and is open to the public.

Watermark Restaurant $$$
Atlantic Station Shopping Center,
MM 3, N.C. Hwy. 58, Atlantic Beach
(252) 240-2811

Insiders looking for a great piece of beef go to the Watermark. Open for dinner only, Watermark specializes in grilled certified Black Angus cuts. Fresh seafood is also offered grilled, fried, baked or panned in butter. With such good food, this restaurant is a very popular spot. However, seating is limited, so call for reservations. Watermark is open for dinner six days a week; the restaurant is closed on Tuesdays. There's live entertainment in season, so be sure to ask about the entertainment schedule.

White Swan Bar-B-Q & Fried Chicken $
2500-A W. Fort Macon Rd., Atlantic Beach
(252) 726-9607
www.whiteswanatlanticbeach.com

White Swan is well known for its eastern North Carolina pork barbecue, fried chicken, barbecue chicken and barbecue pork ribs. The restaurant is also known for excellent cole slaw and hush puppies, seasoned green beans, boiled potatoes, potato salad, baked beans and homemade Brunswick stew. Seating in the restaurant is limited, and take out orders are available. Just call ahead and your order will be ready. The catering service offered by White Swan has a broad selection of entrees, side items and hors d'oeuvre sure to meet your catering needs. Be it for 50 or 2,000 people, White Swan can meet your budget and catering needs. White Swan has been in business since 2004, and Randy and Lill Hingson own the local franchise. There are two convenient locations, one in Atlantic Beach and the newest location in Morehead City.

SALTER PATH

Carltons' Fine Dining $$$$
MM 11, N.C. Hwy. 58, Salter Path
(252) 808-3404

If you're looking for fine dining at the beach, head to Carltons'. This upscale restaurant has been offering delectable dinners in Salter Path since 2003. Dinner entrees focus mainly on steaks and local seafood, but you'll find vegetarian dishes as well as duck and lamb frequenting the menu, too. One of their specialties is an exceptional Maryland jumbo lump crab cake that's sure to become your favorite. The chocolate pudding cake, crème brûlée and Key lime pie are dessert favorites. The atmosphere at Carltons' is elegant yet casual. Carltons' is open year round, sometimes closing for a month or so during the winter, and reservations are suggested.

Frank and Clara's $$
Restaurant and Lounge
MM 11.5, N.C. Hwy. 58, Salter Path
(252) 247-2788

Next to the Salter Path Post Office, Frank and Clara's serves a variety of dinner choices that include fried or broiled seafood and steaks. Insider favorites are jumbo shrimp stuffed with crab meat, char-grilled rib eye or filet mignon, and flounder stuffed with your choice of crab and shrimp or scallops and oysters. Cheese and crackers are on the table to enjoy while you make your selections. Dinner entrees come with either a salad topped with homemade dressings or a cup of clam chowder or she crab soup; a choice of potato, wild rice or cole slaw; and hush puppies or rolls. Special entrees are available for senior citizens and children. Frank and Clara's is open year-round but open only on Friday and Saturday nights during the winter. Reservations are recommended in season.

EMERALD ISLE

Bushwackers Restaurant $$-$$$
100 Bogue Inlet Dr., Emerald Isle
(252) 354-6300

Bushwackers, at Bogue Inlet Pier, is known for its fun wait staff, spectacular oceanfront view and adventurous decor. It is a favorite dinner spot for fresh seafood prepared in a variety of ways, including grilled, blackened, broiled and steamed, all served with a nice variety of fresh vegetables. There are also steaks and inventive pastas and ribs. The appetizer menu is extensive, including gator bites, calamari and a blooming onion. Entrees feature fresh seafood, chicken, char-grilled Angus steaks, prime rib and more. Bushwackers has all ABC permits, serves beer and has an expanding wine selection. The island adventure opens for dinner every night during the season, and winter hours vary.

El Zarape $-$$
8802 Reed Dr., Emerald Isle
(252) 354-1120

El Zarape offers tasty Mexican food at affordable prices. From enchiladas and tacos to shrimp burritos and an array of house specialties, El Zarape brings the taste of Mexico to the old South. There are so many good things to choose from, it's hard to recommend just one. A couple of words of advice: Don't fill up on the freshly cooked tortilla chips and salsa that arrive first, and remember to save room for dessert. El Zarape restaurants are also located in Beaufort and Morehead City.

RuckerJohns Restaurant $$$
Emerald Plantation Shopping Ctr.,
MM 20, N.C. Hwy. 58, Emerald Isle
(252) 354-2413

Bring the whole family to RuckerJohns to enjoy great food in a casual, contemporary atmosphere. Dinner entrees, prepared to order, include fresh seafood, pasta, barbecue shrimp, ribs, steaks, chicken and pork chops. Favorite appetizers include fried calamari, hot crab dip and chicken wings. For lunch, try the grilled Cajun chicken salad, the spinach salad with hot bacon-honey mustard dressing, any of the juicy burgers or a creative sandwich. Or opt for a grilled pizza in distinct flavor combinations. In the warmer months, have lunch on the sunny outdoor patio. Be sure to save room for fresh homemade cakes and cheesecakes for dessert. The lounge (see our Nightlife chapter) is a cozy gathering place enjoyed by the local population, especially on winter nights when there's a crackling fire in the fireplace. RuckerJohns is open for lunch and dinner every day.

 Carteret Catch is a program to sustain the livelihood and heritage of the Carteret County fishing industry. Many of the local restaurants are members.

Beaufort

Aqua Restaurant $$-$$$$
114 Middle Ln., Beaufort
(252) 728-7777
www.aquaexperience.com

Aqua's menu brings you the freshest seasonal items available, all presented with a creative touch. Aqua's small plates offer an exciting array of tastes in "just right" portions that are ideal for sharing or enjoying two or three as a full meal. Aqua's big plates feature choice beef and fresh North Carolina seafood as well as local produce when seasonally available. Aqua is proud to support the local fishermen and farmers. The menu changes frequently and that adds to the excitement of dining at Aqua. You might start your meal with a delicious Caesar salad, fried sesame chicken over arugula or possibly fried goat's cheese over organic greens. For your next course, try a coconut grilled tiger shrimp kebab or jumbo lump crab meat gratinée with Asiago cream, spinach and toasted crostini. And for dessert, enjoy bananas foster, cappuccino mousse or their sinful crème brûlée. Aqua offers an extensive wine and martini list and has all ABC permits. Also try Aqua's food and wine pairing menus. Monthly, the chef pairs four courses from the menu with four half-glasses of wine to give you the ultimate food and wine pairing experience. Friday is Wine Lovers' Night with 33 percent off all bottled wines on their list plus appetizers at the bar until 7 PM. Not a wine drinker? Opt for $5 martinis that night! Aqua is nestled behind Clawson's Restaurant and is open Tuesday through Saturday for dinner. Aqua is a favorite of locals and visitors to the area, so reservations are suggested.

The Beaufort Grocery Co. $$$-$$$$
117 Queen St., Beaufort
(252) 728-3899

Located between Front and Ann streets, you'll find the feel of a country French bistro right in the historic district of Beaufort. At Beaufort Grocery Co. everything served is exquisite, and the service is professional and friendly. Favorite lunch choices might include a

Cobb or Indo Asian Salad or one of their board specials. Their sandwiches are worth trying just for their names alone — the Fuhgeddaboudit, Sumpin's Jumpin' or how about the Sonnamabeach? Dinner starts with such appetizers as seafood burritos, fabulous Carolina crab cakes, or assorted Down East dips and spreads, such as the restaurant's signature pimiento cheese with candied walnuts, pickled Granny Smith apples and Lavosh crackers. Diners may choose entrees of fresh local seafood, choice steaks, chicken, veal and lamb. Each is served with fresh vegetables and delicious breads baked daily. Insiders suggest the grilled pork chop stuffed with fresh mozzarella, roasted tomatoes and pesto with a Marsala demi-glace. Top off your meal with pecan pie or any other dessert, because they are all made on the premises and all are delicious. Beaufort Grocery Co. offers Sunday Brunch, a take-out menu and a full delicatessen with meats, cheeses, homemade salads and breads. Private dining facilities are next door at 115 Queen Street. Beaufort Grocery Co. can cater any event on or off premise for 10 up to 1,000 people. The restaurant has all ABC permits. They close on Tuesdays. Otherwise, it's full speed ahead. Dinner reservations are recommended.

Blue Moon Bistro $$$
119 Queen St., Beaufort
(252) 728-5800

Blue Moon Bistro offers upscale casual dining in a relaxed, historic setting in Beaufort. It's not considered fine dining because there are no coats and ties needed here, but the food, service and experience would make you think otherwise. Offering a laid-back atmosphere, the Blue Moon concentrates on quality food, drinks and service. Dinners are prepared from scratch daily and vary depending on the season and the chef's preparation for the day. You'll always find the best fish, shellfish, poultry and steaks around town. To start your meal, enjoy Blue Moon's mixed green salad with seasonal garnish. Appetizers might include lamb chops, pork pot stickers with tamari-ginger dipping sauce, or seared sea scallops. Entrees change often and could feature Angus rib eye, veal tenderloin with Yukon

Gold mashed potatoes, or locally caught seafood. Guests can also enjoy outstanding soups and a variety of salads. Room for dessert? While the Blue Moon dessert list changes, past favorites have included cheesecake, crème brûlée trio, chocolate torte and fluffy pound cake with fruit. Blue Moon is open for dinner Monday through Saturday in season, and Tuesday through Saturday in the winter months. Reservations are recommended.

Boardwalk Cafe $-$$
510 Front St., Beaufort
(252) 728-0933

Boardwalk Cafe is a wonderful place to have great food in a relaxed atmosphere while learning about the area's history and enjoying the waterfront view. Open at 7 AM, breakfast offerings include waffles, eggs, pancakes, bacon, sausage and more. There's a $1.99 breakfast option and a heart-healthy menu section, too. Lunch is served through 4 PM and features sandwiches, seafood and hamburgers, along with wonderful salads and much more. The cafe serves dinner in the summer with a menu of beef, fish, seafood of all kinds, pastas, salads and homemade soups. An Insider favorite is the creamy clam chowder. The weekend breakfast buffet is served Saturday and Sunday from 7 to 11 AM. Whether you dine inside overlooking the water or outside on the boardwalk, you will enjoy it all. Open every day during the summer, Boardwalk Cafe has a nice selection of beers and wines, all ABC permits, and one great Bourbon pecan pie. Boardwalk features live music Friday and Saturday nights during the summer. They also offer on-site and off-site catering services.

Clawsons 1905 Restaurant & Pub $$
429 Front St., Beaufort
(252) 728-2133
www.clawsonsrestaurant.com

Clawson's 1905 is a favorite destination of Insiders and visitors throughout the day and throughout the year. Clawson's has received recommendations from *Frommer's*, *Fodor's*, and *Traveler Magazine*. An architectural focal point in the middle of downtown, Clawson's 1905 is housed in what was Clawson's General Store back in the early 1900s. While you are there, check out their T-shirts or other Clawson's-branded merchandise, proceed to the living room and catch up with the world according to CNN or watch the big game in HD on their 50-inch Plasma TVs. Then move on to the pub and choose from one of their eight different beers on draft or from the best bottled beer selection in town. Clawson's specializes in North Carolina–crafted brews. Or if you wish, you can be seated upstairs or down for lunch or dinner. Lunch favorites include a long list of sandwiches and burgers and the Dirigible —a hearty baked potato stuffed with seafood, vegetables and meats. Appetizers include seared tuna, seafood creations and more. Dinner always offers fresh seafood, zesty ribs, steaks, chicken and pasta. Whether for lunch or dinner, Clawson's Seafood Bisque is extraordinary and is, singularly, worth a trip to Beaufort. Private banquet facilities are available, and Down East FolkArts Society concerts are performed here in the off-season. Clawson's is open year-round Monday through Saturday for lunch and dinner. From Memorial Day through Labor Day, Clawson's is open on Sunday for dinner. Clawson's gets crowded during the summer months, so reservations are suggested. No matter — it's worth the wait.

El Zarape $-$$
1700 Live Oak St., Beaufort
(252) 504-2004

El Zarape offers tasty Mexican food at affordable prices. From enchiladas and tacos to shrimp burritos and an array of house specialties, El Zarape brings the taste of Mexico to the old South. There are so many good things to choose from, it's hard to recommend just one. A couple of words of advice: Don't fill up on the freshly cooked tortilla chips and salsa that arrive first, and remember to save room for dessert. El Zarape restaurants are also located in Emerald Isle and Morehead City.

Finz Grill $$-$$$
330 Front St., Beaufort
(252) 728-7459

Finz is the perfect place to relax, enjoy good food and visit with friends in a casual atmosphere. Guests may arrive by water or land and are seated inside or on the back porch over Taylor's Creek. The lunch and dinner menus offer sandwiches, burgers, soups (clam chowder is a favorite) and fresh baskets of fried fish. You'll also find crab cakes and oyster burgers and shrimp burgers. Dinner focuses on seafood, especially fresh shrimp and scallops and fish that can be grilled, blackened or fried. Specialties include crab cakes, hot crab dip, spiced triggerfish and Mediterranean fajitas. Steaks and pasta dishes and chef's features are also options. Finz has great homemade desserts, all ABC permits and serves lunch and dinner every day. Finz is closed on Tuesdays off-season; call for winter hours.

Fish Tales at Town Creek Marina
232 W. Beaufort Rd., Beaufort
(252) 504-7263
www.fishtalesattowncreek.com

Steve and Chuck Tulevech, owners of Town Creek Marina, felt there was no better tribute to the boating haven that Beaufort has become than a boathouse-inspired restaurant, and that's exactly why they've poured their hearts and souls into with Fish Tales Waterfront Restaurant. Fish Tales offers genuine hospitality and a place to gather to tell the stories (or perhaps tall tales) of your day at sea. The menu offers the Fish Tales twist on a variety of seafood, chicken and other dishes, guaranteeing something for everyone. Come enjoy the simple, coastal Carolina–inspired fare, unmatched service and endless big fish stories. Open for lunch or dinner, Fish Tales offers patio dining and is family friendly. Enjoy local entertainment on the weekends.

Front Street Grill at Stillwater $$$-$$$$
300 Front St., Beaufort
(252) 728-4956

Front Street Grill at Stillwater is considered one of the premier restaurants on the North Carolina coast. Starters might include such dishes as crispy calamari with ginger aioli, crab spring rolls with plum sauce, baked oysters and goat cheese salad. Favorite dinner entrees focus on fresh seafood and prime choice meats. The lunch menu offers guests large salads, soups, sandwiches and daily seafood specials. All breads and desserts are baked in house. The restaurant's location on the Beaufort waterfront offers spectacular views. The outdoor bar area is called the Rhum Bar, which is perfect for an evening relaxing at the water's edge. The restaurant has all ABC permits and serves lunch, dinner and a Sunday brunch that is not to be missed. Reservations are highly recommended for dinner; however, walk-in guests are welcome. Come by car or boat.

The Net House Restaurant $$$
133 Turner St., Beaufort
(252) 728-2002

If you ask where to go for seafood, many Beaufort residents will send you to The Net House. Just across the street from the Beaufort Historic Site, The Net House specializes in steamed shellfish and broiled and lightly battered fried seafood. Guests enjoy an atmosphere of weathered pine and nautical antiques at this family-owned eatery. Try the Down East clam chowder, she-crab soup or creamy seafood bisque as a dinner appetizer. Dinner focuses on fresh seafood. Local favorites include the fried, overstuffed soft-shell crab and the broiled grouper Dijon. The Net House is also known for its famous Key lime pie. No reservations are taken, but the line starts early. Hours vary according to the season, so call ahead.

No Name Pizza & Subs $
408 Live Oak St., Beaufort
(252) 728-4978

No Name is a great place for pizza and subs (everything from meatball to vegetarian), burgers and spaghetti with meatballs. The Greek salad is loaded with feta cheese and served with a loaf of garlic bread. No Name serves pasta dishes, Greek dishes, sandwiches and chicken. The baklava is a must-have. No Name offers dine-in or drive-through service and is open seven days.

Ribeyes Steakhouse $$-$$$
509 Front St., Beaufort
(252) 728-6105

Ribeyes is a favorite destination in Beaufort. Located on Front Street, the steakhouse offers customers choice Omaha brand grain-fed beef (you guessed

Some things you will see only along the coast.

photo: Carolyn Temple

it, only rib eyes served here), boneless chicken breasts and pork chops. Their seafood includes salmon, tuna and shrimp. Everything here is grilled, not fried, and comes with a fresh salad bar. Entrees also come with a choice of a baked potato or a sweet potato. Manager Mike Lavoy personally takes your order and ensures the meat is cooked to order. Ribeyes has a wonderful lounge and bar area, completed with wide-screen televisions and frequent entertainment. With all ABC permits, Ribeyes offers nightly drink specials. A take-out service is available, as is the use of The Angus Room, which accommodates small and medium-size groups for all types of occasions. The restaurant opens for dinner every night of the week.

Royal James Cafe $
117 Turner St., Beaufort
(252) 728-4573

The Royal James Cafe has a character all its own that keeps people coming back again and again. It offers a simple line of quality fast food, including shrimp burgers, steamed shrimp and Down East clam chowder. The signature sandwich is a 90/10 lean double cheeseburger with secret chili sauce. With an early '50s Formica, wood and neon look, this cafe and pool room has been favorably mentioned in editorial publications from the *Atlanta Constitution-Journal* to *Southern Living*. It draws an interesting mix of locals and tourists, families and singles, and has hours from 9 AM until last call every day except Sunday, when it is open from noon to 7 PM. Sue and Ed Book are celebrating 26 years of ownership in 2009.

The Spouter Inn $$-$$$
218 Front St., Beaufort
(252) 728-5190

A sign with a whale spouting (thus the "Spouter Inn") marks the Front Street entrance to this intimate dining establishment, which is over the water and offers a panoramic view of Beaufort Inlet and Taylor's Creek. The Spouter Inn restaurant offers fresh local seafood, just off the boat.

The lunch menu offers a unique selection of sandwiches, soups, salads and pastas. Sunday Brunch specials include seafood omelets, quiche, eggs Benedict and eggs Orleans. Dinner is as enticing with plenty of seafood. The sesame-seared tuna with a soy glaze, wasabi aioli and pickled ginger is a favorite, but the maple-bourbon barbecue ribs are tempting as well. Fresh-baked breads and desserts are prepared in the restaurant's bakery. The Spouter Inn has a waterfront deck and boat dock; you can come by land or sea. Dinner reservations are recommended. The restaurant is open daily during the summer months. Call for hours during the off-season.

Morehead City

A Taste of Italy $$$
4466 Arendell St., Morehead City
(252) 222-0166

A Taste of Italy offers a real treat — authentic Italian food and continental cuisine right here on the Crystal Coast. Dinner is served with homemade pasta and breads. While there's a variety of options on the menu, many return visitors come back time and time again for the veal you can cut with a fork. As members of Carteret Catch, they offer fresh seafood dishes as well. On- and off-premise catering is available. The restaurant is open for dinner most evenings in season, but it's best to call and check. Winter times vary.

Beach Bumz Pub & Pizzeria $
515 Arendell St., Morehead City
(252) 726-7800

Beach Bumz Pub & Pizzeria is a fun, casual spot with a low-key, coastal decor. Located at the corner of Sixth and Arendell streets, it's not far from the waterfront and is a favorite stop for specialty and build-your-own pizzas. Beach Bumz also offers paninis, burgers, subs, calzones, pasta and more. The warm, extra-thin homemade sea salt chips are available as a side or appetizer and come with a signature dipping sauce that makes them

See this entire guide plus additional content online at insiderinfo.us

irresistible. There's a nice selection of beer, and drafts come served in a mason jar. Beach Bumz is open for lunch and dinner Monday through Saturday and take-out orders are available.

Bistro-By-the-Sea $$$
**4031 Arendell St., Morehead City
(252) 247-2777**

Bistro-By-the-Sea, or as locals call it, The Bistro, is a favorite for both food and hospitality. Regulars love the friendly service, excellent cuisine and distinctive presentations at The Bistro. Enjoy wonderful dinner entrées prepared using fresh vegetables, seafood and tasty cuts of beef. Seafood entrees vary nightly according to freshness and availability. In addition to seafood specialties, locals recommend the char-grilled filet mignon or prime rib or the liver in orange liqueur. We also like the pasta creations. The Bistro offers the freshest of seafoods and is a Carteret Catch participant. They also offer sushi and Japanese bento boxes. A favorite dessert is the mocha ice cream pie. Bistro

By The Sea is open for dinner Tuesday through Saturday and takes the month of January off. Limited reservations may be made for parties of six or more.

Cafe Zito $$$-$$$$
**105 S. 11th St., Morehead City
(252) 726-6676**

Café Zito is a dynamic restaurant serving a fusion of local and Mediterranean cuisine created by Jennifer Kelley and Baptist Knaven. Café Zito has become a local favorite, providing intriguing and excellent food inspired by the best local, seasonal products. Dinner specialties include local organic filet mignon, moussaka, duck breast, grilled lamb and fresh fish specials based on the day's catch. A customer favorite is the Shrimp-Clamzito — little neck clams, shrimp, tomatoes, capers and kalamata olives served over homemade fettuccine. Another favorite is the Parmesan fried olives. Café Zito also offers a creative tapas menu with such features as flatbread pizzas, grilled scallops and stuffed calamari. The restaurant offers a

Shrimp dinners start here.

photo: Peter Doran

wonderful wine list specializing in Mediterranean wines as well as a nice selection of imported beers, ports, sherries and dessert wines. All the desserts served here are homemade and wonderful. Located in the restored historic Bell-Phillips House, the restaurant offers dining inside or on the porch. Patrons will enjoy the personal attention of the owners, who are on hand to ensure a fine dining experience. Café Zito is open for dinner at 5:30 PM; call for more information about opening times. On- and off- premises catering, cooking classes and group lunches can be arranged by reservation.

California Roll Cafe $-$$
909-B Arendell St., Morehead City
(252) 240-1364

If you enjoy fresh sushi, creative salads, soups and nigiri, California Roll is the only place for you. Open for lunch and dinner, this cafe is a local favorite in downtown Morehead City. The menu features a large selection of sushi rolls, including traditional favorites as well as a nice selection of deluxe sushi rolls with a contemporary touch. Try the Caribbean coconut spiced roll, the smokin' eel roll or the wakame tuna roll off the deluxe menu. The cafe also offers a nice vegetarian selection, too. Kids won't be left out; they can have a corn dog or PBJ roll served sushi style. Having a party? Consider a sushi platter or hire a sushi chef to prepare just what your guests would like. California Roll is open Monday through Saturday and is closed Tuesday evenings. Seasonal hours may vary.

Capt. Bill's Waterfront $$-$$$
Restaurant
701 Evans St., Morehead City
(252) 726-2166

Capt. Bill's is the oldest restaurant in Carteret County and it actually sits on pilings over the beautiful waters of Bogue Sound. The restaurant's origins go back to The Atlantic Cafe, which Headen Ballou (later known as Capt. Bill) opened on the corner of Arendell and Ninth Streets in 1938. One year later, he moved his restaurant down the street to the block between Seventh and Eighth Streets (still on Arendell Street) and reopened his restaurant naming it the Morehead Cafe. In 1941,

Mr. Ballou purchased Piner's Fish House on the Morehead City Waterfront and converted the fish house into a restaurant , which he called The Waterfront Cafe and Fish Market. He later changed the name to Capt. Bill's Waterfront Restaurant.

Today owners John and Diane Poag continue to operate a family business. Here you will find fresh local seafood, homemade desserts and wonderful views of the waterway. Dinners begin with such appetizers as homemade hot crab dip or buffalo shrimp, she crab soup or Core Sound clam chowder, or a salad. Entrees highlight seafood — sautéed, baked, broiled, fried or grilled — as well as steaks and chicken dishes. Lunch specials are featured each day. A local favorite is the famous conch stew served each Wednesday and Saturday. Dessert favorites are the Down East Lemon Pie and the 12-inch Hot Fudge Sundae. Capt. Bill's is open daily for lunch and dinner and offers a good selection of beer and wine. They also cater events or host special occasions in their waterfront banquet room.

CC Ralwiggies $-$$
3710 Arendell St., Morehead City
(252) 240-8646

CC Ralwiggies is the place to go for a feel-good, and good for you, lunch. Described as a Vegetarian Playground, this is the place to go for healthy foods. Guests can enjoy a 50-plus item salad bar filled with fresh veggies and more, plus wonderful homemade soups, which vary daily. Fresh breads, a potato bar and fresh fruit and soy milk smoothies are also offered. Chef Toni Oberci and her staff offer a full take-out service with salad platters, hot soups, salad by the pound and platters for events of all types, and they can cater any occasion. Everything prepared is MSG free because, as the menu states — "You are what you eat. Be great!"

Cold Stone Creamery $
4820 Arendell St., Morehead City
(252) 808-2653

For the "Ultimate Ice Cream Experience," it has to be Cold Stone Creamery. The first Cold Stone in the nation opened in 1988, and the Morehead City store is now satisfying the ice cream needs of the

Crystal Coast. The store serves decadent ice cream, ice cream cakes, shakes and smoothies, and offers nuts, fruit and candies to individualize your "creation." Cold Stone's wonderful ice cream and your choice of blend-ins are mixed on its signature frozen granite stone. The store offers gift cards and new to-go containers that can handle up to six servings.

El Zarape $-$$
**4138 Arendell St., Morehead City
(252) 808-2233
Cypress Bay Plaza,
5167 U.S. Hwy. 70 W., Morehead City
(252) 808-3700**

El Zarape offers tasty Mexican food at affordable prices. From enchiladas and tacos to shrimp burritos and an array of house specialties, El Zarape brings the taste of Mexico to the old South. There are so many good things to choose from, it's hard to recommend just one. A couple of words of advice: Don't fill up on the freshly cooked tortilla chips and salsa that arrive first, and remember to save room for dessert. El Zarape restaurants are also located in Beaufort and Emerald Isle.

Floyd's 1921 Restaurant & Bar $$$
**400 Bridges St., Morehead City
(252) 727-1921**

Floyd's 1921 offers creative and tasteful lunch and dinner items. Located in the historic Joseph C. Long house, it's easy to feel right at home in the cozy setting. The lunch menu offers salads, sandwiches and old Southern fixins', as they say, such as High Cotton Crab Cakes, fried chicken, Low-Country Meatloaf, and shrimp and grits. An Insider favorite is the fried oysters and mango spinach salad. Dinner sandwiches and salads are offered, along with a wonderful entree selection ranging from fresh seafood, meats and poultry. Homemade salad dressings and desserts complete an unforgettable dining experience.

Hooters of Morehead City $$
**5050 U.S. Hwy. 70 W., Morehead City
(252) 727-1803**

Hooters has opened a restaurant here on the coast. Like the others in this chain, the restaurant specializes in clams, wings,

shrimp and oyster roasts and is staffed by the "nearly famous Hooters girls."

Kabuto Japanese Steakhouse $$
and Sushi Bar
**5308 U.S. Hwy. 70, Morehead City
(252) 222-3111**

Kabuto has restaurants throughout the state, offering Japanese dishes and a full sushi menu. This restaurant opens for dinner every day of the week to greet guests with a wonderful selection of freshly prepared soups, salads, creative entrees and sushi. Enjoy a hibachi dish prepared right in front of you by a fun, friendly and talented chef. Private party facilities and gift certificates are available. Reservations are accepted.

Kountry Kitchen $-$$
**5380 U.S. Hwy. 70, Unit 1, Morehead City
(252) 240-0046**

Kountry Kitchen offers full breakfast, lunch and dinner menus and is sure to please with new dishes as well as long-time favorites. Kick off the day with a breakfast of eggs, homemade biscuits, grits, waffles, hot cakes and meats. You can even get sausage gravy and fried bologna here. The lunch/dinner menu is available starting at 11 AM. Enjoy burgers, subs, steaks, seafood and fresh vegetables, or try one of the outstanding daily specials. The special might be baked ham, pork chops or a Friday favorite of a fish sandwich and chowder. Kountry Kitchen opens at 6 AM each morning and remains open until 8 PM Monday through Thursday, until 9 PM Friday through Saturday and until 3 PM on Sunday.

Mrs. Culpepper's Crab Cafe $-$$
**5370 U.S. Hwy. 70, Morehead City
(252) 240-1960**

Mrs. Culpepper's Crab Cafe offers wonderful Thai cuisine and fresh seafood in a relaxed diner-type atmosphere. For lunch or dinner, enjoy crab cakes, oysters, shrimp, soft crabs or scallops. You'll also find such creations as pork with ginger, spicy beef with basil, Pad Thai, and oysters with bean sprouts. A favorite is the sampler where you select two or three items served with jasmine rice and a spring roll.

Mrs. Culpepper's also offers retail sales of the uncooked crab cakes that made this place famous. You can also take home fresh shrimp, soft shell and hard crabs, and crab and pork spring rolls. The cafe is open for lunch Tuesday through Saturday, and for dinner Tuesday and Thursday through Saturday.

Mrs. Willis' Restaurant   **$$**
3114 Bridges St., Morehead City
(252) 726-3741

Mrs. Willis' Restaurant has been serving home-cooked meals since 1949. The restaurant actually began in the home of "Ma" Willis as a barbecue and chicken take-out place specializing in mini lemon pies. Customers ate right in the kitchen. In 1956 the restaurant moved into the garage, which is the front of today's restaurant, and additions have been made through the years. We recommend the clam chowder for starters and then the prime rib — for the money, it's one of the best around. Other entrees include the seafood combination plate, chicken livers, pork chops, hamburger steak, stuffed flounder, rib eyes, frog legs, grilled fish, chicken and roast beef. You'll also find plenty of fresh vegetables. Mrs. Willis' offers specials every day and night and accommodates groups of any size. Lunch is served Sunday through Friday and dinner is served seven days a week. The restaurant is open year round.

New Dawn Restaurant   **$-$$**
3010 Arendell St., Morehead City
(252) 726-7472

New Dawn Family Restaurant is a great place for breakfast and lunch. Breakfast is served from 6 AM throughout the day and offers a full menu that includes fresh eggs, locally made sausage

The History Place, the North Carolina Maritime Museum and the Core Sound Waterfowl Museum, in addition to area bookstores and shops, are among the great places to find local cookbooks that bring Crystal Coast cuisine to your kitchen.

and country ham from the N.C. mountains. There's also a build-your-own omelet option. The lunch menu offers an outstanding selection of appetizers, steaks, local seafood and salads. Insider favorites include the oyster po'boy, Maryland-style crab cakes and baby back ribs. New Dawn offers a private party room capable of accommodating 40 to 50 people, and it offers on-site and off-site catering for parties of all sizes.

On A Roll Gourmet Deli   **$**
907 Arendell St., Morehead City
(252) 726-5101

On A Roll starts the day early — at 6 AM — serving breakfast and lunch every day. Breakfast is also served all day on Saturday and Sunday. Breakfast entrees include the favorites of eggs, ham, toast and grits. Enjoy hotcakes, corned beef hash and buttermilk pancakes. Lunches include sandwiches, wraps and more. Try an Italian hoagie with prosciutto, capicola and provolone cheese, or a Jewish hoagie with corned beef, salami, cole slaw and Russian dressing. Favorites include Reubens, burgers, liverwurst and onions, Cubans and paninis. You'll also find Greek and Caesar salads, cold tuna and chicken salad plates, and corned beef specials. On A Roll also offers a full catering service. Closing hours are at 2:30 PM every day except Sunday when they close at 2 PM.

Sanitary Fish Market & Restaurant   **$$**
501 Evans St., Morehead City
(252) 247-3111

Sanitary is a landmark on the Morehead City waterfront. In 1938 Ted Garner and Tony Seamon, both now deceased, opened a waterfront seafood market in a building rented for $5.50 per week, The name Sanitary Fish Market was chosen by the partners to project their compliance with sanitary seafood handling. When 12 stools were set up at the counter, the first seafood restaurant on the city's waterfront was in business. Today's customers find old favorite menu items along with many new additions. Best known for fresh seafood served broiled, steamed, grilled or fried, the Sanitary also offers steaks, poultry and pasta entrees. Lunch always includes a good selection of vegetables and attracts lots of locals. The Sanitary offers a good selection of beer and wine, and lunch and dinner are served every day of the week. The restaurant closes the Sunday after Thanksgiving and reopens the first Friday in February.

Shepard's Point $$-$$$
913 Arendell St., Morehead City
(252) 727-0815

From the crimson walls to the checkerboard floors, Shepard's Point has an urban flair in ambiance and in its cuisine. Shepard's Point is an uptown steak and seafood house in the heart of downtown with a bar specializing in martini cocktails that are second to none. An exposed cellar offers a glimpse of extensive wine selections from around the world, and you can view the chefs in the open kitchen preparing your meal. All breads are baked from scratch daily. Fresh local seafood is the specialty of the house, plus there are ever-evolving entrees that include beef, chicken and pork dishes. The restaurant has added lunch hours this year in addition to adding sandwiches and salads to the menu. Shepard's Point offers affordable dinner specials most nights, which change to reflect the local seafood and produce so there's always something interesting to try. In the spring and summer you may find deep-fried squash blossoms stuffed with ricotta, and in the fall you may find specialties revolving around oysters and collards. Shepard's Point continues its two-for-one specials on Mondays, prime rib specials on Thursdays, free sushi on Fridays until 7 PM and half-price martinis on Saturdays. Private dining rooms are available for up to 90 people. Smoking is permitted in the bar only. On Sundays, a brunch buffet from 11 AM to 2 PM is the order of the day. Shepard's Point is an offshoot from Beaufort Grocery Co., and dinner reservations are recommended.

White Swan Bar-B-Q & Fried Chicken $
4650 Arendell St., Morehead City
(252) 247-3119
www.whiteswanatlanticbeach.com

With an already popular business in Atlantic Beach, White Swan has just opened a new location in Morehead City that offers all of the same Southern favorites. White Swan is well known for its eastern North Carolina pork barbecue, fried chicken, barbecue chicken and barbecue pork ribs. The restaurant is also known for excellent cole slaw and hush puppies,

Want to catch your own game fish dinner? Hire a charter boat to take you offshore fishing.

photo: Peter Doran

seasoned green beans, boiled potatoes, potato salad, baked beans and homemade Brunswick stew. The catering service offered by White Swan has a broad selection of entrees, side items and hors d'oeuvre sure to meet your catering needs. Be it for 50 or 2,000 people, White Swan can meet your budget and catering needs. White Swan has been in business since 2004, and Randy and Lill Hingson own the local franchise.

Swansboro

Capt. Charlie's Restaurant   **$$-$$$**
N.C. Hwy. 24 at 106 Front St., Swansboro
(910) 326-4303

Capt. Charlie's Restaurant specializes in fresh seafood, prime rib and steaks. The traditional menu offers lots of lightly breaded fried seafood, although there are plenty of other choices. Try the stuffed flounder or broiled shrimp and scallops. The steaks have an enormous following too. The desserts here vary and are all wonderful. Well-prepared foods served in ample amounts bring people back to Capt. Charlie's again and again. Have a drink in the lounge while you wait for your table. Capt. Charlie's has all ABC permits and is open for dinner seven nights a week in the summer and every day but Monday in the off season.

Church Street Coffee, Deli   **$**
and Irish Pub
105 Church St., Swansboro
(910) 326-7572

Tucked away on the historic Swansboro waterfront, Church Street Coffee, Deli and Irish Pub began as the first coffee shop in the area, expanded to a deli in 1997, and further expanded to include a pub in 2005. It offers lighter fare with quality Boar's Head meats and cheeses and has a long list of specialty sandwiches. We recommend the Yard Buzzard made with fresh Southern chicken salad topped with lettuce and tomato on your choice of bread. The Church Street Dogs menu section features quarter-pound, all-beef franks served with a lot of different toppings, from the traditional to the adventurous. During the colder months, you'll find

homemade soups to warm your belly. On warmer days, sit outside in the courtyard dining area or on the covered porch and take in the downtown views. Ready to quench your thirst? Whether you're in the mood for espresso drinks (hot or cold), shakes, drafts, imports, micro-brews and even fine wines — they're all here. Church Street is open daily. There is a $20 minimum on all credit card charges.

Yana's Ye Olde Drug Store   **$**
119 Front St., Swansboro
(910) 326-5501

Whether it's the food or the nostalgic '50s music that attracts you, once you've eaten at Yana's you'll go back again and again. Yana's opens every day at 7 AM for breakfast and serves lunch through 3 or 4 PM. Breakfast specialties are cooked to order and served all day. Enjoy a traditional breakfast of eggs and ham, omelets, French toast or pancakes. Their fresh fruit fritters are nationally known and come highly recommended. Lunch can include a variety of gourmet sandwiches, salads or soups. Two of the most popular are the Reuben and the Bradburger, a hamburger with egg, cheese, bacon, lettuce and tomato — it's worth sampling. You'll also want to enjoy the fresh chicken or tuna salad. And the desserts? See for yourself! You'll find everything you'd expect from a 1950s soda shop, including ice cream sodas, root beer floats, milk shakes and old fashioned banana splits.

Down East

Captain's Choice Restaurant   **$-$$**
977 Island Rd., Harkers Island
(252) 728-7122

Captain's Choice is located on Harkers Island and offers a good menu selection and lots of local flavor. There are always lunch specials and plenty of meats, seafood and vegetables, along with chowders and salads. Dinner is a seafood and steak event, all prepared to order. A huge seafood buffet is offered each Friday and Saturday evening and for Sunday lunch. Captain's Choice is open seven days a week in season for lunch and dinner; call for off-season hours.

Driftwood Restaurant $$-$$$
N.C. Hwy. 12, Cedar Island
(252) 225-4861

On the banks of Pamlico Sound, the Driftwood includes a motel, restaurant, campground and gift shop, but locals refer to all those things at the complex by simply saying "at the Driftwood." The restaurant is known far and wide for the weekend prime rib special. Other entrees feature all types of seafood, prepared any way you like, including fresh crab meat, shrimp salad, five seafood combination plates and soft-shell crabs. You'll also enjoy chicken, barbecue, pasta and vegetarian dishes and a children's menu. A full salad bar is offered, and the homemade lemon meringue pie is wonderful. Lunch is offered in the summer months. Beer and wine are available, or you can bring your own liquor and they'll provide the setups. The restaurant is beside the Cedar Island-Ocracoke ferry terminal. Call for hours of operation during the winter. For information about the motel, see our Accommodations chapter; for information about the campground, see our Camping chapter.

Western Carteret County

Mac Daddy's $-$$
130 Golfin Dolphin Dr., Cape Carteret
(252) 393-6565

Located within the large family entertainment center, Mac Daddy's Sports Bar and Grill offers a good selection of food and a full menu from appetizers to desserts. You'll find all your favorite appetizers here like nachos, wings, chicken tenders and more. The onion rings come highly recommended — a huge portion served with three tasty dipping sauces. There's a little something for everyone with entrées that include pasta, ribs, chicken and seafood, and there's lighter fare, such as burgers, sandwiches and pizzas. It's definitely worthwhile to save room for dessert with such decadent choices as the Hershey Bar brownie (this monster feeds two), hot apple cobbler, and raspberry white chocolate cheesecake. The Bar and

Grill offers a large wine and beer selection; ask about their daily specials. Wednesdays are especially popular with Wing and Rib night offering 30-cent wings and 50-cent ribs. Mac Daddy's Bar and Grill opens daily at 11 AM.

Riso's Italian Restaurant $$-$$$
1603 N.C. Hwy. 58, Cape Carteret
(252) 393-8787

Riso's is an authentic Italian restaurant located about 2 miles north of Cape Carteret. This restaurant provides only the finest Italian cuisine and keeps diners coming back again and again. A number of Italian entrees are made with fresh pastas, homemade sauces and seafood. Sandwiches and pizzas are also offered. The restaurant is open year round for lunch Monday through Friday and dinner Monday through Saturday.

T&W Oyster Bar $$
2383 N.C. Hwy. 58, Swansboro
(252) 393-8838

T&W Oyster Bar is an institution for many residents and visitors. The restaurant is back to its original ownership with Earl Taylor and his nephew Ralph Sawyers. As the name implies, T&W specializes in fresh local oysters shucked for you at the oyster bar or your table. You'll also find local seafood of all types, as well as steaks and chicken. An Insider's favorite is the fried shrimp — quickly fried with an extra light batter. T&W opens at 5 PM every day for dinner. Lunch is also served on Sunday, with the restaurant opening at noon. T&W has a good selection of beer and wine.

Really Great Fast Food

Yes indeed, the Crystal Coast does have some really delicious fast food, much of which is homemade and unbeatable in value and taste. We would be remiss if we did not tell you about some of the best establishments — places where you can get a good, quick bite for breakfast, lunch and sometimes dinner. Many are family owned and have stood the tests of time and taste. Our choices are listed in alphabetical order.

Big Oak Drive-In $
MM 10.5, N.C. Hwy 58, Salter Path
(252) 247-2588

Turn on the blinker and pull in here. Big Oak has the best shrimp burger on the Crystal Coast. Other restaurants may serve a good shrimp burger, but Big Oak serves a great one. Other goodies you'll want to sample are chicken and barbecue sandwiches, burgers, hot dogs and BLTs. Big Oak has plates of pit-cooked barbecue, fried chicken and shrimp as well as mighty good french fries, onion rings and slaw. But it's that shrimp burger that will keep you coming back!

Coffee Affair - Talk of the Town $
RBC Centura Plaza,
2302-G Arendell St., Morehead City
(252) 247-6020

There is more than just coffee brewing at Coffee Affair. It is the Talk of the Town, offering a wonderful selection of fresh coffees and teas of all types, fresh-baked desserts, breakfast and lunch items, and catering services. This is a favorite hang-out in Morehead City that has been offering customers a home away from home for several years. Known for fresh-baked scones and homemade chicken salad, it also offers smoothies, cheesecakes and a variety of shakes. Let the friendly folks here cater your next event with breakfast, lunch, appetizers or desserts. The shop offers wireless Internet access, a small meeting room, chess sets and more.

El's Drive-In $
3706 Arendell St., Morehead City
(252) 726-3002

El's has been a Carteret County tradition since 1959. This is an old-fashioned drive-in, which means you are waited on

Sea oats sway in a coastal breeze.

photo: Peter Doran

by a carhop and sit in your vehicle and eat. El's has great burgers, hot dogs, fries and milk shakes. The Superburger, assembled with mustard, onion, slaw and chili, is a Carteret County favorite. Try a shrimp or oyster burger, a BLT, a fish or steak sandwich, a shrimp or oyster tray, or fried chicken. This is a much-enjoyed lunch and dinner spot for locals, so go early to get a parking place. And don't forget to lob a french fry or two out the window to the waiting sea gulls. El's is open from 10:30 AM to around 10:30 PM every day, and usually stays open until midnight on Fridays and Saturdays.

New York Deli $
Causeway Shopping Center,
407 Causeway Rd., Atlantic Beach
(252) 726-0111

This is the place for authentic deli food and we highly recommend the South Philadelphia cheesesteak. The deli serves overstuffed sandwiches, subs, chili dogs, homemade soups, salads and

pasta. There's also an Italian Market with olive oils, roasted peppers, pastas and olives. The deli has a good selection of imported beers and wines. Deli meats and cheeses are available for you to take home and create your own feast. New York Deli offers take-out or eat-in service in an attractive cafe atmosphere; they also offer catering, party trays, gift baskets and homemade bagels. New York Deli is open for lunch Tuesday through Sunday during the season and Tuesday through Saturday in the off season. For something a little different from the regular menu, try the Pasta Night each Friday evening.

Sea Side Galley $
311 Island Rd., Harkers Island
(252) 728-6171

Sea Side Galley offers a variety of foods for eating in or taking out. Enjoy seafood, burgers, subs, pizza and more. The Galley is the first building on the left once you cross the drawbridge on to Harkers Island.

♍ NIGHTLIFE

Don't expect the nightlife here on the Crystal Coast to have a lot of big city offerings, that's just not our style. Instead, expect to find some great local spots that offer everything from casual beach bars, taverns and pubs to more upscale waterfront lounges, martini bars and wine bars. Nightlife comes in a variety of forms on the Crystal Coast and it all depends what you have in mind for the evening. There's something for everyone whether it's sports-related, family-oriented, a place to meet up with friends (or make some new ones) or an intimate setting for two.

Most visitors have a full day of outdoor activities and are happy with quiet evening activities, like a drink after dinner and a walk on the beach or waterfront. Still, the Crystal Coast offers a few spots where you can dance the night away or take in a live band and just enjoy a night of fun. For the more adventurous, there's the chance to show off your mechanical bull-riding skills or showcase your vocals during an ever-entertaining night of Karaoke. The nightlife here welcomes visitors and entertains locals and is quick to accommodate most musical tastes.

Many of the local nightspots offer you a choice of staying inside or enjoying a water view in an outdoor lounge. For those who prefer to be outdoors, which our area's mild climate allows most of the year, there are harbor cruises, the beach and deck bars. Besides the many waterfront bars, several local boats offer sunset trips or dinner cruises. Check our Attractions chapter for more information about entertainment cruises.

Shag dancing to beach music is popular here, and there are clubs that cater to people who enjoy this pastime. The shag is a type of dance that was probably a derivative of the beach bop, although it is smoother and done to rhythm and blues or North Carolina's own beach music. The dance is basically an eight-step, alternate-step that has a definite rhythm and distinct appearance. A few local beach clubs and a few parks and recreation departments offer shag lessons for those wanting to learn.

Here we have listed the spots that cater primarily to nightlife seekers. Some of these close or are only open a few nights each week during the winter so calling ahead is always a good idea in the off-season. If the business is on Bogue Banks, we have used the mile marker (MM) number for easy location.

Bear in mind that many restaurants are considered nightspots because they feature live entertainment on weekends during the season or have a bar, so check our Restaurants chapter for more information on those as well. The local newspaper or any one of the weekly vacation guides might also help you in selecting a nightspot.

If we mention ABC permits, it means that the establishment can legally sell liquor in addition to beer and wine. ABC stands for Alcohol Beverage Control, the state agency that regulates the sale of liquor in North Carolina. At the end of this chapter we have supplied information about movie theaters and a list of ABC stores in the area.

Bogue Banks

ATLANTIC BEACH

When locals think of beach nightlife, they think of Atlantic Beach. It's home to a number of nightspots, but the town retains a family atmosphere and surely doesn't have the night scene other beachfront towns along the East Coast have. Nightspots have come and gone during the years, although there are a number of reputable places that have stood the test of time and continue to offer quality entertainment. There are others, but we'll only tell you about the ones we feel comfortable recommending. New places often open each spring, others close in the fall. If you spot a business we haven't listed, there may be several reasons for its omission — it may not be one we would recommend to a friend; it may have just opened in the spring; or we may have unintentionally overlooked it.

Amos Mosquito's Restaurant & Bar
MM 2, 703 N.C. Hwy. 58, Atlantic Beach
(252) 247-6222

Locally known as a great place to eat, it's also a favorite for its nightlife. Overlooking Bogue Sound, Amos Mosquito's offers a great selection of wines from across the country and around the world at affordable prices, in addition to a nice selection of draft and bottled beers. It has all ABC permits, and the bartender is ready to make your favorite drink. You'll feel love outdoorsy atmosphere and hanging Spanish moss. There's live music on Fridays and Saturdays during the season. Thursday nights are big here, as the res-

taurant offers freshly rolled sushi to order in addition to the regular menu and kicks off karaoke around 9 PM.

Beach Tavern
MM 2.5, N.C. Hwy. 58, Atlantic Beach
(252) 247-4466

Known locally as the BT, this casual tavern is open year round and offers an informal, fun place to hang out. Since 1972 BT has attracted a diverse group of people who aren't looking for anything fancy, so just come as you are. You don't have to leave the family at home since BT allows kids in from 11 AM to 9 PM, and you'll often see families enjoying meals here. You can play pool, darts, Foosball, NTN trivia and pinball, listen to the jukebox and watch sports on a wide-screen TV. The grill serves sandwiches, burgers, hot dogs, salads, subs and good pizza. BT has all ABC permits.

Channel Marker Restaurant
718 Atlantic Beach Cswy., Atlantic Beach
(252) 247-2344

Channel Marker is a mainstay in the summer nightlife of the county and has been for more than 25 years. This is a wa-

Coffee houses are great places to get to know the locals on the Crystal Coast.

photo: Peter Doran

terfront spot that has definitely gained a positive reputation with visitors and locals. You'll find great food, a fun waterfront bar with an atrium lounge, and a beautiful deck overlooking Bogue Sound. There's even dock space available for those who prefer to boat up for their dinner reservations. The bar has all ABC permits and a great selection of beers and wines, and it is a favorite nightspot for people of all ages. Live entertainment is offered on Tuesday nights during the season.

Memories Beach Club
MM 1.5, N.C. Hwy. 58, Atlantic Beach
(252) 240-7424

This is the only Shag Club on the Crystal Coast. During the spring and summer, you'll find Shaggers from all over Eastern North and South Carolina coming here for the best beach music. Memories hosts the Atlantic Beach Shaggers Hall of Fame each year in February, which draws participants from all over the country. Dance lessons are offered year round on the beginner, intermediate and advanced levels. Memories features a number of DJs and hosts many special events. Winter months find Memories open a few nights a week and on weekends. Memories is a private club for members and their guests, so call for membership information or come as a guest with an Insider.

PINE KNOLL SHORES

Cutty Sark Lounge
Clam Digger Inn,
MM 8, N.C. Hwy. 58, Pine Knoll Shores
(252) 247-4155

For a great spot overlooking a calming pool, check out this lounge at the Clam Digger Inn. Cutty Sark opens on weekdays at 5 PM and on weekends at noon. The lounge often features special DJ nights and has all ABC permits. Call for the schedule.

INDIAN BEACH

Frank & Clara's Restaurant & Lounge
MM 11, N.C. Hwy. 58, Indian Beach
(252) 247-2788

The lounge is upstairs over the restaurant and gets in full swing in the summer, offering a DJ playing a variety of music from beach and shag to country and rock.

It opens about 8 PM on Fridays and Saturdays. Call for the entertainment schedule.

EMERALD ISLE

Ballyhoo's Island Sports Grill
140 Fairview Dr., Emerald Isle
(252) 354-9397

Ballyhoo's Island Sports Grill is a great place to go for nightlife. You'll enjoy the food and the fun here. There are two bars at Ballyhoo's, one is nonsmoking until 10 PM and and the other is open later. Ballyhoo's has all ABC permits, a nice selection of wines poured by the glass, and the largest selection of beer in Emerald Isle. Live entertainment is featured Thursday, Friday and Saturday nights in season, but is never so loud you can't enjoy meeting friends or making new ones. Ballyhoo's is open seven days a week during the season and is closed Tuesdays in the off season.

RuckerJohns Restaurant
Emerald Plantation Shopping Ctr.,
MM 20, N.C Hwy. 58, Emerald Isle
(252) 354-2413

This upbeat nightspot is very popular with the Bogue Banks crowd and beyond. You'll find a nice bar separated from the dining area with an extensive selection of draft beer and wines by the glass and all ABC permits. In the summer RuckerJohns often offers entertainment on the outdoor patio, and that's a great place to relax, visit with friends or meet new ones.

Beaufort

Back Street Pub
124 Middle St., Beaufort
(252) 728-7108

This laid-back place is a small little bar housed in a century-old former bakery. Inside, you'll see why it's a favorite among sailors passing through on the Intracoastal Waterway because the walls are covered with their nautical memorabilia. Regulars simply call it Back Street, and there is usually standing room only on the weekends. A little outdoor alley garden directly behind Clawson's Restaurant offers some respite from the crowds. A wide ranging beer selection and an eclectic mix of wine are served at the huge wooden bar.

WELCOME TO BEAUFORT'S NEWEST WATERFRONT DINING EXPERIENCE

The owners of Town Creek Marina felt there was no better tribute to the boating haven that Beaufort has become than a boathouse-inspired restaurant, and that's exactly why they've poured their heart and soul into FishTales Waterfront Restaurant. The menu offers a FishTales twist on a variety of seafood, chicken and other dishes, guaranteeing something for everyone. Bring the whole family and enjoy the simple Coastal Carolina-inspired fare. Open for lunch and dinner daily. We have a seat waiting for you at FishTales!

232 W. Beaufort Road, Beaufort, NC 28516
www.FishTalesAtTownCreek.com
For reservations, call 252-504-7263.

Upstairs is a "sailors' library" where you can bring a book to swap or to read. Back Street Pub has live music year-round; call for details on performers. Wednesdays are Open Mic night. Winter visitors will find a cozy fire and a pot of soup.

Cru Wine Bar and Store
120 Turner St., Beaufort
(252) 728-3066

Cru Wine Bar is the perfect place to meet friends and relax. Within a block of the Beaufort waterfront, this nightspot features a high bar and several living room–type seating areas, perfect for meeting friends or making new ones. It's an intimate place great for enjoying music and sharing conversation. Cru Wine Bar has an outstanding selection of wines and specialty beers and serves them by the bottle or glass. Be sure to ask about their wine tastings and stop in to enjoy live musical entertainment by local artists on Fridays and Saturdays. The Wine Store shares the same space so you can take your favorites home with you. Did we mention it also features sinful chocolates?

The Dock House
500 Front St., Beaufort
(252) 728-4506

The Dock House is easy to find because as you walk the boardwalk off of Front Street on a summer evening, you'll see a large crowd lingering outside of it

enjoying the night's live entertainment. This waterfront bar fronts Taylor's Creek and has long been a favorite of locals and Crystal Coast visitors alike. Space is limited inside, but the upstairs and downstairs deck and boardwalk provide extra room for all the visitors during the summer. The Dock House has all ABC permits, a good selection of pub food and live entertainment on tap during the season.

Fish Tales at Town Creek Marina
232 W. Beaufort Rd., Beaufort
(252) 504-7263
www.fishtalesattowncreek.com

In addition to full lunch and dinner service every day, Fish Tales at Town Creek Marina offers local entertainment on the weekends on their spectacular outdoor patio and bar. Enjoy a view of the harbor, while enjoying music, drink specials and menu specials. Fish Tales can host private parties and events and offers onsite catering.

Front Street Grill at Stillwater
300 Front St., Beaufort
(252) 728-4956

The Rhum Bar at Front Street Grill at Stillwater offers guests spectacular views of Beaufort Inlet, Carrot Island and evening sunsets. This is the perfect place to enjoy selections from an extensive rum list, cocktails, wine, beer and light foods outside. The restaurant has all ABC permits and serves lunch, dinner and a Sunday brunch that is not to be missed. Come by car or boat up to Stillwater's dock.

Royal James Cafe
117 Turner St., Beaufort
(252) 728-4573

Royal James Cafe is the oldest continually existing business in Beaufort's historic district and has a local flavor all its own. With an early 1950s Formica, wood and neon look, this cafe and pool room draws an interesting mix of locals and tourists, families and singles. You'll find regulation antique Brunswick pool tables, an Internet-connected juke box, video games and a flat-screen TV tuned to sports, weather or breaking news. Sue and Ed Book are celebrating 26 years of ownership in 2009.

Morehead City

Crystal Coast Jamboree
1311 Arendell St., Morehead City
(252) 726-1501, (866) 580-7469

Billed as the "Hottest Ticket at the Beach!" this live variety show is filled with great family entertainment. The Jamboree features a two-hour, high-energy show that blends country, oldies, dancers, gospel and outrageous comedy. But don't think there is only one show offered here. The Theater also presents a Concert Series that features top nationally known recording artists; these shows are usually offered once a month. In November and December the Jamboree Cast presents the Jamboree Holiday Show that is filled with all the glitz and glamour that one would hope to find in a Christmas show. This state-of-the-art theater has become another wonderful destination for visitors and group tours that rivals anything in Myrtle Beach and points beyond. Make seating reservations early as most shows sell out early.

Midnight Rodeo
5386 U.S. Hwy. 70 W, Morehead City
(252) 222-0111

This Western nightclub and saloon is a hit in the area and regularly brings in nationally known performers. The club offers live performances for Country Night on Friday evenings and a DJ featuring Top 40 dance music on Thursday and Sat-

Vacation rental prices vary according to their proximity to the water.

photo: Peter Doran

WTKF 107.1 FM
WJNC 1240 AM

THE TALK STATION

The Weekday Line Up

6 a.m.-9 a.m. - Coastal Daybreak with Ben Ball -
Call In Number **1-800-818-2255**
Eastern North Carolina's only radio morning news magazine, with special features,
sports, entertainment and local and national guests.

9 a.m.-12 noon - Laura Ingraham -
Call In Number **1-800-876-4123**
Talk radio just got very interesting. Laura Ingraham is a political pundit with sassy
spice and everything nice.

12 noon-3 p.m. - Rush Limbaugh -
Call In Number **1-800-282-2882**
The Nation's #1 Radio Talk Show. Rush is the Godfather of talk radio and you can
hear him on The Talk Station.

3 p.m.-5 p.m. Dave Ramsey -
Call In Number **1-888-825-5225**
Dave offers life-changing financial advice.

5 p.m.-7 p.m. - VIEWPOINTS with Lockwood Phillips
Call In Number **1-800-818-2255**
Across the street, across the state, across the nation, Viewpoints is where you can
express your point of view.

7 p.m.-10 p.m. Sean Hannity
Call In Number - **1-800-941-7326**
The Legacy lives on.

10 p.m.-1 a.m. - Jim Bohannon -
Call In Number **1-866-505-4626**
Jim goes into in-depth conversations with today's news makers, leading authors
and the latest entertainers.

1 a.m.-6 a.m. Coast to Coast AM, with George Noory -
Call In Number **1-800-825-5033**
America's Most fascinating overnight radio program.

Saturday and Sunday starting at **1 p.m.**
SPORTING NEWS RADIO

www.wtkf107.com

urday evenings. The general store offers Western wear, and there are pool tables, a large dance floor, a mechanical bull, an outside patio and two bars. It's worth stepping outside to enjoy the outdoor tiki bar under the stars. Midnight Rodeo has all ABC permits and offers a variety of beer and wine. Midnight Rodeo is an 18 years of age and older club unless those younger than 18 are accompanied by a parent or legal guardian. It is open to both members and guests.

Raps Grill & Bar
709 Arendell St., Morehead City
(252) 240-1213

Set in a casual pub atmosphere, Raps is a favorite gathering place among locals year round. The roomy bar is often packed during the summer months, but it should definitely be included on your schedule of things to do. The downstairs bar area surrounds a huge oak bar and has tables and plenty of floor space. Raps has all ABC permits and offers a large selection of beers and wines. There are seven televisions total for your viewing pleasure, three of them are big-screen TVs for watching the games. This is the area's hot spot for watching the Super Bowl and other major sporting events. Upstairs are two levels of dining. Be sure to check out Raps' daily drink specials; you'll find a good selection of your favorite beers, shots and mixed drinks at great prices.

Cape Carteret

Mac Daddy's
130 Golfin Dolphin Dr., Cape Carteret
(252) 393-6565

Mac Daddy's is one of the newest spots for nightlife in the area. Also known for its family fun entertainment during the day, it's a great nightspot to find a good mix of fun and relaxation. Challenge your

For a night of fun, locals often travel to Kinston to watch the minor-league Kinston Indians play baseball. See our Sports, Fitness and Parks chapter for information.

friends to a bowling competition, sharpen your pool skills on one of the 7-foot billiards tables or just relax and enjoy Mac Daddy's Sports Bar and Grill. Offering a large selection of beers and wines as well as a full menu, the Sports Bar and Grill has multiple 42-inch TVs, snack-bar seating and a late-night menu. Karaoke Kraze happens on Thursdays from 8 to 11 PM. Mac Daddy's is open year round, seven days a week from 10 AM until midnight with extended hours on the weekends.

Tours

Some visitors and locals like to enjoy the Crystal Coast by day, some want to see it by night. Our recommendation is to do both — you won't be disappointed. Below are a few of the area tours that also offer a bit of nightlife. More information about these tours and others are offered in the Attractions chapter.

Lookout Cruises
Beaufort Waterfront, Beaufort
(252) 504-SAIL (7245)

Steve Bishop captains the *Lookout*, a 45-foot catamaran that can hold 42 passengers. He offers a romantic and relaxing sunset cruise for adults with complimentary beverages served. If you happen to be around during the full moon period, enjoy a moonlit cruise through Beaufort's surrounding waters; just be sure to call and ask for the availability of this tour. It is always best to call ahead to book a cruise on this popular vessel.

Mystery Boat Tours
412 Front St., Beaufort
(252) 728-2527, (866) 230-BOAT (2628)
www.mysteryboattours.com

The *Diamond City* is a floating nightclub. Docked on Beaufort's waterfront, it is available for special charters, wedding cruises, corporate meetings and fun tours. Onboard the 149-passenger vessel you'll find a captain and crew prepared to make your voyage fun and enjoyable. The *Diamond City*'s nighttime "floating party cruise" boards at 9:30 PM for a two-hour cruise each Saturday. With all ABC permits, a state-of-the-art sound system and either a DJ or live entertainment, *Diamond*

City is the place to be for those age 21 and older. Reservations are required, and they offer free soft drinks and coffee to designated drivers. *Diamond City* also offers harbor tours, lunch and dinner cruises, dolphin-watch trips and Sunday brunch rides. Also check out the sister vessel, *Mystery*, which is docked in Beaufort. All cruises require minimum passengers and are subject to cancellation.

TourBeaufort.com
Beaufort
(252) 772-9925

TourBeaufort.com offers several types of tours for visitors and residents of all ages. What better way to spend an evening in Beaufort than to stroll through its historic streets and learn about its haunting tales. The Beaufort Ghost Walk is one of the most popular as it shares the life of Blackbeard and takes tour-goers to his former residence, the Hammock House. This walking tour continues to cover about 10 blocks throughout the historic district, including Beaufort's 300-year-old cemetery, and takes about an hour. This tour is great for families, and kids love it. There are a variety of other tours available, so call for the latest information. Reservations are needed for the tours, which vary in price and point of origin.

Movie Theaters

Movies are a great option for a rainy day or just an evening out-on-the-town. Even better, why not plan for dinner and a movie, and make a full night of it? The movie theaters listed here offer discounts for seniors and children. They also run matinees at reduced prices, but check to make sure which days because off-season matinees are usually restricted to weekends. Movie listings are printed in the *Carteret County News-Times*, published every Wednesday, Friday and Sunday.

Atlantic Station Cinema 4, MM 3, Atlantic Station Shopping Center, N.C. Hwy. 58, Atlantic Beach, (252) 247-7016

Emerald Plantation Cinema 4, MM 20, Emerald Plantation Shopping Center, N.C. Hwy. 58, Emerald Isle, (252) 354-5012

Plaza Cinema One, Two and Three, Morehead Plaza Shopping Center, Bridges St., Morehead City, (252) 726-2081

Liquor Laws and ABC Stores

Though you can buy beer and wine at food and convenience stores, you must purchase liquor in Alcohol Beverage Control (ABC) package stores. Local ABC stores are open Monday through Saturday. Only those 21 years of age or older are allowed in the stores.

Atlantic Beach ABC Store, MM 2.5, N.C. Hwy. 58, Atlantic Beach, (252) 726-3221

Beaufort ABC Store, 1791 U.S. Hwy. 70, Beaufort, (252) 728-2530

Cape Carteret ABC Store, N.C. Hwy. 24, beside the police department, Cape Carteret, (252) 393-2631

Emerald Isle ABC Store, MM 20, Emerald Plantation Shopping Center, N.C. Hwy. 58, Emerald Isle, (252) 354-6000

Morehead City ABC Store, KMart Shopping Center, 4915-D Arendell St., Morehead City, (252) 726-2160

Newport ABC Store, East of U.S. Hwy. 70/Howard Blvd. intersection, next to Subway, Newport, (252) 223-4136

Swansboro ABC Store, N.C. Hwy. 24, west side of town, Swansboro, (910) 326-4810

⊕HOTELS AND MOTELS

Although the beaches are the among the top reasons vacationers come here, the waterfront towns, the history, the natural world and the maritime culture are also big draws to the area. The Crystal Coast is a diverse resort area with a wide variety of accommodations. There are many attractive lodging choices, some rich with history and all full of Southern hospitality. Choose from luxurious oceanfront or sound-side hotels and resorts, family-style motels and efficiency suites. Those looking for something off the beaten path will find even more options in our chapters on Bed and Breakfast Inns, Camping and Vacation Rentals.

On the beach, as in most resort areas, rates vary according to the season and the lodging's proximity to water. If, for economy's sake, you are considering a location away from the water, you may want to ask about access either to the ocean or to the sound and inquire as to whether or not it is within walking distance.

The Crystal Coast is becoming a year-round resort town. We recommend you make reservations in advance no matter what time of year you plan on visiting. During the early spring and late-fall shoulder seasons and in the winter many establishments offer attractive weekend getaways, golf packages and special rates. The area is a popular site for meetings, conventions and fishing excursions throughout the year, and many facilities offer meeting rooms and convention services. The Crystal Coast Civic Center (see our Attractions chapter) in Morehead City accommodates sizable shows and gatherings with hotels and other lodgings conveniently nearby.

Each lodging establishment has a different deposit and refund policy. While some require a deposit equal to one night's stay in advance, others will simply hold your reservation on your credit card. Often a 24-hour notice is sufficient for a full refund, but some require as much as a three-day notice. Because of the area's popularity, extending your stay can be difficult but not impossible. Some places require up to 72-hours notice for extensions past your originally scheduled departure date.

In cases of emergency, we also recommend that you inquire into a hotel's hurricane or emergency policy. Sometimes, hurricane evacuations can mean an abrupt end to a vacation. Most area resorts have policies in place to make refunds available under these conditions, but be sure to ask what that policy is before you pay.

Many of the area's lodgings offer non-smoking rooms by request. The pet policy is the proprietor's option. Most do not allow pets in rooms, although some lodgings do make provisions for them. If your pet will be traveling with you it is best to ask before making reservations. It is also helpful to ask about any extra fees associated with bringing your pet or if there are any size or weight limits.

This guide doesn't attempt to list all the accommodations available on the Crystal Coast. Rather, we've provided a sampling of some of our favorites. For more information about lodging and weekend availability, contact the Carteret County Tourism Development Authority, P.O. Box 1406, Morehead City, NC 28557, (800) SUNNY NC or (252) 726-8148. The Tourism Authority operates visitors centers at 3409 Arendell Street (U.S. Highway 70) in Morehead City and on N.C. Highway 58, just north of the Cameron Langston Bridge to Emerald Isle.

Price Code

For the purpose of comparing prices, we have placed each accommodation in a price category based on the average rate for a double-occupancy room per night during the summer season. There is often a wide range of rates offered at accommodations based on amenities offered. As we have averaged the rate range, you may expect to find rooms at higher and lower prices when you call for reservations. Winter rates can be substantially lower, and holiday rates higher. Rates shown do not include state and local taxes. Amenities and rates are subject to change. It's best to verify information important to you, including credit cards accepted, when making your reservations.

$	$70 and less
$$	$71 to $90
$$$	$91 to $125
$$$$	More than $125

Bogue Banks

All the accommodations we would recommend on the beach are just too numerous to list. In this section we offer a sample range of accommodations from full-service resorts to family and angler favorites with fewer frills. We also suggest you contact condominium developments (see the Crystal Coast Vacation Rentals chapter) because most offer attractive vacation rates.

ATLANTIC BEACH

Bogue Shores Suites $$$
N.C. Hwy. 58 (1918 W. Fort Macon Rd.),
Atlantic Beach
(252) 726-7071

Bogue Shores Suites is located on Bogue Sound in Atlantic Beach. Bogue Shores is a family-oriented establishment and has many wonderful things to offer. The one-room efficiencies are set up to sleep four, and most units have fully equipped kitchens. There are also larger

deluxe accommodations for up to six people. The ocean access is directly across the street. Bogue Shores offers the largest outdoor pool on the island. They also have several picnic areas on the property with boat ramp facilities as well as a dock for fishing.

Caribbe Inn $-$$
MM 1.5 N.C. Hwy. 58
(309 E. Fort Macon Rd.), Atlantic Beach
(252) 726-0051
www.caribbe-inn.com

This clean, cozy, family-owned and operated inn, located on an access channel to Bogue Sound, is an inviting setting for families, fishermen and scuba divers. The friendly hospitality at Caribbe Inn is punctuated by its colorful aquatic decor. Each room is painted in splashy colors with different fish murals and Caribbean designs. All of the rooms have telephones, refrigerators, microwaves and cable. Studio efficiencies with full kitchens as well as some pet-friendly rooms are also available. Guests are welcome to use the complimentary boat slips, picnic areas with grills, dock with a fish-cleaning station and a freezer to store their catches of the day. Caribbe Inn is just a short walk to the ocean and within easy walking distance of restaurants, fishing piers, shopping, shag-dancing clubs and entertainment. Golf and fishing packages are available. Darrel, Trish

and Mike Lawrence look forward to making your visit an enjoyable one.

Clam Digger Inn $$$-$$$$
511 Salter Path Rd., Atlantic Beach
(252) 247-4155

At the Clam Digger Inn every room is oceanfront with a private balcony. Guests will find 102 rooms, each equipped with a microwave, refrigerator, coffeemaker, iron and ironing board. The inn offers direct access to the wide, sandy beach and the ocean. Guests can also enjoy an outdoor pool and hot tub in season, as well as conference and meeting space to accommodate groups made up of 2 to 100 people. The Clam Digger Restaurant is located on the first floor of the inn and is open for breakfast, lunch and dinner. Open year round, the inn has a lounge featuring weekend entertainment. The friendly staff at the Clam Digger Inn can provide all the local information you need to plan your day on the Crystal Coast.

Hollowell's Family Motel $$
MM 1.5, N.C. Hwy. 58, Atlantic Beach
(252) 726-5227
www.hollowellsmotel.com

Hollowell's Family Motel is located two short blocks from the ocean and offers cozy, clean, quiet accommodations. Its location in the heart of Atlantic Beach makes it convenient for guests to enjoy the local restaurants and shopping. All rooms feature a refrigerator, microwave and cable TV. There are a variety of rooms to choose from, including smoking and nonsmoking, as well as rooms with double and king-size beds. Hollowell's offers kitchenettes, two-room efficiencies and an apartment, too. When you're not at the beach, enjoy some more time outside at the pool, eating lunch at one of the picnic spots or cooking out in one of the barbecue areas. Hollowell's has a friendly staff that only complements its affordable prices. Speaking of affordable, the first two children in your family that are ages 12 and younger can stay for free.

Island Inn of Atlantic Beach $$$-$$$$
MM 2, N.C. Hwy. 58 (215 W. Fort Macon Rd.), Atlantic Beach
(252) 726-3780

Island Inn of Atlantic Beach is located in the heart of this beach community, offering guests just a short, easy walk to the beach, shopping and restaurants. The entire inn was renovated in 2007, and the 38 rooms vary from studios to two-room luxury apartments. All rooms feature ceramic tile floors, granite counter tops, microwaves, refrigerators, hairdryers, coffeemakers, free wireless Internet service and expanded cable with HBO. Several rooms include full kitchens. Guests can enjoy the new outdoor pool and outdoor

grills. Open year round, Island Inn is the perfect place to relax for a few nights or the week.

Oceanana Family Resort $-$$$$
MM 1.5, N.C. Hwy. 58, Atlantic Beach
(252) 726-4111
www.oceanana.com

This comfortable motel on the ocean provides many extras. Long a favorite of families with children, the Oceanana offers a pool, a children's play area and equipment, a fishing pier, picnic tables and grills, free pool-side breakfasts in the summer season, beach chairs, and poolside and beach services. Guests are offered the choice of standard rooms, oceanfront rooms or two-room efficiencies, all with refrigerators. The accommodations here are clean and comfortable. Call or visit their website for pricing details. The Oceanana closes for the season in mid-November and re-opens in early April. This motel offers one of the few remaining piers on Bogue Banks, and anglers do not need a saltwater fishing license because the pier provides blanket coverage.

The Palm Suites $$$$
MM 2.5, N.C. Hwy. 58, Atlantic Beach
(252) 247-6400, (800) 972-3297

This premier property is located only blocks from the heart of Atlantic Beach

Your resting spot by the sea awaits.

photo: Peter Doran

and features 90 custom-designed units, each designed with the owner's personal flair to provide you with a tranquil experience. Each unit contains a microwave, refrigerator, coffeemaker, iron, ironing board and hairdryer. Guests will enjoy an outdoor swimming pool, nine soundside boat slips, a boat-launching area and an on-site guest laundry facility. The Palm Suites offers AARP/senior, military, group and wedding discounts. There are no minimum-stay requirements, and units are available on a nightly or weekly basis.

Sheraton Atlantic Beach   **$$$$**
Oceanfront Hotel
2710 W. Fort Macon Rd., Atlantic Beach
(252) 240-1155

The Sheraton Atlantic Beach is a full-service oceanfront resort hotel with 200 ocean-view and oceanfront rooms. Each includes a coffeemaker, refrigerator, hairdryer, iron and ironing board, wireless Internet connection, private balcony and in-room safe. Oceanfront suites with one bedroom, a living room and a whirlpool tub are available. All rooms feature two queen beds or one king Sheraton Sweet Sleeper bed. A summertime children's activities director offers a full schedule of daytime fun. Enjoy a casual dining experience at the Sheraton's restaurant, Milazzo Italian Restaurant, which specializes in seafood and family-style dining and is open for breakfast, lunch and dinner every day of the week. In season, Molly's Oceanfront Bar and Grill serves casual fare and beverages. The lighted fishing pier is complimentary for all guests, and golf and tennis are located near the hotel. The 9,000 square feet of meeting and banquet space includes Sandcastles Oceanfront Clubhouse — a great location for wedding receptions.

PINE KNOLL SHORES

Atlantis Lodge   **$$$$**
MM 5, N.C. Hwy. 58, Atlantic Beach
(252) 726-5168, (800) 682-7057

Set among beautiful live oaks on the oceanside, Atlantis Lodge was among the first hotels built on Bogue Banks. Many of the guests at the Atlantis consider it

their "second home" and return year after year. Most units are arranged as suites, offering efficiency kitchens and dining, living and sleeping areas. All have patios or decks facing the surf, cable TV, wireless Internet and other expected amenities. Recreation areas, equipment, discount golf tickets and complimentary beach furniture and beach services are extended to guests. The outdoor pool is a quiet place for sunning and swimming, and the third-floor lounge has an adjoining library. Unlike most hotels, the Atlantis makes provisions for pets. The lodge proudly sponsors two popular sand-sculpture contests — the Mile of Hope in early May for children with cancer and a competition in August that benefits the Outer Banks Wildlife Shelter. See our Annual Events chapter for details.

Hampton Inn & Suites $$$-$$$$
MM 5, 118 Salter Path Rd., Pine Knoll Shores
(252) 247-5118
www.hamptoninn.com

Formerly known as the AmeriSuites and now a Hampton Inn, this hotel is under construction with completion slated for April 2009. It overlooks the Crystal Coast Country Club Golf Course and is directly across the highway from the ocean. Guests may enjoy the beach via an ocean access walkway. The Hampton Inn is set to offer 109 finely appointed suites and amenities such as a heated outdoor pool, a state-of-the-art fitness center and in-room

plasma TVs, just to name a few. A complimentary Hampton standard breakfast is sure to please. Be sure to ask about the special golf packages. If you need a meeting room, several are available, each with the amenities necessary for conducting successful business meetings.

Seahawk Motor Lodge $$$$
MM 4.5, N.C. Hwy. 58, Atlantic Beach
(252) 726-4146, (800) 682-6898
www.ncbeach-motel.com

This comfortable lodge offers 38 oceanfront rooms with balconies or patios. Each room has a phone, cable TV and refrigerator. Connecting double rooms, a two-bedroom cottage and two three-bedroom, three-bath villas are also available. A pool is situated in the middle of a large, grassy lawn facing the ocean. Guests can use the bicycles and grills. Many guests enjoy relaxing in the hammocks and swings on the oceanfront lawn.

Windjammer Inn $$$$
MM 4.5, N.C. Hwy. 58, Pine Knoll Shores
(252) 247-7123, (800) 233-6466

All of the 46 rooms at the attractive Windjammer Inn are over-sized and oceanfront with a private balcony, refrigerator, microwave oven, cable TV and two telephones. The glass-enclosed elevator is an unexpected surprise and offers a great view of Bogue Sound. Guests enjoy the oceanfront pool, private beach area with beach services and complimentary coffee each morning. There is a two-night minimum during summer weekends and a three-night minimum on holiday weekends. We recommend you get one of the Jacuzzi rooms overlooking the ocean or relax in the hot tub outside by the pool.

SALTER PATH

Oak Grove Motel $-$$
1305 Salter Path Rd., Salter Path
(252) 247-3533

We're impressed by this motel because it's so tidy, and, in the shade of live oaks, it always looks cool, even on the hottest days. It has one- and two-story stone-sided units with 10 standard double-bed rooms and 13 kitchenettes, all with porch rockers for enjoying the shade. This motel is a family facility and has lots of repeat business. Two-night minimums are required on summer weekends, and a three-night minimum is required during major holidays.

William and Garland Motel $
MM 10.5, N.C. Hwy. 58, Salter Path
(252) 247-3733

This small, family-owned motel has eight rooms and three mobile units. Nine are efficiencies. Each room has a refrigerator and microwave. Don't expect anything fancy but do expect a family atmosphere and clean, comfortable surroundings. Guests have ocean access via a short nature trail walkway and access to the 20-acre Salter Path Dunes Natural Area, perfect for swimming, fishing, walking, sunning and picnicking. There is generally a two-night minimum stay on weekends in the summer. The staff welcomes well-behaved pets.

EMERALD ISLE AND CAPE CARERET

Best Western $$$-$$$$
Silver Creek Inn
801 Cedar Point Blvd., Cedar Point
(252) 393-9015

Best Western Silver Creek Inn is located in Cedar Point, just minutes from the beaches, golf courses, historic Swansboro and Hammocks Beach State Park. The inn offers 65 rooms, including mini-suites and rooms with whirlpool baths. Each room offers guests a refrigerator, microwave, coffeemaker, iron and ironing board, hairdryer and free Internet access. Guests can also enjoy an outdoor pool and free continental breakfast. Silver Creek Inn can accommodate group meetings, family gatherings, business meetings and small receptions. Golf packages are available.

The Islander $$$$
102 Islander Dr., Emerald Isle
(252) 354-3464, (800) 354-3464

The Islander, offered by Bluewater GMAC Real Estate, is located on the oceanfront in Emerald Isle. Completely remodeled in 2008, it offers its guests the ultimate experience when staying in an oceanfront condo-tel resort. There are 80 large, well-appointed rooms that include 32-inch plasma TVs and many other amenities. Take a swim in the oceanfront pool or a enjoy a stroll down the beach — the setting is both beautiful and convenient. Within blocks of The Islander, guests have their choice of activities that include family fun, restaurants and shopping. The Islander's website features photos, descriptions, online booking rates and specials.

Parkerton Inn $$
1184 N.C. Hwy. 58 N, Cape Carteret
(252) 393-9000, (800) 393-9909

Parkerton Inn is on the mainland just north of the intersection of N.C. Highways 58 and 24. With 47 rooms, the inn offers several room arrangements, including kitchenette efficiencies and rooms equipped for the handicapped. The inn is dog-friendly. Standard rooms have two queen-size beds, and two executive suites offer king-size beds. The outdoor pool is a popular spot. Golf packages are offered. Every room features a microwave and a refrigerator. Free coffee is available in the lobby.

Beaufort

Most of Beaufort's accommodations are bed and breakfast inns. See our Bed and Breakfast Inns chapter for options other than those listed here.

Beaufort Inn $$$$
101 Ann St., Beaufort
(252) 728-2600, (800) 726-0321

This inn is in the ideal location for lodging in historic Beaufort. Located on Gallant's Channel at the end of Ann Street, it offers 40 rooms and suites with water views or overlooking the town's historic district. All rooms have refrigerators, cable TV, coffeemakers, irons/ironing boards, hairdryers and wireless Internet. The suites also feature microwaves. There is an outdoor hot tub for guests to enjoy. Guests are treated to Katie's special breakfast pie as part of the morning meal. The inn offers on-site bike rentals for guests to enjoy riding along the streets of Beaufort and along the waterfront. Boat slips are available.

The Inlet Inn $$$-$$$$
601 Front St., Beaufort
(252) 728-3600, (800) 554-5466
www.inlet-inn.com

The 36-room Inlet Inn opened in 1985 in the same block of Front Street occupied by the original Inlet Inn of the nineteenth century, which brought guests from across the state to bask in the Beaufort sun. Today's inn, of similar design, is on the waterfront and offers harbor-front rooms on the first and second floor. These rooms have a king-size bed and sofa. Third-floor rooms overlooking the water offer two queen beds and a wonderful window seat for viewing Beaufort Inlet, the waterfront and beyond. Nestled in the heart of the historic district, many rooms open onto private porches and offer bars, refrigerators with ice makers, and built-in hair dryers. Six of the first-floor rooms offer cozy fireplaces, and wireless Internet is available on the premises and at nearby coffee shops. A continental breakfast, served in the rooms, consists of muffins, bagels and juice. Coffeemakers are provided in each room. A courtyard garden, the rooftop Widow's Walk Lounge and an on-site meeting room are also available for guests' use year round.

Morehead City

Buccaneer Inn $$$
2806 Arendell St., Morehead City
(252) 726-3115, (800) 682-4982

Buccaneer Inn has 90 attractive rooms. The majority of the rooms have standard double beds, though some have king-size beds. Guests are offered complimentary hot breakfasts, newspapers, free local calls

HOTELS AND MOTELS

and cable TV. All rooms feature refrigerators, microwaves and hairdryers. Meeting and banquet facilities are available. Special packages include golf, diving and fishing. The inn is beside Morehead Plaza and is a short driving distance from Atlantic Beach.

Econo Lodge Crystal Coast $$
3410 Bridges St., Morehead city
(252) 247-2940, (800) 533-7556

Econo Lodge is two blocks from the Crystal Coast Civic Center and one block from Carteret General Hospital. It offers 56 rooms at reasonable rates and is within easy driving distance of the beaches. The majority of the rooms are furnished with two double beds and a few have king-size beds. Amenities include cable TV, free local calls and complimentary continental breakfast. Some rooms feature refrigerators and microwaves. Restaurants are close by, and there is plenty of parking for cars and boat trailers.

Hampton Inn Morehead City $$$-$$$$
4035 Arendell St., Morehead City
(252) 240-2300, (800) 467-9375
www.hamptoninn.hilton.com/en/hp/hotel

Hampton Inn, overlooking Bogue Sound, offers beautiful views of the Intracoastal Waterway and the island of Bogue Banks. The inn features 119 well-appointed guest rooms with a choice of two doubles or a king-size bed. Two-room suites have a separate living area. Guests enjoy an outside pool and deck area, free continental breakfast served in the sun room, free accommodations for children, an exercise room and complimentary high-speed Internet services. All rooms include a refrigerator, microwave and flat-panel TV. Meeting rooms, plenty of parking and packages for golf and fishing are available. Restaurants and shopping areas are nearby.

> **i** *To catch the Cedar Island Ferry to Ocracoke Island with your vehicle, you must be in line a half-hour before departure time or your reservation will be canceled. No exceptions!*

Holiday Inn Express Hotel & Suites $$$-$$$$
5063 Executive Dr., Morehead City
(252) 247-5001

Holiday Inn Express Hotel & Suites is conveniently located near the beaches and many local attractions. The 75 rooms each feature a refrigerator, microwave, coffeemaker, ironing equipment and hairdryer, as well as free local calls, free wireless Internet access and cable TV with HBO. This hotel offers executive king suites and has several designated pet-friendly rooms. Guests can enjoy an outdoor pool and a sauna as well as a complimentary full breakfast each morning. The fitness room is newly remodeled for the 2009 season with state-of-the-art equipment. Staff at the Holiday Inn Express Hotel & Suites can assist with tour groups and provide area information.

Quality Inn Morehead City $$$-$$$$
3100 Arendell St., Morehead City
(252) 247-3434

Quality Inn, like others in the national hotel chain, offers reliably comfortable rooms with either one king or two double beds. The hotel offers a pool and com-plimentary deluxe continental breakfast served each morning in the guest lounge. Convenient to the Crystal Coast Civic Center and all beach and historic attractions, Quality Inn has 101 guest rooms to accommodate any gathering. Each room has cable TV and includes a hairdryer, coffeemaker, microwave and refrigerator. The entire property features wireless Internet, and the lobby features a business center with computer, fax machine and printer. Golf packages are available, and there are special rates for fishing and diving. Restaurants are within walking distance. The inn neighbors Morehead Plaza. Corporate, AARP and AAA discounts are offered.

Down East

There are a few motels in the Down East area, and we've listed them here. Many people also enjoy the kind of island getaway that is a real back-to-basics experience, so we've also told you about accommodations available on Core Banks (Cape Lookout National Seashore). For information about Down East campgrounds, see our Camping chapter.

Striking scenery is everywhere along the coast.

photo: Peter Doran

Driftwood Motel $$
N.C. Hwy. 12, Cedar Island
(252) 225-4861

Surrounded by beautiful beaches, the Driftwood is the perfect place to escape day-to-day stress and live the island life. Recently remodeled, this 37-room motel is located by the Cedar Island–Ocracoke Ferry terminal. Rooms offer either two double beds or one king-sized bed, and all rooms have cable television with HBO. The fact that there are no phones in the rooms makes the Driftwood the perfect escape. Bring your beach chair, your kayak or your boat and enjoy all the island has to offer. Pets are accommodated at the Driftwood. The motel also has a restaurant known for fresh local seafood and prime rib (call ahead for hours), a gift shop and a campground (see our Camping chapter). The motel is open year-round. A continental breakfast is served to motel guests.

Great Island Cabins $
National Park Service, Harkers Island
(252) 728-2250

Twenty-four rustic cabins are available on South Core Banks at the Great Island area of Cape Lookout National Seashore. These cabins are arranged to accommodate 4, 6, 8 or 12 people and are rented on a per-night basis. The price listed reflects a per-person rate based on full occupancy. The cabins are rustic and include several beds with mattresses, a gas stove with an oven, potable water, sinks, toilets and showers. There are hookups for generators, if you bring your own. Bring everything else you'll need, including cooking utensils and linens. The National Park Service currently operates these cabins and transportation to and from the island is available from the Down East community of Davis. These cabins are very popular, so plan ahead and reserve early. Call the Park Service at the number above for further information or call (252) 241-6783 for reservations.

LO'R Decks at Calico Jack's $-$$
and Ferry Service
1698 Island Rd., Harkers Island
(252) 728-3575

"Lower Decks" is situated right on the water and offers 21 rooms arranged in a variety of ways. Guests can enjoy rooms that include kitchenettes, single beds and double beds. The motel shares the property with a full-service marina that offers a boat ramp, gas, supplies, refreshments and a complete tackle shop. The ferry service provides water-taxi service to Cape Lookout and other locales. Calico Jack's staff can make charter boat arrangements for guests as well.

Morris Marina Kabin Kamps - $
South Core Banks
1000 Morris Marina Rd., Atlantic
(252) 225-4261

Twenty rustic cabins that vary in size to accommodate six may be rented by the day on North Core Banks at the Long Point area of Cape Lookout National Seashore. The price indicated here is a per-person rate based on a full cabin. Some cabins have no electricity, others have solar electricity, and others have electricity and air conditioning. Although water is potable, most visitors bring their own. Pack as you would for a camping trip, and you'll be most comfortable. Long a guarded secret of anglers, this cabin settlement is also the choice getaway for shell-seekers in the spring and bird-watchers in the fall. Ferries run from the town of Atlantic to the cabins several times each day, except from December through mid-March. Making reservations well in advance is recommended. If you take your four-wheel-drive vehicle over on the ferry, you can drive the 22 miles of beach on this island. See our Getting Here, Getting Around chapter for more information on the ferry.

BED & BREAKFAST INNS

Recent travel trends indicate that travelers often seek authenticity from their travel destinations. While location is an important factor, many seek to increase their travel experience by delving deeper and getting to know the area that they are vacationing in and its unique opportunities. Bed and breakfast inns provide an added opportunity to get to know the area because they offer a more intimate setting and are commonly situated at some of the most ideal locations for sightseeing. They reflect the tradition, history and culture of the area with an added focus on providing unmatched hospitality. The innkeepers are a wealth of knowledge and information since most are year-round residents, and they welcome the opportunity to share their knowledge.

Bed and breakfast–style hospitality is available on the Crystal Coast for those who prefer a slower pace, a personal touch and a relaxed atmosphere. Bed and breakfast lodging can be the ideal retreat for those seeking a quiet, stress-free vacation. Room arrangements and breakfast specialties vary at each inn. Most do not have facilities for young children or pets, but some do so be sure to ask. Smoking, if allowed at all, is often restricted to certain areas.

Bed and breakfast lodgings in the county vary from historic inns in Beaufort to a rural inn Down East to beach-focused inns on Bogue Banks. Each offers charming surroundings, memorable views and warm hospitality, and most are within walking distance of area attractions, shops and restaurants. The inns described in this chapter (we list them in alphabetical order within their geographic regions) offer a range of prices based on amenities of each room or suite of rooms.

Coastal scenery is worth a second look.

photo: Peter Doran

PRICE CODE

The price codes reflect an average figure for double occupancy in the peak season from April through October. As always, it's best to verify the information that is important to you — including acceptable forms of payment — when making your reservations.

$	Less than $100
$$	$101 to $125
$$$	$126 to $150
$$$$	More than $150

Beaufort

Captain's Quarters Bed & Biscuit   **$$**
315 Ann St., Beaufort
(252) 728-7711, (800) 659-7111

This two-story home with its luxurious wrap-around porch offers the charm of a Victorian summer at the shore. The interior is decorated with family heirlooms and antiques that reflect the charm of the home. The Captain's Quarters is proud to offer hospitality with "quiet elegance," making guests feel right at home upon arrival. You'll find Ms. Ruby, Capt. Dick Collins and their daughter Polly to be delightful, welcoming hosts. Be sure to ask Capt. Dick Collins about what brought him to Beaufort — his enthusiasm and love for the area are contagious. The three upstairs bedrooms feature private powder rooms and baths. House traditions include Ms. Ruby's fresh "riz" biscuits, full continental breakfasts and complimentary beverages to welcome the sunset each evening. The Collins family will gladly help you with area information and dinner reservations as well as provide you with the use of a computer, wireless Internet service and a fax machine. The Captain's Quarters has been

Hosts at all bed and breakfast accommodations routinely line up adventures and activities for their guests, such as kayaking, Gulf Stream fishing, sailing, golf or tennis. Ask your hosts about setting up activities that interest you.

rated "Excellent" by the North Carolina Bed & Breakfast Association. Payment by personal check is preferred.

County Home Bed & Breakfast   **$$**
299 N.C. Hwy. 101, Beaufort
(252) 728-4611

Located on N.C. Highway 101, a half-mile north of the intersection of U.S. Highway 70 East, County Home B&B is just minutes from Beaufort's famed historic district. Known as the County Home, it is one of the town's most interesting buildings and is Beaufort's only bed and breakfast listed on the National Register of Historic Places. Built in 1913-14, before the days of Social Security and welfare, it was operated by Carteret County for 29 years as a house for the area's "poor, aged and infirm." The building's architectural and cultural interest kept it safe from demolition but not deterioration until it was bought by Terry and Nan O'Pray for restoration into a bed and breakfast. Because of the building's simple yet classic design, don't expect the stereotypical Victorian home most imagine for a bed and breakfast. Instead, you'll find ten private, individually decorated efficiency suites complete with comfortable, charming decor. Its location and backyard pavilion on 2 acres make it an ideal getaway for weddings, family reunions or special weekends. Tell your family and friends you're going to the poorhouse where Southern hospitality is spoken with a Northern accent. Children are always welcome, and pets are allowed in special pet-friendly rooms.

Cousins Bed and Breakfast   **$$**
305 Turner St., Beaufort
(252) 728-3917, (877) 464-7487

Cousins Bed and Breakfast in downtown Beaufort, known for a sumptuous breakfast, is also the only bed and breakfast that allows you to do a little shopping in your nightgown at the on-site shop. Martha and Elmo Barnes offer two air-conditioned rooms with private baths, furnished with an island motif. Located in the Historic District, Cousins resides in the Jarvis-Brown House, circa 1820, and is right across from the historic Carteret County Courthouse. Cousins' tariff covers an incomparable full breakfast prepared by Elmo, who is a master chef and has published his own cookbooks. Cooking classes are also available for small groups, so ask Elmo for details. Whether you're a guest or not, make sure you visit their shop, Martha's Collection of Spices & Gifts, which is full of wonderful items for yourself or to take home as a gift. (See our Shopping chapter for more information.)

The Inlet Inn $$$-$$$$
601 Front St., Beaufort
(252) 728-3600
www.inlet-inn.com

The 36-room Inlet Inn stands in the same block of Front Street occupied by the original Inlet Inn of the nineteenth century, which brought guests from across the state to bask in the Beaufort sun. Today's inn, of similar design, offers harborfront rooms on the first and second floors, each with a king-size bed and sofa. Third-floor rooms overlooking the water offer two queen beds and a wonderful window seat for viewing Beaufort Inlet, the waterfront and beyond. Many rooms open onto private porches and offer bars, refrigerators with ice makers and built-in hair dryers. Six of the first-floor rooms offer cozy fireplaces, and wireless Internet access is available on the premises and at nearby

coffee shops. A continental breakfast, served in the rooms, consists of muffins, bagels and juice. Coffeemakers are provided in each room. A courtyard garden, the rooftop Widow's Walk Lounge and an on-site meeting room are also available for guests' use year round.

Langdon House Bed $$$-$$$$
and Breakfast
135 Craven St., Beaufort
(252) 728-5499
www.langdonhouse.com

The innkeepers and restorers of the Langdon House (c. 1733) extend the hospitality of good friends and provide all the extras that give their guests a personalized experience of Beaufort. Each of the four guest rooms has a queen-size bed and a private bath and is furnished with antiques in keeping with the old Colonial/Federal home. The latest renovation is their "Master Guest Room" with an extra-large whirlpool bath for two and tandem shower with a Grohe Aquatower as well as other surprises. Come here to relax; sleeping late is considered a compliment to the innkeepers. The hallmark of the innkeepers' hospitality is a full breakfast, served until 11 AM. A hearty serving of fresh fruit is followed by one of the house special-

*See this entire guide plus additional content
online at insiderinfo.us*

ties, such as stuffed French toast, Belgian waffles or Mexican cuisine, if your appetite is adventuresome. Credit cards and personal checks are accepted. Bring a change of clothes and a good attitude, and they'll take care of the rest.

Old Seaport Inn **$$-$$$**
Bed and Breakfast
217 Turner St., Beaufort
(252) 728-4300, (800) 349-5823

Old Seaport Inn, located in the Historic District of Beaufort, is just steps away from the Beaufort Historic District and the Beaufort waterfront. From there you can enjoy unique shopping, fine dining or take a trip to the outer islands where you can spend as much time as you like. The Old Seaport Inn offers three uniquely furnished guest rooms, each with a private bath. A full breakfast is served daily. The inn is plaqued by the Beaufort Historic Commission as the Gibble-Delamar House c. 1866. The Old Seaport Inn has two separate porches, one upstairs and one downstairs, that welcome you to relax with a cup of coffee, a glass of wine or a good book along with sea breezes. Located on the first floor is the Cotter Hurst Gallery, where you can view the works of your host, Mary Cotter Hurst BFA, MFA. The gallery includes Mary's limited-edition etchings, wood cuts and original oil paintings. The Old Seaport Inn is one of Beaufort's oldest and finest bed and breakfast inns.

Pecan Tree Inn **$$-$$$**
116 Queen St., Beaufort
(252) 728-6733, (800) 728-7871

This 1860s, two-story Victorian home, complete with gingerbread trim, is a charming bed and breakfast with seven guest rooms. The location is perfect — in the heart of the Beaufort Historic District and just a few steps from the harbor. Each spacious room with private bath has a distinctive character. Two romantic suites have king-size canopied beds and Jacuzzis. A stay at the inn includes an expanded continental breakfast served in the dining room or on the inviting wrap-around front porch. Guests enjoy fresh-baked muffins, cakes and breads, fruit, cereal and fresh-roasted coffee. The hosts can assist with daytrip plans, dinner reserva-

tions or flowers. Beach chairs and bicycles are available. Relax on the cool porches overlooking the inn's expansive herb and flower garden. All rooms have cable TV and wireless high-speed Internet service.

Down East

Otway House Bed & Breakfast **$$$**
368 U.S. Hwy. 70, Otway
(252) 728-5636

Leave the hustle and bustle behind for this bed and breakfast inn, located on 6 acres in the Down East community of Otway. The inn features four private rooms (one king and three queens), each with a full private bath and decorated with antique and reproduction furniture. Rooms have cable TV, hairdryers and other amenities. Guests enjoy a full breakfast of coffee or tea, juice and fruit with their choice of pancakes, French toast or eggs, as well as a choice of bacon or sausage. Pet guests are accommodated in indoor/outdoor kennel facilities with cots, shade screened runs, fans or heat, depending on the weather. Pets can relax in comfort while you go to the beach or play in the new safe, fenced play field. This is a relaxing, quiet place to stay with a wonderful front porch surrounded by mature pecan trees and beautiful butterfly gardens. Located between Beaufort and Harkers Island, Otway House is convenient to the area's beaches, boat-launch sites, historic sites, Cape Lookout National Seashore and the Down East communities. This is the perfect lodging if you like being pampered in the countryside.

Cape Carteret and Emerald Isle

Emerald Isle Inn Bed and Breakfast **$$$**
502 Ocean Dr., Emerald Isle
(252) 354-3222

Elaine and Jim Normile accommodate their island guests in four suites. Two suites are apartments rented by day or week, the other two suites come without kitchen accommodations and can also be rented by day or week. Each suite has a private entrance and a private bath. There are also televisions, VCRs and movie libraries in each suite. Guests enjoy views of the ocean and sound from porches with comfortable swings. Beach accesses are nearby, and beach chairs and umbrellas are available for guest use. A full breakfast is served each morning in the dining room.

Harborlight Guest House $$$$
332 Live Oak Dr., Cape Carteret
(252) 393-6868, (800) 624-VIEW (8439)

With six luxurious suites, Harborlight Guest House is situated on a spectacular peninsula on Bogue Sound just off N.C. Highway 24 near Emerald Isle. This three-story inn offers high-end bed-and-breakfast accommodations in a building that once served as a restaurant for the ferry service. The inn is graced with spectacular views of 530 feet of shoreline and sits in a quiet area close to beaches, Hammocks Beach State Park and all the amenities of the Crystal Coast.

Rocking chairs on the decks are perfect spots to read a good book or just enjoy the wildlife along the waterfront. Suites offer the comforts of fireplaces and whirlpools and the incredible water views that make Harborlight so special. Handicapped-accessible accommodations on the ground level are fully equipped with all necessities. The hospitality of owners Debbie Mugno and Bob Pickens includes a gourmet breakfast served privately en suite or deckside daily. Open year round, the inn offers its 20-person capacity conference room for seminars and other group gatherings. Harborlight Guest House has been featured in *Southern Living* magazine as one of the five outstanding bed and breakfast inns in North Carolina. It has also been named among the "Top Undiscovered Inns in America."

VACATION RENTALS

The Crystal Coast is the perfect place to vacation for so many reasons. There's a little something for everyone when it comes to things to do, see and explore. The same is true for where to stay — there's a variety of choices in that area, too. After all, it will be your home while you're here, so it's important to find the right accommodations for your needs and expectations. With more than 10,000 rooms for rent on the Crystal Coast, according to recent figures from the Tourism Development Authority (TDA), (252) 726-8148 or (800) SUNNY-NC, deciding what best suits your needs is a good place to start. Vacation rental options come in all shapes and sizes. Guests will find everything from small fishing units near the sound or ocean — perfect if you spend all your time fishing — to plush condominiums, quaint cottages and seaside homes with an array of amenities. All you need to do is make a few simple decisions, starting with when you wish to visit the coast. If this is your first visit, you are about to discover why so many people return year after year — if you're a returning guest, the Crystal Coast welcomes you back.

The Rate Season

Since this area offers vacation opportunities throughout all the seasons, the rental rates can run the full spectrum when it comes to pricing. The rates fluctuate according to the season, but what makes it a bit confusing is the definition of "season." The majority of the rental agencies here on the Crystal Coast have the rental seasons defined in their own terms, using a schedule and calendar that reflects their seasonal pricing categories. It's always best to check with each rental company for specific season/rate changes.

As a general guideline, rental agencies on the east end of Bogue Banks and in other areas of Carteret County base rental rates on two seasons: in-season (Memorial Day through Labor Day) and off-season (any other time). On the west end of the island many rental agencies use something similar to a four-season schedule: May through mid-June and mid-August through September are mid-seasons; mid-June through mid-August is prime season; September through November and March through April are shoulder seasons; December through February is off-season or winter. Again, it's best to check with the specific rental company for its seasonal pricing categories. Prime season is the most expensive time to rent a vacation accommodation.

Vacation rentals can vary from $300 to more than $5,000 a week. Don't be surprised to find a few of the premier oceanfront rentals running in the $10,000 a week and higher price range during prime season. You may find rates as much as 20 to 25 percent less in the shoulder season and off-season (after Labor Day and during the winter months) than in-season (Memorial Day through Labor Day). For that reason, many people prefer to vacation during the beautiful weather of the shoulder seasons — April and May and September through November.

Decide what you need and call a rental agency listed in the following pages. Remember, the base rental rate a company lists is not the complete cost of renting, so ask questions. Agencies can add cleaning fees and there are also taxes. In addition to North Carolina's sales tax, Carteret County's occupancy tax is 5 percent. You also will have to provide a security deposit (the amount varies with the rental company), which will be refunded provided nothing is damaged.

Knowing The Beach
is our business.
Helping you find your place at the beach is our pleasure.

Family Owned and Operated

Locations and Types of Accommodations

Rental agencies are a great resource when it comes to finding that cozy beach cottage, upscale oceanfront condo or soundside multi-family house that's perfect for your vacation here on the Crystal Coast. There are a variety of accommodations available, so be sure to investigate your choices. Many rental companies publish an annual vacation rental guide that gives a wealth of information including the location, seasonal costs, amenities, as well as exterior and interior photos of the rentals they have available. Many of the companies also offer an online system through their websites that allows you to be as general or as specific as you like when it comes to searching for the rental that best matches your particular needs. Of course, a phone call to the rental company itself allows you to ask the questions and get the answers you need that you may not get through a brochure, guide or website.

Rental costs vary with the type of accommodation and the location. Always check rental brochures or with an agent about the location. This is very important if you are planning to walk to the beach. Carrying chairs, coolers and an umbrella while watching out for your children can make a short trip seem a lot longer if you are several rows back from the water. Of course, generally speaking, the farther away from the water, the less expensive the rental rate.

At the beach, location is everything, and an understanding of location descriptions can make all the difference in your family's vacation. Imagine a small strip of land, one side facing the sound, the other side facing the open ocean. That makes it easier when deciding what sort of accommodations work best for you. When speaking in terms of accommodation location, oceanfront means facing the ocean with no physical barrier, road or property lines between you and the beach. Oceanside means you can walk to the beach without crossing a major road, but there might be other rows of houses between your cottage and the ocean. Soundfront means the cottage fronts the sound and you have easy access to the water. Soundside means you are on the sound side of the

The *Wind in the Willows* quote holds true here: 'There is nothing – absolutely nothing – half so much worth doing as simply messing about in boats.'

photo: Robert Graves

road and in walking distance of the sound. Often, soundside cottages and developments offer guests access to the ocean and beach by means of a walking path.

If you're vacation rental isn't at the beach, you may want to inquire about your proximity to the beach. The location of your rental and its centrality to shopping, area restaurants and other attractions may be important depending on how you, and those vacationing with you, want to spend your precious vacation time. The more you know in advance, the happier you'll be with your accommodations.

Pets

Many vacationers don't want to have to leave part of the family at home when they travel. For that reason, some of the rental accommodations are happy to offer pet-friendly options. If you do plan to bring a pet with you on vacation, that's one of the first things you'll want to tell the rental agent. There are usually specific requirements when it comes to the number of pets and sometimes there are size limitations. Most places that are pet-friendly allow dogs, but not cats. Be prepared to pay an additional, non-refundable fee. Some places don't allow pets at all and vacationers who violate this rule are subject to eviction, the loss of their deposit and payment of any damages the pet caused. Boarding kennels and many pet services are available in the area. (See the Traveling with Pets section in the Hotels and Motels chapter on our website (www.insiders.com/crystalcoast) for a link to our listing of pet-friendly accommodations.)

North Carolina law bans grilling on the decks and balconies of rental properties. In Carteret County, strong winds can make grilling near cottages a dangerous activity. It is always best to check with your rental agent to find out where to use the grill or review your rental policy for details.

Furnishings and Equipment Rentals

If you are renting an apartment or condo, it will be fully furnished. Most rental brochures list the furnishings (small appliances, TVs, VCRs, stereos, toasters, microwaves, etc.) and other items that are provided, such as beach chairs and umbrellas, hammocks and grills. You might only need to bring your sheets and towels, or you can rent those from your booking agency. If not, there are a few independent agencies that rent linens along with other extras, such as baby furniture and folding beds. (See the Rental Services section in this chapter.)

Length of Stay

Most vacation homes and condos are rented on a weekly basis, particularly in the summer. Some run on a Saturday to Saturday or Sunday to Sunday rental schedule. If you would like just a few days at the beach, check with an agency and see what can be arranged for a two- or three-day rental. Everything is more flexible in the off-season. Each rental unit is governed by rules and regulations spelled out in rental brochures and contracts.

Other Tips

Renting vacation accommodations is a business, so approach it that way. Be sure to read the rental agreement carefully and ask questions if there is anything you don't understand. By getting all your questions answered, you can often reduce the number of items you bring and make it an enjoyable vacation for everyone. If you are a smoker, check to see if smoking is permitted. If you are planning a house party, let the agent know in advance. If large parties are prohibited and you ignore this rule, you could be evicted and lose your money. Rental companies are usually happy to take messages and mail for you. Be sure to let those at home know the name and street address of the unit where you will be staying and the mailing address and phone number of the rental company.

Most rental companies offer travel protection insurance of some type in the event that unforeseen circumstances interrupt or cancel your vacation plans. In many instances, this is the only way of getting reimbursed in the case of a hurricane evacuation, so it's something to consider. When making your reservations, be sure to ask about the company's refund and cancellation policies.

Rental Companies

Rental companies are the local experts when it comes to what's available in terms of weekly and long-term rentals. The Crystal Coast offers numerous rental accommodations, and many places are booked early in the year so it's best to plan as far ahead as possible. Call agencies and request brochures or check their websites to see the available cottages, condos, houses and other available options. These resources can help you make your choice. Up-to-date brochures and websites are a wealth of information, not only about individual rates and policies, but also about area attractions and special events. Generally, agencies will provide a list of items that are provided. All of them clearly spell out the rates and policies of the rental company. Additionally, many agencies are now using online reservations. Here we have listed a few of the many Crystal Coast companies that handle

rentals. We have alphabetically arranged these companies for your convenience. To receive brochures, call the agencies at the numbers listed.

ATLANTIC BEACH

Atlantic Beach Realty - Ocean Resorts
Atlantic Beach Cswy., Atlantic Beach
(252) 240-7368, (800) 786-7368
www.atlanticbeachrealty.net

Atlantic Beach Realty has been offering cottage and condominium vacation rentals on the Crystal Coast for more than 19 years. Specializing in properties in Atlantic Beach and Pine Knoll Shores, this firm's main office is located on the Atlantic Beach Causeway. They offer two on-site offices located at Dunescape Villas and Island Beach and Racquet Club.

Atlantic Sun Properties, Inc.
205 Atlantic Beach Cswy., Atlantic Beach
(252) 808-2SUN (2786)
www.AtlanticSunProperties.com

You're on island time! That's the slogan of Atlantic Sun Properties, where the staff is just waiting to help make your perfect vacation memory happen. Atlantic Sun Properties strives to offer the best of the beach. Each rental cottage, condo and duplex managed by this firm has its own unique offerings, and there is one sure to fit your vacation desires. Let the staff of Atlantic Sun Properties help make your vacation unforgettable.

Beach Vacation Properties
301 Commerce Way, Atlantic Beach
(252) 247-2636, (800) 334-2667
www.beachvacationproperties.com

Whether it is seasonal short-term rentals or off-season long-term rentals, Beach Vacation Properties can find just the right cottage or condominium to suit your needs. This company also handles sales at A Place at the Beach, Sea Spray and Sands Villa as well as offering property-management services. No matter the size of housing you need or the length of your stay, the staff at Beach Vacation Properties can help.

Bluewater GMAC - Atlantic Beach
311-C Atlantic Beach Cswy., Atlantic Beach
(866) 467-3105
www.bluewatergmac.com

Bluewater GMAC Real Estate has four offices to serve you in Atlantic Beach, Beaufort, Cape Carteret and Emerald Isle. They are the winner of the *Coaster Magazine* Readers' Choice Award for both best Real Estate Agency and Best Rental Agency. They offer online booking, spe-

cials and a variety of vacation rentals to fit any budget. This company offers nightly, weekly, monthly and annual rentals. Some of those properties allow pets. They are a full-service company that provides it all, including vacation rentals, real estate sales, builders and aquatics.

Cannon & Gruber Realtors
509 Atlantic Beach Cswy., Atlantic Beach
(252) 726-6600

Cannon & Gruber has a number of cottages and beautiful oceanfront condominiums for rent on Bogue Banks. From Indian Beach to Atlantic Beach and across the bridge along the water in Morehead City, Cannon & Gruber is eager to help vacationers find a perfect site.

Coldwell Banker Spectrum Properties
515 Atlantic Beach Cswy., Atlantic Beach
(252) 247-7610, (800) 334-6390
www.spectrumproperties.com

Spectrum Properties offers the finest selection of vacation rental properties on the Crystal Coast and is unsurpassed in customer service. Choose from oceanfront, oceanside and soundfront homes, condominiums and duplexes of all sizes and prices. Spectrum also offers a wide variety of properties for rental on a long-term basis. Call Spectrum's rental specialists or log onto their website to discuss and/or view great rental properties. Online booking is available.

Deanna Hull Realty
607 Atlantic Beach Cswy., Ste. 103,
Atlantic Beach
(252) 240-0273, (800) 477-4180
www.deannahullrealty.com

Serving timeshare owners since 1984, Deanna Hull Realty offers timeshare rental referral services for owners who can not use their timeshare week at a variety of oceanfront resorts at Atlantic Beach. The company also offers timeshare rental referrals by whole-ownership property owners. Whether you are looking to rent something to enjoy yourself or you are looking for referrals to rent your timeshare week, contact Deanna Hull Realty for assistance.

Realty World First Coast Realty
407 Atlantic Beach Cswy., Ste. 1,
Atlantic Beach
(252) 247-0077

The features of this agency include seasonal rentals of all types — beach cottages and condominiums, oceanfront to soundside — in a variety of price ranges. Realty World First Coast Realty offers rentals on Bogue Banks from Atlantic Beach to Emerald Isle and on the mainland in Morehead City, Beaufort and Newport. This company also offers cottages and condos perfect for a memorable coastal wedding, reception or romantic honeymoon, and it has the resources to accommodate an entire wedding party. The company also has real estate offices in

Be sure to know the times of check-in and check-out. Some rentals may allow early check-ins or late check-outs for a fee, but this usually must be requested well in advance of your stay. **i**

Beaufort, Emerald Isle, Morehead City, Newport and Down East.

SurfSide Realty, Inc.
204 Sandpiper Dr., Newport
(252) 726-0950

SurfSide Realty handles rentals at Atlantic Beach's SeaSpray, Southwinds, A Place at the Beach (APATB) and Tar Landing Villas. These condominium complexes are near Fort Macon State Park and offer miles of beachfront for relaxing and recreation. SurfSide specializes in family rentals and sales.

SALTER PATH, INDIAN BEACH AND PINE KNOLL SHORES

The Ocean Club Spa, Resort and Celebration Center
1700 N.C. Hwy. 58, Salter Path
(252) 247-2035, (888) 237-2035

The Ocean Club Spa, Resort and Celebration Center offers an idyllic vacation experience for families or couples, and it's also the perfect setting for health and wellness retreats, weddings and celebra-

tions, corporate executive meetings and seminars. All the villas are fully furnished. Enjoy The Ocean Club year round with an outdoor heated pool and spa. Guests can also enjoy sound access, small boating and an all-inclusive spa and wellness center.

Sunny Shores
520 N.C. Hwy. 58, Pine Knoll Shores
(252) 247-2665, (800) 624-8978
www.sunnyshoressales.com

Sunny Shores handles many vacation rentals of condos and cottages in Atlantic Beach as well as Beacon's Reach in Pine Knoll Shores. The full-service agency has a variety of lodgings, both large and small, in all price ranges, and offers a property-management service. Contact this firm for information about long-term rentals in the Morehead City area as well.

Whaler Inn Beach Club
323 N.C. Hwy. 58, Pine Knoll Shores
(252) 247-4169, (800) 525-1768

Attractive oceanfront one- and two-bedroom condominiums and efficiencies are the feature here. Completely furnished, the condo units offer fully equipped kitchens. Each unit offers a washer/dryer and a full kitchen. Owners have full access to the ocean beaches in front of the club as well as to the club's heated pool and Jacuzzi. Ownership also allows those living or visiting nearby to continue to use the facility's parking, beach access, showers, swimming, game room and other amenities. Whaler Inn is part of Interval International, allowing owners access to more than 11,000 resorts worldwide.

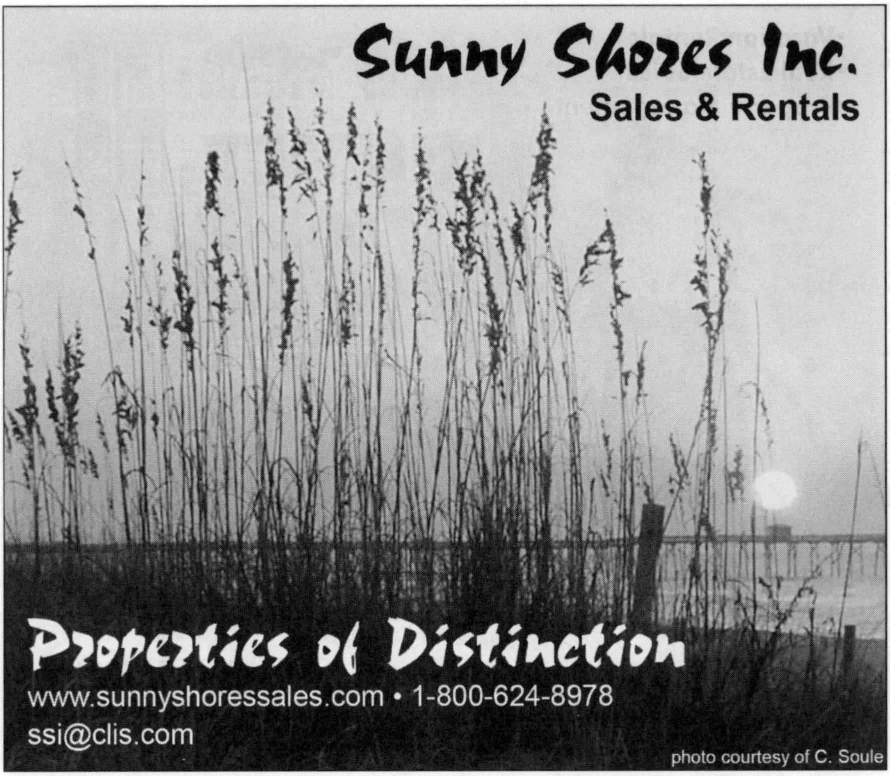

Windward Dunes
801 N.C. Hwy. 58, Indian Beach
(252) 247-7545, (800) 659-7545

Windward Dunes is an eight-story condominium development in Indian Beach and it includes units available for rental. All units are oceanfront with one- or two-bedrooms and include a kitchen and washer/dryer. The facility offers an elevator and indoor and outdoor pools.

EMERALD ISLE

Bluewater GMAC Real Estate-Rentals
200 Mangrove Dr., Emerald Isle
(252) 354-2323, (866) 595-1395
www.bluewatergmac.com

Bluewater GMAC Real Estate has four offices to serve you in Atlantic Beach, Beaufort, Cape Carteret and Emerald Isle. They are the winner of the *Coaster Magazine* Readers' Choice Award for both best Real Estate Agency and Best Rental Agency. They offer online booking, specials and a variety of vacation rentals to fit any budget. This company offers nightly, weekly, monthly and annual rentals. Some of those properties allow pets. They are a full-service company that provides it all, including vacation rentals, real estate sales, builders and aquatics.

See this entire guide plus additional content online at insiderinfo.us

Century 21 Coastland Realty
7603 Emerald Dr., Emerald Isle
(252) 354-2131, (800) 822-2121
www.coastland.com

This full-service real estate company has been in business since 1981. It was the first realty franchise on the beach. The company offers many properties for sale, both new and previously owned homes, condominiums, building lots and commercial properties. The firm specializes in Emerald Isle and the mainland areas of Cape Carteret and Cedar Point. Century 21 Coastland Realty also offers a property management division as well as vacation and long-term rental properties. Call these professionals for your real estate needs at the Crystal Coast.

Emerald Isle Realty
7501 Emerald Dr., Emerald Isle
(252) 354-3315, (866) 689-6327
www.emeraldislerealty.com

Discover first-class Southern hospitality, Crystal Coast style, by calling the knowledgeable staff at Emerald Isle Realty. Located on beautiful Bogue Banks,

Emerald Isle Realty offers vacation rentals for everyone. They specialize in weekly, monthly and annual rentals. Choose from their extensive selection of elegant beach homes, classic cottages, resort condos and pet-friendly vacation homes. Emerald Isle Realty's Reservation Specialists are equipped to take care of every detail of your beach vacation. Call them today to begin planning your "No Worries" dream vacation.

Shorewood Real Estate
7703 Emerald Dr., Emerald Isle
(252) 354-7873, (888) 557-0172
www.shorewoodrealestate.com

Shorewood Real Estate is a family-owned business that specializes in vacation rentals, property management and real estate sales. Celebrating its 13th year of service to property owners and guests of the Crystal Coast, the owners and staff of Shorewood Real Estate pride themselves on the delivery of exceptional customer service, professionalism and courtesy. With a wide selection of vacation rentals with amenities such as private

pools, hot tubs and game rooms, you are sure to find a property to meet your vacation rental needs. Visit their website for online booking and availability.

Spinnaker's Reach Realty
9918 M.B. Davis Ct., Emerald Isle
(252) 354-5555, (800) 245-7746
www.spinnakersreach.com

Spinnaker's Reach Realty offers premiere vacation rentals, sales and property management in beautiful Emerald Isle with personal attention and top-notch customer service. A full-service real estate company, the professional staff of locals helps in the buying, selling or renting of your coastal dream property. Spinnaker's Reach is a gorgeous private rental and long-term community on Coast Guard Road in Emerald Isle with homes and home sites from the sound to the ocean. The on-site office and staff help welcome you home whether you dream of an oceanfront castle or a quaint interior cottage. Spinnaker's Reach welcomes families and their pets to island life by offering several pet-friendly homes. Both small and large rental properties are

available in a private subdivision with reasonable deposits. It is the perfect community for special family gatherings. Whether planning a reunion, a birthday, an anniversary or a wedding, Spinnaker's Reach has an accommodation to fit your needs. Many of the properties feature pools, golf carts and elevators. Visit the website for virtual tours and online booking.

Sun-Surf Realty - Rentals
7701 Emerald Dr., Emerald Isle
(252) 354-2958, (866) 584-5125
www.SunSurfRealty.com

Sun-Surf Realty's slogan "Come for a Week...Stay for a Lifetime" says it all. A family-owned business since 1978, Sun-Surf can help you plan your vacation by offering many choices, including premier homes, modest cottages and beachfront/side condominiums with all the amenities. While here let one of their experienced sales professionals show you how you can make your "place at the beach" a reality. They have a "no-hassle vacation policy" with no reservation or pre-booking fees, buyer representation in real estate sales transactions, and one-on-one, full service property management of both vacation and annual rental properties.

Beaufort

Beaufort offers a limited number of rental units and those are typically advertised with local agents. To find a rental in Beaufort, contact the agents we list here, check *The Carteret County News-Times* or ask an Insider.

Beaufort Realty
325 Front St., Beaufort
(252) 728-5462, (800) 548-2961

Beaufort Realty offers annual and vacation rentals in historic Beaufort. The company offers many unique and historic homes in the historic district and on the waterfront. It also specializes in residential and commercial property in the Beaufort historic district and often has some desirable historic properties for sale. Agents also handle sales in Down East, Morehead City and on the beach.

Eddy Myers Real Estate
131 Middle Ln., Beaufort
(252) 728-1310

In addition to handling sales of historic and waterfront properties in Beaufort, Eddy Myers Real Estate can also help with vacation rentals. Whether it's a historic cottage, waterfront home or harborside suite you desire, let their staff's local knowledge and experience work for you. They also handle vacation rentals in the Down East area.

Down East

A drive Down East, particularly to Harkers Island and Cedar Island, will turn up several nice rental cottages/houses. Some are handled by real estate agencies and many are handled by the property owner. These rentals are popular and are booked year after year by the same people, so we suggest you make arrangements early. The Down East area offers a slower pace for vacationers. Don't look for a vacation that's full of brightly lit stores, bustling hotels or wild night spots. Plan on relaxing, spending time on the water,

enjoying fresh seafood and taking ferry rides to nearby Cape Lookout National Seashore.

Mason's Vacation Rentals
104 Tils Landing, Harkers Island
(252) 728-5870

Mason's offers fully equipped, two-bedroom mobile homes. Pets are welcome. The site is located close to the public boat ramp and ferry services. There is a two-day minimum, and guests get one night free with a week-long stay. Come stay a while with these folks and relax. Larry and Sandy Mason will be happy to see you.

Rose's Vacation Rentals
293 Bayview Dr., Harkers Island
(252) 728-2868

Rose's Vacation Rentals offers four separate units varying from cabins to a mobile unit. Each is priced reasonably, and rates vary depending on the size of the unit and length of stay. During the busy season there is a two-night minimum stay on the larger units. Rose's is located about a half-mile from most of the island's conveniences. Guests will find a grocery store, gift shops, restaurants and passenger ferries located nearby. Overnight docking and a ramp for shallow-draft vessels are available; inquire for the specific details. Rose's also offers two RV hookups and a tent site.

Timeshares

Timesharing may be worth looking into if you love vacationing here year after year. Several developments on the Crystal Coast are set up for timesharing. Billed as a way to have a lifetime of affordable vacations, timeshares allow you to purchase a block of time, usually one or more weeks, for a specific unit. Each year, the time you purchased is yours at that unit. If your plans should change, most of the companies will allow you to exchange your week on the Crystal Coast for another location around the nation or the world — depending on their company's real estate holdings. Check on this before you purchase.

Like any other commitment, be sure to understand all of the terms clearly. Working with a reputable agency will ensure that all of your questions are answered. Before you arrange to buy into a time-share condo, make sure you understand all the extras, including additional fees such as the maintenance fee. Once you pay off the note, you receive the deed to your week in your specific unit. Some organizations do put restrictions on resale, even after you own the time in that unit, so check on that before you put your name on the dotted line.

Convenience is a key factor in time-shares. There's a lot less preparation and a lot more time for easing right into vacation mode. The unit will be completely furnished, down to the linens, dishes and utensils, so you just stop by the supermarket and unload your stuff, and you're set for the duration. Each of the timeshare facilities listed here is loaded with amenities, and each one is different. If you are seriously considering buying into a time-share property, give the resort a call and arrange a tour. For a list of companies that sell timeshares, visit the timeshare section of our Real Estate chapter.

Deanna Hull Realty
607 Atlantic Beach Cswy., Ste. 103, Atlantic Beach
(252) 240-0273, (800) 477-4180
www.deannahullrealty.com

Serving timeshare owners and buyers since 1984, Deanna specializes in Atlantic Beach oceanfront resort property, handles resales with no up-front fee, and works to save buyers on lower-priced homeowners association closeout inventory and time-share resales. Deanna is a licensed Real Estate Broker so whether buying or selling property of any type on the Crystal Coast or surrounding areas contact Deanna for an honest, no-pressure approach. She prides herself on keeping her clients' best interests at heart. Timeshare rentals at A Place At The Beach III, Sands Villa and Peppertree are also available.

Peppertree Atlantic Beach
715 N.C. Hwy. 58, Atlantic Beach
(252) 247-5841

Peppertree Atlantic Beach offers one, two and three-bedroom villas with all the extras. Each unit has a full kitchen and at least one deck. A private boardwalk leads guests from their villa to the wide beach and the Atlantic Ocean. On site, guests can enjoy an indoor and an outdoor pool, a laundry facility, a beauty salon/day spa, a recreation room, a children's playground and pool, grills and picnic areas and a basketball court. Peppertree Atlantic Beach is part of Festiva Resorts, a privately held vacation ownership company that boasts a wide array of resorts throughout the United States and into the Caribbean.

Whaler Inn Beach Club
323 N.C. Hwy. 58, Pine Knoll Shores
(252) 247-4169, (800) 525-1768

Attractive, oceanfront, one- and two-bedroom condominiums and efficiencies are the feature here. Completely furnished, the condo units offer fully equipped kitchens and a washer/dryer. Owners have full access to the ocean beaches in front of the club as well as to the club's heated pool and Jacuzzi. Ownership also allows those living or visiting nearby to continue to use the facility's parking, beach access, showers, swimming, game room and other amenities. Whaler Inn is part of Interval International, allowing owners access to more than 11,000 resorts worldwide.

Rental Services

These rental services make traveling a breeze. You don't have to worry about how you're going to fit everything into your vehicle and still have room for the passengers. There is no need to load up all the extras, such as baby cribs, beach chairs, beach bikes, blankets, towels and linens and bring them from home. Instead, consider renting them from one of the companies listed here. It saves packing,

---

Spring and fall are exquisite at the Crystal Coast. With less humidity in the air, the colors of the coast are incredibly vibrant. The weather is temperate, the beaches have fewer visitors, the restaurants are less hurried, and the roads are less crowded.

---

unpacking and cleanup time, giving you more time for fun.

Beach Wheels Bike Rentals
607 Atlantic Beach Cswy., Ste. 103, Atlantic Beach
(252) 240-BIKE (2453), (800) 504-2450
www.beachwheelsbikerentals.com

Offering "different spokes for different folks," Beach Wheels Bike Rentals provides one of the best and largest selections of bikes on the island. Beach Wheels offers beach cruisers, adult bikes, children's bikes, tag-a-longs, adult trikes, tandems and more. In its seventh year of business, this company provides friendly and convenient service with a free delivery and pick-up service anywhere on the Crystal Coast. Call ahead, reserve your wheels, and when you arrive your bikes will be waiting.

Bogue Banks Beach Gear and Linens Rentals
Bell Cove Village, 9106-C Coast Guard Rd., Emerald Isle
(252) 354-4404
www.boguebanksbeachgear.com

This is the company voted #1 by the Readers' Choice Awards three years in a row. They have two locations to serve your rental needs, one in Emerald Isle and one in Atlantic Beach. Be sure to stop by their Event Rental Showroom located at the Emerald Isle location. Bogue Banks Beach Gear & Linens offers items for daily and weekly rentals. From umbrellas and bikes to their custom beach towels and luxurious linen sets, this company has all your rental needs covered. They offer a wide selection of beach and baby equipment rentals, with free delivery along the Crystal Coast. They also offer a full line of wedding and events rentals with affordable packages and an array of table linens to choose from. These folks provide the largest selection of quality rental items with friendly customer service. Whether you need a crib, high chair, grill or other item, let Bogue Banks Beach Gear & Linen Rentals handle it for you. They're open year-

round seven days a week and they accept VISA/MC with online reservations.

Emerald Isle Baskets and Gifts
7901 Veranda Sq., Ste. 14, Emerald Isle
(252) 354-2350, (800) 653-1585

Emerald Isle Baskets offers creative ways to express your feelings and share special memories. The shop offers custom-made gift baskets of all types, arranged in unique containers and containing special items. Whether it is a university-themed basket or a home theater basket or a vacationers basket, the gift is sure to please the recipient. There are a variety of gourmet foods and gourmet gift baskets to suit any occasion. The shop uses boxes, baskets, tote bags and other containers as the base, and also offers customized embroidery for beach towels, bags and hats. Emerald Isle Baskets also has a nice selection of gifts.

Island Essentials - A Linen and Leisure Rental Company
208-A Bogue Inlet Dr., Emerald Isle
(252) 354-3315

For classic "shore things," such as wooden beach chairs, sun umbrellas and baby gear rentals, look to the welcoming folks at Island Essentials - A Linen & Leisure Rental Company. This company also offers bed and bath linen solutions and bed-making services for vacationers, vacation homeowners and vacation rental managers. They make reserving your rental items easy with online reservations. Delivery and pick-up are always free.

USA Island Rentals
145-C Bogue Inlet Dr., Emerald Isle
(252) 354-8839, (800) 590-1711

USA Island Rentals specializes in items for vacationers. Cottage renters can get rollaway beds, cribs, high chairs, bicycles, beach chairs and umbrellas and other basic beach equipment. The company offers delivery and pickup of items so your vacation can be hassle-free.

CAMPING ⛺

For Insiders who enjoy camping, the Crystal Coast is almost heaven. The area offers excellent camping opportunities, from rent-a-space RV sites with all the conveniences of home to tent camping with no conveniences at all.

Camping along the coast is popular almost year round because of the mild climate. Summer campers may need to create shade with tarps or overhangs to protect themselves from the hot sun.

Campers will find beach camping a little different from mainland camping. You will probably need longer tent stakes to hold things down in the sandy soil. Netting is almost a must, except in the dead of winter, to protect against the late-afternoon and early morning mosquitoes and no-see-ums, those barely visible flying insects that only make themselves known when they bite. A roaring fire and a good insect repellent also help. If you aren't fond of plastering yourself with pesticides, try mixing Avon's Skin-So-Soft with water and spraying it on. This mixture will fend off most insects, and it smells good too.

Primitive camping is available at Cape Lookout National Seashore, Bear Island and in the Croatan National Forest (see our Attractions chapter for more about the National Forest). There are no designated camping sites on Cape Lookout National Seashore, but camping is allowed everywhere except on a small amount of well-marked, privately owned land. Bear Island has quiet, secluded campsites. Croatan National Forest, which includes land in Carteret and Craven counties, offers two options. You can stay in one of the planned campgrounds or pitch a tent anywhere on National Forest land that isn't marked for private use.

Overnight fees vary and usually depend on the location (whether oceanfront or off the beaten path) and the facilities offered. Almost all the commercial campgrounds charge extra for more than two people at one site. Reservations are suggested. Full hookups typically include water, sewer and electricity. There is no charge to camp at Cape Lookout National Seashore or at some sites in Croatan National Forest.

Bogue Banks

Holiday Trav-L-Park Resort
MM 21, N.C. Hwy. 58, Emerald Isle
(252) 354-2250

Located on the oceanside of N.C. 58 at the intersection with Coast Guard Road, Holiday Trav-L-Park offers 375 sites with full hookups along with a host of amenities: cable TV, laundry and shower facilities, an outdoor swimming pool, a recreation room, bicycle and go-cart rentals, a playground and more. The park is also home of the Emerald Isle Wine Market and is within walking distance of grocery stores, a movie theater, golf, shops and restaurants. Reservations are recommended at Holiday Trav-L-Park; nightly fees range from $30 to $85 for up to two people ($5 for each additional person, up to 13 people), depending on location and season. Pets are welcome to stay for an additional $5 per night. Spaces can be rented on an annual basis as well. The park is closed from December through February.

If you're planning to ferry a vehicle to Cape Lookout National Seashore, schedule your trip well in advance to ensure room on the ferry from Davis or Atlantic. (See our Getting Here, Getting Around chapter.)

Western Carteret County

Cedar Point Campground
Cape Carteret
(252) 638-5628

On the White Oak River a mile north of Cape Carteret (follow the signs from N.C. 58), this campground is a good stopover if you want to experience coastal marsh and maritime forest in their truest forms. At Cedar Point, lovers of the outdoors can enjoy many activities — camping, picnicking, fishing, boating and hiking. The site offers 40 camping units with electrical hookups, a bathhouse with flush toilets and warm showers, drinking water and a shallow boat ramp. A fee of $17, for an electrical hook-up, is charged for camping, and Cedar Point is open year-round. The Cedar Point Tideland Trail, an interpretive nature trail at this location, offers a 0.6-mile short loop that crosses the salt marsh and its edges, and a 1.3-mile loop that skirts the edge of the White Oak River and is popular with birders.

Goose Creek Resort
350 Red Barn Rd., Cape Carteret
(252) 393-2628

Goose Creek Resort offers 725 RV sites with full 30- and 50-amp hookups for family camping on Bogue Sound. There is a boat ramp, a pool, a water slide, a game room, a climate-controlled bathhouse, a camp store, tent sites, a 250-foot fishing pier, basketball, crabbing and a dump

> **i** When camping, keep in mind that wild animals, such as skunks and raccoons, are common in this area but are normally cautious and will stay away from humans and their pets. If a wild animal persists in approaching your campsite, particularly during daylight hours, report this to your campground host or the local animal control facility at (252) 728-8585. Do not feed or attempt to touch wild animals.

station. Goose Creek has an amphitheater for dancing and offers church services every other Sunday and on Easter. Open year round, Goose Creek's overnight rates range from $50 to $60 for two adults and kids younger than 12. Call for exact pricing. Water- and power-accessible tent sites cost $41 per night. The resort has accommodations for camping clubs for up to 31 units. Leashed pets are allowed.

Oyster Point Campground
8 miles off Mill Creek Rd., Newport
(252) 638-5628

Oyster Point, a primitive campground with 20 sites, can be found by making a right turn off Mill Creek Road onto Forest Road 181. Amenities are few but include drinking water, restrooms, picnic tables and grills. Campsites are $8 per day. The gate to the campground is locked each night from 10 PM to 8 AM, but a host is available to unlock the gate in case of emergencies. Nearby attractions include hiking on the Neusiok Trail, plus swimming and fishing.

Waters Edge RV Park
N.C. Hwy. 24, Newport
(252) 247-0494

This peaceful, secluded campground on the banks of Bogue Sound is open year round and offers 72 large sites with full hookups and paved roads. There are an additional 14 sites with water and electrical hookups. Folks with tents, campers and RVs can rent a space per night or by the season. Waters Edge amenities include a climate-controlled bathhouse, a 200-foot fishing pier and a dump station. Ask about seasonal and monthly rentals; they are a bargain for those who can get to the Crystal Coast often. Call for rates.

Waterway RV Park
850 Cedar Point Blvd., Cedar Point
(252) 393-8715

This 28-acre park is situated on the Intracoastal Waterway between Cape Carteret and Swansboro. Waterway RV Park offers 350 RV sites with full hookups, and cable TV is available. Open year-round, Waterway RV Park features volleyball and basketball courts, a game room, laundry and shower facilities, two boat ramps, a playground and a swimming pool. Shopping and restaurants are located nearby. This is an annual park. Call for rates.

Whispering Pines Campground
N.C. Hwy. 24, Morehead City
(252) 726-4902

Situated close to Bogue Sound, Whispering Pines has 130 full-hookup sites, a 70-foot swimming pool, a clubhouse with a kitchen, a freshwater pond and fishing. The camp store and the park are open all year. Whispering Pines offers a 10 percent discount to Good Sam and AARP members. Daily rates for pop-ups, travel trailers and motor homes are $44.45 per night. Off-site storage is available for boats and campers. Mail and phone-message services are offered.

Swansboro

Bear Island
1572 Hammock's Beach Rd., Swansboro
(910) 326-4881

Access to Bear Island is provided by ferry from Hammock's Beach State Park (see our Attractions and Getting Here, Getting Around chapters) or by private boat. Tickets are required for everyone riding the ferry, and the fee is $5 for adults and $3 for seniors and children ages 6 to 12. Cash or checks are accepted. Free ferry tickets are available to children age 5 and younger. The 3.5-mile island offers primitive camping at designated spots for $9 minimum per night. For groups, the fee is $1 per person, with a limit of nine campers at each of the three available group sites. The sites don't have water, sewer or electric hookups, although restrooms and showers are available. These facilities are not available from November through March. Campers must register with the park office on the mainland before going over to Bear Island. Campsites for boaters are also offered, but some sites are tricky to get to because of shallow water. Campers traveling by ferry are advised to travel light because it is more than a half-mile

walk from the ferry landing to some sites. Those interested in camping on Bear Island should be aware that alcoholic beverages and open campfires are not allowed. Bring a grill or camp stove for cooking. Although pets are allowed on the island, they are not allowed in the swimming area or on the ferry so you can only get them there by personal boat. Owners also are required to clean up after their pets and keep them on leashes of six feet or less at all times. Be aware that by June 2009, there will be a new reservation system in effect for all North Carolina State Parks. Check this out by going to www.ncparks. gov.

Down East

Cedar Creek Campground and Marina
111 Canal Dr., Sea Level
(252) 225-9571

Owners Catherine and Jerry Nelson cater to family camping with easy access to Core Sound and Drum Inlet. Open April 1 through November 30, the campground offers its guests such amenities as a swimming pool, flush toilets, hot-water showers, a dump station, boating, fishing and horseshoes. There are 35 sites with full hookups, 18 with only electrical and water, and 20 tent sites. Nightly rental for two adults is $25 for complete hookup and $17 without hookup. Extra guests are charged $2 per person. Leashed pets are permitted. Cedar Creek also offers an RV storage area and gives a 10 percent discount to Good Sam and AAA members.

Coastal Riverside Campground
216 Clark Ln., Otway
(252) 728-5155

Open April through December, Coastal Riverside Campground is located on a finger creek of the North River and features 53 RV sites with full hook-ups and 25 additional sites for tents. Campground amenities include laundry facilities, showers, a boat ramp and pier, and cable hookups. Reservations for RV camping are required, and nightly fees are $25 for two people (plus $2 for each additional person) for a full hookup site; $15 for a site without hookups.

Driftwood Campground
N.C. Hwy. 12, Cedar Island
(252) 225-4861

This 65-site, waterfront campground sits next to the Cedar Island–Ocracoke ferry terminal. Overnight fees are $20 with full hookup, $18 for water and electricity only, and $16 for a tent site. A bathhouse and dump station are available. Swimmers and sunbathers will enjoy the camp's sandy beach on Pamlico Sound. Kiteboarding, kayaking and surf fishing are very popular here. The campground is open year-round, although water service is not available December 15 through March 1. It is part of the Driftwood complex, which includes a motel, restaurant and gift shop. Driftwood's restaurant is well known for its great food. (See our Restaurants and Hotels & Motels chapters for more information.)

Core Banks

Cape Lookout National Seashore
131 Charles St., Harkers Island
(252) 728-2250

Cape Lookout National Seashore (see our Attractions chapter), which has four barrier islands and spans 56 miles of remote coastline from Ocracoke Inlet to Beaufort Inlet, offers waterfront camping at its best — and plenty of privacy. You might see a ranger and a few anglers around the cabins or folks around the lighthouse keepers' quarters, but otherwise you are on your own. Imagine sitting around the fire at dusk, listening to the sound of waves and watching the sweeping light of the Cape Lookout Lighthouse, with water as far as you can see in either direction.

This camping area has no developed campsites and no bathhouses (the lighthouse has a toilet and there is a composting toilet near the beach). Because there are no facilities available — not even trash cans — campers must bring in everything they need, including water, and must take their garbage with them when they leave. While there are no fees charged to camp at Cape Lookout, park officials request that campers register either at park headquarters on Harkers Island, the keepers' quarters at the lighthouse or with a park ranger. Campers are not allowed to camp near the lighthouse or the restrooms.

There also are two cabin complexes maintained by private concessionaires and overseen by the National Park Service. They vary greatly in their amenities, although they have cooking facilities, flush toilets and hot showers (see our Hotels & Motels chapter).

So how do you get to this wonderland? By boat or ferry. Ferry service is provided by concessionaires permitted by the National Park Service (see our Getting Here, Getting Around chapter) and numerous privately operated ferry services permitted by the National Park Service. Four-wheel-drive vehicles are permitted in some areas (the ferry services charge an extra fee to transport vehicles to the island). As in all national parks, some restrictions apply, so talk to a ranger before scheduling your trip.

Croatan National Forest

Croatan National Forest
Ranger's Office, 141 E. Fisher Ave., New Bern
(252) 638-5628

Croatan National Forest is made up of 159,866 acres spread between Morehead City and New Bern. Recreational areas are available for a day's outing or for overnight camping. The forest's planned campsites include Cedar Point, Neuse River (Flanners Beach) and Fishers Landing, where you will find drinking water, bathhouse facilities and picnic areas. Primitive camping is permitted all year, and campfires are usually permitted (check with the ranger office during the dry season). For more information on the Croatan National Forest, see our Crystal Coast Attractions chapter or the New Bern Camping chapter.

SHOPPING

When you've had enough of the sand, sun and surf (if that's even possible) or if the weather just isn't cooperating, have no fear — there's always shopping. In fact, many Crystal Coast visitors enjoy the shopping as much as the beach. While the area does not have a large shopping mall, it does have a variety of shopping centers featuring anchor stores and individually owned stores, boutiques and specialty shops. You will find a little of everything — from the necessities to the luxuries and everything in between.

The area has mini-malls, shopping neighborhoods and several good-size shopping centers with some of the major chain stores people are used to. This combination affords you plenty of places to find what you need and want. Since the Crystal Coast is considered a resort area, you'll find dozens of shops that cater to the beachgoer or surfer. Whether you're looking for a beach souvenir, a gift for someone back home, the perfect-fitting swimsuit, a special T-shirt or a beach wrap, you'll find it here. If you need clothing or equipment for your favorite summer sport, you will find many brands of outdoor clothes and sports equipment to choose from — everything from golf apparel and hunting wear to surfboards and kayaks. Be aware, however, that many area shops close or shorten their hours during the winter, so call first to make sure the store you want to visit is open.

We have designed this section to give you a brief look at some of the retail businesses in each Crystal Coast community. Antiques shops are listed separately at the end of this chapter. With such an array to choose from, we can't mention every shop that warrants your attention, so be sure to explore on your own. And, as always, if you're in need of help, other Insiders will be delighted to share information with you.

Bogue Banks

Driving down N.C. Highway 58, the main island road, there's plenty shopping to be had. From individual shops to shopping plazas, there's a store (or two or three) for just about everything. So if it's not the best beach day, take heart and know that there's still a lot to see and do. Most Bogue Banks' shopping is focused on the active lifestyle of both resident and visiting beachgoers. Shops offer swimwear, watersports accessories, casual wear, seashells and souvenirs. There are also some great specialty shops that shouldn't be missed. We offer a sampling of some of the shops you'll find on Bogue Banks, beginning in Atlantic Beach and wandering west to Emerald Isle. We have given the mile marker (MM) number for the shops on N.C. Highway 58. When winter business is slow, Bogue Banks shopkeepers often close early or limit the days they stay open, so call before you head out. You'll find that the huge, specialty stores of Wings and Pacific have found their way to Bogue Banks. These stores are so obvious that you can't possibly miss them, and inside you'll find beachwear, sunglasses, souvenirs, clothing and novelty items. Wings has two stores in Atlantic Beach and one in Emerald Isle, and Pacific has a store in Atlantic Beach and one in Emerald Isle.

ATLANTIC BEACH

Atlantic Beach Surf Shop
MM 2.5, N.C. Hwy. 58, Atlantic Beach
(252) 726-9382

A local business since 1964, Atlantic Beach Surf Shop continues to offer quality beachwear and upscale casual clothes. Footwear, sunglasses, surfboards, T-shirts, sandals and all the accessories are for sale. Pick up a cool sticker for the kids or a chunk of wax for your surfboard. The store carries paddleboards and accessories, too. Looking for surfing lessons? This shop can help you learn to love the waves by offering individual and group surf lessons. Atlantic Beach Surf Shop is open daily year round. Call the shop for the latest surf report.

Beach Book Mart
Atlantic Station Shopping Ctr., MM 3, N.C. Hwy. 58, Atlantic Beach
(252) 240-5655

Beach Book Mart is the perfect place to pick up reading materials whether it's a day at the beach or a rainy day inside. This discount bookstore offers all types of books. Check out their extensive selection of best sellers and their selection of youth and children's books — or maybe some lighter reading material such as comics or magazines. The kids will love their selection of action figures, too. There are lots of cookbooks and books of local interest — all at reduced prices. The store is open daily.

Bert's Surf Shop
MM 2, N.C. Hwy. 58, Atlantic Beach
(252) 726-1730

Bert's has one location in Atlantic Beach and two locations in Emerald Isle. Bert's stocks swimwear, active wear, foot gear, beach T-shirts, sunglasses and a large variety of sports equipment, including surfboards and skateboards. You'll also find some infant and toddler clothing and a youth department. There is a large selection of women's name-brand swimwear and men's sportswear. It's open seven days a week year round.

Captain Stacy Fishing Center Gift Shop
Atlantic Beach Cswy., Atlantic Beach
(252) 247-9551

Located right on the fishing center docks, this gift shop offers jewelry, gifts and flags, many with nautical or beach themes. The shop offers etched glass, crystal and a variety of holiday decorations, as well as T-shirts, casual clothing for men and women, beach bags and hats.

The shop is open year-round, although winter hours are limited.

Coastal Crafts Plus
Atlantic Station Shopping Ctr., MM 3, N.C. Hwy. 58, Atlantic Beach
(252) 247-7210

Coastal Crafts Plus features the work of many crafters, including pottery, jewelry, artwork and woodcrafts. You'll find a large selection of attractive and reasonably priced remembrances of your Crystal Coast vacation. Insiders shop here for gifts, T-shirts, yarn, nautical items and craft supplies. Coastal Crafters is open daily year round.

Hi-Lites
MM 2, N.C. Hwy. 58, Atlantic Beach
(252) 726-3496

Hi-Lites specializes in discounted clothing in juniors, misses and plus sizes with an emphasis on sporty separates. You'll also find swimsuits, belts, earrings, bags and hats and a full line of clothing suitable for the office. The store is open daily year round.

Kites Unlimited and Bird Stuff, Etc.
Atlantic Station Shopping Center, MM 3, N.C. Hwy. 58, Atlantic Beach
(252) 247-7011

Kites Unlimited and Bird Stuff are two stores in one. Kites Unlimited is where you go to find a special kite (and then grin from ear to ear as you get it aloft). The store has hundreds of wind-borne treasures in designs and sizes for all ability levels, including single line and steerable kites. Besides quality kites, take a look at the windsocks, flags, unique games and puzzles. Kites Unlimited is the business that sponsors kite-flying at 10 AM (9 AM in the summer months) each Sunday at Fort Macon State Park. The Bird Stuff part of the store is filled with all things to do with birds, from feeders and seed to baths and houses. It also has a selection of outdoor decor and gardening supplies.

Marsh's Surf Shop
615 Atlantic Beach Cswy., Atlantic Beach
(252) 726-9046

Marsh's is a local favorite known for its knowledgable staff and great selection of clothing and gear. This shop carries everything from quality dresses to shorts and T-shirts to jackets for men, women and children. The upper level was recently updated to offer a full array of ladies' attire. There are plenty of beach items too: sunglasses, surfboards, swimsuits and all types of accessories. Marsh's carries a wonderful selection of active-wear sandals. It's open seven days a week.

Sandi's Beachwear
MM 2.5, N.C. Hwy. 58, Atlantic Beach
(252) 726-4812

Sandi's offers a wide selection of women's specialty swimwear. Shoppers can find the right suit for every size and taste: sizes 4 to 24, long torso, special cup sizes, maternity and mastectomy. Brand-name casual and cruise wear include Athena, Anne Cole, Liz Claiborne and Anne Klein.

Hand-carved decoys and birds are highly collectible local folk art.

photo: Peter Doran

Separates make it easy for all body types to find the perfect suit. Shoes and accessories, cover-ups and sarongs are also offered. Sandi's is open seven days a week in season. Call for winter hours.

SALTER PATH

Watersports Outfitters and Gifts
MM 11, N.C. Hwy. 58 and Headen Ln.,
Salter Path
(252) 247-4386
www.h2osportrentals.com

Watersports Outfitters and Gifts has unique gifts for all of your friends and family members. They carry beach jewelry, fun T-shirts, metal wall art, souvenirs, beach toys, pirate gifts and much more. Check out our front porch deck where there is always a sale going on. The shop is located between the Crab Shack Restaurant and Willis Seafood Market in the heart of Salter Path. They also offer Banana Boat Rides and rentals of Waverunners, kayaks, surfboards, scooters, bicycles and beach equipment.

Wood Artists' Gallery
and Specialty Woods
MM 10.5, N.C. Hwy. 58, Salter Path
(252) 726-1400
www.nicefigures.com

At Wood Artists' Gallery and Specialty Woods, you'll find exquisite handcrafted gifts made from the finest natural woods from around the world created by on-site owners and artists Sharon Barrett and Paula Labelle. It truly is a unique shop that features gifts, a working studio, a gallery and specialty lumber sales. Their motto states "nature makes it beautiful, we enhance it" and that's just what you'll find as you browse their amazing creations and watch firsthand as they develop their masterpieces. You'll find natural-edged tables, platters, vases, boxes, oil lamps, ornaments, bottle toppers, perfume atom-

izers and more in a variety of unusual woods, including Australian Burl, Birdseye Maple, Curly Maple, Redwood Burl, Zebrawood and Purpleheart. In The Wooden Kitchen section of the shop you'll find gorgeous plates and bowls, pepper grinders, spurtles, utensils, cutting boards and oyster knives. They also carry the largest selection of specialty woods and burls in the area. It's worth stopping just for the beauty and smells of the fresh wood and the chance to meet the talented and friendly artisans. Wood Artists' Gallery is open Tuesday through Sunday from 10 AM to 5 PM.

EMERALD ISLE

Bert's Surf Shop
MM 19.5, N.C. Hwy. 58, Emerald Isle
(252) 354-2441

300 Islander Dr. , Emerald Isle
(252) 354-6282

Bert's was Emerald Isle's first surf shop and has two stores in Emerald Isle — one on the main highway and one on Islander Drive. The stores stock just about everything you need for a fun time at the beach. You can always find a good choice of casual clothes, sunglasses, hats, beach T-shirts and bathing suits plus shells and jewelry. Bert's is open seven days a week. Bert's also has a shop in Atlantic Beach.

Carteret Country Store
Emerald Plantation Shopping Ctr., MM 20,
N.C. Hwy. 58, Emerald Isle
(252) 354-3800

The Country Store is a complete souvenir and gift shop where you will find the perfect thing for yourself or for family and friends. The store sells nautical and rare gifts, baskets, windsocks, flags, cards, clocks and frames. The staff is friendly and courteous and more than willing to help you select just what you need. The store is open daily year round.

Devan Lane
MM 19, N.C. Hwy. 58, Emerald Isle
(252) 354-6712

Devan Lane is a favorite for locals and visitors. Inside you'll find unique gifts and collectibles and a creative collection of home decor, including rugs and pillows, in every style imaginable from nautical

 Shopping during the off-season is a great time for sales. Many local stores offer huge discounts during this time of year, so it's worth checking out. Just be sure to call ahead as some of the stores have limited off-season hours.

to tropical to traditional. The shop offers a children's boutique and a nice artwork selection.

Emerald Isle Books & Toys
Emerald Plantation Shopping Ctr., MM 20, N.C. Hwy. 58, Emerald Isle
(252) 354-5323

This store has hundreds of books and magazines for all ages, an extensive collection of regional and travel books, and local interest books. Of course, the store has all the bestsellers in paperback and hard cover. Plenty of kids' toys, from the strictly fun to the educational, are available. Visitors will also find bath items, including Burt's Bees creams and scrubs and Mad Gabs massage oils. Emerald Isle Books and Toys is open seven days a week, all year.

Fran's Beachwear
MM 19, N.C. Hwy. 58, Emerald Isle
(252) 354-3151

For those who dread finding the perfect swimsuit, Fran's is a good place to start. Fran's Beachwear carries an excellent selection of swimwear sure to fit every body type and need, including a nice selection of girls' swimwear and plus sizes. Fran's offers more than 50 lines of suits to choose from with many designer brands such as Ralph Lauren, Guess, Kenneth Cole and Tommy Hilfiger. Beyond swimsuits, there are other types of beachwear from casual to elegant plus a wide range of shoes, bags, jewelry and accessories. Fran's Beachwear is open seven days a week from the middle of February through the end of October. With more than 35 years in business, Fran's has a loyal client base.

J. R. Dunn Jewelers
Emerald Plantation Shopping Ctr., MM 20, N.C. Hwy. 58, Emerald Isle
(252) 354-5074

Dunn's features distinctive jewelry for women, men and children, including many nautical creations. The store will repair and remount your jewelry and watches and gift wrap your purchases. The staff is knowledgeable and very helpful, especially for those of us who can't quite figure out what to select for that special someone.

For a unique gift, be sure to ask about their Atlantic Beach and Emerald Isle destination bracelets. J.R. Dunn also has a shop in Morehead City in the Cypress Bay Plaza on U.S. Highway 70.

Planet Wear
Emerald Plantation Shopping Ctr., MM 20, N.C. Hwy. 58, Emerald Isle
(252) 354-7262

This is a popular store that specializes in tie dye and imported clothing, candles, jewelry, rock and roll collectibles, hemp accessories and more. You'll find beads, incense, stickers and a good selection of Grateful Dead items and beautiful sun catchers. There are always new items, so be sure to stop in. Planet Wear is open every day, although winter hours vary.

The Sweet Spot/Sandpiper Gifts
MM19, N.C. Hwy. 58 (8201 Emerald Dr.), Emerald Isle
(252) 254-6201

The Sweet Spot, located in the heart of Emerald Isle, is loved by locals as well as tourists for their generous scoops of more than 50 flavors of Hershey's Premium Ice Cream. Banana Splits are their specialty — a real treat for all ages. Also a favorite is the fresh, gourmet saltwater taffy — pick and choose your favorites from more than 28 different flavors. They also carry a wide selection of Jelly Belly, fudge, gummies, lollipops and more. While enjoying your ice cream, wander through the Sandpiper Gift Shop and check out the gifts for all ages as well as T-shirts, flags, artwork and jewelry. Be sure to check out the children's area, where the kids can play while you shop. This is a fun shop for all ages.

Tom Togs Outlet
Emerald Plantation Shopping Ctr., MM 20, N.C. Hwy. 58, Emerald Isle
(252) 354-7140

This store sells famous-name clothing at value prices. You will find scores of cotton shorts, T-shirts and tops plus pants, sundresses, hats and outfits for kids. New stock comes in every week. The majority of clothing is for women. The clothing is casual, and you'll also find Flax clothing items here. Be sure to check Tom Togs before you pay full price elsewhere; shopping here is a smart way to save vacation

dollars. The store is open daily; call for off-season hours.

Beaufort

Shopping in Beaufort is easy — a little too easy. Not only are there a variety of shops, but there are some great pit stops along the way like a cup of coffee from Taylor's Big Mug, ice cream from the General Store, fudge from the Fudge Factory or lunch at Clawson's. The shops in Beaufort are sure to suit anyone's taste. Most shops are along or near the downtown waterfront, making it easy to stroll along the scenic Front Street and spend a day visiting the town's shops. The town's many attractions — the waterfront, the Maritime Museum, historic sites and pubs — provide respite for those who find themselves in Beaufort with a born shopper. We couldn't possibly list all the shops, so we encourage you to explore on your own.

We start with shops on Turner Street because Turner is a key access street to Beaufort's historic downtown and the waterfront. Next we cover several shops on Front Street, which faces the water. It offers a nice view of Carrot Island and the boats that are either traveling by or anchored in Taylor's Creek. Then we take you to a few places off Front Street yet still in the historic district and, finally, to a few great shopping spots just outside Beaufort's downtown district.

Parking is at a premium during the summer season. Free parking places are plentiful along the streets of downtown Beaufort, but you may have to walk a few blocks. Don't worry, though; all downtown Beaufort shops and restaurants are within the same couple of blocks, and walking around Beaufort is an activity you'll enjoy.

HISTORIC DOWNTOWN

Turner Street

The Old Beaufort Shop
Beaufort Historic Site, 130 Turner St.,
Beaufort
(252) 728-5225, (800) 575-7483

Located on the Beaufort Historic Site, this store helps finance the educational and restoration programs of the Beaufort Historical Association. Many of the items for sale cannot be found elsewhere because they are made by volunteers. Insiders shop here for local artwork, handmade dolls and books on local history. In summer the shop sells cuttings propagated by the association's Herb Society.

Commercial fishing is alive and well on the Crystal Coast.

photo: Carolyn Temple

Front Street

When you come to the corner of Turner and Front streets, you'll see Somerset Square, a broad, two-story building with white porch railings. It is home to a number of shops and affords a pretty view of the water. Most of Beaufort's stores are within walking distance once you park. A few public parking lots are along Front Street, and street parking is available but limited during the summer months.

Art & Soul
220 Front St., Beaufort
(252) 504-2005

Art and Soul is filled with unique jewelry, art and gifts, and it is simply a fun and uplifting place to shop. The slogan "a handmade marketplace" is perfect. Much of the jewelry is expertly made by owner Jenny Nash-Strickrath, known as the Bead Diva, and includes bead, copper and hand-blown glass items. You'll also find works by locally and nationally known artists and unique gifts sure to surprise and please.

Beaufort Trading Company
Somerset Square, 400 Front St.,
Unit 2, Beaufort
(252) 504-3209
www.beauforttradingcompany.com

Beaufort Trading Company says it "has your family covered," and that is true. In its eighth year on the Beaufort waterfront, Beaufort Trading Company has quite a following of regular customers. You'll find quality Beaufort T-shirts, sweatshirts, hats and caps for everyone from infants to adults. Kevin and Doris Carlin offer Life is Good and Seadog T-shirts and caps, along with Teva and Columbia sandals and sportswear. They also sell kites, sunglasses and leashes, beach cover-ups and more.

Bell's Drug Store
331 Front St. (corner of Turner St.), Beaufort
(252) 728-3810

Bell's Drug Store has been serving Beaufort and its visitors since 1918 and continues the same friendly, professional service today. Along with drugstore items, Bell's has fountain drinks, personal-care items, gifts, cards and a nice collection of glass collectibles. Bell's is open Monday through Saturday.

Down East Gallery
519 Front St., Beaufort
(252) 728-4410, (800) 868-2766

It couldn't even be considered a true tour of Beaufort without a stop in the Down East Gallery. Local artist Alan Cheek displays his work here. Alan's artwork will serve as a lovely reminder of your time spent in the enchanting seaport of Beaufort. Down East Gallery offers works by other local artists and provides custom framing.

Fabricate Apparel
431 Front St., Beaufort
(252) 728-7950

Fabricate specializes in clothes of cool, comfortable natural fibers. It's known for its trendy, expressive clothes for women. You'll find jewelry, bags, hats, scarves and shoes from Naot. Fabricate is open 11 AM to 5 PM (winter), 10 AM to 6 PM (summer) and Sundays 1 to 5 PM from March through December.

The Fudge Factory
Somerset Square, 400 Front St., Beaufort
(252) 728-6202, (800) 551-8066

You guessed it: This store makes fudge — creamy, sinful fudge in many flavors from natural ingredients on marble-top tables right before your eyes. You can buy it by the slice or the pound, to eat or ship anywhere. The Fudge Factory is open daily.

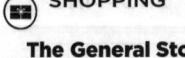

The General Store
515 Front St., Beaufort
(252) 728-7707

The General Store is family owned and operated and is a favorite with locals and visitors alike for its great ice cream and wonderful souvenirs. From hats, T-shirts and shells to saltwater taffy and jewelry, this store has something for everyone. Kids like this place because their spending money goes a long way. You're sure to see a few kids sitting on the bench on the store's front stoop, licking away at a dripping ice cream cone on a warm summer's day. For boaters, food and other staples are available, as are laundry facilities. The store is open Monday through Saturday.

Handscapes Gallery
400 Front St., Beaufort
(252) 728-6805
www.handscapesgallery.com

Handscapes is an Insiders' favorite and the perfect place to find unusual gifts and treasures. The gallery specializes in works by North Carolinians as well as artists and craftspeople from all over the country. Owner Alison Brooks fills the shop with pottery, jewelry, prints, paintings, glass and metal-craft items. More than 200 artists are represented and it is a joy to see their fine workmanship. The store is open year round, seven days a week. Call for winter hours.

Ibis
432 Front St., Beaufort
(252) 728-7220

Next to Fabricate, Ibis features upscale women's clothing such as Eileen Fisher, Nic & Zoe, Citron and Tianello. A large selection of scarves and jewelry flatter every outfit. You will also find hats, bags and shoes by Scala & Yellow Box and San Diego Hats. The store is open Monday through Saturday year round, and Sundays from March through December.

Island Traders
421 Front St., Beaufort
(252) 504-3000

Island Traders is a discount name-brand and catalog clothing outlet carrying ladies', men's and juniors' items at substantial savings off regular retail prices.

You'll also find name-brand footwear as well as other accessories. Island Traders also carries Merrell, Keen, Reef, Bimini Bay, Sanuk, Chaco, Tervis Tumbler, Old Guys Rule and more. The store is open every day, year round, with extended summer hours.

Luna
121 Turner St., Beaufort
(252) 504-3200

Luna is a clothing and craft store with merchandise that is considered either fair trade or eco-friendly — and often times both. Fair trade ensures fair wages for the producers of the items sold at the store (often third-world countries), while eco-friendly merchandise is made from materials that don't negatively impact the environment. Merchandise featured includes clothing, baskets, jewelry, water bottles, salt lamps and much more. Shoppers can feel good about their purchases in a "green" and ethical environment.

North Carolina Maritime Museum
315 Front St., Beaufort
(252) 728-7317
www.ncmm.friends.org

The Maritime Museum Store is where you should buy a memento of your visit to the museum. Excellent books abound: books about maritime habitats, sea creatures, North Carolina cuisine, seashore plants and much more. Look for subjects you or your kids have always wanted to know about but never got around to researching. Many of the books are short, to-the-point and well illustrated. You'll also find outstanding, reasonably priced posters and pictures, plus kids' toys and greeting cards. Boaters will be interested in NOAA navigation charts, topo maps and related publications on navigation, boat-building and ship-model building. The store is open seven days a week all year.

Of Earth and Sea
510 Front St., Unit 1, Beaufort
(252) 504-2050

Of Earth and Sea offers distinctive gifts and home decor, much of it with a nautical or beachy theme. They specialize in Bovano, which is glass-over-copper wall sculptures, and they are the exclusive seller of the new Bovano North Carolina

"Seven Sisters" Lighthouses. They are also a designated SPI Gallery (brass statuary), one of only four in North Carolina. They carry a large variety of items, including shells, candles, Christmas ornaments, pottery and more. They're open seven days a week, though they close on Tuesdays in the winter.

The Rocking Chair Bookstore
Somerset Square, Front St., Beaufort
(252) 728-2671

The Rocking Chair has been in business for more than 30 years, offering a wide variety of books, including regional books, sailing and marine books, cookbooks, children's books, bestsellers, classics, new and used books, hard covers and paperbacks. The store proudly offers books by local and regional authors. The Rocking Chair is under new ownership as of September 2008, but continues its tradition of great customer service. This staff is full of information, and they will order any book for you.

Scuttlebutt
432 Front St., Beaufort
(252) 728-7765

Scuttlebutt specializes in "nautical books and bounty." You'll find an outstanding, high-quality selection of books, clocks, music, games, toys, models and galley ware, along with casual clothing and hats. This is a great store to explore — check out the maps and charts — and it is an Insiders' favorite for unique gifts. The store is open daily year round.

Seagrass Whimsical Gifts
300 Front St., Beaufort
(252) 728-2775

Insiders love Seagrass Whimsical Gifts for its selection of eclectic, sassy and all around unique gifts. The store is filled with items that can please those in the "hard to shop for" category. Seagrass carries conversation pieces and collectibles of all kinds, including Life is Crap T-shirts, Laugh Out Loud tin signs, Whimsy art wall tile, Cat's Meow Village collectibles, Sweet Tea Southern T-shirts, mermaid prints, North Carolina handmade soaps and the list goes on. During checkout, be sure to give either Ham or Gabby a pat on the

head — one of these cute canines is usually on hand to help complete your sale. Seagrass is open year round, seven days a week.

Stamper's Jewelers
435 Front St., Beaufort
(252) 728-4967

Stamper's Jewelers has a full line of jewelry and excellent engraving and repair services. It's a great shop for brides and grooms. You can find diamond bridal jewelry and gifts for the attendants. Stamper's offers popular sterling silver jewelry and name-brand watches. The skilled craftsmen at this store can engrave trophies and plaques.

Taylor's Big Mug Coffee Cafe
437 Front St., Beaufort
(252) 728-0707

Taylor's Big Mug offers 100 percent fair-trade and organic coffee along

Want some free reads for the beach? Collect your old paperback books and visit the Bogue Banks Public Library, 320 Salter Path Road, MM 7, Pine Knoll Shores, (252) 247-4660. You may choose up to 10 paperbacks - all that's required is for you to leave as many books as you take.

with ciders and great espresso drinks. Enjoy a casual cup of joe and a snack at a cafe table or kick back on the sofas. You'll also find bagged coffee to take and enjoy at home or give as a gift. Wireless Internet access is available here, and there are live performances some days and nights. Taylor's Big Mug is open every day at 7 AM, and closing time varies.

Just Off Front Street

Coastal Community Market
606 Broad St., Beaufort
(252) 728-2844

Coastal Community Market offers organic foods and natural products as well as gourmet, Asian and Indian foods. The store offers products for people with food allergies and has wheat-free or sugar-free items for special dietary needs. You'll find bulk food items, all types of cheeses, farm-fresh eggs, locally made breads and granola, natural honey and hundreds of items for your pantry. The market now carries organic wines, as well.

Harbor Specialties
127 Middle Ln., Beaufort
(252) 838-0059, (877) 369-4999

Harbor Specialties offers a variety of "nautical but nice" items, including Sperry deck shoes, Tilley hats and ship's models. This shop features Vera Bradley handbags and offers custom embroidery. You'll also find insulated glassware, clocks and barometers. They also have a large selection of boat bags. For a unique shopping experience, stop by this shop on Middle Lane.

Scott Taylor Photography
214 Pollock St., Beaufort
(252) 728-0900

At Scott Taylor's Photography Gallery and Studio you are sure to find that unique image of Beaufort or the surrounding coastal areas. Scott is well known for his scenic photography and also for exclusive wedding and event photography. He specializes in color, black and white, or split-toned images. If you are looking for a very special gift, let Scott create a family beach portrait that will be treasured for a lifetime. Scott's book, *Coastal Waters - Images of North Carolina,* is available in the gallery and is the perfect way to remember your trip to the coast.

BEYOND BEAUFORT'S HISTORIC DISTRICT

Calypso Cottage
324 Orange St., Beaufort
(252) 728-4299

The Calypso Cottage brings fun yet classic and sophisticated coastal flair to visitors as they step into one of the two shops located in two side-by-side Beaufort cottages. Visitors can find a little bit of everything here. The store offers a bounty of gifts, furniture, accents for the home, bedding and bath, rugs, jewelry, art, books and more — chosen and displayed to bring the feel of the Hamptons right here to North Carolina's coast. Calypso offers an ever-changing inventory of items, so stop by often. Don't forget to check out the Calypso Garden in the back yard, in season. The shop is open year round, seven days a week.

Gaskill's Hardware and Hunting
U.S. Hwy. 70 and Lennoxville Rd.,
900 Live Oak St., Beaufort
(252) 728-3757

Gaskill's Hardware and Hunting is the store that has just about everything. The full-service hardware and hunting store houses everything you'll need for your home and garden, for your animals and your hunting. You'll find paintball supplies along side chainsaws, feed, seeds and plants. Whether you need a simple nut and bolt, a new garden hose, a decorative pot or a screen for your window, the attendants are quick to help as soon as you come in the door. They'll walk you through the store and make it easy to find everything you need. The store carries Carhartt clothing and offers a complete paint store across the street.

Morehead City

Morehead City offers the largest selection of shops on the Crystal Coast. Shopping opportunities are spread from one end of the city to the other and range from clothing boutiques and craft shops to bookstores and marine suppliers. We describe a few of the shops in the city and have arranged them by area. As you read this section of our Shopping chapter, note that Arendell Street, Morehead City's main thoroughfare, is divided by a railroad track that runs from Third Street to the intersection of Arendell and Bridges streets, a distance of about 32 blocks.

WATERFRONT

Morehead's waterfront shopping section has benefited significantly from revitalization. Sidewalks, trees, benches, parks and gazebos invite visitors to take a stroll or sit a spell, and the shops will entice you to come inside. Facing Bogue Sound, most waterfront shopping fronts Evans and Shepard streets. Free parking is available, but it can be hard to find an empty space in the height of the summer. When that's the case, park on Bridges Street, which parallels Arendell Street at this point, and walk across Arendell to the waterfront. Everything is close together, so even if you can't find a parking place on the waterfront, you won't have to walk very far.

Arts & Things
704 Evans St., Morehead City
(252) 240-1979, (877) 640-ARTS (2787)

Owners Porter and Lou Wilson offer the Crystal Coast's finest selection of art supplies and gallery treasures that you don't want to miss. From local art to international artists, Arts & Things offers art for every taste. Paintings, prints, stone and wood sculptures, stained glass, pottery and art glass can be the perfect accent pieces for any home. Bring a favorite painting or print and have it expertly framed on site. For beginner and seasoned artists alike, Arts & Things is stocked with art supplies and a selection of paper, brushes, paints, pastels, throwing clay, clay boards, easels and drawing supplies. This store also offers giclee fine-art printing. A variety of art classes are also offered. Any trip to Arts & Things will brighten your day or palette.

Carolina Artist Studio Gallery, Inc.
800 Evans St., Morehead City
(252) 726-7550

With approximately 30 participating artists, this is a non-profit co-op gallery operated by the artists. Members' work is displayed, and active works in progress are sometimes visible. Members offer classes and workshops in a variety of media for children and adults. The classes vary so it's best to call to see what is available. Visitors are welcome to attend special art openings and exhibits, and the receptions are open to the public. The gallery showcases two-dimensional and three dimensional original artwork, giclee and limited edition prints. Visitors also enjoy the gift gallery that contains a variety of handcrafted items. Hours vary seasonally, so call ahead for specific days and times of operation.

Waterfront Junction
412 Evans St., Morehead City
(252) 726-6283

Waterfront Junction is the place to stop for needleworking tools, kits and accessories. The shop is well known for its custom framing and its large and diverse stock of ready-made frames. Shop at Waterfront Junction Tuesday through Saturday.

DOWNTOWN

As you leave Morehead's waterfront and drive west (toward Newport) on Arendell Street, several shops between 5th and 12th streets are well worth visiting. There is free street parking in front of these stores or you can park on a side street.

City News
514 Arendell St., Morehead City
(252) 726-6320

If you want a copy of the *New York Times*, you will find it here, along with an assortment of local, regional and national newspapers. Greeting cards are available, as are bestsellers and books about local lore. You will also find maps, cold drinks and books for kids. The store is open seven days a week, all year round.

Dee Gee's Gifts & Books
508 Evans St., Morehead City
(252) 726-3314

Dee Gee's Gifts and Books is a tradition on the waterfront and continues to offer a huge selection of books, gifts for all occasions, cards and novelties. Dee Gee's features special sections of local and regional books, children's educational books, toys and games and nautical charts. The staff will be happy to special-order any book. Often Dee Gee's has book-signing parties for local authors or for authors who have written about the area. Dee Gee's carries an excellent selection of decorative pieces for the home and garden. Visitors and locals shop here for special-occasion gift giving, knowing that the just-right serving platter, vase or unique gift will be found here. Anything you select can be gift-wrapped and shipped to your home or to the lucky recipient. As an added bonus, Dee Gee's has a monthly contest to see just how far the store's original newsprint bags can travel. Heading to China or Bermuda or the Grand Canyon this summer? Take a Dee Gee's bag and send them a picture of you with it. You may be the winner of a $20 gift certificate. The store is open daily, and telephone orders are welcomed. You can also order books online and they will delivered to your door or you can pick them up at the store to saving shipping charges. Dee Gee's is a BookSense Store, part of a national affiliation of independent bookstores.

Ginny Gordon's Gifts and Gadgets
1011 Arendell St., Morehead City
(252) 726-6661

Ginny Gordon's shop carries a great collection of cookware, cookbooks from near and far, every cooking utensil imaginable plus gadgets you can't do without. You'll always find good advice about kitchen gadgets, and the helpful staff will demonstrate the workings of anything in the store. The store now features the artwork of Bob Pittman. Ginny Gordon's Gifts and Gadgets is open all year, Monday through Saturday.

Jame's
712 Arendell St., Morehead City
(252) 247-5263

Jame's clothing, accessories & art is a specialty boutique offering the latest in designer jeans, dresses, tops, handbags, shoes, jewelry and more for women. This stylish shop is a local favorite and it reflects the latest trends from New York and California. Jame's carries a variety of designer lines, including Christopher Deane,

Hudson Jeans, Rachel Pally, Tart and Black Halo. Some men's clothing lines are also offered. Owner Jamie Dickinson is an artist herself and offers beautiful original paintings for sale in the boutique.

Parson's General Store
808 Arendell St., Morehead City
(252) 726-8188

Located in an old Victorian home, Parson's is a great place to stop because it has an extensive collection of gifts, nostalgia, home accessories, seasonal decorations and sweets. The shop also offers Hershey's ice cream. It is open all year, seven days a week.

Sew It Seams
905 Arendell St., Morehead City
(252) 247-2114

At Sew It Seams the emphasis is on quilting. The store offers quilting classes with experienced teachers ready to show you how to create your own quilts, whether by machine or by hand. If you're not interested in quilting your own top piece, Sew It Seams can handle the job for you. The store has 1,500 types of fabric, along with sewing patterns, notions, books and a large collection of buttons. Sew It Seams is open Tuesday through Saturday.

AROUND MOREHEAD CITY

As you leave the waterfront and downtown sections of Morehead City and continue driving west on Arendell Street (toward Newport and Havelock), you will encounter a number of small shopping centers. We have listed some of them here, enterprises that are in or just outside the city's limits but not clustered in any single area. The street addresses should make them easy to find.

Just like most areas, major retailers like **Wal-Mart**, **Kmart**, **Sears**, **Best Buy** and **Staples** can all be found, too. Most are easily accessible of off N.C. Highway 70. Although there's not a large shopping mall in Morehead City, the area has slowly been acquiring more of the larger retail stores. The Crystal Coast Plaza off of N.C. Highway 70 is a new addition to the area, which brings some big names in shopping including **Ross**, **Michael's**, **PetSmart**, **TJ Maxx** and **Bed, Bath & Beyond**.

Art Escapes and Frames
Morehead Plaza, 3000 Arendell St., Morehead City
(252) 247-5111

This gallery showcases local and regional artists and emphasizes whimsical artwork. You won't be able to resist the prints, watercolors, sculpture, photographs and other three-dimensional art pieces. If you have in mind a print that isn't in the gallery, ask to see the art catalogs; they will be glad to order for you. The shop provides complete framing services, and stylish gift wrap is available for anything you purchase.

Bell Photography
111 Mansfield Pkwy., Morehead City
(252) 247-1058

Bell Photography has been meeting and exceeding the photography needs of locals and visitors since 1956. Owner David Bell carries on the tradition of quality started by his father, the late Gene Bell. He offers a mixture of photography styles, including contemporary, storybook and journalistic. Whether indoor or outdoor, David strives to keep the rates affordable and to ensure the pictures reflect the beauty of your special day.

Bill's Pet Shop
5370-A Brandywine Crossing, U.S. Hwy. 70, Morehead City
(252) 240-1116

This is a complete pet store, no matter what you need. Bill's Pet Shop sells pets of all types — dogs, cats, birds, ferrets and some reptiles — along with all the supplies and products you need to care for your best friend. This is truly a one-stop, full-service pet shop. You'll find pet crates, cages, leashes, medications and more. Bill's also has a complete tropical and saltwater aquarium section with professional staff ready to guide you in the proper set up and care of your tanks. There are sister stores in Havelock and New Bern.

The Book Shop
Parkway Shopping Ctr., 4915 Arendell St., Morehead City
(252) 240-1163

This bookstore offers a wide selection of new and used paperback, hard-bound and children's books at discounted prices. Any new book not in the store can be ordered and delivered promptly. One side of the shop carries used books, where you will find loads of value-priced novels, cookbooks, history, kids' stories and former bestsellers in both paperback and hardback. You can trade your used books for the store's used books. The Book Shop is open seven days a week.

Captain Jim's Seafood
4665 Arendell St., Morehead City
(252) 726-3454

Captain Jim's Seafood is a fresh seafood market. You'll find fresh shrimp, mahi mahi, tuna, wahoo, triggerfish, scallops and much more. Captain Jim's is one of the cleanest seafood markets in the county, and they'll even pack coolers for free. Stop by and let the staff show you why they're a local favorite.

Coastal Image Photography by Carolyn Temple
3009 Old Gate Rd., Morehead City
(252) 726-7488
www.coastalimagephoto.com

Carolyn Temple and Coastal Image Photography can create a special photographic memory, to be treasured forever, of your family, wedding or event. She has the only lush garden outdoor studio in the area and will schedule location portrait sessions at the beach, at your home or any location of your choosing. She offers a wide variety of services, including black and white portraits, bridal portraits, wedding packages, senior portraits, family and children's portraits.

Dunn's Beds
5360 U.S. Hwy. 70 W, Morehead City
(252) 222-3866

Dunn's Beds is a complete bedroom furniture store sure to have the perfect items to create just the feeling you want in your home. Here you'll find quality beds, night stands, chests, drawers and mirrors by such quality furniture makers as Broyhill, Vaughan-Bassett, Riverside, and Night and Day. The professionals at Dunn's Beds offer mattresses by Tempur-pedic, Simmons, Sensa and Park Place. Dunn's Beds has a nice selection of futons and water beds along with all the water-bed accessories. With delivery and set up offered, this is the place to go for anything in the way of comfortable bedding and bedroom furniture. Dunn's Beds also has a store in New Bern.

EJW Outdoors
4667 Arendell St., Morehead City
(252) 247-4725

EJW Outdoors has been in business for more than 50 years and recently expanded its extensive inventory with a move to its new location. EJW continues to offer all types of outdoor gear — from Columbia and Carhartt clothing and accessories to fishing and hunting gear. The store also sells bikes and services fishing equipment and bikes. EJW also features an archery pro shop with a variety of equipment as well as bow repair and tuning.

General Nutrition Center
Cypress Bay Plaza,
5160 U.S. Hwy. 70 W, Morehead City
(252) 808-3900

GNC is filled with products designed to promote good health. At GNC you will find vitamins and supplements of every type, a wide variety of herbs, items especially for kids, topical books, healthy snack foods and a fully stocked weight-reduction section. The store also has shampoos, scrubs and skin-care products. It is open seven days a week.

The Golden Gull
Pelletier Harbor Shops,
4426 Arendell St., Morehead City
(252) 726-2333

Since 1975 Golden Gull has made sure women in Carteret County are handsomely outfitted in the latest casual wear, sportswear, dresses and after-five ensembles. The store carries a full line of accessories to complement the clothes. Golden Gull also has a Merle Norman cosmetics studio on the premises. The shop is open Monday through Saturday.

The Intimate Bridal and Formal Wear
5370 Brandywine Crossing, Morehead City
(252) 808-2221

Let The Intimate make planning your wedding an enjoyable and fun experience.

The professionals at this shop offer an elegant, friendly atmosphere and will work to ensure you look your best for whatever the occasion happens to be. As a full-service bridal shop, The Intimate offers a tremendous selection of bridal gowns, mother-of-the-bride dresses, bridesmaid dresses starting at $99, prom dresses and social occasion dresses from sizes 2 to 30. There is something to fit every budget, as well as tuxedo rentals and sales. The Intimate is experienced in accommodating large volume tuxedo rentals and out-of-town wedding parties, and they ensure the perfect fit. This shop offers elegance and style for the bride to be and her wedding party. Whether it is that special dress or just the right tuxedo, the friendly staff here can take care of your every need and offer professional advice on clothing, color schemes and sizes. Immediate delivery is available on certain styles, and The Intimate also offers wedding gown preservation. The Intimate has another store at 224/226 Middle Street in New Bern, (252) 638-1220.

J. R. Dunn Jewelers
Cypress Bay Plaza. U.S. Hwy. 70 W,
Morehead City
(252) 726-8700

Dunn's features distinctive jewelry for women, men and children, along with many nautical creations. The store will repair and remount your jewelry and watches and gift wrap your purchases. The staff is knowledgeable and very helpful, especially for those of us who can't quite figure out what to select for that special someone. For a unique gift, the store offers Atlantic Beach and Emerald Isle destination bracelets. J. R. Dunn also has a shop in Emerald Isle.

Knowledge of Christ Books & Gifts
Pelletier Harbor Shops,
4428 Arendell St., Morehead City
(252) 726-7370

This store is filled with books, gifts, stained glass, collectibles, dolls, prints and paintings. You will also find Bibles for adults and children, as well as a nice selection of Christian music and DVDs. The staff here is friendly and knowledgeable, so don't be afraid to ask if you don't find what you're looking for. Shop here Monday through Saturday.

Lynette's Two
Pelletier Harbor Shops,
4426 Arendell St., Morehead City
(252) 726-3733

Lynette's carries distinctive fashions for women from sizes 4 to 20. The shop offers lovely sportswear, jewelry, gift items, hand bags and all the right accessories. It is open Monday through Saturday.

The Parent Trap
Morehead Plaza,
Ste. 20, 2900 Arendell St., Morehead City
(252) 727-0123

The Parent Trap is Carteret County's only "Play Boutique." The store specializes in high-quality toys, games, puzzles and all the latest accessories for new and expectant parents. They also offer nursery and children's furniture. This unique shop offers a play space in the store with a complete activity center. Activities include weekly music class, story time and playgroups. Parent Trap is open Monday through Saturday from 10 AM through 5:30 PM.

The Party Place
4737-A Arendell St., Morehead City
(252) 222-0320

The Party Place offers everything you need to have a party — large or small, wild or intimate. They have a wonderful selection of items for weddings, anniversaries, adult and children's birthday parties and holiday parties. Whether it is paper products, balloons, guest favors or decorations, this store has it all. The store is open Monday through Saturday.

Priscilla's Crystal Coast Wines
5370-K Brandywine Crossing,
U.S. Hwy. 70, Morehead City
(252) 240-3234, (877) 242-7158

This shop has wines for everyday enjoyment or for special occasions. Priscilla offers a wide selection and she can recommend just the right wines to accompany your meals or to be featured at your parties. The shop offers gift baskets, gourmet foods, wine tastings and classes. Be sure to check out the section of the store called The Barn Yard, which offers

quality, inexpensive wines sure to please. Priscilla's also has the largest selection of microbrewed and imported beers in the area. First Friday is a special event that runs from 5 to 7 PM on the first Friday of the month, and Free Fridays happen every Friday.

Remnant City Carpets
7009 U.S. Hwy. 70 E, Newport
(252) 342-2255

A family-owned company, Remnant City Carpets has served the flooring needs of the Crystal Coast area for 35 years. They sell all major brands of hardwood flooring, ceramic tile, laminate flooring and carpet, and they have a large selection of in-stock carpet remnants. Remnant City offers free estimates, and they install and service what they sell. No job is too big or too small, says owner Dean Winchell, The store is located about seven minutes east of Morehead City at the corner of Nine Foot Road and U.S. Highway 70.

Somerset Cellars
3906 E. Arendell St., Morehead City
(252) 725-0029

Somerset Cellars offers a wonderful selection of wines that are sure to please. Favorites include Somerset's Pinot Grigio, Cabernet Sauvignon, Chiaretto and Pinot Noir. Somerset imports crushed grapes and juice to produce custom wines that are available at wholesale and retail. Somerset also offers tours and tastings by appointment. With a few weeks notice, this unique attraction can create personal labels to add a special touch to a wedding, anniversary or birthday, or to add a personal touch to your boat or beach house. Somerset offers 25 different wines. Current hours are 11 AM to 6 PM Wednesday through Saturday, and are subject to change based on demand. Call for hours or a private appointment.

Tal-Y-Bont Interiors
5113-C U.S. Hwy. 70 W, Morehead City
(252) 726-6872

Tal-Y-Bont Interiors is a full-line furniture and interior design store. The 20,000-square-foot showroom contains a wide variety of contemporary and traditional styles, including wicker furniture.

The store will special order items for you, but it carries a large inventory for immediate delivery, which is especially convenient if you are furnishing a Crystal Coast vacation home. Besides furniture, Tal-Y-Bont provides window treatments, bedspreads, wallpaper and a large list of accessories to complete your design scheme. And don't hesitate to call upon the talents of Tal-Y-Bont's professional design staff. They will help you make decisions for your entire home or just the finishing touches. The store is closed on Sunday.

Teacher's Pet
2410 Arendell St., Morehead City
(252) 240-2515

Whether you are the teacher's pet or a teacher, a parent or learning yourself, you are sure to enjoy this store. Teacher's Pet focuses on all types of learning aids — everything from charts and artwork to books and equipment. The shop features educational games and toys for children of all ages. They offer Thomas the Tank Engine trains and building supplies for kids. Teacher's Pet also offers tutoring. Certified teachers are available to tutor one-on-one in the store after school hours and on Saturday; call for fees. Shop here seven days a week during the season.

West Marine
4950 Arendell St., Morehead City
(252) 240-2909,
(800) BOATING (262-8464)

West Marine has everything you need for power and sailboats, with well-marked aisles and friendly, helpful salespeople. West Marine stocks safety and repair equipment, fishing gear, boat electronics, ropes, log books and many other items. It has a good selection of nautical books and charts too. About one-quarter of the store is devoted to men's and women's outdoor clothing, including Topsider and Croc shoes. The store is open daily.

Williams Hardware
Morehead Plaza, 3011 Bridges St.,
Morehead City
(252) 726-7158

Williams Hardware is a family-owned business where customer service is a priority. In business for more than 30 years,

this store has a good reputation and offers the usual items in addition to carrying hard-to-find items. The staff gladly assists in special orders, too. Williams offers specialized services such as repairing window screens, cutting galvanized and PVC pipe, and cutting glass. The store also sells Holland and Wilmington grills. Williams is open year round, seven days a week.

Swansboro

This "friendly city by the sea" is often overlooked when it comes to its quaint, quiet and historical shopping areas, but we think it's a unique treasure. Shops in Swansboro are basically in two areas — along the river on Front Street and its adjoining side streets, and along N.C. 24. We suggest you take some time to walk along the White Oak River, shop a bit, enjoy lunch at one of the restaurants and relax in Bicentennial Park.

Gray Dolphin Boutique & Gift Shop
125 Front St., Swansboro
(910) 326-4444

Established in 1989, the Gray Dolphin Boutique & Gift Shop has been a mainstay in the Swansboro shopping scene for years, and the shop has a loyal following of customers from near and far. Inside you will find fine clothing items, accessories, gifts and more.

Harrika's Brew Haus at 911 Restoration
911 Cedar Point Blvd., N.C. Hwy. 24,
Swansboro
(252) 354-7911

You'll find all sorts of delights in this eclectic shop. This unique shop offers a wide variety of items from cocktail napkins, greeting cards and candles to garden accessories, gourmet kitchen items and pet leashes. Let the friendly staff help you create the perfect custom gift box. New items are always arriving, but you are always sure to find unique sauces, oils, chocolates and other sweet treats. There is a wide selection of teas and over 180 types of beer, the largest selection in the county. The shop now offers inside seating for enjoying your beverage of choice or outdoor seating in the newly remodeled patio area.

The Mercantile
131 Front St., Swansboro
(910) 326-7216

The Mercantile is a unique place to shop. You will find a variety of shopping items for all ages and interests. There are books — cookbooks and bestsellers, local authors and historical sketches — as well as unique gifts of all types and stylish resort wear and casual clothes.

Noah's Ark
201 Front St., Swansboro
(910) 326-5679

Noah's Ark is a wonderful shop to visit. You will find a wide variety of items, including dishes, children's items, books, nautical items and collectibles. You also will find local artwork, gourmet foods and holiday ornaments.

Quilt Cottage
147-3 Front St., Swansboro
(910) 325-1125

If you are looking for a quilt of just about any size, a stop by the Quilt Cottage is in order. This shop offers quilts of all types and sizes, from twin to king. They also offer accessories such as handbags, placemats, pillows, shams, stuffed animals and other toys.

Russell's Olde Tyme Shoppe
116 Front St., Swansboro
(910) 326-3790

At Russell's you'll find country crafts, costume jewelry, handcrafted clothing, pottery, paintings, furniture, baskets, silk and dried flowers, along with kitchen and cooking items. Owner Maxine Russell also offers a wide variety of hand-painted items — from photo albums to glass to wooden items. Each purchase in the store is placed in a hand-painted shopping bag, a gift in itself. The store is open daily most of the year, call ahead for off-season hours.

Through the Looking Glass
101 Church St., Swansboro
(910) 326-3128

When you purchase a gift at Through the Looking Glass, you can be certain it will delight the recipient. This store has an excellent selection of home and garden accessories, fragrances, jewelry, tableware, candles, wines and children's gifts. The Christmas items are extensive and include decorations, nativity scenes, dishes and more. Look for the specialized children's clothing. Need a bouquet of silk or fresh flowers for that special someone? Through the Looking Glass will design an arrangement sure to reflect your feelings. You can shop here daily, but call for winter hours.

Down East

Down East offers only a handful of shops, but each is uncommon and well worth the trip. Because hours vary by season, we suggest you call ahead. As you drive through the Down East area, you will find numerous homes with signs out front welcoming you to stop and consider buying model boats, decoys, crafts and more.

Capt. Henry's Gift Store
1341 Island Rd., Harkers Island
(252) 728-7316

This is a treasure trove of Down East decoys and lots more. Capt. Henry's features nautical items, pottery, prints, jewelry and wonderful decorations. Shoppers will be charmed by the baskets, birdhouses and wind chimes. Capt. Henry's is open for business Monday through Saturday in season and is closed in the winter.

Core Sound Waterfowl Museum Gift Shop
1785 Island Rd., Harkers Island
(252) 728-1500

Located at the end of Harkers Island Road beside the Cape Lookout National Seashore Visitor Center, the Core Sound

Some of the area publications offer coupons for use in local shops and restaurants. These publications can be found in display racks in high-traffic locations throughout the towns or by stopping by one of the two Crystal Coast Visitor Centers at 3409 Arendell Street in Morehead City or off N.C. Highway 58 just before crossing the bridge to Emerald Isle.

Waterfowl Museum is something you do not want to miss. The museum gift shop is filled with Down East gifts, most of which have waterfowl and environmental themes. Decoys are abundant, along with wildlife art, books, cards, house flags, windsocks, T-shirts, birdhouses, bird feeders and much more. The shop also features decoy and local history exhibits. The gift store is open daily. (For more information about the museum, see our Attractions chapter.)

Edgewater Gardens
U.S. Hwy. 70, Smyrna
(252) 729-1842

Edgewater Gardens is a full-service lawn and garden center. This nursery grows its own plants and specializes in herbs and plants of all kinds. This business is located Down East, but it is worth the drive.

Sea Side Stop N Shop
311 Island Rd., Harkers Island
(252) 728-5533

Sea Side Stop N Shop offers a variety of services. Whether you need fuel for your car or boat or convenience store items, this is a great place to stop. You'll also find a gift shop that offers unique nautical items, baby gifts, seasonal items, candles and more. At the other end of the building, Sea Side Galley offers pizzas, burgers, subs, seafood and more to eat in or take out.

Western Carteret County

There are two things to keep in mind while shopping in this area. First, there are quaint, unique shops scattered all along N.C. Highway 24, so be prepared to stop (or turn around, if need be). Second, it's a great area to find locally grown produce and goods. Never tried boiled peanuts? You can find them here, too. Most communities in the western part of the county have a convenience/gas store, a beauty salon and tanning booth, or maybe a craft and flower shop. In addition to the selected stores we describe here, two roadside stands deserve mention — Winberry Farm Produce, on N.C. Highway 24 in Cedar

Point, and Smith's Produce in Ocean, also on N.C. Highway 24. Both offer seasonal local vegetables, Bogue Sound watermelons and cantaloupes, canned food items and crafts. They are usually open for business during the growing seasons of spring, summer and early fall.

Carolina Home and Garden
4778 N.C. Hwy. 24, Newport
(252) 393-9004

Carolina Home and Garden offers a variety of trees, shrubs and plants along with hardware, gardening items and lawn-care supplies at reasonable prices. It is open daily most of the year and is closed on Sunday in the winter.

Redfearn's Nursery
1018 N.C. Hwy. 24, Cedar Point
(252) 393-8243

Redfearn's offers landscaping services and sells potted plants, planters, garden seeds, fertilizers, herbicides and pesticides. The nursery is open daily, except in the winter when it closes on Sunday.

Antiques Shops

The Crystal Coast is home to a number of antiques shops. We highlight a few in this section, and we definitely recommend a day or two of antiquing throughout Carteret County. A popular event for those who love treasures of the past is the Antiques Show and Sale held the last weekend in June at the Crystal Coast Civic Center. The event features more than 40 booths of antiques and collectibles. See our Annual Events chapter for further details.

BEAUFORT

The Marketplace Antiques and Collectibles
131 Turner St., Beaufort
(252) 728-2325

The Marketplace and its companion store across the street, The Marketplace II, display the wares of more than 55 dealers from far and near. It's a must-stop shop for browsers and collectors, with a variety of antiques and collectibles that will keep shopping enthusiasts coming back for more. The Marketplace is open seven days a week. The Marketplace II is located at 126 Turner Street and is also open seven days a week and can be reached at (252) 728-2507.

MOREHEAD CITY

Seaport Antique Market
509 Arendell St., Morehead City
(252) 726-6606

Seaport Antiques is a treat for the senses. Here you'll find the wares of many vendors, giving you an opportunity to see more than one collector's items at a time. You'll find furniture, books, glassware, knickknacks, jewelry and even some household accessories. Keep coming back. The vendors rotate the offerings in their spaces regularly. Seaport is open daily.

SWANSBORO

Swansboro Antique Center
448 Cedar Point Rd., Cedar Point
(252) 393-6003

This rambling building shows the wares of more than 25 dealers in an attractive space. You'll find kitchen collections, decoys, hunting and fishing equipment, furniture, quilts, paintings, toys, books, old radios and cameras, political memorabilia, clothing, tobacco products, old medical items and original stained glass. For the inveterate collector, this place shouldn't be missed. Shop here every day of the week except Monday year round.

🐚 ATTRACTIONS

Traveling along the East Coast, it's difficult to find uncrowded beaches that offer enough flora and fauna in their surrounding areas to truly reflect the natural beauty of the coastal area and its origins. Too often, residential and commercial growth has replaced nearly all of the natural beauty and history that beach towns have to offer. Not so on the Crystal Coast. The beaches and coastal areas here on the Crystal Coast are what attract visitors and keep them coming back year after year. Residents want to both share and protect this beautiful area, working hard to find and maintain that balance. Natural attractions — Cape Lookout National Seashore, Fort Macon State Park, Hammocks Beach State Park, Theodore Roosevelt Natural Area, Rachel Carson Estuarine Research Reserve, Croatan National Forest and Cedar Island National Wildlife Refuge — offer a wide variety of pristine beaches, maritime forests and waterways to enjoy and explore.

This chapter highlights the many attractions of the Crystal Coast, the unique cultural and natural history of the area, natural attractions, the lighthouse and the museums, that enhance the tourists' visits and residents' lives. Some folks come particularly for festivals and events that we discuss in detail in our Annual Events chapter. Other things we Insiders think are particularly attractive about living here, such as parks, we've described in the Sports, Fitness and Parks chapter. For more attractions the whole family will enjoy, see our Kidstuff chapter.

General Attractions

BOGUE BANKS

North Carolina Aquarium at Pine Knoll Shores
MM 7, N.C. Hwy. 58, Atlantic Beach
(252) 247-4003

Experience the thrill of exploring sunken ships — without getting wet — at the North Carolina Aquarium at Pine Knoll Shores. Three shipwreck exhibits re-create the adventure of recreational diving off the North Carolina coast. Visitors also can feel the spray from a mountain waterfall, hold a crab, touch a stingray, see big sharks and watch river otters play. The aquarium, in Pine Knoll Shores near Atlantic Beach, is one of three operated by the state on the North Carolina coast. These aquariums draw hundreds of thousands of visitors each year. The others are at Fort Fisher near Wilmington and Roanoke Island on the northern Outer Banks.

The Aquarium at Pine Knoll Shores recently expanded to 93,000 square feet. The theme, "From North Carolina's Mountains to the Sea," takes visitors on an unforgettable aquatic journey from the state's grand peaks to the open Atlantic, much as a raindrop makes its way to the ocean. Five galleries — Mountain, Piedmont, Coastal Plain, Tidal Waters and Ocean — and more than 3,000 animals depict these aquatic zones. The 306,000-gallon Living Shipwreck, with a 70-foot replica of a sunken, coral-encrusted World War II German submarine, is the

i *Phillips Island, in the Newport River just north of the N.C. State Port in Morehead City, is one of several local islands leased by the National Audubon Society for the protection of nesting colonial water birds. It is visible from the high-rise bridge passing by the port. A brick chimney on the island is all that remains of a defunct fish-processing facility.*

Windblown sand creates fascinating images.

photo: Peter Doran

centerpiece display. Around it glide fierce-looking sand tiger sharks up to 9 feet in length, along with sea turtles, moray eels, giant groupers, schools of fishes and many other creatures that typically congregate around shipwrecks. A 63-foot window offers superb views, and divers in the exhibit can chat with visitors through underwater microphones.

The 50,000-gallon *Queen Anne's Revenge* exhibit duplicates the scene of an eighteenth-century shipwreck in Beaufort Inlet. The wreckage, discovered in 1996, is thought to be from a pirate ship once commanded by the infamous Blackbeard. Nurse sharks, sea turtles, cobia, bluefish, drum and other animals circle replicas of half-buried cannons and other artifacts in this realistic representation.

The shipwrecks are among nearly 40 innovative exhibits. A favorite stop is the River Otter exhibit, where Neuse, Pungo and Eno — a trio of playful North American river otters named for North Carolina rivers — swim and frolic in their Piedmont habitat. Two touch pools allow personal contact with stingrays, whelks, horseshoe crabs and other creatures. Other favorites include the jellyfish, octopus, seahorse and lionfish displays. Diving demonstrations, live-animal programs and animal feedings are among the daily activities free with admission.

The aquarium offers summer camps for children in grades 2 to 7 and many pro-grams, activities and field trips for all ages. Ocean-going collecting cruises, Newport River excursions, snorkeling classes, kayak and canoe trips, crabbing and clamming classes, surfing lessons, interpretive beach walks and forays to remote barrier islands are a few of the choices. These special programs require advance registration, and most charge a small fee. The aquarium also has wonderful settings, a catering kitchen and various rental options for meetings, ceremonies, parties and presentations. Visitors also will find a large gift shop and a snack bar.

The aquarium is open 9 AM to 5 PM daily. The aquarium is closed for Thanksgiving, Christmas and New Year's days. Admission fees are $8 for ages 18 to 61, $7 for age 62 and older, and $6 for ages 6 to 17. Children 5 and younger, registered North Carolina school groups and members of the North Carolina Aquarium Society are admitted free. Admission is free on November 11 each year for Veteran's Day and on the Monday holiday celebrating Martin Luther King Jr.'s birthday. Admission fees are the same at all three North Carolina Aquariums and are used for improvements at all the facilities. Be sure to ask about a membership in the North Carolina Aquarium Society, which offers free or discounted admission to aquariums and zoos across the country, as well as many other benefits. An individual annual membership is $30; a family membership is $50.

BEAUFORT

Beaufort Historic Site
100 Block, Turner St., Beaufort
(252) 728-5225, (800) 575-7483

People come from far and wide to see the Beaufort Historic Site, a 2-acre area attraction made up of ten buildings, six authentically restored, in the center of town. Cared for by the Beaufort Historical Association, the site annually hosts nearly 60,000 visitors, who tour the buildings and participate in the tours, classes, workshops, special events and historical re-enactments scheduled throughout the year. This heritage tourism site, along with the bustling Beaufort waterfront, is part of what makes this little seaport so special and appealing.

Before you begin to look around, go to the **Robert W. and Elva Faison Safrit Historical Center** at 130 Turner Street. The center welcomes and orients visitors to the historic site with free exhibits and demonstrations. If you decide to take any of the guided tours, the Historical Center is where you purchase tickets and meet the tour guide. The **Old Beaufort Museum Gift Shop** is also here, as well as loads of information about the town of Beaufort and other not-to-be-missed attractions. The center is open Monday through Saturday 9:30 AM to 5 PM from March through November and 10 AM to 4 PM Monday through Saturday from December through February. After a visit to the Safrit Historical Center, we guarantee you'll want to spend a few more days in town.

Ongoing preservation efforts have kept Old Beaufort, celebrating its 300th anniversary in 2009, in tune with its treasured history and heritage. Most of the historically important restored buildings you'll see at the Beaufort Historic Site were moved from other locations in town to preserve them for current and future generations. So that visitors get the most from each tour, the BHA has restored and preserved the buildings in award-winning detail. The collections and furnishings, some original to the structure, help interpret a particular period in Beaufort's history. Guided walking tours of the buildings (we describe some of them here) are conducted by costumed and knowledgeable docents Monday through Saturday year-round for $8 per adult and $4 for children.

Josiah Bell House, c. 1825, is a Victorian home with side gardens and served as the residence of the influential Bell family of Beaufort. Josiah Fisher Bell, son of the home's namesake, was a Confederate agent during the Civil War. The home's interior represents the opulent Victorian period.

Samuel Leffers Cottage, c.1778, is a primitive house that was once home to Beaufort's schoolmaster. The house serves as the perfect setting to showcase artifacts relating to the daily Colonial period chores of cooking, spinning, sewing, candle making and weaving.

John C. Manson House, c. 1825, was the first building purchased by the Beaufort Historical Association in the 1960s. Located on its original site, this elegant Federal Period home is an excellent study in the decorative arts, complete with an authentic faux-finished interior. The award-winning home is a testament to the Beaufort Historic Site's dedication to authentic restoration.

The **Carteret County Courthouse** of 1796 has been completely restored to its original governmental glory. It is the only eighteenth-century framed courthouse of its size in North Carolina that has been restored, or is in a condition that would even allow restoration. The authentic preservation project won several local, state and national awards. The courthouse serves as the backdrop for the Beaufort Historic Site's courthouse dramatization, an integral tool for educating today's youth about the early American legal system.

Old County Jail, c.1829, has two cells and a jail keeper's quarters, which were in use until 1954. The Old Jail boasts 28-inch thick walls and legends of ghosts. The jailer and his family coexisted here with the prisoners, though the jailer's quarters were much cozier than those of the inmates.

The **Apothecary Shop and Doctor's Office**, c.1859, features a fascinating collection of medical instruments and memorabilia from the county's early doctors and dentists, most of which are original to the shop. These items make the building very popular with history buffs.

R. Rustell House, c.1732, is home to the **Mattie King Davis Art Gallery**. In its time, the building was a typical Beaufort cottage and was owned by prominent early citizen Richard Rustell, Jr. The gallery is the oldest in Carteret County and is open year round, offering the artwork and crafts for more than 100 local and regional artists for show and sale.

After touring the historic site, hop on the vintage English double-decker bus for a terrific narrated tour of Beaufort's historic district. The tour comes complete with fascinating stories about town residents and noted locations and homes that shaped Beaufort's 300 years of history. Bus tours depart the historic site

CLOSE UP

Beaufort's
Old Burying Ground

As the members of the Beaufort Historical Association are fond of saying, history lives in Beaufort-by-the-Sea. North Carolina's third oldest town has the ability to take history lessons and turn them into something as vivid as a fantasy thriller. Beaufort's Old Burying Ground has the tangible keys to the imagination that can keep that history fresh. From the little girl buried in a rum barrel to the soldier buried standing up, the graveyard is alive with stories.

The town of Beaufort was surveyed in 1713 and incorporated in 1723. The Old Burying Ground was deeded to the town in 1731 by Nathaniel Taylor. According to historical records, the first burials on the site were in 1711 and were marked with wood. Only a handful of the wooden markers remain, but the marble and stone grave markers that were later used have survived the passage of time remarkably well. Nearly 600 gravestones remain today.

Nestled on Ann Street — named for England's Queen Anne — the Old Burying Ground is a feast for the senses. Ancient live oaks offer an eerie shade, cooling the cemetery even on the warmest of days. Sunlight filters through the protective branches, creating a peaceful, almost surreal, atmosphere. A natural sandy path beckons visitors through the iron gates and leads them on a winding trail. The Burying Ground is located close to the Beaufort Historic Site and is guarded by churches on three sides: Ann Street United Methodist Church, circa 1854; First Baptist Church, circa 1854; and Purvis Chapel A.M.E. Zion Church, circa 1820.

The cemetery's layout is haphazard; graves are placed with little rhyme or reason. But that's only one of the things that makes a trip to the site so awe-inspiring. Visitors are invited to meander through the deep recesses of the site to catch a glimpse of all of the stones. Small ones are tucked away in nooks and crannies, while others are large and centrally located, demanding attention. The condition of the stones varies greatly. Some are broken and chipped, while others have begun to lean in the soft sand. Others yet are as imposing as they must have been on the day they were erected. Regardless of their condition, all of the markers speak volumes of what life must have been like for this sleepy seaport village in days of yesteryear. Here you can hear the whispered voices of Colonial life, war and the life on the sea.

And amid the whispers and the inscriptions on the stones, stories start to emerge that paint a picture of the past. It's here that visitors will find the grave of Nathan Fuller, an ensign with the Carteret County Militia during the Revolutionary War. Records show that Fuller sailed from Beaufort to Barbados, England and the West Indies, returning home with supplies. According to the book *Beaufort's Old Burying Ground*, in 1779 Fuller owned "100 acres, two Negroes, 15 cattle, half a lot and 920 pound." In 1784, however, he

Beaufort's Old Burying Ground is a fascinating attraction.

photo: Amanda Dagnino

owned 400 acres and in 1785 he was elected to serve in the North Carolina House. Fuller's home still stands today on Front Street, where most people know it as the Cedars Bed and Breakfast.

Interestingly, Fuller's grave is not far from the resting place of Josiah Fisher Bell, who served as an agent in the Confederate Secret Service. It is said that Bell, whose home still stands on the Beaufort Historic Site, made arrangements for Confederate troops to enter Carteret County, travel to Cape Lookout, and blow up the two lighthouses.

The Old Burying Ground is indeed a place where people have been laid to rest, but it's also a place where history comes to life. It has been listed in *Our State* magazine as one of the top 52 places to visit in North Carolina and has also been featured in Nicholas Sparks' book *A Walk to Remember*. Guests can pick up a map at the Beaufort Historic Site and guide themselves through the graveyard. Guided tours of the Old Burying Ground run from June through September on Tuesday, Wednesday and Thursday at 2:30 PM. Tickets are $8 for adults and $4 for children. Group tours are offered year round. It is best to call for availability.

from April through October on Monday, Wednesday, Friday and Saturday. Bus tour fees are $8 for adults and $4 for children. Groups are delightfully welcomed by reservation.

Don't miss the **Old Burying Ground** on Ann Street. This treasured cemetery, listed on the National Register of Historic Places, was listed in Our State magazine as one of the top 52 sites to see in North Carolina. It was also featured in the Nicholas Sparks book *A Walk to Remember* and is open daily from early morning until dusk as an amazing lesson of our past. The weathered tombstones dating back to the early 1700s chronicle the heritage of Beaufort and the surrounding coast. Stories of military heroes, star-crossed lovers, privateers and noted Beaufort residents of all ages are featured under a protective canopy of live oaks. From June through September, the BHA gives narrated tours of the cemetery on Tuesday, Wednesday and Thursday (fees are $8 for adults and $4 for children). Group tours can also be arranged year round. To take the tour on your own there is a map available at the Safrit Historical Center.

In addition to these activities, the Beaufort Historical Association conducts the fabulous annual Beaufort **Old Homes Tour and Antiques Show** during the last full weekend in June (see our Annual Events chapter). Activities include tours of private and BHA–owned homes and gardens, musical performances, more than 40 antique

dealers from all over the East Coast, re-enactments and more. In case you decide you just can't leave Beaufort (and many have), volunteers are always welcome to become involved in the coastal history presented and preserved through the Beaufort Historic Site and the Beaufort Historical Association (see our Volunteer Opportunities chapter). The Beaufort Historical Association is a nonprofit organization formed in the 1960s by local citizens and is dedicated to the research, education and the preservation of Carteret County's incredible history. Membership at all levels is welcomed. The Beaufort Historic Site also gladly hosts private parties, weddings and receptions by reservation (see our Wedding Planning chapter).

North Carolina Maritime Museum
315 Front St., Beaufort
(252) 728-7317
www.ncmm.friends.org

The North Carolina Maritime Museum's mission is to preserve and interpret all aspects of the state's rich maritime heritage through educational exhibits, programs and field trips. Its exhibits and programming focus on North Carolina's maritime history and coastal natural history.

The museum is located at 315 Front Street in Beaufort in an area immediately adjacent to shops, restaurants and the boardwalk along Taylors Creek. The 18,000-square-foot building is constructed of wood, and some of its design features resemble those of the early life-saving stations that were prevalent along the Carolina coast starting in the late nineteenth century. Public areas, in addition to the exhibit hall, include an auditorium, reference library and the Museum Store.

In the Harvey W. Smith Watercraft Center, located directly across the street, visitors can watch boat restoration and construction from a platform above the boat shop floor. In the John S. MacCormack Model Shop, builders construct scale models of a variety of vessels. Classes in boat-building skills are offered for novices and experienced woodworkers alike. Topics include lofting, boat building carpentry, boat modeling for children, diesel maintenance, plane making and others. Class size is limited, and all tools and materials are provided. Classes are generally offered on the weekends.

Museum exhibits include Coastal Marine Life, North Carolina's Working Watercraft, U.S. Lifesaving Service and Commercial Fishing. Displayed are a typical 1950s outboard motor shop and outboards, ship models, fossil and shell collections, an observation bell, coastal plant and animal life exhibits, indigenous watercraft and more. The museum's library is available for reading and research.

The museum's education staff has provided environmental education programs for the public since 1975. Coastal habitats are highlighted in trips to barrier island beaches, maritime forests, salt marshes and tidal flats. In addition there are trawling trips aboard a research vessel, birdwatching, fossil hunts and kayaking trips. All museum trips and programs are guided and presented by natural science curators with many years of experience in the field.

The museum's annual programs and field trips attract all ages, all interests, all year. The Wooden Boat Show held the first Saturday in May features wooden boats of all kinds, races, workshops and demonstrations for the enjoyment of everyone who appreciates wooden boats. The Junior Sailing Program is a basic-through-intermediate sailing program open to children ages 8 and older. Boat-related program offerings also include Adult Learn to Sail, Beaufort Oars, Sea Scouts, kayaking and Traditional Boat Handling. The Summer Science School for Children offers individual classes and hands-on field trips

Wild bank horses can be seen on Shackleford Banks and Carrot Island.

photo: Peter Doran

for students entering first through tenth grades (see our Kidstuff chapter).

MOREHEAD CITY

Crystal Coast Civic Center
3505 Arendell St., Morehead City
(252) 247-3883

Under a canopy of oaks on the campus of Carteret Community College and overlooking Bogue Sound, the Crystal Coast Civic Center is a multiple-use facility offering 18,000-square-feet of flexible space. The Civic Center can accommodate groups from 10 to 1,000, depending on set-up arrangements. Each year the Crystal Coast Civic Center hosts a variety of events such as exhibitions, trade shows, concerts, banquets, fund-raisers, weddings, receptions and reunions. Events such as the Big Rock Blue Marlin Tournament banquets, Ducks Unlimited Banquet, Numismatic Coin Show/Sale and the Coastal Home & Garden Show are annual favorites. It's a perfect location for private and commercial businesses to hold retreats, workshops and professional development courses, taking advantage of a convenient location and relaxing atmosphere. Accommodations include a full-service catering kitchen, state-of-the-art public address system, wireless Internet, portable staging and a 5,600-square-foot outdoor plaza overlooking the beautiful waters of the Intracoastal Waterway.

The History Place
1008 Arendell St., Morehead City
(252) 247-7533

Everything old is new again at The History Place. This 12,000-square-foot facility houses museum exhibits, the Rodney B. Kemp Gallery with special displays, the Jack Spencer Goodwin Research Library, a classroom, the Les A. Ewen Auditorium/Banquet Hall, the Museum Store and offices. The Tea Clipper, a tea shop and cafe operated by Elaine Gross, is also located in the building. Visitors may enjoy a cup of tea or a light lunch during the day. The History Place houses an extensive collection of textiles, period clothing, furniture, military memorabilia, glassware and artwork, all representing the past of Carteret County. The library has more than 8,000 books and publications and an extensive

photo file documenting the history of Carteret County. The genealogy materials and the Civil War history collections are especially notable. Special exhibits are displayed throughout the year, and year-round programs, seminars and musical events keep Carteret County history fresh and alive. The Lunch with a Dash of History series with local storyteller Rodney Kemp is a crowd pleaser. The History Place is open Tuesday through Saturday 10 AM to 4 PM. The museum is open free of charge to the public, but donations are always welcome. Special guided tours for schools are free. For a unique and memorable event location, The History Place can be reserved for weddings, receptions or other special events. Volunteers are needed to assist with a variety of responsibilities. See our Volunteer Opportunities chapter for more information.

NEWPORT

Outer Banks Wildlife Shelter
100 Wildlife Way, Newport
(252) 240-1200

This indispensable wildlife hospital is located on N.C. Highway 24, 5 miles west of U.S. Highway 70. It's the red brick house with a pond and bridge in the front yard. Outer Banks Wildlife Shelter (OWLS) has become a much-depended-on agency along the Crystal Coast for assistance with wounded wildlife. This nonprofit group cares for more than 1,000 injured or sick birds, mammals and reptiles annually through the efforts of volunteers and licensed rehabilitators. Individuals finding injured or sick wildlife are asked to call and then deliver the animal to OWLS.

Scheduled tours happen on Tuesdays, Thursdays and Saturdays at 2 PM and include a look at the hospital, orphan nurseries and the permanent resident hawks, owls, opossum, vultures and falcons. Groups are asked to call ahead to schedule a tour. The fee is $2.50 per person for scheduled tours with children younger than 2 admitted free. The facility also offers a nature trail open during daylight hours. Check in at the clinic to register for a self-guided tour of the trail. Wildlife outreach programs are available to school groups. Year-round programs for kids include Wild Encounters and the Junior Rehabilitation Program as well as spring, summer and winter camp dates, all of which require preregistration and fees. A gift shop and wildlife reference library are also on site. The sanctuary operates Monday through Saturday from 9 AM to 5 PM.

DOWN EAST

Core Sound Waterfowl Museum & Heritage Center
1785 Island Rd., Harkers Island
(252) 728-1500

Nestled at "the end of the road" on Harkers Island, the Core Sound Waterfowl Museum and Heritage Center was established in 1992 and is a true grassroots partnership. For more than a decade the Waterfowl Museum has been a clearinghouse for heritage, traditions and history of the Down East communities of Carteret County — a hub for heritage tourism. Exhibits and programs focusing on local heritage are offered year round, and the museum houses the area's finest collection of carvings and waterfowl art. The museum archives oral histories and artifacts from the Down East communities. Museum staff offers programs for school groups, bus tours, church trips and others. Call to schedule a tour and plan for a real "Down East" experience with local carvers, boat builders, storytellers and musicians.

Construction on the museum's 22,000-square-foot facility began in 1999, and the Community Hall opened in 2003 with spaces dedicated to demonstrations, community displays and programs and events throughout the year. This area also includes the region's finest selec-

tion of waterfowl art and regional crafts, as well as a wide selection of local history books. Construction is now underway to complete the museum's gallery, library, gathering room, gift shop, archive reading room and Lookout Tower overlooking Core Sound and Cape Lookout. Plans call for a summer 2009 opening with traveling exhibitions and expanded community programs and documentary projects.

During the summer of 2007, the Willow Pond, the 4-acre freshwater centerpiece of the museum's environmental education program, was opened to the public. This interpretive trail and habitat viewing area has been restored in partnership with Ducks Unlimited, the Conservation Fund, N.C. Wildlife Commission, N.C. Wildlife Habitat Foundation and the Cape Lookout National Seashore.

Each December the museum hosts the Core Sound Waterfowl Weekend (see our Annual Events chapter). The weekend celebrates the entire community with preview events ranging from wild-game feasts to boat-building demonstrations, community church services and children's activities along with the mid-Atlantic region's finest carvers, artists and writers. This event has grown to encompass the entire island, beginning with the decoy show at the elementary school and including food sales and bazaars at churches, fund-raising for Scouts and community groups, and an Island Holiday Decorating Contest on Friday night.

There is no admission charge to enjoy the Core Sound Waterfowl Museum and Heritage Center. Hours are Monday through Saturday 10 AM to 5 PM and Sunday 2 to 5 PM. The museum is closed Easter Sunday, Thanksgiving Day and for three days at Christmas. Membership categories start at $30 for individuals, and benefits vary based on the amount of contribution.

SWANSBORO

Burns Racing
915 W. Corbett Ave., Swansboro
(910) 389-7117

Burns Racing & Performance operates from a shop in Swansboro and is home to Burns Racing Team, a successful racing

> *It's true that membership has its privileges. North Carolina Aquarium members gain free unlimited admission for a full year at any of the three North Carolina Aquariums in addition to free or discounted admission at more than 150 zoos and aquariums across the country.*

CLOSE UP

Rachel Carson's Visit to Beaufort

Rachel Carson is best known as the author of the ground-breaking book *Silent Spring* (1962), which exposed the harmful effects of DDT on the natural environment. Carson was a soft-spoken scientist and writer whose voice was — and continues to be — heard around the world.

While she is often called "The Mother of the Modern Environmental Movement," she was first and foremost a lover of nature and an adventurous explorer. She was fascinated with the relationship of people to their environments. In 1938 she came to Beaufort, North Carolina, to visit the U.S. Fisheries Station. Armed with field glasses and flashlight, she boarded a small boat and cast off from Beaufort, crossing Taylor's Creek to the nearby estuarine waters.

Linda Lear's biography *Rachel Carson: Witness for Nature* recounts the scientist's sojourns through the marshlands and her moonlit walks along the beach. Visitors today can still enjoy the splendor of shorebirds taking flight, the mad scramble of thousands of fiddler crabs or the seemingly immobile gaze of periwinkles, snails locked like lookouts on their stalks of saltmarsh cordgrass.

Carson's visit to Beaufort had a powerful impact on her. It inspired passages about shorebirds in her book *Under the Sea-Wind* (1941). In *The Edge of the Sea* (1955), Carson vividly described the estuarine region in Beaufort that now bears her name, the Rachel Carson Reserve.

Some people refer to the reserve as Carrot Island, but Carrot Island is only one piece of a much larger picture. The islands situated at the western end of the site — Carrot Island, Town Marsh, Bird Shoal, and Horse Island — are more than 3 miles long and less than a mile wide, covering 2,025 acres. Middle Marsh, separated from the rest of the site by the North River Channel, is almost 2 miles long and less than a mile wide, covering nearly 650 acres.

The reserve is a safe haven for fish, birds, oysters, crabs, clams and hundreds of plant species. The estuarine region serves as a nursery for juvenile fish, a buffer from storms and as a living laboratory for humans to study the mysteries of life along the coast. Rachel Carson passed away in 1964 after a long struggle with cancer. Her writings serve as inspiration for all generations. Her love of ocean life speaks to all of us. "The edge of the sea is a strange and beautiful place," she wrote.

team on the stock-car circuit. The team can be seen at a number of area tracks, and currently Coastal Plains Raceway in Jacksonville and East Carolina Motor Speedway in Robersonville are the team's home tracks. When the half-mile oval Carteret County Speedway opens in 2009 it will be the Burns Racing Team's home track. The Burns Racing & Performance shop is also the only place to go for anything and everything to do with stock cars and drag racing. Roger Burns and his crew can build your dream car for you or they can find just the right new or used parts for the do-it-yourselfer. This company has

been in business 10 years and specializes in chaisse fabrication and set up.

Mac Daddy's
130 Golfin Dolphin Dr., Cape Carteret
(252) 393-6565

Mac Daddy's opened in October 2008 and offers a variety of activities for people of all ages. This is a complete family entertainment center featuring a 24-lane bowling alley and the largest high-tech arcade on the Crystal Coast. Mac Daddy's is the perfect place for a special celebration such as a birthday party. Mac Daddy's Sports Bar and Grill has a full menu and a great selection of beers and wines. Guests can enjoy a billiard room and snack-bar seating. The conference center can accommodate groups of up to 80 people and offers Internet access. Mac Daddy's is open year round, seven days a week from 10 AM until midnight with extended hours on the weekends.

Tours

There are a number of ways to see all that the Crystal Coast has to offer, including guided and unguided tours. Whether by land, sea or air there's a lot to take in. Ride a bike, book a flight, catch a ferry, take a tour bus, cruise in a catamaran or sail the seas — there's just not enough time to do it all. That's why those who don't live here keep coming back year after year. Guided walking tours are offered by a few businesses and by the Beaufort Historic Site. The site also offers double-decker bus tours of Historic Beaufort. While the majority of guided tours are by water, we start off the list with a business that offers all types of tours.

Diamond City Cruises
412 Front St., Beaufort
(252) 728-2527, (866) 230-BOAT (2628)
www.mysteryboattours.com

Docked on Beaufort's waterfront across from BB&T, *Diamond City* is owned and operated by Mystery Tours and offers tours of the area waterways. While it's available for special charters, wedding cruises, corporate meetings and fun tours, *Diamond City*'s nighttime offerings have gained it an entry in our Nightlife chapter. Saturday nights boarding at 9:30 PM it leaves the dock for a special two-hour party cruise. Call for the schedule and enjoy this ride. This is Carteret County's only floating nightclub, but that's not all. On board the 149-passenger vessel you'll find a captain and crew trained to make your voyage fun and enjoyable. Reservations can be made for a one-and-a-half-hour "ultimate" tour, leaving every Thursday at noon. You'll see wild horses, dolphins, historic Beaufort, Fort Macon, the Outer Banks and more. Lunch is included. *Diamond City* also offers dolphin watches and Sunday brunch with the dolphins. Eve-

Gulls follow ferries hoping for a handout.

photo: Peter Doran

ning cruisers enjoy dinner from 7 to 9 PM, including a captain's dinner and dancing on select evenings; call for reservations. The vessel has all ABC permits, a state-of-the-art sound system and either a DJ or live entertainment. Folks age 21 and older are invited aboard for $10 per person. Also check out *Diamond City*'s sister vessel, *Mystery*, docked in Beaufort. All cruises require minimum passengers and are subject to cancellation.

Good Fortune
Beaufort Town Docks, Front St., Beaufort
(252) 247-3860

If you are fascinated by coastal ecology or want to know more about the subject, arrange to sail with Capt. Ron White, a marine biologist and owner of the 42-foot sailboat *Good Fortune*. This is the largest sailboat for charter in the area, and it is a custom-built craft that accommodates six people. *Good Fortune* is available for full-day and two-hour sojourns, educational trips, group and corporate charters, and evening sails. Capt. Ron can also take you on an ecology tour, a turtle and dolphin watch, snorkeling, a sunset sail, wild-horse watching, birding, shelling and kayaking. This is the only charter that goes to the turtle hole at Cape Lookout in the late spring or early summer. With 30 years experience, Capt. White can customize a package for you and your group. This is a trip that will make your visit to the Crystal Coast a truly memorable one. You'll find Capt. Ron at the docks from April through October. If you want a cruise during the other months of the year, just give him a call.

Island Ferry Adventures
618 Front St., Beaufort
(252) 728-7555
Cape Pointe Marina, Harkers Island
(252) 728-6181

The friendly staff at Island Ferry Adventures is recognized for its outstanding service. Island Ferry Adventures provides services from two locations. The Beaufort location can found across from Inlet Inn on Front Street and operates April through early October and then closes in the winter. During the season, passenger ferry service begins at 9 AM daily with

departures on the top of the hour. The Harkers Island location at Cape Pointe Marina stays open year round. This service operates passenger ferries to Shackleford Banks, Carrot Island, Sand Dollar Island, Bird Shoals and other area islands. Tours and dolphin or horse watches are available during the summer. Private charters are also available with flexibility when it comes to price, time and destination. Call ahead for reservations and departure times.

Lookout Cruises
Beaufort Waterfront, Beaufort
(252) 504-SAIL (7245)

Steve Bishop captains *Lookout*, a 45-foot catamaran that can hold 42 passengers. The vessel operates public tours on a regular schedule from April 1 through November 30 and is available year round for special charters such as parties, birthdays and anniversaries. The regularly scheduled early morning, two-hour dolphin watch is very popular with children and families; the trip is a smooth ride up the Newport River and costs $20 for adults and $15 for kids. If you want to swim, snorkel and look for shells, try the six-hour trip to Cape Lookout. This trip leaves the dock at noon and offers catered lunch, snacks, fresh fruit, shell bags and complimentary beverages. The fee is $60 for adults and $50 for children. A romantic, relaxing, 90-minute sunset cruise is also available for $25 per person. Complimentary beverages are served. It is always best to call ahead to book a cruise on this popular vessel.

Mystery Boat Tours
412 Front St., Beaufort
(252) 728-2527, (866) 230-BOAT (2628)
www.mysteryboattours.com

Docked in Taylor's Creek in Beaufort, the 65-foot, double-decked *Mystery* tour boat offers cruises along area waterways. Complete with a covered cabin, snack bar and a resident pirate who delights all the passengers, especially the kids, the boat provides visitors with a view of Beaufort's historic homes, island ponies, salt marshes, bird rookeries, Morehead City State Port, Fort Macon, Shackleford Banks and other islands along the Intracoastal Waterway. Tours last one and a half hours and are conducted daily at 2, 4:30 and 7 PM from

April through October. The *Mystery* also offers half-day fishing trips from 8 AM to noon. The boat is available for special-occasion charters such as birthdays, weddings and anniversaries. Special-interest trips can be arranged for bird watchers, shell collectors and other groups. Educational trips for school groups are also a specialty. All cruises require minimum passengers and are subject to cancellation.

Segrave Aviation Air Tours
150 Airport Rd., Beaufort
(252) 728-2323

Enjoy views of the Crystal Coast from the air in a Cessna 172. Segrave Aviation, operating out of the Michael J. Smith Airport in Beaufort, offers a bird's-eye view with a choice of two different tours. Rates generally include seating for up to 3 passengers. Tours must be scheduled in advance so call the agency for details. The Cape Lookout Tour runs 30 minutes and starts from the airport and heads over the state port, over Beaufort Inlet, down the main strip of Atlantic Beach and over Shackleford Banks to the Cape Lookout Lighthouse. This tour costs $100. The Beaches and Banks Tour runs 45 minutes and runs the same course as the Cape Lookout Tour but with an extended tour down Atlantic Beach, Pine Knoll Shores and around the southern tip of the Outer Banks up to Drum Inlet. This tour costs $125. The tours operate year-round.

TourBeaufort.com
Beaufort
(252) 772-9925

TourBeaufort.com offers a variety of tours for visitors and residents. The Beaufort Ghost Walk takes guests on a evening stroll through town, with stops at historic sites and the Old Burying Ground.

Both the Rachel Carson Estaurine Research Reserve and the N.C. Maritime Museum schedule guided tours focused on specific ecological environments of the Crystal Coast. Regular calendars of events are available at each facility. All trips require reservations.

They can also arrange ecology and sunset sailing, kayak tours and boat tours. Some tours take guests to nearby Carrot Island and others take guests to Cape Lookout Lighthouse. Reservations are needed for the tours, which vary in price and in point of origination.

Ecology Tours

North Carolina Coastal Federation
3609 N.C. Hwy. 24, Ocean
(252) 393-8185

The North Carolina Coastal Federation (NCCF) is the state's only non-profit organization focused exclusively on protecting and restoring the coast of North Carolina through education, advocacy and habitat restoration and preservation. NCCF headquarters is located in Ocean between Morehead City and Swansboro. The headquarters includes offices, information displays, a nature gift shop, the Daland Nature Library, the Weber Seashell Exhibit, the ShoreKeeper Learning Center and nature trails. They also have volunteer opportunities to plant wetlands plants and restore oyster reefs throughout the year, for those interesting in taking a hands-on approach to coastal restoration.

The Nature Library houses more than 800 nature and coastal titles suitable for all ages, as well as videos and periodicals. Area guests are welcome to browse in the library, and NCCF members can check out books for up to three weeks. More than 300 North Carolina and Atlantic coast seashells are on exhibit at the headquarters as part of the Weber Seashell collection. A printed guide is available. The Nature Shop features environmental and coastal books for readers of all ages, as well as coastal puzzles, games and educational gifts.

Visit NCCF's two Nature Trails in Carteret County, which are open to the public every day during daylight hours. The Patsy Pond Nature Trail in the Croatan National Forest is located directly across from NCCF headquarters in Ocean and features a long-leaf pine forest with spectacular shallow ponds. Visit a globally endangered maritime forest and NCCF's oyster sanctuary while hiking the Hoop Pole Creek

Nature Trail located in Atlantic Beach off N.C. Highway 58 next to the Atlantic Station Shopping Mall. Maps are available at the trail heads.

NCCF'S staffers conduct educational programs throughout the season, including oyster-reef building, shoreline plantings and summertime estuarine ecology trips at Cape Lookout National Seashore. To learn more about any of these programs, call NCCF at (252) 393-8185 or visit www.nccoast.org. NCCF also has an attractive specialized license plate, available through the N.C. Dept. of Motor Vehicles. Purchase of the NCCF license plate gives a $20 donation to NCCF.

Pelican Ecology Tours
Morehead City Waterfront, Morehead City
(252) 504-2447, (252) 241-8601 (cell)

If you really want to get to know the Crystal Coast, you must explore it from the water with a knowledgeable guide. And Pelican Guided Ecology Tours is just the one to call. The *Pelican* is captained by Paul Dunn, an easy-going man with more than 25 years experience fishing and boating in the area waters. Once aboard the 23-foot boat, you will be off for a memorable journey — just be ready to get some hands-on experience! This is a tour that will have you in and out of the boat using seines, dip nets and throw nets to catch and study live specimens. You'll stop on islands and beaches to look for seashells, sand dollars and driftwood or to snorkel. Capt. Paul will show you how to use a clam rake and, hopefully, you'll end up with some bounty for your supper. Along the way, you may see bottle-nosed dolphin, sea turtles, nesting osprey, waterfowl of all types, the ponies of Carrot Island and Shackleford Banks as well as the Cape Lookout Lighthouse and more. Capt. Dunn enjoys many repeat customers, and they continue to recommend Pelican Guided Ecology Tours to others. The *Pelican* can accommodate up to six individuals, and each trip is planned to meet your individual interests. Capt. Paul's fee is $300 for up to six people. The typical trip is six hours of easy-going fun and education. This is a great way to take a close look at the sounds, marshes, barrier islands and beaches that are only accessible by boat. Trips are by reservation only.

State and National Parks

The Crystal Coast is fortunate to have national, state and local parks scattered from one border to the other. Here, we offer a look at national and state parks. County and city parks are described in our Sports, Fitness and Parks chapter. Our coastal parks will fascinate you with historic interest and natural beauty, so get out there and enjoy them.

Cape Lookout National Seashore
131 Charles St., Harkers Island
(252) 728-2250

Cape Lookout National Seashore is one of America's few remaining undeveloped coastal barrier island systems. It encompasses about 28,500 acres of islands, most of which run roughly parallel to the eastern shores of Carteret County. The system is bounded on the north by Ocracoke Inlet and on the south by Beaufort Inlet. Four islands make up the 56-mile seashore: North Core Banks, also known as Portsmouth Island; Middle Core Banks; South Core Banks (including Cape Lookout); and Shackleford Banks. While each of the islands is distinctive in history and characteristics, all four are remote and virtually unspoiled by the hands of man.

Congress authorized Cape Lookout National Seashore to be included in the National Park System in 1966. The National Park Service (NPS) maintains authority over the seashore. Stopping first at Park Headquarters on Harkers Island is a good idea before you take off for the islands. The attractive visitor center, open seven days a week from 9 AM to 5 PM except for December 25 and January 1, provides a wealth of information to visitors. Of particular interest is the video that gives information about barrier islands and their special characteristics. Park rangers and volunteers can answer questions about transportation (only by boat), camping, kayaking and more. You cannot access the seashore from the Park Service Headquarters because the NPS does not provide a ferry service. However, several private ferries operate from Harkers Island, Beaufort, Morehead City, Davis, Atlantic and Ocracoke. Limited ground transportation on the islands can be arranged with the ferry operator prior to departure, as can accommodations. For more information on getting to the islands, see the Ferries section of our Getting Here, Getting Around chapter. For information about the on-island accommodations, see the write-ups for Morris Marina Kabin Kamps and Great Island Cabins in our Hotels and Motels chapter.

Bear in mind, when planning a visit to any of the islands, that they really are undeveloped. No amenities, drinking water, fast-food concessions or places to buy beach umbrellas or suntan lotion are available. Whatever you need for your trip, you must bring with you, and when you leave, you must take everything out with you. See our chapter on Camping for more details.

The seashore's pristine ocean beaches are an incomparable escape for anglers, sunbathers, surfers, snorkelers and shell collectors. Other recreational pursuits in the park include picnicking, primitive camping, migratory waterfowl watching and hunting.

The area is noted for its natural resources. Birds and animals are the only permanent residents. Loggerhead sea turtles nest on the beaches each summer and seldom nest any farther north. The park is an internationally recognized bird habitat area. Raccoons, rabbits, nutria, a variety of insects, snakes and lizards are also among the park's permanent residents. Ghost crabs, mole crabs and coquina clams populate the beaches.

The Cape Lookout Lighthouse, 2 miles from the southern tip of South Core Banks, is still an active aid to navigation. The first lighthouse was built on Core Banks in 1811-12 and was painted with red and white stripes. But the current lighthouse, completed in 1859, wears a distinctive black and white diamond pattern. Visitors are welcome in the restored lighthouse keepers' quarters, which houses a small museum featuring exhibits on the lighthouse and its keepers. Orienta-

tion and information, as well as sales area that carries books, souvenirs and water are also provided at the Light Station Visitor Center. Other associated structures are also preserved near the lighthouse where there are shelters for picnicking, a swimming beach and a boardwalk that leads from the lighthouse area, over the dunes, to the ocean beach. The lighthouse is currently not open to public climbing.

At the northernmost end of Core Banks at Ocracoke Inlet is the Historic Portsmouth Village. The village was established in 1753 to serve as the main port of entry to several coastal communities. Named for Portsmouth, England, the port village was busy with "lightering" incoming vessels, an unloading and reloading process that allowed vessels to pass through the shallow Ocracoke Inlet. During its heyday in the 1860s, the village had a population of 600. After Hatteras Inlet opened, and in the wake of the Civil War, the village became less important in its port services. From 1894 to 1938, the population of Portsmouth centered on fishing and the U.S. Life-Saving Station. After a severe hurricane in 1933, the village population declined, and by the early 1970s, no year-round residents remained. Today, Portsmouth Village looks much like it did in the early 1930s. Some of the homes are still leased by former descendants and a reunion of descendent's, family, friends and the public every other year in Portsmouth Village. Structures that are not under historic leasing are maintained by the Park Service as visitor centers and museums with exhibits to be installed in the summer of 2009 at the Dixon-Salter Visitor Center, school, post office and U.S. Life-Saving Station. Portsmouth Village was placed on the National Register of Historic Places in 1979.

Looking east from Fort Macon, Shackleford Banks is the island across Beaufort Inlet. It stretches 9 miles east to Cape Lookout (South Core Banks) and is bordered by the Atlantic Ocean on the south and Back Sound on the north. The island's sound side has long been a favorite weekend destination for residents escaping the peopled mainland beaches. The rock jetty is a favorite spot for anglers. Shackleford

Banks officially became part of Cape Lookout National Seashore on the first day of 1986. Until then, the island was dotted with cabins or camps that former banks' residents and their descendants used as getaway shelters.

The acquisition of Shackleford Banks meant removing the structures and the livestock that had been left to roam the island. Before 1986, the island was home to hardy herds of wild cattle, sheep, goats, pigs and horses. Only the horses remain today. These famous horses have roamed free for centuries. The exact route of the ancestors of these small, hardy horses to this barrier island is unknown, but genetic research shows evidence of Spanish ancestry in the herd. More than 100 horses roam the island, having divided themselves into harems (one or sometimes two stallions, some unrelated mares and their foals) and bachelor bands (males without harems). These groups of horses find their own food on the island; they are sometimes found in the maritime forest, but mostly graze in the marshes, swales and dunes. Fresh water is available in numerous pools and swales along the length of the island. The horses are managed in as much of a hands-off manner as possible, though some horses are removed for adoption. The horses are co-managed by the National Park Service and the Foundation for Shackleford Horses Inc., an organization formed to protect them on the island. Visitors should remember that they are wild animals and, for your safety and their well-being, the horses should not be approached.

Shackleford Banks was named for John Shackleford, who purchased the land (which became the island) in 1723. Permanent residents once populated communities on Shackleford. New England whaling vessels visited the area as early as 1726. By 1880, six crews of 18 men from Diamond City were whaling off the banks' shores. The whalers were a hardy people and included the Davis, Moore, Guthrie, Royal and Rose families — names still common in Carteret County. Whaling was the backbone industry of this island. Local merchants sold the oil as lamp and lubricating oil or used it to make soap. Whale bone was valuable in making corset stays, ribs for umbrellas and other items. They sold the rest of the whale to be used as fertilizer. The largest community on Shackleford was Diamond City, at the east end of the island. By 1897, about 500 people populated this community, which included church buildings, stores and a school. The population grew in the 1850s because of a boom in the whaling industry. East of Diamond City, across what is now Barden's Inlet, was the Cape Lookout Light Station. West of Diamond City was Bell's Island, a settlement known for bountiful persimmon trees. The western part of Shackleford Banks was known as Wade's Shore. Two hurricanes that closely followed each other in 1896 and 1899 convinced most island inhabitants to move to the mainland. Many moved their homes by boat to Harkers Island or to the Promised Land section of Morehead City. Others resettled in the Bogue Banks community of Salter Path.

Cedar Island National Wildlife Refuge
879 Lola Rd., Cedar Island
(252) 225-2511

This 14,480-acre wildlife refuge on the southern end of Cedar Island is administered by Mattamuskeet National Wildlife Refuge, (252) 926-4021, and provides areas for hiking, bird-watching, launching boats, picnicking and duck hunting. There is a refuge employee on duty, and, while ranger services are not available, the employee can answer questions about the refuge from the Cedar Island number. Waterfowl abundant during the year are mallards, black ducks, redheads, pintails and green-winged teal. Other wildlife at home in the refuge are raccoons, whitetail deer, black bears, woodpeckers and river otters. In the spring and fall, this is a delightful picnicking and bird-watching destination. The Cedar Island Wildlife Refuge was formed in 1964 under the Migratory Bird Act to provide a sanctuary for migratory

CLOSE UP Blackbeard's
Queen Anne's Revenge

It may indeed be the revenge of Blackbeard to be the most remembered of all American pirates. That is probably why the finding of what is believed to be his flagship *Queen Anne's Revenge* is intriguing and has brought thousands of people to Beaufort and the Crystal Coast.

Located by the private firm Intersal in 1996 and currently being excavated by the State of North Carolina, the wreckage is producing strong evidence that the ship found is, in fact, the notorious pirate's doomed vessel. Discovered in 20 feet of water less than 2 miles off historic Fort Macon, the find includes numerous cannon, small arms and other eighteenth-century seafaring items. Some of these items are on exhibit at the North Carolina Maritime Museum in Beaufort. As far as American colonial history is concerned, the *Queen Anne's Revenge* recovery is classified as a major twentieth-century archaeological find.

In some ways, probably more is known of Blackbeard's main ship than of the pirate himself, who despite any legendary portrayal, is not known to have killed a single person. But he captured many a ship in the years from 1716 to 1718 in his short pirate career that ended in November 1718 with his head hanging from the bowsprit of a British ship. That Blackbeard lived in Bath, North Carolina, where he bought a house and filled it with lavish furnishings, is based more on legend than fact. Blackbeard's fierce countenance was a result of burning cannon fuses hanging from his wild beard and broad hat and three sets of pistols in his belt. This is probably the most recorded, and painted, image of the man.

But history and legend often intertwine, and separating fact from fiction is not always easy. For example, you can pick up several biographies of Blackbeard, but where dialogue begins is the end of fact and the beginning of fancy. Besides *Queen Anne's Revenge*, Blackbeard also commanded several additional pirate vessels, including Stede Bonnet's *Revenge* and the sloop *Adventure*.

The excavation for what is dubbed *QAR* has been actively pursued and the diving is continuing. Among the items raised are cannons, shards from large lead-glazed storage containers, salt-glazed stoneware, large iron barrel hoops and several pewter dinner plates and platters with identifying English maker's marks. They also recovered remains of bag shot, wads of lead shot of varying sizes imprinted with cloth fabric. Among the most prized artifacts found was the bronze ship's bell. It bears the date 1705 and the inscription "IHS Maria," which historians believe refers to Jesus and Mary. It is thought that the bell may have been looted from a victim ship. A second unmarked bell was recovered in 2006.

Queen Anne's Revenge was originally a slave ship named Concorde operating out of Nantes, France, as early as 1713. Prior to this there is a good chance the ship was a privateer during Queen Anne's War (1702-1713), making for a very interesting career.

In Blackbeard's time, the days of piracy were numbered. The Caribbean and colonial governments were souring on the common practice of pirating. It had been a lovely arrangement for a while to avoid duty payments to the Crown of England. Everyone profited. Pirates sold stolen merchandise to merchants who were able to make greater profits. But when cargoes that wealthy officials and merchants had invested in were intercepted, that's when the pirates became hunted criminals.

Presumed literate, Blackbeard was a genius at marketing an image. A statuesque man, he wore a full black beard when beards weren't the style. His hair was long and he wore it thickly braided, probably like dreadlocks, at sea. For attacks, he braided his beard, which sprouted from just under his eyes. In his hair and beard, he laced fuse cords used to ignite cannons. When he appeared on the deck of *Queen Anne's Revenge* to demand the surrender of a halted vessel he had guns and knives strapped to himself and was surrounded by smoke like a demon from Hell. So effective was the image that more than 50 ships are known to have surrendered to Blackbeard, as well as one city — Charleston, South Carolina — from which he demanded medicine to treat his crew for various diseases. In fact, there are no recorded battles with ships of Blackbeard's fleet except for the battle at Ocracoke. Ships simply surrendered.

birds. The access is well-marked on Cedar Island. Turn on Lola Road and follow it to the refuge office. One boat ramp is at the end of Lola Road and another is at the base of the Monroe Gaskill Memorial high-rise bridge.

Croatan National Forest
Ranger's Office, 141 E. Fisher Ave., New Bern
(252) 638-5628

Located between New Bern and Emerald Isle, the Croatan National Forest is made up of 161,000 acres and features coastal and inland swamp habitats. The Croatan Forest is home to the largest collection of carnivorous plants in any National Forest and it is near the northern range limit of the American alligator. It also has an amazing collection of bugs. Much of the forest is characterized as swampy with thick underbrush. It is perhaps not a forest suited for everyone, but it is very attractive to area fishermen and hunters and is popular for its hiking trails, boat launches, campgrounds and day-use areas.

The forest spreads in a triangle between Morehead City, Cape Carteret and New Bern. Forest headquarters are on Fisher Avenue, approximately 9 miles east of New Bern off U.S. Highway 70. Well-placed road signs make the office easy to find. Because the Croatan is so expansive and undeveloped, it is best to pick up a forest map from the headquarters if you plan to explore extensively. For short day trips or hiking excursions, site brochures are sufficient.

The name Croatan comes from the Algonquian Indians' name for "Council Town," which was once located in the area. Because of the forest's coastal location,

you'll find many unusual features here. Some of the components of the ecosystem are pocosin, longleaf and loblolly pine, bottomland and upland hardwoods.

Sprinkled throughout the Croatan are 40 miles of streams and 4,300 acres of wild lakes, some fairly large, such as Great Lake, Catfish Lake and Long Lake. Miles of unpaved roads lace through the woodland, providing easy, if at times roundabout, access to its wilderness.

The forest offers excellent hiking, swimming, boating, camping, picnicking, hunting and freshwater and saltwater fishing. Boat access is provided at several locations. Rangers advise that lake fishing is generally poor because of the acidity of the water. All fishing, hunting and trapping activities are regulated by the N.C. Wildlife Resources Commission. A kids' fishing day is generally held in July and specific information is available by calling the Ranger Station. The forest has several camping sites (see our Camping chapter) that are open throughout the year. Primitive camping is permitted all year, and sites are plentiful. Some areas of the forest close seasonally, and fees can vary, so call headquarters for current rates and availability.

As with all national forests, the Croatan's natural resources are actively managed to provide goods and services for the public. Pine timber is harvested and replanted each year, and wildlife habitat for a wide range of animals is maintained on thousands of acres. Endangered and sensitive animal and plant species are protected. The red-cockaded woodpecker is among the endangered animals that find safety here. More common animals are the southern bald eagle, alligators, squirrels, otters, white-tailed deer, black bears, snakes and wild turkeys.

The area is known for its beautiful wildflowers, including five types of insectivorous plants, a combination rarely seen elsewhere. Among the insectivorous plants are pitcher plants, round-leaved sundew, butterworts, Venus flytraps and bladderworts, all of which die if removed from their natural habitat; it is against the law to disturb them. Pamphlets about the wildflowers and insect-eating plants are available at the forest headquarters.

Summer fires, whether spontaneous in nature or controlled for forest nurturing, are common and as a result, few public education programs are offered during the typical tourist season. The insect-eating plants that proliferate in pocosin habitats are actually fire dependent, another reason not to try to take them home. After a good burning, they're well-nurtured and hungry for bugs. Nature is stranger than fiction.

The forest features several trails ranging in length from 1.4 miles to 20 miles. It also offers a 110-mile Saltwater Adventure Trail that offers paddlers a seven-day trip to visit every point of interest or just a one-day trip to visit only a few. Visit the USDA National Forest Service website for recreation overviews, maps and trail information or call the Ranger's Office for further details.

Fort Macon State Park
N.C. Hwy. 58, Atlantic Beach
(252) 726-3775

Fort Macon State Park highlights Fort Macon, one of the most complete forts of the Civil War era in the United States. It is totally intact, covering about five acres on the tip of Bogue Banks, where it was located to protect the channel and Beaufort Harbor from attacks by sea. Structurally, the fort is in great shape following a four-year restoration and renovation that was completed in 2003. The park also offers Fort Macon Beach and is one of the most visited state parks in North Carolina. With an estimated 1.3 million visitors a year, it is by far the most visited site of any attraction on the Crystal Coast.

Walking on the wide path to the fort, a visitor comes to the huge wall and moat, 24 feet deep, that was intended to be flooded with seawater as another obstacle to attackers. Crossing the moat bridge, a visitor is drawn back into the reality

Fort Macon, at the east end of Bogue Banks in Carteret County, was built between 1826 and 1834.

photo: Peter Doran

of what life was like in such forts. Huge cannon emplacements still surmount the ramparts, and two mortars stand out amid the interior, which also has vaulted ceiling casemate rooms where the garrison lived. Reenactments are held in April, July and September.

The critical defense location had been considered before, with Fort Dobbs, named for Governor Arthur Dobbs, begun in 1756 but never completed. In 1808 and 1809 Fort Hampton, a small masonry fort, was built to guard the inlet. Hampton was abandoned shortly after the War of 1812 and by 1825 had been swept into the inlet.

Fort Macon was designed by Brig. Gen. Simon Bernard and built by the U.S. Army Corps of Engineers between 1826 and 1834 at a cost of $463,790. The fort was named for Nathaniel Macon, who was speaker of the House of Representatives and a U.S. Senator from North Carolina. The five-sided structure was constructed of brick and stone with outer walls 4.5 feet thick. The fort was deactivated after 1877 and then regarrisoned by state troops in 1898 for the Spanish-American War. It was abandoned again in 1903, was not used in World War I and was offered for sale in 1923. An Act of Congress in 1924 gave the fort and the surrounding land to the state of North Carolina to be used as a public park. The park, which is more than 400 acres, opened in 1936 and was North Carolina's first functioning state park.

At the outbreak of World War II, the Army leased the park from the state and, once again, manned the fort to protect a number of important nearby facilities. In 1946 the fort was returned to the state, and the park reopened the following year.

Today, Fort Macon State Park offers two great features — beautiful, easily accessible beaches for recreation and a historic fort for exploration. Visitors enjoy the sandy beaches, a seaside bathhouse and restrooms, a refreshment stand, designated fishing and swimming areas, and picnic facilities with outdoor grills. The park is full of wildlife, including herons, egrets, pelicans, warblers, sparrows and other animals.

The fort itself is a wonderful place to explore with a self-guided tour map or with a tour guide. Restored rooms and a bookstore offer exhibits to acquaint you with the fort and its history. The fort and museum are open daily year round. Fort tours are guided through late fall. Reenactments of fort activities are scheduled periodically from spring to fall. Talks on the Civil War and natural history are conducted year round. The fort offers a free summer concert series — call the fort office for this season's schedule. The fort is open daily from 9 AM to 5:30 PM except for Christmas day. Admission is free.

Hammocks Beach State Park
1572 Hammocks Beach Rd., Swansboro
(910) 326-4881

Venture to Hammocks Beach State Park on Bear Island and be rewarded with one of the most beautiful and unspoiled beaches in the area. The park consists of a barrier island off the southernmost point of Bogue Banks and a small area off N.C. 24 just south of the residential area of Swansboro, where the visitors center and ferry landing are located. Watch for state directional signs. The island is accessible only by boat or ferry (see our Getting Here, Getting Around chapter), and camping is allowed (see our Camping chapter). There is a small fee for the ferry to Bear Island, which operates from April through October. Contact the visitors center for the ferry schedule and rates. Ranger programs are conducted for visitors.

Loggerhead turtles come ashore at Bear Island at night during the summer nesting season to make nests above the tide line. Explorers can observe marine life in tidal creeks and mudflats. Outdoor showers, restrooms and drinking water are available to visitors. Go prepared to shade yourself and take along refreshments. It is a half-mile walk from the ferry landing to the ocean beach. Pack light with day packs and beach supplies, since wagons and carts are not allowed on the ferry boats. Whether you spend an hour or a whole day, the trip is always worthwhile.

Rachel Carson Reserve
101 Pivers Island Rd., Beaufort
(252) 838-0883

Just across Taylor's Creek from the Beaufort waterfront is a series of islands approximately 3.5 miles long that make up the Rachel Carson National Estuarine Research Reserve. Most locals refer to the entire chain of islands as Bird Shoal or Carrot Island, although the site is really composed of Carrot Island, Town Marsh, Bird Shoal, Horse Island, Sand Dollar Island and Middle Marsh.

In the early 1970s Congress recognized the need to protect coastal resources from pollution and the pressures of development. The nation's estuaries were particularly vulnerable. Through the Coastal Zone Management Act of 1972, Congress established a National Estuarine Research Reserve System to protect coastal areas for long-term research, education and stewardship. The National Estuarine Research Reserve System is a partnership program between the National Oceanic and Atmospheric Administration (NOAA) and the coastal states. It protects more than one million acres of estuarine land and water, which provides essential habitat for wildlife; offers educational opportunities for students, teachers and the public; and serves as living laboratories for scientists. The island chain across from the Beaufort waterfront is a designated National Estuarine Research Reserve and is named in honor of the famed scientist and author Rachel Carson, who conducted research on the islands in the late 1930s and, through her research and writing, made people aware of the importance of coastal ecosystems. The reserve has many appealing features, including extensive tidal flats, eel grass beds, salt flats and a self-guided trail for visitors, but the site is best known for the horses that live there.

The Rachel Carson Reserve is home to a herd of 42 feral horses. They are descended from domesticated horses taken to the islands in the 1940s to graze. Today they roam the sandy expanse, living in small bands called harems, each consisting of one stallion, several mares and the year's foals. Bachelor males roam the island alone or in pairs. These are either older stallions that have lost their harem to a younger, stronger male or young stallions who have not yet challenged the dominant males.

The Rachel Carson site is a favorite spot for beach combing, swimming, sunbathing and clamming but camping is not allowed and dogs are required to be on a leash. Visitors are encouraged to leave everything — the animals, plants and research equipment — undisturbed.

Reserve education staff and specially trained volunteers conduct tours of the reserve every Tuesday through Thursday from June to September. Tours leave by boat from the Reserve Education Office located on Pivers Island (in west Beaufort). Call (252) 838-0883 to make a tour reservation. School groups are also welcome to arrange for special tours throughout the year. A self-guided trail brochure is available at the Reserve Education office, the N.C. Maritime Museum or ferry service offices. Kayaks are available for rent along the Beaufort waterfront, and many people make a day of paddling around the island. An information sign about the reserve is displayed on Front Street in Beaufort across from the Inlet Inn.

Theodore Roosevelt Natural Area
**MM 7 Roosevelt Dr., Pine Knoll Shores
(252) 247-4003**

This little gem of woods surrounds the North Carolina Aquarium on Roosevelt Drive in Pine Knoll Shores and borders N.C. Highway 58 as it winds through Bogue Banks. Maintained by the aquarium staff and North Carolina State Parks, the 300 acres have extensive maritime forests and freshwater ponds. The family of President Theodore Roosevelt donated the land to the state. The forest attracts naturalists, birders and photographers. There are two trails through the natural area: the Alice G. Hoffman Trail, accessed through the aquarium, and the Theodore Roosevelt Trail, beginning outside the aquarium at the southern end of the parking area. The soundside trails are good places to see land birds. The salt-marsh overlook areas on the aquarium's Salt Marsh Safari boardwalk leading to the Alice G. Hoffman Trail can be good areas for sighting wading birds and migratory waterfowl, depending on the time of year. However, marshes along this section of Bogue Banks are not extensive, so shore and waterbird sightings can be spotty.

KIDSTUFF

What do most kids need at the beach to have fun? Not much! That's why sand and surf are definitely the main attractions of the Crystal Coast for children of all ages. When parents and kids want something different than a day at the beach, not to worry — Carteret County is home to a wide variety of options for families. Set out for fun at one of the amusement areas, visit sea life face-to-face at the aquarium, learn about colonial times at the Beaufort Historic Site, zip down a water slide, take the helm of a bumper boat, putt a round of mini-golf, take a spin in a go-cart or attend a camp. Several summer camps of various styles are offered in the area. If you're interested in how the seashore environment works or want to learn how to sail a boat, make sure you check out the North Carolina Maritime Museum's Summer Science School or Junior Sailing Program. The courses are short, so they won't take up your whole vacation. Many of the sites for adventures that follow are also described in other chapters, and, for further details, we have referred you to them. As always, if you seek other ideas, look in other areas of this book or just ask an Insider kid.

Amusements

Golfin' Dolphin
N.C. Hwy. 24, Cape Carteret
(252) 393-8131

This expansive family entertainment complex, off N.C. 24 in Cape Carteret, is where athletes of all ages and stages can hone their competitive edge. The complex includes a 50-tee driving range, baseball and softball batting cages and an 18-hole miniature golf course. While the bigger kids are sharpening their skills, the little ones enjoy the go-carts and bumper boats

with water-spray attachments. The Golfin' Dolphin also has a snack bar. The complex is open throughout the spring, summer and fall, so call for winter hours. Golfin' Dolphin's new neighbor is Mac Daddy's Bowling Center, complete with 24-bowling lanes, a sports bar and grill, arcade and conference rooms.

Lost Treasure Golf and Raceway
MM 10.3, N.C. Hwy. 58, Salter Path
(252) 247-3024

How about a ride on a train through caves, ancient ruins and under waterfalls to begin the adventure? The family will enjoy an active day at this Salter Path park. You'll love the go-cart ride over bridges and banked curves. You can splash in bumper boats, play games in a high-tech arcade and putt 18 fabulous holes of miniature golf. Ice cream may be purchased. A picnic area can be used for parties, and group rates are offered. Tickets for each activity are sold separately. Call for seasonal hours.

Mac Daddy's
130 Golfin Dolphin Dr., Cape Carteret
(252) 393-6565

OK kids (and kids-at-heart), this is the place you've been dreaming of — there's fun in every corner. Mac Daddy's is a huge family entertainment center that has 24 lanes of bowling, a cutting-edge arcade, a snack bar area and much more. It's a great place to bowl with your family or with a group of your friends. Rack up points in the arcade and bring them up to the redemption counter for the prize you've been working, or rather playing, so hard for. The snack bar has all of the American favorites, including pizza, burgers, hot dogs, fries, nachos and pretzels at an affordable price. It's a great spot for birthday parties, so ask about the packages they offer. Located in the same complex as the Golfin' Dolphin off N.C. Highway 24, Mac Daddy's is open year round, seven days a week from 10 AM until midnight with extended hours on the weekends.

Playland & Lighthouse Golf
MM 20.5, 204 Islander Dr., Emerald Isle
(252) 354-6616

Playland in Emerald Isle has super-fast water slides and several rides for toddlers and youngsters, including bumper cars, bumper boats and grand prix tracks. Adjoining Playland is the Water Boggan and Lighthouse Golf, an 18-hole miniature golf course. Playland also has a snack bar and a picnic area to keep the kids completely happy and give the adults a break. Playland is open seasonally April through September.

Hot To Shop

Bogue Banks Beach Gear and Linens Rentals
Bell Cove Village,
9106-C Coast Guard Rd., Emerald Isle
(252) 354-4404
www.boguebanksbeachgear.com

Whether you need something to entertain the kids or rental equipment for a baby, Bogue Banks Beach Gear and Linens Rentals has what you need. Rent kayaks, umbrellas, beach chairs, Boogie boards and surf gear for the beach or rent bikes for the whole family. You can also rent a crib, high chair, baby gates and other items for the beach house if you don't want to bring them from home. From two locations, one in Emerald Isle and one in Atlantic Beach, Bogue Banks Beach Gear & Linens offers items for daily and weekly rentals. These folks provide the largest selection of quality rental items with friendly customer service. They're open year-round seven days a week and they accept VISA/MC with online reservations.

The Parent Trap
Morehead Plaza, Ste. 20,
2900 Arendell St., Morehead City
(252) 727-0123

The Parent Trap is Carteret County's only "Play Boutique." The store specializes in fine, high-quality toys, games, puzzles, and all the latest accessories for new and expectant parents and babies. The Parent Trap also offers nursery and children's furniture. This unique shop offers a play space in the store with a complete activity center. Activities include weekly music class, story time and playgroups. Parent Trap is open Monday through Saturday from 10 AM to 5:30 PM.

Teacher's Pet
2410 Arendell St., Morehead City
(252) 240-2515

This is a great place for games, toys and things to build, cuddle, paint, put together, discover and, yes, learn. Age-appropriate educational toys run the gamut here, from silly to serious. It's a delightful place to take a kid or to shop for a birthday surprise. The shop also houses educational materials for teachers and conducts workshops in the use of materials. Teacher's Pet offers tutoring services. That's because it's the enterprise of a couple of former teachers.

Lots To Learn

Junior Sailing Program
N.C. Maritime Museum,
315 Front St., Beaufort
(252) 728-7317
www.ncmm-friends.org

The Junior Sailing Program is a basic and intermediate summer sailing program open to children ages 8 to 14. The program uses the fun of sailing and the competition of racing to teach rigging, sailing, seamanship, navigational skills and maritime traditions and history to young sailors. Instructors are certified by the U.S. Sailing Association as Small Boat Sailing Instructors and are certified by the American Red Cross in First Aid and CPR. These programs fill very quickly, and students are accepted on a first-come, first-served basis. Call the N.C. Maritime Museum for class schedules and fee information.

Library Storytime
Carteret County Public Libraries
(252) 728-2050

Throughout the year, the Carteret County Public Libraries offer a number of reading and educational programs. Special programs for young people are offered in the summers as well. Contact the individual libraries for details:

Beaufort — (252) 728-2050

Bogue Banks — (252) 247-4660

Western Carteret — (252) 393-6500

Newport — (252) 223-5108

Storytime is also offered for preschool children ages 2 to 4 years of age at 11 AM in the children's section at the Webb Memorial Library, 812 Evans Street in Morehead City, although it is not affiliated with the county library system. Groups should call ahead to arrange for storytime sessions. Call (252) 726-3012 for details.

North Carolina Aquarium at Pine Knoll Shores
MM 7, N.C. Hwy. 58, Atlantic Beach
(252) 247-4003

Educators at the North Carolina Aquarium at Pine Knoll Shores have designed a number of fun, innovative programs and special activities just for youngsters such as hands-on "Aquarium ABCs" for preschoolers and "Critter Class" for ages 6 to 8. Registration begins April 1 each year for weeklong summer day camps filled with hands-on, feet-wet adventure for kids in grades 2 through 7. Summertime snorkeling outings are geared for ages 5 and older, and surfing lessons are offered for ages 10 and older. Aquarium programs vary with the seasons, and special activity programs require advance registration and fees. To find out what's going on, call the aquarium or see the website for the complete calendar.

Other Good Stuff

Boys & Girls Club of Coastal Carolina, Inc.
601 Mulberry St., Beaufort
(252) 504-2465
3221 Bridges St., Morehead City
(252) 222-3007

The Boys & Girls Club operates a club in Beaufort and a club in Morehead City. The Beaufort Club was the first in the county, opening in 1997 in the former Queen Street School. That facility has seen some renovation since that time, and the membership has grown. The new More-head City Club is on the campus of Morehead City Elementary School. Attendees spend afternoon hours with directed programs of sports and interesting, interactive, positive goings-on. There is also a homework time. Club activities for kids from ages 6 to 18 are available on weekdays from 3 to 7 PM. Summer and holidays bring about expanded hours. Summer camps are also offered in full 10-week sessions or by the week. The Boys & Girls Club also offers after-school programs at several of the county's public schools.

Morehead City Parks and Recreation
1600 Fisher St., Morehead City
(252) 726-5083

This department offers a lot of sports programs designed to teach children the fundamentals of the games and also the value of team participation and sportsmanship with a focus on fun. Team sports include T-ball, basketball and coach-pitch baseball. In addition to sports, the department hosts a number of fun activities for children and adults. Many programs are free, but those with fees are reasonable and well worth the cost for the enrichment they provide. Both city residents and nonresidents are welcome to participate in the department's programs. Morehead City Parks and Recreation sponsors after-school programs for some schools and offers an eight-week summer camp program for children ages 3 to 12. From Memorial Day through Labor Day, the department offers a Saturday in the Park Concert Series at Jaycee Park located at Ninth and Shepard streets. Call for details on the musical performance schedule and times. The department also sponsors the North Carolina Seafood Festival 8K Twin Bridges Road Race that takes place the first weekend of October in conjunction with the Seafood Festival.

Take a field guide to seashells on your beach trips so you can answer "What's this?" each time the kids find a shell. The Discovery Cart of common beach finds at the N.C. Maritime Museum will remind them of all they've learned.

Mystery Boat Tours Treasure Hunt
412 Front St., Beaufort
(252) 728-2527, (866) 230-BOAT (2628)
www.mysteryboattours.com

What kid wouldn't want to hunt treasure on the coast? Mystery Boat Tours offers a Treasure Hunt for children, complete with a pirate. Children and their families are taken to an island and given maps. Then the treasure hunt begins with the pirate at the lead. Everyone finds a treasure chest filled with goods. After the hunt, you can enjoy the beach before heading back to port. Call for information and reservations. All cruises require minimum passengers and are subject to cancellation.

Spinnaker's Reach Realty
9918 M.B. Davis Ct., Emerald Isle
(252) 354-5555
www.spinnakersreach.com

Spinnaker's Reach is a private subdivision of rental and permanent homes built with families in mind. With private beaches, sound access and seasonal activities they have something for every family. Many of the homes offer private pools, golf carts, elevators and media/game rooms. Visit the website for virtual tours.

Outside Fun

Kites Unlimited and Bird Stuff
Atlantic Station Shopping Center,
MM 3, N.C. Hwy. 58, Atlantic Beach
(252) 247-7011

Kites Unlimited is a great store to explore whether you are a kid or an adult. The store sponsors kite-flying events at Fort Macon State Park, and everyone is invited to join in the fun each Sunday at 10 AM, 9 AM in the summer months. Bring a kite because you'll want to try the things you see after the demonstrations, or you can just watch. For truly competitive kite fliers, the Carolina Kite Fest at the Sheraton Atlantic Beach in October is also sponsored by Kites Unlimited (see our Annual Events chapter). Kites Unlimited

has added Bird Stuff to the store, offering feeders, seeds, houses and more.

North Carolina Maritime Museum
315 Front St., Beaufort
(252) 728-7317
www.ncmm.friends.org

For years North Carolina Maritime Museum's education staff has provided environmental education programs for kids and for adults. The programs focus on coastal habitats and are highlighted by trips to barrier island beaches, maritime forests, salt marshes and tidal flats. In the past there have been trawling trips aboard a research vessel, bird watching, fossil hunts and kayak trips. All museum trips are guided. There is a charge for these fun trips, but it is worth it.

North Carolina Seafood Festival
907-B Arendell St., Morehead City
(252) 726-6273
www.ncseafoodfestival.org

Kids have plenty to do during the N.C. Seafood Festival. Young anglers can fish in Atlantic Beach as part of the All Kids' Fishing Classic. Prizes are awarded for the largest of any kind of fish caught, and each angler goes home with a prize. On Saturday during festival, SasSea's Island Playground is jumping with hands-on activities for kids only. Shade trees, a beautiful gazebo and a playground set the backdrop for the fun. With face painting, sidewalk chalk designs, jump rope and story telling, this is a great place for kids and their parents during the festival.

Sea of Dreams
Shevans Park, 16th and Evans Sts.,
Morehead City
(252) 726-5083

This imaginative public playground, designed with input from the kids who are now enjoying it, was constructed by nearly 200 residents of Carteret County. Walk through the entry towers and encounter a maze that sends kids ages 3 and younger in one direction and the older ones in another. Inside, there are slides, swings,

CLOSE UP

The Wild Horses of Carrot Island

Beaufort residents and visitors alike enjoy watching the feral horses as they roam over the inside barrier islands across from the town's main street. These islands are now known as the Rachel Carson Estuarine Reserve. It is easy to see these "ponies" that have never seen a saddle most any day as you drive, walk, run or bike on Front Street along the Beaufort waterfront. These horses range over the small islands across Taylor's Creek, 100 to 200 yards away from the bustling waterfront.

Wild horses roam Carrot Island across from the Beaufort waterfront.

photo: Carolyn Temple

The horses that now call the reserve home are descended from domesticated horses taken to the islands to graze years and years ago. Today they roam the sandy expanse, living in small bands called harems. Each harem consists of one stallion, several mares and the year's foals. Bachelor males roam the island alone or in pairs. These bachelors are either older stallions who have lost their harem to younger, stronger males or stallions who have not yet challenged the dominant males.

For a time in recent years there was a battle over removing the Beaufort horses, with claims made by some officials that they were an "exotic" species and would ruin the islands. The efforts of Beaufort and area legislators won out, and now the horses are protected. For decades, people in Beaufort have kept a watchful eye on them, even taking forage over to the islands in bitter winters.

The islands that make up what is now the reserve are Town Marsh, Bird Shoal, Carrot Island and Horse Island, though folks debate where one leaves off and another begins, depending on the tides. But the tides do not bother the horses, which now number about 40; they will simply swim from island one to another when necessary.

The horses are compact and naturally small, usually less than 14 hands high, and their rugged appearance is a result of living in the wild. The people who work for the estuarine reserve do not feed the ponies because to do so would affect their status as wild animals. The horses must find food and water on their own. Food comes in the form of various salt-marsh grasses that grow on the tidal flats and low dunes. Drinking water comes from temporary freshwater pools. When they have to, the horses sniff out rainwater that's trapped beneath the soil and use their hooves to dig down until they reach the fresh water.

The mainland is not the only vantage point from which to enjoy the feral horses. The best opportunity to come upon one or more of these animals is on the reserve itself. Fortunately, quick trips to the Rachel Carson site are available from several ferry services in Beaufort. While walking about these pristine islands that seem untouched by civilization, you may look up to see a few ponies watching you from just a few yards away, wondering what you are doing there. You can also take a kayak trip around the reserve.

For more about the Rachel Carson Component of the North Carolina Estuarine Research Reserve and nature walks of the islands, see our Attractions chapter.

ladders, spring bridges, a balance beam, a boat, a race car and so much more that it keeps the parking area full every day. Kids younger than 10 must have an adult with them. Groups of 10 kids or more may reserve time to use the playground.

Camps

The Crystal Coast serves as the location for a variety of camps — from day camps to week-long or longer summer camps. And nearby, at the mouth of the Neuse River, are several popular summer camps for youth. Call for program descriptions and prices.

Camp Albemarle
156 Albemarle Dr., Newport
(252) 726-4848

This Presbyterian camp in a beautiful setting on Bogue Sound operates year round and is open to the public. Summer camp sessions are divided into age groups, with weeks dedicated to campers from 2nd through 10th grades. There is also a two-night, three-day mini camp for 1st through 4th graders. Activities include swimming in the pool and sound, basketball, sailing and canoeing, along with other traditional camp activities.

Camp Seafarer and Camp Sea Gull
2744 Seafarer Rd., Arapahoe
(252) 249-1212
218 Sea Gull Landing, Arapahoe
(252) 249-1111

Camp Seafarer for girls and Camp Sea Gull for boys are on the Neuse River in Arapahoe, about 27 miles north of Morehead City and about 25 miles east of New Bern by car. The camps are coastal YMCA

camps with an outpost and docks on the Morehead City waterfront.

The camps focus on strengthening both land and sea skills, but more importantly they emphasize character and skill development. Campers enjoy a nationally recognized seamanship program, including sailing, watersports and ocean excursions from the Morehead City waterfront outpost. The camps conduct environmental education programs that serve schools throughout the state and offer facilities for corporate training and conferences. During the summer, the camps offer weekend and one-week family programs. There are also two-week and three-to-four-week camps for youth. Fall and spring camping programs for families and for kids — both weekend and weeklong — are also available. Contact the camps for details.

Morehead City Parks and Recreation Center
1600 Fisher St., Morehead City
(252) 726-5063

Morehead City Parks and Recreation Center offers an after-school program Monday through Friday from 3 to 6 PM at a rate of $25 per week per child. The program includes homework time, a snack, activities, and arts and crafts. The program is offered on teacher workdays and holidays for special rates.

Summer Day Camps

Dropins Childcare
Cypress Bay Plaza, 5167 U.S. Hwy. 70 W, Ste. 140, Morehead City
(252) 240-DROP (3767)

Dropins Childcare offers hourly drop-in care for children from ages 1 to 11 years. No reservations are required, and children will be in the care of well-qualified, experienced and first-aid–trained staff members. Dropins also offers a preschool and an after-school care program, as well as a school-age summer camp featuring field trips and a variety of activities. The 7,000-square-foot play area is filled with age-appropriate toys, video games, computers and activities. Dropins is open Monday through Thursday from 8 AM to 8 PM, Friday from 8 AM to 10 PM and Sat-

The North Carolina Aquarium at Pine Knoll Shores already offers so much family fun, but in 2010 it is slated to begin construction on an educational pier complex near mile marker 15 in Emerald Isle — with plans to include exhibits, beach access, a soundside dock, fishing pier and much more.

urday from 9 AM to 1 PM and from 5 to 11 PM. From 1 to 5 PM each Saturday Dropins can be rented for birthday parties or other special events, and the staff will handle all the details and all the clean up. Have a no-stress party by leaving the details to the Dropins staff.

Morehead City Parks and Recreation
1600 Fisher St., Morehead City
(252) 726-5083

Youth from across the county can take part in the Morehead City Day Camp. It is open to any child ages 3 to 12 and offers a variety of activities — field trips, arts and crafts, swimming, music, drama and sports games. Campers are divided into different age groups and supervised by a trained staff. The camp operates from 8 AM to 5:30 PM Monday through Friday, and arrangements can be made for parents needing to drop their children off at 7:30 AM. Campers bring their own lunches, and the camp offers an incredibly reasonable price for both city residents and nonresi-dents. In addition to summer day camp, which runs June 15 through August 7 in 2009, they offer pre-camp and post-camp sessions.

North Carolina Aquarium at Pine Knoll Shores
MM 7, N.C. Hwy. 58, Atlantic Beach
(252) 247-4003

The N.C. Aquarium at Pine Knoll Shores offers several sessions of summer day camps from June through August. Each camp runs for five consecutive days. Aquatic Adventures is for children enter-ing grades 2 and 3, Coastal Explorers is for children entering grades 4 and 5, and Sea Scholars is for children entering grades 6 and 7. All the camps provide hands-on, feet-wet learning adventures. The camps require fees and advance registration, which begins April 1. Spaces fill quickly. See the website for the full schedule.

North Carolina Maritime Museum
315 Front St., Beaufort
(252) 728-7317
www.ncmm.friends.org

The Maritime Museum offers a variety of summer programs for students of all ages, from those entering first grade in the fall through tenth graders. The programs planned for 2009 include programs on seashore life, pirates, boats and boat-model building, fishing and crabbing, sailing, coastal photography and saltwa-ter science. Tuitions are charged for the programs, and each is taught by qualified staff members. Friends of the Museum members get discounts on many of the programs.

Sound to Sea Day Camp
Trinity Center, N.C. Hwy. 58,
Pine Knoll Shores
(252) 247-5600

Trinity Conference Center offers an outstanding environmental education day camp. Youth get hands-on exposure to several coastal habitats — the sound, marsh, pond, maritime forest and ocean dunes. They learn about creatures living in each environment, play interesting games, wade in the ocean, make crafts and learn about coastal cultures starting with Native Americans. The youth are with others their age, in groups for rising kindergartners to rising sixth graders. Campers bring their own lunches. Registration for this popular camp usually opens in January.

WEDDING PLANNING

Whether a native of the area or an out-of-towner planning a destination wedding, you cannot go wrong with a Crystal Coast wedding. The Crystal Coast has an ambiance all its own when it comes to romance. With uncrowded beaches, spectacular sunsets over the water, and historic and maritime charm, it's no wonder that love is in the air. Whether the wedding is inside or outside, the beach often plays a part — either in the pre-event parties, the ceremony, the reception or the honeymoon. An added bonus of a Crystal Coast marriage is that members of the wedding party and their guests get to combine celebration with vacation by staying here before and after the big day.

Throughout this chapter you will find lists of vendors who provide wedding-related services, from catering to photography to florals and much more. For a list of spas and salons that provide wedding beauty services, see our Salons and Day Spas chapter.

Wedding Show

Crystal Coast Bridal Fair
3505 Arendell St., Morehead City
(252) 247-3883, (888) 899-6088

An annual Bridal Fair takes place each year in January at the Crystal Coast Civic Center. It is an event the Crystal Coast bride-to-be must attend. Take the groom, the mother, the future mother-in-law and any others involved in the planning. Booths are set up by planners, musicians and DJs, photographers, officiants, honeymoon travel agents and other vendors. You can sample creations by catering companies and wedding cake bakers, plus a fabulous fashion show highlights wedding gowns and dresses for the mothers, bridesmaids and flower girls.

Marriage Licenses

A North Carolina marriage license is a must if you plan to get married on the Crystal Coast. You may get the license in any county in North Carolina, but you must return it to the Register of Deeds in the county where the wedding takes place. This is very helpful for out-of-town couples coming to the beach area to be married, because they can get their license at home (if they live in North Carolina) and bring it with them.

The Carteret County courthouse is in Beaufort. It is located in the historic courthouse, which is about three blocks east of the drawbridge leading into town. The Register of Deeds office is open Monday through Friday but is closed on holidays. Marriage licenses can be obtained from 8 AM to 4:30 PM. Both parties must be present and bring proof of identification and their Social Security cards. Valid forms of identification include a driver's license, passport or military ID. (For those between the ages of 18 and 22, a certified copy of your birth certificate is required along with a driver's license or photo ID.) Applicants under 18 should contact the Register of Deeds before applying. If a person has been divorced, the month and year of last divorce must be provided, and in some instances, you'll be required to show a copy of the divorce decree itself. No blood test, physical exam or waiting period is necessary to obtain a marriage license, which costs $50 and is payable by cash only. The license is valid for 60 days after being issued. Obviously, bring your marriage license to the wedding. Two witnesses must sign the license following the ceremony. The person who performs the ceremony is responsible for getting the license back to the Register of Deeds in the county in which you were married within 10 days. After you're married,

Endless Possibilities

Spinnaker's Reach is beautifully situated on the oceanside of Emerald Isle. It is the perfect tranquil setting for your event... Retreats, Reunions, Weddings or Special Celebrations...

Special Occasions

Weddings

Reunions

WEDDINGS ON BOARD.

LET DIAMOND CITY CRUISES FULFILL ALL YOUR WEDDING DREAMS. IMAGINE, ON YOUR SPECIAL DAY, CRUISING THE SERENE AND SCENIC WATERS OF NORTH CAROLINA'S CRYSTAL COAST! THE DIAMOND CITY, A 149 –PASSENGER CRUISE VESSEL, IS IDEALLY SUITED FOR WEDDINGS AND RECEPTIONS.

THE COVERED UPPER DECK AND ENCLOSED MAIN SALON ENSURE A SUCCESSFUL EVENT NO MATTER WHAT THE WEATHER. ENJOY YOUR UNIQUE WEDDING AND RECEPTION WITH DINING AND DANCING WHILE THE VESSEL IS UNDERWAY. YOU AND YOUR GUESTS MAY SEE THE FABLED WILD PONIES – DESCENDANTS OF MUSTANGS THAT SWAM ASHORE FROM WRECKED SPANISH GALLEONS – ON THE NEARBY BARRIER ISLANDS.

ON BOARD, OUR PROFESSIONAL STAFF IS PREPARED TO MAKE YOUR WEDDING AN EVENT THAT YOU AND YOUR GUESTS WILL CHERISH ALWAYS. YOU CAN PLAN YOUR OWN FESTIVITIES OR ALLOW US TO BE YOUR WEDDING CONSULTANTS. OUR SPECIAL EVENTS COORDINATOR IS READY TO HELP YOU PLAN YOUR DREAM WEDDING.

PLEASE CALL OUR ACCOUNT EXECUTIVE FOR RESERVATIONS AND PRICING.

◆ REHEARSAL DINNERS

◆ WEDDING CEREMONIES

◆ RECEPTIONS

◆ BACHELOR & BACHELORETTE PARTIES

◆ AND ALL OTHER SPECIAL OCCASIONS

DIAMOND CITY CRUISES
252-728-7827
WWW.MYSTERYBOATTOURS.COM

the officiant or magistrate will issue a marriage certificate. Certified copies of the marriage license may be acquired in person or by mail at the Register of Deeds, 302 Courthouse Square, Beaufort, NC 28516. Certified copies cost $10. Specific marriage license questions for Carteret County should be directed to the Register of Deeds, (252) 728-8474.

Wedding Locations and Reception Facilities

The decision of where to hold the wedding ceremony and all the other special events surrounding the day is complicated. There are so many choices on the Crystal Coast — churches, beaches, private gardens, vacation homes, hotels, resorts, parks, historic grounds, maritime attractions, even the aquarium.

Our best advice is to select a few possible dates and start calling places to see if the location you want is available on any of the days you have in mind. Remember, this area has a busy season as a travel and vacation destination, so consider the timing. It's alway best to plan as far in advance as possible.

A list of churches can be found in the Yellow Pages of the local phone book. Also see our Worship chapter. Churches often have rules about their use of their facilities for weddings, such as charging non-members a set fee or only allowing approved pastors to conduct the ceremony in the church.

Fort Macon State Park, N.C. Hwy. 58, Atlantic Beach, (252) 726-3775

The Abilena Mansion
2814 Old Cherry Point Rd., New Bern
(252) 637-3574

Abilena Mansion is a 5-acre riverfront plantation and mansion on the Neuse River in New Bern. The 5,000-square-foot home was built in 1927. It is the area's only riverfront mansion that can be rented for weddings, receptions, vacations, retreats and events. For any event, from a family

reunion to an intimate reception of 20 to a wedding of 150 or more people, Abilena awaits your arrival. Secluded yet only five minutes from town, this is a dream location for many people. There are several acres for parking and events, yet at its core it is still a charming home that will create lasting memories from the moment you drive down the tree-covered lane. In addition to offering a premiere location, owner John Williams can provide professional photography for the big day. A Wedding to Remember Photography services both the New Bern and Crystal Coast areas. In 2009 the Abilena Mansion is host to the New Bern Bridal Fair in March and October. Call or visit the website for information on all the Abilena has to offer.

Beaufort Historic Site, 100 Block, Turner Street, Beaufort, (252) 728-5225

Cape Lookout National Seashore, (reachable by ferry or boat only), Harkers Island
(252) 728-2250

Clawsons 1905 Restaurant & Pub
429 Front St., Beaufort
(252) 728-2133
www.clawsonsrestaurant.com

Clawson's 1905 Restaurant & Pub offers a private dining area for groups of up to 60 people with stunning views overlooking Taylor's Creek. With its historic setting and waterfront view, it is an ideal setting for any big event from receptions to reunions, meetings to parties, and everything in between. Clawson's also offers banquet and catering menus with selections that include breakfast, lunch and dinner offerings and fine dining selections, too.

Core Sound Waterfowl Museum, and Heritage Center, 1785 Island Rd., Harkers Island, (252) 728-1500

Crystal Coast Civic Center, 3505 Arendell St., Morehead City, (252) 247-3883, (888) 899-6088

The History Place, 1008 Arendell St., Morehead City, (252) 247-7533

Diamond City Cruises, Waterfront,, Beaufort, (252) 728-7827, www.mystery-boattours.com

North Carolina Aquarium at Pine Knoll Shores, MM 7, N.C. Hwy. 58, Atlantic Beach, (252) 247-4003

North Carolina Maritime Museum, 315 Front St., Beaufort, (252) 728-7317, www.ncmm.friends.org

Swansboro Rotary Civic Center, 1104 Main St. Ext., Swansboro, (910) 326-6175

Caterers

The Crystal Coast offers many fine caterers. Several operate independently, and the services of others are offered through hotels and restaurants. If you are planning your rehearsal dinner, wedding or reception to take place in an area hotel, check with the events coordinator before you continue planning. The management of some hotels require the use of in-house caterers.

Crab's Claw
201 W. Atlantic Blvd., Atlantic Beach
(252) 726-8222

Crab's Claw offers catering for beach weddings, rehearsal dinners, family reunions and other occasions with a variety of catering packages. Enjoy your occasion at the restaurant, at the site of your choosing or on a boat. Featuring oceanfront fine dining in the heart of Atlantic Beach, the restaurant's location allows patrons to enjoy a panoramic view of the Atlantic Ocean. Dine inside or outside on the deck. The restaurant was recently featured in *Southern Living* magazine and specializes in unique seafood creations.

Floyd's 1921 Restaurant & Bar
400 Bridges St., Morehead City
(252) 727-1921

Floyd's 1921 can serve as the perfect location for your special event or cater an affair at your location. Either way, it will be an event that's remembered for years. Floyd and his staff offer unique creations along with long-time favorites. The professional staff gives their undivided attention to each detail and can help you plan and host special occasions of all types from weddings and receptions to birthdays and anniversaries for any number of people. Floyd's 1921 also caters business events of all types. With all ABC permits and an outstanding wait staff, the folks at Floyd's 1921 can personally handle all your details.

Front Street Grill at Stillwater
300 Front St., Beaufort
(252) 728-4956

Front Street Grill at Stillwater offers full-service catering, specializing in wedding receptions, rehearsal dinners, anniversaries and corporate parties. If your plans call for outdoor dining, Stillwater can accommodate you on the waterfront decks. The decks and restaurant offer sweeping views of Taylor's Creek, Carrot Island, Beaufort Inlet and sunsets over the water, and the outdoor bar is the perfect

place to relax. You'll find innovative menu items paired with special wines that make private dining at Stillwater a special event for everyone.

Roland's Barbecue
1507 Live Oak St., Beaufort
(252) 728-1953

One call to Roland's and you can be assured of a great casual meal. Let Roland cater a fun pig pickin' rehearsal dinner on your deck or a delicious clam bake on the beach. This business offers everything you'll need — pork barbecue (whole hog or chopped), seafood, fried chicken, baked beans, slaw, hushpuppies, tea and lemonade. When Roland's rolls in, everything is provided down to the utensils, napkins and plates.

Somerset Cellars
3906 E. Arendell St., Morehead City
(252) 725-0029

Let Somerset Cellars personalize your event with outstanding wines and custom labels. Whether you are planning a wedding, anniversary, retirement or birthday, or have a need to personalize your boat or beach house, a good wine with a creative personal label adds a special touch. Labels must have federal and state approval so a few weeks notice is needed, but the result is worth the time. Somerset Cellars can also host your special event. With 25 different wines, there is certainly one to please. Favorites include Somerset's Pinot Grigio, Cabernet Sauvignon, Chiaretto and Pinot Noir. Somerset imports crushed grapes and juice to produce custom wines that are available at wholesale or retail. Somerset offers private tours and tastings if the normal business hours are not convenient. Current hours are 11 AM to 6 PM Wednesday through Saturday, and are subject to change based on demand. Call for hours or a private appointment.

White Swan Bar-B-Q and Fried Chicken
2500-A W. Fort Macon Rd., Atlantic Beach
(252) 726-9607
4650 Arendell St., Morehead City
252-247-3119
www.whiteswanatlanticbeach.com

White Swan of Atlantic Beach offers an experienced catering service that can plan your special event, meeting or wedding. These professionals will work within your budget and can cater any size event — be it 50 or 2,000 people. White Swan offers off-site catering services throughout the surrounding counties. The catering menu is broad and includes the popular items of eastern Carolina pork barbecue, fried chicken, roast beef, the famous White Swan honeydew baked ham, and baked or barbecue chicken. They can also prepare seafood cooked on site by special arrangement. They offer a wide selection of side items and hors d'oeuvre. Hours vary seasonally, so it's best to call for specific times, especially in the off-season. White

Swan now has a second location in Morehead City.

Wedding Registries

Wedding-gift registry is available in several local boutiques, major chain stores and jewelry shops. See our Shopping chapter for more about these stores.

Bed, Bath & Beyond, 5160 N.C. Hwy. 70, Morehead City, (252) 726-1170

Belk, Cypress Day Plaza, U.S. Hwy. 70, Morehead City, (252) 726-5121

Dee Gee's Gifts & Books, 508 Evans St., Morehead City, (252) 726-3314

The Crystal Coast provides endless beautiful backdrops for your wedding.

photo: Carolyn Temple

Lowe's Home Improvement Warehouse, 5219 U.S. Hwy. 70, Morehead City, (252) 727-5011

Stamper's Jewelers, 435 Front St., Beaufort, (252) 728-4967

Wal-Mart, 300 N.C. Hwy. 24, Newport, (252) 247-0511

Wedding Planners and Officiants

While many couples opt to have a clergy person perform their wedding ceremony, others seek alternatives. There is often confusion about whether a boat captain can legally marry someone. For the record, this is not true. In North Carolina you must be married by an ordained minister or a magistrate. We have listed some great local resources, including professional event planners, that can help in all stages of the event from planning to finishing touches — and everything in between.

Bridal By The Sea
263 Howard Blvd., Newport
(252) 259-4992
www.bridalbythesea.com

Rachel Munro is passionate about helping the bride and groom make their wedding day an unforgettable occasion and cherished memory. Rachel draws on more than a decade of experience to work with couples and wedding parties throughout the planning process to ensure that time lines and details flow smoothly. She has worked with budgets of all sizes, ranging from backyard barbecues to swanky gala affairs with celebrity guest lists, and she devotes the same amount of enthusiasm and professionalism to each and every one. Rachel offers a number of wedding packages, ranging from simple consultations and contract reviews to a complete coordination package that arranges all the details of the big day, based on the selections and wishes of the bridal couple, including the rehearsal, ceremony and reception. Rachel not only works with vendors of the wedding couple's choice but also can recommend others as needed. Certified by the Association for Certified Professional Wedding Consultants, Rachel offers a complimentary initial consultation. Insiders find her pleasant to work with as well as ardent and professional about planning the perfect wedding. Bridal By The Sea also carries unique rental items in its design gallery that aren't normally available at local party supply stores. Items available include specialty linens, Japanese lanterns, glass vases in all shapes and sizes, and so much more. The inventory is always being updated, so if you don't see it be sure to ask about it.

Dee Gee's Gifts & Books
508 Evans St., Morehead City
(252) 726-3314

Dee Gee's Gifts and Books is a great first stop for wedding planners. You will find all types of assistance and ideas. There are plenty of wedding planning books for the do-it-yourselfer or someone who just needs a few more ideas. Brides can also register at Dee Gee's for table-top dinnerware and serving pieces. Dee Gee's offers a full line of custom wedding and shower invitations and the paper napkins and plates that can personalize any event. Also, you'll find a wonderful selection of unique gifts for all occasions, and a huge selection of books, cards and novelties. Dee Gee's features special sections of local and regional books, children's educational books, toys and games and nautical charts. The store is open daily, and telephone orders are welcomed.

Emerald Isle Realty
7501 Emerald Dr., Emerald Isle
(252) 354- 6155, (866) 388-7208
www.emeraldislerealty.com

Few events are as romantic as a seaside wedding. Let Emerald Isle Realty take care of all the details. Their Events Department offers exclusive wedding packages and services. From rehearsal and ceremony to accommodations and reception planning, Emerald Isle Realty will make your special occasion a memory that will last forever.

TourBeaufort.com
Beaufort
(252) 772-9925

TourBeaufort.Com offers a variety of walking and exploring tours. They can plan, organize and coordinate your wedding or special event. TourBeaufort.com also offers the *Do It Yourself Wedding Guide* for those planning to marry in the area. The guide offers lists of wedding locations and rain locations, pastors/preachers, photographers, caterers, DJs and musicians and videographers/photographers. You'll also find equipment rental companies, marriage licensing requirements and locations, tuxedo rental and dress shops, limousine companies, and rehearsal and reception arrangement information.

Visions Events and Beyond
111 Atlantic Blvd., Ste. 8, Atlantic Beach
(252) 247-3826, (800) 495-3892

Located on the oceanfront of Atlantic Beach, Visions Events & Beyond has a professional and experienced design team that works with couples to bring their wedding visions to life. Visions provides full-service beach wedding packages, catering, floral design, photography, invitations, gifts and accessories, and can pull all the elements of your dream wedding together. Thought about a beach wedding but worried about inclement weather? Visions has an indoor wedding chapel available to ease your mind. Visions can even host receptions with up to 150 guests on the Veranda Deck, which offers panoramic views of the beautiful Crystal Coast. For more intimate gatherings, Visions also offers an indoor location as well as the ability to host your rehearsal dinner or other memorable event right on the beach. After the wedding of your dreams, you'll find the fairytale is far from over. A Walt Disney World® honeymoon surrounds you with an entire world of magic, not to mention an endless array of enchanting possibilities. The travel coordinator at Visions can arrange your Disney honeymoon or any other destination your dreams may take you.

Florists

Whether it be a wedding filled with flowers or just a few simple, elegant arrangements, the local florists professionally handle any request. The local shops have friendly staffs and design professionals on-hand to answer any and all of your questions.

Flowers & Designs by Ernest
1402 Live Oak St., Beaufort
(252) 728-7022

Let Ernest Chiles handle all the details for your special occasion. With more than 35 years of experience, he can provide unique floral designs and superior personal service for any event — whether a wedding, a home party or a business occasion. Ernest and his professional and friendly staff offer all the floral services expected, including fresh and silk arrangements. They also can provide the wedding equipment and props to make your event complete. Flowers & Designs by Ernest has been recognized for its excellence in wedding design and service by local brides.

K.D.'s Florist
1622 Live Oak St., Beaufort
(252) 728-4852

K.D.'s is a local tradition in this area. This is a family-run, friendly place where the staff works to create just the right arrangement to express your feelings for any occasion.

Sandy's Flower Shoppe
4702 Arendell St., Morehead City
(252) 247-3323

Sandy and her staff of professionals can work with your plans — no matter how large or small. They have a nice selection of floral arrangements and can create just the right one for you. The window displays at Sandy's are always beautiful. Sandy's is often the flower shop of choice when it comes to both personal and business needs, and it has a very good reputation in the community.

Through the Looking Glass
101 Church St., Swansboro
(910) 326-3128

Arrangements from Through the Looking Glass are sure to reflect your feelings and are sure to please. The friendly staff offers fresh and silk flowers of many varieties.

Bridal Shops and Formal Wear

Finding the right wedding dress, bridesmaids' dresses or tuxedo style is important, and local shops can provide you with a wide selection sure to please. They have a variety of styles and sizes and can work with you to find the perfect look to reflect the occasion.

The Black Tie
5270-C U.S. Hwy. 70 W, Morehead City
(252) 240-2900

This business offers tuxedo rentals and sales for the gentlemen in the wedding party. The company offers attire for men of just about any age or size.

The Intimate Bridal and Formal Wear
5370 Brandywine Crossing, Morehead City
(252) 808-2221

Let The Intimate make planning your wedding an enjoyable and fun experience. The professionals at this shop offer an elegant, friendly atmosphere and will work to ensure you look your best for whatever the occasion happens to be. As a full-service bridal shop, The Intimate offers a tremendous selection of bridal gowns, mother-of-the bride dresses, bridesmaid dresses starting at $99, prom dresses and social occasion dresses from sizes 2 to 30. There are tuxedo rentals and sales as well. The Intimate is experienced in accommodating large volume tuxedo rentals and out-of-town wedding parties and ensures the perfect fit. The friendly staff can take care of your every need and offer professional advice on clothing, color schemes and sizes. Immediate delivery is available on certain styles, and The Intimate also offers wedding gown preservation. The Intimate also has a store at 224/226 Middle Street in New Bern, (252) 638-1220.

Music

If music is what you want, contact a professional service and let them work

with you to find the right music to suit your wedding theme.

DJ / MC John Drake
Morehead City
(252) 422-4355

John Drake specializes in providing music for all types of events, large or small. With thousands of songs, John can create the perfect party theme for you — whether it be Big Band, top 40, classic, country, Jimmy Buffett, beach music or something in between. Along with his music consultation, John can provide local recommendations for all the details of your wedding, from location to catering to decorations. Interested in a beach or backyard wedding but have no electricity at the site? Don't worry. John now has a portable wireless sound system complete with wireless microphones for the official, readers, singers and others.

Photographers and Videographers

So much time and effort is spent planning for the big event, and it's over so quickly. That's why it's important to capture all of the special moments before, during and after the wedding. Pictures of your wedding will be very special to you for years to come, so hiring a photogra-

pher you can trust is a necessity. Line up a professional photographer well in advance.

A Wedding to Remember Photography
Offices in Emerald Isle, New Bern
(252) 349-2441

A Wedding to Remember Photography makes sure your special day is just that — special. John Williams has been in business for seven years and has photographed more than 450 weddings. He can capture all the events of your day as well as bridal portraits, receptions and family portraits. John offers an indoor studio or can find just the right outdoor location. He offers all types of photography from traditional to photo journalism. A variety of prices and packages are available and listed on the website.

Bell Photography
111 Mansfield Pkwy., Morehead City
(252) 247-1058

Established in 1956, Bell Photography has been meeting and exceeding the photography needs of locals and visitors to the area for years. Owner David Bell now carries on the quality of tradition started by his father, the late Gene Bell. He offers a mixture of photography styles, including contemporary, storybook and journalistic. Whether indoor or outdoor, David strives to keep the rates affordable and to ensure the pictures reflect the beauty of your special day.

Coastal Image Photography
by Carolyn Temple
Morehead City
(252) 726-7488
www.coastalimagephoto.com

Carolyn Temple and Coastal Image Photography can create the perfect portrait or wedding package. She can give you traditional or modern styles in both photography and album presentations. Carolyn specializes in outdoor location photography and weddings. This professional will go above and beyond to meet your photographic desires and create a visual memory to be treasured for years to come.

Deja Vu Multi-Media Productions
(252) 646-3307

Jason Campobasso offers a variety of wedding video packages for your selection. He specializes in video production as well as post-production work, and he works with many local bands. Jason can tape events of all types, adding music and sound to make the creation complete. Jason also offers still photography for weddings or any other special event.

Ellen Le Roy Photography
208 Old Cove Rd., Emerald Isle
(252) 354-3770

Whether it is a wedding, family event or other special occasion, Ellen LeRoy can create the perfect remembrance. She specializes in natural light photography, with a photojournalistic approach. Her professional services include fine art, black and white, and color photography, and she offers retouching and photo restoration services as well. Ellen most enjoys on-location portraits of brides, wedding couples, families, children, babies and pets.

George Mitchell's Photographic Services
Hubert
(910) 326-4425

George Mitchell has extensive experience in all types of photography, from wedding to aerial, in all locations. He offers service from Cape Lookout to Holden Beach. He can professionally capture your special event or your business need with digital imaging, in color or black and white. Whether it is a commercial shot, a wedding package or a family portrait, George Mitchell can capture just the right image you desire. He can also provide you with digital images. George offers large group packages and services corporate events.

Portraits by Angelo
1910 B Glenburnie Rd., New Bern
(252) 633-3755, (866) 801-9493

Portraits by Angelo specializes in location photography and can capture your special occasion, regardless of where

Destination weddings on the coast are all the rage.

photo: Carolyn Temple

it is. When you hire this company to photograph a wedding or special event, you get the services of two professionals —husband and wife John and Brandy Angelo. The Angelos specialize in wedding photography and family and children portraits. They can also photograph the family pet. Portraits by Angelo offers a variety of wedding packages and can provide you with long-lasting memories of your special day in color and black and white.

Scott Taylor Photography
214 Pollock St., Beaufort
(252) 728-0900

For exclusive engagement, bridal and wedding photography, contact the area's premier wedding photographer — Scott Taylor. He offers color and black and white images to complement the wedding day memories and reflect the couple's wishes. Whether he is taking a bridal portrait in his studio/gallery, photographing the wedding party on the beach or traveling to a church or boat wedding, Scott works to capture the candid, intimate images you will treasure for a lifetime. He handles large and small weddings and offers flush-mount, magazine-style wedding albums and full digital wedding packages.

Sunrise Sunset Digital Images
(252) 393-3284

Owner Constance Soule is a photographer, graphic artist and webmistress. She specializes in wedding, beach and portfolio photography. She also offers pet photography, so don't forget to include your pet in all of your special occasion photographs.

Tim Green Photography
Beaufort
(252) 241-4906

Tim Green specializes in wedding photography, family portraits and special occasion photography. His wedding services range from engagement packages to bridal packages to wedding day packages. Tim specializes in studio and beach photography. He offers a wide range of photography services, including school, sports, prom and senior pictures.

Salons and Day Spas

Oasis Day Spa -Salon
5380-E Brandywine Crossing,
U.S. Hwy. 70 W, Morehead City
(252) 726-2600
www.oasisdayspasalon.com

Oasis Day Spa is just the place to send a special friend or just to treat yourself. This is the perfect place to be pampered. Oasis offers a variety of massage therapy techniques, such as deep tissue, hot stone, trigger point, Swedish and the famous Belavi face-lift massage. Oasis also offers facials, microdermabrasion, light therapy, non-surgical face-lifts, waxing and body treatments. Manicures, pedicures and various other types of nail care are also offered. The spa's Hair Salon provides cuts, coloring and styling and specializes in wedding party or special event hair styling. Luxurious spa packages can be designed to meet your special needs.

Transportation

Arranging for the wedding party and bride and groom to arrive in style simply tops off the day. There are several services in the area that can help you set up the right wedding-day transportation.

All Stretched Out Limousine Service
(252) 728-4188

With all amenities, this service is sure to please your wedding party. This company provides full limousine service in Carteret County as well as the surrounding counties.

Diamond Limousine Service
603 Bridges St., Morehead City
(252) 240-1680

When it comes to a special occasion or just a night on the town, Diamond Limousine Service offers luxury, convenience and safety. Diamond Limousine Service has been serving eastern North Carolina since 1955, providing transportation at its finest. The fleet includes a selection of limousines fully equipped with the latest technology, sedans and vintage wedding cars. For larger groups, inquire about a party bus or shuttle bus. The service also offers first-class transportation to all major North Carolina airports.

Sinclair Limousine
1703 Live Oak St., Beaufort
(252) 728-6853

Sinclair Limousine offers modern limousines and a choice of wedding packages to fit any budget. Whether you choose their exclusive "Bridal Edition" Town Car limousine or their ultra-classy Navigator Superstretch, you and your party will arrive in style and comfort. The limousines are clean, smoke-free, well-equipped and always driven by a professional chauffeur. You will appreciate the attention to detail provided by Sinclair Limousine and can rely on dependable service every time. For the ultimate in wedding transportation, their Premiere Wedding Package includes fresh rose petals and a champagne toast. No matter how large or small your wedding may be, their friendly and professional staff will put together a package to meet your needs

Rental Equipment

Why buy things to use only one day, when you can rent quality equipment and have it delivered and picked up? Below is information about several businesses that can save you time, trouble and money.

Bogue Banks Beach Gear and Linens Rentals
Bell Cove Village,
9106-C Coast Guard Rd., Emerald Isle
(252) 354-4404
www.boguebanksbeachgear.com

This rental company offers a full line of wedding and events rentals with affordable packages and an array of table linens

to choose from. These folks provide the largest selection of quality rental items with friendly customer service, and they were voted #1 by the Readers' Choice Awards three years in a row. They have two locations to serve your rental needs, one in Emerald Isle and one in Atlantic Beach. The Emerald Isle location includes an Event Rental Showroom. Bogue Banks Beach Gear & Linens is open year-round seven days a week and they accept VISA/MC with online reservations.

Island Essentials - A Linen and Leisure Rental Company
208-A Bogue Inlet Dr., Emerald Isle
(252) 354-3315

Let Island Essentials put the leisure back into your special day! Whether it's your wedding day, a vow renewal, your annual family reunion or a corporate event, their easy online reservations system and professional event specialists make planning your party quick and easy. Island Essentials offers free delivery and set-up service with every order.

Printers

When it comes to printing invitations for your wedding events, there are some reputable printers in the area who can help you out. They offer a selection of stock invitations to choose from or they can work with you to create a custom design especially for you.

Coastal Press, Inc., 502 Arendell. St., Morehead City, (252) 726-1549

Eastern Offset Printing Company, 410 W. Fort Macon Rd., Atlantic Beach, (252) 247-6791

SALONS AND DAY SPAS

The many local salons and spas attract both returning local clientele as well as out-of-towners to their selection of professional stylists and services. From getting a new look to getting ready for a big event, there are plenty of ways to be pampered. Services range from hair and nail care, tanning and makeup application to massages, facials, manicures and pedicures — the list goes on. Be sure to inquire about the unique offerings at each salon or spa.

A Flair for Hair
8802 Reed Dr., Unit 1, Emerald Isle
(252) 354-3922

A Flair for Hair is a full-service hair salon, specializing in head-to-toe relaxation. The friendly staff here offers spa-style services, including hair and nail design, tanning and spa packages that include massages, facials, manicures and pedicures. Be sure to ask about their specialized wedding services that provide relaxation and pampering to the entire wedding party. They can help you celebrate any special occasion with style and work with you in all your planning needs.

Belk
Cypress Bay Plaza,
5167 U.S. Hwy. 70, Morehead City
(252) 727-0980

The professional consultants at Belk provide tips on cosmetics application and selection. Belk's cosmetic lines include Clinique, Estee Lauder and Lancôme. Let their expertise and product knowledge work for you.

Oasis Day Spa -Salon
5380-E Brandywine Crossing,
U.S. Hwy. 70 W, Morehead City
(252) 726-2600
www.oasisdayspasalon.com

Oasis Day Spa is just the place to send a special friend, loved one or just to treat yourself. It is the perfect place to be pampered. Oasis offers a variety of massage therapy techniques such as deep tissue, hot stone, trigger point, Swedish and their famous Belavi facelift massage. Oasis also offers facials, microdermabrasion, light therapy, non-surgical face-lifts, waxing and body treatments. Manicures, pedicures and various other types of nail care are also offered at Oasis. The spa's hair salon provides cuts, coloring and styling and specializes in wedding party or special event hair styling. Luxurious spa packages can be designed to meet your special needs.

OC Spa
MM 11.5, 1701 N.C. Hwy. 58, Indian Beach
(252) 247-2035, (888) 237-2035

Let the OC Spa become your destination health and wellness spa. This is a full-service European health spa open to the public. Located at The Ocean Club, this spa offers a variety of massage therapies, facials, manicure and pedicure services, wraps, Vichy treatments and sauna steam facilities. The spa features a heated pool along with women's and men's facilities. A vegetarian health and wellness program is also offered. OC Spa provides a wonderful relaxation package for special groups, including wedding parties. OC Spa is part of the The Ocean Club complex and partners with the OC Convention Center for event planning of all types.

The Red Door Hair Salon
1015 Arendell St., Morehead City
(252) 222-4RED (4733)

The Red Door Hair Salon offers the latest looks along with the season's best cuts, color and styles. With friendly and knowledgeable stylists, it's easy to feel at home in this downtown salon. Come alone or bring a friend for a hot new look or just to update and polish an existing style.

Strandz Salon
5053 Executive Dr., Morehead City
(252) 808-2887

Strandz Salon offers complete hair care and has designers on staff to create that perfect look. This full-service hair salon specializes in Framesi color, foil highlights, color corrections and multi-tool cutting. The professional staff can accommodate bridal parties. The salon also offers facial waxing, manicures and pedicures, along with makeup application.

Total Concept Salon Ltd.
4426 Arendell St., Morehead City
(252) 247-5464

This well-established salon offers complete hair care, including the latest cuts, styling, hair color products and more. Ask the color design consultants for the current tips and trends to enhance any look. The salon also provides waxing, cosmetic application and microdermabrasion. Total Concept is just the place to go for bridal styling or to prepare for any upcoming special event.

151

ARTS

The arts are alive and well along the Crystal Coast, and many people choose to journey to the area for its variety of galleries and art shows. Art often imitates life, and much of the local art reflects the relationship of coastal people with the sea. Many artists find the pace of coastal living conducive to developing their talents and move here for that reason. It's not unusual to meet people who were professionals in other locations now earning a living painting, writing or making pottery on the Crystal Coast. The vibrant community of coastal artists is involved in an eclectic array of artistic productions. Arts organizations, especially the Arts Council of Carteret County, actively support artists' endeavors and welcome new members and volunteers. In this chapter you'll find a sampling of the arts groups and galleries in the area. If there is no address for a group, we have listed the name and phone number of a person to contact. Another great source of arts information is the publication *Arts Alive* (see our Media chapter).

Arts Organizations

Arts Council of Carteret County
812 Evans St., Morehead City
(252) 726-9156

The Arts Council of Carteret County was formed in February 1974. The mission is to expand, promote and nurture the arts, honor traditional culture, and welcome creativity. The group strives to accomplish this through organization, communication, facilitation and support of artists and art organizations. The Arts Council works as a distributing agent, funding arts events and education, assisting artists seeking grants and sponsoring a variety of workshops, lectures and classes. Every February it sponsors the Art

From The Heart exhibition, which involves hundreds of artists. The council also sponsors workshops and performances that are announced throughout the year. The addition of programs conducted or assisted by the Arts Council has resulted in a community arts concept that embraces drama, literature, dance, music, traditional crafts, the visual arts and the family. Volunteer assistance and membership support keep the programs of this organization active and growing.

Carteret County Arts and Crafts Coalition
(252) 726-8397

What began as a small group of professionally oriented artists seeking an outlet for their work has grown into a juried, professional art group celebrating its 31st anniversary in 2009. The coalition conducts four major shows each year. Three outdoor shows take place on the Beaufort Historic Site over Memorial Day weekend, Fourth of July weekend and Labor Day weekend. The fourth event is an indoor, three-week show that begins around Thanksgiving each year. New members are welcome, and jurying of new work takes place once each year.

Core Sound Decoy Carvers Guild
1574 Harkers Island Rd., Straits
(252) 838-8818

Born from an idea of seven decoy carvers in 1987, the Core Sound Carvers Guild now has a large membership of active decoy carvers, collectors, breeders, taxidermists and waterfowl artists in more than 25 states. The Core Sound Decoy Festival (see our Annual Events chapter) in December on Harkers Island is an outgrowth of the efforts of the Decoy Carvers Guild. The guild welcomes new members and meets each month on the third Tuesday at 7:30 PM in its new headquarters on Harkers Island Road in Straits. Guild members offer carving classes for adults and other classes for children.

Crystal Coast Quilter's Guild
(252) 393-8032

This energetic group of quilters meets each month on the third Thursday to exchange ideas and learn from presenters. Meetings take place at St. Paul's Episcopal Church in Beaufort. The guild is made up of members who enjoy quilting by traditional and modern methods, including hand piecing, machine quilting and fabric dying. Along with the monthly meetings, workshops take place throughout the year with nationally known quilters and designers. Guild members make and donate children's quilts to the local domestic violence shelter and help with other charitable projects such as donating quilts to wounded military that come back to Camp Lejeune's hospital. Each May the guild hosts a Quilt Show in Morehead City. In 2009 in conjunction with the show, the guild is hosting a large traveling quilt exhibit "Alzheimer's: Forgetting Piece by Piece" to help raise awareness and fund research through art.

Down East FolkArts Society
Beaufort
(252) 504-ARTS (2787)

Folk music comes from the heart and soul of any locale, and its listeners are sometimes travelers with an ear cant to the sea. Between October and May, each month brings a concert to the Crystal Coast. Organized and sponsored by the Down East FolkArts Society, concerts and take place in various locations in the area. In addition, the Down East FolkArts Society sponsors workshops, classes, small concerts, and school and community outreach programs. Call for membership information, to be placed on the mailing list and for concert schedules. All events are open to the public.

Dance

Private dance studios on the Crystal Coast offer classes in ballet, tap and modern dance for everyone from toddlers to adults. Students perform recitals and often participate in area festivals, group functions and parades. Dance organizations are also active in community events.

Many ballet students from local studios audition each year for the North Carolina School of the Arts, the American Ballet Theatre and the Joffrey Ballet.

photo: Peter Doran

Spice up life, meet new people and get some fun exercise by learning some new dance moves — Salsa, Mambo and ballroom classes are offered, too. Group lessons of varying skill levels are available and private lessons can also be arranged. Class offerings and schedules change throughout the year and some classes fill quickly, so calling in advance is best.

The Carolina Strut
Performing Arts Centre
303 N. 35th St., Morehead City
(252) 726-0431

Carolina Strut is under new ownership by Lyndsay Loveland so keep an eye out for new programs and classes as they are offered throughout the year. This studio offers classes for adults and children in such areas as tap, ballet, pointe, modern, lyrical and jazz styles, as well as tumbling and music lessons. Other popular favorites include ballroom, Salsa and Mambo classes. The studio offers a Wiggles class for children as young as 2 years old and continues classes through adults.

Dance Arts Studio
123 Bonner Ave., Morehead City
(252) 726-1720
1390 Lennoxville Rd., Beaufort
252-728-1855

Dance Arts Studio offers classes in such arts as tap, ballet, pointe, modern dance, jazz and creative movement in classes for ages 3 through adult. Special classes are offered for adult beginners. Tumbling and piano classes are also offered at their Beaufort facility.

Music

The Crystal Coast is home to several choral groups that perform often and occasionally audition new prospects. We are fortunate to host an extraordinary concert series, a wonderful music festival weekend in the spring, and active jazz and folk art music societies that promote, in concerts and education, America's most innovative music styles. The summer season brings additional concert series to the area that showcase various musical styles and genres, many of which are offered free of charge.

American Music Festival
The History Place, 1008 Arendell St., Morehead City
(252) 728-6152
www.americanmusicfestival.org

The American Music Festival is a nonprofit chamber music series featuring concerts performed from September through May. The 2009–10 series marks the 20th season of quality performances. The series is supported by subscription ticket purchase, grants, donations and donor sponsorships and is managed by a volunteer board of directors. Donations to the fund further promote music with an educational outreach program that takes the gifted musicians into area schools. Past concerts included world-class performances by musicians of the Alexander Quartet, Nicholas Duchamp, Carolina Piano Trio and Daedalus Quartet. Series subscriptions for five concerts start at $100. Individual performance tickets are $25 for adults and $15 for students and military. Performances usually take place on Saturdays at 8 PM at The History Place in Morehead City.

Beaufort By-the-Sea Music Festival
(252) 422-8365

Beaufort's Music Festival takes place in May each year and is a local favorite that draws crowds from Beaufort and beyond. The event features multiple stages with live musical performances. Enjoy music and fun for the whole family for free at venues all throughout the town, including the waterfront, Beaufort Historic Site, N.C. Maritime Museum and local restaurants and pubs. Other fun events surround the festival. See our Annual Events chapter for more about this event.

Carteret Chorale
(252) 726-6193

This group of talented vocalists from Morehead City, Newport, Beaufort and the surrounding areas has performed together for more than 30 years, creating a chorale known widely for its top-notch performances. The chorale performs benefit concerts regularly in Carteret County and has taken its talent to Williamsburg, Carnegie Hall, the National Cathedral, Yugoslavia and Russia. Director Laurence

THE AMERICAN
MUSIC FESTIVAL
CONCERT SERIES

2009-2010 Season

Fry Street Quartet, Degas Quartet, Nicolas Duchamp, Barbara Mckenzie, Emanuel Gruber, And Others.

8 PM @ The History Place, September-May
1008 Arendell Street, Morehead City, NC | Tickets @ 252-728-6152
www.americanmusicfestival.org

ARTS

Stith, retired professional pianist, vocalist and educator, is also a composer, and the group often performs his original music.

Crystal Coast Choral Society
(252) 247-5929

The Crystal Coast Choral Society is made up of members from several counties and is under the direction of Finley Woolston. The group generally meets for weekly rehearsals each Tuesday evening from 7 to 9 PM at the United Methodist Church in Swansboro. This is a non-audition chorus and welcomes new members. This chorus offers local concerts and often travels to perform. For further information, call the number above or Finley Woolston, director, at (910) 324-3684.

North Carolina Symphony
(252) 637-9400, (877) 627-6724

The North Carolina Symphony is a full-time, professional orchestra which performs across the state with the highest artistic standards to enrich, entertain and educate the people of North Carolina. The Symphony performs four concerts at the New Bern Riverfront Convention Center, including a Holiday Pops concert in December. Enjoy a free concert scheduled in early summer at Tryon Palace Historic Sites & Gardens in New Bern. Tickets are available by calling the Symphony Box Office at (877) 627-6724 in Raleigh or the Craven County Convention and Visitors Center at (252) 637-9400.

Writers' Organization

Carteret Writers
(252) 504-2968

This group of professional and aspiring writers gathers at 11:30 AM sharp on the second Tuesday of each month at Captain Bill's Restaurant in Morehead City. Meetings include lunch, friendly conversation about the art of writing, and a scheduled speaker to further inspire the writers. The group often takes a break during the summer. They also conduct special workshops, seminars and contests, which are open to everyone. The door is always open to new members and to those simply curious about honing their writing skills with the support and camaraderie of fellow scribes.

Creativity abounds in many coastal regions, the Crystal Coast especially.

photo: Peter Doran

Public Art Exhibitions

Art can be enjoyed in a number of places on the Crystal Coast, from museums and libraries to waterfronts and post offices. The **North Carolina Maritime Museum**, 315 Front Street, Beaufort, (252) 728-7317, exhibits work of state and local artists. These works complement the museum's maritime focus. Monthly exhibits are shown at **Carteret General Hospital**, 3500 Arendell Street, Morehead City, (252) 247-1616, sponsored by the Arts for the Hospital committee. **The History Place**, 1008 Arendell Street, Morehead City, (252) 247-7533, features works of various local artists. The **Carteret County Public Library** branches in Beaufort, Pine Knoll Shores and Newport and the Western Library sponsor artists in displays that change monthly and often include the work of adults and students. **Carteret Community College**, 3505 Arendell Street, Morehead City, (252) 222-6000, displays the work of students in the college library. The Upstairs Gallery at the college also features work by students and other local and regional artists. The Morehead City Waterfront and Downtown area is home to a **Fish Walk** where local artists have created a number of two to three foot columns that feature fish of various types. On Harkers Island, the **Core Sound Waterfowl Museum and Heritage Center**, (252) 728-1500, exhibits the best of hand-carved decoys and wildlife art.

Four beautifully restored murals depicting local scenes may be admired in the **Beaufort Post Office** on Front Street. Russian-born artist Simka Simkovitch painted these oil-on-canvas paintings in 1940. He was engaged by then-postmaster W. H. Taylor and paid $1,900 for his work. Simkovitch's fee was funded by the Fine Arts Program, a federal project that provided work for artists during the Great Depression. The large oils, ranging from 10 to 12 feet, show the Cape Lookout Lighthouse, the *Orville B.* mail boat, the wreck of the Crissie Wright, and a stunning scene of Canada geese. All were recently restored by conservator Elizabeth Speight of Philadelphia.

Art Lessons

Carteret Community College and the Arts Council continuously offer art lessons and classes to residents and visitors. Additionally, many of the art galleries listed in this chapter offer art lessons and workshops on various types of art — from watercolor and drawing to pottery and stained glass. The Core Sound Decoy Carvers Guild, listed in Arts Organizations, also offers carving lessons for adults and children.

Continuing Education Department
**Carteret County Community College,
3505 Arendell St., Morehead City
(252) 222-6200**

The Corporate and Community Education Division at Carteret Community College offers courses in various arts techniques each semester. There often is no tuition charge for county residents age 65 or older. For those under age 65, the fees are nominal. Call for more information and for details on the current listing of courses offered each semester.

Art Galleries

The number of galleries in Carteret County continues to increase. Many of our local artists have decided to dedicate their lives to the business of art, showcasing not only their own work but also the work of others. What follows is merely a sampling of some of the area's tried-and-true galleries. As you tour the area, we promise you'll find a treasure chest of other galleries to visit too.

ATLANTIC BEACH

Vision Gallery
**407 Atlantic Beach Cswy., Atlantic Beach
(252) 247-5550**

Since 2002 Vision Gallery has operated as one of the premier art galleries in the state. Original paintings and sculpture from established North Carolina and southeastern United States artists are the gallery's focus. The gallery mounts exhibits in the spring and summer months, and new work from gallery artists is displayed on a year-round basis.

 ARTS

SALTER PATH

Wood Artists' Gallery and Specialty Woods
MM 10.5, N.C. Hwy. 58, Salter Path
(252) 726-1400
www.nicefigures.com

At Wood Artists' Gallery and Specialty Woods, you'll find exquisite handcrafted gifts made from the finest natural woods from around the world created by on-site owners and artists Sharon Barrett and Paula Labelle. It truly is a unique shop that features gifts, a working studio, a gallery and specialty lumber sales. Their motto states "nature makes it beautiful, we enhance it" and that's just what you'll find as you browse their amazing creations and watch firsthand as they develop their masterpieces. You'll find natural-edged tables, platters, vases, boxes, oil lamps, ornaments, bottle toppers, perfume atomizers and more in a variety of unusual woods, including Australian Burl, Birdseye Maple, Curly Maple, Redwood Burl, Zebrawood and Purpleheart. In The Wooden Kitchen section of the shop you'll find gorgeous plates and bowls, pepper grinders, spurtles, utensils, cutting boards and oyster knives. They also carry the largest selection of specialty woods and burls in the area. It's worth stopping just for the beauty and smells of the fresh wood and the chance to meet the talented and friendly artisans. Wood Artists' Gallery is open Tuesday through Sunday from 10 AM to 5 PM.

BEAUFORT

Down East Gallery
519 Front St., Beaufort
(252) 728-4410, (800) 868-2766

Visiting Down East Gallery is an experience you must have. This gallery represents the paintings and prints of local artist and Beaufort resident Alan Cheek. Viewing his work takes you to Beaufort and the coast immediately. If you are searching for that special piece to always remind you of this area, or for a special gift, Down East Gallery is just the

place to find it. The gallery also features the work of other local artists, and framing services are available.

Handscapes Gallery
400 Front St., Beaufort
(252) 728-6805
www.handscapesgallery.com

Handscapes is an Insiders' favorite and the perfect place to find unusual gifts and treasures. The gallery specializes in works by North Carolinians as well as artists and craftspeople from all around the country. Owner Alison Brooks fills the shop with pottery, jewelry, prints, paintings, glass and metal-craft items. More than 200 artists are represented, and it is a joy to see their fine workmanship. The store is open year round, seven days a week. Call for winter hours.

Mattie King Davis Art Gallery
Beaufort Historic Site, 130 Turner St., Beaufort
(252) 728-5225, (800) 575-7483

Carteret County's oldest art gallery sells the varied works of many local and regional artists. Paintings, basketry, glass, wood, pottery and textiles are represented. A different artist is featured every few months with artist openings and receptions regularly held at the site. The gallery is a great place to not only see some outstanding artwork but also to receive an introduction to the Beaufort Historic Site.

Scott Taylor Photography
214 Pollock St., Beaufort
(252) 728-0900

At Scott Taylor's Photography Gallery and Studio you are sure to find a unique image of Beaufort or the surrounding coastal areas. Scott is well known for his scenic photography, and also for exclusive engagement, wedding and event photography. He specializes in color, black and white, or split-toned images. Let Scott create a family beach portrait that will be treasured for a lifetime. Scott's book titled *Coastal Waters - Images of North Carolina* is available in the gallery and is the perfect way to remember your trip to the coast.

MOREHEAD CITY

Art Escapes and Frames
Morehead Plaza, 2900 Arendell St., Morehead City
(252) 247-5111

For bright colors, movement and a flair for fun, Art Escapes and Frames is the place to go. The gallery features original artwork in a variety of media by North Carolina and regional artists. The gallery specializes in open and limited-edition prints and has a large selection for special orders. Custom framing is also offered. Whether it is acrylics, oils, watercolors or pottery, this gallery has quality items you are sure to enjoy.

Art Studio 500
500 Arendell St., Morehead City
(252) 726-3704

Art Studio 500 is an art gallery and more. Owner Richard Farrell is in the process of expanding the gallery, which is housed in a 100-year-old building. In addition to the gallery, Art Studio 500 offers a wide range of artistic services that include reproduction work, giclee prints, photography and illustration. The studio also specializes in graphic design, advertising, digital printing, all types of large format graphics and custom signage. Art Studio 500 is an all-in-one creative resource that provides a wide range of artistic and marketing services.

Arts & Things
704 Evans St., Morehead City
(252) 240-1979, (877) 640-ARTS (2787)

Arts & Things on the Morehead City waterfront has something for all art enthusiasts. With a very knowledgeable and helpful staff, this gallery offers a diverse and large collection of original art, along with limited-edition and open-edition prints. Arts & Things also features stone sculptures, art glass, pottery, shorebird carvings and stained glass. They offer framing, art supplies and workshops in a variety of media.

Bridges Street Pottery
1910 Bridges St., Morehead City
(252) 342-1134

Once a church, now a gallery and working potters' studio, Bridges Street Pottery displays and sells functional and decorative raku, porcelain and stoneware pottery made by local artists. Artists also create art tile for residential and commercial use. Potter Scott Haines, an instructor at Carteret Community College, teaches private lessons and hosts workshops here.

Carolina Artist Studio Gallery, Inc.
800 Evans St., Morehead City
(252) 726-7550

With approximately 30 participating artists, this is a nonprofit co-op gallery operated by the artists. Members' work is displayed, and active works in progress are sometimes visible. Members offer classes and workshops in a variety of media for children and adults. The classes vary so it's best to call to see what is available. Visitors are welcome to attend special art openings and exhibits, and the receptions are open to the public. The gallery showcases two-dimensional and three-dimensional original artwork, giclee and limited-edition prints. Visitors also enjoy the gift gallery that contains a variety of handcrafted items. Hours vary seasonally, so call ahead for specific days and times of operation.

Carteret Contemporary Art
1106 Arendell St., Morehead City
(252) 726-4071

This gallery specializes in paintings and shows an extraordinary selection. Visitors will also find works by national, regional and local artists in frequently changing exhibits. Some of the 2009 artists featured include Jimmy Craig Womble, Richard Fennell, Kyle Highsmith and Richard Garrison. Carteret Contemporary Art also provides quality custom framing at the gallery.

 ANNUAL EVENTS

The events that take place in any given region provide insight into what that area is all about, what it's founded upon, what it's proud of and what makes it unique. Traditions, history and community are very important on the Crystal Coast, and many events take place each year to celebrate these very things. From the American Music Festival concert series beginning each fall and the famous Newport Pig Cookin' Contest each April to the numerous athletic events and the Core Sound Decoy Festival in December, you'll find that Carteret County events are excellent ways to enjoy yourself and learn a little about the area. The area's traditional festivals, even the large N.C. Seafood Festival, have a sense of warmth reflective of a small-town, coastal region. You'll find a coming together of first-time visitors and long-time residents, young and old, family and friends, those just passing through — and everything in between. Fold in with the crowd and feel right at home. The simple pleasures of just being on the Crystal Coast provide a full plate, but including any of the following events in your plans expands a sample taste of the area into a real feast. Nearby communities host great events as well. Check our New Bern Annual Events chapter and the Havelock and Oriental chapters for more events.

> **i** *Many of the local events offer free admission, but you'll want to have some cash with you just in case. There's usually an opportunity to spend a little when it comes to food and drink, crafts, souvenirs or other tempting items. And remember: Vendors appreciate small bills!*

January

Bridal Fair
Crystal Coast Civic Center, 3505 Arendell St., Morehead City
(252) 247-3883, (888) 899-6088

This is an event the bride-to-be must attend. Take the groom, the mother, the future in-laws and any others involved in the planning. Booths are set up by planners, DJs, photographers, officiants, honeymoon travel agents and more. You can sample creations by catering companies and wedding cake bakers, plus see a fabulous fashion show highlighting wedding gowns, dresses for the mothers of the bride and groom, bridesmaids and flower girl dresses, and much more. Tickets are $5 and are available at the door or in advance by calling Pam Kaiser (252) 240-3256.

New Year's Day Kite Fly
Atlantic Beach
(252) 247-7011

Go fly a kite — or just come and watch as kite fliers kick off the New Year. The high-flying action begins around noon at The Circle area in Atlantic Beach. If you don't bring a kite, at least bring a camera and capture a fun way to bring in the New Year. For those who decide to participate, this event is good practice for the annual Carolina Kite Fest in October. The event is hosted by Kites Unlimited; call the number above for details.

Penguin Plunge
The Circle area, Atlantic Beach
(252) 808-7485

The 2009 Penguin Plunge marked the sixth year friends gathered to dip into the ocean on New Year's Day, and more than 120 people took part in the event. The fun starts at 1 PM. Plungers are asked to donate $5 to help with a local charity.

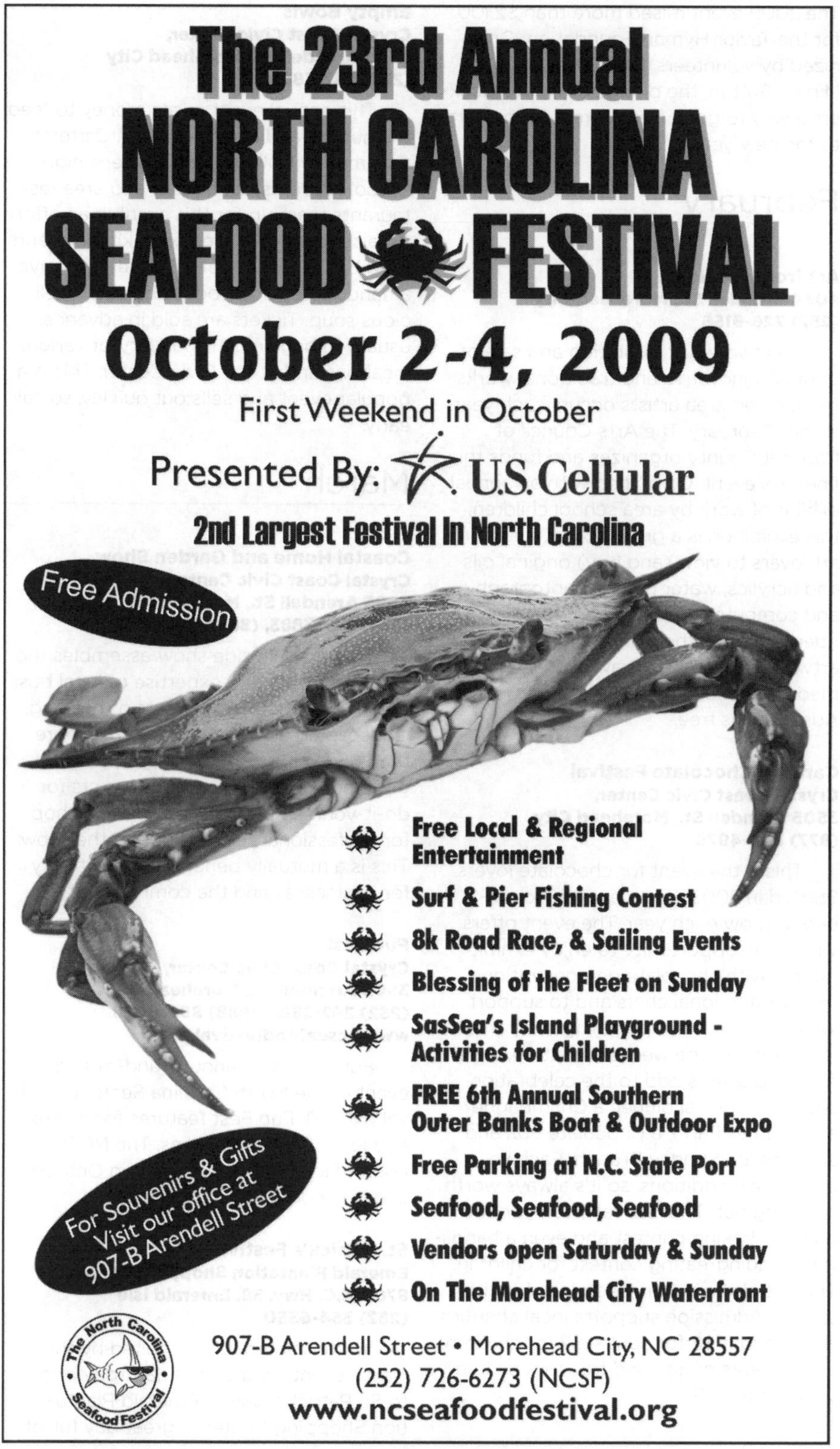

The 23rd Annual
NORTH CAROLINA
SEAFOOD  FESTIVAL
October 2-4, 2009
First Weekend in October

Presented By: ⭐ U.S. Cellular

2nd Largest Festival In North Carolina

Free Admission

🦀 **Free Local & Regional Entertainment**

🦀 **Surf & Pier Fishing Contest**

🦀 **8k Road Race, & Sailing Events**

🦀 **Blessing of the Fleet on Sunday**

🦀 **SasSea's Island Playground - Activities for Children**

🦀 **FREE 6th Annual Southern Outer Banks Boat & Outdoor Expo**

🦀 **Free Parking at N.C. State Port**

🦀 **Seafood, Seafood, Seafood**

🦀 **Vendors open Saturday & Sunday**

🦀 **On The Morehead City Waterfront**

For Souvenirs & Gifts Visit our office at 907-B Arendell Street

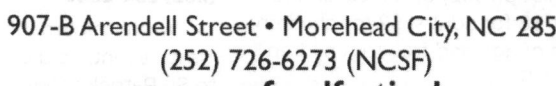

907-B Arendell Street • Morehead City, NC 28557
(252) 726-6273 (NCSF)
www.ncseafoodfestival.org

The 2009 event raised more than $2,100 for the Taylor Hyman Foundation. Organized by volunteers Tabbie Nance and Miriam Sutton, the plunge offers fun seekers a way to get a fresh, a real fresh, start to the new year.

February

Art from the Heart
4034 Arendell St., Morehead City
(252) 726-9156

This two-week exhibition and sale of original, innovative and traditional works by selected area artists occurs each year in mid-February. The Arts Council of Carteret County organizes and funds this fine-arts event. Combined with an annual exhibit of work by area school children, this exhibition is a great opportunity for art lovers to view (and buy) original oils and acrylics; water media; photography and computer generated art; glass, stone, fiber arts and other three-dimensional artwork; pastels and drawings; and mixed media. Proceeds benefit the Arts Council. Admission is free.

Carolina Chocolate Festival
Crystal Coast Civic Center,
3505 Arendell St., Morehead City
(877) 848-4976

This is the event for chocolate lovers. Started in 2003, the event has continued to grow each year. The event offers visitors an opportunity to enjoy exhibit booths with chocolate demonstrations from professional chefs and to support local nonprofit groups selling tasty treats. In addition to the weekend festival, other fun-filled events add to the celebration, such as a special dinner, a Champagne and Truffles Party, a Chocolate Spa and a Chocolate Sunday Brunch. Each year brings new additions, so it's always worth checking out. The festival offers fondue, music, a baking contest and even a hands-free pudding-eating contest for children. There is also a supervised place for kids to play. Admission supports local charities and is about $8 for adults, $2 for children 5 to 12 years of age and free for children younger than 5.

Empty Bowls
Crystal Coast Civic Center,
3505 Arendell St., Morehead City
(252) 247-3883

This annual event raises money to feed the hungry and is very popular. Carteret Community College, local potters, high school students, art classes and area restaurants team up for this event in an effort to raise money for area soup kitchens and food banks. For about $15, guests receive a handcrafted soup bowl and some delicious soup. Tickets are sold in advance, usually in beginning in January, at various locations and at the Civic Center. This is a popular event and sells out quickly, so call early.

March

Coastal Home and Garden Show
Crystal Coast Civic Center,
3505 Arendell St., Morehead City
(252) 247-3883, (888) 899-6088

This annual trade show assembles the services, wares and expertise of local businesses that focus on aspects of building, landscaping and decorating. With more than 65 exhibitors you can gather ideas, good advice and the right products for do-it-yourself projects. Or you can shop for professional services during the show. This is a mutually beneficial opportunity for businesses and the community, too.

Fun Fest
Crystal Coast Civic Center,
3505 Arendell St., Morehead City
(252) 247-3883, (888) 899-6088
www.ncseafoodfestival.org

Fun Fest is an annual fund-raising event of the North Carolina Seafood Festival (NCSF). Fun Fest features food, music and lots of fun for families. The NCSF takes place the first weekend in October and is a wonderful coastal event.

St. Patrick's Festival
Emerald Plantation Shopping Center,
8700 N.C. Hwy. 58, Emerald Isle
(252) 354-6350

Winter hibernation is halted by this March event, held on the Saturday prior to St. Patrick's Day at Emerald Plantation Shopping Center. A great day full of fun and games for the entire family, the event includes corned beef and cabbage, traditional beverages and music. Green is plentiful when it comes to attire and decorations, so be prepared to join in the fun — and even join in a jig. The festival features everything from arts and crafts vendors to children's amusement rides to live entertainment for all to enjoy. Other events surrounding the festival include an 8K road race and the Little Ms. and Mr. Leprechaun Contest. Sponsored by the Emerald Isle Parks and Recreation Department and the Business Association, the festival supports local craftspeople and civic organizations. It's free and loads of fun for the entire family.

Swansboro Oyster Roast & Pig Out
Swansboro Rotary Civic Center,
1104 Main St. Ext., Swansboro
(910) 326-6175
www.swansbororotary.com

This is an event not to be missed if you enjoy oysters or a pig-pickin'. And while you are enjoying all the food and having fun, you are helping the community. The event funds scholarships awarded each year by the civic organization. From Swansboro through Emerald Isle and beyond, the population turns out for all-you-can-eat oysters, flounder, clam chowder, hot dogs or a pig-pickin' with traditional slaw and hushpuppy trimmings. The event usually happens around St. Patrick's Day on the third Saturday in March. Tickets are $40 in advance and $45 at the door. The event takes place from 5 to 8 PM.

April

Beaufort Wine and Food Weekend
Various locations, Beaufort
(252) 728-5225, (800) 575-7483

This Beaufort Wine and Food Weekend is a five-day event showcasing wine makers, local and celebrity chefs, and other notable personalities. It pairs great wine with great food, and the proceeds benefit local non-profits that draw tourism into the area. This year's event supports the Beaufort Historical Association, the Friends of the North Carolina Maritime Museum and the Carteret County Commu-

nity College Culinary School. There is an ever-growing list of events for both wine lovers and food lovers (or in most cases, both). The weekend includes wine luncheons and dinners, seminars, art, music and tastings. The main event takes place in Beaufort; however, various events are conducted at restaurants and other locations in nearby towns. Vin De Mer Grand Tasting Village is the highlight of the weekend. It takes place on Saturday in Beaufort and features a huge tasting tent filled with wines and foods. Tickets are available at the Beaufort Historic Site Visitor Center, 130 Turner Street and online.

Easter Egg Hunt
Beaufort Historic Site,
100 Block Turner St., Beaufort
(252) 728-5225, (800) 575-7483

On the Saturday before Easter Sunday, the Beaufort Historic Site is the perfect setting for a traditional Easter egg hunt for the younger members of the family up to age 7. It's a BYOB event, bring-your-own basket that is, heaped with small-town warmth and charm. The hunt begins at 11 AM with hundreds of hidden eggs to be found. There are prizes and refreshments, too. Admission is free, and everyone is welcome.

Easter Sunrise Services

The dawning of Easter morning is celebrated in services at several locations across the county, many on the waterfront or beach. The *Carteret County News-Times* lists service locations and times the week before Easter.

Emerald Isle Homes Tour & Art Show
Western Carteret Public Library,
230 Taylor Notion Rd., Cape Carteret
(252) 393-6500

The Emerald Isle Homes Tour and Art Show, in its 12th year in 2009, is sponsored by the Friends of the Western Carteret Public Library. Tour hours are 10 AM until 4 PM, and hostesses at each home welcome visitors. Tickets can be purchased at the library, the Visitor Center on N.C. Highway 58 and other various other locations throughout the area, including the Carteret County Library. Tickets are $12 in advance, $15 the day of the show, and come with a self-guided tour map to the homes and gardens found in Emerald Isle and Cape Carteret. The art show features works by local artists and is held at the Lands' End clubhouse in Emerald Isle. Money raised benefits the library.

Fort Macon Civil War Reenactment
Fort Macon State Park, Atlantic Beach
(252) 726-3775

This event features Civil War–period activities performed by members of the 1st N.C. Volunteers. Similar events take place in July and September. Talks on flags, uniforms and Civil War dress are held, as well as musket firings and drills. Admission is free.

Lookout Spring Road Race
Sports Center, 701 N. 35th St.,
Morehead City
(252) 726-7070

This annual family fun and fitness road race in Morehead City is sponsored by the Lookout Rotary Club and takes place on the last Saturday of April. This is a flat and fast course with an event for every age and every skill level. The road race begins and ends at the Sports Center, and participants can run a 10K, 5K or 1 mile, or take part in the baby-jogger race. Proceeds from the event benefit local charities and civic organizations. There is an entry fee,

and families get a price break. Prizes are awarded.

Newport Pig Cookin' Contest
Newport Park, Howard Blvd., Newport
(252) 223-PIGS (7447)

The annual Newport Pig Cooking Contest is one of the largest whole-hog, pig-cooking competitions in the state. This huge barbecue competition is held on the first Friday and Saturday in April and draws folks from all along the Eastern seaboard for the best barbecue on earth. You'll find great food, baked goods, live entertainment, rides and children's activities. Delicious Down East barbecue goes on sale around noon on Saturday, as soon as judging has been completed. Drive-up service is even available for those who want a great lunch but don't want to wade through the crowds. The event benefits numerous civic organizations. The winning cooks go on to the state championship.

Portsmouth Island Homecoming
(252) 728-2250

This heritage event celebrates the history of Portsmouth Village on the Core Banks and is usually celebrated on even-numbered years on the Saturday after Easter. Now an Historic District in Cape Lookout National Seashore, Portsmouth is

The ocean is the top attraction for everyone on the Crystal Coast.

photo: Carolyn Temple

just south of Ocracoke Inlet. Access is only by boat. The event provides a unique look at early island life. Friends and descendants of island residents get together for an old-fashioned church homecoming and dinner on the grounds. Call for details and the latest information.

Publick Day
**100 Block Turner St., Beaufort
(252) 728-5225, (800) 575-7483**

This annual event features a Colonial-style flea market with the outdoor sale of varied merchandise and crafts, along with entertainment, mock trials and exhibits. The day recalls Colonial excitement generated by the arrival of the circuit court judge to Beaufort. Proceeds benefit the restoration efforts and educational programs through the Beaufort Historical Association. Admission is free, but expect to have your wallet tempted by the array of crafts and goodies available. You'll find everything from antiques, collectibles, fine arts and crafts, wood turnings and toys, books, herbs, handmade jewelry and more. The kids can enjoy children's colonial games with a living history demonstration from 1 to 3 PM and there are opportunities to ride the vintage English double-decker with a narrated tour of the Beaufort Historic District for a small fee. Hours are from 9 AM to 4 PM.

May

American Music Festival
**The History Place, 1008 Arendell St., Morehead City
(252) 728-6152
www.americanmusicfestival.org**

The American Music Festival is a non-profit chamber music series featuring concerts performed from September through May. The 2009 - 2010 series marks the 20th season of quality performances. The series is supported by subscription ticket purchase, grants, donations and donor sponsorships and is managed by a volunteer board of directors. Donations to the fund further promote music with an educational outreach program that takes the gifted musicians into area schools. Past concerts included world-

class performances by musicians of the Alexander Quartet, Nicholas Duchamp, Carolina Piano Trio and Daedalus Quartet. Series subscriptions for five concerts start at $100. Individual performance tickets are $25 for adults and $15 for students and military. Performances usually take place on Saturdays at 8 PM at The History Place in Morehead City.

Beaufort By-the-Sea Music Festival
**Waterfront and Downtown Venues
(252) 422-8365**

Music flows along Taylor's Creek and through downtown Beaufort each year during the Music Festival. Multiple stages are set up throughout town, and a variety of music is offered, with something sure to suit the ears of all ages. On Saturday, the Beaufort Historic Site features a family fun area that showcases performers and all kinds of fun activities for the kids. The is a free community event, and volunteers do all the work.

Carteret County Arts and Crafts Coalition Spring Show
**Beaufort Historic Site,
100 Block of Turner St.
(252) 728-5225, (800) 575-7483**

This under-the-tent event is an outdoor exhibition and sale of arts and crafts by juried coalition members and is held three weekends a year on Memorial Day, Fourth of July and Labor Day. There's also a holiday show that runs at another location for a three-week show between Thanksgiving and Christmas. With an average of 40 local artists featured, it's a great venue to view and purchase the work of these local artists and craftsmen. With many of the artists on site, it offers the opportunity to meet and talk with them in person and get insight into their work. The event runs Saturday from 10 AM to 5 PM and Sunday noon to 5 PM. Admission is free.

Crystal Coast Quilt Show
**Crystal Coast Civic Center,
3505 Arendell St., Morehead City
(252) 247-3883, (888) 899-6088**

Quilts and all things to do with quilting are what you will find at this annual event. Sponsored by the Crystal Coast Quilt

Guild, the show is a wonderful opportunity to see quilts made by local artists as well as artists from across the country. Each year the talented members of the guild make a quilt to be raffled off at the show. They also exhibit their creations in a judged show. Last year's show included more than 100 quilts. Vendors are on hand to offer quilting and sewing supplies and materials. The show runs from 9 AM until 5 PM on both days. Admission is $5 and is good for both days, with children under the age of 12 admitted free.

Marine Corps Air Station Cherry Point Air Show
Cherry Point
(866) WINGS NC (946-4762)

Marine Corps Air Station Cherry Point Air show is the state's largest air show on the East Coast's largest Marine Corps air station. The 2009 show features the aerobatic jet team, the Canadian Snowbirds, renowned for their thrilling performances. Friday's Night Show features afterburners, rocket trucks, sky divers and fireworks. The Saturday and Sunday day shows feature military and civilian aerobatic demonstrations, historic and modern displays, the Blue Angels, F-18 Hornets, AV-8B Harrier demonstrations and flybys. The show features plenty of activities for children. The show and parking are free, with preferred seating available for purchase. Of course, bring some extra cash for some souvenirs, food, drinks and more. It's also helpful to bring lawn chairs or a blanket.

Morehead City Family Boating and In-Water Boat Show
Morehead City
(252) 808-0440

Always held the third weekend in May, the Downtown Morehead City Revitalization Association launched the Morehead City Family Boating and In-Water Boat Show in 2008. The event showcases boat sales of all types plus family boat programs, educational events, entertainment and plenty of vendors. Take advantage of the opportunity to tour in-water and on-shore power boats, view Coast Guard exhibits, catch up on the latest boating technology and learn more about boating safety through the show's exhibits

and programs. With a gala celebration on Friday, the show runs from 10 AM to 5 PM on Saturday and 11 AM to 4 PM on Sunday.

Swansboro Rotary King Mackerel Bluewater Tournament
Swansboro
(910) 326-3474
www.swansbororotary.com

Swansboro Rotary Club's King Mackerel and Bluewater Tournament is held each May and offers some big prizes. Registration takes place on the first day. The 2008 event drew a field of 165 king mackerel boats and 40 bluewater boats, and a total purse of nearly $250,000 in cash and prizes, with the first place taking home a guaranteed $25,000 in cash. Proceeds from the tournament benefit the Swansboro Rotary Scholarship Program for deserving seniors in Onslow and Carteret counties. Participants pay category fees to compete in the tournament.

Women's Fair
Crystal Coast Civic Center,
3505 Arendell St., Morehead City
(252) 247-3883, (888) 899-6088

Women's Fair is a trade show that focuses on women's lives. The show features booths and demonstrations on health, well-being, fashion, careers and more. Fashion shows and seminars take place during the expo.

Wooden Boat Show
N.C. Maritime Museum, 315 Front St.,
Beaufort
(252) 728-7317
www.ncmaritimemuseum.org

The Wooden Boat Show of the North Carolina Maritime Museum in Beaufort was the first and is the largest gathering of wooden watercraft in the Southeast. This fascinating event takes place the first Saturday in May. This is not a commercial show. Instead it is a full day of scheduled demonstrations, talks and races that attract people who share an interest in the art, craftsmanship and history of wooden boats. Enthusiasts race radio-controlled boats in the pool on the Maritime Museum patio, and the public is given an opportunity to sail in traditional North Carolina boats. The show also offers music, a naval re-enactors encampment and a shipwreck

exhibit. This show has something fun for all ages, so be sure to bring the whole family. The museum offers wooden boat–related exhibits and events the week leading up to the show. Since some of the events and exhibits take place at the museum's expansion site at Gallants Channel in Beaufort, there are free park-and-ride services offered, including a ground shuttle and water ferry service from downtown Beaufort. Admission is free.

June

Antiques Show and Sale
Crystal Coast Civic Center,
3505 Arendell St., Morehead City
(252) 728-5225, (800) 575-7483

This show is held in conjunction with the Beaufort Old Homes and Gardens Tour on the last weekend in June each year. You'll find plenty of interesting antiques and collectibles at the show with more than 40 booths for your viewing (and shopping) pleasure. Tickets usually cost $5 and are good Friday through Sunday of the Old Homes and Gardens Tour weekend. A combo ticket for the tour and show/sale is offered. Tickets are available through the Beaufort Historical Association by calling the number listed above.

Beaufort Old Homes and Gardens Tour
Beaufort Historic Site, 100 Block Turner St.,
Beaufort
(252) 728-5225, (800) 575-7483

The Old Homes and Garden Tour has become a favorite of visitors from around the world, and in 2009 Beaufort marks

Happy 300th Anniversary Beaufort-by-the-Sea! Founded in 1709, North Carolina's third-oldest town celebrates in 2009 with two weeks of homecoming celebration activities slated for September 7th through the 13th and September 21st through the 27th. For information, as well as monthly activities leading up to the big celebration, call (252) 241-1259.

its 300th anniversary so there's a lot to celebrate. During the last full weekend in June, the tour opens some of the county's oldest private homes and buildings for narrated tours on Friday and Saturday. New restorations and those in progress keep the tour fresh. This year marks the 49th annual walking tour, selected as a Southeast Tourism Society Top 20 Event for the month of June 2009. Tour-goers enjoy a self-paced tour of private historic homes, gardens, churches and meeting halls. Private homes including the circa 1709 Hammock House, the Beaufort Historic Site buildings, the Old Burying Ground, narrated bus tours of the historic district, music concerts and an antique car show are all slated for this year's event. Tickets are $16 in advance and $20 on tour days. Children age 12 and younger get in for half price, and a combo ticket for the Antiques Show and Sale is available. This fund-raising activity benefits the Beaufort Historical Association.

Big Rock Blue Marlin Tournament
Various locations, Morehead City
(252) 247-3575
www.thebigrock.com

Big Rock — one hardly needs to say more. The tournament celebrated its 50th anniversary in 2008 and is one of the oldest and largest sport-fishing tournaments in the country. It involves fishing, fishing-related events, parties and daily public weigh-ins on the Morehead City waterfront during the week and uses the Civic Center for various events. The tournament benefits charities and nonprofit organizations. Of course, the tournament winners benefit from a handsome monetary reward.

Concert at Fort Macon Series
Fort Macon State Park, Atlantic Beach
(252) 726-3775

The Concert in the Park Series begins June 5 and continues on various Friday evenings through August 7. Concerts are scheduled for the following dates: June 5, June 19, June 26, July 10, July 24 and August 7. This is one of the many outreach projects of the Friends of Fort Macon, and admission is free. Each concert begins at 7 PM and ends around 8 PM.

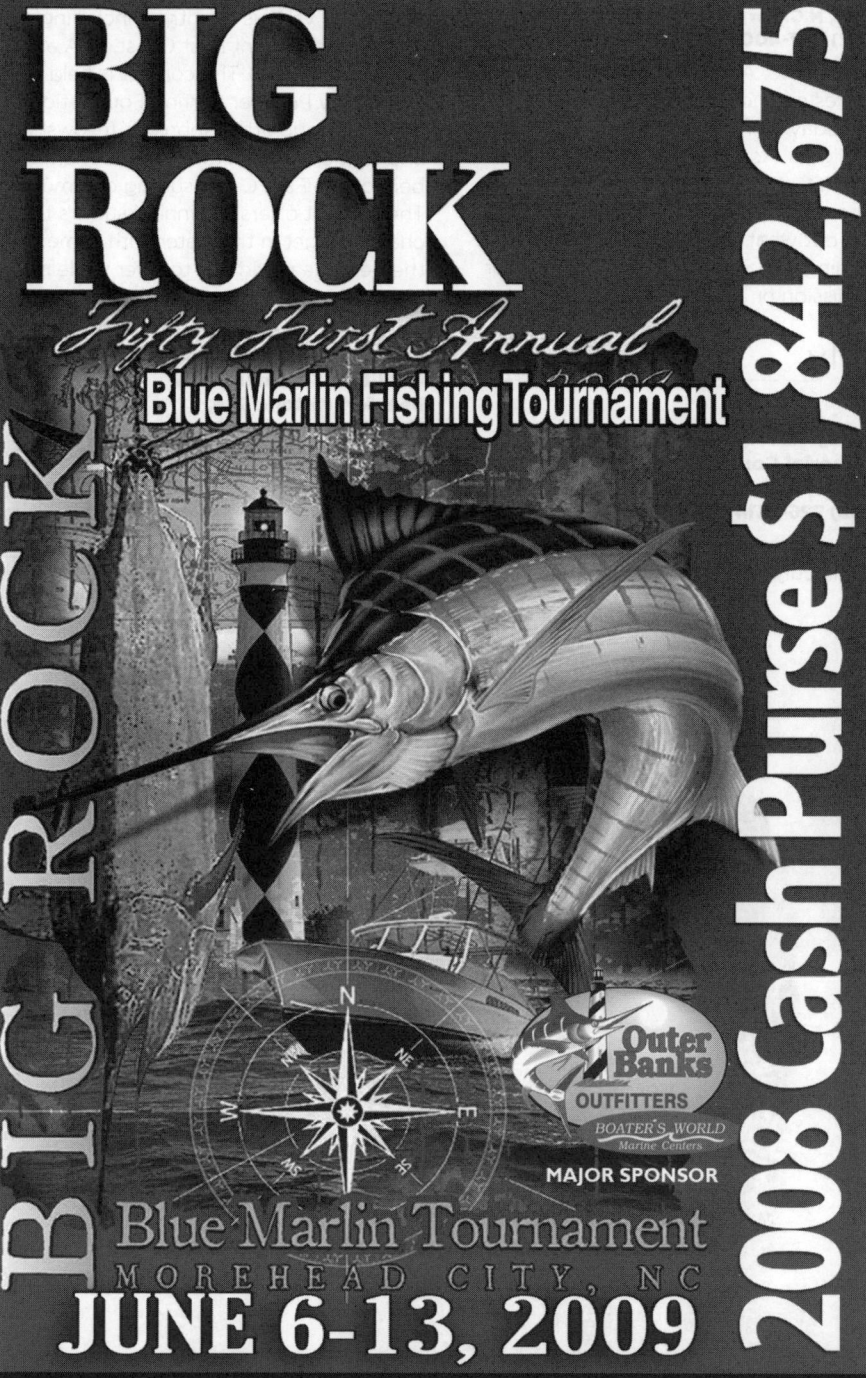

The Big Rock Blue Marlin Fishing Tournament
PO Box 1673, 405 Evans St., Morehead City, NC 28557
252-247-3575 • director@thebigrock.com
thebigrock.com

Family Nights at The Aquarium
MM 7, N.C. Hwy. 58, Pine Knoll Shores
(252) 247-4003

The N.C. Aquarium at Pine Knoll Shores extends its hours on various Thursday nights in the summer for Family Nights. Activities for all ages begin at 5 PM, with a different theme chosen for each Thursday night. Call ahead to find out what the theme will be for the evening. Programs are free with regular admission or a membership.

July

Buddy Pelletier Longboard Memorial Contest
Atlantic Beach
(252) 726-2314

Held annually during the last full weekend in July, this event attracts amateur and professional surfers from the East Coast and various countries, including former and current East Coast, ESA and world champions. The contest is held by the Buddy Pelletier Surfing Foundation, an organization that sponsors fellowships and renders humanitarian aid to members of the East Coast surfing community. The contest offers beginning surfers the chance to get in the water with some of the best the world has to offer while raising funds to help fellow surfers.

Carteret County Arts and Crafts Coalition Summer Show
Beaufort Historic Site,
100 Block of Turner St., Beaufort
(252) 728-5225, (800) 575-7483

This under-the-tent event is an outdoor exhibition and sale of arts and crafts by juried coalition members and is held three weekends a year on Memorial Day,

Family time is what a beach vacation is all about.

photo: Carolyn Temple

Fourth of July and Labor Day. There's also a holiday show that runs at another location for three weeks between Thanksgiving and Christmas. With an average of 40 local artists featured, it's a great venue to view and purchase the work of these local artists and craftspeople. With many of the artists on site, it offers the opportunity to meet and talk with them in person and get insight into their work. The show runs Saturday from 10 AM to 5 PM and Sunday noon to 5 PM. Admission is free.

Fort Macon Civil War Reenactment
Fort Macon State Park, Atlantic Beach
(252) 726-3775

This July event features Civil War–period activities performed between 10 AM to 4 PM by members of the 1st N.C. Volunteers. Similar events take place in April and September. Talks on flags, uniforms and Civil War dress are held, as well as musket firings and drills. Admission is free.

Historic Beaufort Road Race
Front St., Downtown Beaufort
(252) 222-6359

This popular road race takes place on the third Saturday in July, and 2009 marks its 30th year. The morning event includes a certified 10K run, a certified 5K run and walk, and a 1-mile run and walk. There are also 10K and 5K wheelchair events and a 5K baby-jogger race. All the events start and end on the Beaufort waterfront. The race is organized by Beaufort Ole Towne Rotary to benefit area youth and community projects. There is an entry fee, and families get a price break. Prizes are awarded.

Independence Day Celebrations
Various locations
(252) 726-8148

Fourth of July fireworks and festivities take place throughout the Crystal Coast. Morehead City, Atlantic Beach and Emerald Isle regularly have evening fireworks, and Beaufort has a great "small-town" morning parade that is followed by a community picnic on the courthouse lawn with free ice cream and live music. Consult the local papers for times and festive locations before the weekend, or call the Crystal Coast Visitor Center, (252) 726-8148.

Fireworks also light up the Swansboro waterfront every Fourth of July.

August

Outer Banks Wildlife Shelter Sand-Sculpting Contest (Sculpt for Wildlife)
On the Beach at Atlantis Lodge,
123 N.C. Hwy. 58, Pine Knoll Shores
(252) 240-1200

Held on the first Saturday in August, this popular event helps support the efforts of the Outer Banks Wildlife Shelter. The sand-sculpture competition brings out the best and the brightest in Carteret County and beyond. What began as one energetic family's pastime at a reunion now draws some serious competition for adults and children. The creations are spectacular every year, and it's well worth the trip. Repeat competitors and new entries are always welcome. The professional sand sculptors known as Sandy Feat are usually on hand to provide the centerpiece for the contest as well as give out tips on sculpting and design. The competing sand-sculpting teams raise contributions to benefit the Outer Banks Wildlife Shelter.

September

American Music Festival
The History Place, 1008 Arendell St.,
Morehead City
(252) 728-6152
www.americanmusicfestival.org

The American Music Festival is a nonprofit chamber music series featuring concerts performed from September through May. The 2009 - 2010 series marks the 20th season of quality performances. The series is supported by subscription ticket purchase, grants, donations and donor sponsorships and is managed by a volunteer board of directors. Donations to the fund further promote music with an educational outreach program that takes the gifted musicians into area schools. Past concerts included world-class performances by musicians of the Alexander Quartet, Nicholas Duchamp, Carolina Piano Trio and Daedalus Quartet.

CLOSE UP
The Fabulous
North Carolina Seafood Festival

Imagine for a moment the sounds of music. In front of you two men sit under a large tent, both strumming guitars and singing quiet folk songs in unison. The sound is broken on occasion by the beat of a rock band two blocks away and the laughter of children nearby. You can hear wind chimes tinkling from a craft booth and the squeals of children on the merry-go-round. And then you take a breath and the smell permeates the air — ahhh, seafood. That's what the N.C. Seafood Festival is all about. The rides, musical entertainment and crafts are a merely a bonus. You're here for the seafood.

The story of how North Carolina's second largest festival came to be is somewhat of a legend in Carteret County. As the story (or fish tale, if you prefer) goes, the idea originated as a lunchtime joke in 1986 while several locals ate at a restaurant. One would simply not let the idea of a festival die, and that festival is alive indeed.

Always taking place the first weekend in October on the Morehead City Waterfront, the festival will celebrate its 23rd year in 2009. The first N.C. Seafood Festival saw 35,000 people flock to Carteret County, astounding the organizers. And if they thought that was something, they probably could have never fathomed the three-day event would draw more than 225,000 in 2005.

With a dedicated volunteer board of directors, a small paid staff and lots of volunteers, the N.C. Seafood Festival focuses on promoting the Crystal Coast, emphasizing the seafood industry that has sustained the area since its birth. It also offers an ideal outlet for area nonprofit organizations to raise needed funds. You'll find high school band boosters frying shrimp, Rotarians grilling hot dogs and football teams selling T-shirts. If they don't have something to vend themselves, the festival board allows non-profit groups to sell festival mementos, keeping a portion of the funds for themselves. Through the years, the number of commercial food vendors has been lowered to allow the nonprofit groups the opportunity to reap the benefits of the community festival. In past years, over $150,000 has gone back into county non-profits such as churches, schools, and youth and civic groups. The N.C. Seafood Festival has become a true community event.

Local music and culture is mixed with well-known contemporary artists. The N.C. State Port, one of only two industrial ports in the state, opens its gates for vessels tours and provides free parking with shuttle service. The festival now includes a family fishing tournament, an 8K road race, a photo contest, a sailing regatta, the Southern Outer Banks Boat Show, a Cooking with the Chefs Tent, fireworks and more.

Numerous stages are set up throughout the waterfront area and offer everything from country music and storytellers to children's performances and sing-a-longs. On Sunday morning at the Port, commercial fishermen are honored with the annual Blessing of the Fleet, a commemorative religious ceremony that recognizes fishermen who have passed away. In addition to the great seafood, the outstanding music and the wonderful crafts, Coastal Yesterday is one area that features the traditional crafts of the past — boat building, decoy carving, net mending along with environmental education displays and hands-on activities.

Above all, the N.C. Seafood Festival is a great introduction to the culture and seafood of the Crystal Coast. It is an ideal way to see what Carteret County is all about. Come and have a look, or a taste, for yourself.

Series subscriptions for five concerts start at $100. Individual performance tickets are $25 for adults and $15 for students and military. Performances usually take place on Saturdays at 8 PM at The History Place in Morehead City.

Atlantic Beach Saltwater Classic
Atlantic Beach
(800) 546-4622
www.bluewaterpromo.com

The Atlantic Beach King Mackerel Tournament is a huge event and is one of the nation's largest all-cash king mackerel fishing competitions. The tournament benefits the Atlantic Beach Volunteer Fire Department. Registration and all events are at Atlantic Station Shopping Center, with weigh-ins on the Atlantic Beach Causeway.

Carteret County Arts and Crafts Coalition Fall Show
Beaufort Historic Site,
100 Block of Turner St., Beaufort
(252) 726-8397, (800) 575-7483

This under-the-tent event is an outdoor exhibition and sale of arts and crafts by juried coalition members and is held three weekends a year on Memorial Day, Fourth of July and Labor Day. There's also a holiday show that runs at another location for three weeks between Thanksgiving and Christmas. With an average of 40 local artists featured, it's a great venue to view and purchase the work of these local artists and craftspeople. With many of the artists on site, it offers the opportunity to meet and talk with them in person and get insight into their work. The show runs Saturday from 10 AM to 5 PM and Sunday noon to 5 PM. Admission is free.

Carteret Numismatic Coin Show
Crystal Coast Civic Center,
3505 Arendell St., Morehead City
(252) 247-3883, (888) 899-6088

This event is usually held the last weekend in September and attracts dealers and the public alike. Coins collectors from near and far travel to this annual event to view, sell, swap and trade coins of all types. You'll find everything from currency to ancient coins including medals, tokens, U.S. and world coins, and more. There are books, educational supplies and other publications on hand, too. This show

is hosted by the local Numismatic Coin Club and is a popular event. Admission is a $1 raffle ticket with hourly drawings and the chance to win a gold coin.

Fort Macon Civil War Reenactment
Fort Macon State Park, Atlantic Beach
(252) 726-3775

This September event features Civil War–period activities performed by members of the 1st N.C. Volunteers. Similar events also take place in April and July. Talks on flags, uniforms and Civil War dress are held, as are musket firings and drills. Admission is free.

October

American Music Festival
The History Place, 1008 Arendell St.,
Morehead City
(252) 728-6152
www.americanmusicfestival.org

The American Music Festival is a nonprofit chamber music series featuring concerts performed from September through May. The 2009 - 2010 series marks the 20th season of quality performances. The series is supported by subscription ticket purchase, grants, donations and donor sponsorships and is managed by a volunteer board of directors. Donations to the fund further promote music with an educational outreach program that takes the gifted musicians into area schools. Past concerts included world-class performances by musicians of the Alexander Quartet, Nicholas Duchamp, Carolina Piano Trio and Daedalus Quartet. Series subscriptions for five concerts start at $100. Individual performance tickets are $25 for adults and $15 for students and military. Performances usually take place on Saturdays at 8 PM at The History Place in Morehead City.

Carolina Kite Fest
Sheraton Atlantic Beach,
MM 4.5, N.C. Hwy. 58, Atlantic Beach
(252) 222-4012

This is a family fun flying event for kite fliers and spectators alike. On this weekend, the sky fills with kite demonstrations, competitions and night kite flying. Most of the action takes place during the hours of

10 AM and 4 PM, with the night fly usually taking place at 8 PM on Saturday. Come as early as you can with camera in hand as there's a lot to see. As long as the wind cooperates, you'll see everything from colorful kites to team flying to mass ascensions of every size and shape kite imaginable. Kids' activities such as candy drops and kite building are also part of the event. Admission is free. The event is sponsored by Kites Unlimited; contact them at (252) 247-7011 for more information.

Annual Emerald Isle Triathlon
Emerald Isle
(252) 354-6350

Emerald Isle Parks and Recreation and the Emerald Isle Business Association sponsor this triathlon that has competitors taking a 750-meter swim in the ocean, biking 19.3 kilometers on N.C. Highway 58 and running a 5K neighborhood course. This is a small local race that is quickly becoming a favorite event. Contact the Parks and Recreation department for details or to register.

Mullet Festival
Downtown Swansboro, Swansboro
(910) 326-1174

This is the area's oldest festival, started about 55 years ago to celebrate the completion of the new bridge over the White Oak River in Swansboro. The first festival was so fun that it has been celebrated ever since with a parade, a street carnival, arts and crafts, music, food and vendors of all types. Held the second weekend in October, the event centers around lots of fried mullet, of course, and it benefits local civic organizations. Admission is free.

N.C. Big Sweep
(252) 222-6352

N.C. Big Sweep is a statewide effort to clean trash from waterways, beaches and roadsides. The annual event involves many volunteers as individuals and as groups, and their hard work pays off in the beautification of the area. The event is coordinated through the North Carolina Cooperative Extension Service. October 10, 2009, is the official local date of Big Sweep, but volunteers can participate a few weeks before or after.

North Carolina Seafood Festival
907-B Arendell St., Morehead City
(252) 726-6273
www.ncseafoodfestival.org

The North Carolina Seafood Festival takes place the first weekend in October on the Morehead City waterfront. The average attendance for the Seafood Festival is 125,000 during the three days of this mammoth outdoor annual festival. The second largest festival in North Carolina, its highlights are an endless variety of seafood prepared in a multitude of ways, street dances, concerts, crafts, educational exhibits, programs and a fair with rides and games. Be sure to visit a new feature in this year's festival at the Cooking with the Chefs Tent where the motto is "Learn it, Taste it, Love it! " This new area of the festival serves fresh-from-the-North-Carolina-waters seafood samples prepared by area chefs. A free taste of Texas Pete Zestier Seafood Cocktail Sauce awaits you as you enter into this fantastic area of the festival, so come with an appetite. The festivities are spread from the North Carolina State Port to Ninth Street. Free parking is available at the port, and shuttles transport festival-goers to the fun. Festival headquarters and a gift shop are located at 907-B Arendell Street in Morehead City, and a staff works all year planning and conducting festival-focused activities, like the photographic and art contests that select poster art for promoting the event. There's also a scholarship golfing extravaganza. Admission to the festival is free.

Surf Fishing Workshop
MM 7, N.C. Hwy. 58, Pine Knoll Shores
(252) 247-4003

Experienced anglers share their techniques in the N.C. Aquarium's annual Surf Fishing Workshop on a weekend in October. Topics and instruction include information on rods, reels, weights, line, tackle, bait, fish identification, catch and release, cast netting, "reading" the surf, locating fish from the beach and caring for the catch. The course culminates with a fishing excursion to Cape Lookout. Beginners will find the lessons especially helpful, but all anglers are welcome. Call or check the website for fees and age requirements.

Trick or Treat under the Sea
MM 7, N.C. Hwy. 58, Pine Knoll Shores
(252) 247-4003

The N.C. Aquarium hosts a bewitching event of family-oriented Halloween fun with an aquatic twist. Originally a one-night-only event, its popularity with the community has allowed the aquarium to offer it for two nights. Children trick-or-treat at booths set up among the galleries and exhibits. Visitors of all ages enjoy "spooky" fun and games. The Halloween hijinks are a crowd pleaser. Special admission fees apply; call ahead for times and additional details closer to the event.

November

Annual Antique-A-Thon
The History Place, 1008 Arendell St.,
Morehead City
(252) 247-7533

The annual Antique-A-Thon is scheduled on the first Saturday in November at The History Place in downtown Morehead City. People are invited to bring antiques and consult with a panel of experts about

their treasures. A silent auction is also held. This event is very popular.

Carteret County Arts and Crafts Coalition Holiday Show
Location varies(252) 726-8397

This three-week show and sale of original juried artwork by members of the Carteret County Arts and Crafts Coalition opens each year in alternating locations. Local artists combine their work to create the show for Christmas shopping opportunities and, because of the outstanding works, it is truly an event not to be missed.

Community Thanksgiving Feast
Beaufort Historic Park,
100 Block Turner St., Beaufort
(252) 728-5225, (800) 575-7483

On the Sunday before Thanksgiving, a traditional Thanksgiving feast is served at the Beaufort Historic Site. Area restaurants contribute the lunch-feast fixings, and the community gathers together in thanks. Proceeds from this ticketed event benefit preservation efforts of the Beaufort Historical Association. A limited number of tickets are sold at the Beaufort Historic

Sand fences help establish protective dunes by catching blowing sand.

photo: Peter Doran

Site and usually sell out before the day of the event. Dinners are available for takeout or can be enjoyed in the warmth of the heated tent.

Ducks Unlimited Banquet
Crystal Coast Civic Center,
3505 Arendell St., Morehead City
(252) 247-3883, (888) 889-6088

The annual fund-raising benefit for the preservation of waterfowl habitat is eagerly anticipated each year, and it takes place on the first Thursday in November. Ticket price includes membership, a wonderful dinner and an evening at the Crystal Coast Civic Center with others committed to waterfowl-habitat preservation. There are also live and silent auctions.

Jumble Sale
Beaufort Historic Site,
100 Block Turner St., Beaufort
(252) 728-5225, (800) 575-7483

This is a shopper's delight and a little bit of everything can be found here. The Jumble Sale turns the Beaufort Historic Site into a community market with art, handmade crafts, holiday gifts, pre-loved treasures, antiques, clothing, food and much more. Admission is free.

December

Christmas Flotillas
Morehead City and Beaufort waterfronts,
Swansboro
(252) 728-5806

On the Crystal Coast, Santa arrives by boat. Evening parades of decorated and lighted boats bring him in to kick off the Christmas season celebration on the coast. During the first Saturday in December on both the Morehead City and Beaufort waterfronts at sunset, families gather to ring in the season as the brightly decorated boats slowly drift by in the Crystal Coast Christmas flotilla. In Swansboro, the lighted celebration starts a little bit earlier in the year — on the Friday after Thanksgiving. Call the various town halls for the

most up-to-date information including flotilla times: Beaufort, (252) 728-2141; Morehead City, (252) 726-6848; Swansboro, (910) 326-4428.

Coastal Carolina Christmas Walk
Beaufort Historic Site, 100 Block Turner St.,
Beaufort
(252) 728-5225, (800) 575-7483

Beaufort decorates for Christmas in traditional styles and invites the public to take part in the Coastal Carolina Christmas Walk. Beaufort Historic Site, historic bed and breakfast inns and other structures open their doors for this annual holiday tradition. The afternoon event generally takes place from 2 to 4:30 PM and offer tours with entertainment and refreshments. The event is free to the public. There is a fee to ride the double-decker bus or to purchase raffle tickets to benefit preservation of historic structures through the Beaufort Historical Association.

Core Sound Decoy Festival
Harkers Island Elementary School,
Various locations, Harkers Island
(252) 838-8818

The Core Sound Decoy Festival is a coastal tradition. Held the first full weekend in December on Harkers Island, this two-day festival includes competitions in carving and painting decoys, exhibits and sales of old and new decoys, a loon-calling contest, a children's painting contest and other special competitions. There are additional activities for children, educational exhibits and an auction. The festival benefits the Core Sound Decoy Carver's Guild and Harkers Island Elementary School and is the area's largest off-season event.

Train Show
Train Depot, Broad and Pollock Sts.,
Beaufort
(252) 728-4027

Trains, trains and more trains. This exhibit of trains is set up in Beaufort's old Train Depot and is for the young and young at heart. Organized by Beaufort residents John and Virginia Costlow, the exhibit offers a glimpse into the past with antique working model trains.

Waterfowl Weekend
Core Sound Waterfowl Museum,
1785 Island Rd., Harkers Island
(252) 728-1500

The Core Sound Waterfowl Museum opens its doors the first weekend in December and offers a slate full of tradition-al, down-home fun. Educational exhibits, competitions, retriever demonstrations, arts and crafts and food can be found at the museum's Shell Point headquarters, near the very end of Island Road on Harkers Island. There are many other special events — such as the preview party and seafood extravaganza — associated with this weekend, so call the museum for the latest information.

🎣 FISHING, BOATING AND WATERSPORTS

The Crystal Coast is the perfect place for water-related activities. Surfers searching for ocean waves, windsurfers and water-skiers looking for calm sound waters, and anglers hoping for something in between will find exactly what they want along the Carteret County coastline. A wonderful bonus for all water enthusiasts is the generally mild climate, which allows folks to participate in their favorite sports nearly all year. In this chapter we offer a look at fishing, boating, equipment rentals and places where you can access our beautiful beaches. For businesses and beach access areas on Bogue Banks, we have given the mile marker (MM) to help you find them.

Fishing

The Crystal Coast hosts numerous fishing tournaments. The Swansboro Rotary Club hosts its King Mackerel/Blue Water Fishing Tournament in May, and one of the nation's largest king mackerel tournaments, the Atlantic Beach King Mackerel Tournament, is held in October. The Big Rock Blue Marlin Tournament, one of the largest and oldest blue marlin tournaments in the country, is held each June. For details and dates, see our Annual Events chapter.

Federal government studies report that your chances of catching fish in North Carolina waters are unsurpassed along the entire East Coast. Of the 21 recorded catches of Atlantic blue marlin in excess of 1,000 pounds, five have been caught off the North Carolina coast. In fact, a 1,002-pounder is on display in the parking lot behind the Crystal Coast Visitors Center in Morehead City.

Seasoned anglers know a secret: Year-round fishing is a reality here. Saltwater anglers have access to miles and miles of fishing from the ocean, sounds, bays,

rivers and creeks that define the natural wonderland of our coastal county. Inlets offer passages to ocean waters and deep-sea fishing. Ten miles east of Morehead City and Atlantic Beach is Cape Lookout, which offers some of the best fishing on the East Coast.

Weather permitting, local fishing is soul-satisfying in the spring, summer, fall or winter. Consult our Sportfishing Guide in this chapter to find out which months are best for catching particular fish species. Whether you surf fish from the barrier island beaches or charter a private boat or head boat, you're sure to have the time of your life. If you desire a remote fishing experience, try vacationing at the fishing camps out on the Core Banks. You'll find more information about these hideaways in our Accommodations chapter.

A license is required for anyone 16 years or older to harvest fin fish in the sounds, rivers and tributaries, to three miles out into the ocean. If you are fishing from three to 200 miles offshore, this license will be required to bring your catch back to shore. Before you fish, get a fishing license from a local tackle shop or at www.ncwildlife.org. Contact the N.C. Division of Marine Fisheries, (252) 726-7021, for a list of size and catch limits and harvest restrictions.

FISHING SCHOOL

North Carolina Aquarium at Pine Knoll Shores Surf Fishing School
MM 7, N.C. Hwy. 58, Pine Knoll Shores
(252) 247-4003

Most anglers come to the Crystal Coast equipped with fishing skills and knowledge, but a growing number of people want to know more about fishing in area waters or want to improve their chances of hooking the big one. The North Carolina Aquarium at Pine Knoll Shores conducts a surf-fishing workshop every

fall during the second weekend in October. It's taught by experienced fishing guides and is designed for novice surf fishermen, but all anglers are welcome.

FISHING REPORTS

What's biting when and where is as important to avid anglers as the world news is to the rest of us. Information about catches is available at most bait and tackle shops, marinas, piers or charter boat rental offices. To get the inside track on where to fish, read the *Carteret County News-Times*. Every Friday it publishes "On the Line," a column by fishing writer Capt. Jerry Dilsaver.

FISHING GEAR

Now that you've boned up on how to fish, it's time to get your gear. Local tackle shops not only have the fishing stuff you'll need, but they also offer bits of advice about what fish are biting and where. We've listed just a few of the many good shops in the area.

EJW Outdoors
4667 Arendell St., Morehead City
(252) 247-4725

EJW's has been in business for more than 50 years and recently expanded its extensive inventory with a move to its new location. EJW's continues to offer gear for a variety of sports, including hunting, biking, paint ball and archery. Fishing, however, is its primary focus, and you can find an assortment of rods and reels along with all kinds of bait and clothing. The store also services fishing equipment and bikes.

Freeman's Bait & Tackle
Atlantic Beach Cswy., Atlantic Beach
(252) 726-2607

Freeman's is easy to find — just look for the big sign that says "Fish Tales Told Here." This complete saltwater tackle shop sells rods, reels, bait, clothing and other supplies and offers a repair and cleaning service. Freeman's has been in business for more than 42 years and knows the ins and outs of fishing along the Crystal Coast. Feel free to ask questions, but, remember, you may hear a fish tale or two along the way.

K&V Grocery
K&V Plaza, 307 Mangrove Blvd., Emerald Isle
(252) 354-1949

K&V Grocery is a convenience store and gas station as well as a bait and tackle shop. At this year-round shop anglers will find groceries, all kinds of bait, crabbing supplies and tackle boxes. Also for sale are rods and reels and rain gear for those dedicated to fishing no matter what the weather. K&V also can hook you up with a charter boat.

FISHING PIERS

Fishing and crabbing from piers is a favorite pastime along the Crystal Coast. While hurricanes in recent years have wreaked havoc on several favorite spots, there are still two piers open for business. These piers are popular spots during the spring, summer and fall. Take along your kids or anyone who has never fished — it's fun!

Bogue Inlet Fishing Pier
MM19, N.C. Hwy. 58, Emerald Isle
(252) 354-2919

This 1,000-foot, lighted pier is a popular spot for anglers and beachgoers. Parking in the large lot is free weekdays if you are fishing and $5 on Saturday and Sunday; from there access to the ocean beach is a short walk through the lot and down some wooden stairs. People who want to fish may do so from the pier all day at rates starting at $8.50. Bathrooms, a fish-cleaning station, tackle, bait and a snack bar are on the premises.

Oceanana Family Resort Pier
MM 1.5, N.C. Hwy. 58, Atlantic Beach
(252) 726-4111
www.oceanana.com

This lighted pier is part of the Oceanana Family Resort Motel, but you don't have to be a motel patron to fish here — the pier is also open to the public. You will find the lowest cost fishing passes on the Crystal Coast, and motel guests fish for free in the off-season. No saltwater fishing license is necessary; a blanket pass is provided by the pier, which remains one of the last fishing piers on the Crystal Coast. The Oceanana also sells bait, rents rods and reels and has an arcade, a tackle and snack shop, plus plenty of parking. The pier's grill offers delicious breakfast and lunch menus.

Head, Charter and Tour Boats

Fortunate anglers can fish from their own boats, but lacking your own (or a friend's) you can choose from the dozens of commercial rentals and charters. One good way to enjoy a day of inexpensive fishing is on a head boat. These large vessels take as many as 50 people out into the Gulf Stream for a day's worth of deep-sea fishing. The name came about because you pay by the head, or per person, for the trip. You don't hire the entire boat, just a spot on the deck. The crew provides the rods, reels and bait; you just take your personal belongings, such as a cooler of drinks and snacks, seasickness prevention, weather gear and sun protection.

Charter boats are smaller vessels hired by a private party of four to six individuals. A typical half-day excursion will take you bottom fishing offshore where grouper, red snapper, triggerfish and grunts are plentiful. A whole day of deep-sea fishing involves motoring some 40 miles offshore to the Gulf Stream. Chartering a boat to troll the Gulf Stream is what you want if you hope to catch tuna, wahoo, dolphin, marlin and sailfish. Offshore charters are expensive — daily fees can top $1,200 or more for a full party — but if you split the cost between six anglers it's a pretty good deal. If you don't have a complete group, a charter captain may be able to hook you up with another half-party willing to share the expenses of chartering the boat.

Most head and charter boats operate year round, with less frequent trips in the dead of winter. For more information about head and charter boats, we recommend you walk along the Morehead City and Beaufort waterfronts, check out the marinas on the Atlantic Beach Causeway or talk with other anglers.

More than 70 licensed charter boats and head boats operate year-round on the Crystal Coast so we can't list them all

here. Our descriptions are representative samples of the vessels available for hire.

Captain Stacy Fishing Center
Altantic Beach Cswy., Atlantic Beach
(252) 247-7501

Capt. Stacy's fleet consists of more than 14 vessels, including everything from 35-foot sport-fishing boats to an 83-foot head boat. The head boat offers half- and full-day trips along with a 24-hour trip. The fleet's charter boats can be hired for half- and full-day trips year-round.

Carolina Princess
Sixth St., Morehead City
(252) 726-5479, (800) 682-3456
www.carolinaprincess.com

Fishing at its best! Half-day, full-day and 18-hour deep sea bottom fishing, affordable standup sportfishing, and private charters are available for all of your special events (catering available). Capt. Terrell Gould is one of the area's best known captains, and the *Carolina Princess* has been fishing around the Carolinas since the 1950s. They provide the fishing on a modern 95-foot boat that has A/C and heat and is equipped with up-to-date electronics. The *Carolina Princess* provides your rod and reel and bait and keeps your fish iced until you return to the dock. There is a full galley on board where a chef prepares tasty food cooked to order at reasonable prices. Fish cleaning is available on return to the dock. The upper sundeck is great for those that just want to bask in the warm Gulf Breeze and dolphin, whale or bird watch.

Continental Shelf, Inc.
406 Evans St., Morehead City
(252) 726-7454, (800) 775-7450

The *Continental Shelf* has an ideal charter for the fisherman who wants to have something to talk about for years to come. Select from a half-day adventure

---

To get the inside track on where to fish, read the Carteret County *News-Times. Every Friday it publishes "On the Line," a column by fishing writer Capt. Jerry Dilsaver.*

---

that includes pirate tales, dolphin watching and near-shore fishing on the Crystal Coast or try a full-day of fishing for grouper, triggerfish or vermillion snapper. For the more adventuresome, head out overnight for some fast-paced excitement hunting the big fish offshore. All you have to bring is your good luck and a big cooler. The *Continental Shelf* provides rod and reel, bait and tackle, and they will ice the fish for the trip home. A snack bar aboard the boat has sandwiches and snacks to sustain you during a long day of reeling. The *Continental Shelf* is a 100-foot sportsfisher and can easily handle 40 or more anglers. She has three V-8 turbo diesels and enough electronics to find the wiliest fish. You can fish in comfort from

the boat's upper or lower deck or stern as the *Continental Shelf* has a broad beam and plenty of elbow room. The boat docks on the Morehead City waterfront next to Olympus Diving.

Fishead Charters
Swansboro
(910) 459-2257

With 22 years of boating and fishing experience, Captain Chris Sewell of Fishead Charters can make your day a truly enjoyable experience. Offering inshore and near-shore fishing charters, Chris can customize your half-day (four hour) or full-day (six hour) trip to be exactly what you want. Chris supplies rods and reels, tackle, ice and bait. He will clean the fish

Sailing is king along the coast, especially in Beaufort, New Bern and Oriental.

photo: Tom Sapp

and can offer quite a few recipes on how to cook them. If you want to go clamming, crabbing, cast netting or are interested in a brief history of Swansboro, Emerald Isle or Cape Carteret, Chris has got you covered. You will not need a fishing license — he has a blanket license for his boat, a 21-foot Bay boat.. All you need to bring are sodas, water, snacks and sunscreen. Chris keeps his charters clean and non-smoking and he operates in a Christian environment. Year round, depending on the weather and the season, you can catch flounder, speckled trout, redfish, sheepshead, bluefish, Spanish mackerel, black drum, spot and croaker. If the fish aren't biting, Fishead Charters is also available for eco-tours. Explore the local islands or hunt for fossilized shark's teeth. Chris likes to keep his tours to two passengers, but if you need more room, he can help you find what you need. He is U.S. Coast Guard certified and fully insured.

Mystery Boat Tours
600 Front St., Beaufort
(252) 728-2527
www.mysteryboattours.com

Enjoy inland bay fishing aboard the *Mystery*. The trip includes your rod, reel, bait, tackle and ice, and no individual fishing license is necessary as the *Mystery* maintains a license for the boat. Mates onboard help bait hooks and remove fish so it couldn't be easier to try your hand at catching flounder, blues, croaker and sharks. The *Mystery* will have you to your first fishing spot within 15 minutes of leaving the dock. There is also an on-board snack bar with light snacks, cold drinks and hot coffee. All cruises require minimum passengers and are subject to cancellation.

Nancy Lee Fishing Center
N.C. Hwy. 24 E, Swansboro
(252) 354-3474

Three miles from Emerald Isle, Nancy Lee Fishing Center offers five-hour head-boat fishing charters for adults and children as well as five-, eight- and 11-hour private charters that consist of bottom fishing and trolling. All of Capt. Lee Manning's vessels are Coast Guard inspected and equipped with the latest safety and electronics gear. The boat has an on-board fishing license so no individual licenses are needed. Private dolphin-watch cruises are also available.

Boating

MOTOR AND SAILBOAT RENTALS AND SAILING INSTRUCTION

There's nothing finer on a bright, breezy, sunny day than taking to the water in a boat, particularly a sailboat. You'll often hear sailing enthusiasts quote *The Wind in the Willows*: "There is nothing — absolutely NOTHING — half so much worth doing as simply messing about in boats." Kids ages 8 and older who want to learn how to sail should check out the North Carolina Maritime Museum's summertime Junior Sailing Program, (252) 728-7317.

Watersports Rentals
MM 12, N.C. Hwy. 58,
1960 Salter Path Rd., Indian Beach
(252) 247-7303
www.h2osportrentals.com

Watersports Rentals, with locations at MM 11, Salter Path, (252) 240-4FUN, and at MM 12, Indian Beach, (252) 247-7303, offers sailboats for rent as well as sailing instruction.

KAYAKING

With hundreds of miles of inland and coastal waterways, kayaking along the Crystal Coast gains in popularity yearly. As interest in kayaking grows, so do the number of businesses offering rentals and tours. Unlike the wild, crashing rides through roiling river waters, kayaking along the coast is a peaceful, safe way to explore the naturally shallow waters of our abundant inlets, creeks and estuaries, which are home to an incredibly rich diversity of wildlife.

Bogue Banks Beach Gear
& Linens Rentals
Bell Cove Village,
9106-C Coast Guard Rd., Emerald Isle
(252) 354-4404
www.boguebanksbeachgear.com

Bogue Banks Beach Gear is the place to find fun. From beach-ball–colored umbrellas to bikes for cruising around

the island and kayaks for paddling the waterways, their huge inventory and great selection of rental gear is like no other on the Crystal Coast. Their watersports rentals, including kayaks and surf gear, come with free delivery. Reservations can be made on-line. The shop is open seven days a week.

Core Sound Kayaks and Touring Co.
Harkers Island Rd.,
3.7 mi. off U.S. Hwy. 70, Harkers Island
(252) 728-2330

Kayakers now have easy access to the beautiful waters Down East, thanks to Core Sound Kayaks and Touring Company and Cape Lookout Outfitters. Here you can rent a kayak from Core Sound native Capt. Dennis Chadwick and his wife, Robin, plus find some basic instruction and gain some Insider knowledge on the most picturesque areas for a day of paddling. Go at it alone or let the Chadwicks give you a tour of local destinations such as Cape Lookout Lighthouse. Kayaks are rented by the half-day and full day. Drinks and snacks are available on-site. Core Sound Kayaks is an authorized dealer of Wilderness Systems Kayaks. Capt. Chadwick also offers birding and sight-seeing tours around Harkers Island, Cape Lookout, Shackleford Banks and the Rachel Carson estuary for groups up to six aboard his Harkers Island–built, flared-bow wooden skiff.

DolphinMoonKayak
(252) 808-7485

DolphinMoonKayak specializes in individual and small-group touring and instruction to assist in your exploration of the pristine Crystal Coast region. This company is the one to contact to learn about the history, environment and geology of the coast as you glide past the shorebirds, horses, dolphins and sea turtles that inhabit this barrier island region. Local touring favorites include trips to the Rachel Carson Reserve, Cape Lookout, the Beaufort waterfront, Shackleford Banks, Core Banks and Hammock's Beach. Half-day, full-day and extended trips are available, and custom trips can be designed just for you.

Watersports Rentals
MM 12, N.C. Hwy. 58,
1960 Salter Path Rd., Indian Beach
(252) 247-7303
www.h2osportrentals.com

Watersports Rentals offers Waverunner rentals by the half-hour or hourly and kayak rentals by the hour, day or week. Experienced staff members will provide you with lessons and guidance. If you are looking for family adventure consider embarking on a Banana Boat Ride that accommodates up to eight people. It's fun for ages 4 and older.

Watersports Rentals friendly staff invites landlubbers to enjoy their 180-foot pier and two-level observation deck. Also, don't forget to check out the Dolphin Deck Tiki Bar for the best sunsets on the Crystal Coast. Sit, relax and have a cold beer or soft drink with your family and friends.The public is always welcome. It's located at Mile Marker 12 on the border of Emerald Isle and Indian Beach. Call for further information and reservations.

BOAT RAMPS

Catering to water lovers is something the Crystal Coast does best, and you'll find a variety of boat ramps in Carteret County to get you on your way. Whether you've rented a boat or have your own, you'll need to know where you can launch it. Private ramps are in every part of the Crystal Coast, and most marinas and campgrounds have boat ramps. For a list of the free municipal- or county-maintained ramps, see our Crystal Coast Marinas chapter or call the marina closest to you. Chances are you won't have to drive far to put your boat in the water.

Watersports

PERSONAL WATERCRAFT RENTAL

The popularity of one-person (or sometimes two- or three-person) watercraft is growing quickly, and shops renting Jet-Skis and Waverunners are keeping up with that popularity. Some local townships have placed regulations on the use of such watercraft, so be sure to ask your rental or service agent about current rules before hitting the water for a day of fun.

Watersports Rentals
MM 12, N.C. Hwy. 58, Indian Beach
(252) 247-7303
www.h2osportrentals.com

Water Sports Rentals offers Waverunner rentals by the half-hour or hourly, and kayak rentals by the hour, day or week. Experienced staff members will provide you with lessons and guidance. Looking for family adventure? Consider embarking on a Banana Boat Ride, fun for ages 4 and older, that accommodates up to eight people. Water Sports Rentals' friendly staff invites landlubbers to enjoy their 180-foot pier and two-level observation deck. Don't forget to check out the Dolphin Deck Tiki

Bar for the best sunsets on the Crystal Coast. Sit and relax and have a cold beer or soft drink with your family and friends. The public is always welcome. Call for further information and reservations.

Watersports Outfitters and Gifts
MM 11, N.C. Hwy. 58 and Headen Ln., Salter Path, (252) 247-4386
www.h2osportrentals.com

Watersports Outfitters offers Banana Boat Rides and rentals of Waverunners, kayaks, surfboards, scooters, bicycles and beach equipment. The store has unique gifts for all of your friends and family members. They carry beach jewelry, fun T-shirts, metal wall art, souvenirs, beach toys, pirate gifts and much more. Check out their front porch deck where there is always a sale going on. The shop is located between the Crab Shack Restaurant and Willis Seafood Market in the heart of Salter Path. Be sure to stop by and say hello.

SCUBA DIVING AND SNORKELING

The Crystal Coast has been named one of the ten best diving locales in North America by several popular dive magazines. And with the number of shipwrecks located off Carteret County's coastline, wreck diving is growing in popularity. Local businesses are quick to keep up with demand. Diving is an all-year activity thanks to the Gulf Stream's warm waters, which are about 40 miles offshore. In summer, water temperatures average in the 80s, with visibility of 75 feet to as much as 150 feet. The best dive months are June through September, when the most tropical fish are present. Since 1994, readers of *Scuba Diving* magazine have consistently ranked North Carolina as one of the Best Diving Destinations in North America. It's also been recognized by Scuba Diving readers as the top spot for Wreck Diving and Big Animal Life Diving.

Discovery Diving Company
414 Orange St., Beaufort
(252) 728-2265

When you're ready to learn, Discovery can teach you to scuba dive or snorkel. On the water on Orange Street, the company offers Professional Association of Diving Instructors (PADI) Open Water Diver training ranging all the way to instructor courses. Discovery has an in-house repair shop and rents and sells just about everything you need for diving: tanks, regulators, masks, fins, snorkels, wet suits and digital cameras suitable for underwater photography. The shop is a Nitrox facility. With three charter boats, the company arranges and conducts dive trips to fascinating sites: submerged submarines, ocean liners, tankers, freighters and armed trawlers. If you're not part of a group, Discovery will set you up with other interested divers.

Olympus Dive Center
713 Shepard St., Morehead City
(252) 726-9432

In business since 1976, Olympus is operated by the Purifoy family. With two custom dive boats, it is a full-service shop offering full- and half-day dive charters, equipment rental and instruction. The shop is also a Nitrox facility. Beginners can take National Association of Underwater Instructors (NAUI) and Professional Association of Diving Instructors (PADI) entry-level courses. For the advanced diver, the center offers specialty certifications such as night diving and wreck diving. Equipment rentals and sales, charters and instruction are available for everyone from the novice to the serious diver. Olympus also has some interesting dive artifacts on display, and it's worth a trip to check these out.

WINDSURFING

To many, windsurfing is the thrill of thrills, and wave sailors are discovering that the Crystal Coast is a nearly perfect place for the watersport. The mild temperatures, miles of open water and windy conditions windsurfers need are right here on the Crystal Coast. Insiders know the shallow, protected waters of Bogue Sound are ideal for the neophyte windsurfer, while the more exposed areas, such as Beaufort, Bogue, Shackleford and Drum inlets, offer exciting challenges for experienced sailors. Comfortable water temperatures and steady winds year round add to the attraction of windsurfing in our area.

SKIING

We're talking water-skiing here. Most surf shops carry water skis and will provide you with information on where to ski. Favorite water-skiing spots are Bogue Sound west of the Atlantic Beach high-rise bridge, the waters of Back Sound between Beaufort and Shackleford, and Core Creek north of Beaufort. These areas are typically free from no-wake zones and are wide enough to allow for skier safety.

SURFING

Surfing is and always has been very popular along the North Carolina coast. There are plenty of places to catch the swell on the Crystal Coast. Any of our surf shops can provide information about wave conditions and surf contests, and local surfers along the Atlantic Beach oceanfront are great sources of information. Most local outfits also rent surfboards and body boards. Listed below are some of the surf shops that can fulfill your needs.

Action Surf Shop
5116 U.S. Hwy. 70 W, Morehead City
(252) 240-1818

Action Surf Shop has whatever you need from wetsuits to surfer clothing, hats, shoes and swimsuits. Need a custom board? This is the place. Check out Action's up -to -the-hour surf report on all the good surfing locations in Carteret County.

Bert's Surf Shop
MM 2, N.C. Hwy. 58, Atlantic Beach
(252) 726-1730
300 Islander Dr.,
across from Bogue Inlet Pier, Emerald Isle
(252) 354-2441
MM 19, N.C. Hwy. 58, Emerald Isle
(252) 354-6282

If you came into the surfing/body boarding/skateboarding world naked, Bert's Surf Shop would be the place to go. They have the locations — two shops in Emerald Isle, one in Kinston (just in case

See this entire guide plus additional content online at insiderinfo.us

you're driving to the beach and think of something you need) and places up and down the coast (Atlantic Beach, Carolina Beach, Surf City, Wilmington and Myrtle Beach). Outfit yourself from head to toe — clothing, hats, shoes, jackets, sweats, surfboards, surfboard wax, leashes, skateboards and body boards, swimsuits, wetsuits and accessories (watches, jewelry, luggage, canholders). If you can't find the perfect gift, Bert's has gift cards.

Hot Wax Surf Shop
200 Mallard Dr., Emerald Isle
(252) 354-6466

Hot Wax Surf Shop offers on-line and in-store kayaks, surfboards, Action Sports accessories and other watersports equipment. Hot Wax T-shirts and sweats are the highest quality and are their best sellers. They also carry gift items and active wear. Ask about their Hot Wax Surf Camps to learn the basics of surfing, marine life and water safety. Daily, weekly or private lessons are available. The shop also carries rental equipment.

Marsh's Surf Shop
Atlantic Beach Cswy., Atlantic Beach
(252) 726-9046

This shop carries a bit of everything, from quality dresses to shorts and T-shirts to jackets and sweats for men, women and children. There are plenty of beach items too — sunglasses, surfboards, swimsuits and all types of accessories. Marsh's carries a wonderful selection of active-wear sandals. The store is open seven days a week

SWIMMING

You can swim just about anywhere along the Crystal Coast, with the exception of a few posted areas. But even the most skilled pool swimmer may have difficulty dealing with ocean waves and undertows, so be careful and never swim alone. Rip currents are very common along the North Carolina shoreline. If you find yourself being pulled by frightening currents, the most important thing to do is to stay calm. Never swim against the currents. If you are caught in a rip current, relax and let it carry you toward the sea. Eventually it will dissipate. Swim parallel to the shore

to get out of the rip current, and then swim diagonally toward the shore instead of straight in. Be aware that only a handful of beaches employ lifeguards. Areas along Bogue Banks, such as the Atlantic Beach Circle area and Fort Macon State Park, post lifeguards during the summer season. Swimming is not allowed around Fort Macon's rock jetties or on the inlet side. There are no public pools on the Crystal Coast, only those at hotels, condominiums, private communities and fitness centers. (Read our chapter on Sports, Fitness and Parks to learn more about fitness center swimming pools.)

Beach Access

If you want to swim, walk or run, surf fish, collect shells or sunbathe, how do you get onto our marvelous Crystal Coast beaches? As is true in many coastal areas, getting onto the beach can be confusing. It can be difficult to tell where the private property ends and public access begins. Parking can also be difficult at times.

Towns along Bogue Banks, including Indian Beach, Pine Knoll Shores and Emerald Isle, are currently working on making the beach more accessible to visitors and locals. Until then, Insiders know where to go. In this section we list many of the spots that will take you directly to the ocean or sound. We also tell you which places have parking and bathroom facilities and are disabled accessible. Public Beach Access areas are marked with signs that feature blue letters and a sea gull flying in an orange circle. These signs are not large, so keep your eyes open for them.

For the Bogue Banks areas we cite the mile marker (MM) and we begin with one of the area's most popular public beach playgrounds, the access at The Circle. Then we work from east to west (from Fort Macon to Emerald Isle). Some access areas have gates that are opened at first light and closed at dusk; others allow driving on the beach with certain restrictions.

ATLANTIC BEACH

When you crest the Atlantic Beach bridge you know you've reached the beach at last. Beautiful Bogue Sound spreads out before you, busy with boats and the beckoning spray of their wakes. The all-embracing horizon, whether sun- or cloud-filled, promises ocean waves and sandy beaches. As you descend the bridge, you can detect the colorful beach structures that characterize The Circle. At the intersection of Atlantic Beach Causeway and N.C. 58, The Circle is directly in front of you. Three big flags — American, State of North Carolina and Atlantic Beach — wave in greeting.

Traffic signs on The Circle advise vehicles to bear right on West Drive. A half-block down this street is the West **Atlantic Boulevard Regional Access**. There are bike racks, bathrooms, a bathhouse with outdoor showers, drinking fountains, faucets for cleaning fish and a covered gazebo should you wish to stay out of the sun. The beach is easily reached by a wooden ramp, suitable for disabled persons. Vehicular access to the ocean is just off The Circle, at the south end of Raleigh Avenue. Atlantic Beach closes the beach to vehicles between Good Friday and Labor Day.

Fort Macon State Park, at the eastern tip of Bogue Banks, offers miles of beaches on which to roam, swim and sunbathe. The park has two popular access areas. The one at the west end, before you pass by the park office, is a Regional Public Beach Access area (look for the inconspicuous Bath House sign on the right side of N.C. 58 as you approach the fort). These popular family beaches are disabled accessible and feature a large bathhouse, outdoor showers, a seasonal refreshment stand, picnic shelters, outdoor grills and ample parking. Here you can indulge in all the beach activities you wish. The other Fort Macon beach access is a sandy track leading from the southwestern corner of the parking lot that serves visitors to the fort. This pathway takes you over the dunes to a wide stretch of beach facing Bogue Inlet. Visitors cannot swim, wade or surf at this access, but walking, observing shore and sea life and basking in the sunshine are permitted. The only restroom is at the entrance to the fort. (For more information about Fort Macon State Park, see the Crystal Coast Attractions chapter.)

The Crystal Coast is known for sparkling waters and miles of beaches.

photo: Peter Doran

The Les and Sally Moore Public Beach Access at MM 1 offers toilet facilities, outdoor showers, a covered gazebo and a boardwalk over the dunes to the beach. It is equipped for the disabled and offers parking for about 50 cars. Once on the beach, the young and not-so-young will find swings at the foot of the primary dunes. Farther west on Salter Path Road near MM 4, the Sheraton Atlantic Beach Oceanfront Hotel maintains a parking lot. The Sheraton charges a fee for all-day parking during the season; otherwise, this public access is available to pedestrians only. Look for the access sign on the east side of the lot.

PINE KNOLL SHORES

Pine Knoll Shores has worked diligently over the past few years to provide more public beach access points throughout the town. One of the town's largest public access points is located at Memorial Park, MM 6, with 40 parking spaces, an overlook deck and a picnic table; another is adjacent to the Iron Steamer, MM 7, featuring a restroom and parking spaces for about 60 cars. Parking only is available at these access points: 25 spaces along the western boundary of the Ramada Inn near MM 8, and 20 slots underneath the water tower at the Indian Beach/Pine Knoll Shores town boundary, right past MM 9.

SALTER PATH

Carteret County maintains the Salter Path Regional Public Beach Access, MM 10 off Salter Path Road. It's a 22-acre park with paved parking for 75 cars plus a boardwalk over the dunes to the ocean, a picnic area, bathrooms and outdoor showers. It is equipped for disabled persons. Needless to say, this is a very popular spot and is usually full from dawn to dusk.

INDIAN BEACH

Trinity Center parking (20 spaces) is located underneath the water tower at the Indian Beach/Pine Knoll Shores town boundary, MM 9.5. Sea Isle Plantation West parking (10 spaces) is located in wooded area just east of MM 10. Salter Path Regional Access includes 75 parking spaces, outside showers, picnic tables and bathrooms located within the Roosevelt State Park area. Indian Beach Access includes

36 parking spaces and a four-wheel-drive access ramp. Ocean Club parking (10 spaces) and access are located at the border of the Salter Path Campground and the Ocean Club Townhouses, MM 11.5. Baptist Church Gazebo is an oceanfront facility with 10 parking spaces located at MM 12.

EMERALD ISLE

Emerald Isle features quite a few public beach access points, many of them handicapped-accessible. Be aware that parking at many of the access points may be limited or non-existent. We've listed a few of the largest ones that offer public parking.

Third Street Ocean Access, located just west of the Indian Beach line near MM 12, offers parking for 12 cars, an overlook picnic area and a ramp that goes over the dunes to the beach. The Eastern Ocean Regional Access is located at 2700 Emerald Drive between Pier Point and Ocean Reef Condominiums. The parking lot can accommodate 250 cars, and daytrippers will appreciate the picnic gazebo, outdoor showers, bathrooms and drink machines. The Western Ocean Regional Access is located just over the B. Cameron Langston Bridge near the Islander Motor Inn at 299 Islander Drive. This access area features sand volleyball courts, restrooms, outdoor showers and parking for 200 cars.

Emerald Isle Parks and Recreation loans out four beach wheelchairs for disabled persons. The wheelchairs have great big tires for negotiating the sandy beaches, and they break down to fit into a car trunk. You can borrow one for a day for free; pick them up at the Emerald Isle Fire Department on N.C. 58. Pick up

---

In Crystal Coast waters, the best fish to catch in the surf are striped bass, bluefish, summer flounder (also known as fluke), weakfish, speckled trout, red drum, kingfish, croaker, spot, pompano and Spanish mackerel. (Source: Surf Fishing–Catching Fish from the Beach, *by Joe Malat.)*

after 8 AM and return by 8 PM. A driver's license is required to borrow a wheelchair. Handicapped-accessible beach access points include Randy's Way Access at 9519 Ocean Drive and Wyndtree Access at 10535 Wyndtree Drive; both feature a single handicapped parking space.

BEAUFORT

The Newport River Park is on the east side of the Beaufort-Morehead City high-rise bridge, off the causeway on U.S. 70. It has a pier, sandy beach, picnic area, bathhouse and launching ramp sufficient for small sailboats. This is a popular spot for fishing. The park entrance is directly across from Radio Island. Radio Island, off the causeway on U.S. 70, is the largest island between the Beaufort-Morehead

City high-rise bridge and the drawbridge into Beaufort. It is home to a variety of businesses — marinas, boat builders, a fuel terminal and a condominium complex. The beach access is a favorite spot for locals because it fronts Beaufort Channel and affords an impressive view of Beaufort and the surrounding islands. Swimmers are advised to stay close to shore when swimming due to dangerous currents in the deeper water. Portable toilets are provided, grills and picnic tables are available, and there's plenty of parking.

HARKERS ISLAND

Located on the southeast side of the Harkers Island drawbridge, a beach access point offers 20 parking spaces but no facilities.

MARINAS ⚓

North Carolina has the largest area of inland waters on the East Coast. The Outer Banks enclose several large inland sounds: Currituck, Albemarle, Pamlico, Core and Bogue, which are laced together north to south by 265 miles of the Intracoastal Waterway (ICW). This liquid highway of inland waters makes the numerous coastal resorts and historical points of interest easily accessible by boat.

Of Carteret County's total 1,063 square miles, 531 miles are water. The bountiful brine giving definition to the Crystal Coast challenges the greater portion of the populace and most annual visitors to see the area by water. The weather lures pleasure boaters and sailors almost year round. Even in the coldest months, you'll find a few days that are too pretty to stay ashore.

Because many boaters enjoy the shallow, protected waters along the Crystal Coast, numerous marinas are available to serve the fleet of water traffic. There are more than 35 marinas, most on or just off the ICW. And, via the ICW, boaters can sojourn to nearby Oriental (see our chapter on Oriental) and New Bern, where a number of marinas serve power and sailing vessels. See the Marinas section of our New Bern On the Water chapter for those marina listings.

Crystal Coast marinas have varying water depths, services, amenities, transient

A boat rests in the harbor.

photo: Peter Doran

accommodations and proximity to sights and services. Many condominium developments and campgrounds provide private docks for their owners and renters.

In this chapter we list many of the Crystal Coast's marinas. Please call to inquire whether a marina offers the specific services you'll need. For you boaters who don't leave home without your craft trailing behind, we've also given the locations of public launch ramps. There is no launch fee at these locations. At most of the marinas we've listed, launch ramps are available. In general, marinas charge a small fee for use and to leave your vehicle and trailer while your boat is in the water.

Marinas

BOGUE BANKS

Anchorage Marina
517 E. Fort Macon Rd., Atlantic Beach
(252) 726-4423

Anchorage Marina is convenient for anglers and pleasure boaters. It has 130 slips, rented on an annual basis, for boats up to 60 feet. It also has a launch ramp and gas and diesel fuel. Anchorage Marina is located within walking distance of motels and restaurants.

Captain Stacy Fishing Center
Atlantic Beach Cswy., Atlantic Beach
(252) 247-9551

Known for its charter boats and deep-sea fishing trips led by highly experienced and respected captains, Capt. Stacy Fishing Center also has 15 permanent slips with deep-water access. Diesel fuel and electrical services are available, and a gift, tackle and bait shop are located on-site. For more information about Capt. Stacy Fishing Center, see our Fishing, Boating, Watersports & Beach Access chapter.

Island Harbor Marina
510 W. Marina Dr., Emerald Isle
(252) 354-3106

With channel access off the ICW, Island Harbor Marina has wet slips for boats up to 25 feet, three launch ramps, a ship's store, gas and diesel fuel, fenced storage for boats on trailers and boat rentals.

Sea Water Marina
400 Atlantic Beach Cswy., Atlantic Beach
(252) 726-1637

A favorite of sport-fishing boats, Sea Water Marina on the Atlantic Beach Causeway has 25 wet slips, on-site gas and diesel fuel stations, and a complete ship's store.

Triple S Marina Village
1511 E. Fort Macon Rd., Atlantic Beach
(252) 247-4833

Near Fort Macon State Park, Triple S Marina Village has 65 slips and a launch ramp often used by weekend anglers. Restaurants are nearby.

BEAUFORT

Boaters who arrive in Beaufort via the ICW may drop anchor in Taylor's Creek in the designated anchorage on the south side of the channel. A number of moorings are privately owned, and boaters are asked to respect waterway courtesies of space and anchorage. There is no charge for anchoring and no limit for length of stay. A public dinghy dock and restrooms are available. The dock master at the Dock House is available to answer questions. Town Creek on the north side of Beaufort is also a designated anchorage with a dinghy landing.

Airport Marina
294 W. Beaufort Rd., Beaufort
(252) 728-2010

At the north end of Turner Street on South Creek, Airport Marina has 17 wet slips, a launch ramp and restrooms. Boaters also can purchase snacks, cold sodas and beer, ice and fishing tackle.

Beaufort Docks
500 Front St., Beaufort
(252) 728-4129

The marina most frequently visited by transient boaters visiting the Crystal Coast has gas and diesel fueling services. Behind Finz's Restaurant in downtown Beaufort, the marina also offers snacks and ice.

Beaufort Town Dock
330 Front St., Beaufort
(252) 728-2503

Beaufort Town Docks has 100 slips and gas and diesel fueling. It accommodates boats up to 250 feet. Right on the Board-walk in downtown Beaufort, the marina is convenient to restaurants and lodging, and it offers a courtesy car to use for supply runs.

Radio Island Marina
156 Radio Island Rd., Beaufort
(252) 726-3773

Radio Island Marina, located on the Morehead City-Beaufort Causeway, has 38 dry stack rentals and eight wet slips, lift-out dry storage and gasoline. It offers repairs and sells boats and fishing supplies.

Sea Gate Marina
729 Sea Gate Dr., Beaufort
(252) 728-4126

Off N.C. Highway 101, 1 mile north of Core Creek Bridge on the ICW, Sea Gate is a development with a 72-slip marina used for both residents and non-residents. Gas and diesel fuels and a launch ramp are also available, as are 24-hour laundry facilities, a boaters' lounge, a small ship's store and showers.

Town Creek Marina and Yacht Sales
232 W. Beaufort Rd., Beaufort
(252) 728-6111

Just north of the Beaufort drawbridge, Town Creek offers many services, including a complete boat yard with a 50-ton lift, 88 wet slips with floating docks, transient dockage for boats up to 140 feet, dry storage, and gas and diesel fuels.

MOREHEAD CITY

70 West Marina
4401 Arendell St., Morehead City
(252) 726-5171

Visible as you drive through Morehead City, this marina on Pelletier Creek is centrally located with easy access to a variety of shops and restaurants. 70 West Marina offers dry storage for 350 boats and is a dealer for the sale and repair of Mercury, Volvo and Yamaha outboards.

Coral Bay Marina
4531 Arendell St., Morehead City
(252) 247-4231

On Pelletier Creek, Coral Bay Marina offers 20 slips for boats up to 50 feet and dry-storage services for boats of 36 feet

and less. Slips are rented by the month. Gasoline, diesel fuel and engine repair services are available.

Harbor Master
4408 Central Dr., Morehead City
(252) 726-2541

On Pelletier Creek, Harbor Master has 30 slips rented by the year. It offers haul-out and dry storage in a working boat yard, which includes a propeller shop. Harbor Master also offers hurricane haul-out services.

Morehead City Yacht Basin
208 Arendell St., Morehead City
(252) 726-6862

Famous in Carteret County as the spot where Ernest Hemingway once docked his boat, the Yacht Basin, as it's known around town, is just off Calico Creek north of the Morehead City high-rise bridge. Eighty-seven slips are available for monthly and transient dockage for boats up to 150 feet. Gas and diesel fuels are on site. Internet service is available for customers, as are laundry facilities, showers, a pump-out station, a ship's store and an observation deck. Sea Tow is located on the premises.

Morehead Gulf Docks
608 Evans St., Morehead City
(252) 726-5461

This dock offers gas and diesel fueling, 30/50-amp electric service, and four spaces accommodating boats up to 120 feet. It is within walking distance of a ship's store, a gift shop and several restaurants.

Portside Marina
209 Arendell St., Morehead City
(252) 726-7678

Dry stack and out-of-water storage are available at Portside Marina, located between the North Carolina State Port and the Morehead City waterfront. Gasoline, diesel, 15 slips and repair services are offered. Boaters will also find showers, laundry service and 30/50 amp power.

WESTERN CARTERET AND SWANSBORO

Almost every home or business on the White Oak River or Bogue Sound has a dock, boat ramp or both. But the commercial docks, particularly the ones big

enough and with channels dredged deep enough to accommodate a very large motor or sailing yacht, are few.

Casper's Marina
301 S. Water St., Swansboro
(910) 326-4462

Conveniently located on the Intracoastal Waterway in Swansboro, Casper's has dry storage of boats up to 150 feet, and 180 feet of open dock for transient boaters. Haul-out repairs, gas and diesel fuel also are available.

Dudley's Marina, Inc.
N.C. Hwy. 24 E, Cedar Point
(252) 393-2204

North of Swansboro off the ICW, Dudley's is a working boat yard and marina with 25 slips, overnight dockage at the fuel dock, repair services, and gas and diesel fuels. It services Mercruiser, Mercury and Volvo Penta marine engines.

DOWN EAST

Calico Jack's Inn & Marina
1698 Island Rd., Harkers Island
(252) 728-3575

Calico Jack's offers 50 slips by the month or night. Slips accommodate boats up to 30 feet long. Calico Jack's also offers a launch ramp, a supply store and a motel.

Harkers Island Fishing Center
1002 Island Rd., Harkers Island
(252) 728-3907

A full-service marina with 70 slips for boats of 30 feet or less, Harkers Island Fishing Center has a launch ramp, repair services, a lift for dry storage, a supply store, and gas and diesel fuel service. Efficiency motel rooms, rental cottages and ferry service to Cape Lookout also are available.

Morris Marina Kabin Kamps and Ferry Service, Inc.
1000 Morris Marina Rd., Atlantic
(252) 225-4261

You can launch your boat and store it in or out of the water at Morris Marina in

Atlantic. The marina has a grill and fishing supply store on site and ferry service to its fish camps on Core Banks.

Boat Sales and Service

For boat and motor sales and service, one of these businesses should be able to help. In the previous discussion of marinas, we've mentioned the authorized dealers and repair services if they are on site at the marina. Other dealers of boats and motors are listed below.

Jones Brothers Marine
5437 U.S. Hwy. 70, Morehead City
(252) 726-8404

This Yamaha dealership is also headquarters for the Jones Brothers Bateau, Cape Fisherman, Southport and Scout Boats. They also repair Yamaha engines.

Morehead Marine, Inc.
4971 Arendell St., Morehead City
(252) 247-6667

This is an authorized sales and service dealer for Yamaha outboards as well as Parker and Grady White boats.

Public Boat Ramps

The Crystal Coast has many boat ramps, large and small, public and private. Below is a short list of just a few of the state-maintained public ramps. Because most ramps don't have names, we've listed them alphabetically according to location. You won't have to pay a fee to launch your boat at any of these ramps.

BEAUFORT

Curtis A. Perry Park is a public ramp with four launching areas into Taylor's Creek. The park is at the east end of Front Street near the tennis courts. Two ramps and docks, as well as a fishing pier and comfort station, are offered at the Town Creek Water Access at Turner Street and West Beaufort Road. These are maintained by Carteret County Parks and Recreation Department. The Grayden Paul Jaycee

See this entire guide plus additional content online at insiderinfo.us

Town Park, on Front Street at the south end of Pollock Street, provides a short, wide pier. Boats may be launched from a soft-sand area and docked on the west side of the pier. Diagonal parking is available on Front Street.

DOWN EAST

The Salters Creek Wildlife Ramp is available on the east side of the high-rise bridge on U.S. Highway 70 just before you get to the Down East community of Sea Level. Access to the Oyster Creek Wildlife Ramp at the Oyster Creek Bridge just northeast of Davis is also available from U.S. 70.

HARKERS ISLAND

At the Cape Lookout National Seashore Picnic grounds, there is a small sand beach adequate for launching canoes and kayaks. Let the park rangers in the Visitors Center know that you're going out on a trip. A public launch ramp is located on the Straits at the north side of the Harkers Island bridge. Another small launch site with a parking area is at the western end of Harkers Island at Fisherman's Inn fish camp. Fees are charged for overnight parking.

CEDAR ISLAND

A ramp is beyond the Cedar Island National Wildlife Refuge office on Lola Road at the south end of the island. The refuge also maintains a ramp on the west side of (and almost below) the high-rise bridge, on N.C. 12, just west of the island.

CEDAR POINT

A ramp maintained by the N.C. Wildlife Commission is on the south side of N.C.

Highway 24 between Cape Carteret and Swansboro. The Cedar Island National Wildlife Refuge maintains a boat ramp on the west side of the high-rise bridge (on N.C. 12) that crosses Thorofare Bay.

MOREHEAD CITY

Municipal Park, behind the Crystal Coast Visitor Center at 3409 Arendell Street (U.S. 70), has several launching areas and lots of parking. While swimming is not allowed, a shady picnic area with grills and tables offers a nice resting spot to enjoy a view of the sound. The park is just east of Carteret Community College.

A boat ramp at 10th and Shepard streets in Morehead City serves as the nearest launch location to Sugarloaf Island, the undeveloped island across from the city waterfront. The launch ramp accommodates boats 16 feet or less, and parking is available. Sugarloaf Island is a nice place to get away from it all while being close to everything.

Boating Emergency Numbers

Coast Guard Information, (252) 257-4598

Search/Rescue Emergencies, (252) 247-4544, (252) 247-4545

Swansboro Lifeboat Station
Emerald Isle
(252) 354-2719

Use the number above in an emergency. To contact the Lifeboat Station in a non-emergency, dial (252) 354-2462.

SPORTS, FITNESS AND PARKS

There never seems to be enough time to experience all that the coast has to offer, especially when it comes to being out in the sand, the sea and the salt air. North Carolina's Crystal Coast has plenty to offer in the way of sports — in and out of the water. The mild weather along North Carolina's coast makes people want to spend as much time as possible outdoors. Whether it's walking on the beach, running, basketball, beach volleyball, boating, bicycling, wind-surfing or kayaking, the wonderful coastal scenery makes any activity more fun. If the weather just won't cooperate or you need some equipment, you can visit one of the local fitness centers. In this chapter, we offer a brief introduction to some of the area's most popular sports and give you a contact for how to participate. At this chapter's end, we list some of the county and city parks on the Crystal Coast. Information about state and national parks is given in our Attractions chapter. Watersports, such as wind-surfing, kayaking and sailing, are described in our Fishing, Boating and Watersports chapter.

Sports

Sports and other avenues of recreation abound in the Crystal Coast area. With a good deal of sports enthusiasts who participate in their favorite events casually or as part of an organized team, there are a lot of options and resources that can be found locally. Here is our list of some popular sports, along with helpful informa-

> **i** *The beaches and most of the park areas are canine-friendly. Just remember that there are leash laws and that owners are expected to clean up after their pets.*

tion on how to contact someone in the know. If you can't find what you're looking for, ask around and someone will point you in the right direction.

BASEBALL AND LITTLE LEAGUE

Youth and adult teams are sponsored by the Carteret County Parks and Recreation Department, (252) 808-3301. Watching the Kinston Indians, a minor-league professional baseball team, is always exciting. Games are played on weeknights and weekends during the season in the newly renovated, historic Grainger Stadium — a ballpark with all the extras. Special promotions are offered daily, so be sure to ask for details. Kinston is less than a two-hour drive from Morehead City. For ticket information and a game schedule, call (252) 527-9111 or (800) 334-5467.

BASKETBALL

Many of the Crystal Coast parks have basketball courts, as do a few of the area fitness centers. The Carteret County Parks and Recreation Department, (252) 808-3301, sponsors a basketball league, and many school gyms are used for play.

BICYCLING

Whether it's on the beach at low tide, in the residential back streets of Bogue Banks, along historic waterfronts or on several of the towns' bike paths — there is an abundance of choices when it comes to having some two-wheel fun. Although bikers in the area would agree that bike lanes would be a welcome addition to the roadways, that is not yet the case. Salter Path Road (N.C. Highway 58) is a widely traveled route by cyclists. You'll find that it runs most of the length of Bogue Banks, known here as "the island," which allows travel from Emerald Isle to Fort Macon — and everything in between. The town of Emerald Isle has a bike path that wanders off the main route in town to include green grassy areas and shady wooded sections, as well as parts of the downtown district. Look for additional miles of biking and running paths in the coming years.

Morehead City provides a multi-use trail that accommodates both pedestrians and cyclists, providing a safe alternative from the high-traffic area of Bridges Street. It runs along Bridges Street, between Country Club Road and North 35th Street and offers both a practical and recreational connection between West Carteret High School and the businesses located in that area. For a look at beautiful Beaufort, try the Beaufort Bicycle Route, a cruising loop around town that includes the waterfront and parts of the historic district. Pick up your route map at the Safrit Visitors Center at the Beaufort Historic Site on Turner Street.

The Swansboro Bicentennial Bicycle Trail offers miles of good biking that begins in historic Swansboro and follows roadways throughout the area. The loop path crosses the White Oak River to Cape Carteret, winds through the Croatan National Forest, crosses the river again and returns to Swansboro.

North Carolina's Division of Bicycle and Pedestrian Transportation offers a color map showing bicycle enthusiasts where to cycle on the Outer Banks, in addition to other useful information and resources. Three loop and two linear bicycle routes are highlighted and include portions of the mainland as well as the barrier islands. Contact the Division of Bicycle and Pedestrian Transportation, N.C. Department of Transportation, 1552 Mail Service Center, Raleigh, NC 27699, (919) 807-0768.

FITNESS CENTERS

Morehead City

Gold's Gym
Cypress Bay Plaza,
U.S. Hwy. 70, Morehead City
(252) 247-4653

Gold's Gym is part of a nationwide franchise and has been flexing its muscles in the fitness community for five years. The gym offers unlimited mutual use of its facilities for those with annual or bi-annual memberships and a travel exchange program for other Gold's Gyms across the country. Memberships vary in price and

can be arranged by the week or month. Guest visits are $10, or just $5 when accompanied by a member. Equipment includes Life Fitness, Hammer Strength and a wide variety of cardiovascular equipment and world-class group exercise programs, including body pump and body flow, as well as a wide variety of free weights. Gold's offers free child care for ages 6 months to 11 years, tanning facilities and a pro shop with apparel, supplements and smoothies. Gym hours are Monday through Thursday from 5 AM to 10 PM, Friday from 5 AM to 8 PM, Saturday from 8 AM to 5 PM and Sunday from 9 AM to 5 PM.

Morehead City Community Center
1600 Fisher St., Morehead City
(252) 726-5083

This is a popular place with many city residents and guests. Members have use of the fully equipped weight room, loaded with free weights and machines, a gym with a full-size basketball court, and a game room with pool and Ping-Pong tables. The center also offers floor aerobics classes and yoga classes. Managed by the city's Parks and Recreation Department, this facility is likely the area's most affordable fitness center. Individual rates are $30 for city residents and $60 for non-residents. Family rates are $45 and $90. There are also special rates for use of the gym and game room, and those vary from $10 to $30 per year. High school and college students 16 years of age and older, regardless of where they live, can join the gym for $20 per year. Senior citizens age 62 and older who are residents can use the gym free of charge; non-city residents pay $20. The gym operates Monday through Friday from 8 AM to 8 PM and Saturday from 1 to 6 PM. It is closed Sunday.

Sports Center
701 N. 35th St., Morehead City
(252) 726-7070

This large fitness center offers a holistic approach to family fitness. The center was recently renovated and has a knowledgeable staff ready to assist members and guests. It offers a fully equipped weight room, Nautilus and fitness equipment, racquetball courts, and an indoor walking/running track. Many group classes are offered, including Pilates, yoga, water aerobics, cycling and sport conditioning. Personal trainers are also available. Sports Center has a tanning salon, stair climbers, treadmills, spinning cycles, basketball/volleyball courts, an Olympic-sized outdoor pool and an indoor pool. The center also offers a snack bar and child-care services. Annual and monthly memberships are available as well as temporary and guest options. The center is open Monday through Thursday from 5 AM to 10 PM, Friday from 5 AM to 9 PM, Saturday from 8 AM to 6 PM and Sunday from 1 to 6 PM.

Beaufort

Curves for Women
1726 Live Oak St., Beaufort
(252) 728-1444

112 Queens Creek Rd. , Ste.2 , Swansboro
(910) 326-1200

4219 Arendell St., Morehead City
(252) 247-5239

Curves for Women is part of a nationwide franchise, although each gym is locally owned and operated. Join one Curves and you can get a travel pass to use at any Curves in the country or abroad. Workouts are based on 30-minute total body circuit training with a combination of aerobics and strength training. All equipment is hydraulic to be easy on your joints. Individuals rotate from upper-body workout equipment to lower-body workout equipment with recovery/spring board stations in between. The workouts are done based on time and are fast moving. There is a membership fee and a one-time sign-up fee.

Eastern Athletic Club
105 Professional Park Dr., Beaufort
(252) 728-1700

This fitness club offers a full line of Nautilus workout equipment, a free-style weight room with quick-change collars, treadmills, EB Power Ride bikes and much more. The gym offers a variety of classes, including water and floor aerobics, spin

classes, yoga, body pump and more. It also includes a 25-foot, heated junior Olympic swimming pool, a steam room, tanning beds and a large, tiled hot tub spa. Memberships include an enrollment fee and then $45 per month for a single person, $50 for a couple and $60 for a family. Student discounts are available. Club hours vary depending on the season, so call ahead.

Snap Fitness
1718 Live Oak St., Beaufort
(252) 728-3357

Are you always ready to exercise just when the gyms are closing? Snap Fitness has answer for you. Here you have access 24 hours, seven days a week, 365 days a year with a simple card key access. There are no contracts, and rates are $34.95 a month for an individual and $49.95 for families. Snap offers the latest in fitness equipment with plenty of treadmills, strength-training machines, free weights and more.

Bogue Banks

Emerald Isle Parks & Recreation Community Center
7506 Emerald Isle Dr., Emerald Isle
(252) 354-6350

The center is open to residents and nonresidents, offering a full-size gym for indoor tennis, basketball, volleyball and soccer. Classes vary and often include aerobics — both step and step-free — classes, karate, Pilates and yoga. The facility also features a weight room, a game room with Ping-Pong and card tables, restrooms with showers and a fully equipped kitchen. Space for meetings and parties is available. Outside you will find tennis courts, a basketball court and a children's play area. Rates are $5 per day or $20 for a week of fun. Annual memberships are also available for Emerald Isle residents and nonresidents. The center's hours are Monday through Friday 8 AM to 9 PM from Labor Day to Memorial Day and 8 AM to 8 PM from Memorial Day to Labor Day, and all

See this entire guide plus additional content online at insiderinfo.us

Saturdays from 9 AM to 4 PM. The center is closed on Sunday.

Western Carteret County

Cape Carteret Aquatics and Wellness Center
**300 Taylor Notion Rd., Cape Carteret
(252) 393-1000**

Open seven days a week, this full-service wellness center takes its summer visitors into account. The club offers an indoor, 25-yard competition heated pool, hot tub and steam room, an indoor full-size basketball court, and a fully equipped weight room. Classes of all varieties, including Pilates, yoga and reformer sessions as well as water and floor aerobics, offer members a variety of workout choices. Licensed professionals ensure that quality guidance and instruction are given to members. The club also offers kids' programs, personal training, swim lessons and therapeutic massage. Day passes are available for $12 per day or $100 for 15 visits, and weekly passes are $50. The center offers many discounts for corporate memberships, medical professionals,

education professionals, students and active military, so be sure to inquire about them. The center is open Monday through Friday from 5:30 AM to 9 PM, Saturday from 8 AM to 4 PM and Sunday from 1 to 6 PM, with the pool area closing 30 minutes earlier.

FLYING

Michael J. Smith Airport
**180 Airport Rd., Beaufort
(252) 728-1928**

The Crystal Coast's sole airport, located in Beaufort, offers only chartered or private aircraft service. A modern facility, it is the sixth busiest municipal airport in North Carolina. Here you can arrange the services of private planes for trips or sightseeing or you can line up private flying lessons. The airport is named in memory of Capt. Michael J. Smith, a Beaufort native who served as pilot of space shuttle *Challenger*, which exploded January 28, 1986. Navy Capt. Smith learned to fly at this airfield. More complete details of the airport are in the Getting Here, Getting Around chapter.

Surfboards are available for rent along the coast.

photo: Peter Doran

GOLF

Ready to tee it up? Golf can be played on the Crystal Coast just about 365 days a year. Golfers who know the area know the local courses offer some of the best golf bargains around. With courses designed with both the novice and professional in mind, you'll find a level of challenge that's enjoyable for all. Add in some exquisite coastal and inland scenery with some well designed courses, and you're ready for a day on the links. Just remember that most courses require scheduling a tee time, so be sure to call ahead. Information about golf courses in the area is provided in our Golf chapter.

GYMNASTICS

Cedar Point Gymnastics Training Center
135 Sherwood Ave., Cedar Point
(252) 393-7778

Cedar Point Gymnastics is a U.S.A. Gymnastics Member Club. It is open year round and provides classes for those interested in gymnastics and tumbling. The center offers a complete girls' and boys' gymnastics program for preschool age and older. Training for beginners through advanced students is provided by certified coaches. Full-day and half-day summer camps are offered for ages 4 and older. A registration fee is charged, and other fees vary. A cheerleading group is also based at the center. The center is available for birthday parties with a reservation.

Dance Arts Studio
123 Bonner Ave., Morehead City
(252) 726-1720
1390 Lennoxville Rd., Beaufort
(252) 728-1855

At both of its locations, Dance Arts Studio offers a variety of classes such as gymnastics, tumbling, ballet, jazz, pointe and tap. Classes are offered for young children, teenagers and adults. The studios have floating wood dance floors, private dressing rooms and a parent lobby. The Beaufort location is also equipped with tumbling mats, a low balance beam, a mini-trampoline and a vault for gymnastics. Piano lessons are also offered at the Beaufort location.

HORSEBACK RIDING

Acha's Stable
1341 Nine Mile Rd., Newport
(252) 223-4478

Acha's Stable is a family business that provides lessons and offers boarding and stall rentals for horse owners. The stable is just west of Morehead City.

By The Sea Farms
380 Pigott Rd., Gloucester
(252) 729-1756
www.bytheseafarms.com

By The Sea Farms is a breeding farm of Andalusian horses. The farm focuses on producing high-quality horses with willingness, intelligence and correct movement for multi-disciplines. Some of their offspring are winning multiple Res. Grand Championship and more. These horses are perfect for dressage, three-day eventing, driving, jumping, reining or even cow work. By The Sea Farms offers a family-oriented yet professional touch to horse training, imprinting and ownership. By The Sea Farms offers horses for sale or lease as well as breeding. This farm is home to Ladino TG, a dark bay Andalusian stallion who stands at stud on the farm. He produces blacks, bays, buckskins and chestnuts foals. You can learn more by visiting the farm's website or visiting the farm itself.

Cedar Island Stables
120 Driftwood Dr., Cedar Island
(252) 225-1885

Cheryl McMahon, owner and operator of Cedar Island Stables, calls this "the most beautiful place to ride on the planet." Cedar Island Stables offers beach rides on well-trained horses that provide an up-close look at the beautiful landscapes and seascapes of Cedar Island. One-hour rides with a guide cost $55 per person and cross the beautiful 1,000-foot river to the next island. One and half hour rides cost $85. Shorter rides of a half-hour are $35. Anyone older than 3 without fear of horses is welcome. Pony rides in a fenced area cost $1 per minute. Call ahead and make reservations. Cedar Island Stables is open year-round.

Zeigler's Stables and Cross Country Tack
**144 Mason Ln., off Howard Blvd., Newport
(252) 223-5110**

The stable offers riding lessons, boarding and a tack shop. Cross Country Tack is a part of the stables and can be reached at (252) 223-0311.

HUNTING

Hunting along the Crystal Coast is very popular with locals, and many visiting hunters make Carteret County their hunting destination. Guide services have long been a popular means for duck and goose hunters to experience new locales. Using knowledgeable guides cuts down on your chances of spending time in the wrong spot.

Brown's Hunting & Guide Service
**Davis
(252) 729-1578**

Capt. Kyle Brown is an excellent guide and strives to put you right on the action. He lives in the Down East community of Davis and, as a local man, knows the area waterways and gamelands well. Duck hunting is his specialty, and he is a licensed captain.

KARATE

Karate lessons are often offered by the Morehead City Parks and Recreation Department, (252) 726-5083, and also at several of the local fitness centers (see the Fitness Centers section previously in this chapter).

Elite Martial Arts Academy
**4907-C Bridges St., Morehead City
(252) 808-2400**

Previously known as Lewis' Tae Kwon Do Center, this business has a reputation for providing quality instruction and for students placing high in competitions. The academy is owned and operated by two-time World Champion Russell Lewis — a fifth-degree black belt with more than 20 years of experience and a long list of accomplishments — and his wife, Jennifer, also a black belt. The academy offers instruction for beginners through advanced for ages 5 through teens and adults with focuses on building physical fitness,

mental discipline and self-confidence. Group and private lessons are offered in a patient, supportive atmosphere.

KITE FLYING

Fort Macon State Park, on the eastern end of Bogue Banks, is the most popular location for everyone to fly kites. Every Sunday morning folks meet there at 9 AM in the summer and 10 AM in the winter. The annual Carolina Kite Festival, which takes place on the last weekend in October that is not Halloween, features high-flying excitement happening outside of the Sheraton in Atlantic Beach. The festival is sponsored by Kites Unlimited, (252) 247-7011.

RUNNING AND WALKING

Grab your iPod, your dog or a group of friends and hit the streets, sidewalks and sand for some breathtaking sights — and get some exercise, too. Running and walking are favorite forms of exercise along the Crystal Coast. Because of mild year-round temperatures, one seldom has to miss a day of exercise and outdoor enjoyment. The Beaufort and Morehead City waterfronts and the beaches continue to be the most favored running and walking spots, and they are heavily traveled by early morning and evening exercisers. Those runners who like to test their skills or run with a group can participate in the races described below. Most of them include walks, too.

Beach Run Series
**Atlantic Beach
(252) 808-3301**

This series of seven runs sponsored by the Carteret County Parks and Recreation Department begins in the spring. This low-key weekday series attracts lots of local runners and walkers for evening runs. The 1-mile run/walk, 5K and 10K are on the beach and begin and end at the main beach access area, formerly known as The Circle, in Atlantic Beach. Dates vary depending on the tides. A fall run mini-series has also been added as a fundraiser for the Special Olympics.

SPORTS, FITNESS AND PARKS

 **CLOSE UP** Dolphins are
a Wonderful Sight

Catching a glimpse of bottlenose dolphins traveling, feeding, resting or so-cializing along the Crystal Coast is a wonderful treat, and not so rare. From the beaches, bridges and riverbanks, locals and visitors alike can often see dolphins. If you are boating, dolphins can be seen in most waterways.

There is a difference between dolphins and porpoises, and many people get them confused. What you will see in this area are dolphins. Porpoises do not gener-ally venture into North Carolina waters. The only porpoise species that occurs near the U.S. East Coast is the harbor porpoise, and it typically ranges from Virginia to Canada.

Bottlenose dolphins are long and streamlined, with a distinct blunt beak and a prominent dorsal fin that curves toward the tail. They are bigger than their por-poise cousins, with adults generally ranging in length from 8 to 10 feet (males are slightly larger than females) and weighing between 500 to 800 pounds. Dolphins' teeth are sharp and shaped like cones, not flattened like those of a porpoise. These aquatic creatures are cetaceans, the taxonomic order of marine mammals that in-cludes all "the great" whales, dolphins and porpoises.

Dolphins are also members of the suborder *odontocetti*, meaning toothed whales. More than 70 species of toothed whales live in the waters of the earth, many of which are found in relatively shallow, temperate coastal waters. It's not un-usual to spot bottlenose dolphins in groups of about a dozen, fairly close to shore. They usually have light-colored bellies and dark backs — colors that help them blend in with their surroundings. These graceful creatures are powerful swimmers and often frolic in the bow waves of boats or surf on large waves.

Bottlenose dolphins along the East Coast of the United States are severely and negatively impacted by human activities. After a die-off that killed up to half of the population, the National Marine Fisheries Service in 1993 listed them as depleted under the Marine Mammal Protection Act. Dolphins have washed ashore dead with evidence of having been struck by boats, entangled in fishing nets, and with for-eign material (human trash) in their stomachs. Yet little basic information that is critical for their conservation is known, such as reproductive rates, residency and migration patterns, and habitat needs.

That information is being gathered by a small group of dedicated professionals. Keith Rittmaster, Natural Science Curator at the North Carolina Maritime Museum, directs a program that identifies local dolphins and records their movements, as-sociations and reproduction information. The process used is called photo-identifi-cation and involves the use of photographs of the scars and notches that dolphins ac-quire on their dorsal fins to recognize and verify resights of known individuals. Ritt-master, along with his wife, Victoria Thayer, have been studying the bottlenose dolphins in this area since 1985. Individually identi-fied dolphins that they first photographed in 1985 are still seen regularly in the waters around Beaufort. They have also matched dolphins identified in Beaufort with photo-graphs from study sites as far south as cen-tral Florida, as far north as New Jersey and

Watch for dolphins in the waterways of North Carolina.

photo: Keith Rittmaster, NC Maritime Museum.

many sites in between. This collaboration is critical to the study, and researchers from the Virginia Marine Science Museum, National Marine Fisheries Service, Duke Marine Lab, Nags Head Dolphin Watch and UNC-Wilmington all share photographs and data.

In addition to studying the live, free-swimming dolphins, Rittmaster is authorized under the Marine Mammal Protection Act to respond to strandings of whales and dolphins as part of the Marine Mammal Stranding Network. Examining carcasses of beached dolphins has shown him many negative effects of human interactions. Dolphins tangled in fishing nets and lines die trapped in the debris. Dolphins are also sliced by boat propellers and ingest litter that can often be lethal.

People have fed wild dolphins, and Rittmaster cites reports of people even giving the dolphins Twinkies, sunglasses or whatever is in the boat with them when they run out of fish. Lens caps, fishing hooks and other litter have been found inside of dead dolphin stomachs. Dolphins are wild animals, and if they get used to coming to people, it can create danger to the animals as well as to humans. Some wild dolphins have come to expect the handouts, and have been known to become aggressive and bite. It is against federal law to feed or harass wild dolphins, punishable by imprisonment and/or fines.

To raise money to help protect and increase understanding of dolphin behavior and human impact on them along the North Carolina coast, the N.C. General Assembly approved the sale of a $30 special license plate with all revenues going to support the education, conservation and research programs of the N.C. Maritime Museum. For more information about the research program or the license plates, visit www.capelookoutstudies.org.

One more thing — the "dolphin" on a restaurant menu or for sale in a fish market is not the marine mammal. Instead it is the dolphin fish that is commercially fished in local waters. Insiders usually call that fish by its Hawaiian name — *mahi mahi*.

Historic Beaufort Road Race
Front St., Downtown Beaufort
(252) 222-6359

Sponsored by Beaufort Ole Towne Rotary Club, this is the area's most popular race and it always takes place on the third Saturday of July. Participants are promised a scenic course that is "hot, flat and fast." Hundreds turn out to tackle the 1-mile run/walk, or the certified 5K run/walk and 10K courses. This is such a popular race that families from across the country plan their vacations around it. Race proceeds fund youth scholarships and programs and many community needs.

Lookout Rotary Spring Road Race
Morehead City
(252) 726-7070

This race kicks off the local race season and takes place on the last Saturday morning in April with a flat 10K, 5K and 1-mile run/walk beginning and ending at the Sports Center, N. 35th Street in

Morehead City. The race is sponsored by the Lookout Rotary Club of Morehead City and is an event for every age and skill level. For more information, call the Sports Center at the number above.

Twin Bridges 8K Road Race
Beaufort to Atlantic Beach
(252) 726-6273

You have two choices with the Twin Bridges Race: You either run the 8K or stay on the porch. Because there aren't any hills on the coast, the race directors throw in two high-rise bridges. The race, slated for the first Saturday in October, is the kickoff for Saturday's events at the

---

Use a fishing reel to hold your kite string. Some say that's cheating, but a reel sure makes it a breeze to bring a high-flying kite back to earth.

N.C. Seafood Festival on the Morehead City waterfront. The race begins at the drawbridge in Beaufort and ends on the Atlantic Beach Causeway.

SOCCER

There's a lot of action on the soccer fields across the area for children and adults. Carteret County Parks and Recreation Department, (252) 808-3301, sponsors leagues for younger players and for women and men. Rotary Park and Soccer Complex features lighted soccer fields and many extras. Information about that park is listed in our Parks section.

SOFTBALL

The Carteret County Parks and Recreation Department sponsors a men's, women's and coed softball league each year. The teams are usually sponsored by local businesses and are very competitive. Call (252) 808-3301 for information.

TENNIS

Tennis is another one of those not-so-well-known Crystal Coast treasures. The Crystal Coast has really good places to play tennis, just not many of them. As with golf, you can play tennis almost all year round. Emerald Isle Parks and Recreation keeps a list of people who share the love of tennis and are interested in getting together to play singles, doubles and mixed games. Call (252) 354-6350 and let them help you find a perfect match. (Some parks that aren't mentioned in this section have tennis courts too. See the Parks section at the end of this chapter.)

The Country Club of the Crystal Coast
152 Oakleaf Dr., Pine Knoll Shores
(252) 726-1034

This semi-private club features four beautifully maintained clay courts along with a picturesque 18-hole golf course. Members and non-members are welcome, and memberships are available. A certified USTA pro is on hand, and group and private lessons can be arranged. A game-matching service is also available.

VOLLEYBALL

Beach volleyball is a classic beach event — and what better way to get some exercise, have some fun and get a tan all at the same time? Volleyball nets can be found at some of the parks in the area as well as on the beach. Tournament nets are put out during the season on the main beach in Atlantic Beach, formerly known as The Circle. They are there for public use so join in on a game or just sit by and watch the action. For details, call the Atlantic Beach Town Hall, (252) 726-2121.

YOGA

Yoga For You
2900 Arendell St., Morehead City
(252) 247-9642

Yoga for You is not a one-size-fits-all yoga center; instead, it is a welcome respite from the usual gym-like atmosphere. The peaceful, pristine studio is dedicated solely to yoga instruction with a warm, calming atmosphere that eases the mind, spirit and body. The professional teachers are all yoga certified to make practice both safe and effective. A wide range of instruction includes gentle and introductory yoga, advanced levels and yoga tailored specifically for men, seniors, children and teens. With a variety of weekday and weekend classes, including a "Lunch and Learn" series and other specialized workshops, there's something for everyone. In addition to the wide range of class times and days, there is also pricing to fit every budget, including drop-in rates, five and ten class passes, and monthly options. Be sure to ask about free-class passes for military service and for cancer survivors. The retail section sells Fair Trade items from all over the world as well as exercise apparel made in the Carolinas, gifts, teas, books and other interesting things. Find out for yourself why locals come here to find the gentle way to well-being.

Parks

COUNTY PARKS

The Carteret County parks system offers visitors and residents more than 150 acres of open space for recreational enjoyment. The system of parks, ball fields, beach accesses and fishing piers are managed by the county's Parks and Recreation Department. The parks and ball fields offer picnic areas and parking access. Here we briefly describe each of these facilities.

(Beach accesses and fishing piers are detailed in our Fishing, Boating and Watersports chapter.) Along with maintaining the parks, the county also offers a variety of programs, from summer camps to recreational teams, Senior Games to Special Olympics. Call the Parks and Recreation Department, (252) 808-3301, for the latest schedule.

Eastern Park
450 U.S. Hwy. 70, Smyrna

This 30-acre facility has lighted adult and youth fields, basketball courts, lighted tennis courts, lighted multi-purpose fields, a playground, horseshoe pits, beach volleyball courts and a walking trail. Visitors to the park will also find a picnic area, restrooms and a large parking area.

Harkers Island Beach Access
Southeast Side of Drawbridge, Harkers Island

This area offers parking space and a beach access. Across the road is a nice public dock for fishing. No restroom facilities are offered. There are no lifeguards, so visitors swim at their own risk.

Leon Mann Jr. Enrichment Center
3820 Galantis Dr., Morehead City (252) 247-2626

This county-operated center offers facilities for seniors ages 50 and older and hosts a variety of recreational activities, health and wellness classes, nutrition programs and various other services. The center has a fully equipped kitchen, physical fitness rooms with showers and lockers, a game room, three classrooms (one with microwave, stove/oven and refrigerator), a health room, all-purpose rooms and a library. Outdoor facilities include shuffleboard courts, patio areas and horseshoe pits. The center is open Monday through Friday, 8 AM to 5 PM. The center is available for rental on nights and weekends.

Manley Gaskill Field
Next to Harkers Island Elem. School, 1163 Island Rd., Harkers Island

The facilities available here include one large lighted ballpark, one youth ball field, a concession stand and a storage shed.

Mariners Park
201 East St., off U.S. Hwy. 70, Sea Level

This park consists of 20 acres, including lighted adult and youth athletic fields, tennis courts, a basketball court, a playground and restrooms.

Marshallberg Picnic Area
Marshallberg Rd., at the Harbor, Marshallberg

These picnic shelters are situated overlooking the water and provide a beautiful water view for visitors.

Newport Ball Field
Next to Newport Elem. School, 219 Chatham St., Newport

This park has three ball fields and a storage shed.

Newport River Park
East of the Beaufort-Morehead City bridge

The park's 4 acres encompass an island of sand, a sunning area, picnic tables, a new 300-foot fishing pier and a boat ramp sufficient for launching small boats. The entrance is directly across from the entrance to Radio Island.

Radio Island Water Access
501 Marine Dr., off U.S. Hwy. 70, Beaufort

This area offers wading, swimming, picnic tables, grills, restrooms and outdoor showers. Be aware that there are dangerous currents in deeper water and it is best to stay close to the shore when swimming. There is no lifeguard on duty, so keep a watchful eye on the kids when they're in the water.

South River Park
1030 South River Rd., Beaufort

This area provides a playground, parking spaces, a basketball court, a picnic shelter/comfort station and restrooms. It is nicely landscaped and has some nice shady areas.

West Beaufort (Town Creek) Water Access
298 W. Beaufort Rd., Beaufort

This facility has floating docks, a fishing pier, two boat ramps and a comfort station. It offers boat access to the water just north of the Beaufort drawbridge. This facility is undergoing renovations to build new boat ramps, but access is expected to be ready by the spring.

Western Park
275 Old N.C. Hwy. 58, Cedar Point

This park's 34 acres include lighted adult and youth fields, a lighted multi-purpose field, restrooms, playgrounds, a basketball court, lighted tennis courts and a picnic shelter. The park also includes a community center featuring two small classrooms, one large meeting room and a kitchen.

MUNICIPAL AND CITY PARKS

Bogue Banks has a few parks and the majority of those focus on access to the beach. For descriptions of the beach access areas, see our Fishing, Boating and Watersports chapter.

Emerald Isle

Emerald Isle Parks and Recreation Department, (252) 354-6350, maintains several public parks and continues to increase the number and quality of these facilities. To learn about the numerous beach access areas in Emerald Isle, see our Fishing, Boating and Watersports chapter.

Blue Heron Park & Tennis Courts
behind Emerald Isle Town Hall, MM 19, Emerald Isle

Located behind the Emerald Isle Town Hall, this park features tennis courts, a basketball court, a picnic shelter and a children's playground. Use of the tennis courts requires reservations, which must be made in person. There is a small fee for use of the tennis courts.

Emerald Isle Woods
Coast Guard Rd., Emerald Isle

Located along Coast Guard Road, this soundside, 41-acre park features walking trails and sound access in addition to a birding trail, grills, a picnic pavilion, restrooms and a pier.

Merchants Park
Emerald Dr., MM 19.5, Emerald Isle

Merchants Park is on the south side of Emerald Drive and offers parking, picnic tables, a shelter and restroom facilities.

There is no public beach access from this site.

Salter Path Beach Access
MM 10, 1025 N.C. Hwy. 58, Salter Path

This facility offers beach access for swimming, picnic tables, grills, a 465-foot boardwalk and a restroom with outside showers.

Salter Path Park
Ballpark Dr., Salter Path

This area provides a ball field, playground, basketball court, parking lot and picnic shelter.

Beaufort

Curtis A. Perry Park
East end of Front St.
adjacent to the boat ramp, Beaufort

You'll find a basketball court, two lighted tennis courts, restroom facilities, a dock and a waterfront picnic area complete with grills. The park was built around the four boat ramps provided by the N.C. Wildlife Service and named in memory of the town's former public works director.

Freedom Park
201 Freedom Park Rd.,
S.R. 1412 off Lennoxville Rd., Beaufort

This 15-acre tract is surrounded by woods and is a popular place for all types of activities. It has lighted regulation adult and youth fields, a play lot, basketball courts, a picnic shelter and restrooms.

Grayden Paul Jaycee Park
Front St. at the south end of Pollock St., Beaufort

Located on Front Street across from the post office, this pretty little park offers a grassy picnic spot, a gazebo, a dock and a swimming area. It's a great place to sit and read a book or to just watch the boats going by in Taylor's Creek. The park was named for the late Grayden Paul and it is maintained by the local Rotary Club.

Morehead City

Morehead City Parks and Recreation Department oversees the city's parks and the Morehead City Community Center at 1600 Fisher Street. (The center also houses the department's offices.) Directly behind the community center are multi-purpose sports fields used primarily for softball and baseball. Each of the city parks offers different amenities. The department offers all types of programs, from aerobics and dance and karate classes to special holiday events and youth sports programs. For the latest information about what's going on, call Parks and Recreation at (252) 726-5083.

City Park
10th and Arendell St., Morehead City

This is a shady city park with playground equipment and a few picnic tables. Additional parking has recently been added, making City Park a great place to stop for lunch or play time while cruising the Morehead City waterfront shops. This park is equipped with a large gazebo and bathroom facilities and is beside the recently restored Train Depot. Reservations for large groups and shelter use is required. There is a small charge for residents to use the gazebo.

Jaycee Park
9th and Shepard St., Morehead City

This is the site of the city's Summer in the Park concert series hosted by the

Parks and Recreation Department on Saturday evenings during the summer months. You'll find parking, picnic tables, a gazebo, swings and a short pier at this park.

Municipal Park
3409 Arendell St.,
behind Visitors Center, Morehead City

Visitors will find plenty of parking, picnic areas and a very popular boat ramp. The park borders Bogue Sound, just west of the Atlantic Beach high-rise bridge. This park is an attractive place to eat lunch and watch the boats and sea birds. Restroom facilities are available in the Visitor Center. If you plan to launch your boat, get there early for a parking place.

O'Neal Field
off 20th St. and Mayberry Loop,
Morehead City

O'Neal Field was dedicated in the spring of 2007 and is adjacent to the Rotary Park Soccer Complex. Both are operated by the Morehead City Parks & Recreation Department. O'Neal Field offers a lighted, full-size American league baseball field as well as restroom facilities.

Bicycling is a popular form of transportation in the area.

photo: Peter Doran

Piney Park
27th and Bridges St., Morehead City

This tiny green space offers a quiet respite to anyone who feels like getting outdoors. You'll find pine-tree shade and picnic tables.

Rotary Park-Soccer Complex
off 20th St. and Mayberry Loop, Morehead City

This park and soccer complex is a wonderful addition to the city's park system. It was paid for with a combination of federal and state grant money and support from county Rotary Clubs and other community organizations. The site features several regulation, lighted soccer fields that are often converted to make seven fields for play by younger athletes. The park has picnic shelters, lighted basketball courts and restroom facilities. A walking trail around the perimeter of the park features a boardwalk through the woods and ties into the city's sidewalk system.

Shevans Park
16th and Evans St., Morehead City

Shevans Park has lighted tennis courts, shelters with picnic tables and restroom facilities. There is also a large, impressive children's maze called Sea of Dreams. Based on kids' ideas, the playground's basic theme is a castle. Inside, kids can play on cable ladders, spring bridges, a balance beam suspended from chains, a boat, a race car, rings, musical chimes, a wooden-horse ride, a pirate's ship and a playhouse complete with a toy stove and kitchen. This community project was financed by

private donations of cash and materials and built by volunteers. Reservations are required to reserve the shelters. There is no fee to reserve the small shelter and a minimal fee to reserve the larger one.

Sugarloaf Island
Evans St., Morehead City
(252) 726-5083

Sugarloaf Island is across the waterway from the Morehead City waterfront and is accessible only by boat. Once on the 22-acre island, visitors can enjoy an island habitat park with a nature trail, beach areas and restroom facilities.

Swinson Park
4319 Country Club Rd., Morehead City

This 34-acre park is located beside Morehead City Primary School and is a popular spot for sports and family outings. Visitors will find lighted and unlighted adult and youth athletic fields, lighted tennis courts, basketball courts, play lots, a picnic shelter and a comfort station. This park also provides access to Morehead City's trail system for biking, running and walking.

Swansboro

Bicentennial Park
N.C. Hwy. 24,
at the base of the bridge, Swansboro

The park contains a life-size statue of Otway Burns, Swansboro's favorite privateer from the War of 1812, and a memorial to Theophilus Weeks, founder of the town. It's the perfect place to fish from the sea wall, play or simply sit and enjoy the beauty of the White Oak River.

GOLF

From the beach to the driving range, eastern North Carolina's temperate climate makes it an ideal location for all sorts of outdoor activities, including golf. The Crystal Coast has a variety of scenic and challenging courses awaiting golf enthusiasts, and most of the area's exceptional courses are open to the public. Courses are busy year round, and many Insiders consider fall the most favorable time to play. However, golf can be played here practically 365 days a year, if you wish.

It's best to call ahead to reserve tee times, especially on weekends. Golfers who know the Crystal Coast know it is one of the best golf bargains around. Several local hotels offer golf packages that include accommodations, meals, guaranteed starting times, greens fees and a few extras; call the businesses listed in our Hotels and Motels and Bed and Breakfast Inns chapters and ask about special incentives for golfers.

Where possible, local courses take full advantage of the area's natural beauty. Many greens and tees offer glorious views of waters and wildlife, so the intrepid golfer gets a chance to experience a little something extra as the game unfolds. Several of the courses listed have recently completed multi-million dollar makeovers that bring them into championship form. The courses we recommend will bring you many enjoyable rounds of golf. All fees are for 18 holes of play unless noted otherwise, and be sure to ask about seasonal rates since these may vary from course

Crystal Coast golf courses are known for thier spectacular views.

photo: Peter Doran

to course. We've also listed a local driving range.

Courses

Brandywine Bay Golf and Country Club
N.C. Hwy. 24 and U.S. Hwy. 70,
Morehead City
(252) 247-2541

West of Morehead City, this 18-hole, par 71 championship course was ranked among the area's best places to play by *Golf Digest* in 2006. A very popular course, it is set in dense woods laced with streams and ponds. Indeed, water and woods are part of the play for every hole. Designed by Bruce Devlin and Bob Von Hagge, Brandywine plays 6609 yards from the championship tees, 6150 from the regular tees, 5390 yards from the gold, and 5192 yards from the women's. Improvements recently have been made to greens and fairways, and the installation of cart paths is ongoing. Golfers will find a pro shop, a snack bar, putting greens and a chipping area with practice bunkers. Greens fees (including carts) are $51 in season and $40 off season. Walkers may play for a reduced fee, but Insiders recommend that you call ahead for time limitations and pricing. June through September golfers can take advantage of the twilight special. Check with the pro shop for pricing. A junior program and group rates also are available.

Carolina Pines Golf and Country Club
390 Carolina Pines Blvd., Havelock
(252) 444-1000

On the scenic Neuse River just west of Havelock and about 10 miles east of New Bern, this challenging 18-hole, par 72 course is everything the golfer could want. The course features elevated greens, bermudagrass fairways, abundant sand traps and ample water that rewards the accurate shotmaker on seven of 18 holes. Tim Dupre, the club pro, will arrange lessons for those who are interested. Golfers also will find a pro shop, a driving range, target

greens and a clubhouse with a lounge and patio that overlooks freshwater lakes and the golf links. Fees are $33 weekdays and $36 weekends, including cart. Carolina Pines is directly off U.S. Highway 70; look for the signs. The Flounder Jubilee, held the second weekend in June, is the course's big event tournament.

The Country Club of the Crystal Coast
152 Oakleaf Dr., at MM 5, N.C. Hwy. 58,
Pine Knoll Shores
(252) 726-1034

Formerly known as Bogue Banks Country Club, this 18-hole course is the only golf course on the island. Nestled among the sand dunes and maritime forests of Pine Knoll Shores, the course has four holes that overlook Bogue Sound. Beautiful water oaks, lofty pines and abundant wildlife enhance the appeal of this course. The course is par 70 from the blue tees, and par 72 from the white and red tees, measuring 6022 yards from the blue tees, 5644 yards from the white tees, and 4986 from the red tees. In-season rates are $54 for 18 holes before 3 PM and $38 after 3 PM. Off-season rates are $40 for 18 holes before 2 PM and $32 after 2 PM. Greens fees include a $1 Daily Club Green Fee. All rounds include the use of a cart. Tee times are required seven days a week and may be made one week in advance. Golfers will also find a fully stocked pro shop and clay tennis courts on the club grounds. A new clubhouse and lounge were constructed in 2007.

The Links at Plantation Harbour
1885 Adams Creek Rd., Havelock
(252) 444-4653

The Links is a USGA–regulation size, 18-hole, par 72 course with a total of 5994 yards from the championship tees. Golfers play on a combination of continuous single and double fairways, with nine holes returning to the clubhouse. The course's topography is basically level, but a few major slope changes take advantage of the natural ridges and valleys that enhance the beauty of the pine and hardwood

roughs. Surrounding many greens are bunkers composed of moderately packed loose sand, 4 to 5 inches deep. Several ponds, lakes and canals offer additional challenges to players. The Links is open year round, seven days a week, from sun up to sun down. The club has a pro shop, a clubhouse, a snack bar and a large practice putting green and a driving range. Tee areas are well marked with signs that note yardage and describe each hole. Fees to play 18 holes, including cart, are $25 on weekdays and $28 on weekends and holidays year round. On Wednesday, the fee is only $18. If you choose, you may walk the course for $15 during the week and $18 on Saturday and Sunday. Call for tee times.

Silver Creek Golf Club
N.C. Hwy. 58 N, Cape Carteret
(252) 393-8058

On N.C. Highway 58 just north of Cape Carteret, the Silver Creek Golf Club is a 7005-yard, par 72 championship course, renovated with Tif Eagle greens and beautiful fairways and tees. Designed for championship play by Gene Hamm, Silver Creek is the longest course in Carteret County, and it is known for the gusty winds that challenge golfers year round. Year-round rates are $40 to $52, depending on season, and include the use of a cart. Walk-ins are allowed year-round at a rate of 18 holes for $36. Call in advance for tee times. Special twilight rates are avail-

able from late May to mid-September after 1 PM. The Southern-style clubhouse and snack bar has a wide porch overlooking the course. The pro shop carries a good selection of merchandise. A pool and tennis courts are available, as are a practice green and driving range for pre-game warm up. A bucket of balls costs $3.

Star Hill Golf Club
202 Club House Dr., Cape Carteret
(252) 393-8111

Star Hill offers 27 holes in a wooded, hilly setting. Opened in 1965, it is one of the area's finest championship courses. At the junction of N.C. Highways 24 and 58 between the Intracoastal Waterway and the Croatan National Forest, Star Hill offers the Sands (3244 yards), the Pines (3270) and the Lakes (3381). Star Hill's rate structure is $69 for 18 holes in season, $48 off season. Reserved tee times are recommended throughout the year. Star Hill also offers three-play and 10-play passes. While the three-play pass is offered for in-season use only, the 10-play pass is good year-round. Junior and active-duty military discounts also are available. Patrons will find a pro shop offering rental clubs, a full line of clothing, accessories and professional equipment. Other amenities include a Cayman driving range, a total short-game practice area and a swimming pool. The attractive, casual-atmosphere Champions Room lounge is open daily, as is the Sandbar Grill, which offers breakfast and lunch daily. Those arriving by air will enjoy the use of Star Hill's private airstrip.

Driving Range

Golfin' Dolphin
N.C. Hwy. 24, Cape Carteret
(252) 393-8131

This business offers fun for serious golfers — and for their companions who would rather do something else. People who want to practice their golf swing can use the 250-yard driving range. Buckets

of balls cost $4 for 40, $6 for 60 balls, $8 for 80 balls and $15 for 200 balls. Not-so-serious grown ups and kids will get a charge out of the 18-hole mini-golf course (with elevations up to 22 feet), batting cage, go-cart track, Water Wars and bumper boats. The batting cage is for softball and baseball, and the go-cart track and bumper boats are a great way to give vent to the competitive spirit in all of us. Golfin' Dolphin is behind Hardee's in Cape Carteret and is open from 9 AM to 11 PM every day during the summer. Fall hours through December are 10 AM to 5 PM. Winter hours vary.

REAL ESTATE 🏠💲
AND NEIGHBORHOODS

The Crystal Coast has always been a great place to live, work and play, and the area continues to be discovered by those wanting to relocate, retire or find a second home. If you want to join those who call this area home, or "second home," this chapter is just for you. It is specifically designed to assist you in searching for an existing home or property in the area.

In this chapter we introduce you first to the areas and neighborhoods that make up the expansive Crystal Coast and then to some of the area's real estate companies. Our lists are by no means complete, but they will serve to familiarize you with neighborhoods, businesses and services. The realty firms recommended here are listed in the area of their home office and then alphabetically. These are not the only reputable firms in the area, but we simply couldn't list them all. We revise this book annually, and we welcome your comments concerning additions or omissions in the next edition.

One invaluable source of free information for anyone interested in purchasing property is *HOMES Magazine* of the Crystal Coast. This free monthly guide, published by NCCOAST Communications, contains descriptions and photos of residential and commercial property currently on the market in Carteret County. The guide also lists e-mail and homepage addresses for many of the individual Realtors. You can pick up a free copy at supermarkets, drug stores, restaurants and hundreds of local commercial establishments.

We begin our review of the area by looking at beach neighborhoods. When we talk about the beach we are referring to the island of Bogue Banks, which encompasses the townships of Atlantic Beach, Pine Knoll Shores, Indian Beach, Salter Path and Emerald Isle. From there we move to historic Beaufort, then to the central town of Morehead City, westward to Swansboro and finally to the Down East reaches of Carteret County.

As our 18th edition goes to press, the current economic situation has created many wonderful real estate bargains on the Crystal Coast. The average inland neighborhood home currently sells for about $200,000 to $300,000. Waterfront homes can go for $400,000 to $2 million or more. Like everywhere else, homes on the Crystal Coast vary tremendously in price, and proximity to water, historic districts, golf courses and upscale subdivisions accounts for pricier real estate. Significant development has taken place away from the water recently, and a wide range of housing is available.

There is no specific relocation service on the Crystal Coast; however, rest assured that most real estate agents go to great lengths to ensure their clients have a smooth transition and move. The Crystal Coast Chamber of Commerce, (252) 726-6350, can also provide you with some information about the area.

If the property you are considering is not in an incorporated city or subdivision, ask your real estate agent or the county planning office what uses are permitted in that area. Large portions of Carteret County are not zoned and may permit certain uses you have not considered — for your lot as well as your neighbor's. As with

view, a fact that increases the price of the property tremendously.

If searching for a summer or vacation home at the beach, note that most of the condominium complexes have rental units managed by area realty companies. Not sure which site fits you best? Spend a week or a weekend there and see if the site is what you had in mind.

Atlantic Beach

There's change happening here, offering residents and visitors alike a nice blend of old and new. With a remaining hint of a nostalgic air about it, Atlantic Beach is seeing its 1950s beach houses change to modern structures. There are still plenty throwback-to-the-1950s rambling beach houses and small cottages, but they are nudged right up next to ponderous two-story clapboards on narrow streets running parallel to the ocean. Atlantic Beach continues to be primarily made up of "local" residents — people who have lived here most of their lives and wouldn't dream of living anywhere else. The demographics at this end of Bogue Banks are slightly different than the rest of the island. Expect a younger crowd at Atlantic Beach instead of the large concentration of retirees found at other beach locations. Families in their 30s and 40s are commonplace, probably because of the small, affordable, near-beach cottages that allowed these couples to purchase their homes at a reasonable price in years past.

Today, transition can be seen as Atlantic Beach is making great strides to revitalize itself. The Circle, a once-popular family amusement area, is being renovated and plans are well underway for major developments and improvements to the area. Condos, restaurants and shops will soon fill the area that once was home to a Ferris wheel, go-cart tracks and amusement arcades.

Private homes, vacation rentals and mobile homes are mixed throughout this small oceanfront town, and over the years building has extended several blocks back from the water to N.C. Highway 58 (Salter Path Road). Most of the dwellings in Atlantic Beach are within walking distance of the ocean or sound, and the majority of new homes are concentrated on the east-

all major purchases, ask questions so you'll know before you commit.

Neighborhoods and Developments

BOGUE BANKS
THE BEACHES

Driving the length of Bogue Banks on N.C. Highway 58, you'll see what the island has to offer when it comes to its real estate and its neighborhoods. Like most beach resort areas, the Crystal Coast has a wide variety of real estate options — everything from small cottages and huge oceanfront homes to condominiums and mobile homes. We mention a few of the communities on Bogue Banks here; however, for a more complete list of what is available, check with a real estate agent. Also, for information on timeshares, check our Crystal Coast Weekly and Long-Term Vacation Rentals chapter.

Many newcomers move to the Crystal Coast for one reason: to live by the water. Atlantic Beach, Pine Knoll Shores, Indian Beach and Salter Path often have existing homes on the market. However, new construction has been a constant during the last several years, and there is an array of newer homes, condominiums and townhouses. Keep in mind that homes in this part of the county generally have a water ern end of the island, along Fort Macon Road.

Here, too, are a number of developments, such as **Sea Spray**, **A Place At the Beach** and **Southwinds**, with prices ranging from $195,000 to $400,000. **Sands Villas Resort** offers resort condominiums in the range of $345,000 to $500,000. **Island Quay** is a development of homes that average about $500,000.

By far Atlantic Beach's most colorful development is **Sea Dreams** at MM 1.5. Built on a high dune with views of the ocean and sound, this small development offers bright, cheery homes and a clubhouse, playground and pool. An oceanfront home here is in the $1.5 million range.

Pine Knoll Shores

Pine Knoll Shores is a planned community that combines coastal living with the harmony of nature, and the original developers deserve credit for their farsightedness. Built in a maritime forest, the town has done an admirable job of trying to lessen the impact of development on the natural environment. Drive through town and you will see what we mean. Trees are everywhere and are protected by restrictive covenants. Pine Knoll Shores is proud of its "Tree City" designation, which is a national recognition from the Arbor Day

Foundation for the town's commitment to preserving its community forestry.

Pine Knoll Shores is nearly 90 percent developed, but both large and small homes come on the market fairly regularly. Prices on home sites and homes vary greatly, depending on proximity to the ocean, the sound, the many canals or the 18-hole golf course located in town. Within the central portion of the town, many homes are built on canals, with the option of private docks. You will find homes from $300,000 to well over $1 million.

Bogue Shores Club and **Beachwalk at Pine Knoll Shores** are townhouse and condominium developments between MM 6 and 7 on N.C. 58. All are on the ocean and in nice maritime forest settings. Design features include courtyards, sun porches, gourmet kitchens, private balconies and other upscale luxuries. Prices can start at $399,900 and go up.

The **McGinnis Point** subdivision is a Bogue Sound community, with homes on, near or removed from the water. As with all property on Bogue Banks, prices for single-family homes vary widely, depending on location, and vary between $300,000 to $900,000.

Beacon's Reach, MM 8 through 9, is a large village-type development in a maritime forest on land once owned by

Beautifully twisted live oaks are everywhere in this region.

photo: Carolyn Temple

the Roosevelt family. It includes both multi-family and single-family dwellings, and prices vary greatly. An interior lot could sell for $450,000, and homes on the sound could bring in $1 million. Residents have access to lighted tennis courts, swimming pools, a marina and parks on the ocean and the sound. Meticulously landscaped, the villages include **Ocean Grove**, with three- and four-bedroom units; **Westport**, with one-, two- and three-bedroom units and both soundfront and freshwater lagoon-front units; the **Breakers**, with oceanfront condominiums; **Fiddlers' Walk** with sound-side condominium units; and **Maritime West**, with oceanfront units.

Salter Path and Indian Beach

There's a lot of local history in Salter Path and Indian Beach. Many of the longtime residents in the two small communities are descended from fishermen, and some still make their living on the water. You'll find a variety of homes here. Some homes are low, rambling structures, nestled under windswept live oaks bent from prevailing winds. Others are mobile homes, and many are large, new homes. Hurricane Ophelia in the fall of 2005 damaged many homes and businesses in these two communities.

The town of Indian Beach has seen the development of upscale residential communities. **Sea Isle Plantation** and **Sea Isle** are two examples, and prices can range from $700,000 to $1.5 million. At MM 10, Sea Isle offers home sites and custombuilt residences on both sides of Salter Path Road, and on Bogue Sound and the ocean.

The **Summerwinds** condominium complex is a large, oceanfront complex offering spacious living quarters with prices

ranging from $330,000 to more than $1 million. Recreational facilities include an indoor, heated swimming pool, a whirlpool, saunas, exercise rooms, a spa and racquetball courts. Outside are three oceanfront pools with sun decks and a boardwalk.

Kiawa (kee-wah) is another Indian Beach soundfront community, off N.C. 58 between the towns of Atlantic Beach and Emerald Isle. Interior lots can start at $54,000, and homes can go for more than $1 million. Individual soundfront docks are available. Sea Ridge Townhomes in Indian Beach offers oceanfront and ocean-view two-bedroom townhouses.

The Ocean Club is billed as a luxury family resort and conference center and offers condominium homes in a beautifully landscaped environment. Each mid-rise building has condominium homes with elevator service. The site has an oceanfront pool, picnic areas, an exercise room, a spa and more amenities. Soundfront homes start around $300,000 and oceanfront can start around $900,000. **Grande Villas at the Preserve** is in Indian Beach and prices start at $600,000 and go up. **The Nautical Club** is underway with plans to offer 217 luxury condos on the oceanside and the soundside. Prices will start at around $400,000.

Grande Villas at Indian Beach
**1435 Salter Path Rd., Indian Beach
(877) 845-4438**

Grande Villas at Indian Beach is scheduled for completion in spring 2009 and offers 86 expertly appointed residences ranging from about 1,400 to nearly 3,000 square feet. These oceanfront luxury condominium residences feature unique interiors, state-of-the-art appliances and oceanfront balconies. The Grande Villas offers owners many amenities, including a lounge, outdoor living areas, a seaside stone fire pit, a pool, a fitness center, a sauna and a pet park.

Emerald Isle

The western end of Emerald Isle is family-oriented with a growing number of permanent year-round residents. Originally, the only access to the western end of the island was by boat and, later, ferry. It wasn't until the 1970s that the B. Cameron

i *The* Island Review *is a local magazine for the Bogue Banks area that features a Property Watch section each month. This section provides a listing of recent area property transfers that occurred as recorded at the Carteret County Registrar of Deeds.*

Langston high-rise bridge opened the area to tourists and newcomers. Emerald Isle is now one of the fastest-growing areas of the county. Sections along Coast Guard Road, off N.C. 58, have seen an astounding amount of development in recent years.

You'll find many of the town's recently built residences quite impressive. Homes and cottages come in all styles, but most are multi-storied with wide porches and decks, so residents can take advantage of the beach view and sea breezes. Although some developers have bulldozed dunes and cleared much of the natural vegetation, others have left stands of maritime forest. There are a number of condominium and town-home developments as well.

Lands End is an exclusive gated residential community on Coast Guard Road off N.C. 58 near the Point in Emerald Isle. Ownership includes use of a spacious clubhouse, a pool, four lighted tennis courts, stocked freshwater lakes and a lighted boardwalk to the beach. All roads are private, and utilities are underground. Prices can range from $393,000 to more than $2 million.

Emerald Plantation is a sound-side subdivision that extends from N.C. 58 to Bogue Sound. A mixed-use development with single-family homes, townhouses and patio homes, amenities include a clubhouse, a pool, a boat ramp, tennis courts and a security gate. Sound-side homes here could sell for $1.5 million, while interior homes could range between $330,000 to $500,000.

The Point on Coast Guard Road off N.C. 58 at the westward tip of the island is one of the most established areas and has a wonderfully wide beach. The **Wyndtree** subdivision is a large tract near Emerald Isle Point that offers a wide diversity of sites from oceanfront to ocean view. Prices for homes in The Point area range from $600,000 to $1.5 million.

Deerhorn Dunes, **Sea Dunes** and **Ocean Oaks** are three well-planned subdivisions that are almost indistinguishable from one another. On Coast Guard Road off N.C. 58, all are relatively new and were built around the same time. They are made up primarily of single-family homes, nicely landscaped

on spacious lots. Homes range from $270,000 to more than $2.5 million.

Cape Emerald off N.C. 58 on the sound side of Coast Guard Road is a subdivision of primarily permanent residents, with homes averaging from $400,000 to more than $1 million. Amenities include a clubhouse, a heated pool and spa, two tennis courts and a security entrance.

Emerald Landing, **Royall Oaks**, **Dolphin Ridge** and **Pointe Bogue** are beautifully landscaped developments that offer peace and privacy in a verdant, spacious, wooded setting. Lots vary from 75-feet wide to 30-feet wide on ocean- and road-fronts. Interior lots also vary in size due to efforts to preserve the area's wetlands. Emerald Landing, Pointe Bogue and Royall Oaks have soundfront sites, and Dolphin Ridge has oceanfront building sites. Homes in these areas can start at $550,000 and go to more than $3 million.

Also off Coast Guard Road is **Spinnaker's Reach**, an area described as a "sound to sea community." These investment properties can range from $500,000 to $2.5 million. It is tucked into the maritime forest and features a community pool, guarded entrance and a sound-side pier and nature trail. Single-family dwellings and oceanfront duplexes are part of this community.

BEAUFORT

Beautiful Beaufort-by-the-Sea offers its residents a quaint maritime environment coupled with lots of history. Everything in Beaufort revolves around the historic district or the water — sometimes both. The town's geographic design lends itself to small residential areas built around roads and water. The older and more established neighborhoods and developments are in the historic area. Most new development is east of Beaufort along U.S. Highway 70 or north along N.C. Highway 101.

This small port town is a haven for boaters and is a hub of activity during the summer months. Many of the historic homes have been restored as residences or bed and breakfast inns. Its breathtaking waterfront is a natural setting for listening to live music and socializing at outdoor cafes. The town's many shops, restaurants and tourist attractions give Front Street a festive air. Runners, strollers, walkers and bike riders flow constantly along the main Front Street thoroughfare, and the Historic District can easily be covered on foot.

Beaufort's Historic District is the one of the oldest residential areas in the state and covers about 15 square blocks. Homes here date back to the 1700s, and exterior characteristics are governed by guidelines of the Beaufort Historic Preservation Commission. Charged with assuring the integrity of the area, the commission reviews all proposals for exterior changes such as paint color, siding, window treatments, redesign and other building changes. Businesses and signage in the historic district are also regulated. The historic commission was not formed until the 1980s, so you will see a few things that would not meet their standards today but were "grandfathered" in. Property prices vary greatly in the historic district, depending on distance from the water, size and age of the house or building and its condition and could range from something in the $500,000s to more than $2.5 million.

Beaufort homes outside the historic district also carry a variety of price tags, again depending on the distance from the water as well as size, age and condition.

Deerfield Shores, north of Beaufort off N.C. 101, is an attractive area on the Newport River and Intracoastal Waterway. Central to the development is the Carolina Marlin Club, a private boating (sail and motor) club complete with a 73-slip marina, a clubhouse and a swimming pool. Slip owners own the marina and clubhouse, which is also used by the Morehead-Beaufort Yacht Club. While a handful of lots are still on the market, re-sale homes in Deerfield are just beginning to pop up. Homes here could start around $275,000 and increase to around $950,000 as you get closer to the water.

Gibb's Landing is a small subdivision on North River, reached by following U.S. 70 east of downtown Beaufort and turning right on Steep Point Road. Subdivision amenities include a community dock, pool and gazebo, and prices start in the mid-$300,000s.

Howland Rock is a small subdivision that offers residents such amenities as a boat ramp, docks, a recreational area and a homeowners' association. The entrance road is on U.S. 70, just across from the

Waterfront property is at a premium on the coast.

photo: Peter Doran

Food Lion grocery store. Most of the homes were custom-built with attention to detail, and home prices could start around $350,000.

Jones Village is in the Beaufort town limits and is one of the area's oldest subdivisions. There are several entrances from Live Oak Street (U.S. 70) to the subdivision, which wraps around behind Jones Village Shopping Center. The development is a quiet, well-settled area that seems to attract a good mix of people. Prices average about $150,000 to $350,000.

Tiffany Woods is a newer development about 4 miles east of Beaufort on U.S. 70. Several cul-de-sacs extend from the lighted main road, giving the neighborhood a feeling of privacy. Prices here vary from $275,000 to $375,000.

Sea Gate is a waterside resort community 7 miles from Beaufort on N.C. 101 at Core Creek. The development is on the Intracoastal Waterway with a deep-water marina, a ship's store, gas and diesel fuel, a clubhouse, a playground, a swimming pool, tennis courts, a boat ramp and a security entrance. There is a wide range of prices here — from $175,000 to $600,000 for homes and building lots available from $60,000 and higher. Waterfront and water-view lots are more expensive.

The Oaks at Beaufort offers a real community feeling and seeks to replicate the look and feel of old Beaufort, particularly the front porches and alley-accessed garages. Although it's not in the historic district, a short footpath provides homeowners quick access to Front Street and then an easy mile-and-a-half walk to downtown Beaufort. The 42-lot, single-family subdivision offers eight basic home styles, each with many interior and exterior variations. Prices are around $290,000 to $340,000.

The east end of Lennoxville Road features wonderful views of the water and Cape Lookout. A large lot here could be priced around $1 million.

Graystone Landing is located about 3 miles up N.C. 101 from Beaufort. This neighborhood offers about 60 building lots. A few waterfront lots are available, although the majority are wooded interior lots in quiet surroundings. The houses in

Graystone are custom-built and vary in style. Pricing can range from $275,000 to $950,000.

Other relatively new neighborhoods are **Old Beaufort Village**, **Palmetto Place** and **The Courtyard East**. Prices in these three areas range from $135,000 to $200,000. The development fills Professional Drive, off of U.S. 70 East on the outskirts of Beaufort. Residents can easily walk to stores and the post office.

North Harbor is located off U.S. 70 about three miles east of Beaufort and offers homes around $150,000 to $250,000.

Construction of **North River Club** is underway. This planned community is laid out in villages that feature designed homes, bungalows, patio homes and condominiums. Nestled between Highway 70 and Highway 101 and just five miles from historic downtown Beaufort, North River Club is made up of about 620 acres and features a championship golf course and will later include a swimming and tennis center for property owners. Home packages start around $300,000, and vacant lots are also available.

Eastman Creek Landing is one of the area's newest developments north of Beaufort between N.C. 101 and the Intracoastal Waterway. This neighborhood offers a clubhouse, pool, docks and boat slips. Sites start around $61,900, and new homes begin at $199,990.

Stanton Landing is a gated waterfront community on the Intracoastal Waterway. Located north of Beaufort on N.C. 101, the subdivision offers two-thirds-acre lots, some with deep-water docks, and all owners can enjoy the clubhouse, pool and docks. A waterfront lot could go for around $250,000, with larger lots available off the waterfront.

Sandy Point on the north shore of Carteret County along the Intracoastal Waterway is a Weyerhaeuser community that prides itself on its white sandy beaches. Amenities include a beachfront gazebo, a boardwalk, large recreation areas, underground utilities and paved streets. Sandy Point's wooded home sites range in size from 1.4 to 10.9 acres, and waterfront lot prices could be around $200,000.

Olde Towne Yacht Club is situated on Radio Island, between Beaufort and Morehead City. With condo units arranged in high-rise buildings, owners have outstanding views of the surrounding waterways, islands and Cape Lookout National Seashore. The yacht club offers owners a gated entry, a water slide swimming pool, a hot tub and fitness facilities. The marina features deep-water boat slips and floating and fixed docks. A three-bedroom condominium sells for about $500,000 to $650,000. Boat slips are available for sale or lease.

Olde Towne Yacht Club
100 Olde Towne Yacht Club Rd., Beaufort
(252) 726-3066

Olde Towne Yacht Club is a gated community located on Radio Island and offers residents unprecedented views of Taylor's Creek and Carrot Island, as well as Shackleford Banks and the Atlantic Ocean. This waterfront condominium development features several floor plans, each with a private balcony. Amenities include a clubhouse, fitness facilities, a steam room, a water-side swimming pool with a whirlpool, and a private beach. Olde Towne offers a full-service marina, the closest one to the Beaufort Inlet. Call for information about condominium and boat slip sales and vacation rentals.

Morgan Creek Landing
200 Old Causeway Rd., Beaufort
(252) 726-2060, (800) 379-2955

Located on Old Causeway Road between Morehead City and Beaufort, Morgan Creek Landing is a private waterfront community designed for boaters, anglers and those who simply enjoy living on the water. A project of Waterfront Lifestyle Properties, Morgan Creek Landing features 30 luxury condominiums completed in 2007. Each condominium comes with a 35-foot boat slip and lift and features a private balcony overlooking the water, an entry balcony and exterior storage.

MOREHEAD CITY

Morehead City is the area's largest city, and it has the most neighborhoods. Like most early communities, it began at the water's edge because that's where the work was. Morehead City's earliest

inhabitants lived near what is now the N.C. State Port, bounded by Bogue Sound, the Newport River and Calico Creek. As the area filled up, homes were built farther west. Today people continue to live by the water, but not so much for the work as for the beauty of the views and the breeze.

Morehead City's downtown is seeing many improvements and an active Revitalization Committee is hard at work. Between Arendell Street and Bogue Sound, from about Ninth to 14th streets, is a neighborhood of small, wood-sided homes known as the Promise Land. Some of these houses were moved to the mainland on sailing skiffs at the turn of the last century when severe storms almost destroyed the once-flourishing fishing village of Diamond City on Shackleford Banks. Homes were dragged out of the water and rolled on logs to their new foundation. As the story goes, one spectator commented on the sight, "It looks like the Children of Israel coming to the Promise Land." The name stuck.

More and more developments are popping up in Morehead City and along the outskirts of town. Prices vary greatly depending on the proximity to the water.

The Shores at Spooners Creek features condominiums and individual home sites. Prices start at around $750,000. The Shores is a gated community featuring a marina, floating docks and boat slips.

Park Villas will be a 72-unit condominium complex across from Brandywine Bay. The complex will consist of nine buildings with eight units per building — four on the ground floor and four on the second level. The community will feature a community pool and an area for boat and/or RV storage. Expected to open in late 2007, prices will start at $149,900.

Joslyn Trace is a peaceful subdivision on N. 20th Street at the junction of Country Club Road. Homes here are both one and two stories. Creek Pointe and Mandy Farms are two neighborhoods just off Country Club Road. Expect prices in these communities to be around $225,000.

South Shores is an established waterfront community off Country Club Road on the Newport River. It offers members of its homeowners association lighted streets, curbs and gutters, a swimming pool and tennis courts. Across Country Club Road is Brookewoods subdivision, a neighborhood with lots of friendly families. Homes in these areas start around $270,000 and go up.

Country Club Road is a main thoroughfare along the north side of Morehead City. West Carteret High School is at the western end, and the Morehead City Country Club is toward the eastern end. In between are mostly long-settled neighborhoods, although a few new developments have gone up in recent years. In most areas the lovely old trees have been left in place, and most homes are suitable for retirees or young families. Homes along Country Club Road average around $250,000 to more than $300,000.

Country Club East is a development across from and fronting the golf course. Two- and three-story homes are the norm. Prices vary, depending on the size, features and distance from the golf course, and are from just under $300,000 to more than $500,000.

River Heights lies to the east of the country club and is one of the older suburbs. Homes here are rarely on the market, and when they are, they are sold relatively quickly at affordable prices. Hedrick Estates on the west side of Country Club Road features nice one-and two-story homes with well-landscaped yards. Homes here being in the mid-$100,000s and go to just over $200,000. Adjacent to Hedrick Estates is Westhaven Village, made up of one- and two-story homes on large wooded lots. Homes in this area start at around $220,000 and range to more than $400,000.

West-Car Meadows off Country Club Boulevard is a well-established, affordable development, backed by Swinson Park and close to Morehead City Primary School, the high school and shopping areas. This is a good location for families with children. Homes here are rarely available, but would begin around $200,000. Northwoods is a nice development off Country Club Road, with single-family and two-story dwellings on large tree-covered lots. Homes in these areas can start around $225,000 and go up to $400,000.

Justin's Corner is an attractive community of starter or retirement homes on Mandy Lane, just off 35th Street, south of the Sports Center. These houses are 1,200 to 1,700 square feet, with attached garages, fully equipped kitchens and no interior steps to climb. Prices are about $210,000.

Blair Pointe is a waterfront development located at the eastern end of Country Club Road. This subdivision has building lots situated on an artificial pond, Dill's Creek and on the Newport River. The development has sidewalks, pedestrian bridges, lighted-curbed streets and private docks. A wide price range is found here, depending on proximity to water and water depth. Lots are about $300,000 and homes can go for well over $1 million.

Just west of Blair Pointe is **Blair Farm**. This large development is tucked away by Blair Pointe off of Country Club Road. Blair Farm offers something for everyone — single family homes, patio homes and large homes — depending on which neighborhood you choose. A few building sites are still available, with one last section yet to be offered. Amenities include a clubhouse, a community swimming pool, a playground and tennis courts. More new areas are being developed. Prices for lots range from $120,000 to $250,000 and homes range from the high $200,000s to more than $500,000.

Bonham Heights, **Mansfield Park** and **Mitchell Village** are older, spacious, well-established neighborhoods along Bogue Sound off U.S. 70. Homes vary from modest bungalows to two-and three-story residences. Most residents have lived in these areas for a number of years; however, homes do occasionally go on the market. Prices can start at $250,000 and go up depending on their location to the sound. The Landings at Mitchell Village is a townhome community with two- and three-bedroom units, each with a garage. The prices start at $230,000 to $260,000. **The Bluffs** is a condominium development at the end of Mansfield Parkway, overlooking Bogue Sound. Units are individually owned townhouses or condominiums, most with a sound view, and prices range from $400,000 to $710,000.

Morehead City's selection of neighborhoods is quite good. There are many areas available in a variety of price ranges. There is something for everyone, if you're willing to search. Or contact a local real estate agent and let them find something that fits your needs and budget.

Country Club Run
224 Brandywine Blvd., Morehead City
(252) 240-5000, (800) 523-4612

Country Club Run is being developed and, when completed, will include 171 single-family homes and 70 duplex-style townhomes. Located between the Newport River and Country Club Road in Morehead City, Country Club Run offers residents easy access to schools, shopping and the beaches. Residents can enjoy a clubhouse and pool. Prices here start in the low $200,000s.

Park Villas
224 Brandywine Blvd., Morehead City
(252) 240-5000, (800) 523-4612

Park Villas is currently being developed and when completed will be a 72-unit condominium complex located across from Brandywine Bay in Morehead City. The complex will consist of nine buildings with eight units per building, four on the ground floor and four on the second floor. The community will be nicely landscaped and feature a community pool, as well as an area for boat and/or RV storage. Prices start at $139,900.

The Shores
Morehead City
(252) 726-2060, (800) 354-5631

The Shores features 34 condominiums and 10 individual home sites. Condominiums feature three bedrooms and three baths, large balconies, deluxe kitchens, elevators, vaulted ceilings and much more. Owners enjoy a clubhouse, a pool and an 88-slip marina with Brazilian hardwood floating docks with slips ranging from 35

Lighthouses protect mariners, warning of treacherous coastline or shoals.

photo: Peter Doran

to 100 feet in length. Located next to the Intracoastal Waterway in a private, gated community, The Shores offers residents the ultimate year-round or second home in a low maintenance neighborhood on the water.

WESTERN CARTERET COUNTY

As the county's population increases, development in the western part of Carteret County continues. This area has some long-established neighborhoods, but many new ones are springing up along N.C. Highway 24 between Morehead City and Cape Carteret and along U.S. 70 between Morehead City and Havelock.

Spooner's Creek and **Spooner's Creek East** are long-standing neighborhoods built around the marina at the mouth of Spooner's Creek and along Bogue Sound. The area features large homes, many with their own private docks, and you can expect to pay in the neighborhood of $750,000 for a home here. Spooner's Creek South is a new development in the area, offering many lots with boat slips.

Brandywine Bay is an exclusive planned subdivision, stretching from Bogue Sound to U.S. 70. Begun in 1972, the project was built around the Earle Webb estate. The waterfront portion of Brandywine Bay consists of a noncommercial marina with a community boat ramp surrounded by residential building lots. Marina slips are individually owned. Three townhouse projects surround the harbor with homes attractively placed, creating the image of a village. There are single-family residences, and lots available on either side of the townhouses and harbor. The project continues across N.C. 24, where it surrounds a beautiful 18-hole championship golf course. Some homes were built in the 1970s, and there is usually a nice selection of re-sales. Brandywine North is the subdivision's newest neighborhood. Prices vary greatly in Brandywine based on the relationship to water and the golf course. A starting price would be $250,000 and up.

Village Green at Brandywine Bay offers duplex-style homes arranged with two units per building. There you will find one- and two-story units starting around $200,000 or $250,000.

The Village at Camp Morehead by the Sea is on the site of the former Camp Morehead between N.C. 24 and Bogue Sound. This waterfront development offers residents a clubhouse, a pier, tennis and basketball courts and a swimming pool, and prices can start around $450,000 and go up to $1.5 million.

Gull Harbor, **Soundview**, **Ho-Ho Village** and **Barnesfield** are all established developments along Bogue Sound on N.C. 24. While some homes are quite large and elaborate, others are moderate in size and style. Many have deep-water docks. **Somerset Plantation** is off N.C. 24 and features a swimming pool, tennis courts, a boat ramp, a residential day dock, boat slips and a secured entrance. Homes in these neighborhoods range from $200,000 to more than $1 million, depending on how close the land is to the water.

In the Broad and Gales Creek areas are **Bluewater Banks**, **Fox Lair** and **Rollingwood Acres**. These are subdivisions close to Broad Creek Middle School. Bluewater Banks is a soundfront development, and Rollingwood Acres is on Broad Creek. Home prices vary greatly, depending on location and water access. Fox Lair is a non-waterfront development. Prices in these communities can range from $200,000 to more than $1.5 million.

Bogue Watch and **Cannonsgate** are under construction off N.C. 24. These communities are surrounded by Croatan

National Forest and the Intracoastal Waterway. Homesites vary in cost depending on their location. Bogue Watch is a gated community with 287 homesites. Residents can enjoy a pool, deep water access, parks and much more. Waterfront and waterview homesites range from $160,000 to $800,000. Cannonsgate is also a gated community and offers a 75-slip marina, clubhouse, swimming pool, tennis courts and a boat launch. Homesites start at $155,000 and go up.

Bluewater Cove is located off West Firetower Road, just outside Cape Carteret. This community offers residents a deeded water access, community daydock, boat ramp, pool and clubhouse. Lot prices vary and start around $115,000.

Marsh Harbour is a new community in Cedar Point featuring a community pool, pavilion and boat/RV storage areas. Lots start around $65,000 and go up. Quailwood Village is off Taylor Notion Road, near the golf course. Homes here start at $245,000 and go up.

Farther up N.C. 24 toward Swansboro are **Bogue Sound Yacht Club** with homes in the $350,000 to $490,000 range; Blue **Heron Bay**, where homes can range from $250,000 to $780,000; and **Hickory Shores**, with prices between $379,000 and $600,000. Homes vary from spacious and elaborate to small and practical.

In Cedar Point, at the intersection of N.C. 58 and N.C. 24, is **Magen's Bay**. This is a residential, soundfront area with homes selling from $350,000 to $1.3 million. Magen's Bay features private-gate entry, a pool and a bathhouse, tennis courts, deeded water access and a 100-foot pier to Bogue Sound.

Four miles east of Cape Carteret is **Cedar Key**. Nestled along Bogue Sound,

Stop by the Crystal Coast Visitors Center, 3409 Arendell Street (U.S. Highway 70 E.), Morehead City, to pick up a free street map of Morehead, Beaufort, Swansboro, Atlantic Beach, Down East, Newport and many of the area's other towns.

this development offers beautiful views of Carolina sunsets. Water access is available, and a pier, park and picnic areas are open for residents. Prices here can start around $100,000 for a homesite.

Bluewater Cove is located off N.C. 58 on West Fire Tower Road across from Silver Creek Golf Course. The subdivision offers residents water access, a pool and clubhouse, and a boat ramp and day dock. Prices start at $350,000.

SWANSBORO

Historic Swansboro offers a variety of housing opportunities, including historic houses near the business district, mobile homes on the outskirts of town and charming new homes on unbelievably beautiful lots overlooking the water. Swansboro attracts those seeking to relocate to a quiet, coastal area, and the waterfront offers outstanding restaurants and shops of all types.

In the town itself, there are basically three types of homes. In the oldest part of town are the historic homes, some rehabilitated and restored and others in need of attention. Around the fringes of the business district and extending several blocks in all directions are houses that were built about 50 years ago. They, like the older homes, are a mix of beautifully restored and maintained residences, with some that would be on the market as fixer-uppers. Closer to the city limits are homes built within the past 25 or 30 years. Most are still in good condition but not particularly distinctive in design.

In recent years, new developments have been opening, bringing a totally new look to Swansboro's housing picture. **The Hammocks** at Port Swansboro is a gated community offering townhomes ranging from $170,000 to $250,000. This community features private day docks and a boat ramp. The **River Reach** development brought a dramatic change in Swansboro's real estate market, with properties ranging from $300,000 and up.

The Villages at Swansboro is a development on Mount Pleasant Road, and it is especially for seniors 55 years of age and older. This single-family, one-story condominium community is set in a park-like area. Exterior home and yard maintenance

are taken care of so seniors can live a care-free life. Homes here sell for around $200,000.

Plantation Estates is a waterfront subdivision on the White Oak River with homes starting at $400,000. **Hurst Harbour** is an exclusive subdivision near the ferry landing at Hammocks Beach State Park. Here homes start at $400,000 and go up. **Oyster Bay** offers homes in the area of $300,000. **Walnut Landing** was designed for more economical residences with prices starting at $225,000.

Port West Townhouses are beside Swansboro Primary School and are made up of 13 buildings with four units each. Most units are rentals; however, some are owner occupied. The townhouses feature one, two or three bedrooms and sell for about $80,000 to $100,000.

Swann Harbour is a waterfront development off N.C. 24 on the White Oak River offering one- and two-story homes with two or three bedrooms. The condominiums here sell for about $250,000, and the patio homes go for about $275,000 and up. There are three floor plans available ranging from 1,300 to 1,700 square feet. Many units face the river, which is accessible by a boardwalk; other units face Swansboro town park. Community amenities include a swimming pool, a boat-landing gazebo and a dock.

Pirates Cove is a townhome subdivision with a pool and clubhouse environment.

These properties are being purchased for investment or by people looking for low-maintenance housing centrally located in Swansboro for around $125,000. **Deer Run** is also another town subdivision and prices start at $175,000 and go up.

DOWN EAST

Down East communities themselves make up the neighborhoods. The communities string along U.S. 70 and the waterfronts and revolve around the churches or the volunteer fire/rescue departments. You should keep in mind that Down East living isn't for everyone. The conveniences of town living are quite a few miles away, but there are certainly many of life's simple pleasures here.

Many of the county's traditional fishermen and boat builders live Down East, an area along U.S. 70 that merges into N.C. 12 and extends from Bettie to Cedar Island. As you cross the many Down East bridges, it is not unusual to see clammers hip-deep in the water. Boat sheds are more common than garages, and the whir of saws and smell of wood chips are sure signs of boat builders. Fishing and shrimp boats ply the waters year round, and egrets, herons, ospreys and other shorebirds live in the marshes and wetlands along the highway.

As more people move to Carteret County, its eastern sector has seen the development of a few subdivisions outside the small communities. Homes and acreage are becoming increasingly available and, although prices vary widely, they are going up — especially properties situated on the many creeks, inlets, bays, marshes and rivers that are the beauty of Down East. But if you want to get away from it all, for now this is the place to do it.

None of the Down East area is zoned, and therefore the area falls under Carteret County jurisdiction. Because of current regulations and coastal development requirements, land suitable for development is sparse in the Down East portion of Carteret County. This is a treasured area that many people seek to call home so land is in great demand. Land prices vary greatly depending upon location, view, elevation and amenities. Most Down East residents, both natives and newcomers to the beautiful area, do not want new high-density development approved. Concentrated development would change the quiet way of life and harm the area's fragile environment, and some citizen groups continue to work to have the Down East areas protected.

Still, there are a number of neighborhoods and subdivisions in the Down East area. **Harbor Point** in Straits was established several years ago. With home sites on a secluded peninsula, the development offers a park area and boat ramp and is completely sold out. Resales are infrequent and when a property is available the range could be $200,000 to $750,000.

Midden's Creek is a waterfront community about 15 minutes east of Beaufort in the Down East town of Smyrna. Waterfront lots are about $200,000 and offer direct boat access to Cape Lookout and Drum Inlet by way of Core Sound. These lots are in excess of an acre and each has a septic permit.

Ward's Creek Plantation and **Tranquility Estates** are both in Otway and offer houses in the range of $175,000 to $300,000. Ward's Creek offers waterfront, water-view and water-access lots. Tranquility Estates offers waterfront lots on Ward's Creek and all interior lots have water access to Ward's Creek. **Jade Point** is a developing waterfront community located off Crow Hill Road in Otway.

There are a few developments on Harkers Island, including **Harkers Point** and **Harkers Village**. These two areas are sold out, and if a lot resale does open up it goes quickly. Prices in these two developments could range from $750,000 to $1 million. **West Bay** is a new development on the north side of Harkers Island with lots ranging from $150,000 to $450,000.

Real Estate Companies

ATLANTIC BEACH

Al Williams Properties
300 Atlantic Beach Cswy., Atlantic Beach
(252) 726-8800, (800) 849-1888
www.alwilliamsproperties.com

The company slogan states Al Williams Properties has been a coastal tradition for more than 20 years. Agents offer a strong knowledge base of the area. Listings often include exclusive condominium properties and waterfront homes on the beach and in Morehead City as well as building lots and acreage. Al Williams' Realtors are available to show you any type of property.

Alan Shelor Real Estate
407 Atlantic Beach Cswy., Ste. 3, Atlantic Beach
(252) 247-7700, (800) 849-2767

This company offers properties all around the Crystal Coast and has been in business for more than 35 years. Five Realtors are on staff to help clients find just the right residential, resort or commercial property. Alan Shelor is a general contractor and can provide local appraisal services as well as residential construction services. Feel free to contact him personally at (252) 723-1467.

Atlantic Beach Realty
Atlantic Beach Cswy., Atlantic Beach
(252) 240-7368, (800) 786-7368
www.atlanticbeachrealty.net

Owners Charles and Mary Duane Hale are longtime residents of the area and have extensive knowledge of properties on the Crystal Coast. Atlantic Beach Realty is a full-service real estate firm, handling condominiums and cottage rentals of all types. With a primary office in Atlantic Beach, the firm also offers an

office at Dunescape Villas and another at Island Beach & Racquet Club.

Beach Vacation Properties
301 Commerce Way, Atlantic Beach
(252) 247-2636, (800) 334-2667
www.beachvacationproperties.com

This company handles sales at A Place at the Beach in Atlantic Beach, Sea Spray and Sands Villa, as well as offering property-management services. They also offer short-term seasonal rentals or off-season long-term rentals and can find just the right cottage or condominium to suit your needs. No matter the size of housing you need or the length of your stay, the staff at Beach Vacation Properties can help.

Bluewater GMAC - Atlantic Beach
311-C Atlantic Beach Cswy., Atlantic Beach
(866) 467-3105
www.bluewatergmac.com

With four sales offices strategically placed along the Crystal Coast in Atlantic Beach, Beaufort, Cape Carteret and Emerald Isle, this full-service real estate firm can assist you with your dream of owning coastal real estate. Whether it be a quaint cottage, an elegant oceanfront home, a carefree condo or an undeveloped home site, the Bluewater GMAC real estate sales team has the Crystal Coast covered. Bluewater GMAC offers friendly, knowledgeable and professional Realtors ready to assist you. The sales team can also show you the wisdom of vacation ownership by

renting to others as an easy way to help pay for your beach property.

Cannon & Gruber Realtors
509 Atlantic Beach Cswy., Atlantic Beach
(252) 726-6600

Formed in 1995, Cannon & Gruber offers many enviable listings not often found on the market. This firm offers residential listings, with beach and soundfront condominiums as a specialty. It also handles commercial properties and property management. Contact them for a listing of properties that are currently available.

Coldwell Banker Spectrum Properties
515 Atlantic Beach Cswy., Atlantic Beach
(800) 237-7380, (252) 247-7600
www.spectrumproperties.com

Coldwell Banker Spectrum Properties is a full-service agency that has been serving all of Carteret County for more than 30 years. The Realtors specialize in residential home and condominium sales, home-site sales and commercial sales throughout the area. They also offer long-term and seasonal rentals and professional property-management services.

Deanna Hull Realty
607 Atlantic Beach Cswy., Ste. 103, Atlantic Beach
(252) 240-0273, (800) 477-4180
www.deannahullrealty.com

Owner Deanna Hull is a native of Carteret County and has 25 years of experience in the real estate business. Her agency handles all types of properties for buyers and sellers on the Crystal Coast and surrounding area. She also handles timeshare re-sales with no up-front fee. Whether buying or selling, stop by and visit for an honest, professional approach. Deanna prides herself on keeping her clients' best interests at heart. The office is located in the big yellow building on the Atlantic Beach Causeway.

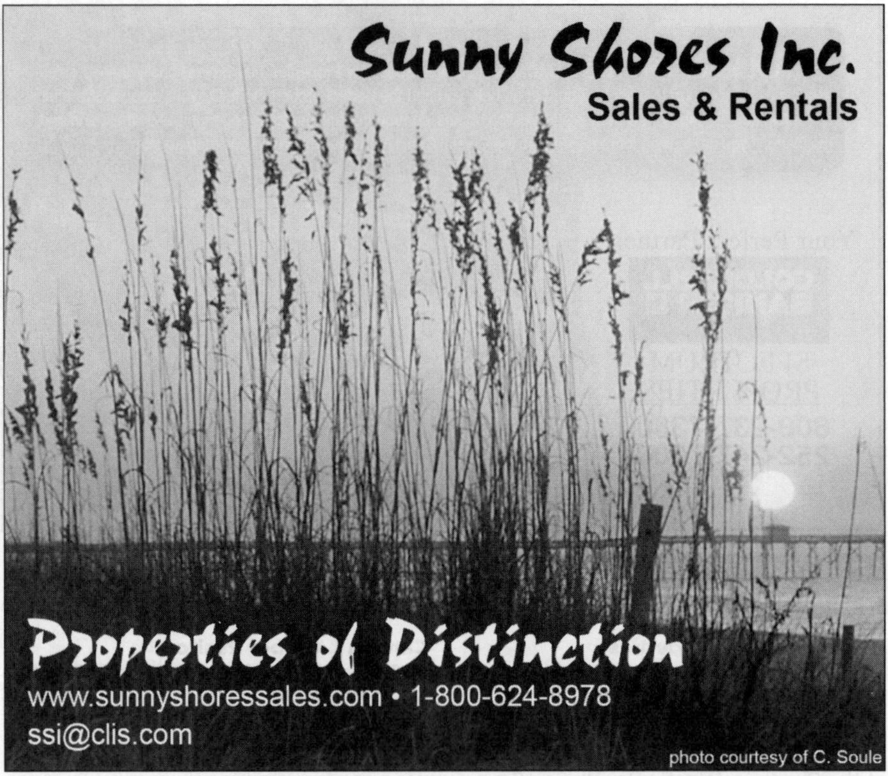

Gull Isle Realty
611 Atlantic Beach Cswy., Atlantic Beach
(252) 726-7679, (800) 682-6866

In business since 1971, Gull Isle Realty handles appraisals as well as sales of

condominiums, homes, building lots and investment properties. Gull Isle Realty also handles a number of long-term rentals and provides rental management. The firm has a state-certified appraiser. Call Owner-Broker David Waller for any real estate need.

Realty World First Coast Realty
407 Atlantic Beach Cswy., Ste. 1,
Atlantic Beach
(252) 247-0077

This full-service agency provides an extensive inventory of homes, condominiums and building lots. Knowledgeable agents match new homeowners with affordable property in the right locations. Realty World First Coast Realty has offices in Atlantic Beach, Beaufort, Emerald Isle, Down East, Newport and Morehead City. The firm has an outstanding reputation for its property-management program and its vacation and annual rental department, (252) 247-5151, (800) 972-8899. This company also offers cottages and condominiums perfect for a coastal wedding, reception or romantic honeymoon.

---

i *In addition to the real estate companies we recommend, the Carteret County Association of Realtors can assist in answering questions about reputable local real estate companies at (252) 247-2323.*

Sound 'N' Sea Real Estate
205 Atlantic Beach Cswy., Atlantic Beach
(252) 726-1239

Owned and managed by Ellen and Demus Thompson, Sound 'N' Sea Real Estate specializes in the sale of homes and condos on the island and mainland. The Thompsons' firm is the oldest continuously owned and operated full-service real estate business in the Atlantic Beach–Pine Knoll Shores area.

The Star Team Real Estate
201 W. Fort Macon Rd., Atlantic Beach
(252) 727-5656

Sally Smith and Louis Weil have formed a comprehensive real estate company that carries the slogan The Star Team - Coastal Property Specialists. This firm offers properties of all types, from first and second homes and investment properties to new construction and commercial. They handle residential properties throughout Carteret County and also specialize in primary, vacation, retirement and second-home properties.

PINE KNOLL SHORES AND INDIAN BEACH

First Commercial Properties
1700 N.C. Hwy. 58, Salter Path
(252) 247-2035, (888) 237-2035

First Commercial Properties offers development acreage, building lots and private residences throughout Bogue Banks, Crystal Coast, Newport, Morehead City and the surrounding area. This firm's market niche is commercial ventures and exclusive vacation residences. In business for more than 23 years, it has solid expertise in handling commercial transactions and consulting with coastal investors. The company has helped create and market such developments as The Ocean Club Resort, Sea Isle Plantation and Kiawa.

Pine Knoll Shores Realty
320 Salter Path Rd. (N.C. Hwy. 58), Ste. Y, Pine Knoll Shores
(252) 727-5000, (800) 605-8598

Share your real estate dreams with these professionals and let them go to work. Pine Knoll Shores Realty has the slogan "Your best friend at the beach" and they live up to that by focusing on your specific needs. The company specializes in properties on Bogue Banks but it handles listings throughout the county. Whether you are interested in a primary home, a second home, a condo or a lot, the company's brokers can find just the right property.

Sunny Shores
520 N.C. Hwy. 58, Pine Knoll Shores
(252) 247-2665
www.sunnyshores.com

Sunny Shores is a full-service company operated by experienced Realtors. The company offers sales, vacation rentals and property management, along with maintenance and cleaning services. Sunny Shores' specialty is meeting unique rental requirements. For rental information, call (800) 626-3113. The office is across from the Clam Digger Inn.

EMERALD ISLE

Advantage Coastal Properties
301 Mangrove Dr., Ste. 1-A, Emerald Isle
(252) 354-9000

Ed and Mac (Margaret) Nelson work as a team to offer the Nelson Advantage for Advantage Coastal Properties. They offer full real estate services and a low commission of 3.9 percent to all their clients. The Nelson team specializes in handling the needs of out-of-town buyers and sellers, and they offer residential and second-home properties. Whether along Bogue Banks from Atlantic Beach to Emerald Isle,or across the bridge on the mainland, the Nelson Advantage is sure to fulfill your real estate needs.

Angelfish Properties
7601 Emerald Dr., Emerald Isle
(252) 354-8984
www.angelfishproperties.com

Angelfish Properties is a full-service agency that specializes in oceanfront, waterfront and investment properties. While their main focus is on Emerald Isle, Swansboro and Cape Carteret, Brian Peele and his five agents can locate just the property you are seeking anywhere in the surrounding area as well. This knowledgeable and friendly agency handles the sale of homes, lots and condos as well as commercial properties.

and long-term rental properties. Call these professionals for your real estate needs at the Crystal Coast.

Emerald Isle Realty
7501 Emerald Dr., Emerald Isle
(252) 354-4060, (866) 515-0043
www.emeraldislerealty.com

Emerald Isle Realty is a family-owned and operated company offering sales, property management and vacation rental services. Their knowledgeable and courteous sales staff will guide you in the selling and buying process of your family vacation home, beach residence or investment property. They specialize in resort sales on Bogue Banks, as well as residential and commercial listings on the mainland. Their sales team is ready to work with you.

Bluewater GMAC - Emerald Isle
200 Mangrove Dr., Emerald Isle
(888) 354-2128
www.bluewatergmac.com

With four sales offices strategically placed along the Crystal Coast in Atlantic Beach, Beaufort, Cape Carteret and Emerald Isle, this full-service real estate firm can assist you with your dream of owning coastal real estate. Whether it be a quaint cottage, an elegant oceanfront home, a carefree condo or an undeveloped home site, the Bluewater GMAC real estate sales team has the Crystal Coast covered. Bluewater GMAC offers friendly, knowledgeable and professional Realtors ready to assist you. The sales team can also show you the wisdom of vacation ownership by renting to others as an easy way to help pay for your beach property.

Realty World First Coast Realty
7413 Emerald Dr., Emerald Isle
(252) 354-3070

This full-service agency provides an extensive inventory of homes, condominiums and building lots. Knowledgeable agents match new homeowners with affordable property in the right locations. Realty World First Coast Realty also has offices in Atlantic Beach, Beaufort, Down East, Newport and Morehead City. The firm has an outstanding reputation for its property-management program and its vacation and annual rental department, (252) 247-5151, (800) 972-8899. This company also offers cottages and condominiums perfect for a coastal wedding, reception or romantic honeymoon.

Century 21 Coastland Realty
7603 Emerald Dr., Emerald Isle
(252) 354-2131
www.coastland.com

This full-service real estate company has been in business since 1981. It was the first realty franchise on the beach. The company offers many properties for sale, including new and previously owned condominiums, building lots and commercial properties. The firm specializes in Emerald Island and the mainland areas of Cape Carteret and Cedar Point. Century 21 Coastland Realty also offers a property management division as well as vacation

Shorewood Real Estate
7703 Emerald Dr., Emerald Isle
(252) 354-7858, (888) 557-0172
www.shorewoodrealestate.com

A full-service, family-owned business, Shorewood Real Estate specializes in real estate sales, property management and vacation rentals. Celebrating their 13th year of service to property owners and guests to the Crystal Coast, the owners and staff of Shorewood Real Estate pride themselves on the delivery of exceptional customer service, professionalism and courtesy. Whether your interests are in real estate as an investment, a second home or a primary residence, their sales team is ready to assist you in your purchase.

Spinnaker's Reach Realty
9918 M.B. Davis Ct., Emerald Isle
(252) 354-5555
www.spinnakersreach.com

Spinnaker's Reach Realty offers pre-miere vacation rentals, sales and property management in Emerald Isle with personal attention and top-notch customer service. A full-service real estate company, the professional staff of locals helps in the buying, selling or renting of your coastal dream property. Spinnaker's Reach is a private rental and long-term community on Coast Guard Road in Emerald Isle with homes and home sites from the sound to the ocean. Many of the properties feature pools, golf carts and elevators. Visit the website for virtual tours and online book-ing.

Sun-Surf Realty
7701 Emerald Dr., Emerald Isle
(252) 354-2958, (866) 584-5124
www.SunSurfRealty.com

Sun-Surf Realty's slogan "Come for a Week...Stay for a Lifetime" says it all. A family-owned business since 1978, Sun-Surf can help you plan your vacation by offering many choices, including premier homes, modest cottages and beachfront/side condominiums with all the amenities. Let one of their experienced sales profes-sionals show you how you can make your "place at the beach" a reality. They have a "no-hassle vacation policy" with no reser-vation or pre-booking fees, buyer repre-sentation in real estate sales transactions, and one-on-one, full-service property management of both vacation and annual rental properties.

Watson-Matthews Real Estate
9102 Coast Guard Rd., Emerald Isle
(252) 354-2872

This business has been active since 1979 with sales of condominiums, single-family dwellings and investment and commercial property. Watson-Matthews offers homes and home sites in prestigious Lands End, Cape Emerald and other Em-erald Isle developments as well as along Bogue Banks and on the mainland.

BEAUFORT

Beaufort Realty
325 Front St., Beaufort
(252) 728-5462, (800) 548-2961

This company specializes in residential and commercial property in the Beaufort historic district and it often has some desirable historic properties for sale. Beaufort Realty also handles sales in Down East, Morehead City and on the beach. The company is one of the few firms that offers annual and vacation rentals in historic Beaufort.

Bluewater GMAC - Beaufort
601 Cedar St., Ste. 5, Beaufort
(252) 504-3334, (866) 803-0073
www.bluewatergmac.com

With four sales offices strategically placed along the Crystal Coast in Atlantic Beach, Beaufort, Cape Carteret and Emerald Isle, this full-service real estate firm can assist you with your dream of owning coastal real estate. Whether it be a quaint cottage, an elegant oceanfront home, a carefree condo or an undeveloped home site, the Bluewater GMAC real estate sales team has the Crystal Coast covered. Bluewater GMAC offers friendly, knowledgeable and professional Realtors ready to assist you. The sales team can also show you the wisdom of vacation ownership by renting to others as an easy way to help pay for your beach property.

CENTURY 21 Down East Realty
415 Front St., Beaufort
(252) 728-5274, (800) 849-5795

CENTURY 21 Down East Realty specializes in Down East and Beaufort properties. It also handles property in Morehead City and is affiliated with the CENTURY 21 Newsom-Ball office in Morehead City. The firm handles residential and commercial sales as well as appraisals. It is Beaufort's oldest full-service real estate company.

Core Sound Realty
2622 U.S. Hwy. 70 E, Beaufort
(252) 728-1602

Core Sound Realty handles all types of real estate — residential, commercial, acreage and home sites — all over Carteret County. It specializes in waterfront, water-view and water-access properties in Beaufort and Down East and acts as agents for buyers and sellers.

Eddy Myers Real Estate
131 Middle Ln., Beaufort
(252) 728-1310

Eddy Myers Real Estate specializes in a selection of waterfront and water-view properties in historic Downtown Beaufort and in surrounding areas of the North Carolina Central Coast. They can help with waterfront estates, historic or commercial properties, condos, beach homes, vacation cottages or year-round residences.

The Holland Group Real Estate
113 Turner St., Beaufort
(252) 504-2400, (888) 879-7790

Owned by owner/agent Jeanette Holland, this agency is a quickly growing company that handles property throughout the county. Whether it is a first home, a second home, a retirement home or an investment property, this company's agents can act for the seller or buyer. The company also offers commercial real estate and property-management services.

Realty World First Coast Realty
100 Cedar St., Beaufort
(252) 728-6455

This full-service agency provides an extensive inventory of homes, condominiums and building lots. Knowledgeable agents match new homeowners with affordable property in the right locations. Realty World First Coast Realty also has offices in Atlantic Beach, Emerald Isle, Down East, Newport and Morehead City. The firm has an outstanding reputation for its property-management program and its vacation and annual rental department, (252) 247-5151, (800) 972-8899. This company also offers cottages and condominiums perfect for a coastal wedding, reception or romantic honeymoon.

MOREHEAD CITY

Advantage One-Tom Saunders Realty
100 N. 28th St., Morehead City
(252) 247-7444, (800) 587-2549

This company offers a great variety, from homes in some of the area's most exclusive residential districts to fixer-uppers with investment potential. It offers lots, acreage and commercial properties and specializes in waterfront and residential properties and a few long-term rentals. The firm can provide appraisals, property management and relocation services.

CENTURY 21 Newsom-Ball Realty
4644 Arendell St., Morehead City
(252) 240-2100, (800) 849-5794

CENTURY 21 Newsom-Ball Realty has an office in Morehead City and a sister office in Beaufort. The agents at both offices are well-rounded and knowledgeable of the area. The company offers complete services, emphasizing the sale of homes, businesses and acreage throughout the county. CENTURY 21 also provides appraisals and commercial leasing services.

Chalk & Gibbs Realty
1006 Arendell St., Morehead City
(252) 726-3167, (800) 849-3167

Chalk & Gibbs Realty has been serving Carteret County since 1925 as a full-service, independent real estate agency. Agents assist with sales of new construction projects, resales, commercial and investment properties, as well as homes and acreage. Chalk & Gibbs offers property management services. The company also is a full-service insurance company.

Exit Realty Seaside
7009-A U.S. Hwy. 70 E, Newport
(252) 342-5557, (252) 342-2220
www.coastalhomesource.com

Exit Realty Seaside represents both buyers and sellers in Carteret and Craven counties from Atlantic Beach, Morehead City, Beaufort and Newport to Havelock and New Bern. Let Teresa and Stacy Winchell share their real estate expertise with you whether you're looking for an affordable first home, a beach vacation home or a retirement home in a quiet subdivision. They are proud to specialize in working with young military families in an effort to meet all their housing needs.

Golf & Shore Properties
224 Brandywine Blvd., Morehead City
(252) 240-5000, (800) 523-4612

Golf & Shore Properties specializes in properties in Brandywine Bay. The company also represents properties throughout the county, and the experienced agents

can help you select lots, single-family homes and townhomes. The office is right inside the U.S. 70 gate to Brandywine. Their slogan, "Live Where You Play!", is a perfect fit.

Home Finders Robinson and Associates
106 Industrial Dr., Morehead City
(252) 240-7653

Alan and Sharon Robinson own and operate this family business. Alan Robinson has been in the real estate business since 1979, and his wife joined him in 1988. The company handles single-family homes from Morehead City to Newport plus lots and acreage. It also offers property-management services, works with several builders and offers long-term rentals.

Kivett's Happy House Realty
1205 Arendell St., Morehead City
(252) 342-4444
www.happyhouserealty.com

Kivett's Happy House Realty serves as a selling or buying agent for property throughout Carteret County and the Crystal Coast, including the beaches, mainland, islands and Down East. The company specializes in homes and land, and sells for as low as 3.9 percent. These helpful professionals offer customers the use of a moving truck for local moves, and you can view the Crystal Coast video on the company's website.

Linda Rike Real Estate
1410 Arendell St., Morehead City
(252) 247-6922, (800) 240-6922

Linda Rike has been providing real estate services in the county for more than 24 years. With that experience, this firm knows the county well and handles new construction, re-sales, condominiums, homes and lots. The company specializes in waterfront and second homes, resort and recreational properties and retirement relocations. It also offers a few long-term rentals.

N.C. Coastal Properties -
Gena Gilbert Real Estate
4219-H Arendell St., Morehead City
(252) 240-0259, (877) 240-0259

Gena Gilbert , owner/operator, and her agents handle residential listings of homes and condos, as well as investment properties. They specialize in waterfront property, working as both seller's and buyer's agents.

Putnam Real Estate
3800 Arendell St., Morehead City
(252) 726-2826

Putnam Real Estate is a full-service agency that specializes in the sale of new and established homes, commercial properties and building lots throughout the county. In business since 1972, the company offers full appraisal services, property management and long-term rentals.

RE/MAX Ocean Properties
1305 Arendell St., Morehead City
(252) 222-3222, (866) 910-3222

Alton Best and Serena Sullivan of RE/MAX Ocean Properties have more than 40 years of combined real estate experience to provide trusted services for both buyers and sellers. Multi-million dollar producers, Best and Sullivan live in Harkers Island and Beaufort, respectively, and know the entire Central Coast area very well. Their listings range the entire Crystal Coast region, including many waterfront properties.

Realty World First Coast Realty
4747 Arendell St., Morehead City
(252) 222-4747

This full-service agency provides an extensive inventory of homes, condominiums and building lots. Knowledgeable agents match new homeowners with affordable property in the right locations. Realty World First Coast Realty also has offices in Atlantic Beach, Beaufort, Emerald Isle, Salter Path and Newport. The firm has an outstanding reputation for its property-management program and its vacation and annual rental department, (252) 247-5151, (800) 972-8899. This company also offers cottages and condominiums perfect for a coastal wedding, reception or romantic honeymoon.

Waterfront Lifestyle Properties
5113-B U.S. Hwy. 70, Morehead City
(252) 726-2060, (800) 254-4217

Waterfront Lifestyle Properties, LLC is developer of premium waterfront locations along North Carolina's central coast. This firm focuses on offering gated communities for single-family homes, luxury condominiums, clubhouses, pools and private marinas.

DOWN EAST

Many of the real estate agencies throughout the county handle property in the Down East area, which is east of Beaufort. There are only a few real estate companies with offices actually in the Down East area.

Golden-Lew Realty
383 U.S. Hwy. 70 E, Otway
(252) 728-3974

Owner-broker Catherine Golden has handled sales of residential, commercial and waterfront properties for more than 20 years. Golden-Lew specializes in properties Down East and in Beaufort.

Realty World First Coast Realty - Gateway
535 U.S. Hwy. 70, Bettie
(252) 728-7790

Realty World First Coast has expanded to include an office in the Down East area. Formerly known as Eastern Gateway Realty, this office offers plenty of knowledge of the Down East area and what it has to offer. This full-service agency provides an extensive inventory of homes, condominiums and building lots. Knowledgeable agents match new homeowners with affordable properties in the right locations. Realty World First Coast Realty has offices in Atlantic Beach, Beaufort, Emerald Isle, Down East, Newport and Morehead City. The firm has an outstanding reputation for its property-management program and its vacation and annual rental department, (252) 247-5151, (800) 972-8899. This company also offers cottages and condominiums perfect for a coastal wedding, reception or romantic honeymoon.

Sea Level Real Estate at The Holland Group Real Estate
113 Turner St., Beaufort
(252) 504-2400, (252) 504-7177 (direct)

Danielle Taylor, a Down East native and owner of Sea Level Real Estate for 10 years, has taken her years of real estate experience and joined forces with the locally owned Holland Group Real Estate. Servicing both buyers and sellers, Sea

Level Real Estate still maintains its interest and service to "the Original Down East." Top-quality service is a primary focus, and clients have the added bonus of the experience and exposure of two companies working for them.

WESTERN CARTERET AND SWANSBORO

Bluewater GMAC - Cape Carteret
415 W. B. McLean Blvd., Cape Carteret
(800) 752-3543
www.bluewatergmac.com

With four sales offices strategically placed along the Crystal Coast in Atlantic Beach, Beaufort, Cape Carteret and Emerald Isle, this full-service real estate firm can assist you with your dream of owning coastal real estate. Whether it be a quaint cottage, an elegant oceanfront home, a carefree condo or an undeveloped home site, the Bluewater GMAC real estate sales team has the Crystal Coast covered. Bluewater GMAC offers friendly, knowledgeable and professional Realtors ready to assist you. The sales team can also show you the wisdom of vacation ownership by renting to others as an easy way to help pay for your beach property.

CENTURY 21 Waterway Realty
406 Corbett Ave., Swansboro
(910) 326-4152, (877) 326-4152

An established agency in Swansboro, CENTURY 21 Waterway sells building lots, new homes and re-sales in the Swansboro/Cape Carteret/Emerald Isle area. Most of the company's agents are longtime residents of the area. The company also handles commercial properties, lots and acreage along the White Oak River and the Intracoastal Waterway and offers long-term rentals and property management.

Racing Realty
911 W. Corbett Ave., Swansboro
(910) 326-7222
www.racingrealty.net

Racing Realty is your one-stop source for real estate services covering the Swansboro, Hubert, Stella, Cedar Point, Cape Carteret and Emerald Isle areas. With 25 years combined experience in the local market, Georgia Powell and Can-

dace Burns are the ones to locate just the right home, commercial property, land or investment property for you. Their goal is to provide you with superior service. The agents can represent the buyer or seller. Racing Realty also offers property management services and many year-round rental properties.

Realty World First Coast Realty
2946 N.C. Hwy. 24, Newport
(252) 247-2946

This full-service agency provides an extensive inventory of homes, condominiums and building lots. Knowledgeable agents match new homeowners with affordable property in the right locations. Realty World First Coast Realty also has offices in Atlantic Beach, Beaufort, Emerald Isle, Down East and Morehead City. The firm has an outstanding reputation for its property-management program and its vacation and annual rental department, (252) 247-5151, (800) 972-8899. This company also offers cottages and condominiums perfect for a coastal wedding, reception or romantic honeymoon.

SurfSide Realty, Inc.
204 Sandpiper Dr., Newport
(252) 726-0950

SurfSide Realty, Inc., focuses on finding just the right property for each client. Whether that is an island home, a house on the mainland, a vacation place or a condo, this mother-daughter team can find just the place. Both are brokers and licensed Realtors and act as agents for buyers or sellers. SurfSide also handles rentals.

Timeshare Sales

Deanna Hull Realty
607 Atlantic Beach Cswy., Ste. 103, Atlantic Beach
(252) 240-0273, (800) 477-4180
www.deannahullrealty.com

Serving timeshare owners and buyers since 1984, licensed real estate broker Deanna Hull specializes in Atlantic Beach oceanfront resort property, handles resales with no up-front fee and works to save buyers on lower-priced homeowners association closeout inventory and timeshare resales. Whether you're buying or selling property of any type on the Crystal Coast or surrounding areas, contact Deanna for an honest, no-pressure approach. She prides herself on keeping her clients' best interests at heart. Timeshare rentals at A Place At The Beach III, Sands Villa and Peppertree are also available.

Real Estate Services

Advanced Water Systems - Kinetico
5633 U.S. Hwy. 70 E, Newport
(252) 223-4444

Kinetico provides residents of Carteret County with an important commodity: treated water. Much of the county's water comes from private wells, and much of the local well water contains iron and calcium. Kinetico sells water-treatment equipment that continuously delivers high-quality drinking water.

Brown & Curtis Home Services, LLC
104 Stuart Ave., Emerald Isle
(252) 354-2861

Brown & Curtis Home Services offers professional property-management services for non-renting second-home owners. They can make life easier in so many ways by making all the arrangements you need for your home. Let this firm contact and supervise licensed, bonded contractors as they work on your home. Brown & Curtis offers a variety of services from roofers and electricians to plumbers and pest-control experts. They can also arrange to be on site to accept deliveries.

Carteret-Craven Electric Cooperative
1300 N.C. Hwy. 24 W, Newport
(252) 247-3107

Providing electrical service to much of western Carteret County, this member-owned corporation has more than 37,500 accounts. It services all residents of Bogue Banks except those living in Atlantic Beach; all residents in Cape Carteret, Cedar Point and along N.C. Highway 58 to Maysville; residents along N.C. 24 from the Swansboro line to Gull Harbor and down

Nine Foot Road to the bridge at Rams Horn Drive and Lake Road to Havelock; residents along old Highway 70 to Havelock; and Morehead City residents in some areas of Country Club and Crab Point. It also serves residents in Cedar Island, South River, Merrimon, Harkers Island and along N.C. Highway 101 to the outskirts of Beaufort. The cooperative also provides service to portions of Havelock and small areas in Jones and Onslow counties. A deposit may be required when making an application, or a letter of good credit from another utility company may waive that deposit requirement.

Embarq
New Bern
(252) 633-9011

While many people may recognize Embarq as a long-distance carrier, in this area it's also the local telephone company. Depending on your previous record, you may be asked to pay a deposit before service is initiated. The deposit usually is refunded after a year. Connection can take three or four working days, longer if there has not been telephone connection at that address before. Embarq also offers unlimited long distance, high-speed Internet, satellite TV service and bundled packages.

Progress Energy Carolinas
1099 Gum Branch Rd., Jacksonville
(888) 534-8946

Progress Energy has headquarters in Raleigh. The customer service number is (800) 452-2777, and the number to report outages is (800) 419-6356. All required city and county inspections must be completed prior to connecting your permanent electric service. An electrical inspection is required for newly constructed homes or manufactured homes. Since electricity is billed after it is used, Progress Energy may require a security deposit before completing your application for service. If a deposit is required, the company will contact you either by e-mail or phone to provide additional instructions.

Green Building Services

Accredited Solar & Wind
Emerald Isle
(252) 389-8208,
(877) SAFE PWR (723-3797)

If you are seeking solar or wind alternatives for your home or business, contact Accredited Solar and Wind. Specializing in photovoltaics (electricity generated from the sun), solar thermal (hot water from the sun), solar pool heating and wind power, Accredited Solar and Wind can design and install all products that are currently available. They also service and troubleshoot existing systems throughout North Carolina. Whether it is new construction or retrofitting an older home, if you would like to take advantage of the state and federal tax incentives, call for a free, no obligation, on-site evaluation.

Starfire Solar
Hubert
(910) 326-6136

Contact Starfire Solar for the latest and most efficient solar-energy equipment. The company focuses on solar-thermal applications, such as supplying hot water and space heating, along with other applications of solar energy to reduce energy costs, reduce greenhouse gas emissions and provide for a sustainable energy future. Let these professionals help you earn tax credits and reduce your bills with quiet, virtually maintenance-free equipment.

Apartments

The apartment complexes along the Crystal Coast offer a nice selection for renters. This coastal area is not filled with a large number of apartment complexes like other beach areas, so once the nicest ones are filled, there is a often a slow turnover rate. Area real estate companies often manage apartments for the owners, and rentals are also listed in the classified section of the *Carteret County News-Times*. We have listed a few of the larger apartment complexes here.

Beaufort Town Apartments I, II & III
201 Glenda Dr., Beaufort
(252) 728-2940

Located about 2 miles from the waterfront, Beaufort Town Apartments offers units with two bedrooms and one and half baths or units with two bedrooms and two and a half baths. Residents can enjoy a pool and a small playground area. The complex allows children, and cats and small dogs are allowed with a separate deposit.

Country Club Apartments
4600 Country Club Rd., Morehead City
(252) 726-2389

Country Club Apartments are centrally located in Morehead City and less than 15 minutes from the beach. The complex features many trees on the property, a nice playground and offers a quiet setting for its residents. Maintained by a friendly staff, they offer apartments with one, two or three bedrooms. Children are welcome, and pets are permitted with some stipulations regarding size, number and fees.

Kings Mill Apartments
1200 Daughters Dr., Newport
(252) 223-6311

Built in 2000, Kings Mill offers affordable housing to individuals 55 years of age or older. One- and two-bedroom apartments are offered in this complex, and there is an income restriction for residents. Its location is convenient to downtown Newport.

Orlandah Court Apartments
Chalk & Gibbs Realty, 3115 Bridges St., Morehead City
(252) 726-3167

Orlandah Court Apartments features units with one or two bedrooms. This quiet complex allows children but not pets. Centrally located in town, it offers convenience and fair pricing in the rental market.

🌴RETIREMENT

As the number of older residents increases, the county and its various towns develop more activities directed toward suiting the needs and interests of the senior set. With the variety of sports, hobbies, volunteer opportunities and entertainment available, most retirees stay as busy as they want to be.

Housing requirements can change quickly during the retirement years. Townhouse and condominium developments are perfect for retirees who also decide to retire from house and lawn maintenance. All real estate companies can guide you toward more simplified living arrangements in beautiful locations. See the Crystal Coast Real Estate chapter for more about the housing alternatives available.

Housing exclusively for older citizens on the Crystal Coast is available in a variety of settings, from federally subsidized accommodations for the elderly and disabled on fixed incomes to exclusive retirement complexes where you buy the unit and pay a monthly maintenance fee

i

Retirees love the Crystal Coast. It doesn't snow all winter, it's not excessively hot all summer, golf and gardening are great nearly year round, the fishing is fantastic, and the people are charming. Adding to the attraction are the relatively inexpensive property costs, compared with other popular retirement areas. Because of the large bang for the retirement buck, the Crystal Coast enjoys a fast-growing population of highly educated, well-traveled and active retired citizens.

that includes taxes, meals, laundry and around-the-clock security service. In addition, there are nursing homes, rest homes and family-care centers for those who need extra attention. If you need information about any or all of the nursing-care facilities in the Crystal Coast area, call the Department of Social Services at (252) 728-3181. If you are shopping for a nursing-care facility, be sure to make several visits to the places you are considering so you can make the very best choice.

Services and Organizations

Area Agency on Aging/
Eastern Carolina Council
233 Middle St., New Bern
(252) 638-3185

Based in New Bern but serving the elderly throughout eastern North Carolina, this agency helps adults 55 years or older maintain and improve their quality of life by addressing their needs and concerns. Programs include adult day care, care management, disaster preparedness and assistance, a family caregiver support program, information and referral, in-home aid, transportation and more. New programs are always in development; call for more information. See our New Bern Retirement chapter for more information about this agency.

Help-At-Home Senior Care
1202 S. Glenburnie Rd., New Bern
(252) 672-9300

Providing in-home care 24 hours a day, seven days a week, Help-At-Home allows seniors throughout eastern North Carolina who need just a little bit of "help at home" to stay in their homes and enjoy their independence. This service matches caregivers to senior clients and provides services such as meal planning and preparation, light housekeeping, medication reminders, bill-paying assistance, bathing-safety monitoring, errand running and local transportation.

Leon Mann Jr. Enrichment Center
3820 Galantis Dr., Morehead City
(252) 247-2626

The Leon Mann Jr. Senior Enrichment Center, operated by the Carteret County Senior Services Department, is a multi-purpose center for seniors age 50 and older. It is open weekdays from 8 AM until 5 PM and sponsors a senior dance on Friday evenings from 7:30 until 11 PM. The center is fully disabled-accessible, bright and well-designed, and includes large meeting rooms, classrooms, a library, a billiards room and a fully equipped fitness room. Classes, workshops, seminars and entertainment events include lively lessons in line dancing, yoga, computer skills, bridge and the arts. The facility is also used for a variety of visiting community services, including legal aid, financial counseling, pharmacy assistance and blood-pressure checks. Transportation to and from the center and hot lunches are available for seniors age 60 and older. A representative from the New Bern Social Security office is available at the center the first Wednesday from 8:30 AM until 2:30 PM. No appointment is necessary.

Meals on Wheels
(252) 726-4654

Meals-On-Wheels programs provide home delivery of hot meals, usually one a day, five days a week. The program is designed to help the elderly, shut-ins, those recuperating from surgery and disabled persons. Some systems require full payment for meals, some seek contributions and others operate entirely on donations. Contributions come from area churches and people within the community.

Senior Games
Carteret County Parks and Recreation Dept., 801 Arendell St., Ste. 8, Morehead City
(252) 808-3301

Carteret County has a year-round Senior Games program designed to keep

residents age 55 and older healthy, active and involved. Local games are held each May, and a year-round program leads up to the annual state Senior Games held in Raleigh in September. Competitions include tennis, golf, swimming, biking, table tennis, horseshoes, croquet, track, billiards, bowling and more. Get the picture? It's active. Games also include Silver Arts competitions in painting, sculpture, writing, heritage crafts, and instrumental and vocal music. Local winners compete in the state Senior Games during the fall and can advance to the nationals. The Senior Games committee sponsors workshops to prepare prospective athletes or artists. Registration is required to participate.

Senior Pharmacy Program
502 Middle St., New Bern
(252) 638-3657

The Senior Pharmacy Program assists eligible seniors, ages 60 and older in Craven, Jones, Pamlico and Carteret counties, with costs for prescription medications. An outreach of Catholic Charity, it helps pay for prescriptions that treat chronic diseases such as cancer, high blood pressure, heart disease, diabetes, glaucoma, acid reflux, arthritis and clinical depression. Post-hospitalization medications may be covered on a limited basis. Sites for the monthly distribution of vouchers, to be used toward the prescription costs, are generally at area senior centers. Call ahead for an appointment. The program's mailing address is P.O. Box 826, New Bern, NC 28563.

Housing Options and Facilities

Ekklesia I and Ekklesia II
405 Barbour Rd., Morehead City
(252) 726-0076

Ekklesia I and II is a HUD–subsidized retirement complex in a quiet part of town off Barbour Road. About two blocks from Morehead Plaza Shopping Center, Ekklesia I and II includes 94 one-bedroom units and six two-bedroom units, all arranged in clusters around the community center, which houses laundry facilities, a mail room and a large meeting room with a kitchen. The offices of the site manager and activities director are also in the community center. Regular activities include monthly birthday parties, holiday parties, bingo, club meetings and such special events as an annual bake sale. A service coordinator also is available to help residents find community programs that may be of assistance to them.

Harborview Towers
812 Shepard St., Morehead City
(252) 726-0453

Locally owned and operated, Harborview Towers is in a downtown residential neighborhood on the Morehead City waterfront overlooking Bogue Sound. The modern 10-story, 50-apartment complex is adjacent to Harborview Health Care Center, a skilled-nursing and intermediate-care facility for 122 patients. Residents purchase lifetime rights, with deeds of trust, to live in the Towers' efficiency apartments and one- and two-bedroom units. A monthly fee includes maintenance, housekeeping, laundry, emergency and scheduled transportation, one meal a day in the dining room, property taxes and all utilities except telephone, Internet ac-

cess and cable. All but the smallest units have balconies providing views of either Newport River or Bogue Sound. There is outdoor parking, with some covered parking on the building's ground floor. The facility has an activities director and full-time security.

Snug Harbor on Nelson Bay
272 U.S. Hwy. 70 E, Sea Level
(252) 225-4411

Snug Harbor is the only retirement community in Carteret and Craven counties to offer three levels of care: independent living, assisted living and skilled-nursing care. Originally built for retired Merchant Marines and opened to the public in 2001, the retirement community of Snug Harbor offers rich maritime history and the picturesque surroundings of Nelson Bay. Medicare rehabilitation and respite care are available. Private accommodations, including suites for couples, are available. Fine cuisine is prepared and served three times a day in the elegant dining room. Medical care and a full-scale activity calendar ensure that residents can stay as healthy and active as possible. Overnight accommodations are available for visiting family members.

Some of the best times on the coast involve simply relaxing.

photo: Peter Doran

Somerset Court of Newport
3020 Market St., Newport
(252) 223-2600

Somerset Court offers 16 beautifully furnished, two-bedroom apartments, each accommodating four residents who are able to live independently with some assistance. Assistance includes three nutritious meals a day (with special diet considerations) served in the dining room; laundry and housekeeping services; medication monitoring and administering; scheduled transportation; and a variety of social, recreational and educational opportunities. The community-within-a-community complex is designed around an exterior courtyard with a gazebo-style bandstand for special performances and events and a village green for community gatherings. Each apartment has a courtyard patio. Monthly rental includes all services, and an enthusiastic staff is available at all times.

Taylor Extended Care Facility
468 U.S. Hwy. 70 E, Sea Level
(252) 225-4611

This facility was named in honor of the four brothers who donated it to the county: Daniel, William, Alfred and Leslie Taylor. Opened in 1953, Taylor Extended Care is a 104-bed, long-term care facility offering skilled nursing as well as custodial care for the aged. A primary-care clinic and pharmacy are located on the premises.

Family Care Centers

Family-care centers provide a home-like atmosphere for those who need some care but can basically live independently. Residents must be ambulatory and perform some light-housekeeping duties. They usually have kitchen privileges. Residents generally live in semi-private bedrooms with a shared bath, have meals together and use the living room or other facilities jointly with other residents. There is a resident supervisor who does the heavy housework and cooking and, in general, looks after the residents. Transportation for medical attention, worship and shopping is provided. Medicine is under lock and key and is dispensed by the supervisor according to doctors' directions.

Crystal Coast Family Care Home
107 Graham Ln., Beaufort
(252) 728-4422

In a quiet, rural setting off N.C. Highway 101, Crystal Coast Family Care Home offers private rooms with shared baths and common-use living areas for 12 residents. Each of the two homes in the facility has a live-in supervisor to prepare meals, dispense medicines or give any needed attention 24 hours a day. Meals are served family-style. Planned activities include cookouts, transportation, worship and shopping. The Crystal Coast Family Care Center for ambulatory and semi-ambulatory residents has been operating since 1991.

Veterans Groups

Because of the proximity of several military bases and military hospitals, Carteret County is home to many veterans. The more than 9,000 veterans living on the Crystal Coast make up nearly one-fifth of the permanent population. There are numerous veterans' organizations in the area, and all welcome new members. The **Veterans' Service Office** at 613 Cedar Street in Beaufort, (252) 728-8440, offers problem-solving services to veterans. The **Carteret County Veterans Council**, (252) 393-6178, is the coordinating body for member veterans' organizations of Carteret County. The council sponsors the Morehead City Veterans Day Parade and Carteret County Memorial Day Ceremony and promotes exhibits and issues relevant to veterans.

The **Morehead City VA Outpatient Clinic**, (252) 240-2349, operated by the

---

There's no need to drive all *the way to New Bern to visit the Social Security office. A representative from the office is available at the Leon Mann Jr. Enrichment Center for Senior Services on Wednesdays from 8:30 AM to 2:30 PM. The representative takes lunch from noon until 1 PM. No appointment is necessary.*

Durham VA Medical Center, is located at 5420 U.S. Highway 70 West. The clinic, which is open Monday through Friday, provides primary care, mental health, immunizations, dental and blood-drawing services by appointment to VA–enrolled patients in Carteret, Craven, Jones and Pamlico counties. Walk-in and emergency services are not available.

Other veterans' organizations in the area include **Military Order of the Purple Heart Chapter 639**, (252) 808-3766; **Veterans of Foreign Wars Post 2401**, (252) 728-4390; **Veterans of Foreign Wars Post 9960**, (252) 393-8053; **Veterans of Foreign Wars Post 8986**, (252) 726-8806; and **Vietnam Veterans of America Chapter 749**, (252) 393-6178

SCHOOLS AND CHILD CARE

Educational opportunities in the area include public, charter and private schools. This section gives you information about schools and child-care facilities on the Crystal Coast. Our Higher Education and Research chapter contains information about community colleges and research facilities in the area.

Public Schools

CARTERET COUNTY SCHOOLS

Providing a rigorous and relevant curriculum delivered by faculty and staff in caring relationships with students — that is the key to a quality education. And that is the focus of the Carteret County Public School System. Students across the grades continue to achieve top scores in this system, and, of the state's 115 public school systems, Carteret County ranks in the upper 10 percent. Carteret County Public School System focuses on providing a quality education to its approximately 8,500 students enrolled in 17 schools. The schools are located throughout Carteret County, from Atlantic to Cape Carteret.

With about 1,218 employees, the school system is the largest employer in the county. County residents recently approved $50 million in school bonds to provide for major renovations at 14 of the county's 17 schools. The majority of the work is complete and all work will be finished by 2010. These renovations will address health and safety issues for students and staff and provide for new classroom construction at four schools.

Carteret County public schools are governed by an elected seven-member board of education. Members serve four-year staggered terms and are chosen in county-wide, nonpartisan elections. School board members meet in open session each month.

For information about the public school system, including information about curriculum, testing, transportation, employment and more, visit www.carteret-countyschools.org or contact the Carteret County Public School System's Central Services office (Board of Education), 107 Safrit Drive, Beaufort, NC 28516, (252) 728-4583. There are also two publicly funded charter schools in the county that offer an alternative educational approach.

ONSLOW COUNTY SCHOOLS

Onslow County School System is one of the largest school systems in the state, with a 2008-09 student enrollment estimated to be about 22,500. The system has several educational facilities — 19 elementary schools, eight middle schools, seven high schools and one alternative school. Five of these schools are in the Swansboro area, just west of the Carteret County line.

Onslow County is the home of Camp Lejeune, the largest amphibious Marine base in the world, and the Onslow County School System's student population is indicative of the transient nature of the military community. Approximately one third of the students move into or out of the system or between schools within the system during the school year. Much of this movement is attributed to the percentage of students from military or military-connected families, and that number will continue to grow as more and more troops are scheduled to arrive in the area. As with the student population, the professional personnel of the Onslow County School System is also impacted by the military community. The system hires about 350 new teachers each year. Approximately 25 percent of the classroom teachers in Onslow County Schools hold a graduate license. For information about the Onslow County Public School System, call (910) 455-2211.

Charter Schools

Two charter schools offer educational alternatives to students in Carteret County. Charter schools are considered public, as they receive public funds, yet by virtue of their charters with the State Board of Education, they are free from many rules and regulations that public schools must follow. Admission is by application and lottery selection. For more information on charter schools, call the N.C. Department of Public Instruction, (919) 807-3722.

Cape Lookout Marine Science Charter High School
**1108 Bridges St., Morehead City
(252) 726-1601**

Cape Lookout is a charter school serving students in grades 9 through 12. The school offers a regular high school curriculum. With a maximum number of 150

Kids naturally love being outdoors.

photo: Carolyn Temple

students, the school strives to provide one-on-one services to students.

The Tiller School
1950 U.S. Hwy. 70, Beaufort
(252) 726-1826

The Tiller School is a public charter school that serves students in kindergarten through 5th grade. Originally a private school founded in 1992, Tiller was granted charter status in 1998. The school offers limited transportation in the Morehead City area.

Private Schools

There are several private schools located in Carteret County. The grade level served varies by organization, and many are faith-based schools. There are also some home-school families in the county. For information about home schools, contact the N.C. Department of Non-Public Instruction, (919) 733-4276, or the Carteret County Schools Central Office, (252) 728-4583.

Beaufort Early Education Programs
(BEEPs)
1390 Lennoxville Rd., Beaufort
(252) 504-3797

Beaufort Early Education Programs (BEEPS) provides high quality preschool education and care for children from ages 3 to 5. The program involves phonetics-based instruction, early math and science awareness, dramatic play, fine and gross motor skill development, physical activity, socialization and self-help skills development. The dedicated and highly trained staff provides a nurturing environment that inspires creativity and enthusiasm for educational exploration. BEEPS is committed to a low student to teacher ratio (10:1), which helps provide each child with focused individual attention. Their goal is to see that each child involved with BEEPS meets his/her potential and is prepared to excel in a kindergarten program.

Crystal Coast School of the Arts
4907 Bridges St., Morehead City
(252) 726-5050

Crystal Coast School of the Arts is a professional institution offering a variety

of classes. Tap, jazz, ballet and ballroom lessons are offered for all ages. Tiny Tots tumbling and dance instruction is offered along with Mom & Me and Kindermusik programs.

Gramercy Christian School
U.S. Hwy. 70, Newport
(252) 223-4384

Gramercy Christian School is a ministry of the Faith Evangelical Bible Church. The school provides a traditional Christian educational program for a growing number of students in kindergarten (at least age 5) through 12th grade. Some transportation is provided.

Newport Developmental Center
903 Church St., Newport
(252) 223-4574

The Newport Developmental Center provides training for children from birth through young adult who need help because of developmental and language disorders, mental retardation, autism, emotional handicaps or learning disabilities. The program operates during daytime hours Monday through Friday and also provides day care for children.

St. Egbert's Catholic School
1705 Evans St., Morehead City
(252) 726-3418

St. Egbert's Catholic School is affiliated with St. Egbert's Roman Catholic Church. Located in Morehead City, the church serves students from the surrounding area and provides a Catholic-based education. St. Egbert's offers classes for students in kindergarten through 5th grade.

Child Care

Child care fees vary and are usually based on the child's age, the number of hours the child spends at the facility or the number of children in the same family attending the facility. Many child-care centers provide transportation to and from school (if needed), summer programs and extended hours on weekends. Carteret County and the State of North Carolina regulate day-care homes and day-care centers through the issuance of registrations and licenses. Regulations call for all such facilities to meet health and safety standards. In the case of nonsectarian child-care institutions, standards for children's learning and play programs must be met. For a complete list of regulated day-care homes and licensed day-care centers, call the Carteret County Department of Social Services, (252) 728-3181.

DAY CARE

Morehead City

Dropins Childcare
Cypress Bay Plaza,
5167 U.S. Hwy. 70 W, Ste. 140,
Morehead City
(252) 240-DROP

Dropins Childcare offers hourly drop-in care for children from ages 1 to 11 years. No reservations are required, and children will be in the care of well-qualified, experienced and first-aid–trained staff members. Dropins also offers a preschool and an after-school care program, as well as a school-age summer camp featuring field trips and a variety of activities. The 7,000-square-foot play area is filled with age-appropriate toys, video games, computers and activities. Dropins is open Monday through Thursday from 8 AM to 8 PM, Friday from 8 AM to 10 PM and Saturday from 9 AM to 1 PM and from 5 to 11 PM. From 1 to 5 PM each Saturday Dropins can be rented for birthday parties or other special events, and the staff will handle all the details and all the clean up. Have a no-stress party by leaving the details to the Dropins staff.

Excel
601 N. 35th St., Morehead City
(252) 247-4831
103 Fairview Dr., Beaufort
(252) 728-2223
700 N. 35th St., Morehead City
(252) 247-4831

Excel offers a variety of child-care services with two locations in Morehead City and one location in Beaufort. The two locations in Morehead City combine to offer child care for children from ages 1 through 12. A pre-kindergarten program through the More at Four partnership with the Carteret County Public School System is offered, as is after-school care. Summer camps are offered for children from

3 through 12 years of age. The Beaufort location provides professional care for children from 6 weeks of age through 12 years, including after-school and summer camp programs. All three Excel sites are open from 6:15 AM to 6 PM, and some transportation is provided.

First Presbyterian Church
1604 Arendell St., Morehead City
(252) 247-2202

This church program offers morning preschool and half-day kindergarten for children ages 3, 4 and 5. Call the office to find out the times and months care is offered.

Kids Junction
4907 Bridges St., Morehead City
(252) 726-5502

Kids Junction offers child care for children from two years old through eighth grade. Half-day preschool classes are provided for youngsters from two through four years old. After-school classes are offered for those in kindergarten through eighth grade. Kids Junction provides transportation for children from area schools.

My School Child Care
3415 Eaton Dr., Morehead City
(252) 247-2276

My School serves youngsters from age 6 weeks through age 10 and provides a preschool program, before- and after-school care and a summer program. My School provides van transportation to and from the Morehead City schools. The center is open from 6:30 AM to 6 PM.

Beaufort

Ann Street
United Methodist Church Preschool
500 Ann St., Beaufort
(252) 728-5411

Ann Street United Methodist Church Preschool offers a very popular program, and there is always a waiting list for enrollment. The church facility has been providing child care since 1972. Ann Street offers programs for children ages 2 through 5 from 7:30 AM to 5:30 PM. Parents can select the full-day program or the half-day program, and a special pre-kindergarten program is offered.

Beaufort Child Development Center
201 Professional Park Dr., Beaufort
(252) 728-2786

Beaufort Child Development Center serves children from 1 to 5 years of age, with a special focus on students who qualify for the Head Start program. The center offers after-school care for children from kindergarten through early elementary age. Summer programs are also offered. The center is open from 6 AM to 6 PM.

Beaufort Christian Academy
U.S. Hwy. 70 E, Beaufort
(252) 728-3165

Beaufort Christian Academy offers day-care services during the day for children ages 2 through 5, including pre-kindergarten and kindergarten programs. After-school care is provided for students up to age 12.

Western Carteret County

The Sandbox Child Care
130 Fort Benjamin Rd., Newport
(252) 223-3432

In the heart of Newport, just off Old U.S. Highway 70 E, The Sandbox serves children from ages 2, if potty trained, to 9 with full day-care service, morning preschool, and before- and after-school programs. The Sandbox also offers a complete summer program. It is open from 6:30 AM until 5:30 PM weekdays.

St. James Day Care and Preschool Center
1011 Orange St., Newport
(252) 223-3191

St. James offers care for children from ages 6 weeks to 11 years. A day-care program is offered during the day, and before- and after-school care is provided. It's open 6:30 AM to 6 PM Monday through Friday, and school buses from Newport

Elementary School pick up and drop off children at St. James. The center also offers summer programs.

White Oak Christian Day Care
U.S. Hwy. 24, Bogue
(252) 393-7808

In Bogue near Cape Carteret, White Oak Christian Day Care offers day care and preschool activities for children from ages 1 through 4 and after-school care for children up to 5th grade. White Oak Christian also offers a complete summer program.

Swansboro

Swansboro United Methodist Child Care
665 W. Corbett Ave., Swansboro
(910) 326-3711

This center accepts children from ages 6 weeks to 10 years. The younger children are offered day-care services, and there is an after-school program for children up to the age of 10. Swansboro Elementary School buses provide transportation for the children.

Private, In-Home Care

Nancy's Nannies
Morehead City
(252) 726-6575

Reliable, experienced sitters are available on the Crystal Coast through this service. Nancy's Nannies is used widely and offers responsible adult babysitters for in-home child care. This is a trusted service for visitors staying in rentals and hotels. This service provides sitters for a day, night, weekend or longer. Sitters can also be arranged to care for children during special events, such as weddings. Nancy's Nannies has been in business since 1991 and provides services to the coastal area, New Bern, Topsail Island and Raleigh.

🎓 HIGHER EDUCATION AND RESEARCH

Several higher-education institutions are accessible to Crystal Coast residents interested in pursuing additional education or seeking enrichment. The area is also home to many well-known and respected research laboratories. Many residents of the Crystal Coast commute to Greenville to earn degrees from East Carolina University. (For more information about ECU, see our New Bern Schools and Child Care chapter.)

Higher Education

Carteret Community College (CCC)
3505 Arendell St., Morehead City
(252) 222-6000

Carteret Community College is located on the shore of Bogue Sound off U.S. Highway 70 in Morehead City. The college offers the latest vocational-technological training and features programs that prepare students for the skills they need in the fast-paced information age, where computers and the Internet have changed the way business is done.

Students can pursue Associate in Science, Associate in Arts and Associate in Fine Arts degrees as well as associate degrees in programs for business and computer technologies, health sciences, vocational licensure fields, and public and legal services. In addition, a variety of shorter diploma and certificate programs also enable Carteret Community College to provide students with the training needed to find employment in a changing workforce.

With programs like aquaculture technology, cosmetology technology, Internet technologies, paralegal technology, culinary technology, hotel and restaurant management, marine propulsion systems, and boat manufacturing and related marine trades, CCC students have a wide range of options. Additionally, students can work toward careers in interior design and a variety of health science related fields, including the new associate's degree in nursing program.

As an authorized academic training partner of the Microsoft Corporation, the college has the Microsoft seal of approval to teach students how to use its software products. Students can also test for Microsoft and Cisco certifications, which tell prospective employers they have mastered their technical specialties.

In the Corporate and Community Education Division, the college provides businesses and industries with training opportunities for employees in a variety of subjects. Supervision, leadership and customer-service training can be customized to meet an organization's needs. Seminars addressing the needs of small business and entrepreneurs are available to the public.

With occupational training courses such as electrical, plumbing, HVAC and carpentry, students are taking advantage of the flexible training opportunities available at the college. Furthermore, the Basic Skills Department provides students with an opportunity to obtain their GED, attend Adult High School or improve their English if it is their second language.

The Corporate and Community Education Division also offers pre-licensing courses for insurance, real estate, general contractor and marine captain. From a public safety training standpoint, students can enter the six-month Basic Law Enforcement Training Program or participate in shorter emergency medical training and fire-fighting programs.

Carteret Community College has expanded training opportunities in aquaculture, business technologies, health sciences and marine trades.

The college's library is open to the public and has one of the fastest Internet connections in the region. CCC was the first community college in North Carolina to be connected to the University System's North Carolina Research and Educational Network. From audio books and best sellers to an interlibrary loan program with colleges and universities throughout the state, the college's library is an excellent research facility as well as quiet place to get away.

Coastal Carolina Community College
444 Western Blvd., Jacksonville
(910) 938-6394

Coastal Carolina Community College is a fully accredited state institution with more than 50 curricular programs in college transfer, general education and vocational and technical training programs. Many of these programs are available during the daytime, evening, at specially scheduled times and online.

While the main campus is located on Western Boulevard in Jacksonville, the college also offers classes at Camp Lejeune and Marine Corps Air Station New River. More than half of the college's students are enrolled in the college transfer curriculum. Business and marketing, education and engineering are just a few of the many areas of study available to transfer students. Military family members, regardless of their state of residency, receive in-state tuition rates. Active-duty military are eligible for tuition assistance from the military. Many students enroll in the college's continuing education courses. These practical academic and technical programs are designed to increase an individual's employment opportunities and performance.

Craven Community College
800 College Ct., New Bern
(252) 638-4131

Like Carteret and Coastal Carolina Community Colleges, Craven Community College offers a variety of two-year degrees at its New Bern and Havelock campuses. (For more information, see our New Bern Schools and Child Care chapter.)

Mount Olive College at New Bern
2131 S. Glenburnie Rd., Ste. 6, New Bern
(252) 633-4464, (800) 868-8479

Mount Olive College (MOC) at New Bern offers convenient, flexible programs for working adults. Mount Olive College is geographically distributed in six eastern North Carolina communities, including Mount Olive, Research Triangle Park, Goldsboro, New Bern, Washington and Wilmington. The college provides degree programs in locations, times and formats that fit the busy lifestyles of working adults. Through MOC's innovative approach to education, working adults have the opportunity to earn a degree while continuing their employment. Students enter a class (called a cohort), meet four hours one night a week and complete a sequence of courses that lead to an associate's or bachelor's degree.

Mount Olive College at New Bern offers both associate's and bachelor's degree options. The Heritage Plus Program, designed specifically for working adults who have little or no college experience, leads to an associate's degree and provides the core courses for admission to the bachelor's degree programs. Mount Olive College at New Bern offers the following bachelor's degree programs: criminal justice and criminology, early childhood education, healthcare management, management and organizational development, and modular religion major.

Mount Olive College at New Bern has a tradition of student-focused, supportive programming and teaching styles. Courses are experiential, emphasizing self-directed study, critical thinking and writing skills. Classes are small, allowing students and faculty the opportunity for personal interaction. Students pre-register a semester at a time. Classes meet from 6 to 10 PM one night a week and are guaranteed to be the same night throughout the program's duration. Books are delivered to the student. Financial aid is available.

Research Facilties

The Crystal Coast is home to numerous research facilities and has one of the largest concentrations of marine scientists

on the East Coast at the North Carolina State University Center of Marine Sciences and Technology. All of the research facilities discussed here have something to do with the surrounding water and water-related resources. They offer research, product development and personnel training for corporations around the world. Area laboratories have been involved in developing many products. Contract research has included work with companies such as Strohs Brewery, W. R. Grace, Hercules Chemical, Biosponge Aquaculture Products, International Paint, Allied Chemical, Sunshine Makers, Aquanautics, Mann Bait Company, 3M Corporation and General Dynamics.

Duke University Marine Lab
135 Duke Marine Lab Rd., Piver's Island
(252) 504-7503

This inter-disciplinary facility has three objectives — research, teaching and the translation of sound science into effective environmental policy. The laboratory's large resident academic staff and visiting professors and researchers from throughout the United States and abroad have contributed to its worldwide reputation.

The laboratory maintains a full-service campus, two large research vessels and a fleet of smaller boats. The largest is the R/V *Cape Hatteras*, a 135-foot ship owned by the National Science Foundation and run by Duke on behalf of the Duke University-University of North Carolina Oceanography Consortium.

This 72-year-old lab, located adjacent to the Rachel Carson Estuarine Research Reserve and Cape Lookout National Seashore, has a long and productive relationship with the Town of Beaufort and surrounding areas, and the faculty serve on many local, state and national scientific and environmental boards and commissions. Founded by zoology professor A. S. Pearse in 1937, the laboratory began with seven cottages and two six-week terms for college seniors and graduate students. Now the lab consists of 23 buildings —

research facilities, dormitories, shore installations to support research vessels, a library and an auditorium with year-round classes for undergraduate, professional masters and Ph.D. students. Tele-video links connect the lab to learning centers and collaborators worldwide.

North Carolina Division of Marine Fisheries
3441 Arendell St., Morehead City
(252) 726-7021

This large facility is charged with stewardship of marine and estuarine resources in coastal creeks, bays, rivers, sounds and the ocean within 3 miles of land. This state agency carries out the policies set by the nine-member Marine Fisheries Commission and the Secretary of the Department of Environment and Natural Resources.

The DMF has a marine patrol section that works in law-enforcement districts along the North Carolina coast. Their job is to protect the state's fisheries resources and to make sure people comply with conservation regulations. Officers also inspect seafood houses, fish dealers and restaurants that buy or sell North Carolina seafood.

Artificial reefs have gained popular support in recent years — artificial reef organizations, sport-fishing clubs, local governments and civic organizations are all interested in their construction, management and evaluation. The DMF is in charge of the state's Artificial Reef Program, which has 40 ocean sites and seven estuarine sites ranging from a half-mile to 38 miles from shore. It is one of the most active artificial reef programs in the country and receives funding from the groups noted above as well as from the state legislature.

Other sections of the DMF conduct fisheries and gear research, collect and process the catch statistics of all commercial and recreational fisheries and do shellfish mapping, shellfish leasing and shellfish disease work. The DMF also administers the popular North Carolina Saltwater Tour-

See this entire guide plus additional content online at insiderinfo.us

nament and the Governor's Cup Conservation Billfish Tournament series.

North Carolina State University Seafood Laboratory
303 College Cir., Morehead City
(252) 222-6334

Established in 1970, the N.C. State University Seafood Laboratory is an applied research and extension education unit of the Department of Food, Bio-Processing and Nutrition Sciences. Located in the Center for Marine Sciences and Technology, the Seafood Lab focuses on seafood safety and technology, seafood product development, and seafood marketing. Personnel work with seafood-related industries, public health professionals and consumer groups on seafood quality and safety issues, nutrition and utilization, innovative processing technologies and value-added fishery products. Support is provided through the N.C. Cooperative Extension Service, N.C. Agricultural Research Service and N.C. Sea Grant Program.

Rachel Carson Reserve
135 Duke Marine Lab Rd.,
Pivers Island, Beaufort
(252) 838-0883

The Rachel Carson Reserve, part of the four-component North Carolina National Estuarine Research Reserve, is just across Taylor's Creek from Beaufort. It may look like just a collection of small marshy islands — including Town Marsh, Bird Shoals, Carrot Island, Middle Marshes — but the reserve is an active field research and classroom site.

The program is a joint program through the National Oceanic and Atmospheric Administration and North Carolina State Division of Coastal Management. The reserve system was created to maintain undisturbed estuaries for research on the natural and human processes that affect the coast, and the Rachel Carson site serves that purpose well.

Field trips by foot and by boat are offered Memorial Day through Labor Day. Insiders recommend a visit; there are many fascinating things to be observed while touring the reserve's 2,600 acres of uplands, marshes and intertidal/subtidal flats. The site is always open to the public and is accessible only by boat. Trail brochures are available. For more information about the Rachel Carson component, call the number above and also see our Attractions chapter.

University of North Carolina Institute of Marine Sciences
3431 Arendell St., Morehead City
(252) 726-6841

The Institute of Marine Sciences (IMS) is an off-campus research, training and service unit of the University of North Carolina at Chapel Hill. Its mission is to serve the state and nation by conducting high-quality basic and applied marine sciences research, by training young scientists to continue this tradition and by providing professional expertise and leadership in marine issues ranging from local to global scale. Resident faculty are actively involved in addressing important scientific questions related to the nature, use, development, protection and enhancements of marine resources, as well as communicating research results and information about new technologies to professional and public audiences.

COMMERCE AND INDUSTRY

Tourism and commercial fishing are big parts of the area's economic picture, but a number of domestic and international companies call Carteret County home. The **Carteret County Economic Development Council, Inc.**, (252) 222-6120 or (800) 462-4252, and the **Carteret County Chamber of Commerce**, (252) 726-6350, can provide detailed information about area businesses and industries.

The **North Carolina Port at Morehead City** is the county's most visible industry. Situated on the east end of Morehead City, the 116-acre main facility is just 4 miles from the open sea. The port includes part of Radio Island, the body of land on the southeast side of the Morehead City–Beaufort high-rise bridge. With a 45-foot-deep entrance channel and equally deep bulk berths, the Morehead terminal can accommodate the biggest ships in the industry. Its turning basin is one of the deepest in any East Coast port. Established in 1945, the Port of Morehead offers a foreign trade zone and direct rail service through Norfolk Southern Corporation. It is one of two state-owned ports; the other is in Wilmington.

North Carolina's ports link the state's citizens, businesses and industry to world markets. From Morehead City, PCS Phosphate (Potash Corp. of Saskatchewan) exports phosphate-based materials throughout the world and utilizes the Intracoastal Waterway to barge these materials to the port from the company's mine in Aurora, North Carolina. Recycled steel for the Nucor mill in Hertford County arrives at the port via ship or ocean-going barge and is transferred to barges for transport up the Intracoastal Waterway to the mill at Tunis. Regional tire manufacturers rely on imports of raw rubber through Morehead City from Southeast Asia and Indonesia. Manufacturers whose rubber passes across the docks at Morehead City include Goodyear, Cooper, Michelin, Bridgestone and Continental. Agribusiness in the region receives fertilizers through the port. Ore used to manufacture fiberglass products is also imported through Morehead City.

Atlantic Veneer Corporation in Beaufort is the world's largest manufacturer of hardwood veneers in North America, with manufacturing facilities on three continents. It exports about half of its products. Atlantic Veneer also operates a local retail outlet, which is an important source of lumber and hardwoods for boat builders and cabinet makers. With approximately 327 area employees, this corporation is the county's largest private employer.

Veneer Technologies has operated a plant in Newport since 1993. It makes three main products: face veneers, flexible-sheet veneers and edge banding. Its products are sold throughout the United States and around the world.

SPX Dehydration & Process Filtration, formerly Hankinson International, is a manufacturer of compressed-air treatment products, which are used in a variety of industries, such as furniture finishing and painting. The company has substantially expanded its plant, which is located in Newport on N.C. 24.

Bally Refrigerated Boxes Inc., located off U.S. 70 in Morehead City, manufactures walk-in refrigerated units, coolers and freezers. Bally specializes in custom cooler units ranging from 6 to 28 feet high. Its

See this entire guide plus additional content online at insiderinfo.us

freezers are designed to be stacked to create coolers as much as 100 feet high and as long as a football field. Hospitals, restaurant chains, restaurant equipment dealers and refrigeration wholesalers make up most of Bally's customers, and about 30 percent of its business is exported. Recent developments include the addition of mortuary units to the product line and the purchase of the largest lot in the Business Park for future expansion.

Creative Outlet Inc., a family owned-and-operated firm in Morehead City, makes a wide variety of apparel for the healthcare industry — hospital gowns, scrubs, bed sheets, pajamas — that are sold throughout the nation. One of a dwindling number of apparel manufacturers in this textile state that was once home to many, this aggressive small manufacturer is growing to retrieve exported jobs still needed at home. Creative Outlet has retail stores in Morehead, Kinston and Fayetteville.

Carteret County's largest single landowner is a farming company. Of the 90,000 acres of farmland here, 44,000 acres make up **Open Grounds Farm**, one of the largest farms east of the Mississippi. The Italian-owned farm tills about 35,000 of these acres, producing corn and

wheat for the poultry-feed and hog-feed industries, soybeans for instate processing plants and cotton for North Carolina gin mills. The farm, which stretches north from Merrimon Road outside Beaufort to U.S. 70 east near Sea Level, also raises some livestock. You can get a look at the farm by checking in at the main gate on Merrimon Road. Permission to enter is most often granted, although visits are not recommended on Sundays or during busy planting or harvesting times.

Parker Marine Enterprises Inc. specializes in the construction of fiberglass fishing and pleasure boats. The company plant is on N.C. 101 outside Beaufort and recently underwent a significant expansion. Boats are sold through authorized dealers. The company has recently expanded and anticipates further development in the near future.

Another boating enterprise is **Jarrett Bay Boatworks Inc.**, founded in 1986, located in the heart of the 175-acre JBBW Marine Industrial Park six miles north of Beaufort on N.C. Hwy. 101 by land and ICW MM 198 by water. The JBBW Park is a public-private partnership among Jarrett Bay, the town of Beaufort and the Economic Development Council of Carteret County. It is a one-of-a-kind, full-service

Most of the shrimp in North Carolina are caught with trawl nets in the sounds and rivers.

photo: Peter Doran

facility specializing in the building of custom Carolina sport-fishing boats, servicing boats up to 220 tons and brokering new and pre-owned boats. The JBBW Park features on-site marine businesses such as Covington Detroit Diesel, Gregory Poole Caterpillar, Bansch American Towers, Offshore Marine Electronics, ZF Marine and the JBBW Ship Store with dockage and fuel.

Just as fishing is big business in Carteret, fishing gear grows annually as a significant part of its economy. **Henry's Tackle**, a division of the international Big Rock Sports company, is the 10th largest privately held company in the state. Growing also is **Sea Striker**, a locally owned and operated manufacturer of fishing tackle.

New employment opportunities arrive with regularity. The stretch westward continues in Morehead City. New chains and businesses move to the area on an almost monthly basis, offering residents a variety of options when seeking employment.

As the natural westward progression into open land continues, Morehead City is working to make its downtown area more attractive. Business and property owners formed the **Downtown Morehead City Revitalization Association** in the late 1990s to help maintain the vitality of the downtown area. The group's goal is to improve the physical appearance of downtown, beautify Arendell Street, preserve historic buildings and provide better transportation to and around Morehead City. It also helps foster current businesses in the area and helps promote the downtown area as a great place for new business. The DMCRA promotes festivals and special events in pursuit of its goals. It is the sponsor of the annual Blackbeard Festival (see our Annual Events chapter).

To help attract new industry, Carteret County has developed the **Crystal Coast Business Park**, a 58-acre park located west of Morehead City on U.S. 70. The park is zoned for industrial purposes, including warehousing and distribution facilities. It offers 11 parcels ranging in size from 1.84 acres to 13.78 acres. Morehead City provides the water, sewer and utilities. With proximity to railroad service, the N.C. State Port and U.S. 70, the park promises to be an excellent location for business and light industry.

As with any seasonal community, unemployment rates peak in December and January in Carteret County. The December 2009 unemployment figure was 7.8 percent , a slightly lower rate than the state and national average of 7.9 percent. Carteret's labor force of 33,505 people has 2,613 unemployed. It ranked the 24th lowest in unemployment of the state's 100 counties.

The military continues to be a major factor in the county's economic well-being (see our Military chapter) with 1,685 Carteret County residents, about 30 percent of the civilian workforce, employed at **Marine Corps Air Station Cherry Point and the Fleet Readiness Center**. Carteret County is also home to a number of the active-duty military personnel and their families. In addition, the U.S. Coast Guard has a strong presence in Carteret County as it helps monitor the area's waterways and state port.

While continuing to depend on service industry jobs to support its robust tourism industry, the economic base for Carteret County continues to diversify and remain healthy. Wages do not compete with those in metropolitan areas, but compare well when held against the cost of living. Many Insiders find Carteret County and its small-town, laid-back way of doing things to be the ideal place to live, work and play.

Business Services

The UPS Store
4915 Arendell St., Morehead City
(252) 726-4433

The UPS Store, the world's largest pack-and-ship business service, has a location in Morehead City at 4915 Arendell Street, where it offers all the conveniences you need. Services include packing and shipping, fax sending and receiving, color and black and white photocopying, as well as computer station rental. They now offer notary, laminating and blueprint copy services.

HEALTHCARE Ⓗ

The healthcare field in the Crystal Coast area offers the best of both worlds. The comforting, small-town feel of its caring and friendly physicians and medical staff is enhanced by the latest technology, equipment and treatments. Routine and specialized medical care, diagnostic procedures, treatment and surgery are available along the Crystal Coast. Carteret County, with the help of nearby universities, is staying on the cutting edge of medical care. In cases of emergency, residents and visitors receive medical attention on a walk-in basis at several locations around the county during weekday business hours, and a few even offer weekend hours. At other times Carteret General Hospital's emergency room provides excellent care. In most towns or communities throughout the county, there are clinics or specialized practices that are willing to work in appointments for urgent care. And, of course, asking an Insider is also a great way to find a new family physician. Various home healthcare services help to bring people home earlier from surgeries, injuries and illnesses that have traditionally required hospital recoveries.

As Carteret County's population continues to grow, the healthcare community strives to keep pace. Some of the area's medical facilities are in the process of expansion or have recently opened newly built extensions or additions.

Alternative healthcare options available on the Crystal Coast facilitate healing in nontraditional ways. Practitioners of a variety of holistic approaches to well-being include preventative medicine and the relief of pain in ways that include massage therapies, acupuncture, yoga and herbal remedies.

Hospitals

Carteret General Hospital
3500 Arendell St., Morehead City
(252) 808-6000

Carteret General Hospital is a 135-bed, not-for-profit community hospital serving eastern North Carolina. With commitment to excellence and advanced technology, the hospital offers educational and excellence programs that enhance its specialty services to a level that you would expect at larger facilities. Since opening its doors in July 1967, Carteret General has grown from a small organization to a full-service hospital. The physicians and staff are among the finest healthcare providers in eastern Carolina. As the second-largest employer in Carteret County with 1,100 employees, the hospital has remained committed to improving the community's health. In addition, the hospital works with 65 active physicians and many consulting physicians to meet the community's growing healthcare needs. Educational programs are available for total joint and spine orthopedic surgery, heart failure, stroke, diabetes care and breast cancer care.

Several of the hospital's excellence programs have been recognized for the commitment to quality patient care. The Carolinas Center for Joint & Spine surgery received the Ralph E. Snyder Innovator Award for Total Joint. The Cancer Clinic provides cutting-edge medical oncology, radiation therapy and chemotherapy for cancer patients in Carteret County. Breast

Cancer services include digital mammography, MRI Breast Coil and Breast Excellence Program. Additionally, Carteret General Hospital has been named among the nation's top five percent in general surgery for the nation, according to one of the nation's leading healthcare ratings companies. Patients remain loyal to Carteret General by ranking it above the 90th percentile of all hospitals nationwide in patient satisfaction surveys.

Carteret General is fully accredited by the Joint Commission for the Accreditation of Healthcare Organizations (JCAHO). More than just a hospital for the sick, Carteret General has focused on reaching out to the community to promote health and wellness. Outpatient services include Parish Nursing, Imaging Center, Sleep Diagnostic Lab, Cardiac Rehabilitation, Hospice, Home Health, Raab Oncology (Cancer) and a Learning Center. The hospital also operates Taylor Extended Care in Sea Level for residents who require specialized long-term care or short-term rehabilitation. Continual additions of facilities, services and state-of-the art equipment keep Carteret General Hospital abreast of the latest developments in medical diagnosis and treatment. Carteret General Hospital prides itself on being committed to providing excellent service and treating every individual with respect, compassion and dignity, while constantly striving to exceed the expectations of its customers.

Craven Regional Medical Center
2000 Neuse Blvd., New Bern
(252) 633-8111

This major, 350-bed regional medical facility provides a full complement of inpatient and outpatient services for its tri-county service area. Specialized care areas include intensive and intermediate care, oncology, adult mental health, women's and pediatric care. The hospital's centers of excellence include comprehensive cardiac care, including leading-edge open heart surgery, and cancer care featuring state-of-the-art radiation therapy and rehabilitation in a modern, 20-bed facility. Care is prescribed by a medical staff of more than 230 board-certified physicians representing nearly all medical specialties supported by 1,800 professional employees. The center provides 24-hour emergency services, including Express Care for minor illness and injury and outpatient surgery and diagnostic imaging in free-standing facilities in the thriving McCarthy Square medical community. PET CT imaging, magnetic resonance imaging (MRI) and 64 slice CT scanning confirm the medical center's commitment to staying at the forefront of technology. For more information see our New Bern Healthcare chapter.

Onslow Memorial Hospital
317 Western Blvd., Jacksonville
(910) 577-2345

Onslow Memorial Hospital is a large medical facility that is accredited by the Joint Commission on Accreditation of Healthcare Organizations. With more than 100 physicians on its medical staff, Onslow Memorial Hospital provides a wide range of specialties, including cardiology, (Cardiac Cath Lab), ENT, family practice, general surgery, orthopedic and pediatric surgery, internal medicine, OB-GYN, neonatal intensive care, neurosurgery, pain management, urology, a heartburn center and the Women's Imaging Center. A $45 million surgery center and emergency room have recently been completed to accommodate the expanding needs of this community. The addition provides more private rooms and technology while also allowing the operating rooms to have surgical navigation systems.

Pitt County Memorial Hospital
2100 Stantonsburg Rd., Greenville
(252) 847-4100

Pitt County Memorial Hospital provides comprehensive acute, intermediate, rehabilitation and outpatient health services to more than 1.3 million people in 29 counties. In an average year, about

i

The Broad Street Clinic in Morehead City offers medical treatment for chronic illnesses for the non-insured who meet the agency's income criteria. The clinic can be reached at (252) 726-4562.

37,000 inpatients and more than 228,000 outpatients are treated at Pitt Memorial. In a typical year, more than 3,000 babies are born at the hospital. The clinical staff includes more than 600 physicians and 1,400 nurses. Pitt Memorial is one of four academic medical centers in North Carolina and is the flagship hospital for University Health Systems of Eastern Carolina and serves as a teaching hospital for the Brody School of Medicine at East Carolina University. Pitt Memorial is considered a regional resource for all levels of health services and information.

The East Carolina Heart Institute, a collaboration between Pitt County Memorial Hospital and East Carolina University, is the first of its kind in North Carolina devoted exclusively to the prevention and treatment of cardiovascular diseases at all levels. With the patient at the center, the Heart Institute employs a fully integrated approach to cardiovascular care that combines education, research and the practice of medicine and surgery.

Home Healthcare

Several home healthcare businesses are located in Morehead City and provide services to patients in the Crystal Coast area. Each offers varying degrees of nursing, rehabilitation therapies, medical social work, in-home aides, medical equipment and supplies that allow patients the opportunity to live comfortably within their own homes. Many of the services are reimbursable through insurance, so be sure to ask. For additional providers, contact your physician.

Carteret Home Health
302 Medical Park, Morehead City
(252) 808-6081

As a service of Carteret General Hospital, Carteret Home Health allows patients to receive the highest quality professional medical care while still being able to enjoy the familiar surroundings of home. The services they provide include professional nursing care, physical therapy, speech therapy, personal care and family aides, and medical social workers. The service also works with special needs including

colostomy care, IV therapy, tube feedings and diabetic instruction. A 24-hour on-call nurse is available as well. For terminally ill patients, Carteret Home Health works closely with Hospice of Carteret County.

Hospice of Carteret County
302 Medical Park Ct., Morehead City
(252) 808-6085

Hospice of Carteret County is a not-for-profit agency that helps terminally ill patients and their families by providing hope, care and dignity through professional support and care at home. Hospice's goal is to work with their patients as they spend their last days in the comfort of their own home, alert and pain-free, while being surrounded by familiar faces and the things they love. Hospice offers a team approach that includes all ranges of care from medical and nursing to social and spiritual. Life-limiting illnesses such as cancer, Alzheimer's, end-stage heart and respiratory diseases are addressed with services such as caregiver teaching, assistance and support; nursing services; medical social worker and chaplain services; physical, occupational and speech therapy services; pain and symptom management; medical equipment and supplies; and so much more.

Liberty Home Care & Hospice
1206 Arendell St., Morehead City
(252) 247-4748

Liberty Home Care is a private business that offers a range of home-care services aimed at speeding recoveries and shortening hospital stays. It offers skilled nursing care, physical and occupational therapies and other services and supplies as needed. Liberty Home Care has offices throughout North and South Carolina.

Professional Nursing Service
212 N. 35th St., Morehead City
(252) 247-6911

Professional Care Service is a private firm that provides professional aid care. A professional will assess the needs of the individual in his or her home. Sitters and certified nurse assistants can then, based on need, assist with bathing, transfers from bed to chair, meal preparation and light housekeeping.

Physical Therapists

Physical therapy is often just the thing individuals need to fully recover from surgery or an injury. Physical therapists determine the best and most appropriate techniques for their patients, working to restore movement and function, relieve pain and prevent further injury. The techniques are varied depending on the needs of the patient, but most include education that helps patients even after physical therapy has ended. The list below provides a few options; check with your physician for further options.

Beaufort Physical Therapy
106-A Professional Park Dr., Beaufort
(252) 838-0222

This team provides physical therapy and outstanding care. These professionals offer rehabilitation services as well as treat muscular-skeletal disorders and sports-related injuries. They also provide stroke rehabilitation services.

Carteret Physical Therapy
3700 Symi Cir., Morehead City
(252) 247-2738

This firm has provided care for area residents and visitors for years. With licensed physical therapists and assistants, it specializes in physical medicine, rehabili-

tation, work conditioning, women's health, aquatic therapy and orthopedics/sports physical therapy.

Alternative Healthcare

In addition to traditional healthcare resources, the Crystal Coast offers a wide variety of alternative resources when it comes to health and wellness. Alternative healthcare includes massage and body-work therapies; herbs, nutrition, food and health products; stress, pain and energy therapies and more. Alternative healthcare also provides counseling, pharmacy, medical, chiropractic and nursing resources. Finding and maintaining wellness is the primary goal of alternative healthcare. Practitioners in the Crystal Coast community offer holistic, integrated, natural healthcare methods to relieve stress, ease pain and move patients toward self-healing. A variety of massage and movement therapies are offered for stress reduction, pain relief, better posture and flexibility, recovery from surgery and accidents, and relief of migraines, carpal tunnel and repetitive-stress syndrome. Area practitioners of varied specialties form the Whole Health Resource Network. The Whole Health Resource Network provides copies of its annual directory free-of-charge at many area locations. Additional

Swimming, snorkeling or scuba diving, the coast has something for everyone.

photo: Tracy Turpen

information about alternative services is also available at the Coastal Community Market, 606 Broad Street, Beaufort, (252) 728-2844.

Yoga for You
2900 Arendell St., Morehead City
(252) 247-YOGA (9642)

Yoga for You is not a one-size-fits-all yoga center; instead, it is a welcome respite from the usual gym-like atmosphere. The peaceful, pristine studio is dedicated solely to yoga instruction with a warm, calming atmosphere that eases the mind, spirit and body. The professional teachers are all yoga certified to make practice both safe and effective. A wide range of instruction includes gentle and introductory yoga, advanced levels and yoga tailored specifically for men, seniors, children and teens. With a variety of weekday and weekend classes, including a "Lunch and Learn" series and other specialized workshops, there's something for everyone. In addition to the wide range of class times and days, there is also pricing to fit every budget, including drop-in rates, five and ten class passes, and monthly options. Be sure to ask about free-class passes for military service and for cancer survivors. The retail section sells Fair Trade items from all over the world as well as exercise apparel made in the Carolinas, gifts, teas, books and other interesting things. Find out for yourself why locals come here to find the gentle way to well-being. Yoga for You is also a center for the Whole Health Resource Network and can provide information on other area alternative healthcare services.

MASSAGE THERAPISTS

Massage therapy benefits include everything from relaxation, rejuvenation and refreshment to the reduction of pain from injury, surgery or certain types of disease. Massage therapy can provide relief and rehabilitation for physical injury as well as provide relief from day-to-day stress. Carteret Community College offers courses in therapeutic massage therapy, and often students provide discount massages as a practicing service. There is nothing as relaxing as a complete massage from a qualified and knowledgeable therapist.

Whether you select a full-body massage, a back massage or a foot and hand massage, the results are always worth the time and money spent. We have listed here a few of the licensed therapists practicing in the area. Day spas providing massage therapy treatments are listed in the Salons and Day Spas chapter.

Elizabeth Hawkes
121 Queen St., Beaufort
(252) 728-2741

Elizabeth Hawkes is well-known throughout the area and specializes in therapeutic massage and reflexology. If Elizabeth is not available, she is happy to refer clients to other local outstanding licensed therapists.

Therapeutic Massage,
Jaya Jean Sarnacki, BS
Morehead City
(252) 726-8419

A therapeutic massage therapist and certified yoga instructor, Jaya Jean Sarnacki offers a variety of massage therapy types. Clients can enjoy Reiki, deep tissue, Swedish, craniosacral and hot stones. Jaya Jean has been a certified yoga instructor since 1992. Using intuition, training and 13 years of experience, Jaya Jean focuses on facilitating the body in reaching its own healing. She offers services in her office or in the client's home.

ACUPUNCTURE

Acupuncture has been accepted as an important treatment for many physical conditions as well as for stress relief and improved health. It is particularly noted for providing pain relief without the side effects of traditional medications. It is becoming more available in conventional medical settings and can be used as a stand-alone treatment or as a complement to other treatment methods. However, services have been slow in coming to the

Located on Bridges Street in Morehead City, the Carteret County Health Department, (252) 728-8550, offers a variety of healthcare options and screening programs for citizens of all ages.

Crystal Coast. Here are some of the options in our area.

Acupuncture Point
3110 Arendell St., Morehead City
(252) 726-1100

Stephanie Kaplan is a licensed acupuncturist with more than 20 years of experience.

Mental Health

Brynn Marr Behavioral Healthcare System
192 Village Dr., Jacksonville
(910) 577-1400, (800) 822-9507

Brynn Marr Hospital extends comprehensive services throughout eastern North Carolina in treatment of emotional and behavioral problems, mental illness and chemical dependencies for individuals of all ages through full hospitalization and residential care programs. Brynn Marr's Help Line is a free confidential crisis and referral service.

Onslow Carteret Behavioral Healthcare Services
3820 Bridges St., Morehead City
(252) 726-0707

Onslow Carteret Behavioral Healthcare Services assists individuals in need of services for mental health, developmental disabilities or substance abuse. This service is provided through a wide variety of individually tailored methods, including handling emergency situations. It supports both insured and uninsured individuals. Patients may refer themselves or can be referred by a family member, school, court system representative, minister, physician or other area agency. The services also offers a 24-hour emergency response line.

Urgent and General Medical Care

Beach Care East
106-D Professional Dr., Beaufort
(252) 728-2205

Beach Care East is a newly opened urgent and primary care center in Beaufort. The center focuses on keeping Carteret County healthy and is open Monday through Friday 9 AM to 5 PM.

Beach Care Medical Care Center
5059 U.S. Hwy. 70 W, Morehead City
(252) 808-3696

From colds to cardiac problems, Beach Care treats emergencies, offers primary care and performs minor surgery. The center has in-house lab and X-ray services. It is staffed by a full-time physician and a physician's assistant and is open Monday though Saturday 9 AM to 9 PM and Sunday 9 AM to 5 PM.

The Doctor's Office
Veranda Square, 7901 Emerald Dr., Ste. 7, Emerald Isle
(252) 354-6500

Although not an urgent care center, this facility offers primary care to its patients and accepts walk-ins. The Doctor's Office has convenient hours that run 9 AM to 6 PM Monday through Saturday with lab hours from 8 to 9 AM. The facility is open on Saturdays from 9 AM to 2 PM for walk-ins, not appointments.

Eastern Carteret Medical Center
U.S. Hwy. 70, Sea Level
(252) 225-1134

Eastern Carteret Medical Center, a subsidiary of Carteret General Hospital, provides treatment of minor emergencies and illnesses and offers complete family care. Appointments are available and walk-ins are worked in as quickly as possible. It is open from 8:30 AM until 4:30 PM on Monday, Tuesday, Wednesday and Friday. The center closes for lunch from noon to 1 PM.

ECIM Private/Urgent Medical Care
906 W. B. McLean Dr., Cape Carteret
(252) 393-9007

The ECIM office in Cape Carteret provides primary care along with urgent medical care for patients in Carteret County and surrounding areas. Emergency-trained physicians and physician assistants at ECIM Urgent Medical Care, part of the ECIM network based in New Bern, provide treatment for minor emergencies and family medical needs. Hours of operation are Monday through Friday 8:30 AM to 5

PM. Appointments may be scheduled for primary care; however, no appointment is necessary for urgent medical care.

The Heart Center of Eastern Carolina
3332 Bridges St., Ste. B, Morehead City
(252) 808-0145

The Heart Center of Eastern Carolina is a full-service cardiology practice featuring the most up-to-date services in the diagnosis, treatment and prevention of cardiac and vascular diseases. These cardiologists offer patients many kinds of non-invasive and invasive treatments: diagnostic catheterization, balloon angioplasty, nuclear cardiology, peripheral vascular disease treatments, atherectomy, stent placement, pacemaker implant and follow-up echocardiology, hypertension treatment, ECP therapy and lipid management. Electrophysiology, nutrition consultations as well as clinical research trials are also included in their services. Patients are seen by referral and appointment. The Heart Center of Eastern Carolina also has an office in New Bern (see our New Bern Healthcare chapter).

Med Center One
600 Atlantic Beach Cswy., Atlantic Beach
(252) 247-2464

This privately owned facility treats minor emergencies and offers primary general medical care. The facility offers an in-house X-ray service and a dispensing pharmacy for patients of record. Med Center One can provide services for vacationers on a walk-in basis and also accepts patients for primary care. Hours are Monday through Saturday 9 AM to 6 PM. Seasonal Sunday hours are noon to 4 PM.

Newport Family Practice
338 Howard Blvd., Newport
(252) 223-5054

Since the nearest emergency room and hospital facilities are in Morehead City or New Bern, Newport Family Practice Center offers a needed service in the Newport community. This privately owned clinic, which has in-house X-ray and lab facilities as well as a pharmacy next door, is open from Monday through Friday 8 AM to 4:30 PM and Saturday from 8:30 to 11:30 AM. The center prefers seeing patients who have made appointments in advance but will accept walk-ins in an emergency.

Nova Pain Management
1815 S. Glenburnie Rd., New Bern
(252) 672-0095

This business is in New Bern, but many Crystal Coast residents are willing to make the drive for its services. Licensed acupuncturist Toni Rittenberg began studying acupuncture at the age of 11 in her hometown of Beijing, China. After graduating from medical school in China, she moved the United States to complete her post-doctoral work at Harvard University. Toni served as Dean of Facility at an acupuncture school in Oakland, California, before moving to New Bern. She has been engaged in private practice in New Bern for 11 years. She offers authentic Chinese acupuncture as a proven and effective way to treat many medical conditions. A full Chinese herbal pharmacy is also located on-site. Toni Rittenberg can be reached at Nova Pain Management at the number above.

Seaside Family Practice of Beaufort
407 Live Oak St., Ste. 1, Beaufort
(252) 728-2328

Seaside Family Practice of Beaufort offers a variety of healthcare services for children and adults of all ages. Included in those services are full physicals, commercial drivers license (CDL) physicals, school physicals and women's health physicals. It also provides a wide range of sick care, injury care and suture care and removal. The practice specializes in management of chronic diseases and provides cryotherapy and respiratory treatments. Seaside Family Practice is currently accepting new patients and accepts most insurance coverage. Hours of operation are Monday through Friday 8:30 AM to 4:30 PM with extended hours on Tuesday until 6:30 PM.

Support Groups and Services

In Carteret County there are a number of active support groups with concerns related to children and family difficulties, mental and physical health, lifestyle changes and substance abuse. Many support groups meet at Carteret General Hospital or at area churches, but that certainly doesn't cover all of the locations. Following are some of the groups who meet regularly in the area. If the list doesn't include a group related to your concern, contact Carteret General Hospital, (252) 808-6000, or ask an Insider.

Better Breathers, (252) 808-6195

Cancer Support Group, (252) 808-6177

Fresh Start - Stop Smoking Program, (252) 808-6611

Heart Healthy Support Group, (252) 808-6454

Hospice of Carteret County, (252) 808-6085

Look Good Feel, Better for Female Cancer Patients, (252) 808-6642

Meals on Wheels, (252) 726-4654

National Alliance for the Mentally Ill, (252) 728-5298

Parkinson's Disease Support Group, (252) 808-6000

Potters for Parkinson's, (252) 728-3988

Prostate Cancer Support Group, (252) 808-6177

Emergency and Other Phone Numbers

Dial **911** from anywhere in the area for emergencies (police, sheriff, fire and rescue services).

Alcoholics Anonymous/AL-ANON, (252) 726-8540

American Red Cross, (252) 637-3405

Carteret County Department of Social Services, (252) 728-3181

Carteret County Domestic Violence Program, (252) 728-3788

Carteret County Health Department, (252) 728-8550

Carteret County Humane Society and Animal Shelter, (252) 247-7744

Outer Banks Wildlife Shelter (OWLS), (252) 240-1200

Rape Crisis Program, (252) 504-3668

VOLUNTEER 👥
OPPORTUNITIES

O ne of the treasures of this area is the support and involvement of those in the community. Volunteers make up the core of many organizations on the Crystal Coast. These individuals of all ages render their time, talents, experience and services. Through a variety of volunteer opportunities, residents donate their talents in gardening, narrating historical tours, helping students, directing tourists, preserving the natural environment, building houses, offering tax preparation assistance and assisting hospital patients and underprivileged families. Volunteering brings satisfaction to many people's lives and offers the chance to not only give back to the community but also meet other people with common interests.

For those with time to share, volunteering will open new doors through many worthwhile organizations that always welcome and train new volunteers. Volunteering offers an opportunity to learn something new or teach others, and groups such as these will welcome the call. For those who may not have the ability to volunteer their time, there are other ways of helping out such as giving monetary donations, donating goods or services, or participating in various fund-raising events that benefit these local organizations and the community.

Public Sites and Parks

Beaufort Historic Site
100 Block Turner St., Beaufort
(252) 728-5225, (800) 575-7483
Beaufort Historic Site is a large preservation organization that relies heavily upon its volunteers. From docents and tour guides, to English double decker bus drivers and office staff, there are literally hundreds of unique and enjoyable volunteer opportunities for people of all ages

at Beaufort Historical Association (BHA). The site maintains Beaufort's oldest art gallery, the Mattie King Davis Art Gallery, and a fund-raising thrift shop staffed by volunteers. Members of the community are also encouraged to volunteer to provide information to visiting school groups. Scripts and other materials are provided in advance. Whether you want to volunteer on a regular basis, or just offer your expertise or help during a special season or event, the BHA is always appreciative of its volunteers.

Cape Lookout National Seashore
131 Charles St., Harkers Island
(252) 728-2250
Volunteers provide valued skills and assistance for many programs at Cape Lookout National Seashore. At the Harkers Island headquarters, volunteers can help at the Visitor Center to greet visitors, provide information and operate the bookstore. There are also many programs for those volunteers who like to be outside and active. As caretakers and keepers, volunteers live and work for six weeks at a time at the Cape Lookout Light Station, Cape Lookout Village, the Great Island Cabin area and Portsmouth Village. Other volunteers help with special projects such as photography, monitoring wildlife or presenting school programs. Whatever your interest, there are many rewarding opportunities to help protect the National Seashore and to facilitate visitor understanding and enjoyment of its resources.

Carteret County Public Library
210 Turner St., Beaufort
(252) 728-2050
Each of the four Carteret County public libraries has an active volunteer group that helps with all types of library programs, from Storytime for Kids to adult

reading groups to book sales. Contact the individual libraries in your area for details:

Beaufort — (252) 728-2050

Bogue Banks — (252) 247-4660

Western Carteret — (252) 393-6500

Newport — (252) 223-5108

Carteret County Public School System
107 Safrit Dr., Beaufort
(252) 728-4583

Volunteer opportunities in the public school system are many and varied. Each of the county's 17 public schools seeks individuals interested in tutoring students, helping with special projects, working with band programs or assisting in the office. Whether you are interested in listening to a first grader read, helping a fourth grader with multiplication, having lunch each week with a special student or working out chemistry problems with a tenth grader, the school system would be excited to have your help. The school system requires a background check and provides mandatory training for all its volunteers.

Core Sound Waterfowl Museum and Heritage Center
1785 Island Rd., Harkers Island
(252) 728-1500

Core Sound Waterfowl Museum depends on volunteer help for daily carving demonstrations and special programs year round. Demonstrations, revolving local exhibits and programs focusing on local heritage are offered year round. The museum houses the area's finest collection of carvings and waterfowl art and archives oral histories and artifacts from the Down East communities. Volunteers are needed to help with programs for school groups and bus tours, to assist staff with administrative duties and to serve on committees and boards. For more information on the museum, see our Attractions chapter.

Down East Library
Corner of U.S. Hwy. 70 and Whitehurst Rd., Smyrna
(252) 729-0281

This small library was formed based on the need to have library services in the Down East area of Carteret County. Founded, supported and staffed by volunteers, this library is offering a wonderful

service to the area. Volunteers of all types are needed — from those interested in answering the phone or shelving books to those interested in helping with the children's reading program. There are many community programs and classes developing, including after-school homework help, knitting and scrapbooking classes, and book clubs. All the books in the library are by donation, so book donations are always needed and appreciated.

Fort Macon State Park
N.C. Hwy. 58, Atlantic Beach
(252) 726-3775

Volunteers, working through the Friends of Fort Macon, act as guides at this historic site throughout the year. Training is usually conducted in February of each year. Volunteers help park rangers with special group tours and presentations. Fort Macon is one of the busiest state parks in North Carolina, and volunteers play an important role in facilitating visitation. A Coastal Education Center is in the process of being built with completion slated for late summer or early fall of 2009. Volunteer opportunities, such as meeting and greeting visitors and assisting in the overall operation of the center ,are forthcoming; contact the park for details.

The History Place
1008 Arendell St., Morehead City
(252) 247-7533

The History Place has become a landmark of Morehead City. It focuses on Carteret County through exhibits and displays in a 12,000-square-foot facility that includes a museum, research library, museum store, classroom and auditorium/learning center. Docents are the backbone of this organization. The History Place has only one full-time paid staff member and one part-time paid library director. The rest of the "staff members" are volunteers. Docents greet visitors and answer questions, with shifts usually set at three hours either once a week or once a month, generally from 10 AM to 1 PM or 1 to 4 PM. Museum hours are 10 AM to 4 PM Tuesday through Saturday. Docents assist visitors in the gallery, museum store or library. Docents also assist, on occasion, with folding brochures and newsletters or helping keep the museum scrapbook up to date. There is always a need for volunteers to assist in preparing for events and programs. Training for volunteers is provided.

North Carolina Aquarium at Pine Knoll Shores
MM 7, N.C. Hwy. 58, Atlantic Beach
(252) 247-4003

The aquarium relies upon a large force of cheerful volunteers to help visitors enjoy the many exhibits and programs and to assist the staff with a variety of tasks. Volunteers interpret exhibits, discuss marine life in the touch pools, staff the discovery carts, greet school groups and help with kids' crafts and activities, among other things. The information desk and the sport-fishing gallery also offer volunteers a chance to work closely with aquarium visitors.

North Carolina Maritime Museum
315 Front St., Beaufort
(252) 728-7317
www.ncmm.friends.org

North Carolina Maritime Museum volunteers are renowned for their hospitality and helpfulness. They work at the museum's information desk, serve as interpreters at displays and as guides for school and other groups, do restoration and construction work in the museum's Watercraft Center and ship model shop, serve on the Board of the Friends of the Museum, assist with the Cape Lookout Studies and Junior Sailing Programs, maintain the reference library, perform clerical duties and help at special events and programs.

Animal Care Services

Humane Society of Carteret County
853 Hibbs Rd., Newport
(252) 247-7744

Members provide staffing for administration and animal-care services, usually for dogs and cats that are in between homes. Volunteers are needed at the shelter primarily to help clean up the facilities and care for animals. Donations are accepted for yard sales held annually during the summer months. There is an ongoing wish list of items for the shelter, such as monetary donations, dry food for dogs

Homes along the Central Coast may date to the 1700s.

photo: Peter Doran

and cats, non-scoopable litter, bleach, paper towels, dish soap, laundry detergent, copy paper, index cards and more. Volunteers are also needed to operate the Humane Society Thrift Store in Morehead City, (252) 726-1399.

Outer Banks Wildlife Shelter
100 Wildlife Way, Newport
(252) 240-1200

This shelter for injured wildlife is operated with volunteer help, including the help of licensed rehabilitators. Funding efforts include daily aluminum-can recycling, an annual benefit dinner, an art auction and contributions of visitors and rescuers of injured animals. Feeding and animal care is volunteered. Volunteers are always needed and must be 18 years of age or older. The Baby Bird Feeders program offers opportunities for those 13 years of age and older. On-the-job training is provided to all volunteers.

Pet Adoption and Welfare Society (PAWS) of Carteret
1211 Bridges St., Morehead City
(252) 247-3341

PAWS focuses on animal adoption, health and safety, and community education and participation. PAWS offers an adoption program in which pets are spayed, neutered and healthy for their placement. PAWS rescues and vets pets regularly in addition to expanding and partnering with other community organizations. PAWS partnered with Carteret County Emergency Management and County Animal Control to provide a pet-friendly hurricane shelter for Carteret County. In another partnership with the Boys and Girls Club of Coastal Carolina, PAWS offers fun and educational pet care clinics throughout the year. Annually, PAWS hosts the Sunday Brunch fundraiser during the Carolina Chocolate Festival, hosts the OktoberPets event at the Crystal Coast Civic Center, and participates as Pets for Vets in the Morehead City Veteran's Day parade. Plans are in the works for a Pet Adoption Center, which will house the administrative and educational facility. Volunteers are always needed to assist through participation in adoption programs, foster care, the thrift store,

membership, the hurricane shelter, education and fundraising. The website provides a wealth of information and showcases adoptable pets.

Human Care Services

American Cancer Society
(252) 247-3230

The American Cancer Society plans the annual Relay for Life, a 24-hour fund-raising event each year in Carteret County. The event takes place on a high school track in the county, bringing groups from churches, businesses and families together in the fight against cancer. Volunteers not only participate in the relay but organize it as well. Help is always needed.

Boys & Girls Club of Coastal Carolina
3221 Bridges St., Morehead City
(252) 222-3007
601 Mulberry St., Beaufort
(252) 504-2465

The Boys & Girls Club of Coastal Carolina includes clubs in Morehead City, Beaufort and Havelock. The club relies on volunteers in all aspects of its operation, including tutoring, special-skills training, fund-raising, homework help and administrative support. Volunteer positions vary and include art program volunteers, handyman volunteers, homework helpers, social recreation area volunteers and technology lab volunteers just to name a few. Best of all, they provide positive role models for kids. After-school programs are also in place in several elementary schools in the area. They are always in need of additional help. Specific volunteer positions that need to be filled can be found on the club's website.

Broad Street Clinic
534 N. 35th St., Ste. K, Morehead City
(252) 726-4562

The Broad Street Clinic offers medical treatment for chronic illnesses for the non-insured who meet the agency's income criteria. Volunteers help in administrative capacities and as receptionists, and medical professionals donate their time to offer services. There are volunteer opportunities during the day and evening, and training is provided.

Carteret County Domestic Violence Program
(252) 726-2336

Volunteers help in a variety of capacities for the Carteret County Domestic Violence Program. An upscale resale shop, Caroline's Collectibles, 3716 Arendell Street in Morehead City, is completely staffed by volunteer help. Additional volunteers serve on the board, assist at the program's center for non-violence, help in Caroline's House and help raise funds for this deserving organization. Volunteers are also needed to provide transportation and to serve as child-care sitters.

Carteret County General Hospital
3500 Arendell St., Morehead City
(252) 808-6046

The Carteret County General Hospital volunteer program began in 1977 and today has a vital group helping in 30 different areas of the hospital. In addition to providing support for the hospital, the volunteers also raise funds for the Hospital Foundation through various fundraising activities held throughout the year. The largest fundraiser is The Gift Gallery, the hospital gift shop, which is staffed by volunteers. For more information about the Carteret General Hospital Volunteers, call the Volunteer Office.

Carteret Literacy Council
Morehead City
(252) 808-2020

This program matches tutors with students, often adults, who need help with reading, writing or math. Private sessions are arranged by the tutor-student team who meet once or twice a week at a location convenient to both parties. Volunteer training is coordinated by the Literacy Council every three months. In addition, the program offers an annual business spelling bee each year in October and an outreach program that offers free presentations on literacy, storytelling for the

Head Start program, and Bringing Books to Babies in cooperation with Carteret General Hospital.

Crystal Coast Habitat for Humanity
5898 U.S. Hwy. 70 W, Newport
(252) 223-2111

Habitat for Humanity provides volunteer labor to build homes for qualified families, and volunteers support the program every step of the way. Volunteers serve on the board and are involved in administrative functions, in the hands-on acts of building and in fund-raising efforts. Call the office for volunteer forms. The program's resale home store also relies on volunteer labor. Donations and purchases from the store help the funding of the materials they need to build the homes. You can call them at (252) 223-4493 and arrange for them to pick up large item donations.

Down East Council of Hispanic/Latino Affairs (DECHLA)
503 Guion St., New Bern
(252) 672-8667

DECHLA provides services to the Hispanic and Latino community in Carteret, Craven, Jones and Pamlico counties, including free community English classes, Spanish and English interpretation, computer education, and referral information and services. The New Bern center is always in need of help in the upkeep and maintenance of the premises, basic clerical tasks and data entry. There are ongoing volunteer opportunities available; contact the director at the New Bern office for the most current opportunities.

Foster Grandparent Program
301 McQueen Ave., Newport
(252) 223-1650

The Foster Grandparent Program, administered by Coastal Community Action, serves Carteret, Craven, Pamlico and Jones counties. It provides a stipend for limited-income participants ages 60 and older who offer 20 hours a week for one-on-one extra assistance of children in school, libraries or in the hospital, where they must annually meet safety training requirements of hospital employees. Volunteers must apply.

Guardian ad Litem
Courthouse Square, Beaufort
(252) 838-8145

After training, Guardian ad Litem volunteers are assigned by the juvenile court to investigate cases of child neglect or abuse and to report their findings to the court. This advocate for the child ensures that the child's interests are properly presented to the court.

Hope Mission of Carteret County, Inc.
1410 Bridges St., Morehead City
(252) 240-2359

Hope Mission exists to meet the immediate needs of people requiring help. At the mission's soup kitchen, volunteers assist in serving food provided by area churches, restaurants and private donations. Lunch is served daily Monday through Saturday from 11 AM to 12:30 PM to people in need, and special dinners are served during the holiday season. The soup kitchen often needs volunteers Monday through Friday from 8 AM to 2 PM and welcomes church groups and organizations. The mission also offers a men's shelter and a men's and women's recovery home.

Hospice of Carteret County
302 Medical Park Ct., Morehead City
(252) 808-6085

A division of Carteret General Hospital, Hospice of Carteret County trains volunteers to serve patients and care-giving

Volunteers operate thrift shops for the Carteret County Humane Society, the Domestic Violence Program of Carteret County, the Beaufort Historical Association, and the Pet Adoption and Welfare Society (PAWS). Each is a great place to donate clothing or household items. And don't forget to check these places for bargains!

families. They provide relief and support for family members by keeping the patient company, running errands and serving as a vital link between the family and Hospice staff.

Martha's Mission Cupboard
901 Bay St., Morehead City
(252) 726-1717

This is an emergency food pantry for families in crisis in Carteret County. Every month, the mission provides food for more than 300 families, senior citizens and mentally and physically challenged persons. Martha's Mission operates strictly on donations, and volunteers help to sort and distribute the incoming food. The Mission Cupboard is open Monday, Wednesday and Friday from 10:30 AM to 3 PM.

Meals on Wheels
Morehead City
(252) 726-4654

Meals on Wheels volunteers are always needed to help deliver meals to homebound individuals. Meals on Wheels also has groups in the surrounding areas, including Beaufort.

Project Christmas Cheer
(252) 247-7275

Project Christmas Cheer began in 1985 when a group volunteered their time to assist an overflow of families seeking assistance from the Carteret County Department of Social Services. Volunteers take applications and match the applicants with donors. Donors make arrangements to deliver Christmas gifts such as food, toys, blankets, fuel oil and things that would really help during Christmas of a difficult year. The offices are open from October through December.

Retired and Senior Volunteer Program (RSVP)
301 McQueen Ave., Newport
(252) 223-1630

RSVP strives to meet vital community needs by providing volunteer opportunities for seniors. Members of RSVP are age 55 and older and pledge to perform at least one hour of service each week. These active, energetic volunteers are matched with tasks that suit their abilities, interests and experience. RSVP volunteers tutor in schools, help homebound seniors with meal delivery, compile mailings and make visits at nursing homes.

Environmental Services

N.C. Big Sweep
Morehead City
(252) 222-6359

N.C. Big Sweep is a statewide effort to clean trash out of the waterways. It's a one-day effort that occurs in Carteret County annually on a Saturday in October following the North Carolina Seafood Festival. Big Sweep is locally coordinated through the N.C. Cooperative Extension Service office in Morehead City.

North Carolina Coastal Federation
3609 N.C. Hwy. 24, Ocean
(252) 393-8185

This coastal environmental protection organization offers education, restoration and preservation, environmental information and legislative accountability and is

funded through membership contributions. Volunteers are needed to help with marsh-grass plantings in the late spring, oyster shell baggings and reef creation, and trail maintenance days. Volunteers are also needed in the office to type, file, answer phones and more. Help with membership drives and fund-raising is always needed. Specific expertise is welcomed, as NCCF coordinates special projects and events.

Rachel Carson Reserve
101 Pivers Island Rd., Beaufort
(252) 838-0883

Volunteer opportunities at the Rachel Carson National Estuarine Research Reserve in Beaufort include: collecting water samples, clearing trails, assisting with the annual horse and bird censuses, guiding visitors on nature walks, leading canoe or kayak trips, helping in the headquarters office, participating in periodic beach sweeps or reserve clean-ups, and assisting the education staff with summer camps. Volunteers gain firsthand knowledge of estuarine ecology and enjoy the beautiful islands that comprise the Rachel Carson National Estuarine Research Reserve.

MEDIA

With each passing year in Carteret County, there seems to be more and more media coverage, especially in the avenue of printed media and the web presence that often accompanies that media. New publications continually spring up throughout the year, giving readers the opportunity to experience all that the Crystal Coast has to offer. It's no wonder — and no secret — that there continues to be interest and continuing growth in this area of the state. Although there is no daily newspaper printed in the county, the *Carteret County News-Times*, a local news tri-weekly, is published here, and a neighboring county daily, the *Jacksonville Daily News*, has a bureau in the county. A state daily, the Raleigh *News and Observer*, also circulates here, as do several local weekly papers. Several radio stations are based in the area, and the Fox Network has a local affiliate based in Morehead City. Other networks have television stations close by to cover local news. Time Warner Cable, located in Newport, offers the full spectrum of cable channels as well as digital service and Road Runner cable modem service.

Print

Arts Alive
4206 Bridges St., Morehead City
(252) 726-7081

Arts Alive is a regional magazine designed to showcase the arts of Carteret, Onslow, Craven, Pitt, Beaufort and Pamlico counties. *Arts Alive* is a key resource for everyone interested in enjoying, participating in and preserving the arts. Local arts councils use *Arts Alive* as a forum to promote coming exhibits, concerts, classes, contests and plays. *Arts Alive* is published monthly, though the January and February issues are combined. *Arts Alive* is distributed free through racks and stands in the six counties.

The Beaufort Gam
Beaufort
(252) 728-2435

The Beaufort Gam is a free weekly newspaper focusing on local news, including municipal and county governments, information on school and community events, and informative columns. *The Gam* distributes more than 12,000 copies every Thursday to more than 300 distribution outlets throughout Carteret County and extending into Swansboro. Out-of-the-area mail delivery is also available.

Carteret County News-Times
4206 Bridges St., Morehead City
(252) 726-7081
www.thenewstimes.com

The county happenings can be found on the pages of the Carteret County News-Times, published Wednesday and Friday afternoons and Sunday morning. Produced by a staff of local writers, this newspaper is a good source of information for vacationers who want to know the schedules of tours, festivals, kids' programs, seminars, exhibits and events of all types within the county and the surrounding area. The paper has an expanded area sports section and entertainment section, and a business portion is included each Wednesday. The *News-Times*, which has been in business for more than 95 years, is available by subscription and in vending machines throughout the county. The *News-Times* also publishes the *Tideland News* based in Swansboro and the *Topsail Voice* in Hampstead.

271

Coaster
201 N. 17th St., Morehead City
(252) 240-1811

Now in its 25th year, *Coaster* is called the Guide to the Crystal Coast for a reason — because it provides such a great overview of area happenings and attractions. This seven-issue magazine is a comprehensive, full-color guide and offers needed information to residents, visitors, retirees and second homeowners. You'll enjoy the features, the area attraction information and guides of all types. Maps, ferry schedules and tide tables are offered, and the calender of events offers the latest Crystal Coast happenings.

Crystal Coast Parent
Morehead City
(877) 219-1403

Crystal Coast Parent strives to bring information about family events and news to one publication. This free bi-monthly magazine is made available to families who live in and visit Carteret, Craven and Onslow counties. Its goal is to be a one-stop parenting resource for information about family-oriented local events, opportunities, products and services with a focus on raising balanced, healthy and happy children.

HOMES Magazine
201 N. 17th St., Morehead City
(252) 247-7442

HOMES real estate magazines are a must-have to locals who are looking to buy real estate or search rental listings in the area. Additionally, *HOMES* are a helpful resource for those living out of the area looking to permanently relocate or for those searching for a second home in the beautiful central coast region. Four area-specific *HOMES* magazines are published and distributed monthly for the Crystal Coast, Jacksonville/Onslow, Topsail and Craven/Pamlico areas plus a regional military edition.

The Jacksonville Daily News
Jacksonville, (910) 353-1171, Morehead City
(252) 808-2275

The Daily News is a daily morning paper that covers state and national events,

Jacksonville, Onslow County and Marine Corps Base Camp Lejeune. The paper also has a Carteret County bureau with writers and a photographer who provide coverage of Carteret County activities and county-wide issues. One reporter also focuses on fisheries and environmental issues in eastern North Carolina. Home delivery is available to Carteret County subscribers.

North Carolina Coastal Homes & Design
Beaufort
(252) 838-1280

North Carolina Coastal Homes & Design magazine features homes and decor throughout the coastal region and also highlights information on real estate trends, building and design products and more with a focus on the natural beauty of the local coastal communities. Readers gain informative advice on home decorating, become acquainted with new and up-and-coming products for the home, and visually benefit from the professional photography that brings these homes and design trends to life — all with a coastal flair.

This Week Magazine
4206 Bridges St., Morehead City
(252) 726-7081
www.thenewstimes.com

This Week Magazine (TWM) is considered the ultimate authority on entertainment for the Crystal Coast and has been for 30 years. Locals and visitors alike turn to TWM to find out what is happening in the area and region. Each Thursday, 20,000 free copies are distributed to racks and stands throughout eastern North Carolina. *TWM* offers a comprehensive calendar of events spotlighting festivals, concerts, theater, fishing, NASCAR news, book reviews, the arts and dining out. *TWM* is the entertainment and TV section of the Friday edition of the *Carteret County News-Times*.

Tideland News
774 W. Corbett Ave., Swansboro
(910) 326-5066

Tideland News is published each Wednesday from its office in Swansboro. Owned by Carteret Publishing Company of Morehead City, which also publishes the *Carteret County News-Times*, the paper covers news and activities in Swansboro, the eastern portion of Onslow County and western Carteret County. The communities covered by this weekly include Hubert, Bear Creek, Stella, Peletier, Cedar Point, Cape Carteret, Emerald Isle, Bogue and Ocean.

Television Stations

Headline News
Beaufort
(252) 838-0006

Operated by Doug Raymond Productions, Headline News Local Edition is featured at 24 minutes after each hour and six minutes before each hour on Channel 49. Headline News offers coverage of local events and the meetings of the county commissioners, town boards, the board of education and more. This newscast provides viewers a chance to see what is really happening in their community.

Time Warner Cable Channel 10
U.S. Hwy. 70, Newport
(252) 223-6410

With an office and studio in Newport, Time Warner Cable Channel 10 is the area's community channel. Its programming includes a variety of topics, from schools and health issues to sports and talk shows. The station also broadcasts tapes of the meetings of county commissioners and boards of education from Carteret County and neighboring Craven County. Locally produced programs focus on community events and disseminate information about community projects and community-service activities.

UNC Center for Public Television
Research Triangle Park, Raleigh
(919) 549-7000

North Carolina public television is broadcast locally on Channel 13. Viewers may choose from the public television programs to which they are accustomed along with regional features tailored to the interests of North Carolina residents.

WCTI-TV 12 ABC
225 Glenburnie Dr., New Bern
(252) 638-1212

Television Channel 12, the local ABC affiliate, provides comprehensive local coverage as well as ABC programming. Channel 12 produces local programs, including "Good Morning Eastern Carolina" and "Community Spotlight." The station offers local news, sports and weather each weekday at noon, 5, 6 and 11 PM. This station has a reporter and photographer dedicated to covering events in Carteret County.

WFXI-TV 8/14 FOX
5441 U.S. Hwy. 70, Morehead City
(252) 240-0888

Television Channel 8 and Channel 14 show the regular Fox programming and offer a local news show each night at 10 PM. With an office in Morehead City, the channel offers some local television coverage.

WITN-TV 7 NBC
U.S. Hwy. 17 S, Washington
(252) 946-3131

Television Channel 7 is the local NBC affiliate. Along with NBC programming, the station has area news coverage, including high school and college sports. News is broadcast at 5:30 AM, noon, and at 5, 6 and 11 PM.

WNCT-TV 9 CBS
3321 S. Evans St., Greenville
(252) 355-8500

Television Channel 9 is the regional CBS affiliate and carries all of the network's programming. Local news, sports and national news are shown at 5 and 6 AM, noon, and 6 and 11 PM. A WNCT reporter is assigned to covering the Crystal Coast.

Cable Television

Time Warner Cable
500 Vision Cable Dr., Newport
(252) 223-6400

Time Warner is a franchised cable provider for Carteret County as well as Craven and Onslow counties. This company provides digital cable services, high-speed Internet and digital phone service. For hookup service or additional information, call the office.

Radio Stations

Lite 98.7 FM
Jacksonville

This is the station locals prefer for on-the-job easy listening. You can enjoy this type music all through the day. Weekday evenings from 7 PM to midnight, on-air radio personality Delilah offers advice along with caller dedications and requests.

Public Radio East
800 College Ct., New Bern
(252) 638-3434

With studios on the Craven Community College campus, Public Radio East offers listeners two distinct formats. The news and classical music format is heard on 89.3 FM and presents nearly 120 hours of classical music each week plus in-depth news weekday mornings and afternoons during NPR's "Morning Edition" and "All Things Considered." "The News & Ideas Network" — heard on 88.5 FM in New Bern, 90.3 FM in Goldsboro-Kinston, 91.5 FM Atlantic Beach and 88.1 FM in Greenville — offers those NPR signature programs and more, including news from the BBC, live national call-in programs "The Diane Rehm Show" and "Talk of the Nation" as well as "The Sound," a weekday evening program of roots rock, Americana and contemporary folk. During weekends on all the Public Radio East frequencies, it's America's favorite mechanics Tom and Ray Magliozzi during "Car Talk" Saturday at 10 AM, music and storytelling Saturday evening at 6 PM during "A Prairie Home Companion" and five hours of jazz Sunday

at 6 PM during "An Evening with the Jazzman."

Thunder Country 96.3 and 103.7
New Bern
(252) 672-5900

Thunder Country plays continuous new country music for its country music fans. The station also brings everything NASCAR to country radio.

WSFL 106.5
New Bern
(252) 633-1500

WSFL plays classic rock all day and features the "John Boy and Billy Show" from 6 to 10 AM each weekday. This station offers local, national and financial news, as well as sports, rock and NASCAR coverage.

WTKF 107.1 FM
U.S. Hwy. 70, Morehead City
(252) 247-6343
www.wtkf107.com

North Carolina's first FM talk station, WTKF 107.1 exclusively offers "Coastal Daybreak" with Ben Ball, the area's only morning show that's all talk. Ball taps into all the area happenings, history, book reviews, hot health issues and more, keeping eastern North Carolina citizens up to date. On The Talk Station you'll also find Rush Limbaugh, Laura Ingraham, Michael Reagan and other talk-radio favorites. These include many locally produced programs like "Viewpoints," "Youthpoints," "Positive Living" and "The Wine and Dine Radio Show." Sports coverage includes the Tar Heels of North Carolina, the Carolina Panthers, local high school games and Sporting News Radio. News and weather are broadcast every 30 minutes. The station is also heard in Jacksonville on WJNC 1240 AM.

WORSHIP

Whether you're a resident, visitor or newcomer, you have hundreds of worship options on the Crystal Coast. You can attend a service, admire the architecture or learn about local history by visiting the local churches. Many of the area's community activities and volunteer efforts are spearheaded by local houses of worship.

Churches are around every corner, but that's not unusual for an area many refer to as the "Southern Bible Belt." Baptist, Methodist and Pentecostal churches predominate. Episcopal, Presbyterian, Friends, Unitarian/Universalist and Catholic churches are also represented, along with many other denominations. Visitors who choose to worship at a synagogue may visit Temple B'Nai Sholem Synagogue, 505 Middle Street, New Bern.

Many of the area's oldest churches are in Beaufort. For the most part, these are wooden structures preserved to look just as they did hundreds of years ago. Each church is distinct — some are modern structures, some are classic brick designs, others are weathered and vine-covered. Each has its own legends and stories held dear by its congregation.

It's not possible for us to list the hundreds of worship centers located around the Crystal Coast. We have described a few of the churches that are noted for their historic buildings, the sizes of their congregations or their convenient locations. For more information about other churches in the area, check the Yellow Pages or the Friday evening edition of the *Carteret County News-Times*, where you will find a directory of local churches.

Ann Street United Methodist Church, on Ann and Craven Streets in Beaufort, (252) 728-4279, was built c. 1854. The church features curved wooden pews, beautiful

Churches are plentiful throughout the area, which is part of the 'Southern Bible Belt.'

photo: Peter Doran

stained-glass windows and hand-carved rosettes in the ceiling. The steeple, stretching high above the houses on the low coastal land, was shown on old mariners' charts as a point of reference, a beacon to aid those at sea. It is one of three churches surrounding the Old Burying Ground (see our Crystal Coast Attractions chapter). The church's modern educational building stands across the street and is used for community events.

Purvis Chapel AME Zion Church, 217 Craven Street, (252) 504-2605, is Beaufort's oldest continuously used church. Built in 1820, it stands on the same block as the Ann Street United Methodist Church. Originally built by the Methodist Episcopal Church, Purvis Chapel was later deeded to the AME Zion congregation and is still owned by that group. The church's bell was cast in Glasgow, Scotland, in 1797. The building is listed on the National Register of Historic Places, and in 1998 the Purvis Chapel was recognized with a second Kathryn Cloud Historical Preservation Award. The church you see today, though modified somewhat, closely resembles the original structure.

The area's oldest Episcopal church is **St. Paul's Episcopal Church**, c. 1857, located at 209 Ann Street, (252) 728-3324, in Beaufort. Local shipbuilders built the church in two years. Visitors will notice that the interior of the sanctuary bears a striking resemblance to an upside-down ark. It is reported to be one of the ten most acoustically perfect buildings in North Carolina. Holy Eucharist is on Sunday and a midweek Eucharist is conducted each Wednesday.

St. Stephen's United Church of Christ, 500 Cedar Street, Beaufort, (252) 728-4918, was built in 1867, along with the neighboring two-story school building that housed the Washburn Seminary. Records show the lot was purchased for $100 in 1867, and the seminary served as a school for many years. St. Stephen's pews are the original dark mahogany and still have the center railing that separated families and Sunday school groups. Through the years, no major modifications have been made to the church's exterior.

The **First Baptist Church of Morehead City**, 810 Bridges Street, (252) 726-4142, is one of the town's oldest churches. The congregation first met in July 1873 and originally shared a small building near the waterfront with the town's Methodists. After the Civil War, the congregation built the current structure. An adjacent 18,000-square-foot Family Life Center was dedicated in 1994 and is available for community activities, meetings and weddings.

Located at 900 Arendell Street in Morehead City, the **First United Methodist Church**, (252) 726-7102, was founded in 1879 but has roots that go back to Shepard's Point in 1800. Today's sanctuary was dedicated in 1952.

St. Egbert's Catholic Church, 1706 Evans Street, (252) 726-3559, had its start in Morehead City in 1929. Community service is an important part of this church, and support and Bible study groups regularly meet in church facilities. Parish services are offered Saturday and Sunday, and mass is held daily. The church also operates a private school for students from kindergarten through fifth grade.

The **Unitarian Coastal Fellowship**, 1300 Evans Street in Morehead City, was organized in Carteret County in 1980 and promotes religious diversity. Services are held in the fellowship hall on Sundays at 10:30 AM. Religious education and child care are available. Call (252) 240-2283 for more information.

Glad Tidings Pentecostal Holiness Church, 4621 Country Club Road in Morehead City, (252) 726-0160, grew from a 1930s tent revival. In 1997 the church dedicated a 20,000-square-foot worship and outreach center, which seats 1,200 and features a state-of-the-art sound and lighting system and a catwalk for theatrical and musical productions. The building also contains a main floor with a balcony, a bridal-hospitality room for weddings and welcoming first-time visitors, and a bookstore, Inspiration Station. Glad Tidings has a 10,000-square-foot family life center, with a large open area, classrooms, a kitchen and offices. The center is available for weddings, conferences and meetings.

MILITARY

Military bases and training facilities dot North Carolina's Crystal Coast, but they have not spoiled its beauty. They have just added a few more people, a little noise, extra traffic every now and then — and a lot of patriotism.

Occasionally, residents express concern about low-flying aircraft, the noise caused by a night-training flight or the increased traffic on the roads, but all in all the military bases are excellent neighbors. They provide employment and income and contribute to the community through uncountable volunteer hours. Military personnel often volunteer to tutor students, clear and construct school athletic fields, help nonprofit groups with projects and raise funds for holiday programs. We're glad to have them in Carteret and Craven counties.

Of the surrounding bases, the **Marine Corps Air Station (MCAS)** base at Cherry Point in Havelock has the greatest impact on the Crystal Coast. One of the most valuable assets is the base's Fleet Readiness Center (FRC) East. The command employs nearly 4,000 civilian, military and contractor personnel, who work in a wide variety of skilled technical and professional positions. FRC East's customers include: 202 different Navy and Marine Corps activities, 24 foreign nations, five U. S. Air Force activities, three U.S. Army activities and two other federal agencies. As a service provider specializing in support

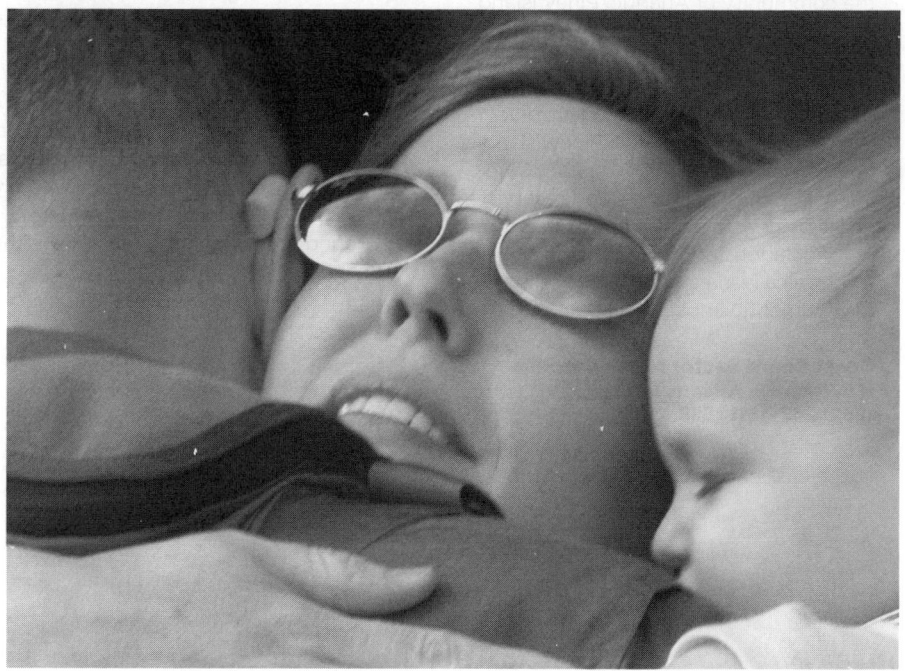

Military family reunions are a common and happy sight in Havelock.

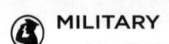

of Marine Corps aircraft, engines and components, FRC is the only source of repair within the continental United States for many jet engines and rotary wing engines, as well as turbofan vectored thrust engines. See our Havelock chapter for more information on MCAS Cherry Point.

Camp Lejeune Marine Corps Base is located in nearby Jacksonville. The Port of Morehead City is the port of embarkation and debarkation for the Second Division of the U.S. Marine Corps at Camp Lejeune. Military troops from Camp Lejeune often travel N.C. Highway 24 from Swansboro to Morehead City. Another nearby military establishment is Seymour Johnson Air Force Base in Goldsboro, which is about a two-hour drive from the Crystal Coast.

What follows is information about some of the other military establishments in the area.

Atlantic Outlying Field and Piney Island (Marines)

These two training facilities are in the Down East area of Carteret County. Atlantic Outlying Field is a 1,514-acre facility in the community of Atlantic. Piney Island, or BT-11 as the military refers to it, is a 10,000-plus-acre electronic practice range at the eastern tip of Carteret County. As part of the Mid-Atlantic Electronic Warfare Range (MAEWR), Piney Island is used by various military groups, including active-duty personnel and reservists. While planes do fly over the area, bombing simulations are recorded and scored electronically via computers to lessen the environmental impact.

Coast Guard Sector North Carolina
N.C. Hwy. 58, Atlantic Beach
(252) 247-4511 x538

Coast Guard Sector North Carolina at the east end of Bogue Banks is the

home port of one large cutter and several smaller vessels. The base is charged with overseeing the waters from Virginia to the North Carolina–South Carolina border. Coast Guard missions include homeland security, search and rescue, and law enforcement.

Coast Guard Station Emerald Isle
Station St., Emerald Isle
(252) 354-2462

The vessels of this station, located at the west end of Bogue Banks in Emerald Isle, patrol about 50 nautical miles of the Atlantic Intracoastal Waterway, including Bogue Inlet, New River Inlet, White Oak River and New River all the way down to Surf City and 30 miles offshore. The primary focus is on homeland security, search and rescue, and law enforcement.

Marine Corps Auxiliary Landing Field
Bogue Field, off N.C. Hwy. 24

This 875-acre landing field fronts Bogue Sound. It is primarily used for field carrier landing practice, and pilots perform many of these landings at night to simulate landing on an aircraft carrier. It serves as the Marines' only East Coast site for such training and includes the maintenance and operation of an expeditionary airfield. This capability helps ensure success for the Corps. It provides the force with the means to forward deploy its aviation assets in order to have a more readily accessible aviation punch for the Marine Air Ground Task Force commander on the battlefield.

NEW BERN 🐾

New Bern is a unique town. It is a product of 1700s Swiss heritage, augmented by the fact of escaping intact as a Southern city taken hostage by the North during the Civil War. New Bern's location on two rivers, its relatively short distance from the coast and the existence of its railroad made it a valuable commodity to the Union Army until the end of the war, thereby preserving New Bern's architecture and way of life. With its Southern gentility intact, this river town maintains its heritage of Colonial, Georgian, Federal, Greek Revival and Victorian architectural styles.

Early in the area's history, this site on the Neuse and Trent rivers captured the interest of the Tuscarora Indians. It is believed the Indians may have had hunting camps and villages here for thousands of years.

Swiss and German immigrants originally settled New Bern in 1710, naming the settlement after Bern, the Swiss capital. The town was officially founded by Swiss Baron Christoph deGraffenried. As in "old" Bern, New Bern is distinguished by its imposing clock tower above City Hall. The clock was repaired in 2008 in preparation for New Bern's 300th birthday celebration, which will take place in 2010. The city emblem is a black bear going up a golden road, and this symbol appears frequently throughout the city.

New Bern's history contains chapters written by Native Americans, Swiss, British, Colonials, Yankees and Rebels. With each intrusion, the city moved forward. The resulting microcosm of American history today flourishes along New Bern's tree-lined streets, creating a picturesque town proud of its rich history.

Historic markers point out the houses where the first elected assembly in the colonies met in defiance of the crown in 1774, where a signer of the U.S. Constitution lived, and where George Washington slept — twice. Markers also point out the office of jurist William Gaston, the first chief justice of the state Supreme Court and composer of "The Old North State," the state song.

The second-oldest city in North Carolina, New Bern is the site of many firsts. The first state printing press was set up and the first book and newspaper were published here. The state's first public school opened here. The first official celebration of George Washington's birthday was held in New Bern, and it was here that the world's first practical torpedo was assembled and detonated. In the 1890s C. D. Bradham, a New Bern pharmacist, invented Brad's Drink, now known as Pepsi-Cola (see our Close-up on Bradham and Pepsi-Cola in our New Bern Restaurants chapter).

Without question, New Bern's centerpiece is **Tryon Palace**, the lavish Georgian brick mansion named after William Tryon, the British Colonial governor who had it built in 1770. After the Revolutionary War, the palace served as the home of the state capital until 1795. The original palace burned in 1798. The current establishment is a reproduction built in the 1950s from the original plans, which were found in England. It is a sumptuous showplace inside and out.

Downtown New Bern sits on a point of land at the confluence of the Neuse and Trent rivers. Once the heart of the city, the downtown area fell into great disrepair in the early 1970s due to the development of shopping malls and suburban housing outside the business district.

That all changed in 1979 when local government gave Swiss Bear Downtown Development Corp — a nonprofit corporation of civic leaders — the authority

In an area with so much water, boats are important to nearly everyone.

photo: Peter Doran

and responsibility to bring the downtown area back to life. Today, art galleries, specialty shops, antiques stores, restaurants and other businesses have resurrected downtown and the waterfront, turning it into a bustling hub of activity.

Progressive improvements are continuously underway. Built and dedicated in 1995, James Reed Lane is a lovely downtown mini-park and pedestrian walk-through on Pollock Street across from Christ Church. The pleasant respite amid downtown activity was planned and funded through efforts of Swiss Bear, in honor of the first rector of Christ Church. Private restoration efforts return many of the downtown buildings to their turn-of-the-last-century elegance.

New Bern will begin the celebration of its upcoming 300th birthday with a First Night Celebration on December 31, 2009. The New Bern Board of Aldermen passed a resolution establishing a committee to plan the year-long Tercentenary Celebration that takes place in 2010. (Read more about New Bern's 300th Celebration in our Close-up in the New Bern Attractions chapter.)

The Neuse and Trent rivers converge at downtown's Union Point Park, the city's major celebration spot for events, such as Neuse River Days and the Fourth of July. The Neuse, with headwaters in the central part of the state, takes a lumbering left turn and widens to 6 miles across, making it the widest river in the United States. The 1954 Alfred Cunningham drawbridge into downtown New Bern was closed in May 2007 and will remain closed while a new Bascule drawbridge is built. This is part of a $40 million demolition and building project. The new bridge is scheduled for completion by November 2009, in time for the year-long New Bern 300th anniversary celebration. Downtown New Bern is now accessible on U.S. Highway 70 from the Pembroke exit.

New Bern's proximity to the broad, shallow Pamlico Sound and the Atlantic Ocean helped shape its destiny. The town long thrived on the richness of its waterways and the fertile soil surrounding them. In Colonial times, West Indian and European vessels would dock here to trade merchandise. The river led inland to pitch, tar and tobacco and, of course, to local hospitality. Today, the rivers serve as the focus of the area's recreational activities: water-skiing, sailing and fishing. Hotel-based marinas for modern-day skippers edge toward the Trent River channel from Union Point Park and also front the Neuse. New Bern's rivers are a tremendous source of local pride, and pollution in the past decade stirred tremendous state and local efforts in restoring their health.

New Bern's southeastern boundary is only a few miles from the Croatan National Forest, a 157,000-acre preserve that shelters deer, bear, alligator and the rare Venus flytrap, a carnivorous plant. Canada geese and osprey are common sights along the rivers, as are the resident great blue herons. Given the right weather conditions and saltwater intrusion, the Neuse River has been known to hide 8-foot bull sharks. In November 2004 a 300-pound Mola Mola, perhaps better known as a giant ocean sunfish, was found in the Neuse River five miles from New Bern.

New Bern has four historic districts with homes, stores and churches dating back to the early eighteenth century. Within easy walking distance of the waterfront are more than 164 homes and buildings listed on the National Register of Historic Places. Also nearby are several bed and breakfast inns, hotels, restaurants, banks, antiques stores and specialty shops.

The historic districts also are home to many of the town's 2,000 crape myrtles — New Bern's official flower. New Bern has some glorious gardens. Led by the example of the professionally pampered Tryon Palace gardens, the town's residents have a yen to make things grow. During the spring explosion of dogwoods and azaleas, a ride through many neighborhoods can be breathtaking.

 **CLOSE UP**

The Battle of New Bern

Heavy rain fell on New Bern the night of March 13, 1862. February and March had been miserably wet months. The next morning, March 14, dawned wet with heavy fog, particularly where the Confederates were encamped, along the railroad to the east of town. The area was a pocosin — one of the swampy areas of eastern North Carolina. And the rain didn't help. Soaking into the woolen uniforms of the soldiers, it made movement unpleasant and the chill of a spring morning inescapable.

Reenactors help us remember the Battle of New Bern.

photo: Martha L. Hall

For the Confederates, the object of the battle was to keep New Bern and the rail line from falling into Union hands. The railroad, carrying men, supplies and ammunition through New Bern, was on a direct route to the Army of the Confederacy in Virginia. Disruption of this major conduit would make the war more difficult for the South.

The Battle of New Bern was only six hours long and the Union Army won — with 1,080 total casualties. The Confederates suffered 68 killed, 116 wounded and 400 captured or missing, compared to the Union's 90 killed, 285 wounded and a single man captured. The Federals captured nine New Bern–area forts and 41 heavy guns and occupied a base that they would hold to the end of the war, in spite of several Confederate attempts to recover the town. Union officers wasted no time taking up residence in many of the city's finest buildings, and New Bern became the hub for Federal activity in North Carolina during the war.

One hundred and thirty-seven years later, the Battle of New Bern is still remembered. On October 19, 2001, the battlefield was listed on the National Register of Historic Places. The site is located 5 miles east of the city. Much of the land near the battlefield now is home to Taberna, an upscale residential neighborhood. The 24.65 acres of land where the battle took place was donated to the Civil War Trust and the New Bern Historical Society by Weyerhaeuser Real Estate Development Co.

An additional 2.4 acres was purchased with the help of a grant from the Craven County Tourism Development Authority, and a Visitors' Center has been constructed on this parcel of land. The battlefield area is heavily wooded but there are accessible trails, and some of the original Confederate redans (fortifications) are in decent condition.

On March 10, 2007, an 11.5-ton granite and bronze monument, donated by the 26th North Carolina Regiment Reactivated, was dedicated at the site in memory of the 26th North Carolina Regiment, who fought and died at the Battle of New Bern.

Guided tours are available through the New Bern Historical Society Foundation, (252) 638-8558, for a fee of $5. You may e-mail the Historical Society for more information at nbhistoricalsoc@newbernmail.com or stop by the New Bern Riverfront Convention Center, 203 South Front Street, (252) 637-1551, for printed material and maps.

For more information on the Civil War in New Bern, you can go to www.civil-waralbum.com/misc3/newbern1.htm for pictures of the battlefield, houses in New Bern that were important during the war and links to other New Bern Civil War websites.

Gardens, both public and private, extend throughout the city and its suburbs. Summertime brings day lilies, dahlias, zinnias, black-eyed Susans and petunias. Home gardens produce tomatoes, herbs, squash, corn and other favorites. In fall it seems everyone goes slightly crazy for chrysanthemums. (See our New Bern Annual Events chapter for information about the fall Mumfest.) Flowering cabbage and pansies brighten the winter.

Besides the downtown historic district, New Bern also has the Ghent, DeGraffenried and Riverside neighborhoods, which carry official historic neighborhood designations. Ghent, across Trent Road from the DeGraffenried neighborhood, was the town's first suburb, and its flowering-tree-planted median on Spencer Avenue was once a trolley bed. The neighborhood displays an eclectic collection of architectural styles. DeGraffenried Park, bounded by Trent and Neuse roads, is well known for its beautiful large lawns and brick Colonial Revival-style houses. Its sidewalks make it a grand place for walking. This neighborhood came into its glory days pre-World War II. Ride down Lucerne Way or Queen Anne's Lane and look for the wrought-iron gates on many homes.

Riverside, developed at the turn of the twentieth century, runs between the Norfolk Southern railroad tracks and the Neuse River to Jack Smith Creek. The neighborhood has imposing mansions along National Avenue giving way to more modest residences on neighboring streets.

Tucked between New Bern and the Trent River is Trent Woods, one of the wealthiest of North Carolina's incorporated towns. Here is the New Bern Golf and Country Club, the Eastern Carolina Yacht Club and some of the area's priciest real estate. Trent Woods' costly, pine-shaded real estate is, more and more, in similar company within New Bern's housing market. About 5 miles south of town off U.S. Highway 17 is River Bend, which began as a planned development but later incorporated. Like Trent Woods, it has its own country club, golf course, tennis club, marina and waterfront acreage along the Trent River and the canals that lead to it.

Both River Bend and Fairfield Harbour, another planned community about 8 miles east of New Bern on the Neuse River, have attracted retirees primarily from the Northeast. Fairfield Harbour's amenities include a couple of golf courses, two swimming pools, tennis courts, a marina, a restaurant and lounge, horseshoe pits, and walking and riding paths.

Five miles east of downtown New Bern on U.S. 70 E, lies Taberna, a 1,100-acre golfing community with single-family and patio homes as well as townhouses. The site is centered around an 18-hole golf course, designed by Jim Lipe, a head architect for Jack Nicklaus. The clubhouse includes a restaurant and lounge and swimming pool. Just past Taberna is Carolina Colours, a new 2,000-acre development consisting of single-family homes, condominiums and town homes. Carolina Colours' new pavilion opened in 2007, with a 18-hole golf course, designed by William R. Love, tennis courts, a fitness center and swimming pool. The planned community also has a 25-acre lake, and walking paths and sidewalks are everywhere. New Bern's newest elementary school, Creekside, just opened in this area.

If all this sounds too boringly nice, take heart. There are a few trouble spots. Insiders' brows furrow when they talk about the town's traffic lights and its lack of nightlife.

First, the traffic lights. New Bern has an overabundance of them on U.S. 17, which is called Broad Street downtown and Dr. M. L. King Jr. Boulevard as you head south toward Jacksonville. With the closing of the bridge at the foot of Broad Street, several traffic lights downtown were removed. But if you're headed south and don't catch the lights just right, once you hit Dr. M. L. King Jr. Boulevard expect plenty of stops along U.S. 17. And, at the peak hours of 8 AM, noon and 5 PM, you can expect bottlenecks around the road's intersections with Simmons Street, U.S. 70, McCarthy Boulevard and Glenburnie Road.

Until December 2009 the main thoroughfare through downtown New Bern is receiving a $2.5 million improvement that will change the face of Broad Street from the Sudan Shrine on E. Front Street to the traffic light beside the fire station on Broad and First streets. The street is being converted into a two-lane road complete with grading, drainage, paving, curb, sidewalks and signals on the the 1.1 mile length of road leading into downtown New Bern. A center island will be constructed all along the renovation, complete with the planting of trees, and each main intersection will have a turn lane. This has been tagged as part of the 300th celebration to spiff up the city's interior.

Downtown's traffic woes were eased with the opening of the high-rise Neuse River Bridge in late 1999. The bridge spans the Neuse River and goes from Bridgeton on U.S. 17 to James City on U.S. 70. The bridge replaced the John Lawson drawbridge that connected directly to Broad Street and almost always caused major traffic back-ups when opened. The old bridge was dismantled.

As for New Bern's nightlife, there are a few lounges, some live music in restaurants, wine bars and coffeehouses and two movie theaters, but those with a hankering for more need to hit town at the right time. New Bern has good professional and amateur acting groups (including the annual Shakespeare festival), several subscription performance seasons, an annual Chamber Music festival and an annual Sunday Jazz Showcase worth the wait. The town also has wonderful festivals and shows. Mumfest, New Bern Preservation Foundation's Antique Show and Sale, the Spring Homes and Gardens Tour, Ghostwalk and Tryon Palace Christmas Candlelight Tours are among the favorites (see our New Bern Annual Events chapter). Residents also gather for special occasions on the Trent River waterfront — on July Fourth for the fireworks and in early December for the Christmas flotilla. But, otherwise, the town's social life takes place in private homes and social clubs and at various civic and charity functions that are staged on an annual basis.

To really get to know New Bern, you have to get personal. Come visit. Think of the river city as a tantalizing treasure hunt where gems are revealed as you walk its streets. It's there that you will discover the real New Bern. Take time to read the historic markers and talk to the people in their gardens and on their porches. You're likely to find a sailor from California, a cyclist from New Zealand, an urban refugee from New York or a retired shop owner from Honolulu sharing your park bench. Ask them why they chose to live here. New Bernians like to talk about their town.

New Bern is a gentle place, a place where one can truly enjoy the passing scene, where people know how to appreciate a pretty day or the slow journey of the rivers. This is the real treasure of New Bern. Come share with us.

Eastern North Carolina
1450 AM in New Bern

Radio Free ENC - 1450 AM in New Bern, NC

This is the sportstalk radio station specifically designed to complement the Radio Free ENC 105.7 FM / 1490 AM ESPN here in New Bern. We bring you hourly regional newscasts from the North Carolina News Network as well as local weather and local Sportscenter updates from WCTI Channel 12's Brian North and Derek Bayne. Finally, both stations bring you the best in play by play live sports from national pro, local college, and high school football, baseball, hockey, and basketball.

 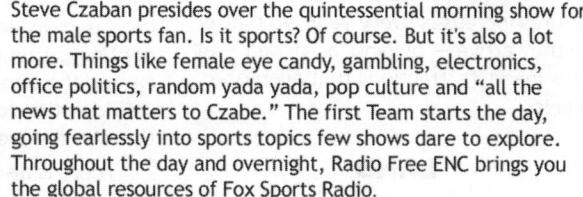

6 AM - 8 AM

Steve Czaban presides over the quintessential morning show for the male sports fan. Is it sports? Of course. But it's also a lot more. Things like female eye candy, gambling, electronics, office politics, random yada yada, pop culture and "all the news that matters to Czabe." The first Team starts the day, going fearlessly into sports topics few shows dare to explore. Throughout the day and overnight, Radio Free ENC brings you the global resources of Fox Sports Radio.

8 AM - 9 AM

The Daily Neuse Show w/ Phil Knight is the only news, interview, and opinion show local to New Bern and Craven County. Join Phil live Monday thru Friday as we simulcast the C-TV 10 Daily Neuse Show and listen to what your friends and neighbors are up to OR what they are thinking.

dan patrick
9 AM-12 Noon

Dan Patrick is known for his wry, irreverent interviews, often asking humorous hypothetical questions and occasionally making bets with them. Dan Patrick regularly hosts high-profile guests including athletes Charles Barkley, Reggie Miller, and John Smoltz; writer Peter King and sportscasters Bob Costas and Rich Eisen. Patrick is joined on the air by producers Paulie and Seton, talent coordinator Fritzie, and official show blogger McLovin. As he did during his ESPN tenure, Patrick regularly chats with his crew about sports, as well as current events, entertainment, and their personal lives.

12 Noon - 3 PM

It's been said that Miller is "One of the premiere comedy talents in America today..." While others are blunt assessing Miller's comedic stature, Dennis himself makes a virtue of understatement, but there is nothing low key about his career. For two seasons, Miller called the plays alongside Al Michaels and NFL Hall of Fame quarterback Dan Fouts on ABC's "Monday Night Football." He was also the "Weekend Update" correspondent on "Saturday Night Live" for six years, before exiting in 1991.

11 PM - 1 AM

Tony Bruno's success in radio isn't one of those reality show contestant, overnight sensation, or flavors of the month. His diversity, pop culture knowledge, love of wine and fine dining, world travel, varied musical tastes and being very handy around the house keep him very active, healthy and strong. Tony is now focusing on being married to his loving, caring and supportive radio show audience and having some loyal friends to balance out a great career and life.

NEW BERN
GETTING HERE, GETTING AROUND

New Bern is growing with new restaurants, new shops and new living spaces. The number of retirees and new residents moving in and the number of tourists coming to explore the area's many treasures increases every year. No matter how they arrive — by land, air or sea — all routes lead to attractions that everyone will enjoy.

LAND

From the north, U.S. Highway 17 leads directly into the heart of New Bern. From the west, Interstate 95 leads to U.S. Highway 70, which continues straight into New Bern. From the north or south, U.S. 17 is the most direct route to the area. From the east, the drive here is along U.S. 70 from the Morehead City area.

The $93 million Neuse River Bridge, the costliest in North Carolina's history, opened in late 1999. The 1.9-mile, four-lane bridge spans the Neuse River from Bridgeton to James City, connecting U.S. 17 to U.S. 70. At its highest point, the bridge arches 65 feet above the Neuse River. It replaced the two-lane John Lawson drawbridge, which was dismantled shortly after the opening of the new bridge. The Neuse River Bridge allows travelers heading directly to the beaches from the south or north to bypass the heart of New Bern. Exit ramps along U.S. 70 can take you into the downtown his-

toric district, to Trent Woods (Pembroke), to U.S. 17 N. or to Glenburnie Road.

The Alfred Cunningham Bridge, which once spanned the Trent River and connected the downtown historic district with the Neuse River Bridge and U.S. 70, has been dismantled and construction continues to replace that span by 2009. During the two-year construction period, traffic to the downtown area will be routed through the Trent Woods/Pembroke exit.

There is also construction being done on Broad Street from the circle on E. Front Street to the fire department on First Street. The approach to downtown is undergoing repaving, curb and guttering, the creation of a tree-lined center island, planting of a grass strip between the curb and sidewalk, extension of pedestrian lights to First Street, parking on both sides of the street and a bike path. This construction has been tagged as part of the 300th anniversary effort to beautify New Bern. Completion date on the contract is December 2010. Your best bet is to take Pollock Street, past Tryon Palace, downtown from First Street after coming off the Trent Woods/Pembroke exit.

Bus Service

Greyhound Lines, Inc./New Bern
W. C. Convenience Store,
4010 Dr. M. L. King Jr. Blvd, New Bern
(252) 633-3100, (800) 231-2222

Greyhound Lines, Inc. provides bus service to and from New Bern. Four buses depart daily. Two buses depart for Raleigh — one at 11:20 AM and one at 7:05 PM. Two other buses are bound for points south: Jacksonville, Wilmington and Myrtle Beach, S.C. The southbound bus leaves at 7:45 AM, and a 4:45 PM bus goes only to Camp LeJeune. Someone is available to handle phone calls and ticket sales from

The Neuse River Basin is identified by signs at bridge crossings on highways in eastern North Carolina. These signs are reminders of the numerous sources and vast area that influences the waters of the Neuse River.

9 AM to noon and 3 PM until the last bus leaves.

Taxi and Shuttle Services

New Bern offers several professional taxi franchises that run 24 hours a day. The cars are clean, the drivers are courteous and the fares are moderately priced. If you need a cab, try those listed here.

New Safeway Taxi Service, New Bern, (252) 633-2838

Tryon Cab Co., New Bern, (252) 636-9335

Car Rental

You will need a car if you plan to see more of the area than downtown New Bern. A few car rental businesses are based at the Craven County Regional Airport, 200 Terminal Drive in New Bern.

Avis Rent-a-Car, New Bern, (252) 637-2130

Hertz Rental Car, New Bern, (252) 637-3021

AIR

Daily US Airways Express flights to and from Charlotte are available at the Albert J. Ellis Airport, located 30 miles south of New Bern and at Coastal Carolina Regional Airport in New Bern. The Ellis Airport also has Delta flights to Atlanta. Call to make your most advantageous connection. Car rentals are located at both airports.

Albert J. Ellis Airport
264 Albert J. Ellis Airport Rd., Richlands
(910) 324-1100

Seven daily US Airways Express flights to and from Charlotte are available at the Albert J. Ellis Airport, as are four flights daily to Atlanta on Delta. The airport is located 30 miles south of New Bern. Parking prices range from $1.50 for the first hour in

short-term parking to $7 a day for long-term parking. Car rentals are available. A restaurant and gift shop are located on-site. Fixed-base services are available through Jacksonville Flying Service, (910) 324-2500.

Coastal Carolina Regional Airport
200 Terminal Dr., New Bern
(252) 638-8591

New Bern offers the convenience of the Coastal Carolina Regional Airport, 2 miles southeast of downtown New Bern off U.S. 70. The airport offers as many as 12 daily nonstop flights to Atlanta or Charlotte with one-stop connections to more than 300 destinations worldwide via US Airways Express and Delta Connection. Food is available in the terminal, and airport parking is available for 50¢ per half-hour or $6 daily.

Michael J. Smith Airport
180 Airport Rd., Beaufort
(252) 728-1928

Within an hour's drive of New Bern, this airport only offers chartered or private aircraft service. The fixed-base operator is Segrave Aviation, (252) 728-2323, which handles fueling, car rentals, flight instruction, charters, sightseeing flights, pilot supplies and charts, maintenance and more.

Raleigh-Durham International Airport
Exits 284B and 285, Morrisville
(919) 840-2123

Raleigh-Durham (RDU) is the major international airport serving North Carolina from the Research Triangle Park area. RDU, a two-hour drive from New Bern, is a major hub for domestic and international travelers, serving 36 domestic and international destinations. RDU has 10 major and 17 regional airlines. Car rental services are available at the airport.

SEA

Boaters arriving on the water come up the Intracoastal Waterway and then travel

See this entire guide plus additional content online at insiderinfo.us

the Neuse River to New Bern. The Neuse River flows into the Pamlico Sound and has well-marked channels. New Bern also fronts the Trent River, which flows into the Neuse. A complete description of the rivers, bridges, ferry schedules and marinas is offered in our New Bern On the Water chapter.

ONCE YOU'RE HERE

If you arrive by air or water and are interested in exploring all that New Bern has to offer, a rental car would be a good investment. There is no public transportation in New Bern.

Bikes are a wonderful way to get around the downtown and waterfront areas. However, because of the narrow shoulders and increasingly heavy traffic, we wouldn't recommend biking along the highways that immediately lead to and from New Bern.

Walking is the most interesting way to travel in the downtown area, so park the car in any of the well-planned downtown parking areas and see New Bern at a slower pace.

Tourism and Relocation Information

New Bern Area Chamber of Commerce
316 S. Front St., New Bern
(252) 637-3111

If you are exploring the possibility of opening a new business or relocating to New Bern or the surrounding area, contact the New Bern Area Chamber of Commerce for specific information to help with your considerations. Chamber hours are Monday through Friday 9 AM to 5 PM.

New Bern Riverfront Convention Center
203 S. Front St., New Bern
(252) 637-1551, (800) 437-5767

The New Bern Riverfront Convention Center features 28,000 square feet of meeting and special event space, including a 12,000-square-foot ballroom. It is within walking distance of nearly all downtown accommodations and shopping. Businesses and groups can take advantage of the center's many amenities to host successful meetings and conventions. The center offers a large waterfront veranda overlooking the Trent River and in-house kitchen facilities for on-site catering. Handicapped accessible and with ample parking, the center is home to a number of great annual trade shows and special events, many of which are open free to the public. Insiders consider the New Bern Riverfront Convention Center a great asset to the downtown historic district.

New Bern-Craven County Convention and Visitor Center
203 S. Front St., New Bern
(252) 637-1551, (800) 437-5767

If you are a visitor, here's your first stop — the friendly staff would love to help you prepare for your stay in New Bern and Havelock. Located in the New Bern Riverfront Convention Center, the New Bern-Craven County Convention and Visitors Center staff will equip you with maps, brochures and suggestions that will get your visit off to a fantastic start. You'll be greeted warmly Monday though Friday from 8 AM to 5 PM and Saturday from 10 AM to 4 PM. The center is closed on Sundays.

RESTAURANTS 🍴

A delightful variety of dining options is available to New Bern residents and visitors. Restaurants feature culinary fare from around the world, and you'll find everything from traditional Southern home cooking to fine European cuisine. If you're looking for good seafood, you'll love dining out in New Bern. In fact, you would be hard-pressed to find a restaurant that does not offer some type of shellfish or other seafood. The following guide alphabetically highlights some of the Insiders' favorite local restaurants. We did not list popular chain and fast food restaurants; you are probably familiar with those in your own hometown. We encourage you to ask locals for other recommendations and to call ahead for hours of operation.

PRICE CODE

The price code we use for our restaurants reflects the average price of a dinner for two. Because entrees come in a wide range of prices, our price code reflects an average cost of entrees, not the most expensive item or the least expensive item. For restaurants that do not serve dinner, the price code reflects the cost of lunch fare. Price code averages do not include appetizers, drinks, desserts, gratuity or the state's 6.75 percent sales tax. Prices are also subject to change. Unless otherwise noted, all of these establishments accept credit cards.

$	Less than $20
$$	$20 to $30
$$$	$31 to $40
$$$$	$41 or more

Almond Tree Cafe & Ice Cream Shop $
208 Middle St., New Bern
(252) 637-9307
2116 Trent Road , New Bern

Enjoy a meal at Almond Tree Cafe & Ice Cream Shop. Open daily, Almond Tree offers breakfast treats such as chocolate-chip Belgian waffles, pancakes, scrambled eggs, omelets made to order and croissant or bagel sandwiches featuring egg and cheese and your choice of ham or bacon. For lunch or dinner, enjoy shrimp, turkey, chicken, roast beef, ham and more, all creatively prepared and served in pitas and wraps. You can also get hot soups or a salad here. Almond Tree also features specialty coffees, cappuccinos and low-fat frappuncinos. A children's menu features PB&J, a pita cheese melt, hot dogs and yummy offerings of ice cream, sundaes, milk shakes and cookies.

The Baker's Square $$$
227 Middle St., New Bern
(252) 637-0304

The Baker's Square is a favorite among Insiders for its generous portions, fantastic prices and outstanding service for breakfast, lunch and dinner. The Baker's Breakfast platters feature pancakes, French toast, biscuits and gravy or eggs with your choice of sausage or bacon. Or you can create your own combination from a list of breakfast items. For lunch, enjoy a home-cooked meal of beef, chicken or seafood, and for dinner choose from selections including prime rib, shrimp, soft-shell crabs, catfish and pork, all prepared in tantalizing ways and served with sides of vegetables, cole slaw and Baker's rolls. Insiders highly recommend the country fried steak.

See this entire guide plus additional content online at insiderinfo.us

Salads and sandwiches also are offered on the lunch and dinner menus. You'll definitely want to top off your dinner with a tempting dessert of pie, cheesecake or pastries. The Baker's Square is a very popular restaurant, and Insiders recommend you time your visits to miss the crowds, particularly on Friday and Saturday nights. It's open Monday for breakfast and lunch and on Tuesday through Saturday for breakfast, lunch and dinner.

Capt. Ratty's Seafood & Steakhouse $$$
202 Middle St., New Bern
(252) 633-2088

Open daily, Capt. Ratty's menu features a variety of seafood and steaks cooked just about any way you like. Owner Tom Ballance says the restaurant serves some of the best steak in the state, due partially to Capt. Ratty's high standards in selecting steaks for its customers. Crab, shrimp and oysters come prepared in a variety of dishes sure to please even the pickiest eaters. Our seafaring Insider recommends the Peck of Oysters and Captain's Platter with its generous servings of crab legs, oysters, clams, shrimp and mussels — but not on the same night, of course. The price of the oysters depends on whether you shuck or the Capt. Ratty's staff shucks. Bring your shucking knife, just in case. A children's menu features favorites such as grilled cheese and hamburgers. Clam chowder, sandwiches and salads round out the menu. Beverages include soft drinks, tea, coffee, beer and mixed drinks. Capt. Ratty's also is noted for its excellent selection of wines.

Carolina Bagel and Deli Company $
Village Square Shopping Center,
3601 Trent Rd., New Bern
(252) 636-0133

Carolina Bagel Company, open Monday through Saturday, may be one of New Bern's best-kept breakfast and lunch secrets. Tucked away in Village Square on Trent Road, Carolina Bagel offers fresh-baked bagels all day, and you can top those with your pick of homemade cream-cheese spreads. In addition, Carolina Bagel makes delicious pastries and homemade brownies from scratch daily. For lunch, choose from the salads, platters and

sandwiches. A kids' menu features a PB&J, BLT and grilled cheese. Catering also is available.

Chadwick House Cafe $$
712-B Pollock St., New Bern
(252) 637-2018

Insiders like the Chadwick House Cafe because of its delicious food and relaxing atmosphere. Although small in size, the cafe is big on service. Owners Amy and John Faulkenberry provide a simple but tasty menu that includes Southern staples such as chicken salad and pimiento cheese. You can have either those or your turkey, ham and roast beef sandwiches prepared on white or wheat bread or croissants. You can choose one of the salads to go along with a cup or bowl of soup and top off your lunch with a slice of pie or cheesecake. (Insiders highly recommend the chicken salad sandwich, the Senate bean soup and the chocolate chip cheesecake.) Chadwick House Cafe also features a daily special and a soup of the day. Weather permitting, the cafe has outdoor seating. The cafe sells many of its menu items by the pound or half-pound, and pies and cakes are available with advance notice; just call or stop by for details. Chadwick House Cafe does not serve alcohol nor does it accept credit cards. Off-street parking is available. It's open for lunch Tuesday through Saturday.

The Chelsea Restaurant $$$
335 Middle St., New Bern
(252) 637-5469

Come to The Chelsea for the delight of good food. Fine detail is apparent in every preparation from the kitchen. Among the varied selection of appetizers try the Shrimp and Crab Toast — shrimp, crab and a blend of cheese on French bread, pan fried in butter and served with a port wine reduction. For an exciting blend of tastes, try the turkey pita club sandwich, combining smoked turkey, bacon, Monterey Jack cheese, lettuce and tomato in herbed pita bread and served with raspberry mayonnaise. For lunch or dinner, try the Southern Osso Bucco — roasted pork shank braised with olive oil, red wine, fire-roasted tomatoes, olives and capers. Served with garlic smashed potatoes and seasonal vegetable, it is a particular favorite of Insiders all over town. The Shrimp and Grits, a combination of shrimp, smoked sausage, cheese and the Southern staple of grits is also pleasing fare. Surprises are mixed with traditions on the menus that are nicely varied. The Chelsea offers a wide selection of domestic or imported beers and wine and mixed drinks. This also is a popular nighttime gathering place (see our New Bern Nightlife chapter). The restaurant serves lunch and dinner daily except Sunday. The Chelsea is housed in the restored 1912 building, which was the second drugstore of pharmacist Caleb Bradham, the inventor of Pepsi-Cola.

China Wok $$
**3321 Dr. M. L. King Jr. Blvd.,
McCarthy Crossing, New Bern
(252) 636-5288**

Insiders like China Wok because of the speed and efficiency involved in getting their food. Whether you choose to eat in or take out, your wait is never a long one. Located in McCarthy Crossing Shopping Center, China Wok does not have lavish decor or fancy dinnerware, but what it lacks in atmosphere, it more than makes up for in scrumptious food and over-sized portions. Its menu features nearly 100 possibilities in pork, chicken, seafood and beef, some available in hot and spicy combinations. China Wok is open daily, with lunch specials available Monday through Saturday.

Christoph's Restaurant $$-$$$
and Lounge
**100 Middle St., New Bern
(252) 638-3585**

Christoph's on the Water, located at the Sheraton New Bern, is open daily for breakfast, lunch and dinner. The restaurant offers a contemporary casual dining experience on the beautiful Trent River waterfront. Christoph's features hand-cut steaks and seafood to tempt any palate and offers the only outdoor waterfront dining in all of New Bern. Christoph's Lounge is the only place to meet your friends, unwind with your favorite libation and enjoy the live entertainment every Friday and Saturday evening.

Country Biscuit Restaurant $
**809 Broad St., New Bern
(252) 638-5151**

Early birds will appreciate Country Biscuit's opening hour of 5 AM. Eat your breakfast on a biscuit — your choices are steak, ham, tenderloin, sausage, bacon and cheese. Breakfast plates with your choice of the above and eggs also are available. Country Biscuit also has a lunch menu with plates and sandwiches. Insiders recommend the baked ham if you're in the mood for a plate or the cheeseburger if you want a sandwich. Breakfast choices come with a side of grits or hash browns; lunch with your choice of vegetable. No time to stop? Swing through Country Biscuit's drive-through window.

The Cow Cafe $
**319 Middle St., New Bern
(910) 672-9269**

Here's a restaurant not only for the young but also the young at heart. The Cow Cafe — New Bern's only "Four Hoof" restaurant — is in the historic downtown area. Its delicious menu features such delights as the Moo-chos, Save-A-Cow barbecue baskets, Grazin' Garden Salad, El Moo's Chili and other sandwiches, soups and salads. Of course, you'll want to save some room for gourmoo popcorn, ice cream and tasty milk shakes. The cow boutique features plenty of cow-inspired items, where you can find the perfect gift for all ages that says "I love moo." The Cow Cafe is open Monday through Saturday for lunch and dinner.

El Cerro Mexican Bar and Grill $$
**1331 E. Main St., Havelock
(252) 444-5777**

For authentic Mexican food, El Cerro has an extensive Mexican menu that includes combination, vegetarian and children's dinners. The combination dinners give you not only a great bargain, but also the opportunity to sample a variety of dishes, including chalupas, chile rellenos, enchiladas, tacos and burritos, with the diner's choice of chicken or beef as filling. El Cerro offers Mexican and domestic beers, wine by the glass, margaritas (also available by the pitcher) and mixed drinks. It is open daily for lunch and dinner.

 **CLOSE UP** The Birthplace
of Pepsi-Cola

You never know what legacy you might leave the next millennium. When New Bern's would-be pharmacist Caleb Bradham concocted what he called Brad's Drink in 1898, he couldn't possibly have guessed what impact it would have on twentieth-century culture and beyond. The ultimate fate of his peppy solution, which he later named Pepsi-Cola, would have seemed as far-fetched to him as satellite TV or computers.

In 1998 Pepsi-Cola, now an international corporation, celebrated its 100th anniversary, and the local Pepsi-Cola Bottling Company of New Bern opened The Birthplace of Pepsi Cola at the corner of Middle and Pollock Streets, (252) 636-5898. This shop includes a reproduction of the soda fountain where Bradham first served his popular drink and includes local Pepsi memorabilia. You also can purchase a variety of merchandise emblazoned with the Pepsi logo. Outside, a historical marker on Pollock Street also marks the spot where Brad's Drink was invented.

New Bern is the birthplace of Pepsi-Cola.

photo: Janis Williams

Caleb Bradham, born in 1867 in Chinquapin, North Carolina, just wanted to be a pharmacist. He graduated from the University of North Carolina and started medical school. Due to family finances, he had to leave school. Bradham then relocated to New Bern and became a high school teacher. When Bradham learned that a drugstore was being offered for sale at the corner of Middle and Pollock streets, he bought it with the help of investment partners. Bradham worked at the drugstore and studied until he passed the Board of Pharmacy examination in 1895 with the highest score that year.

Soon thereafter, Bradham concocted a new drink for his soda fountain that he called Brad's Drink. His advertising described Brad's Drink as "exhilarating, invigorating and aids digestion." By 1898, young Bradham had bought the store from his partners and he named the new carbonate Pepsi-Cola. Bradham began his cola operation on an organized basis in 1903. The company packaged the syrup for sale to other soda fountains. The bottling process was on the rise and, by 1910, had exceeded sales at soda fountains. Business boomed until right after the World War I years, when sugar jumped from 5.5¢ a pound to 22.5¢ a pound. For Pepsi-Cola, which was retailing at 5¢ per bottle, this spelled financial disaster. After collapsing into bankruptcy, the company changed hands four times before winding up in 1931 as a subsidiary of Loft, parent company of today's internationally known Pepsi-Cola.

Bradham continued to run the Bradham Drug Company until his death in 1934, but he never saw any of the media frenzy surrounding his drink, such as Michael

Jackson dancing with a Pepsi or Ray Charles crooning about the right thing. You can see Caleb Bradham's home, which still stands on the corner of Johnson and E. Front streets. You can also visit the building at the corner of Broad and Middle streets that was leased by the Bradham Drug Company for the second location of its state-of-the-art drugstore pharmacy. The building now houses The Chelsea restaurant, which features a wall mural depicting the Pepsi-Cola story. At Middle and Pollock streets, near the historical marker, you're going to find it hard to resist ordering Brad's Drink at the Pepsi store — or anywhere else in New Bern.

Flounders Seafood and Smokehouse $$
425 Hotel Dr., New Bern
(252) 636-1200

Flounders Seafood has built a reputation for providing excellent service and savory food. Owner Chris Tompkins utilized his 18-plus years of experience in the restaurant industry to create a family-friendly establishment that features daily specials and moderate prices. From appetizers to dinner platters, Flounders offers all of your favorites in shrimp, scallops, flounder, catfish, trout, crab, clams, oysters and more. Steak and pork entrees are available for those in the mood for something other than seafood. The delicious menu is rounded out with homemade desserts, and the sweet iced tea should be your beverage of choice. Flounders has all ABC permits and is open daily.

Gina's Pizza $
1904 S. Glenburnie Rd., New Bern
(252) 633-9000

Looking for something quick but delicious? Give Gina's a call. New Bern Insiders recommend the Veggie Gourmet Pizza, The Works Gourmet Pizza (sampling of all the toppings), and the stromboli and lasagna dinners. Gina's offers a fairly extensive menu, including salads and hot wings. Best of all, Gina's prices are a bargain, and daily specials are offered as well. It's open Monday through Saturday until 10 PM, and Gina's delivers with a minimum order of $7.

Harvey Mansion Historic Inn $$$
& Restaurant
221 S. Front St., New Bern
(252) 635-3232

Harvey Mansion Historic Inn & Restaurant offers three great locations in one beautiful setting: a classy restaurant, an elegant bed-and-breakfast and a fun nightclub. The 9,000-square-foot house, built from 1797 to 1804, is the last remaining structure fronting the Trent River from New Bern's time period as a thriving colonial seaport. On the first and second floors, diners will enjoy their selections of seafood, beef, poultry or lamb dishes in one of six dining rooms, including the green room which originally was the house's formal parlor and still features its ornate woodwork and molding. All dishes, from the menu created by chef Scott Weiss, come with a house salad and fresh dinner rolls. Specialties include such favorites as beef and Brie en croute, lamb osso bucco, Asian ahi tuna stack, chicken Chesapeake and coastal Carolina crab cakes. Delicious appetizers, homemade desserts, an extensive wine list and nightly specials are also among the items that have made the Harvey Mansion a great destination for dinner.

MJ's Raw Bar & Grille $$$
216 Middle St., New Bern
(252) 635-6890

With its good prices and excellent portions, MJ's Raw Bar & Grille makes a great stop for lunch and dinner. From its daily specials to its homemade soups and desserts to its famous Maryland crab cakes, MJ's has something to please every palate. Insiders recommend you try the crab meat-stuffed mushrooms as an appetizer, but a variety of other options are available too. Enjoy shrimp, oysters, clams, crawfish, scallops and mussels from the raw bar, or feast on a blackened Angus burger, the Mellow Mushroom burger or a Buffalo fried chicken sandwich. Homemade delicacies include the soup of the day and a yummy array of desserts. MJ's also stocks a full-service bar and offers a fine selection of wines with an international flair. MJ's is open daily.

Moore's Olde Tyme Barbecue $
**3621 Dr. M. L. King Jr. Blvd., New Bern
(252) 638-3937**

Since 1945 Moore's has specialized in eastern North Carolina chopped barbecue pork, but it offers more than that. Whether you eat in or take out, the food at Moore's is good, home-style cooking. A meal of pork or chicken barbecue is served with cole slaw, french fries and hush puppies. There's also a seafood plate with shrimp, flounder and trout. And Moore's serves an honest-to-goodness shrimpburger. But before you decide what you want, check the specials, including the St. Louis–style ribs on Saturdays. Moore's can cater small, large or huge events or put on a North Carolina–style pig pickin'. The restaurant is open for lunch and dinner every day but Sunday.

Mustard's Last Stand $
**E. Front St., New Bern
(252) 638-1937**

Mustard's Last Stand is a concession stand that offers the very best in Sabrett hot dogs and Polish sausages on buns.

It's the perfect place to stop while on a walking tour of downtown New Bern. Mustard's also serves foot-long hot dogs and jalapeno and cheese dogs, and you can get those served with the works — chili, mustard, ketchup, sauerkraut and cooked onions. Mustard's offers drinks, chips and more. The hot dogs are better than those at any ballpark, and you don't have to fight for a parking space. Mustard's is open 10:30 AM until 2:30 PM Monday through Saturday at its long-time stand on E. Front Street across the street from Union Point Park.

Stacia's Lieu Secret $$$-$$$$
at A Catered Affair
**3402-B Trent Rd., New Bern
(252) 637-7331**

Stacia's Lieu Secret is an inviting dinner stop for New Bern Insiders and a favorite location for special-occasion dinners and private parties. Diners will enjoy the romantic atmosphere created by a combination of the beautifully decorated dining room and pleasant staff. Owner Stacia Reid's culinary creations always include the freshest ingredients prepared in creative and tasty ways. Stacia's Lieu Secret at A Catered Affair is open for

Sit and relax – that's what you do on vacation.

photo: Peter Doran

dinner Thursday through Saturday nights. Reservations are recommended. Stacia and her crew have been providing professional catering services through A Catered Affair for 20 years in the New Bern area. Catered lunches are available for groups of 10 or more.

Stompin' Grounds $
1706 U.S. Hwy. 70 E, New Bern
(252) 672-5282

Stompin' Grounds is a coffee bar, a wine shop, a great place for lunch and one of those places where you could just settle in and stay for a while. Whether your choice is a frappuccino or a cappuccino, a latte or a cup of Stompin' Grounds regular, the staff can fix you right up. If you want to try a new wine, you can discover that here as well. Stompin' Grounds also caters dinners and lunches in your office, your home or on site, and it is available for private wine tastings. Try a flight of wines at the Friday night wine bar with one or two of the delicious hors d' oeuvres. Stompin' Grounds is open Monday through Thursday from 6:30 AM until 6 PM, on Fridays from 6:30 AM until 10 PM and on Saturdays from 7:30 AM until 4 PM.

Trent River Coffee Company $
208 Craven St., New Bern
(252) 514-2030

This complete coffee bar and retail coffee shop is the social gathering place for locals on most weekday mornings for endless coffee or hot chocolate and a selection of breakfast breads and pastries. Looking for something a little cooler? Trent River Coffee Company also serves ice cream and milk shakes. On announced evenings, this is the staging place for the

Down East FolkArts Society live performances and other performing musicians. Coffee and a world of other things are brewing every day.

Tryon Palace Seafood $
520 S. Front St., New Bern
(252) 638-2280
Stingray Cafe, 520 South Front St., New Bern
252-638-2280

Open Monday through Saturday, Tryon Palace Seafood is a great stop to pick up fresh selections — shrimp, oysters, flounders, scallops and more — to prepare at home. But this South Front Street treasure also offers a restaurant, The Stingray Cafe, next door where you can pick up orders of tasty shrimp and oyster burgers, soft-crab and crab-cake sandwiches, fish and chips, and more with sides of fries, slaw and hushpuppies.

NEW BERN
ⓨ NIGHTLIFE

Although it isn't overrun with entertainment spots — a refreshing factor for a riverfront city — New Bern offers a nice variety of nightlife. Nighttime entertainment here mainly revolves around smaller gathering places where friends meet to mix and mingle.

New Bern also has an active cultural arts scene. The city is home to three theater organizations. Two of these groups stage a number of performances throughout the year, and there are several performances for children, while the other offers a new Shakespeare presentation every summer. See our New Bern Arts chapter for more information.

As for the wander-in, sit-down-and-enjoy-yourself type of nightlife, New Bern has that to offer too. Not all of New Bern's nightspots are listed here for several reasons — it may have just opened, was unintentionally overlooked or may not be a place we would recommend to a friend. So although there may be others, the nightspots that follow are among the more popular with Insiders. Some of New Bern's bars are private and require membership fees and a waiting period before the memberships become valid.

1797 Steamer Bar
221 S. Front St., New Bern
(252) 635-3232

This nightclub, which Insiders love for its *Cheers*-type atmosphere, is located in the cellar of the Harvey Mansion. It features the house's original kitchen fireplace and andirons, as well as a copper-top bar, exposed beams and a low ceiling to complete its casual and cozy environment. The bar serves wine, domestic and imported beer and mixed drinks, along with chicken wings, sandwiches and other snacks. Live entertainment is offered on occasion.

Capt. Ratty's Seafood & Steakhouse
202 Middle St., New Bern
(252) 633-2088

The upstairs bar of Captain Ratty's is open all week, but on Thursday through Saturday evenings this is a great place to unwind after work, enjoy a drink and dinner, and listen to free live entertainment. Capt. Ratty's is well-known to Insiders for its great wine selection. Sandwiches and generous salads are popular items on the menu. Seafood and steaks are the prime choice for evening dining. The price of oysters depends on whether you shuck your own or have the staff do it for you.

The Chelsea Restaurant
335 Middle St., New Bern
(252) 637-5469

The Chelsea is a popular downtown gathering place for those interested in mingling with friends or soon-to-be friends. The bar is in the restaurant area (see our New Bern Restaurants chapter) and serves mixed drinks, beer and wine. The building and the decor are interesting in themselves. This historic structure was first used by local pharmacist Caleb Bradham, inventor of Pepsi-Cola, as his second drug store.

The Ice House
3709 Trent Rd., New Bern
(252) 637-3780

Celebrate with other fans as you watch seasonal sports and NASCAR racing on The Ice House's 52-inch color television. Open seven days a week year round, the club offers snacks, mixed drinks and beer.

The Ice House is a private club; call for membership information. The Ice House features darts, pool tables, golf games and pinball machines. Music favorites are available on the jukebox, and Saturday night features karaoke.

Mr. Stix Billiards
2724 Neuse Blvd., New Bern
(252) 638-2299

Practice your shots in a quiet, inviting place where, after warming up, you can always find a challenging game. Bring your own stick, or you can buy or borrow one. The 9-foot regulation tables in the back are rented by the hour; those in the front operate on quarters. Open daily, Mr. Stix is a beer-only club.

Movie Theaters

Discounts for children and matinees are available at New Bern's movie theaters. For what's showing, call the theaters or check listings in the local newspaper.

Neuse Boulevard Cinema, 2500 Neuse Blvd., New Bern, (252) 633-2438

Southgate Cinema 6, 2806 Trent Rd., New Bern, (252) 638-1820

Liquor Laws and ABC Stores

ABC stores are the only establishments in the state allowed to sell liquor by the bottle. Beer and wine are sold in grocery and convenience stores and in specialty food shops throughout the area. New Bern's three ABC stores are open Monday through Saturday, but the hours vary. No personal checks are accepted, and only those age 21 and older are allowed in the stores.

ABC Store No. 1, 318 S. Front St., New Bern, (252) 637-3623

ABC Store No. 5, Harris Teeter Shopping Ctr., 2003 S. Glenburnie Rd., New Bern, (252) 638-4847

ABC Store No. 6, Trent East Crossing Shopping Ctr.,off U.S. Hwy. 70 E, James City, (252) 633-2246

NEW BERN
HOTELS
AND MOTELS

Overnight lodgings in New Bern present a delightful variety of vantages from which visitors may enjoy the town. The river city has several major hotels silhouetting its skyline and a number of excellent bed and breakfast inns. One inn is said to be inhabited by a friendly ghost, but if you're seeking less spiritual digs, you may choose from a nice variety of options. Many visitors choose the advantages of packages that offer discounted rates at lodgings and golf courses or dinner plans and a therapeutic massage. Hotels positioned along the city's picturesque waterfront offer lovely views of the Trent and Neuse rivers, and a number of economy and budget motels are near the downtown or outlying commercial areas. Cozy and architecturally interesting bed and breakfast inns are sprinkled throughout the historic district (see our New Bern Bed and Breakfast Inns chapter). The alphabetical listing of hotels, motels and condominiums in this section is not intended to recommend one lodging over another. We feel comfortable recommending all of the accommodations listed in this chapter.

PRICE CODE

Room prices fluctuate with the seasons, but for the purpose of reflecting rate information, we have shown high-season (summer) rates for double occupancy. Winter rates may be substantially lower. Rates are subject to change; therefore, we urge you to verify rate information when making your reservations. All hotels accept most major credit cards.

$	$59 and less
$$	$60 to $79
$$$	$80 to $124
$$$$	$125 and more

Abilena Mansion $$$$
2814 Old Cherry Point Rd., New Bern
(252) 349-2441

Abilena Mansion is a 5-acre riverfront plantation and mansion on the Neuse River in New Bern. The 5,000-square-foot home was built in 1927. It is the area's only riverfront mansion that can be rented for weddings, receptions, vacations, retreats and events. For any event, from a family reunion to an intimate reception to a wedding of 250 people, Abilena awaits your arrival. Secluded yet only 5 minutes from town, this is a dream location for many people. There are several acres for parking and events, yet at its core it is still a charming home that will create lasting memories from the moment you drive down the tree-covered lane. Visit the website or schedule a tour of the property to see why this may be the perfect location for your riverfront event.

BridgePoint Hotel And Marina $$
101 Howell Rd., New Bern
(252) 636-3637

The 115-room BridgePointe Hotel and Marina is just across the Trent River from New Bern's historic downtown area. Top-floor guest rooms have a beautiful water view of either the Neuse River or Trent River. Coffeemakers, refrigerators, microwaves, ironing equipment, Wi-Fi and satellite television with four movie channels are standard in every room. Room choices include a king bed, two double beds or a Jacuzzi suite. Meeting and banquet facilities are available. Guests of the BridgePointe Hotel are allowed to use the amenities available at Courts Plus, located off Glenburnie Road (see our New Bern Recreation and Parks chapter). In season, you also can relax at the BridgePointe Hotel's outdoor pool, and vacation and golf packages are available. The Outback Steakhouse is next door.

Comfort Suites $$$-$$$$
Riverfront Park
218 E. Front St., New Bern
(252) 636-0022
www.comfortsuitesnewbern.com

Located in New Bern's Historic District, this newly renovated hotel won the 2006 award for the best Comfort Suites in North and South Carolina as well as a Platinum Hospitality Award. This is nothing new for this fine hotel. In 2000 it garnered the Comfort Suites of the Year award and has been a Gold Hospitality Award winner for 12 consecutive years. Featuring a Colonial look and a warm, friendly atmosphere, the Riverfront Park hotel has 100 suites, many with waterfront balconies that offer beautiful views of the mile-wide Neuse River and others with views of Union Point Park. All suites have traditional furnishings and your choice of two double beds or a king-size bed, all with down pillow-top bedding. All rooms are equipped with a refrigerator, microwave, coffeemaker, iron and ironing board. Whirlpool suites are also available. Other amenities include a 32-inch, high-definition TV in each room, free local calls and high-speed Internet access, an outdoor pool with a waterfront courtyard, an outdoor heated whirlpool, a waterfront gazebo, a fitness center, a guest laundry room, a board room and meeting facilities. Complimentary deluxe continental breakfasts are served each morning, and a complimentary evening guest reception is held nightly Monday through Thursday. The hotel is within walking distance of New Bern's downtown area and historic sites, as well as the New Bern Riverfront Convention Center. Significant discounts on room rates are available, so be sure to ask about the options.

Days Hotel - New Bern $$$
925 Broad St., New Bern
(252) 672-0222

The Days Hotel offers Southern hospitality at its best with a newly renovated facility offering 110 rooms, three of them handicapped accessible. The hotel has a swimming pool, three meeting rooms that can cater and serve up to 300 people, a complimentary business center for business travelers, wireless Internet access and the Sugar Bear Grill and Bar, a full-service restaurant open every day except Thursday and Sunday. All guests enjoy a complimentary breakfast consisting of Minute Maid juices, Kellogg's cereals, fresh fruits and an assortment of muffins, bagels or pastries, served with fresh-brewed Folger's coffee. The hotel is pet-friendly. Guests receive a complimentary copy of *USA Today* and are within walking distance of Historic Downtown New Bern. The management promises that you can expect warm hospitality and clean, comfortable rooms where everything works, so that your stay is trouble-free and enjoyable.

Hampton Inn - New Bern $$
200 Hotel Dr., New Bern
(252) 637-2111, (800) HAMPTON

At the intersection of N.C. Highway 17 and U.S. Highway 70, the award-winning Hampton Inn New Bern offers 101 rooms in a park-like setting among nearby restaurants and shopping. Guests are offered tastefully furnished rooms with flat-screen TVs, Hampton's "Cloud Nine" bedding, and thoughtful amenities, including hairdryers, coffeemakers and ironing equipment. The hotel also offers an outdoor seasonal pool, a hot tub, a fitness center and complimentary wireless Internet throughout the hotel and public areas. The "On the House Hot Continental Breakfast" is available every day from 6 to 10 AM. Ninety percent of the guest rooms are designated nonsmoking. Nearby attractions include the New Bern Historic District and Tryon Palace, which are a couple of miles away. Hampton Inn New Bern offers a 100 percent satisfaction guarantee.

Hilton New Bern Riverfront
100 Middle St., New Bern
(252) 638-3585

The Hilton New Bern Riverfront, located in historic downtown New Bern

See this entire guide plus additional content online at insiderinfo.us

and within easy walking distance of the area's shops and restaurants, has something for everyone. The hotel features newly renovated guest rooms, suites and condominiums overlooking the Trent River and a 250-slip marina in scenic downtown New Bern. The Hilton New Bern offers 15,000 square feet of flexible meeting and banquet space for your next conference, meeting, wedding reception or special event

The Hilton's restaurant, Christoph's on the Water, is open daily for breakfast, lunch and dinner. Enjoy the beautiful views along with hand-cut steaks, seafood and an extensive wine list. Christoph's Lounge offers a comfortable place to unwind with your favorite drink, meet some of your friends or enjoy the live entertainment each Friday and Saturday evening. Beginning in April, and continuing through the warm summer months, The Deck offers the place to cool off and begin your weekend enjoying live entertainment while overlooking the beautiful New Bern Grand Marina.

Holiday Inn Express - New Bern $$
U.S. Hwy. 17 S. at Glenburnie Rd., New Bern
(252) 638-8266

New Bern's Holiday Inn Express offers the comfortable standards of Holiday Inn at a no-frills price. The hotel has no on-site restaurant; however, it is in an area with bountiful restaurant options, and it offers a morning breakfast bar for guests. The hotel has a pool and a fitness room. All guest rooms have two double beds. The Holiday Inn Express is within easy access from U.S. 70 at the U.S. 17 S. exit, on Dr. M. L. King Jr. Boulevard, where there are also numerous shopping opportunities. Transportation is necessary to see New Bern's attractions.

The Sparrow House $$$$
220 E. Front St., New Bern
(252) 637-3574

The Thomas Sparrow House is the only accommodation of its kind in Downtown New Bern. It's a vacation home that al-lows a family or a group to rent the entire home. The Sparrow House can be rented for your wedding party or family reunion. The house sleeps 12 with four large bedrooms, six queen beds and adjoining full baths. The fourth floor bedroom has a two-person Jacuzzi. Air mattresses are available for children or an increased number of guests up to 20. Catering is available, or you may prepare your own meals in the full kitchen and enjoy them in the formal dining room. If you would rather dine out, the restaurants of historic New Bern are on your doorstep. The house has parking for 12 vehicles. Five flat-screen televisions, cable television, wireless Internet, DVD players in each room, and a washer and dryer are available. Small receptions or rehearsal dinners of up to 50 people can be held at the home as well. See our New Bern Wedding Planning chapter for more about renting this house for weddings and events.

Vacation Resorts $$$-$$$$
International
1141 Broad Creek Rd., New Bern
(252) 633-1151

A professional management company since 1964, Vacation Resorts International manages properties in the Fairfield Harbour community, offering fully furnished one- to three-bedroom condominiums on a daily or weekly basis. The price code shown is based on four people sharing a two-bedroom unit during the summer. All units at Fairfield Harbour accommodate six to eight people, and guests are extended all development amenities, including the recreation center's two swimming pools and two golf courses. For rentals on a daily basis, a minimum of two days is required; for holiday weekends, a minimum of three days is required.

NEW BERN
BED & BREAKFASTS AND SMALL INNS

Staying in one of New Bern's historic bed and breakfast inns provides a close-up view of Southern hospitality. For travelers who enjoy a unique experience, the warm welcome of your hosts offers you a home away from home. The comforts and decor of these historic homes make for a relaxing getaway in the context of an interesting historical town. Add to that the option of antiques shopping, mystery weekends or fine dining and pampering, and choosing among the bed and breakfast accommodations in New Bern is an enviable task. When you reserve, ask the innkeepers about anything that may concern you, such as smoking, handicapped accessibility or pets. Also ask about the inn's credit card, reservation and cancellation policies. The inns listed here accept credit cards unless noted otherwise.

PRICE CODE

The codes indicated here reflect an average price for a night's stay for two people in the high season (summer). Each inn's amenities vary, depending on the rooms, suite of rooms or packages offered. Be sure to ask what your price includes.

$	Less than $85
$$	$85 to $100
$$$	$101 to $140
$$$$	More than $140

The Aerie Bed and Breakfast $$$-$$$$
**509 Pollock St., New Bern
(252) 636-5553, (800) 849-5553
www.aeriebedandbreakfast.com**

Experience the warmth and charm of historic New Bern by day and relax in comfort by night in The Aerie, an 1882 Victorian bed and breakfast located just one block from Tryon Palace. The Aerie features period furnishings in seven gracious guest rooms, each with a private bath. Some have a whirlpool tub for a truly luxurious experience. Cable TV, a VCR/DVD player, a CD player, a movie library and free wireless high-speed Internet all help make your stay at The Aerie one you will not forget. A full breakfast, with your choice of three entrees, and evening

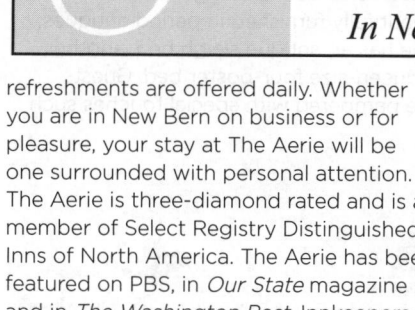
refreshments are offered daily. Whether you are in New Bern on business or for pleasure, your stay at The Aerie will be one surrounded with personal attention. The Aerie is three-diamond rated and is a member of Select Registry Distinguished Inns of North America. The Aerie has been featured on PBS, in *Our State* magazine and in *The Washington Post*. Innkeepers Michael and Marty Gunhus invite you to come and experience the quintessence of charm that is The Aerie Bed and Breakfast.

Hanna House Bed & Breakfast   **$-$$$**
218 Pollock St., New Bern
(252) 635-3209

Located in the Rudolph Ulrich House (c. 1896) in New Bern's historic district and listed on the state Register of Historic Places, Hanna House's five guest rooms are tastefully furnished in period antiques. Each has its own private bath, two with Jacuzzis. Guests are offered unique, gourmet breakfasts at their choice of time. The house and grounds are available for small weddings and other special occasions. Special packages are available. Hanna

House is conveniently located within walking distance of many New Bern attractions. Hosts Camille and Joe Klotz are dedicated to making your stay a comfortable one.

Harmony House Inn B&B   **$$-$$$$**
215 Pollock St., New Bern
(252) 636-3810, (800) 636-3113
www.harmonyhouseinn.com

The rocking chairs and swing on the long front porch and the two front doors (you'll see what we mean) distinguish this Greek Revival–style bed and breakfast in the historic district. The original part of the house was built sometime before 1809, and additions and porches have been added. Around 1900, the house was sawed in half, and the west side was moved nine feet to accommodate a new hallway and staircase. The inn now has seven guest rooms and three romantic suites, all furnished with antiques and homemade crafts. Two of the suites have heart-shaped Jacuzzis, and all rooms have private baths and decorative fireplaces. A full breakfast — which may include house specialties such as stuffed French toast with homemade blueberry maple syrup, cheese strata, potato, bacon and cheese casserole, and homemade coffeecake — is served each morning in the dining room. Another Harmony House specialty is the Toffee Bar Coffeecake, which was featured in the December 1999 issue of *Bon Appetit*. Owners Ed and Sooki Kirkpatrick host a social hour each evening, offering wine and cheese or other hors d'oeuvres. The Harmony House was voted best Best Bed and Breakfast for 2005 and 2006 by the *Sun-Journal* Readers' Choice Awards. The bed and breakfast has also been featured on the PBS show "Carolina Weekends."

Harvey Mansion Historic Inn & Restaurant $$$
221 S. Front St., New Bern
(252) 635-3232

The Harvey Mansion Historic Inn & Restaurant offers three great options in one beautiful setting: a classy restaurant, an elegant bed-and-breakfast and a fun nightclub. The 9,000-square-foot house, built from 1797 to 1804, is the last remaining structure fronting the Trent River from New Bern's time period as a thriving colo-

nial seaport. The inn features three guest rooms with king or queen accommodations available. The inn has several private bathrooms — one includes a Jacuzzi bath and shower combination. All rooms share a common living area with a balcony that overlooks Union Point Park and the Neuse and Trent rivers. Rooms also have telephones and dataports should you wish to stay in touch with the modern world while feeling so comfortably away from it.

Howard House Victorian Bed & Breakfast $$$-$$$$
207 Pollock St., New Bern
(252) 514-6709, (800) 705-5261

Howard House, a restored Victorian home in the heart of the New Bern historic district, was built between 1888 and 1893 and reflects the detailed craftsmanship of the period. Owners and hosts Steven and Kimberly Wynn offer six lovely guest rooms, each with a private bath. The house's five-sided turret encloses an upstairs guest room that has an antique queen-size bed. Other guest rooms are beautifully furnished in period antiques; one has an antique sleigh bed, another, a queen-size four-poster bed. Guests are pampered with special touches such

Many open spaces await your discovery in New Bern.

Photo courtesy of NC Division of Tourism, Film and Sports Development as desserts every evening and a social hour. Attention to special occasions like birthdays and anniversaries is easy to arrange; simply ask your hosts. Bicycles are available for seeing the town, and complimentary airport transportation is available upon request. A full and scrumptious breakfast served each morning may include apple-pecan pancakes, Canadian bacon, homemade breads, muffins and fresh-ground coffee, teas and juice.

Meadows Inn $$$
212 Pollock St., New Bern
(252) 634-1776, (877) 551-1776

The home of the Meadows Inn was a private residence until 1980. The c. 1847 structure is named for its original owner, New Bern merchant John Alexander Meadows. Meadows Inn has seven guest rooms, each with a television, VCR, private bath and antique and reproduction furniture. The third floor, two-bedroom suite is perfect for families traveling together, as children are always welcome at Meadows Inn. Phones are available in each room, and local calls are free. Wireless Internet access also is available at no charge. A full breakfast is served every morning in the breakfast room, including hot entrees, fruits, breads and a choice of coffee or tea. Complimentary soft drinks and tea

are always on hand. Romantic getaways, business meetings, destination weddings, family reunions, small group retreats and conferences at the nearby New Bern Riverfront Convention Center are but a few of the ways to make some new memories at Meadows Inn and experience hospitality with history.

New Berne House Inn $$$
709 Broad St., New Bern
(252) 636-2250, (866) 782-8358

This Colonial Revival–style bed and breakfast, located about a block from Tryon Palace, dishes up "Sweet Revenge" several times each month with its popular mystery weekend, full of intrigue and wonderful food at one price per couple. But staying here any time can be a real treat. All six guest rooms are air-conditioned and have private baths. Rooms accommodate two people and are furnished with twin, queen or king beds (one even features a "notorious" brass bed said to have been rescued from a burning brothel in 1897). Guests always have access to the house library. Host Barbara Pappas serves refreshments and beverages and treats her guests to full, home-cooked breakfasts served on her collection of vintage dishes, featuring many distinctive and striking patterns.

NEW BERN

CAMPING

I f you enjoy communing with nature, you're in for a treat when camping in the New Bern area. Nature enthusiasts can rough it at Croatan National Forest campsites that are off the beaten path. If you prefer modern camping comforts, you'll find commercial campgrounds that provide a number of services.

The Croatan National Forest allows primitive camping anywhere except picnic areas and parking lots. Reservations are not accepted for any recreation area in the Croatan. The Croatan National Forest has several camping areas with various kinds of facilities and can accommodate any size recreational vehicle. For detailed camping information, call the district ranger's office, (252) 638-5628, or stop in and pick up maps at the office at 141 E. Fisher Avenue, 9 miles south of New Bern off U.S. Highway 70 E. Office hours are 8 AM to 4:30 PM Monday through Friday. The office is closed weekends and holidays. A map of the Croatan National Forest is on sale at the office for $9. For a complete description of this magnificent forest, see our Crystal Coast Attractions chapter.

Fishers Landing
**Croatan National Forest, U.S. Hwy. 70 E,
Riverdale
(252) 638-5628**

Perched on a bluff above the Neuse River about 8 miles south of New Bern, Fishers Landing is found by turning left across U.S. 70 East at the Riverdale Mini-Mart. This recreation area offers only the barest of amenities, but what it lacks in creature comforts is more than compensated for by the chance to be among nature's creatures. Take an early morning walk along the crescent-shaped sandy beach, accessible by wooden stairs set into the cliff, and you'll see ospreys, egrets, sea gulls and herons. Between the small parking lot and the bluff is a wide, grassy

area backed by a row of trees. You can swim in the Neuse River here, but we suggest wearing shoes for protection against the rocks and tree stumps on the river bottom. The wheelchair-accessible site offers unimproved walk-in tent camping and picnicking, non-flush toilets, grills and drinking water. Fishers Landing is open year round.

Moonlight Lake RV Park
**180 Moonlight Lake Dr., New Bern
(252) 745-9800**

Located within 10 minutes of historic downtown New Bern, Moonlight Lake RV Park has 27 RV lots and 10 tent sites, including 50/30 amp electrical hook-ups, water and sewer service, garbage disposal, horseshoe pits, picnic tables, laundry facilities and a bathhouse. Five of the tent sites are primitive. Ask about tent camping rates. RV rates for sites are $30 daily, $125 weekly, $375 monthly and $3,900 yearly, not including electricity. Cable TV, phone service and wireless Internet are available at an extra charge on all lots. With a monthly or yearly rental, cable TV is free. The facility accepts Passport America and Camp Club USA for a 50 percent discount Sunday through Thursday. Also available is a 550-square-foot guest house that sleeps four and has many amenities.

Neuse River (Flanners Beach)
Recreation Area
**Croatan National Forest, U.S. Hwy. 70 E,
Riverdale
(252) 638-5628**

Locals call this area Flanners Beach. Open March through November, it is 10 miles south of New Bern off U.S. 70 along the Neuse River. The site has 42 units (14 with electrical service), flush toilets, warm showers, drinking water and a dump station. A nightly fee of $12 is charged for campsites; sites with electrical hook-ups cost $17. Daytrippers can enjoy the area's free public facilities, including a swimming area, toilets, cold showers, drinking fountains and a picnic spot with 44 tables. Visitors also will enjoy the 3-mile hiking/biking trail. A 1-mile loop of the trail goes around the campground and is paved for easy handicapped access.

New Bern KOA
1565 B St., north of New Bern
on U.S. Hwy. 17, New Bern
(252) 638-2556

Nestled on the tranquil banks of the Neuse River 5 miles north of New Bern, the New Bern KOA is the perfect setting for a peaceful retreat, particularly for those campers who are used to the high standards KOA sets for its campgrounds. The campground offers full and partial hook-ups for RVs, patio sites with special amenities and 50/30 amp hook-ups on long, level sites. Tent sites are available with or without electric hookups. Also available for rental are Kamping Kabins,

Lodges and a Kottage, which takes the rough out of roughing it with heat, air conditioning, and beds with soft mattresses.

Site amenities include clean restrooms, hot showers, a swimming pool, laundry facilities, a full-service camp store, propane, cable TV, a playground, storage and broadband or wireless Internet access. Pets are welcome at KOA and will enjoy their very own Bark Park. On the banks of the Neuse River, there is a pier with 10 boat slips and a ramp. Fishing and crabbing from the pier while the sun sets over the river is always a nice way to end the day. KOA offers Value Season, Adventure Season and holiday rates. Monthly rates are possible based on availability. Children younger than age 6 camp free when accompanied by an adult. Reservations can be made by phone or online with a deposit using Visa, MasterCard and American Express.

N ew Bern offers many shopping opportunities, from large department stores to specialty shops and boutiques. Scattered among the streets in New Bern's Historic Downtown, you'll discover a distinctive selection of shops that make anyone's must-shop list. For a pleasant meander, stroll along Middle, Pollock, Hancock, Craven and South Front streets. We've highlighted a few of the shops you'll find along the way and a few others around New Bern. These shops are certainly not the totality of the New Bern shopping experience, but they'll whet your spending appetite. Because shops can — and do — change their hours to accommodate the needs of their customers, and because many have seasonal hours, you should call ahead to check what days and hours they are open. Antiques shops are featured at the end of this chapter. And don't forget to also check out our listing of art galleries in the New Bern Arts chapter.

The Downtown New Bern map (at the front of this book) shows the four free public parking lots in historic downtown. New Bern imposes a two-hour parking limit, and public employees are always on the move checking for time-limit violators.

Downtown New Bern

Art of the Wild
218 Middle St., New Bern
(252) 638-8806

Art of the Wild is a magical mix of local and imported art objects. The artwork is predominantly birds and animals in the wild, sculpted and carved in wood, marble resin, water buffalo horns, driftwood and tree roots. You'll find the carvings of the late Jeth Lindsey as well as the work of his sons, Arden and Vol, and other local artists. Art of the Wild sells framed and unframed prints, jewelry and decorative wall objects.

Bear Essentials
309 Middle St., New Bern
(252) 637-6663

Pamper yourself at Bear Essentials, which offers an attractive and useful array of organic and natural personal-care products, including soaps, lotions, cosmetics, balms and more. This Insider was particularly drawn to apricot soap that includes honey in every bar — it not only smells good but makes skin feel silky smooth. Located in downtown's Kress Building, Bear Essentials also features a selection of cute baby clothing made from all-natural cotton and a line of women's clothing made from hemp. Custom gift baskets can be created from your selections. It's open Monday through Saturday.

The Birthplace of Pepsi Cola
256 Middle St., New Bern
(252) 636-5898

Come see where this popular soft drink got its start and enjoy an ice-cold Pepsi at the reproduction of pharmacist Caleb Bradham's soda fountain. Bradham invented what was first known as "Brad's Drink" in 1898. A gift shop offers a plethora of Pepsi merchandise, everything from bags, books and bears to shirts, toy trucks and limited-edition collectibles. The shop is open every day.

Branch's
309 Pollock St., New Bern
(252) 638-5171

For more than 50 years, Branch's has offered New Bernians a unique shopping experience. A third-generation, family-owned business, Branch's now focuses on providing quality furniture for the home and office, accessories, prints, mirrors, lamps and more in over 200 product lines. Branch's features fine gift items such

The Four C's
COASTAL CASUAL CLOTHING COMPANY
252 Middle St
New Bern, NC 252 636-3285
www.thefourcs.com

*Casual Clothing, Comfortable Shoes
Travel Accessories, Unique Jewelry
Great Gifts, Science Toys
Books & Guides, Equestrian Supplies*

as Howard Miller clocks; Gibson photo albums, scrapbooks, address and guest books; Michael Healy doorbell covers and door knockers; and Yankee Candles.

Carolina Creations
317-A Pollock St., New Bern
(252) 633-4369

Carolina Creations is an art, craft and gift gallery par excellence. Many potters, glass blowers, woodworkers and jewelers are represented, and the result is a broad selection of practical and decorative art for the home, including works by resident potter Michael Francoeur and others. Stop and see the local art — Carolina Creations features a unique collection of original art, prints and note cards by local artists, as well beautiful paintings and delightful pen-and-ink drawings by resident artist Janet Francoeur. Free gift wrapping, layaway plans, a bridal registry and online shopping are offered.

Farmer's Market
421 S. Front St., New Bern
(252) 633-0043

This terrific market, housed in a large, airy building, is the place to go for fresh vegetables and fruits, flowers and crafts and free-range meats. On any given

weekend, you also might find jams, jellies, pickles, preserves and vinegars, along with home-baked cakes, breads and pastries. The market runs year round; from March through December it's open on Saturdays from 7 AM to 1 PM; from January to March, it is open from 8 AM to noon. A word to the wise: Go early when the market first opens, before all the good stuff is gone. Entertainment and demonstrations are also featured on selected weekends.

The Four C's
252 Middle St., New Bern
(252) 636-3285

Open seven days a week, Four C's is an adventure in itself. You'll find a mix of gifts and sportswear for men and women, plus camping gear, travel accessories and equestrian supplies. The shop carries a nice variety of active wear made by Columbia, Royal Robbins, The North Face and other well-known brands. For your feet, choose trendy sandals by Keen and Naot, clogs by Dansko, plus athletic shoes and hiking boots. Besides all this, you can buy hats, books, toys and jewelry — great gifts for all ages. Four C's even throws in the gift wrapping for free.

*See this entire guide plus additional content
online at* insiderinfo.us

Fraser's Wine, Cheese, Chocolate and More
210 Middle St., New Bern
(252) 634-2580

Fraser's is an extraordinary shop that features, much as its name implies, wine, cheese, chocolate and more, including specialty foods and imported and domestic beer. Also available are whimsical yet classy wine accessories, home decor items and Fraser's Fantasy Bags.

The Galley Store
300 E. Front St., New Bern
(252) 633-4648

Located in historic downtown New Bern on the waterfront, The Galley Store is convenient whether you're traveling by land or by river. Stop in for a "Special of the Day" complete meal or just grab a restaurant-quality sandwich. Try the Weekly Meal Planner and forget about the stress of shopping and cooking. The Galley Store accepts grocery and provisioning orders by phone or online as an added convenience for boaters and downtown residents. The Galley offers name-brand, choice-cut steaks, meat, fruit, vegetables, basic groceries and home supplies, along with local baked goods and seafood, coffee, wine and beer. Visitors can find a wide variety of North Carolina products from peanuts to ham, whether they're planning a party, an extended stay or a gift basket to take home from vacation.

Stop by and fuel up at The Galley's BP fuel station (including on-road diesel) or pull up to the dock fueling stations. The Galley Store has 100 percent gas; no ethanol. In addition to food, beverage and fuel, The Galley also sells hunting and fishing licenses, tackle and bait for those eager to enjoy the great outdoors. There are plenty of places at The Galley to just sit or stroll along the beautiful waterfront of New Bern and soon there will be a dock restaurant, bar and lounge with the best river views found in the area.

Middle Street Landing
225 Middle St., New Bern
(252) 514-0000

At Middle Street Landing you enter an explosion of color into the world of Vera Bradley handbags and accessories.

Then you are enveloped in the fragrant world of Crabtree & Evelyn, Camille Beckman, The Thymes, Archipelago and Lady Primrose. You will also discover the fine sterling and gold jewelry of Pandora and the Swarovski crystal jewelry of Emily Ray. Surprises abound at Middle Street Landing with the reversible coats of Mycra Pac, and the Christmas ornaments of Old World and Christopher Radko. There are also gift baskets for all occasions. The sales staff offers exceptional customer service.

Mitchell Hardware
215 Craven St., New Bern
(252) 638-4261

This is a place you have to experience first-hand. The window display is like a historic showing of farm and garden equipment. Step inside to find an eclectic offering of traditional hardware items in a turn-of-the-century setting. Mitchell's carries a complete line of hardware, garden and yard equipment, practical gifts, cast-iron and enamelware and garden seeds. There is also a large country store section with everything from country hams to crockery and pottery. But Mitchell's, which has been in business for more than 100 years, is an honest-to-gosh, no-nonsense hardware store that opens at 6:30 AM Monday through Saturday. It's the place Insiders depend on to get those difficult-to-find items they remember from Grandma's kitchen and Grandpa's tool shed.

Rosemary St. Clair Originals
711-B Pollock St., New Bern
(252) 636-3589

Rosemary St. Clair Originals, which offers a truly unique shopping experience, has moved to a new location —"The Red House" next door to the Museum Store at Tryon Palace. Rosemary creates hand-painted, appliquéd, quilted and embroidered clothing for regular and plus-size figures. Many of these Art-to-Wear clothing items and purses are one-of-a-kind collectibles. Rosemary also features hand-painted T-shirts, patchwork vests and quilted jackets, along with a wonderful line of costume and handmade jewelry. Gift certificates and free gift wrapping are available, and layaways and special orders are always welcome.

Snap Dragon Way Cool Toys
214 Middle St., New Bern
(252) 514-6770

How long has it been since you truly had fun shopping? Try Snapdragon Way Cool Toys for an inviting selection of baby items, crafts, games, dolls, science kits, outdoor products and a variety of neat stuff. Snapdragon has Melissa and Doug, Corolle (dolls), Playmobil, puppets and far too many nifty and inspiring things to list here. You just have to visit the nooks and crannies full of bright colors, jumbles of toys and fun. Every corner you turn reveals something exciting. Snap Dragon is open Monday through Thursday from 10 AM until 5 PM, Friday 10 AM until 8 PM, Saturday 10 AM until 5 PM and Sunday noon until 4 PM.

Treasures on the Trent
309 Middle St., New Bern
(252) 637-7900

Treasures on the Trent specializes in gifts for the hard-to-please. You'll always find something unique, whether you are looking for a goodie for the golf enthusiast, a distinctive present to celebrate a wedding or housewarming, or a special gift for the new baby in the family. Decorative glass, leather jewelry cases, fine jewelry and sterling silver, artwork and more are but a few of the items you'll enjoy browsing through with a stop at Treasures on the Trent. A bridal and gift registry service is available. It's open Monday through Saturday.

Tryon Palace -
Museum Shop and Garden Shop
613 Pollock St., New Bern
(252) 514-4932

Tryon Palace has two shops, one featuring New Bern and Colonial memorabilia and gift items, and the other devoted to garden things and local crafts. The Museum Shop, in the historic Daves House on Pollock Street, carries distinctive jewelry; fine home-decor items in glass, paper, porcelain, silver and other materials; books on the history of New Bern, Craven County, North Carolina, the South and decorative arts; and much more. The Garden Shop features a selection of heirloom plants, crafts, books and tasty sauces and jellies. Both shops offer a wonderful selection of souvenirs for children. If you are not buying a general admission ticket to tour

When visiting Tryon Palace, be sure to stop by their Museum Shop and Garden Shop.

 **CLOSE UP**

The Bears
of New Bern

The showpieces of Bear Plaza, located on Middle Street between South Front and Pollock streets, are its towering wooden black bear sculptures. The black bear is the symbol of the City of New Bern, and the bears of Bear Plaza are a nod to the city's heritage.

Woodcarver Tom Penney carved the original bears for a business in Pamlico County. When that business went under before the bears were delivered, Penney offered to sell them to the city. It was the spring of 1994.

"Once we saw them, we had to have them," said Susan Moffat-Thomas, executive director of the downtown revitalization group Swiss Bear. "They were perfect for Bear Plaza, which was basically empty at the time."

A fund-raising campaign to buy the bears didn't take long. By November of that year, Swiss Bear had raised the necessary funds, even a bit extra for the plaza's lights. Local people contributed to the effort to bring the bears to Bear Plaza, the majority of them contributing in the names of their grandchildren, whose names are memorialized on a plaque located in the plaza. Since New Bern is a retirees' haven, the majority of the children listed on the plaque do not live in New Bern. It's a special treat when they come to town to visit their grandparents and see their name on the Plaza wall.

The bear is the official mascot of New Bern.

photo: Janis Williams

Unfortunately, it didn't take long for the bears to fall victim to termites. The late Jeth Lindsey of Art of the Wild did his best over the years to save the bears, but despite his constant patching and valiant efforts, the bears continued to deteriorate. By spring 1998, the truth was apparent: No amount of patching could fix the damage caused by termites, and the bears would need to be replaced. And in September 1999, one of the bears toppled, either due to gusting winds or vandalism.

When a Mumfest trivia contest asked the question "What animals live in the downtown plaza?" no one was surprised to see, and contest organizers were amused by, such answers as "wooden bears and termites." By the time that bear toppled, however, Swiss Bear had received the necessary funds from the Municipal Service District Advisory Committee (a group of downtown property owners) to replace the bears. Swiss Bear tracked down Penney, now a resident of Myrtle Beach, South Carolina.

"We really like his work and wanted him to do the very same bears," Moffat-Thomas said.

In October 1999, Penney returned to New Bern and carved the biggest of the new bears during Mumfest. He later completed the other two. The new bears, carved from cypress and thoroughly pretreated to prevent termite damage, were placed on Bear Plaza in spring 2000. The new bears are so life-like, you almost expect Goldilocks to scamper through at any moment.

Tryon Palace and its gardens, you'll need to pick up a pass at the Visitors Center or the Museum Shop in order to get to the Garden Shop because it is located inside the gate on palace grounds. Both shops are open daily.

Around New Bern

Outside of the historic district, New Bern has several shopping centers and one mall. The stores we mention in this chapter are by no means all there is to New Bern shopping; we've chosen ones throughout the area to give you an idea of what's available.

As you bear west on U.S. Highway 70, the second exit after the Historic District is the U.S. Highway 17 exit. In New Bern, U.S. 17 is named Dr. M. L. King Jr. Boulevard. Many stores and shopping centers are found on King Boulevard, which runs north to south. Twin Rivers Mall is on King, at the end of the U.S. 17 exit from U.S. 70. Anchor stores Belk and JCPenney have outside entrances. Inside, shoppers have access to about 30 stores, ranging from a video arcade, electronics boutique and pizzeria to jewelry shops and shoe stores. Across King Boulevard from Twin Rivers Mall is Rivertowne Square, anchored by Books-A-Million and Wal-Mart. Continue south along King Boulevard to the intersection of McCarthy Boulevard, and you'll find Staples, Target and New River Pottery.

Bill's Pet Shop
2636 Dr. M. L. King Jr. Blvd., New Bern
(252) 637-3997

Pet lovers will enjoy this shop at Berne Square Shopping Center. It's worth a stop just to see the adorable puppies and kittens on display. There are plenty of other pets available as well, including birds, ferrets, some reptiles and a wide variety of fish. This full-service, one-stop shop carries food, treats, pet-care products, toys, leashes, crates, medications and everything else you'll need to care for your best friend. Bill's features a complete tropical and saltwater aquarium section with a professional staff ready to guide you in the proper set up and care of your tanks. There are sister stores in Havelock and Morehead City.

Books-A-Million
Rivertowne Square, Dr. M. L. King Jr. Blvd., New Bern
(252) 635-6963

Books-A-Million (a chain store with locations in the South and West) offers every genre of book you can think of (at discounted prices), a large number of magazines and newspapers, and an impressive children's book section as well as reading activities scheduled throughout the week for various age groups. The Rivertowne Square store is huge, attractive and hard to leave. Customers are encouraged to relax in the comfy chairs and linger over the books or join friends in the store's coffee shop, Joe Muggs, which features espresso, pastries and more. Members of the Millionaire's Club — requiring an investment of $20 a year — entitles you to a 10 to 40 percent discount on everything in the store, even sale items. You can even use your card for online purchases.

Cooks & Connoisseurs
1907 S. Glenburnie Rd., New Bern
(252) 633-2665, (800) 540-COOK

This wonderful specialty food store carries gourmet and international foods from around the world. A variety of coffees and cheeses, necessary cooking tools and gadgets, and an extensive selection of wines are for sale. You'll also find impressive glassware and gourmet cookware. Cooks & Connoisseurs prepares gift baskets. Cooking classes are available; call for a current schedule.

Dunn's Beds
2703 U.S. Hwy. 70 E, New Bern
(252) 636-2216

Dunn's Beds is a complete bedroom furniture store sure to have the perfect items to create just the feeling you want in your home. You'll find quality beds, night stands, chests, drawers and mirrors by such quality furniture makers as Broyhill, Vaughan-Bassett, Riverside, and Night and Day. The professionals at Dunn's Beds offer mattresses by Tempur-pedic, Simmons, Sensa and Restonic. Dunn's Beds has a nice selection of futons and water beds along with all the water-bed accessories. With delivery and set up offered, this is the place to go for anything in the way of comfortable bedding and bedroom furniture. Dunn's Beds also has a store in Morehead City.

Flythe's Bike Shop
2411 Trent Rd., New Bern
(252) 638-1544

Why buy a bike in a box and endure the frustration of putting it together when Flythe's can offer you a quality bike already assembled? Insiders like this place because of the selection of bikes and recumbents available for adults and kids. You'll also find scooters, baby bike seats, baby joggers and strollers, bike trailers and more. If you just need a bike while you're in town for a visit, Flythe's has bike rentals (a credit card is required for rentals), including free pickup and delivery. Flythe's also is a complete repair shop, and you just can't beat the friendly customer service. Layaway and gift certificates are available.

Hearne's Jewelers
Rivertowne Square, 1331 McCarthy Blvd., New Bern
(252) 637-2784

Hearne's offers quality men's and women's jewelry and is a trusted, well-established company. Founded in 1972 by Mickey Hearne and now run by his sons Mike and Jimmy, the business combines courtesy with integrity. Hearne's offers exquisite rings, earrings, necklaces and bracelets as well as a fine line of watches, including those made by Seiko and Citizen. This is the place to go for jewelry and watch repair and to have stones mounted.

KabOOdles
755 McCarthy Blvd., New Bern
(252) 514-0300

KabOOdles is New Bern's fabulous toy store with more than 3,000 square feet of unique toys. Browse a large variety of toy lines including Melissa and Doug, Corolle, Bruder Trucks, Alex, Webkinz, Breyer, Calico Critters and more. You can also stuff your own animal in the Bears & Buddies center. Got a sweet tooth? Don't miss out on the 12-foot Wall of Candy and the Pucker Powder center. Free gift wrapping and free Birthday Box registry are available.

New Bern Fabric Center
1218 S. Glenburnie Rd., New Bern
(252) 633-4780, (877) 327-7076

New Bern Fabric Center offers a large selection of reasonably priced fabric, notions and supplies for quilting, smocking, heirloom and embroidery projects. New Bern Fabric Center also carries a full line of Bernina machines, products and accessories. Clubs devoted to utilizing the machines to their full potential meet on a monthly basis. Classes are offered for adults and children; call the store for a complete schedule. It's open Monday through Saturday.

Party Suppliers
2648 Dr. M. L. King Jr. Blvd., New Bern
(252) 637-7722

Make your next occasion a memorable one with a stop at Party Suppliers. While a couple of aisles are always devoted to upcoming holidays (and you definitely won't want to miss stopping by here at Halloween and Christmas), Party Suppliers always offers the latest trends, designs and colors in invitations, decorations, table settings, party favors, banners and more. Birthday party themes range from Scooby Doo and Clifford the Big Red Dog (for the younger set) right on up to the Aged to Perfection and Over the Hill collections (for the young at heart).

Red Willow's Gift Shoppe and Art Gallery
130 West Jones Street, Trenton
(252) 448-1138

Red Willow's offers garden giftware and local craftsmen's wares such as hand-made afghans, jewelry, boiled wool pocketbooks, recycled chair frames with new knitted webbing, seasonal wreaths, soaps and candles. There is a farmers' market Friday and Saturday for the local farmers to sell their produce. While you're downtown, drive around the corner to the Trenton Millpond for a spectacular and scenic end to your shopping experience.

Sewing Solutions
1505 S. Glenburnie Rd., New Bern
(252) 633-1799

This shop, owned by Debbie Woods-Tyer, doubles as a display room for her many projects. Decorative embroidery work, home crafts and decorations and quilt squares are among the many creations you can see. Debbie offers Pfaff sewing machines, sergers and embroidery machines, as well as a wide variety of sewing notions, patterns, quilting supplies and books on sewing and quilting. Debbie also teaches sewing classes for all levels and produces a free quarterly newsletter with new product listings, sewing tips and class schedules.

Antiques

New Bern offers plenty of antiques shops to nose around in and discover lost treasures. Although for several years New Bern's wonderful antique shops tended to cluster in the downtown area, over the past few years old favorites have relocated and new ones have popped up all over town. We've included a few of our favorites to get you started. If you're interested in antiques shows, the New Bern Preservation Foundation, (252) 633-6448, hosts an antiques fair showcasing invited dealers every February (see our New Bern Annual Events chapter).

Andrea's Attic Antiques
2104-B Trent Blvd., New Bern
(252) 633-5656

Andrea's Attic Antiques offers a fine and wide selection of antiques and collectibles, so much we'd be hard-pressed to even begin to list all the great things shoppers can find here. Insiders particularly love to browse the incredible selection of antique and vintage jewelry, although collectors who specialize in a niche will want to explore the cut glass, hats, dishes, cookie jars, books, art and prints, Pepsi and Coke items, and even more on display. Andrea's is open Monday through Saturday.

Habitat for Humanity Resale Store
930 Pollock St., New Bern
(252) 633-5512

While the Habitat for Humanity Resale Store is not an antiques store, it's one of those cool shops that offers a lot of "stuff" you can't find anywhere else. The store regularly features an assortment of quality furniture, tested appliances, household furnishings and fixtures, office equipment and building materials. The Resale Store is a terrific place to visit when you are remodeling, furnishing a college dorm room, or looking for that special accent piece for your home. Twice a year, the store also features fantastic Progressive Clearance Sales, where merchandise is progressively marked down 35 to 50 to 65 percent off in order to clear the floor for new items. The Resale Store supports the mission of Habitat for Humanity of Greater New Bern: to provide safe, decent housing for all families in New Bern and around the world. The store is open Monday through Saturday.

Jane Sugg Antiques
228 Middle St., New Bern
(252) 637-6985

Here you will find high-quality period and reproduction furniture, lamps, crystal and rugs. Jane Sugg also features some exquisite sterling tea sets and flatware. It's open Monday through Saturday.

JL Kirkman's Antique Flea Mall
1198 U.S. Hwy. 17 N, Bridgeton
(252) 634-2745

JL Kirkman's is located across the Neuse River Bridge just five minutes from downtown New Bern. The flea mall, right off the highway in Bridgeton in the old Eagle Supermarket building, prides itself on having the highest quality solid-wood used furniture in the area at the most affordable prices. With more than 48 vendors in its 10,000 square-foot showroom, JL Kirkman's has a tremendous variety of furniture, glassware and home decor.

Middle Street Antiques & Flea Market
221 Middle St., New Bern
(252) 633-4876

Insiders love the selection of antique and reproduction stained glass available at Middle Street Antiques. Hanging in the front window of the shop, these pieces of art frame an enticing invitation to come in and browse the antique and reproduction furniture, dishes, toys, books and more that are arrayed in ever-changing displays. Open daily, Middle Street Antiques is a must-see for those interested in old-time collectibles.

New Berne Antiques & Collectibles
1000 Greenleaf Cemetery Rd., New Bern
(252) 637-0206

To find New Berne Antiques & Collectibles, just make a left off Dr. M. L. King Jr. Boulevard one traffic light south of the turn to New Bern High School. They're in the old Sunshine Gardens building. If you love old stuff, you'll love browsing their many booths. You're bound to see a "thingy" grandma used to have or a toy that brings to mind memories of your childhood. Just about everything you can imagine is for sale, including toys, Pepsi memorabilia and antique tools, in more than 12,500 square feet of space.

Poor Charlie's Flea Market and Antiques
208 Hancock St., New Bern
(252) 672-0208

Poor Charlie's dealers offer just about everything a nostalgia buff could want. The old warehouse that houses the dealers suggests long-ago places; it's complete with a dimly lit interior and that alluring smell of old, stored-in-the-attic stuff. Patrons will find antiques, collectibles, home accessories, heirloom jewelry, furniture and household items.

Seaport Antiques
504 S. Front St., New Bern
(252) 637-5050

This market is a multi-dealer shop specializing in quality antiques and collectibles, including china, furniture, chandeliers, art, jewelry and more, at very reasonable prices. Insiders find Seaport Antiques a great place to browse and look at all the treasures.

Tom's Coins & Antiques
244 Middle St., New Bern
(252) 633-0615

As the name implies, this shop sells coins and all manner of antiques. It has beautiful antique and reproduction furniture, estate jewelry, crystal, china, stamps and sports cards. There are lots of nostalgic items and collectibles. Owner Tom Faulkenberry is an appraiser and auctioneer.

NEW BERN
ATTRACTIONS 👥

The importance of New Bern's history cannot be overemphasized. The city of New Bern was settled in 1710 (New Bern celebrates its Tercentennial in 2010) at the confluence of the Neuse and Trent rivers and began to flourish as a farming and shipping community. The city soon became an important port, exporting naval stores and, later, tobacco and cotton. The captains of the ships that hauled these high-demand products used the spires of New Bern's churches to guide them up the Neuse River, which at the time had few navigational aids or other landmarks. Several of the older homes in New Bern have widow's walks projecting above the roofs, where wives would watch for their husbands' ships returning from long sea voyages.

Pirates also found the dark coves and creeks along the rivers ideal for subversive activities and, of course, for hiding treasures. Blackbeard supposedly stayed in a huge house by the Neuse, where he planned his raids on oceangoing ships carrying rich cargo between the American colonies, England and the West Indies.

New Bern can credit its gentility to its once-thriving plantations that produced exportable products to be shipped around the world. The plantations themselves often became small towns, but today little remains of the beautiful estates that depended on the dark waters of the Neuse and Trent rivers for livelihoods. What does remain are the moss-hung oak and cypress trees guarding the many creeks and sloughs along the winding Trent and broad Neuse.

Like other cities, New Bern endured the pangs of growth and change, eventually developing a character all its own. It did not, however, forget its past. History taught New Bern many hard lessons, one of which was to value its heritage. To that end, a great number of old homes

and churches have been restored, and, in cases of potential loss, relocated, thanks to groups such as the New Bern Preservation Foundation. Salvaged structures now number more than 150, and restoration efforts are continuous. For more about the city's history, see our New Bern chapter.

While the historical sites, homes and buildings are the focal points of New Bern, the art and cultural events of the town are constant attractions. A large community of reputable visual artists grace New Bern with their work, which is often exhibited at the Bank of the Arts, the public library and commercial art galleries (see our New Bern Arts chapter). Performing arts events and festivals occur year round (see our New Bern Annual Events chapter).

Not listed in many guidebooks (except this one) but known to New Bernians are the town's churches, each distinctive and worthy of a sightseeing visit. Of the area's many historic houses of worship, it is perhaps Christ Episcopal Church on Pollock Street that has the most interesting lore. Included in the church's regalia is a silver communion service donated by King George II. The service survived two fires and reconstruction. According to local history, the communion service was stolen in the 1960s or '70s. The thief, so goes the tale, fenced it with a man who recognized it for what it was and returned it to the church. For more information on New Bern's churches, see our New Bern Worship chapter.

In addition to the official sights of New Bern, walking tours of the historic district are very popular. Attractions open to the public primarily focus on the town's history; however, many of the historic homes are private residences and are closed to the public. Nonetheless, walking the streets and viewing the architecture and landscapes of these grand old homes will give you the feel of the city's Colonial heritage.

Most of the attractions are within walking distance of each other, and we have listed a number of the sites here. For heritage walking tour information, including maps focusing on historic homes, the Civil War, New Bern's African-American heritage, and historic churches and cemeteries, let your first stop be the **New Bern-Craven County Convention and Visitors Bureau**, located in the New Bern Riverfront Convention Center at the corner of East and South Front Streets, (252) 637-9400 or (800) 437-5767. Everyone there is very helpful with orienting you to the town. Hours are Monday through Friday 8 AM to 5 PM, Saturday 10 AM to 4 PM and

---

 *Much has been done to preserve the area where the Battle of New Bern took place in March 1862 during the Civil War. (The Union forces triumphed and occupied New Bern for the rest of the war). The New Bern Historical Society now owns 25 acres of the original battlefield, located near Taberna, and preserves this acreage in its natural state. The battleground's major annual event is Civil War Adventure Day, which is March 14, for about 50 children ages 6 to 11 and their parents. The youngsters participate in a small-scale reenactment and go on an educational tour of the battlefield. A visitor center was dedicated in January 2008 and will provide a base site for individual visitors and tours such as school and civic groups. The battlefield is open to the public, and $5 tours are available with a trained guide. In the immediate future, battlefield tours will continue to be on a call-and-reserve basis through the Historical Society. Call (252) 638-8558.*

(between Memorial Day and Labor Day) Sundays from 10 AM to 2 PM.

For those who enjoy the woodlands as well as the city, nearby Croatan National Forest provides a close-up look at coastal marshes, estuaries and forest. The 157,000-acre preserve is home to insectivorous plants, uncommon wildflowers, marsh and shore birds, and a variety of forest animals such as black bears, alligators, deer and wild turkeys. Forest hiking trails and overnight campsites are popular with nature lovers. For a detailed description, see our Crystal Coast Attractions chapter.

WALKING TOUR ATTRACTIONS

As we mentioned in the introduction, many of New Bern's historic homes are private residences and therefore not open to the public. However, a leisurely stroll along riverwalks through the historic district will allow you to observe the landscapes, architecture and gardens of these vintage homes. Walking also will give you a real sense of the many Old World customs that characterize this Colonial town.

The New Bern-Craven County Convention & Visitors Bureau, located in the New Bern Riverfront Convention Center at the corner of East and South Front Streets, has several self-guided walking tour maps covering different aspects of New Bern's long and interesting historical heritage, including the Civil War era and the town's historic churches and cemeteries.

New Bern Tours offers guided walking tours for 10 or more people by reservation, (252) 637-7316. A few of the town's more notable residences and buildings are listed here. Please note that most of these homes are private residences and are not open to the public.

• The **John Horner Hill House**, 713 Pollock Street, is a Georgian-period dwelling built between 1770 and 1780. It is noted for its rare nine-over-nine sash at the first-floor windows.

• The **Henry H. Harris House**, 718 Pollock Street, was built in 1800 and is a well-preserved example of vernacular Federal-period architecture.

• The **Anne Green Lane House**, 804 Pollock Street, is a transitional late-Georgian-early Federal house built between 1790 and 1800. It was remodeled during the Victorian period.

•The **John H. Jones House**, 819 Pollock Street, is a small Federal house with an unusual central chimney. Its original separate kitchen remains at the rear.

•The **White House**, 422 Johnson Street, is a simple sidehall Federal house built c. 1830–40. It is noted for its two end chimneys with a small pent-roofed closet in between.

•The **Cutting-Allen House**, 518 New Street, is a transitional late-Georgian–early Federal sidehall house built in 1793. It is considered unusual because of its flanking wings and large rear ballroom. It was saved from demolition in 1980 and moved to its present location.

•The **Hawks House** at New and Metcalf Streets offers a side-by-side comparison of styles. Dating from the 1760s, the western part of the house is Georgian, and the eastern section is Federal, added by Francis Hawks, son of John Hawks, architect of Tryon Palace.

•The **Clark House**, 419 Metcalf Street, was built between 1795 and 1804. It is one of several gambrel-roofed houses in the historic district.

•The **Attmore-Wadsworth House**, 515 Broad Street, is an unusual one-story, Italianate-style house built c. 1855. Several Italianate-style homes are part of the city's historic architecture.

•The **Thomas McLin House**, 507 Middle Street, is a Federal-style cottage unique for its strict symmetry and diminutive scale.

•The **W. B. Blades House**, 602 Middle Street, was built in 1903 and is noted for its elaborate Queen Anne design.

•The **Jerkins-Duffy House**, 301 Johnson Street, was built c. 1830 and is unusual because of its exterior Federal design and interior Greek Revival elements. It is also noted for its captain's walk and exposed-face chimneys.

•The **George Slover House**, 209 Johnson Street, was built c. 1894 and is an eclectic combination of Queen Anne and shingle-style architecture.

•The **Charles Slover House**, 201 Johnson Street, is a stately brick townhouse built in 1848–49 that was selected as headquarters by Gen. Ambrose Burnside during the Civil War. C. D. Bradham, inventor of Brad's Drink (now known as Pepsi-Cola), purchased the house in 1908.

•The **Eli Smallwood House**, 524 E. Front Street, is one of the finest of New Bern's Federal brick sidehall houses, built c. 1810. It is noted for its handsome portico and elegant interior woodwork.

•The Federal-style **Dawson-Clarke House**, 519 E. Front Street, was built c. 1807–10 and enlarged in 1820. It is one of several historic homes exhibiting the use of double porches, a popular style in the coastal region.

•The **Gaston House**, 421 Craven Street, is a Georgian home (c. 1770) built by architect, builder and patriot-statesman James Coor. It was purchased in 1818 by Judge William Gaston and was the scene of the founding of St. Paul's Roman Catholic Church. Gaston was a brilliant orator, lawyer, member of Congress, State Justice and author of the state song. The house was enlarged c. 1850.

•The **David F. Jarvis House** (c. 1903), 220 Pollock Street, is a good example of neoclassical revival architecture.

•The **Edward R. Stanly House** and Dependency, 502 Pollock Street, was built c. 1849 in the Renaissance Revival style. The cast-iron grills over its windows are unique in New Bern.

•The **Wade House**, 214 S. Front Street, was built in 1843 and remodeled before 1885 in the Second Empire style. The cast-iron crest on the mansard roof and the iron fence are notable surviving features.

AFRICAN-AMERICAN WALKING TOURS

Tryon Palace Historic Sites & Gardens offers a monthly African-American walking tour in spring, summer and fall. The walking tour, which lasts about 90 minutes and covers 16 blocks, features 300 years of African-American history. There is a fee charged for this tour, and reservations are required. For information, call (252) 514-4900 or (800) 767-1560.

CLOSE UP

New Bern's 300th Birthday Celebration

In 2010, New Bern, the second oldest town in North Carolina, will turn 300 years old. A year-long slate of events is scheduled, geared toward celebrating each of the 365 days of the year.

The year-long festivities kick off on December 31, 2009, with New Bern's First Night celebration. The downtown area will welcome patrons from afternoon until midnight to bring in the New Year with music and entertainment galore.

Some of the year's activities will involve the opening of the new Alfred Cunningham Bridge across the Trent River and the debut of the new 48,000-square-foot N.C. History Center at Tryon Palace Historic Sites and Gardens. Other events will focus on history through reenactments and re-creations, lectures and movies.

In March, to celebrate the Battle of New Bern (March 14, 1862) and the resulting Northern occupation, Tryon Palace will present "A Union City in the Midst of the Confederacy: New Bern Occupied." In May, there will be a Civil War naval bombardment at Union Point Park. The national assembly of the U.S. Colored Troops will convene in New Bern that same month. A production of 1776 will be mounted by the New Bern Civic Theatre in April. July brings a special Independence Day celebration. The African-American community will celebrate Juneteenth with a choral festival, a homecoming and a ball in June. Each month will have something going on that is geared historically to that time.

The 300th celebration events calendar is available at www.newbern300th.com and, according to the organizers, will continue to be updated.

It will be a great year for New Bern. Come and share.

Here is a sampling of events for the New Bern 300th Celebration.

December 31, 2009

• First Night Celebration

New Bern's 300th Celebration kicks off with a spectacular public party. Ticketed events will also be available. Buttons for the event are $8 in advance, $10 at the event.

March 13-15, 2010

• A Union City in the Midst of the Confederacy: New Bern Occupied

A Civil War weekend at Tryon Palace, concentrating on the Union occupation of New Bern and the civilian aspects of the Civil War.

June 18, 2010

• Juneteenth Celebration at New Bernian Heritage Ball

June 19, 2010

• Juneteenth Choral Festival of African-American Music

June 20, 2010

• Juneteenth Homecoming Picnic and Family Gathering

September 16-19, 2010

• 300th Jubilee Weekend

September 16, 2010

• Rededication of the Federal Courthouse
• Reenactment of Bayard vs. Singleton

September 17, 2010
- Official Welcome Ceremony
- Activities throughout downtown area
- Family Picnic
- North Carolina Symphony
- Fireworks

September 18, 2010
- Heritage Parade
- Cultural Street Festival
- Flotilla
- Street Concerts
- Jubilation Ball (Ticketed Event)

September 19, 2010
- Pancakes in the Park (Ticketed Event)
- Synchronized Church Bells
- Closing Ceremony

The Craven County Tourism Development Authority offers a series of self-guided walking tours, one of which covers New Bern's African-American history. The tour sheet is available at the Craven County Convention and Visitors Center at the corner of East and South Front Streets and it details historic sites important to local African-American heritage. These include churches, businesses, residences and social organizations, a few of which are described below.

•The **George H. White House** at 519 Johnson Street was the home of lawyer George H. White, who was elected to the U.S. House of Representatives in 1897. He later fled to Philadelphia and was the last African American in Congress from the South until the 1960s.

•Built in 1923, the **Rhone Hotel**, 512 Queen Street, was not only the first African-American owned hotel in town but also the home of Charlotte Rhone, New Bern's first black registered nurse and Craven County's first social worker. (Charlotte's sister Henrietta owned the hotel.) The Rhone Hotel was in business from the 1920s to the 1950s.

•**Dr. Fisher's Office**, 830 Queen Street, was the office of Dr. Hunter Fisher from 1920 to 1947. When the building was being constructed with its soaring false front, it was surrounded by other commercial buildings; now it stands alone.

•The **First Baptist Church** at 819 Cypress Street is the oldest African-American church building standing in New Bern. Its congregation was established in 1869, and the current building was built in 1906. Booker T. Washington lectured here in 1907. In 1922 the church's brick walls protected it from the Great Fire of that year, and it served as a shelter for victims left homeless.

Attmore-Oliver Civil War House Museum
511 Broad St., New Bern
(252) 638-8558

The Attmore-Oliver Civil War House Museum was originally built in 1790 by prominent New Bernian Samuel Chapman. Today, it serves as a house museum for the New Bern Historical Society. It was enlarged to its present size in 1834 and houses eighteenth- and nineteenth-century antiques, a doll collection and Civil War memorabilia. Of particular interest are the fine Greek Revival portico and two-story porches at the rear of the house. The house is open in April on the weekends; call for times and days. The house can be shown to groups by appointment and can

Don't feel embarrassed to wander residential streets or stop and gaze at any of the houses in the historic district. Everyone appreciates your admiration.

be rented for private functions. Be aware, however, that it is not handicapped accessible.

Cedar Grove Cemetery
Queen and George Sts., New Bern

If you're one of those people who loves wandering through old graveyards, you'll not want to miss this one. Statuary and monuments beneath Spanish moss–draped trees mark burial traditions from the earliest days of our nation. One smallish obelisk lists the names of nine children in one family who all died within a two-year time span. The city's monument to its Confederate dead and the graves of 70 soldiers are also here. The cemetery's main gate features a shell motif, with an accompanying legend that says if water drips on you as you enter, you will be the next to arrive by hearse.

Centenary United Methodist Church
309 New St., New Bern
(252) 637-4181

First organized as a congregation in 1772, the current Centenary United Methodist Church was designed by Herbert Woodley Simpson and completed in 1905. Its rounded walls and turrets have an almost Moorish look. Guided tours, which are available weekdays between 9 AM and 4 PM, begin with a stop by the church office.

Christ Episcopal Church
320 Pollock St., New Bern
(252) 633-2109

More than 260 years old, Christ Episcopal Church is the oldest in New Bern and one of the oldest in North Carolina. This is actually the third church building to stand in this area. The first was completed in 1750 and was later destroyed by fire. The foundation of that first church is on the current church grounds. The second church was completed in 1824 and destroyed by fire in 1871. The church you see today was completed in 1875; it is a Gothic Revival building that incorporates surviving walls of that second church. The steeple, with its four-faced clock, is one of the identifying marks of the downtown skyline. Among the treasures on display are a 1752 Book of Common Prayer, a huge

1717 Bible and a five-piece silver communion service given to Christ Church by King George II. Each bears the royal coat-of-arms. Call for a tour of the church.

Craven Arts Council & Gallery
Bank of the Arts
317 Middle St., New Bern
(252) 638-2577

Built in 1911, this interesting granite structure once served as a bank but now houses the headquarters for the Craven Arts Council and Gallery. The classical facade of the building features Ionic columns leading into the open, two-story gallery. Changing exhibits of various media — painting, sculpture, photography, pottery, fiber art and other art forms — showcase the work of local and Southeastern artists. Many special events, such as concerts, lectures and receptions are offered here throughout the year. The Bank of the Arts does not charge an admission fee (donations are welcome), and visitors are welcome to browse. It is open Tuesday through Saturday from 10 AM to 6 PM. The building is handicapped accessible.

Croatan National Forest
Ranger's Office, 141 E. Fisher Ave., New Bern
(252) 638-5628

Croatan National Forest is an expansive nature preserve bordered by New Bern, Morehead City and Cape Carteret. The district ranger's office is on Fisher Avenue, which is approximately 9 miles south of New Bern just off U.S. Highway 70 East. Well-placed road signs make the office easy to find.

Due to its coastal location, the forest has many unique features. Some of the ecosystems present include pocosins, longleaf and loblolly pine, and bottomland and upland hardwoods. Sprinkled throughout the Croatan are 40 miles of streams and 4,300 acres of wild lakes. Black bears, otters, deer, raptors and many other forest creatures live in this coastal woodland. Within the forest's boundaries are insectivorous plants such as the Venus flytrap, butterworts, pitcher plants, sundews and bladderworts, which find the forest an ideal habitat. These rare plants are protected by law. The forest is also well-known for its beautiful wildflowers. Pamphlets on the wildflowers and insectivorous plants are available at the district ranger's office.

The forest areas are excellent for hiking, swimming, boating, hunting, fishing and picnicking. Miles and miles of unpaved roads lace through the woodland, providing easy if sometimes roundabout access to its wilderness. Recreation areas are available for a day's outing or for longer visits. Camping fees vary, so call the district ranger's office for seasonal rates. Because the Croatan is so expansive and undeveloped, it is best to stop in at the district ranger's office on Fisher Avenue and pick up a forest map before heading out. The best times for venturing into coastal woodlands are fall, winter or early spring. Summer can be very hot and buggy, so prepare yourself with insect repellent. For more information on the Croatan National Forest, see our Crystal Coast Attractions chapter.

The Firemen's Museum
408 Hancock St., New Bern
(252) 636-4087

The New Bern Fire Department is one of the oldest in the country, still operating under its original 1845 charter as the Atlantic Hook and Ladder Company. The museum houses steam pumpers and an extensive collection of other early firefighting equipment. Also on exhibit are rare photographs, Civil War relics and even the mounted head of Fred, the faithful old fire horse who, according to legend, died in his tracks while answering what turned out to be a false alarm. The museum is open year-round Monday through Saturday from 10 AM to 4 PM. Admission is $5 for adults and $2.50 for children. Children younger than 6 get in free.

First Presbyterian Church
418 New St., New Bern
(252) 637-3270

The oldest continually used church building in New Bern, First Presbyterian

was built in 1819–22 by local architect and builder Uriah Sandy. The congregation was established in 1817. The Federal-style church is similar to many built around the same time in New England but is unusual in North Carolina. Like that of Christ Church, the steeple on First Presbyterian is a point of reference on the skyline. The church was used as a Union hospital and lookout post during the Civil War, and the initials of soldiers on duty in the belfry can still be seen carved in the walls. Tours between 9 AM and 2 PM weekdays are self-guided, but visitors should stop by the church office first.

George W. Dixon House
609 Pollock St., New Bern

The Dixon House, built in 1828, epitomizes New Bern's lifestyle in the first half of the nineteenth century, when the town was a prosperous port and one of the state's largest cities. The house, built for a New Bern merchant, is a fine example of neoclassical architecture. Its furnishings, reflecting the Federal period, reveal the changing tastes of early America. The house was converted into a regimental hospital when Union troops occupied New Bern during the Civil War. Admission is included in the Tryon Palace Complex ticket.

John Wright Stanly House
307 George St., New Bern

On his Southern tour in 1791, President George Washington dined and danced at Tryon Palace, but his two nights in New Bern were spent at the nearby home of John Wright Stanly. Stanly died of yellow fever in 1789, but New Bern residents reopened and refurnished the residence, then located on Middle Street, just for Washington's visit. Washington described his overnight accommodation as "exceeding good lodgings." During the Revolutionary War, Stanly's merchant ships plied the waters as privateers, capturing British ships to aid the American cause. The elegance of Stanly's house, built in the early 1780s, reflects the wealth of its owner.

See this entire guide plus additional content online at insiderinfo.us

Distinctive American furniture of the period complements the elegant interior woodwork. The Stanly family history provides a fascinating chronicle of father and son, epidemic and duel, war and wealth. Admission is included as part of the Tryon Palace Complex admission.

New Bern Academy Museum
New and Hancocks Sts., New Bern
(252) 514-4900, (800) 767-1560

Founded in 1764 and built in 1809, New Bern Academy is the oldest public school building in North Carolina and one of the oldest in America. It was still used as a school recently enough to have been attended by some of New Bern's current residents. After it closed, it sat vacant for several years before being purchased and renovated in the 1980s by Tryon Palace. Today, the museum houses exhibits illustrating the 300-year-old history of New Bern and eastern North Carolina, including exhibits on architecture, education and the Civil War (during which it was used as a hospital). The academy is open Monday through Saturday from 1 to 4:30 PM, with admission charged as part of the Tryon Palace Complex admission.

New Bern National Cemetery
1711 National Ave., New Bern

Encompassing nearly eight acres, New Bern National Cemetery was established in 1867 as a final resting place for veterans. The grounds where the cemetery was established were once the site of military drills by occupying forces during the Civil War. Once inside the gates, visitors are impressed by row after row of matching government standard-issue white marble gravestones, precisely lined. Also on the grounds are Civil War monuments dedicated during the early twentieth century to the fallen of companies of New Jersey, Rhode Island, Connecticut and Massachusetts. The cemetery is the site of a Memorial Day service every year.

New Bern Trolley Tours
333 Middle St., New Bern
(252) 637-7316, (800) 849-7316

Touring the town by trolley is a comfortable and interesting alternative to a walking tour. Narrated 90-minute tours

depart the corner of Pollock and George Streets, and tickets can be purchased either on the trolley car or at the trolley office at 333 Middle Street. During the months of January and February, call for tour times. April through October, tours are scheduled for 11 AM and 2 PM Monday through Saturday and 2 PM on Sunday. In July and August, tours are set for 9 AM and 11 AM Monday through Saturday and 2 PM on Sunday. Tours or charters for special groups or occasions may also be arranged. Professional guides narrate the tours with attention to historical and architectural interests and spice the narrative with folklore and local knowledge. Special 90-minute tours focusing on Civil War history and African-American history are available by charter. Trolley tours cost $15 for adults and $7 for children 12 and younger.

Robert Hay House
Eden St., New Bern

The tour of the Robert Hay House provides insight into the lives and society of middle-class craftsmen and artisans essential to everyday life in the early nineteenth century. Scottish-born Robert Hay was a skilled craftsman of carriages and riding chairs. He purchased the house in 1816 and lived there until his death in 1850. The original structure, purchased for $1,000, was a single heated room on the first and second floors, with a cellar kitchen and large cooking fireplace. Hay enlarged the house between 1820 and 1830 with a rear addition consisting of a double porch and two small heated rooms. The house gives visitors a firsthand experience with early nineteenth-century methods of climate control. Winter heating is provided by working fireplaces in the parlor and working kitchen, and summertime cooling is provided by using the open doors and windows to harness the breeze off the nearby Trent River. In addition, louvered shutters on the sunny sides of the house are closed to block the sun's hot rays. The Robert Hay House, which was opened to the public in late 1998, has been restored to the appearance it had between 1830 and 1850. The house is furnished with accurate reproductions made by skilled woodworkers using traditional hand methods, a tactic necessary because the house is not equipped with the modern climate controls needed to protect the antiques. Admission to the Hay House is included as part of the Tryon Palace Complex ticket.

Tradewind Aviation Scenic Rides
820 Aviation Dr., New Bern
(252) 636-0716

What could be a more interesting and unusual way to see New Bern than to see it from the air? Tradewind Aviation, based at Craven Regional Airport, offers reasonably priced, 30-minute and one-hour tours for one to three passengers aboard a Cessna 172.

Tryon Palace Historic Sites & Gardens
610 Pollock St., New Bern
(252) 514-4900, (800) 767-1560

Tryon Palace, built in 1770 by Royal Governor William Tryon, was known at the time as one of the most beautiful buildings in America. After its use both as a Colonial and state capitol, the palace fell into disrepair. The main building burned in 1798 and the kitchen office was dismantled in the early nineteenth century. When reconstruction was undertaken in the 1950s, only one wing — the stables — remained standing. The palace now houses an outstanding collection of antiques and art, and the grounds are devoted to extensive landscaping, ranging from English formal gardens and a kitchen garden to wilderness garden areas.

Included as part of the main palace complex are the John Wright Stanly House (1783) on George Street, the George W. Dixon House (1828) on Pollock Street and the Robert Hay House (1810) on Eden Street. The Stanly home, which was originally on New Street and moved to its present location in the 1960s, was built by a Revolutionary War patriot. George Washington stayed in this house for two nights in 1791. The Dixon House is a prominent Federal-style home noted for its rare neoclassical antiques. The restoration of the 1810 Robert Hay House on Eden Street

is an accurate reflection of the lifestyle technology of its period.

Palace tours take place daily, with special tours added during the Christmas season. A self-guided interior tour of the Kitchen Office focuses on the behind-the-scenes tasks necessary to maintain the daily eighteenth-century operations of the palace and its occupants.

Annual events include the colorful Colonial Christmas and candlelight tours in December, the Decorative Arts Symposium in March, Gardener's Weekend during New Bern's Historic Homes and Gardens Tour in the spring, and the July Independence Day Celebration (see our New Bern Annual Events chapter for more about these events). The African-American Lecture Series and the African-American Walking Tours run monthly from spring through fall. Blacksmithing and weaving are also among regular crafts demonstrations.

The palace gift shop in the Jones House and the crafts and garden shop behind the palace west wing are open during regular palace hours. An audiovisual orientation program is shown at the visitors center.

The palace is open year round, Monday through Saturday 9 AM to 5 PM and on Sunday from 1 to 5 PM. The last tour begins at 4 PM. The palace is closed on Thanksgiving Day, December 24 through 26 and New Year's Day. A number of tour options are available, including two-day and annual passes, and group discounts are extended to pre-arranged groups of 20 or more. General admission is $15 for adults and $6 for students in grades 1 through 12. These tickets are valid for two consecutive days. Active-duty military families get a discount. Children in kindergarten or younger get in free. For specific tour price information or group reservations, call the numbers above. The historic sites and gardens are partially equipped for disabled visitors.

O nce upon a time, there was a beautiful place at a point where two rivers met. It was such a beautiful place that even the first person who ever saw it — a Tuscarora Indian — wanted to live there. In fact, the entire tribe decided it was a good place to live. There were lots of fish in the two rivers, game to hunt in the forest and many trees that the Native Americans could use to build all the things they needed.

One day, some other people arrived in the beautiful place. Their leader was from a far-away place called Bern, Switzerland. The people saw the two rivers that came together and admired the big forest that had what they needed to build things. They also decided that this was the best place in the New World to live. They called the place New Bern to remind them of their old city. Except for once or twice, the people of New Bern got along pretty well with the Tuscarora Indians, but that's another story.

The people of New Bern built a fine town with pretty houses, and their town became a capital where the king sent a governor to rule the whole land. The people built a fine house in New Bern for the governor -- a palace. Everyone loved the palace, and people came from all over the land to see and enjoy it. Even pirates came up the river from the sea to see the town with the palace. And because it was always a beautiful place to live, people kept coming to New Bern.

Over the years, the people of New Bern got together to build a fort for their children to play in and places where their children have parties, eat ice cream and purchase toys. Today, they bring wonderful performers from far away to teach and entertain the children. They even have a variety of summer and day camps where children can feed farm animals, experience colonial life or just have fun being a child. From near and far, visitors still bring their children to New Bern to enjoy the town with a real palace, and the people of New Bern continue to live happily ever after. Read on for the details. This is hardly The End.

Arts

The Accidental Artist
220 Craven St., New Bern
(252) 634-3411

You might think The Accidental Artist is a great place to spend a rainy afternoon when the kids have decided there's nothing else to do. Actually this is a great place to have fun no matter what the weather is like. At this studio, you can showcase your creativity by selecting and painting your own pottery. The Accidental Artist will then fire your one-of-a-kind masterpiece. Come relax in the informal atmosphere and give your artistic impulses free reign. If you are feeling creatively challenged, the in-house artist can create an item for you. You can even book studio space for birthday parties, club meetings and other special occasions. The Accidental Artist is open daily.

Art & Materials
219 Middle St., New Bern
(252) 514-2787

Art & Materials is a great place for kids (of all ages) to feed their artistic impulses. It is the only place in New Bern to purchase the supplies for whatever art form one wishes to pursue. The shop features a variety of workshops in painting, drawing, pottery and more. Owners Chris and Shelley Mathiot bring in some of the finest local artists to teach summer camps, after-school art lessons, special holiday sessions and classes for home-school students.

Craven Arts Council
317 Middle St., New Bern
(252) 638-2577

The Craven Arts Council & Gallery sponsors two week-long fun and educational Summer Arts Camps for children ages 4 to 12 (morning and afternoon sessions). Day campers strengthen their creativity in process-oriented activities in arts disciplines such as creative drama, music, creative movement and visual arts. Classes for particular age groups are limited, so early registration is a good idea. Scholarships are available through school art teachers.

Eats

Almond Tree Cafe & Ice Cream Parlor
208 Middle St., New Bern
(252) 637-9307

Almond Tree Cafe & Ice Cream Parlor (used to be Marina Sweets) has long been an Insider kids' favorite because of its baked goods and ice cream. Milk shakes, banana splits and sundaes are cool treats you must try during a busy expedition in New Bern. Parents will appreciate the opportunity to introduce their children to the old-fashioned atmosphere of an honest-to-goodness ice cream shop.

Bear City Fudge Company
244 Craven St., New Bern
(252) 670-8675

What better way to treat the kids — and yourself — than with a delicious piece of homemade fudge? Bear City Fudge Company offers at least 25 flavors. Some days there are more to enjoy. Sample tastes are offered to help you decide between the classic flavors and the more exotic ones. Platters, special orders and other services also are available. While you're waiting for your order, you'll enjoy looking at the many teddy bears on display and the mural that depicts the Craven Street of days gone by. Bear City Fudge Company is open Monday through Saturday.

Surf fishing is a popular pastime on the Outer Banks.

photo: Peter Doran

327

The Cow Cafe
319 Middle St., New Bern
(910) 672-9269

The Cow Cafe is not only for the young but also the young at heart. New Bern's only "Four Hoof" restaurant is in the historic downtown area. Its delicious menu features such delights as the Save-A-Cow barbecue baskets, the Grazin' Garden Salad, El Moo's Chili and other favorites among the sandwiches, soups and salads offered. Of course, you'll want to save some room for gourmoo popcorn, ice cream and tasty milk shakes. The cow boutique features plenty of cow-inspired items, where you can find the perfect gift for all ages that says "I love moo." The Cow Cafe is open Monday through Saturday for lunch and dinner.

Farms

A Day at the Farm
183 Woodruff McCoy Rd., Cove City
(252) 514-9494

For an "udderly" good time, visit A Day at the Farm, located 20 minutes west of New Bern off U.S. Highway 70. A Day at the Farm, a former dairy that operated from 1947 to 1993, offers kids a chance to see an old-time dairy farm and explore old barns, an old kitchen and other outbuildings dating back to 1896. One of the most popular events is the Easter Egg Hunt. Other group activities may include butter-making the old-fashioned way. The Pack House is a great place for a sleepover in the loft or a special party event. A Day at the Farm also sponsors a week-long summer camp that gives young people (and the young at heart) an idea of the fun and chores of farm life. Prices vary depending on activity; call ahead for more information and for an appointment or for

 The Festival of Fun, hosted every April by the New Bern Recreation and Parks Department, features amusement rides, games, clowns, hands-on educational activities, exhibits and other activities for children and families.

information about special events. Gifts and treats are available in the ice cream parlor and gift shop.

Kirkman's Farm and Petting Zoo
5255 N.C. Hwy. 55 W, Cove City
(252) 638-1847

A family-run operation located about 20 minutes west of New Bern, Kirkman's Farm is a real working farm where visitors can see many of the day-to-day activities that go along with growing crops such as corn, wheat, rye, oats, hay and pumpkins. In addition to seeing the farming activities, children will enjoy the opportunity to feed and pet the farm's many barnyard buddies, including goats, potbelly pigs, rabbits, ponies, cows, a miniature donkey, ostriches, an emu, a rhea and more. In season, the farm offers hayrides and a pumpkin patch. At Christmas, hayrides tour the farm's lights and decorations. School groups and Scouts are welcome. Anytime you plan to visit, be sure to call ahead for an appointment.

Learning

Build and Grow Program
Lowe's, 150 Lowe's Blvd., New Bern
(252) 638-6777

Build and Grow is a free program held once a month for children grades 2 through 5. Lowe's provides all materials and supplies, and each child is given his or her own work apron and safety goggles. As children complete a project, they are awarded a certificate, as well as a patch for their apron. A parent must accompany the child throughout the activity. A word to the wise: Pre-registration is absolutely required at the Customer Service Desk as Lowe's only receives enough kits for the number of children who are pre-registered.

New Bern Historical Society
512 Pollock St., New Bern
(252) 638-8558, (800) 849-7316

Every spring, the New Bern Historical Society hosts a Civil War Adventure Day for boys and girls at the location of the Battle of New Bern, which took place in 1862. This event brings history to life in an encampment-style environment that features authentic drills, musket-shooting demonstrations and more. While these programs are fee-based, members of the historical society receive a discount.

New Bern-Craven County Public Library
400 Johnson St., New Bern
(252) 638-7815

The children's library at the New Bern-Craven County Public Library is well-organized for toddlers through sixth-graders to enjoy selecting from the collection of books, videotapes and audio cassettes. Stories on CD-ROM are available for use in-house on the department's computers. Help is plentiful. Weekday programs for children include Time Out For Toddlers on Friday at 9:30 AM, featuring stories, songs and finger plays for children ages 3 and younger. Preschool Storysteps for ages 3 to 5 takes place Tuesdays at 9:30 AM, offering stories, puppet plays, music and other fun. The Children's Story Hour is held Thursday at 4 PM for children between the ages of 5 and 10 and involves storytelling, movies and creative activities. The Story Seekers program fosters the imaginations of children ages 10 and older through puppetry and storytelling. (Pre-registration is required for Story Seekers.) The library hosts a number of other special programs throughout the year, including the Summer Reading Book Club.

Tryon Palace Historic Sites & Gardens
610 Pollock St., New Bern
(252) 514-4900, (800) 767-1560

Besides the standard tour (admission fee of $5 for children grades 1 to 12 and free for children kindergarten-age and younger), Tryon Palace offers a number of pint-sized programs designed to foster an interest in history, among them the summer Camp Yesteryear, the Colonial Fife & Drum Corps, and holiday day camps, concerts, films and more. Information on age limitations, registration and fees, where applicable, is available by calling the number above.

Parks

Creekside Park
Craven County, Old Airport Rd., New Bern
(252) 636-6606

Creekside Park is located on 111 acres next to Craven Regional Airport. Developed by the Craven County Parks and Recreation Department, it features 12 athletic fields, perfect for soccer, baseball, softball and football; a large playground where children ages 5 to 12 will enjoy climbing, swinging and sliding; a sand volleyball court; and a quarter-mile paved walking trail. Another fun area is the park's waterfront, which has a fishing dock, playground, nature trail and a gazebo. Restrooms and picnic shelters also are available. Reservations for these facilities can be made by calling the department at the number above; rental fees apply to the picnic shelters and athletic fields.

Fort Totten Park
New Bern Parks and Recreation,
Fort Totten Dr. & Trent Blvd., New Bern
(252) 639-2901

Let your kids burn some energy jumping, climbing, swinging, spinning and sliding in Fort Totten Park's fantastic playground. (Meanwhile, parents can relax on one of the many park benches located beneath shady trees.) The park also features a lighted baseball diamond, public restrooms and a picnic shelter with two grills and street-side parking. It is located close to New Bern's downtown historic district.

Kidsville Playground
New Bern Parks and Recreation,
1225 Pine Tree Dr., New Bern
(252) 639-2912

Kidsville, a beautifully planned active and interactive fort-like play environment that captivates both children and adults, is located next to the West New Bern Recreation Center on Pine Tree Drive near the intersection of U.S. Highway 70 and N.C. Highway 17. With or without a kid, Kidsville

See this entire guide plus additional content online at insiderinfo.us

merits a visit. Whether you choose to slide, swing, climb, clamber or scamper through its interesting twists and turns, Kidsville will wow you and is the perfect place for a sunny afternoon picnic. Groups of 15 or more must make reservations by calling ahead.

Recreation

Craven County 4-H
300 Industrial Dr., New Bern
(252) 633-1477

4-H is a volunteer-based, skill-building organization for children and teens ages 5 to 19. Children participate in 4-H community clubs, after-school workshops, field trips and other special events and hands-on activities taking place on weekends, evenings and school holidays. There are currently five active 4-H clubs in Craven County, and children participate each year in 4-H sponsored educational activities. These activities focus on a wide range of interests, including camping, cooking, horses, the environment, computers, sports, recycling, wildlife and more.

Craven County Recreation and Parks Department
406 Craven St., New Bern
(252) 636-6606

The Craven County Parks and Recreation Department offers programs and classes for preschool and school-age kids throughout the school year and in summer day-camp programs. Karate is instructed year round for ages 3 and older. Tennis lessons, baton twirling, soccer, Pop Warner football and basketball for girls and boys are among the sports activities organized and supervised seasonally.

New Bern kids enjoy being close to the Crystal Coast beaches — they're less than an hour away.

photo: Molly Harrison

New Bern Gymnastics
260 Kale Rd., New Bern
(252) 259-5734

New Bern Gymnastics offers classes for ages 18 months through 16 years. Classes range from beginner to advanced gymnastics and tumbling. NBG offers a competitive Junior Team (Level 2/3) and an upper level team (Level 4 and up). Located in a brand-new, 10,000-square-foot facility, NBG has an abundance of new and kid-friendly equipment along with an experienced and certified staff.

New Bern Parks and Recreation Department
248 Craven St., New Bern
(252) 639-2901

The New Bern Parks and Recreation Department offers a number of children's sports programs throughout the year, including cheerleading, baton twirling, fencing, baseball, soccer, basketball, track and field, karate, tennis, wrestling and football. Recreation centers are located at 901 Chapman Street, (252) 639-2919, and 1225 Pine Tree Drive, (252) 639-2912. For teens the department hosts Young Adults Active in the Community (YAAC), a teen council that gives local teens a place to share ideas and bring new recreational opportunities to town. Scheduled events and clubs such as CHOICES, Saturday Night Madness and Teen Night also give local teens opportunities to socialize and share their thoughts and opinions. In addition to its programs and clubs throughout the year, the department also offers the BEAR After School Program for ages 6 to 14 during the school year and the Bern Bear Bunch Day Camp during the summer. Offered 9 AM to 4 PM weekdays for three two-week sessions, the Bern Bear Bunch Day Camp is open to children ages 6 to 12. Residents living within the city limits are allowed to register two weeks earlier than everyone else. Campers participate in games, contests, arts and crafts, swimming, water games, movies, sports, field trips, cookouts and much more.

Strike Zone Family Fun Center
3550 Dr. M. L. King Jr. Blvd., New Bern
(252) 637-6033

Strike Zone Family Fun Center offers hours of entertainment for kids and their parents. It offers 24 bowling lanes, a full-service snack bar and a fantastic arcade. Family Special Mondays through Wednesdays features a game of bowling, a large pizza, a pitcher of soft drink and 16 arcade tokens for $30 for up to four people. Strike Zone is the perfect place to host a birthday party. Call to schedule your party. See our New Bern Parks and Recreation chapter for more information about Strike Zone.

Swing Zone
4605 U.S. Hwy. 70 E, New Bern
(252) 634-GAME

This entertainment complex offers plenty of family fun for all ages. The 18-hole miniature golf course includes sand traps, rough turf and plenty of water among its many challenges that will keep your game interesting. The park also features four batting cages and the area's only paintball course. Paintball participants must buy their paintballs from Swing Zone, which offers equipment rentals. Indoors, Swing Zone boasts the largest arcade in Craven County with more than 25 action and redemption games, a snack bar featuring freshly baked pizza and cookies, plus ice cream and that hometown favorite, Pepsi. Swing Zone can book parties for seven to 50 people and can customize packages to include indoor and outdoor activities. Season passes and re-loadable gift cards also are available.

Twin Rivers YMCA
100 YMCA Ln., New Bern
(252) 638-8799

The YMCA's Aquatic Center features lots of room for kids to swim and play and includes water slides, a splash park and a zero-entry section. To keep all play safe, the YMCA also specializes in swimming instruction ranging from beginning lessons to Water Safety Instructor certification. With the emphasis on fair play, participation and fun, the YMCA offers year-round sports activities for all age groups in gymnastics and competitive swimming, as well as seasonal basketball, flag football and more. Summer day-camp programs offer a terrific range of sports activities for all age groups. The Youth Center for ages 6 to 18 years provides supervised gaming such as bumper pool and table tennis. Child-care services are available for parents using the YMCA facilities.

Shopping

Snap Dragon Way Cool Toys
214 Middle St., New Bern
(252) 514-6770

If you have a child with you while you're shopping the historic downtown district, reward yourselves with a play break at Snapdragon Way Cool Toys, which has the coolest in specialty toys. Featuring toys for children ages newborn and older, Snapdragon offers an inviting selection of crafts, scientific and magic kits, as well as dolls, plush toys, books, Playmobil sets, action figures and a variety of just fun stuff. This is a fascinating store to explore and a must-stop on any downtown excursion. Snapdragon is open Monday through Thursday 10 AM until 5 PM; Friday 10 AM until 8 PM; Saturdays 10 AM until 5 PM, and Sunday noon until 4 PM.

NEW BERN
WEDDING
PLANNING

Getting married is a monumental event, and the idea is to make it as special as possible. From historic churches to stately homes, lovely waterfront locales to contemporary settings, New Bern offers a number of exciting locations to make your wedding day an extraordinary one. In this chapter, we highlight just a few of the locations and services available in the New Bern area, including information on where and how to obtain the marriage license.

Wedding Show

New Bern Bridal Expo
New Bern Riverfront Convention Center,
New Bern
(252) 638-8101

Those planning a wedding in the New Bern area will want to mark their calendars for this show, held annually on the last weekend in January. The expo highlights services available locally, including catering, photography, musicians and more.

It also includes a fashion show and prize drawings. Admission is $5.

Marriage Licenses

North Carolina requires that all couples get a marriage license before the marriage takes place. Licenses are available at any Register of Deeds office in North Carolina. The Craven County Register of Deeds office is located at 226 Pollock Street, (252) 636-6617.

To obtain a marriage license, those age 21 and older need to come in together and bring their driver's licenses, Social Security cards and $50 in cash; those 18 and 19 years of age also need to bring along certified copies of their birth certificates. (Those 17 and younger should call the registrar's office for more information about other requirements they need to meet.) If you have been divorced within six months, bring your divorce papers.

The Register of Deeds office issues marriage licenses Monday through Friday between 8 AM and 4 PM. The license is

valid for 60 days in any county in North Carolina. After the wedding, certified copies of the marriage certificate are available from the Register of Deeds for $10 each.

In North Carolina, you can be married by a magistrate — the Magistrate's Office is located in the Craven County Law Enforcement Center at 411 Craven Street, (252) 639-9015, next door to the courthouse. You'll need to bring two witnesses (at least 18 years of age), your marriage license and $20 in cash for state fees; otherwise, the magistrate typically does not charge anything for performing the ceremony, although tipping is permitted. The Magistrate's Office is open 24 hours a day, seven days a week (but keep in mind that jail visitation takes place between 11 AM and 4 PM on Saturdays and Sundays, so the lobby of the office can get crowded).

The Register of Deeds office, (252) 745-4421, in neighboring Pamlico County has a few different requirements. Located on the first floor in the courthouse on N.C. Highway 55 in Bayboro, the office requires that couples who have ever been divorced at any time should bring in a copy of their divorce decrees. Marriage licenses are issued Monday through Friday from 8 AM to 4 PM; the bride and groom will both need to be present in order for the license, which costs $50 in cash, to be issued. Those 18 and older should bring along their driver's licenses and Social Security cards, although the Pamlico County office allows the use of a W-2 or tax return in lieu of a Social Security card. (Those 17 and younger should call for more information.) The license is valid for 60 days. After the marriage, the couple can pick up one free certified copy of the marriage certificate; copies after the first one are $10 each. The Magistrate's Office, (252) 745-6010, also is located in the courthouse.

Wedding and Reception Locations

New Bern has many beautiful old churches that provide exceptional locations for your wedding. A list of churches is available in our New Bern Worship chap-

ter. You will need to call for more information as each church has its own policies and fees concerning weddings. Other sites are listed below.

Attmore-Oliver House
512 Pollock St., New Bern
(252) 638-8558

Looking for a beautiful and historic location for your wedding? The 1790 Attmore-Oliver House is available for special occasions, and its size allows for large weddings and receptions (and for parties and business functions as well). Call the New Bern Historical Society at the number above for fees and other information.

Hilton New Bern Riverfront
100 Middle St., New Bern
(252) 638-3585

Experience the wedding of your dreams at The Hilton New Bern Riverfront, newly renovated and located in historic downtown on the scenic Trent River. The experienced staff will ensure that every detail of your special day is handled with creativity and ease. The flexible banquet space and beautiful outdoor area plays a perfect host to ceremonies, receptions, luncheons and dinners. Contact the catering coordinator today to let them help you plan your dream.

Inns of New Bern
Downtown New Bern, New Bern

Downtown New Bern's seven bed-and-breakfast inns offer unique settings for small weddings, bridal showers, honeymoons and overnight accommodations for wedding guests. See our New Bern Bed and Breakfasts chapter for names and complete descriptions of the inns.

New Bern Riverfront Convention Center
203 S. Front St., New Bern
(252) 637-1551

With its 12,000 square feet in the Colonial Capital Ballroom downtown, along with smaller spaces upstairs in the Tryon Rooms, Berne Room and Craven Boardroom, and a beautiful waterfront veranda, the New Bern Riverfront Convention Center has the flexibility to host groups from 50 to 1,350. Its proximity to three hotels and numerous bed-and-breakfast inns downtown makes it a good location for weddings and reunions with a number of out-of-town guests. The center also maintains a preferred caterers list, making the hunt for that service a bit less stressful.

Accommodations

See our New Bern Hotels and Motels and New Bern Bed and Breakfast Inns chapters for listings of hotels and bed and breakfast inns in the area.

The Sparrow House
2814 Old Cherry Point Rd., New Bern
(252) 637-3574

Abilena is a 5-acre riverfront plantation and mansion on the Neuse River in New Bern. The 5,000-square-foot home was built in 1927 and is the area's only riverfront mansion rented for weddings, receptions, vacations, retreats and events. Abilena awaits your arrival for anything from a family reunion to an intimate reception for 30 to a wedding party of 250 people.

A wedding photographer for seven years, John Williams, and his wife, Mary Ann, purchased this magnificent property and have opened the house and grounds to allow you to have the wedding of your dreams. This is the ultimate location … secluded, yet only five minutes from town. There are several acres for parking and events, yet at its core Abilena is still a charming home that will create lasting memories from the moment you drive down the tree-covered lane.

The amenities include a 20-by-40-foot in-ground private pool and a Jacuzzi for eight persons complete with fireplace and a river view. Inside the home, there is a full kitchen with washer and dryer, coffeemaker, refrigerator, stove, dishes and silverware, as well as a formal dining room. Five comfortable queen-size beds and two sleeper sofas will sleep 14 people, with the availability of two air mattresses for children and a private nursery off one

of the bedrooms with a crib and rocking chair. Cable TV/VCR/DVD with access to a movie library of more than 100 titles and wireless high-speed Internet are available. A stainless steel gas grill is accessible for a family cookout or a romantic steak dinner. There is off-street parking for up to 75 cars. A two-person kayak and a 14-foot Hobie Cat sailboat are included with the house and may be used free of charge. Jet Skis are available for rent as well as a four-wheeler (riders must be 16 years of age).

Wedding Planners and Officiants

Bridal By The Sea
263 Howard Blvd., Newport
(252) 259-4992
www.bridalbythesea.com

Rachel Munro is passionate about helping brides and grooms make their wedding day an unforgettable occasion and cherished memory. Rachel uses her 11 years of experience along with full hands-on service to work with couples and wedding parties throughout the planning process to ensure that details flow smoothly. She has worked with budgets of all sizes, ranging from backyard barbecues to swanky gala affairs with celebrity guest lists, and she devotes the same amount of enthusiasm and professionalism to each and every one. Rachel offers a number of wedding packages, ranging from simple consultations and contract reviews to a complete coordination package that arranges all the details of the big day. Rachel not only works with vendors of the wedding couple's choice but also can recommend others as needed. She is the exclusive, full-service coordinator for China Grove Plantation, a lovely wedding venue in Pamlico County on the banks of the Neuse River. Bridal-by-the-Sea offers a wonderful bridal showcase at the Maritime Museum and on the historical grounds in Beaufort to benefit local non-profit organizations. Certified by the Association for

Certified Professional Wedding Consultants, Rachel offers a complimentary initial consultation. Insiders find her pleasant to work with as well as ardent and professional about planning the perfect wedding.

Occasions to Celebrate
2500 Trent Rd., Ste. 30, New Bern
(252) 637-9100, (866) 576-9100

The event planning professionals at Occasions to Celebrate can turn your vision of a beautiful wedding into a reality. With more than 20 years of experience, Occasions to Celebrate can take the stress off you and handle everything from set up to clean up. They specialize in exceptional balloon and floral arrangements and will work with your caterer, facility and entertainment to ensure that your wedding and reception run as smoothly as possible. Occasions to Celebrate also offers tuxedo and equipment rentals and carries a selection of beautiful invitations. Call for a free consultation.

Reverend Bonnie Compton
125 Canebrake Dr., New Bern
(252) 638-2358

Rev. Bonnie is available to make your wedding-day experience special by creating a ceremony that reflects the caring you feel in your hearts for each other. If you wish to include family, children, pets,

The coast is a favorite location for destination weddings.

photo: Carolyn Temple

music, special readings or religious traditions, Reverend Bonnie will be pleased to accommodate you. You can write your own vows or choose from her selection. Whether your wedding is a simple elopement or an elaborate formal affair, Rev. Bonnie enjoys working with each couple to create a special and unique ceremony for their special day in New Bern, Kinston, Emerald Isle, Jacksonville, Greenville, Oriental, the Crystal Coast and surrounding areas. There are many options available that can be included in your ceremony to personalize it, including unity candles, sand ceremonies, blessing for an unborn child, blessing of the hands, rose ceremony and poetry. She also performs renewal of vows ceremonies as well as life commitment ceremonies. Fees for the service depend on the location of the wedding, the services provided and the distance traveled. A signed contract and up-front payment are required to reserve your wedding date and to get started on writing your ceremony. You can meet her in person, by telephone or do everything by e-mail.

Florists

Greenleaf Park Florist
4090 Dr. M. L. King Jr. Blvd., New Bern
(252) 638-5156

The staff at Greenleaf Park Florist is ready to sit down with everyone involved with planning the wedding to answer questions and provide other guidance on the important decisions of flowers. Greenleaf, which prefers planning to take place at least three months prior to the wedding, can deliver fresh and silk flowers in beautiful arrangements to the wedding site, as well as provide flowers for the wedding party, parents, grandparents and other important guests.

Wiley's Flowers & Gifts
2100 Trent Blvd., New Bern
(252) 637-4133

This full-service florist is well-known in New Bern for providing distinctive and beautiful floral arrangements, silk or live, for every occasion. From the wedding to the reception, Wiley's can provide flowers,

bouquets, corsages and boutonnieres for the wedding party. They also provide wedding equipment such as candelabra. Delivery and set-up services are available. Wiley's prefers to have at least two months' notice, if not more, depending on the size of the wedding and the reception. Call for a consultation.

Catering and Cakes

A Catered Affair Cafe Catering
3402-B Trent Rd., New Bern
(252) 637-7331

Owner Stacia Harris-Reed and her crew can add a special touch to your bridal shower, bridesmaids' luncheon, rehearsal dinner and reception with the same marvelous and delicious food that has made her restaurant such a favorite in New Bern. A Catered Affair Catering is a preferred caterer for the New Bern Riverfront Convention Center, and the restaurant's beautifully decorated dining room also is available to rent for special occasions.

The Chelsea Restaurant
335 Middle St., New Bern
(252) 637-5469

The Chelsea can bring the fusion cuisine that New Bernians love so much to your rehearsal dinner and reception. The Chelsea is able to provide catering services for any venue in the area. Housed in Pepsi inventor Caleb Bradham's second pharmacy, The Chelsea also has wonderful banquet facilities located upstairs (an elevator is available) and can seat up to 120 guests. Call for more information and available booking dates. The Chelsea is a preferred caterer for the New Bern Riverfront Convention Center.

Rental Equipment

Country-Aire Rental
1253 S. Glenburnie Rd., New Bern
(252) 638-6000

Country-Aire Rental offers a complete line of equipment for weddings and receptions, everything from the big items such as archways and candelabra for the ceremony right down to the bud vases for the reception tables. A staff wedding and event coordinator is on hand to assist in handling everything you need for the big day, including decor items, glassware, china, flatware, linens, tents, tables, chairs and more. Pickup and delivery services are available for Country-Aire's diverse rental selection of wedding items in brass, silver, white lattice, wood and wicker. Tuxedo rental also is available.

Photographers and Videographers

A Wedding to Remember Photography
220 E. Front St., New Bern
(252) 349-2441

John Williams has been a professional wedding photographer for more than seven years, shooting more than 450 weddings. The owner of A Wedding to Remember Photography, he employs two other photographers to make sure that all the romantic and wonderful memories of your special day are preserved. Specializing in all types of wedding photographs,from traditional to modern,

the services are affordable, and Williams will arrange a package to suit your needs and budget.

After the wedding, Williams will assign the wedding photo copyrights to the bridal couple. Most wedding photographers retain the copyright, preventing couples from making copies or changes. A Wedding to Remember Photography offers you the opportunity to use your precious keepsakes as you choose. Your photos can be printed, re-printed, e-mailed or enlarged. Along with the photographs that are printed as part of your package, all of the photos taken of your event are placed on full-resolution DVDs, and copies are given to the bridal couple and their parents for safekeeping. Friends and family can view and order these lasting and timeless mementos through A Wedding to Remember's website. Williams is available to shoot weddings, family pictures and portraits anywhere in eastern North Carolina.

Adrian Henson Photography Inc.
2718 Neuse Blvd., New Bern
(252) 638-5607

Adrian Henson redefines the wedding experience with quality photographs

If you have a special request or idea for your wedding, talk to your wedding planner.

photo: Tracy Turpen

of your special day. He creates traditional photos as well as a few "out of the box" shots of your precious wedding memories. You may choose the location or Adrian may suggest one for you — Tryon Palace and the beaches are two popular venues. Albums, coffee-table books and slide shows set to music are available through Adrian's business. Photos are available in color and black and white and may be saved on high-quality paper or canvas. Adrian and his wife, Heather, do their own framing and cutting. Their motto is "Photography is a part of our lives, let us make it part of yours!" Give them a call to discuss times and rates.

Portraits by Angelo
1910 B Glenburnie Rd., New Bern
(252) 633-3755, (866) 801-9493

Portraits by Angelo offers the skilled services of husband and wife photography team John and Brandy Angelo, who specialize in weddings and portraiture. Both John and Brandy are members of the Professional Photographers of North Carolina, an organization whose members are willing to uphold a strict code of ethics in behavior and quality of work. As your wedding photographers, John and Brandy will tell your unique story through the images they create without ever being intrusive. Wedding images are posted online so the couple can choose their memories together. Portraits by Angelo offers a choice of coffee-table–style books to preserve the images of your day. The Angelos specialize in location photography — downtown, at the beach, Fort Macon or Tryon Palace and numerous other locations. They also offer custom studio portraits.

Formal Wear

The Intimate Bridal and Formal Wear
230 Middle St., New Bern
(252) 638-1220

Now with two great locations (the other is in Morehead City), you'll see why brides-to-be consider The Intimate eastern North Carolina's premier bridal shop. The Intimate features the latest styles, accessories and shoes for brides, with gown sizes ranging from 2 to 30. Come shop the selection of exclusive brand names, including 2Be Bridal, Jasmine, Venus Bridal, Private Label by G, Maggie Sottero and others. The shop also carries a selection of fashions and dye-able shoes and accessories for the bridal party and the mother of the bride and groom, and it offers tuxedo rentals and sales as well. You'll also enjoy shopping The Intimate's selection of cocktail dresses and prom apparel for those other special occasions.

Tuxedos Too
4167 Dr. M. L. King Jr. Blvd., New Bern
(252) 633-5292
www.webebridal.com

Tuxedos Too offers a huge selection of designer styles, including Calvin Klein, After Six, FUBU, Perry Ellis, Ralph Lauren and Ecko. There is a wide variety of vests, colors, accessories and shoe styles perfect for a wedding, prom, quinceanera, cruise or upcoming special occasion. Tuxedos Too has the perfect tuxedo for you and promises that you'll look your best at any formal occasion. Tuxedos Too has free consultations and free measuring.

The Wedding Shop
4163-4165 M. L. King Jr. Blvd., New Bern
(252) 514-0446
www.webebridal.com

The Wedding Shop is New Bern's newest bridal and prom store, located conveniently on U.S .17 South, 3 miles south from U.S. 70 and about 3/4-mile from New Bern High School. Claudia and her friendly staff, with 15 years of experience, will help you select a dress that embodies romance on your wedding day. They carry bridal gowns, mother's dresses, bridesmaids and flower girl dresses, prom gowns, tiaras, veils, shoes and accessories. There's no appointment necessary to try on bridal and bridesmaid gowns by B2, Belsoie, Casablanca, Dessy, Eden, Emerald Bridal, Ella Rosa, Moonlight, Jordan and Raylia Designs, just to mention a few. Check out their fantastic prices and take advantage of their Bridal Special. Details are posted on the website. The shop does alterations and will customize gowns. Need a tuxedo? Tuxedos Too is right next door.

Jewelry, Gifts and Bridal Registry

Carolina Creations
317-A Pollock St., New Bern
(252) 633-4369

For the bride and groom who might already have an established household, a distinctive piece of art from Carolina Creations will make a memorable and appreciated wedding gift. Whether it be a work by resident potter Michael Francoeur, a beautiful painting or pen-and-ink drawing by resident artist Janet Francoeur, or artwork by other local artists, Carolina Creations always has something new and unique to offer. Brides may indicate their preferences by using Carolina Creations' bridal registry service both in the gallery and online for out-of-town guests.

Hearne's Jewelers
1331 McCarthy Blvd., New Bern
(252) 637-2784

Founded in 1972 by Mickey Hearne and now run by his son Mike, Hearne's combines courtesy with integrity. It has one of the area's largest and best selections of loose diamonds, ready to mount in exquisite rings, earrings, necklaces and bracelets. Brides and grooms also will want to check out the selection of Benchmark rings, available in gold and platinum with distinctive designs and diamonds. Hearne's offers the stackable rings by Hidalgo, which offer couples the opportunity to create one-of-a-kind rings in gold and platinum with diamonds, precious stones and enamel.

Treasures on the Trent
309 Middle St., New Bern
(252) 637-7900

Treasures on the Trent is one of Middle Street's more popular gift shops. Shop here for a wonderful selection of gifts, including leather full-size and travel-size jewelry boxes, desk accessories, clocks and beautifully crafted game sets by Wolf Designs, and men's fashion products such as grooming sets, valet trays, cuff links and more. You'll also find Peggy Karr glass, Caswell-Massey bath and body products, Baldash crystal and many other distinctive gifts for the bride, the groom and their new home. Treasures on the Trent also offers a selection of wedding invitations, and the Imprintables line of invitations, which are perfect for bridal showers, bridesmaid luncheons, rehearsal dinners and other wedding occasions.

Invitations and Supplies

Party Suppliers
2648 Dr. M L. King Jr. Blvd., New Bern
(252) 637-7722

Party Suppliers carries a full aisle of wedding supplies, including cake toppers, personalized albums and guest books, garters, printed napkins, toasting glasses, unity candles and more. Its aisle of plastic and paper table settings, napkins, serving pieces and more will ensure that you can find the wedding supplies you need in the colors of your choice. Helium tank rentals and balloons of all colors are available for those who plan to use balloons as part of the celebration. Party Suppliers also offers custom-made banners, a complete line of printable papers (which can be customized on the spot with your message or invitation) and beautiful custom invitations discounted 30 percent off the manufacturer's list price.

Treasures on the Trent
309 Middle St., New Bern
(252) 637-7900

Treasures on the Trent offers a selection of wedding invitations, including the Imprintables line of invitations, which are perfect for bridal showers, bridesmaid luncheons, rehearsal dinners and other wedding occasions.

NEW BERN
DAY SPAS
AND SALONS

Looking your best is an important part of feeling your best. New Bern is fortunate to have some very creative talent available to help you achieve both of these ideals. From the top of your head to the tip of your toes, you can maximize your looks through skin-care products, tanning techniques, the latest hairstyles, manicures and pedicures offered at salons and spas in New Bern. And, of course, some businesses offer the ultimate in relaxation — therapeutic massage. While New Bern has a plethora of beauty-related businesses, Insiders recommend these to help you get started.

Advanced Attractions Salon
204 Craven St., New Bern
(252) 638-6191

Advanced Attractions Salon, located in New Bern's historic downtown, features a full range of services. Its stylists, who train extensively each year to keep up with the latest skills, offer shampoos, cuts, styles and permanent waves and specialize in highlighting and color services. Facials, manicures and pedicures are also available. Advanced Attractions carries a full line of Aveda and Redkin hair-care products. Services are available either by appointment or on a walk-in basis.

Coastal Cuts Tanning & Day Spa
3336 Wellons Blvd., New Bern
(252) 637-9295

The stylists at Coastal Cuts Tanning & Day Spa can offer you a great shampoo, cut and style, even new color or a permanent wave if you'd like to make a major change. But they also go the extra step. You can get longer or straighter hair with Great Length hair extensions and the Bio-ionic hair-straightening system. The salon also can wax away unwanted facial hair and help you have your best tan ever, via the tanning bed or spray tanning. Coastal

Cuts Tanning & Day Spa has a nurse on staff who can use micro-dermabrasion to exfoliate your face, giving your skin a healthy glow. For hair services, the salon provides service either by appointment or on a walk-in basis; tanning and micro-dermabrasion are available by appointment only. Hair-care products, including Nexxus, Redkin and the Coastal Cuts Tanning & Day Spa line also are available. This unisex salon is open Monday through Saturday.

The Comfort Zone Massage & Day Spa
714 Pollock St., New Bern
(252) 638-1616

If you are working too hard and need to relax, The Comfort Zone can help. With appointments available Tuesdays through Saturdays, The Comfort Zone specializes in aromatherapy massages, hot stone massages, facial rejuvenation (a non-surgical facelift) and hand massages. Ask about Hypnossage, the ultimate in comfort and relaxation. Spa products and gift certificates are available.

Dun'Artie Salon & Day Spa
1706-C U.S. Hwy. 70 E, New Bern
(252) 637-5507

Prepare to be pampered at Dun'Artie Day Spa, where "your robe and slippers are waiting." Massage therapy and body treatments are designed to relieve muscle tension and leave you feeling refreshed and renewed. Facials and chemical facials are customized to your skin type and condition. Also available are hair-care services, including coloring and permanent wave styling, plus nail services and waxing. Dun'Artie features several special spa packages, such as the Cinderella's Ball for ages 15 and younger, Mommy & Me prenatal massage and bridal party packages. Gentlemen's spa services include massage, body and face treatments, manicures and pedicures, and a barber is on staff to provide haircuts, beard trims, shaves and more. Although Dun'Artie accepts walk-ins, appointments are highly recommended. Dun'Artie is open Tuesday through Saturday.

Fantastic Sam's
1505 S. Glenburnie Rd., New Bern
(252) 636-1144

Locally owned, this Fantastic Sam's franchise features salon-quality cuts and styles for adults and children at affordable prices. Those opting for a new look will benefit from texturizing, coloring and highlighting services. Hair conditioning, beard and mustache trimming, facial waxing and hair straightening are but a few of the many services available. The salon carries a great selection of hair-care products, including Nexxus, Bedhead and the Fantastic Sam's brand. Walk-ins are always welcome at Fantastic Sam's, which is open Monday through Saturday.

Leigh & Co. Hair Salon
1503-D S. Glenburnie Rd., New Bern
(252) 635-9255

Located near Market Place Shopping Center, Leigh & Co. is more than your standard beauty salon. Leigh Broome and her stylists keep up with education and training to offer women, men and children the latest in progressive cuts, styles, permanent waves, foiling techniques, hair conditioning and more. Leigh & Co. also offers its customers spa manicures and pedicures. Another great service is the Princess Party for little girls, where up to 10 divas-in-training are pampered with hair updos and manicures. In business since 2000, Leigh & Co. sees clients by appointment or on a walk-in basis Tuesday through Saturday.

Merle Norman Cosmetic & Nail Salon
3601 Trent Rd. #8, New Bern
(252) 638-3665

Discover the beauty in you with the aid of Merle Norman cosmetics and accessories. At "The Place for the Beautiful Face,"

you'll enjoy free makeovers, skin-care lessons, five-minute hydrating facials, waxing, manicures, pedicures and nail enhancements. You can even try out up to 24 new hairstyles via the shop's Styles on Video. Merle Norman offers the area's largest selection of magnifying mirrors and a small gift section that includes cosmetic bags and candles. Merle Norman is open every day but Sunday. It's located in the Village Square shopping complex.

Supercuts
2027 Glenburnie Rd., New Bern
(252) 672-5611

If you'd like a hip hairstyle at an affordable price, Supercuts is just the place for you. Insiders really like Supercuts because of their call-ahead service for walk-in customers. You simply call in and the staff will add your name to its waiting list and give you an idea of how long the wait will be, usually between 15 to 45 minutes. All you have to do is show up, hop in the stylist's chair and enjoy Supercuts' many services, including cutting, styling, coloring and more. Supercuts also offers a wide selection of high-quality hair products. The salon, located in the Harris Teeter shopping plaza, is open every day.

Totally Tan & More
2704 Neuse Blvd., New Bern
(252) 635-1189

In business for more than 12 years, Totally Tan & More uses Wolff Tanning Systems to help you safely achieve that summery golden glow. In addition to tanning beds, the full-service salon also features spray-on tanning via a self-contained unit. Hair, nail and massage services are available as well. The business, a state training facility for other salons, also offers tanning bed sales and service. Totally Tan & More accepts appointments Monday through Saturday during the summer season, but is closed weekends during the winter. Try the new Ultra-Bronze high-pressure tanning system that maintains your tan every two weeks.

NEW BERN
ARTS

For the first three decades of the twentieth century, New Bern was known as the "Athens of North Carolina" because of its many artistic and educational endeavors. While the Great Depression put a halt to much of the activity, a rebirth occurred in the 1970s, and today locals enjoy performances and exhibits from an ever-increasing number of local and touring artists.

The Craven Arts Council and Gallery, located in the Bank of the Arts on Middle Street, supports and features all art disciplines and sponsors the popular New Bern Sunday Jazz Showcase and many other visual and performing arts events throughout the year. In addition, the New Bern-Craven County Public Library at the corner of Johnson and Middle Streets selects an artist of the month and displays his or her work in its attractive building.

The evidence that the arts are treasured in New Bern is most apparent on a walk through the city's historic downtown. Galleries are proliferating in renovated buildings, and murals on the walls of public buildings reflect the work of varied artists interpreting New Bern's history.

New Bern is also home to active community theater groups, the New Bern Civic Theatre and the RiverTowne Repertory Players, which stage and sponsor a number of productions annually. The Carolinian Shakespeare Festival puts on impressive performances for three weekends in August. The Coastal Carolina Chamber Music Festival features world-class musicians for a two-week appearance in the fall, and numerous musical groups and dancers, including historical dancers, stage other performances throughout the year. Vocal musicians will not be left out. Several communities and Craven Community College have musical groups featuring excellent singers who perform concerts during the year. There is also a community band

consisting of music instructors, students and the best and brightest citizens of New Bern and surrounding communities who play because they love the music.

In this chapter we describe our arts organizations. If a group doesn't have a street address or regular office, a phone number is given, sometimes in addition to a contact name.

Visual Arts

The Accidental Artist
220 Craven St., New Bern
(252) 634-3411

At this studio, you can showcase your creativity by painting your own pottery, which The Accidental Artist will then fire for you to complete your one-of-a-kind masterpiece. Come relax in the informal atmosphere and give your artistic impulses free reign. You can even book studio space for birthday parties, club meetings and other special occasions. The Accidental Artist is open daily but may be closed on Sundays in the winter; call for hours.

American Needlepoint Guild, Crystal Coast Chapter
New Bern
(252) 636-0065

The Crystal Coast Chapter of the American Needlepoint Guild is an educational, nonprofit organization dedicated to the art of needlepoint. Experienced and beginning stitchers are invited to attend

Local artist Doug Alvord painted the murals in the New Bern Riverfront Convention Center. The four murals depict four essential eastern North Carolina elements: fishing, farming, forestry and faith.

the group's meetings, held at 10 AM the first Monday of each month at the West New Bern Recreation Center on Pinetree Drive. Programs consist of stitching projects, instruction and demonstrations as well as fellowship.

Art & Materials
219 Middle St., New Bern
(252) 514-2787

Art & Materials sells paints, brushes, how-to books and other supplies for those who work in oils, acrylics, pastels and watercolors as well as paper and pottery. The business, owned by the Mathiot family, features the works of local artists. They schedule a variety of workshops and classes for adults and children who want to explore their artistic talents. There is a complete pottery studio offering pottery classes. The shop also sponsors summer camps, after-school art lessons and special classes for home-school students. The Flying Cat Bead Shop is located inside Art & Materials for those interested in creating their own distinctive jewelry. Gallery Arts, a giclee printing gallery, is found here, as is Asian Artifacts for the Art of Living, featuring art items, paintings and cards with an Oriental flair.

Coastal Photo Club
New Bern

The Coastal Photo Club meets the third Saturday at 9:30 AM every month at Centenary United Methodist Church. The club is open to people of all ages and skill levels who are interested in photography. In-club photo competitions, field trips, photography-related lectures and other activities provide club members with opportunities to share knowledge and learn new skills. Club dues are $20 a year for single members and $30 for family.

Craven Arts Council and Gallery / Bank of the Arts
317 Middle St., New Bern
(252) 638-2577

Besides nurturing local artists, this organization provides exhibition space for local, regional and national artists in the Bank of the Arts, a reclaimed 1911 bank building that also houses the arts council's administrative offices. The large, open main gallery, open Tuesday through Saturday 10 AM to 6 PM, is the staging area for a variety of exhibits. Popular traveling exhibits are often featured, and overall works include a variety of media, ranging from traditional to contemporary. The Pottery Vault and Gift Shop, the council's gallery shop, features the work of Carolina artists and is open year-round. Craven Arts Council is a membership organization with various sponsorship levels available. Members are entitled to ticket discounts and receive a monthly newsletter, *The Luminary*, that announces upcoming arts events. The Bank of the Arts facility is available for rental for your party or meeting. Call the Craven Arts Council and Gallery for more information.

Red Willow's Gift Shoppe and Art Gallery
130 West Jones Street, Trenton
(252) 448-1138

Red Willow's Gallery — "The Arts" Downtown Gallery — adjoins the gift shop with watercolors, oils and photography by local artists. An artist works in house on certain days of the week; call to inquire about the schedule. The gallery is open Monday through Saturday from 9 AM to 7 PM.

Theater

Carolinian Shakespeare Festival
New Bern
(800) 346-2770

Carolinian Shakespeare Festival (CSF) performances are presented the first three weekends of August at the New Bern Civic Theatre in downtown New Bern. This professional theater company has staged some of the Bard's most well-known works, including *Romeo and Juliet*, *A Midsummer Night's Dream*, *Hamlet* and *Macbeth*. The goal of CSF is to make the classics entertaining and accessible to everyone. Discounts are available for students and seniors. Tickets are sold by phone and at various locations around town, including the Bank of the Arts on Middle Street. Auditions usually take place in March each year for the upcoming season, with rehearsals scheduled for the month of July.

New Bern Civic Theatre
414 Pollock St., New Bern
(252) 633-0567

A nonprofit organization, New Bern Civic Theatre (NBCT) was organized in 1968 to provide community theater for area adults and children. The group's theatrical productions range from serious drama to lively musicals, including original works. NBCT also offers a number of art education opportunities for children, including StageHands, a performing group of the civic theater that annually stages a special production by children for children. Its unique performances are presented simultaneously in sign and spoken language. The theater also hosts a popular two-week Children's Acting Workshop in the summer.

RiverTowne Repertory Players
Sudan Shrine Auditorium,
403 E. Front St., New Bern
(252) 637-2662

This nonprofit community theater group, formed in 2001, is dedicated to encouraging, promoting and practicing the theatrical arts in the community. RiverTowne's performances take place at the Sudan Shrine Auditorium downtown. Membership in the Players is open to anyone 16 years and older with a desire to be involved in the organization's operation, including acting, singing, directing, lighting, producing and more. Annual dues are $15 per person. Tickets are available for productions at the Bank of the Arts Tuesday through Saturday and at the door at the time of performance.

Dance

Baroque Arts Project
724 Pollock St., New Bern
(252) 636-0476

The Baroque Arts Project, under the direction of Paige Whitley-Baugess, combines music and dance in exciting and innovative performances to bring the rich tapestry of the Baroque period to life. The project specializes in the music

and dance of the seventeenth and eighteenth centuries, offering many engaging educational programs in addition to its public performances and tours. Season tickets are available.

Craven Historical Dancers
724 Pollock St., New Bern
(252) 636-0476

This unique dance troupe performs, in costume, eighteenth-century social dances, including reels, country dances, minuets, cotillions and jigs. They entertain at holiday performances, festivals and other events. The group meets periodically and each fall accepts new members. Director Paige Whitley-Bauguess also directs the New Bern Dancing Assembly, a costumed Baroque dance performing group for boys and girls in 4th through 12th grades. Baroque dance classes and workshops are offered at Down East Dance.

Dance Theatre
Performing Arts Studios, Inc.
2107 S. Glenburnie Rd., New Bern
(252) 637-1818

Open since 1990, Dance Theatre Performing Arts Centre, under the direction of Veronica Sabiston, is a training ground for dance students of all ages and skills, from the absolute beginner to the very advanced. Dance Theatre's comprehensive program offers a diversified curriculum, including classical ballet and pointe, lyrical, jazz, hip hop, tap and jumpstart. This dance school also features classes for adults and offers multiple classrooms for personalized attention. The award-winning Dance Theatre offers opportunities for students to participate in regional and national competitions and, on the local level, to take part in mall shows, festivals, parades, telethons and more. The studio conducts a local school performance tour and

---

Looking for a great rainy day outing with children? Try The Accidental Artist at 220 Craven Street. Just buy a piece of pottery and let the kids paint it any way they want, and the shop will fire their finished products for later pick-up.

hosts many performances throughout the year, including its annual Spring Performance in May. Excerpts are aired on local television Channel 10 each summer. Dance Theatre prepares students for auditions each year for the North Carolina School of the Arts (NCSA), American Ballet Theatre (ABT) and Joffrey Ballet. It's also proud to have directed many of its students toward roles in national television, major motion pictures and music videos as well as dance-related presentations for Walt Disney World, Kings Dominion and Busch Gardens.

Down East Dance
2500 Trent Rd., Ste. 4, New Bern
(252) 633-9622

Down East Dance prides itself in educating students of all ages in the art of dance. Classes in ballet, pointe, jazz, hip hop, tap and Baroque are designed to create positive, joyful learning experiences that encompass coordination-building skills, flexibility, strength, technique, correct alignment and creativity. Every other year, the Down East Dance ballet faculty and students stage an impressive performance of *The Nutcracker* with guest artists. Down East Dance also showcases two youth performance groups.

Rivertowne Ballroom
305 Pollock St., New Bern
(252) 637-2003

Want to learn how to swing, cha cha or tango? Maybe the fox trot and the waltz are more your speed. If you've ever had an interest in learning ballroom dancing, this is the place to go. Private and group lessons are offered, and dance students get an opportunity to practice their skills at weekly parties.

Wanda Kay's School of Dance
801 Cardinal Dr., New Bern
(252) 636-2811

Wanda Kay offers tap, jazz and ballet for ages 3 through adult in her specially designed studio. The Wanda Kay Dancers, a group of advanced dance students, perform at fairs and festivals throughout the area, including MUMfest. Wanda Kay's Troupe opens the New Bern Christmas Parade every year.

Music

Coastal Carolina Chamber Music Festival
New Bern
(252) 626-5419

The Coastal Carolina Chamber Music Festival, now in its seventh season, features two fall weekends of beautiful classical music performed by world-class musicians at a variety of locations throughout downtown New Bern. Each year's roster includes talented professionals who perform internationally as soloists and members of the country's finest ensembles, such as the Boston Symphony Orchestra, the Boston Pops and the Metropolitan Opera Orchestra. Festival events include not only musical performances but also interactive and entertaining social events that combine to create an up-close and personal concert experience. Season, individual and mix-and-match ticket options are available.

Craven Community Chorus
New Bern
(252) 638-7357

This large choral group, formed in 1985, performs locally as well as in surrounding counties and out of state. There are no auditions, and membership is open to anyone from 18 to 80 who can carry a tune and enjoys singing. The 60-member group likes to include instrumentalists whenever possible and usually plans its shows around a theme. Past performances have featured Dixieland standards, Old West favorites, Big Band hits and classic 1950s rock 'n' roll in the annual spring and Christmas productions. Weekly practices take place from 6:30 to 8:30 PM Tuesdays at Craven Community College's Orringer Auditorium.

Craven Concerts Inc.
New Bern
(252) 637-1119

This organization, in its 26th consecutive season, schedules five concerts each year, staged at Grover C. Fields Performing Arts Center on Dr. M. L. King Jr. Boulevard. Season tickets cost $75 for non-reserved seating and $90 for reserved seating. Pro-

CLOSE UP

The Three
(Copper) Bears

New Bern has a number of distinctive bears around town, the bear being the city's symbol as homage to its Swiss roots. Three of the more unusual bears — two of them on City Hall facing Craven and Pollock Streets, and the other on the old fire department on Broad Street — date from 1914, when they were purchased for around $75 each.

What is not commonly known is that these three copper bears were unofficially named in tribute to three city leaders. The bear on the old fire department building is King William I and was named for William Ellis, who served as mayor from 1903-05 and alderman from 1909-17. Ellis also was a fireman with the Atlantic Fire Company. The bear facing Pollock Street is King William II, named for William Blades, who served not only as alderman from 1913-17 but also on the Building Committee when City Hall was renovated in 1913-14. The bear facing Craven Street is Crown Prince Albert, named for Albert Bangert. He

One of the Copper Bears on display in New Bern.

photo: Vina Hutchinson Farmer

served as the city's mayor from 1913-17 and 1925-29 and as an alderman from 1903-07, 1911-13, 1917-19 and 1921-25.

The bears were originally located on the old City Hall on Craven Street and were apparently moved to their current locations when City Hall moved to the old Federal building in 1936.

(Insiders' Guide thanks John Leys and Victor Jones of the New Bern-Craven County Public Library for providing this information.)

ductions feature a variety of performances as well as the staging of an annual live opera performance. Season ticket holders are entitled to admission to reciprocal concerts in nearby communities. Membership applications and additional information are available by calling the number above or writing to P.O. Box 12213, New Bern, NC 28561-2213.

Fairfield Harbour Chorus
(252) 638-8470

This chorus began with 24 enthusiastic members in 1984. Today, membership totals approximately 65 vocalists. The group performs about 15 concerts each year, featuring all types of music, including show tunes, gospel, Broadway hits, holiday arrangements, pop and contemporary. It has given numerous performances in area churches, rest homes and retirement

homes and has combined talents with other choruses at Cherry Point and Craven Community College. Members must be residents of Fairfield Harbour. Rehearsals are conducted on Monday evenings at 7 PM at the Fairfield Community Center. Rehearsals begin the first Monday after Labor Day and continue until mid-May.

Fuller's Music
2310 Trent Rd., New Bern
(252) 638-2811

Fuller's Music carries a complete inventory of instruments, sheet music and other items for both beginning and experienced musicians. Talented instructors teach lessons on a variety of instruments, including guitar, piano, drums, flute, clarinet, saxophone, trumpet, trombone, banjo, mandolin, fiddle, violin and dulcimer.

North Carolina Symphony
(252) 637-1551

The North Carolina Symphony comes to New Bern with an outstanding series of concerts featuring classical and popular favorites. Several seating options and price ranges are available. Four performances take place at the New Bern Riverfront Convention Center, including a Holiday Pops concert in December, with a free concert scheduled during early summer at Tryon Palace Historic Sites & Gardens. Season tickets are available by calling the symphony office at (877) 627-6724. Individual tickets may be purchased at New Bern/Craven County Convention and Visitors Center, (252) 637-1551.

Commercial Galleries

ART Gallery Ltd.
502 Pollock St., New Bern
(252) 670-4000/636-2120

On the second floor of the Edward Stanly House, this gallery offers fine works in contemporary North Carolina arts, including paintings, art glass, sculpture, jewelry, porcelain and tapestry. It is open daily by appointment.

Carolina Creations
317-A Pollock St., New Bern
(252) 633-4369

An artist-owned studio and gallery open since 1990, Carolina Creations offers handcrafted American and North Carolinian fine art and contemporary craft by more than 250 professional artists. The gallery represents potters, glass blowers, woodworkers and jewelers, as well as original art and prints by owner Janet Franceour and pottery by her husband, Michael. You'll also find the painted furniture line Sticks as well as sculpture and prints by StoryPeople. Carolina Creations is open daily, and there is always something new to discover.

Framing Fox Art Gallery
217 Middle St., New Bern
(252) 635-6400

The Framing Fox Art & Custom Picture Framing Gallery has been serving the public for more than 30 years with creative custom picture framing and a large selection of collectible fine art. Framing Fox specializes in collectible signed and numbered limited-edition prints, canvas and giclees by the leading artists in the United States, and they are authorized representatives for these artists. Custom framing, fine art, free location of hard-to-find prints and shipping anywhere are all part of Framing Fox's excellent service.

New Bern ArtWorks
323-B Middle St., New Bern
(252) 634-9002

Want a little adventure in your life? Enter New Bern ArtWorks, located in historic New Bern and accessible through the Bank of the Arts or the parking lot behind the Chelsea Restaurant on Middle Street. The studio is actually behind Port City Java. Here, 30 local artists create beauty using one uniting factor — a box. Each artist begins with this three-dimensional form and using various sizes, designs or creates his/her vision of what goes in the box. Owner Martha Williams says "thinking outside the box" has become a working motto. Some artists paint inside the box; others have done boxes within boxes. Some boxes may contain linings to provide a backdrop for other art forms — a marble sculpture or a painted canvas. All of the boxes are original art. The boxes can be hung on the wall or stacked on a desk or table. There are no rules, just ideas. Although the box is the signature of the shop, you will find other artworks such as jewelry, pottery and sculpture. The New Bern ArtWorks is open Tuesday through Friday from 10 AM until 6 PM and Saturday from 10 AM until 4 PM. It's closed on Sundays and Mondays.

Weavers Webb Gallery
602 Pollock St., New Bern
(252) 514-2681

Featuring a wide selection of hand-woven items, such as baby blankets and table linens, this gallery offers an expanded selection of knitting and needlepoint supplies, as well as crochet and cross-stitch items. Classes are available in needlepoint, weaving, crochet and knitting.

NEW BERN
ANNUAL EVENTS

The town of New Bern does an incredible job of entertaining and educating throughout the year. Tryon Palace Historic Sites & Gardens hosts special events, and the Craven Arts Council and Gallery and other arts organizations sponsor art exhibitions, music and dance performances year round. Several concert series and performing artists provide musical and visual entertainment around town. The New Bern Civic Theatre and the RiverTowne Repertory Players schedule a variety of dramatic and comedic presentations, and numerous musical and art organizations annually schedule shows and perform at city functions and festivities. Current calendar information may be obtained through the New Bern-

Craven County Convention & Visitors Center, (252) 637-9400 or (800) 437-5767.

January

Shriners' Parade
Sudan Shrine Center/Winter Ceremonial, New Bern
(252) 637-5197

The Shriners host a colorful and entertaining parade in downtown New Bern, featuring clowns, horses, mini-cars, bands and more. Shriners' parades, wherever performed, are fun, funny and as festive as a fez. The parade is part of the Winter Ceremonial, which occurs annually during the fourth weekend of January, bringing in thousands of Shriners from all over North

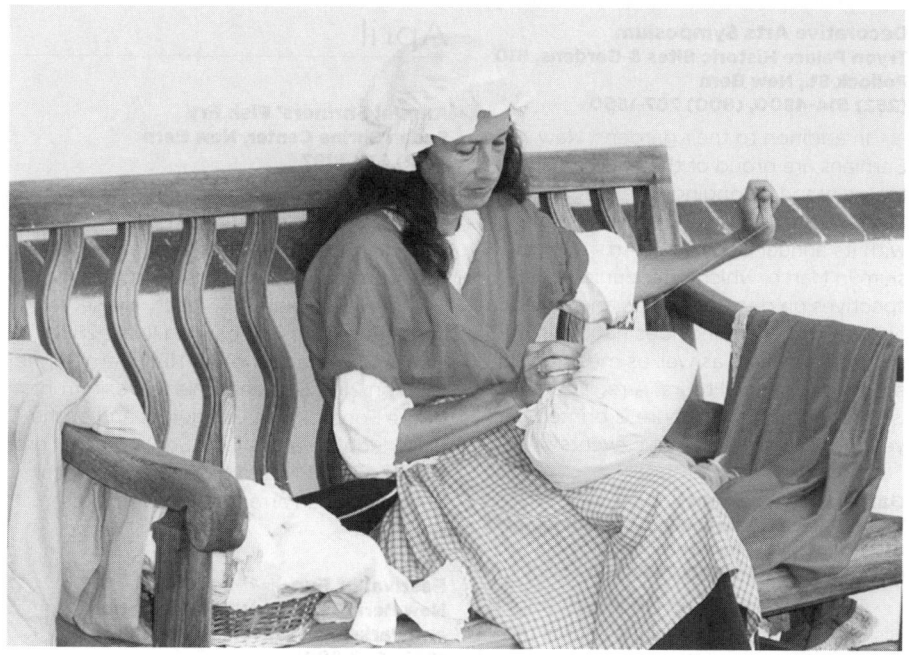

See life as it happened in Colonial America when you visit Tryon Palace Historic Site in New Bern.

photo: Vina Hutchinson

Carolina for events centered at the Sudan Shrine Center at the corner of Broad and E. Front Streets.

February

New Bern Preservation Foundation
510 B Pollock St., New Bern
(252) 633-6448

Antiques take the stage in early February when the New Bern Preservation Foundation sponsors its annual three-day Antiques Show & Sale at the New Bern Riverfront Convention Center. The show hosts more than 60 dealers who sell, demonstrate, instruct and exhibit eighteenth- and nineteenth-century and early twentieth-century American antiques. Experts also are on hand to identify whether your items are "antique or junque." Tickets cost $5 for all three days. Proceeds from the show benefit the Preservation Foundation's restoration projects and help fund programs and education.

March

Decorative Arts Symposium
Tryon Palace Historic Sites & Gardens, 610 Pollock St., New Bern
(252) 514-4900, (800) 767-1560

In addition to their gardens, New Bernians are proud of the authenticity of their vintage belongings. Here again, Tryon Palace Historic Sites & Gardens fills the bill with its annual Decorative Arts Symposium in March, which offers unique perspectives on decorative arts and American history. This event includes nationally recognized speakers as well as meals, social events and special tours. A registration fee is charged, and a brochure is printed each year outlining the thematic events.

Gardeners' Weekend
Tryon Palace Historic Sites & Gardens, 610 Pollock St., New Bern
(252) 514-4900, (800) 767-1560

The weekend of the New Bern Spring Historic Homes and Gardens Tour is the same as Gardeners' Weekend at Tryon Palace Historic Sites & Gardens. Palace gardens are open free throughout the weekend. The 14 acres of gardens are planted with more than 30,000 bulbs and spring flowers, resulting in a riot of lovely colors. Thousands of gloriously colored tulips are in bloom, along with expansive plantings of blazing daffodils and pansies. All of this is set against a luxurious background of azaleas and dogwoods. It's quite a sight. The palace also hosts a Heritage Plant Sale, which features perennials, herbs, annuals, trees and shrubs as well as a collection of rare and historic plants, all available for purchase.

Model Train Show
Coastal Carolina RailRoaders, New Bern
(252) 638-8872

February and March brings the annual weekend Model Train Show of the Carolina Coastal Railroaders. The dates at this point are not final as they involve the New Bern High School calendar. The interesting collection of miniatures and model trains shown in the New Bern High School auditorium is a great stop for kids 11 and younger, who are admitted free with an adult. Admission for ages 12 and older is $6.

April

Annual Shriners' Fish Fry
Sudan Shrine Center, New Bern
(252) 637-5197

In 2010 this annual tradition celebrates 43 years of providing New Bernians with delicious fish plates. Proceeds from the event benefit Shriners' Hospitals for Children. Fish plates, $6 each, are served in the Furniture Fair parking lot at 2880 Neuse Boulevard and the New Bern Shrine Club on 2102 S. Glenburnie Drive, in front of the Food Lion in Bridgeton, and at the Food Lion in James City. Serving times are 11 AM to 1:30 PM and 4:30 to 7 PM. Local businesses can arrange to have plates delivered.

Festival of Fun
New Bern Department of Recreation and Parks, 248 Craven St., New Bern
(252) 639-2901

This fun-filled day of entertainment for children and their families includes amusement rides, games, clowns, hands-on educational activities, exhibits, pony rides and lots of other fun activities. Organized by the New Bern Recreation and Parks Department, the festival takes place at beautiful Union Point Park on E. Front Street.

Spring Historic Homes and Gardens Tour
New Bern Historical Society,
512 Pollock St., New Bern
(252) 638-5773

Many people enjoy visiting New Bern in April for the New Bern Spring Homes and Gardens Tour. The event is cosponsored by the New Bern Historical Society and the New Bern Preservation Foundation, and the town puts on its prettiest face to welcome visitors. The tour includes private homes, gardens and churches in the historic district, with guides and location maps provided. The tour can best be enjoyed on foot and is an ideal opportunity to explore selected homes and landmarks in this river city. During the two-day event, Tryon Palace also opens its gardens for free. Historic Homes and Gardens Tour tickets, $20 on tour days or $15 in advance, may be purchased at the New

Bern Historical Society office. Tickets are available for $13 for groups of 20 or more, or the active military. Tickets can also be ordered in advance by mail.

May

New Bern Jazz & Blues Fest
New Bern Riverfront Convention Center,
New Bern
(252) 634-3261

Though there will be no festival in 2009, the New Bern Jazz Preservation Society hosts two nights of hot jazz and cool blues during its festival. This popular two-day event features nationally known headliners. The 2010 celebration will be a special celebation in honor of New Bern's 300th anniversary.

Strawberry Festival
Vanceboro
(252) 244-0017

Celebrating this delicious, locally grown fruit, the Strawberry Festival features food, rides, music, games and much more, all in a family-friendly atmosphere. The festival is sponsored by the Vance-

Many New Bern residents travel to the nearby coast to pursue their passion for surfing.

photo: Peter Doran

boro Rescue Squad. To get to Vanceboro, located 20 miles from New Bern, cross the Neuse River Bridge and take U.S. Highway 17 north to N.C. Highway 43 and follow the signs.

Tryon Palace Concert Series
Pollack and George Sts., New Bern
(252) 514-4900

This four-concert series of free evening performances on the palace's South Lawn runs from mid-May through late June each year and includes concerts by a broad range of ensembles, including the North Carolina Symphony.

June

Neuse River Days
Neuse River Foundation, New Bern
(252) 637-7972

Sponsored by the Neuse River Foundation, this festival is designed for people who enjoy outdoor activities. Kayak and canoe races, including the Neuse River Classic and the River Dog Relay Race, are among the festival's most popular features for all levels of competitors. The not-so-serious are invited to race homemade rafts in the Great Twin Rivers Raft Race. Every year participants are entertained by the unusual entries, some of which actually float. Of course, Neuse River Days also offers music, crafts, games and other festival favorites.

July

Fourth of July Celebrations
New Bern/Craven Co. Convention & Visitors Bureau, New Bern
(252) 637-9400, (800) 437-5767

As one of America's first towns to have a Fourth of July celebration, New Bern still enjoys a well-turned-out celebration with traditional hot dogs and fireworks. Swiss Bear coordinates the impressive fireworks display that takes place at Union Point Park on the downtown waterfront. Bands

traditionally perform patriotic music to complement the event. Additional holiday activities take place at Tryon Palace Historic Sites & Gardens, where the gardens are open for free.

August

Carolinian Shakespeare Festival
New Bern
(800) 346-2770

Carolinian Shakespeare Festival performs the works of the Bard in a three-week run the first three weekends of August. Discounts are available for students and seniors.

Greater New Bern Business Expo
New Bern Area Chamber of Commerce, New Bern
(252) 637-3111

The Greater New Bern Business Expo, hosted by the New Bern Riverfront Convention Center and presented by the New Bern Area Chamber of Commerce, demonstrates the diversity of the business community in the Craven County area. Businesses and non-profit organizations set up displays, offer free samples, discounts and door prizes, and share information about their products and/or services. Admission is $1.

September

Coastal Carolina Chamber Music Festival
New Bern
(252) 626-5419

The Coastal Carolina Chamber Musical Festival brings some of the nation's most talented musicians to eastern North Carolina for concerts that are entertaining, educational and interactive. Taking place at various locations over two weekends, the festival includes special open rehearsals that offer behind-the-scenes peeks and opportunities to meet the artists, as well as a free family concert that offers discovery and adventure for all ages. Fes-

See this entire guide plus additional content online at insiderinfo.us

tival packages as well as individual concert tickets are available.

DUFFEST
Henderson Park, New Bern
(252) 639-7586

DUFFEST is short for Greater Duffy-field Unity Family Festival. It celebrates the heritage of this historic African-American neighborhood with a parade, live music, food and other cultural activities. Sponsored by the Greater Duffyfield Residents Council, the festival is designed to foster community pride and unity.

October

Coastal Carolina Fair & Expo
Craven County Fairgrounds, U.S. Hwy. 70 E, New Bern
(252) 636-0303

Livestock and produce events are always interesting to see at this fair, sponsored by the Craven County Jaycees, but most folks come for the midway. Admission is available at the gate and includes all rides, special events, exhibits and parking, but the midway has lots of ways to entice more money from your pockets, including food, games and concessions.

Mumfest
Swiss Bear, 316 S. Front St., New Bern
(252) 638-5781

Swiss Bear Downtown Development Corp. has organized and coordinated the annual fall event now known as Mumfest for the past 27 years. In cooperation with the City of New Bern, this celebration, always the second weekend in October, highlights the city's assets and attracts more than 80,000 visitors to the downtown area and its waterfront. Mumfest, one of the top 10 festivals in the state, kicks into high gear on Saturday and Sunday, with an endless diversity of festival foods, arts and crafts, corporate exhibits, and a kids' corner with amusement rides, fun activities, puppets, rock climbing and more. Those attending also can enjoy such attractions as live-stage and roving entertainment; a model railroad exhibit; military vessel tours; flower and art shows; and a boat show. Tryon Palace Historic Sites &

Gardens features free admission to its gardens. A free trolley shuttle makes parking easy — just park at Twin Rivers Mall or one of the other convenient locations and ride the trolley into the downtown area.

New Bern at Night Ghostwalk
New Bern Historical Society, 512 Pollock St., New Bern
(252) 638-8558

In late October, the New Bern Historical Society conducts its New Bern at Night Ghostwalk, complete with ghosts from New Bern's past. Walking tours feature historic homes, churches and the Cedar Grove Cemetery. (Insiders recommend you attend all three nights. Attend the cemetery tour the first night, which is the only attraction open the first day of the tour, and then divide up the rest of the attractions over the next two nights. This will give you more time to enjoy the walk.) Ghostwalks focus on historic events particular to New Bern, and ghosts from historic occasions are present in homes and historic buildings on the tour to tell how the times affected them. Tickets are available at retail locations and the historical society's headquarters at 512 Pollock Street.

November

Craven Arts Council Holiday Showcase and Sale
317 Middle St., New Bern
(252) 638-2577

The Craven Arts Council's annual Holiday Showcase and Sale kicks off in November. Shoppers will find many unique handcrafted gift items, including jewelry, pottery and stoneware, floral arrangements, birdhouses, fine knitted baby wear, stuffed animals, toys and more. Admission to the sale is free.

December

Coastal Christmas Celebrations
Various locations, New Bern
(252) 637-9400, (800) 437-5767

You can easily catch the spirit of the season in New Bern. Annual events of New

Bern's Coastal Christmas Celebration during the month of December include the Craven County Jaycees' festive parade the first Saturday of the month in downtown New Bern, and the Craven Regional Medical Center Foundation's Festival of Trees gala, including the popular Breakfast with Santa for children. Downtown merchants host a special First Friday event, staying open late and offering fantastic bargains. Caroling, musical performances, prize drawings and other events round out this event. The New Bern Women's Club hosts its annual "The Holly and the Ivy" Homes Tour. Santa Claus also hears the Christmas wishes of good little boys and girls in his Santa House on the corner of Broad and Middle streets. Performers from Down East Dance offer *The Nutcracker* ballet every other year.

Coastal Christmas Flotilla
New Bern
(252) 639-2902

Santa arrives in downtown New Bern in style aboard a Hatteras yacht as part of the Coastal Christmas Flotilla, which takes place the first Saturday in December and is organized by New Bern Parks and Recreation. The flotilla of gaily decorated boats of all sizes proceeds down the Trent River and passes Union Point, giving spectators a long, lingering look at the boats festooned with sparkling lights, diving dolphins and red-nosed reindeer.

Handel's Messiah
Centenary United Methodist Church,
309 New St., New Bern
(252) 637-4181

A local favorite since 1981, performances of this classic around the time of "Old Christmas" in early December combine 150 community voices and North Carolina Symphony musicians with conductor James Ogle, conductor emeritus of the Boise Philharmonic Association and a former associate conductor of the North Carolina Symphony. Tickets are available for two afternoon and two evening performances.

Tryon Palace Christmas Celebration
Tryon Palace Historic Sites & Gardens,
610 Pollock St., New Bern
(252) 514-4900, (800) 767-1560

Staff and volunteers prepare for weeks for the Tryon Palace Holiday Celebration. By the beginning of December the palace looks much as it did during the holidays in 1770 when Governor William Tryon hosted a "very grand and noble Entertainment and Ball" to celebrate the opening of his sumptuous home and the Royal capital. The palace is lighted and adorned with fresh fruit and fragrant greenery. Cooks are busy in the kitchen preparing confections and delicacies, and the air is filled with holiday aromas. The tours run throughout the month of December and include all of the site's historic homes. Special events include Candlelight Tours, fireworks displays and the Jonkonnu celebration. Admission prices are $15 for adults and $6 for children.

NEW BERN
ON THE WATER ⛵

With New Bern's location at the confluence of the Neuse and Trent rivers, it's not surprising that its citizens take to the water like, well, ducks. The weather is mild enough year round to entice the locals into kayaking, sailing, skiing, fishing or relaxing on or around the rivers.

Waterways

Boaters, fishing enthusiasts and out-doorsy types in the New Bern area have two waterways to explore: the expansive Neuse River that flows into Pamlico Sound or the slow, meandering Trent River that flows into the Neuse.

The Neuse River is ideal for cruising by sail or power, with miles of sandy beaches, clearly marked channels, easy access via the Intracoastal Waterway (ICW) and Pamlico Sound and many marinas and protected anchorages. The Trent River is deep, has a marked channel and is navigable by small boat. Its lower reaches are fine for uncrowded water-skiing. Brices Creek, a tributary of the Trent, winds far into the Croatan National Forest and offers excellent fishing and wildlife observation.

The bridge over the Trent River leading into downtown New Bern is now closed, undergoing a two-year project by the North Carolina Department of Transportation to replace the Alfred Cunningham Bridge, which once spanned the Trent River and connects downtown New Bern to U.S. Highway 70. While the project is underway, traffic is being diverted to the Trent Woods/Pembroke exit, located just minutes from downtown. The bridge is scheduled to be replaced by 2010 in time for New Bern's 300th anniversary.

National Oceanic and Atmospheric Administration (NOAA) stations in the area are New Bern and Beaufort, WX-2 (162.475 MHz) and Hatteras, WX-3 (162.40 MHZ).

A clearly marked channel up the Neuse from the Intracoastal Waterway will bring you into historic New Bern. The natural channel depths generally run between 8 and 12 feet, with little noticeable tidal effect. A strong easterly or northerly wind will raise the level, while a sustained westerly breeze, say 25 knots, can lower this level by as much as 2 feet. Also noteworthy to boaters are the sapling stakes dotting the river. The stakes are strung with nets in the early spring and late fall. The nets are usually buoyed by corks or plastic bottles or marked by white flags.

The Neuse is a wide river, which invites sailing in addition to motor-cruising and water-skiing. The many wandering tributaries promise scenic canoeing and exciting fishing. Much of the Neuse River's shoreline south of New Bern forms one of the boundaries of the vast 157,000-acre Croatan National Forest. Here, locals and visitors enjoy public recreation areas, with swimming and picnic facilities near the Minnesott ferry terminal and at Flanner's Beach south of New Bern.

Fishing

Expect to hook bass, bream, flounder and many more fish in local waters. The Neuse River is also home to many crabs, and catching them provides tasty and profitable rewards. Nearby Croa-

See this entire guide plus additional content online at insiderinfo.us

tan National Forest permits fresh- and saltwater fishing; however, fishing in the forest's freshwater lakes is poor because of the acidity of the water. But along its river shoreline, oystering, crabbing and flounder-gigging can be worthwhile efforts. To find out about the best fishing spots, talk to a ranger at the ranger office at 141 Fisher Avenue, 9 miles south of New Bern just off U.S. Highway 70 E. The office is open weekdays from 8 AM to 4:30 PM.

If you just like to cruise backwoods waters, several forest locations have fishing piers and boat ramps, including Brices Creek, Cahooque Creek, Catfish Lake, Great Lake and Haywood Landing. Some of these sites are deep in the Croatan National Forest, so it's best to check with a ranger for specific directions. Better yet, stop by the ranger office and pick up a forest map. (For more information on places to fish in the park, see our New Bern Parks and Recreation chapter.)

Boating

MARINAS

Boats of all sizes can find berthing space in downtown New Bern and nearby marinas. Whether you're just cruising around or wish to launch your boat at one of the many local ramps, most locations have similar facilities. In the downtown area especially, it is not unusual for leisure yachters or sailors to arrive for what they thought would be a short visit only to find themselves living aboard their vessels, staying weeks, sometimes months, even years. If you're traveling to New Bern from some distance, it is wise to call ahead to ensure docking space availability, especially during the warmer months. Here, we list the local marinas in alphabetical order.

BridgePoint Marina
101 Howell Rd., New Bern
(252) 637-7372

BridgePointe Marina is located within walking distance of downtown New Bern's attractions, shopping and dining. BridgePointe is across the Trent River from the New Bern Riverfront Convention Center. Open year round, BridgePointe serves sail and power vessels up to 150 feet. It

has 125 floating laminated cedar slips, a marked entry channel with 12-foot approach depth, and a dockside depth of 8 to 16 feet. Amenities include a pump-out station, ice, electricity, showers, laundry facilities, a patio, grills and Wi-Fi. Marina guests also are allowed full use of the hotel pool. Outback Steakhouse is located next door.

Duck Creek Marina
699 Galloway Rd., Bridgeton
(252) 638-1702

At the head of Duck Creek on the north side of the Neuse, this marina is open year round and serves sail and power vessels up to 46 feet. It has 55 slips, a marked entry channel with an approach depth of 6 feet, a dockside depth of 6 feet, a 35-ton lift, a storage yard for do-it-yourself repair work, marine supplies, electricity and showers. There are no transient slips. Because the marina is across the river from New Bern, you will need transportation for shopping or visiting the city's attractions.

New Bern Grand Marina
100 Middle St., New Bern
(252) 638-3585

The New Bern Grand Marina, located on the Trent River, offers the ultimate in dockage on North Carolina's Inner Banks. The marina is located in historic downtown New Bern with its quaint shops and local restaurants — all within easy walking distance — and adjacent to the Hilton New Bern with full hotel amenities, including a state-of-the-art fitness center. The fully renovated floating dock system can easily accommodate yachts up to 200 feet and offers a pump-out station, Wi-Fi, water, cable, phone hookups, showers and a laundry facility.

Northwest Creek Marina
104 Marina Dr., New Bern
(252) 638-4133

Northwest Creek Marina is on the north side of the Neuse River, near the Fairfield Harbour resort development. Open year round, the marina serves sail and power vessels up to 75 feet. It has 272 slips, a marked entry channel with 8 feet of water depth and dockside depth of 12 feet. Amenities include gas and diesel fuel, a pump-out station, a launching ramp, electricity, showers and laundry facilities. Marina patrons can pay special rates to use the resort's amenities, including the indoor and outdoor pools and lighted tennis courts. Transportation will be needed to visit New Bern's attractions.

Public Docks - Union Point Park/ Lawson Creek Park
Downtown, New Bern
(252) 639-2900

Union Point Park and Lawson Creek Park serve as city parks and public docks. Boaters can anchor at either park to orient themselves to the area and locate more permanent moorings. The parks feature boat ramps and public facilities; however, a city ordinance prohibits overnight dockage.

Tidewater Marine Co.
300 Madame Moore Ln., New Bern
(252) 637-3347

On the Trent River, Tidewater Marine Co. is open year round and serves sail

and power vessels up to 40 feet. It has 30 slips, three transient slips, a marked entry channel with controlling depth of 21 feet, 15 feet at dockside, a railway and lift, a launching ramp, some supplies and electricity. It also offers repairs on propellers and hulls. Because it is away from New Bern's hub, you will need transportation to see the sights.

NEARBY MARINAS

Nearby marinas at Clubfoot Creek and Minnesott Beach, on the Neuse River, are destinations for enjoyable day sails or cruising trips from New Bern. (See our separate chapter on Oriental for details about the marinas there.) In addition, many marinas along the Crystal Coast are easily accessible from New Bern via the Neuse River and the ICW. (See our Crystal Coast Marinas chapter for listings.) For the convenience of boaters, we provide information on marinas near New Bern that you can visit as you make your way up and down the Neuse River or toward Pamlico Sound.

You can find work boats like these everywhere on the Central Coast.

photo: JoAnn Bristol

Matthews Point Marina
2645 Temples Point Rd., Havelock
(252) 444-1805

Matthews Point Marina is off the beaten track on Clubfoot Creek on the south side of the Neuse River, 10 miles east of Cherry Point. Nestled comfortably in a safe harbor, the year-round marina serves sail and power vessels up to 45 feet. It has 106 slips, six of which are transient berths. It has a marked entry channel, approach depth of 7 feet and dockside depth of 6.5 feet, gas and diesel fuel, electricity, a pump-out station, laundry facilities, showers and ice. A clubhouse, cook-out area and upper-deck lounge are available to boaters. A yacht sales brokerage also is located on-site.

Wayfarers Cove
1107 Bennett Rd., Arapahoe
(252) 249-0200, (800) 922-1424

This waterfront community in Minnesott Beach, on the north side of the Neuse River between New Bern and Oriental, offers a true hurricane hole in Wayfarers Cove Marina, formerly known as the Minnesott Beach Yacht Basin. The year-round marina is scheduled for a state-of-the-art Sound Marine floating dock and slip system, serving sail and power vessels up to 60 feet. It has 150 slips, with transient berths available, and a marked entry channel, approach and dockside with depths of 8 feet. Amenities include a 60-ton lift, dockside utilities, a pump-out station, ice, showers, laundry facilities and wireless Internet. Full-service marine repairs are available. The marina is also contiguous to a championship golf course.

Sailing

Various sailing competitions take place throughout the year in the waters around New Bern. For more information, check the annual events calendar maintained by the **Visitors Center**, (252) 637-9400 or (800) 437-5767. Or call **Blackbeard's Sailing Club**, (252) 633-3990, or **On The Wind Sailing Cruises at Northwest Creek Marina**, (252) 322-5804.

On the Wind Sailing Cruises
Northwest Creek Marina, Fairfield Harbour, New Bern
(252) 322-5804

On the Wind offers a variety of charters, including day, evening, sunset and live-abroad cruises to the Outer Banks. All cruises depart from Northwest Creek Marina at Fairfield Harbour, and complimentary soft drinks are served. Call for prices. Sailing instruction also is available.

Paddling

If you want to explore some interesting places by canoe, try the two open-water lakes in the Croatan National Forest. Both Great Lake, 2,809 acres, and Catfish Lake, 962 acres, are home to osprey and alligators, and black bears might be within sight. They are unusual bodies of water because they are surrounded by pocosin, the Indian name for "swamp on a hill." Pocosin is an impenetrable jungle of pond pine, titi, zenobia and greenbriers, but it supports fragile ecosystems that add to the beauty and wildness of the Croatan National Forest. If you prefer to canoe in enclosed waters, take your canoe to the smaller creeks: Brices, Hadnot, Hancock, Cahooque, Hunters and Holston. In these waters, you can observe a rich variety of plants and wildlife. If you want to canoe in moving waters, paddle in the White Oak, Neuse and Newport rivers. Many varieties of birds show themselves in these waters, and watching them in their natural habitat is a fascinating experience.

Brices Creek Canoe Trail
Craven County Parks &
Recreation Department, 406 Craven St., New Bern
(252) 636-6606

For a map of this canoeing adventure, call the Craven County Parks and Recreation Department at the number above, or pick up a map at the park office, 406 Craven Street in New Bern. The trail is about 12 miles long, beginning at the bridge on State Route 1111 and ending at Lawson Creek Park on the Trent River. There are five access points, and the trail is clearly marked by directional signs. Hours of operation are dawn to dusk.

New Bern is surrounded by water and great open spaces, making it an unbeatable location for all kinds of recreational activities. Adults and children will find numerous places to exercise and take part in sports programs. For those who want to sample a variety of athletic pursuits, the City of New Bern and Craven County offer year-round recreation programs and public areas for tennis, power walking, running, baseball, basketball, softball and soccer. Both the county and city maintain public boat ramps and fishing piers. Hiking trails are maintained by the Forest Service in the Croatan National Park, and the Brices Creek canoe trail is coordinated by Craven County Recreation and Parks Department (see more about that in our New Bern On the Water chapter). Golfing is a favorite pastime around here; for a list of courses see the New Bern Golf chapter.

Recreation and Fitness Centers

Courts Plus
2911 Brunswick Ave., New Bern
(252) 633-2221

The Broadcast Vision cardio exercise equipment at Courts Plus ensures a good workout, as do the expanded free-weight facilities and state-of-the-art weight-training equipment. A staff of personal trainers can provide additional assistance and motivation. After your workout, you can wind down in the saunas, steam room or whirlpool. Lockers, towels and a tanning booth are also available. The pro shop offers apparel, equipment and accessories for your fitness needs. You can play racquetball on one of the four indoor courts, or go swimming and take part in aqua aerobics in the indoor and outdoor pools. You also can participate in organized basketball, karate and aerobics, and child care and special programs for children are available. Courts Plus does not have trial memberships, but visitors may purchase a one-month, temporary membership.

Craven County Parks and Recreation Department
406 Craven St., New Bern
(252) 636-6606

The Craven County Parks and Recreation Department offers a variety of programs and facilities for citizens of all ages. Activities and events vary according to age, season and interest levels. Youth programs held throughout the year feature baton twirling, karate, tennis, soccer, baseball, girls softball and youth basketball. Youth camp opportunities include summer day camps and environmental education camps. Other special events scheduled for youth are a fishing derby and tennis lessons.

Adults will enjoy such activities as flag football, co-ed softball, road races, tennis lessons and tournaments, golf classes, dog-obedience instruction, senior archery and kayak lessons. The recreation department is also a lead agency for the Neuse River Senior Games, an Olympic-style event for competitors ages 55 and older. The recreation department also sponsors the Craven County Special Olympics for ages 8 and older. Sports include basketball, bowling, aquatics, equestrian events, cycling, track and field, golf and bocce. More than 400 athletes compete and 500 volunteers assist in this program every year.

The department has canoes, kayaks and other sports equipment available to the general public on a rental basis. Picnic shelters and ball fields can be reserved for exclusive use through the recreation department. Rental fees and deposits are required. Since many events and activities vary according to season and available resources, you might want to visit the department to see what's offered when. Office hours are Monday through Friday 8 AM to 5 PM.

Gold's Gym
3340 Dr. M. L. King Jr. Blvd., New Bern
(252) 634-9499

Located at the corner of McCarthy Boulevard and Dr. M. L. King Jr. Boulevard, Gold's Gym has more than 300 pieces of user-friendly exercise equipment. Cross-training and bike machines, Cybex, Life Fitness and Hammer Strength machines, free weights and more are ready to help you get fit and stay fit. New members are given fitness assessments and assistance with setting realistic fitness goals by one of the gym's personal trainers, who also are available to work with members one-on-one. Group classes are offered in Body Attack, Body Pump, Body Step, Body Flow, yoga, Tai Chi, kickboxing, floor and senior fitness, weight training, spinning and more. Other amenities include a juice bar, a nutrition center, tanning beds, a stand-up booth for tanning, free child care and more. A variety of membership options are available at Gold's Gym, which is open daily.

New Bern Parks and Recreation Department
248 Craven St., New Bern
(252) 639-2901

The New Bern Parks and Recreation Department operates most of its programs from three centers: Stanley White Recreation Center at 901 Chapman Street, (252) 639-2919; West New Bern Recreation Center, 1225 Pine Tree Drive, (252) 639-2906; and the Community Resource Center, 908 Bloomfield Street, (252) 636-4127. For details about seasonal programs, call the New Bern Parks and Recreation Department and ask for brochures or visit one of the three recreation centers. Each is staffed by a center supervisor, an athletic supervisor and program directors. They will be happy to answer your questions.

Programs include youth lessons in tennis, cheerleading, baton twirling, golf and football. Tee-ball and baseball are offered to youths between the ages of 6 and 12. Babe Ruth baseball is played by youths ages 13 through 18. Girls' softball, soccer, basketball and wrestling also are offered. Adult leagues cover softball, basketball, flag football and volleyball. For tennis lovers, the department operates four public courts, all of which are lighted for night

There's more to time on the water than work hours.

Photo courtesy of NC Division of Tourism, Film and Sports Development play. Other classes for all ages include ceramics, creative writing, aerobics, bridge and martial arts.

There are three after-school programs for ages 6 to 13 at the two recreation centers and the Community Resource Center; these offer computers, help with homework, and games. There are a number of clubs devoted to special interests, such as outdoor adventure, miniatures, model airplanes, embroidery and more. Special programs include billiards, softball, table tennis and other tournaments, as well as a ceramic and hobby show each May. The department also offers a number of programs for seniors, detailed in our New Bern Retirement chapter.

Twin Rivers YMCA
100 YMCA Ln., New Bern
(252) 638-8799

At the Twin Rivers YMCA, you'll find a variety of programs for the entire family, including preschool swim lessons, youth progressive swim lessons, lifeguard classes, adult swim lessons, competitive swimming, aqua aerobics and arthritis aquatics. The YMCA provides youth sports programs for flag football, basketball and soccer. The YMCA directs an after-school enrichment program for children during the school year, a summer sports camp and a day camp over the summer months.

Adult programs include low-impact aerobics, step aerobics, aerobics for older adults, Pilates, Silver Sneakers and yoga. Other adult programs consist of volleyball, basketball and racquetball. A weight room and wellness center allow teens and adults ages 16 and older the opportunity to increase fitness through strength training and the use of a variety of cardiovascular equipment such as treadmills, stair-climbers, cross-trainers and exercise bicycles. An indoor walking track allows walkers to get in their daily exercise no matter what the weather outdoors. The YMCA's Aquatics Center offers water slides, a spray park, a zero-entry section, plenty of deck space, and lots of room for lap swimming, playing and fun. The outdoor pool is available for use during cooler months, thanks to its "bubble roof."

Bowling

Strike Zone Family Fun Center
3550 Dr. M. L. King Jr. Blvd., New Bern
(252) 637-6033

This state-of-the-art, smoke-free recreational facility features 24 lanes of bowling fun. Cost is only $4.75 each game; shoe rental is a separate cost. Scheduled for Saturday nights is the spectacular, lights-out Big Bang Cosmic Bowling, complete with satellite radio, a laser show and glow-in-the-dark bowling balls and pins for a special price from 9 PM until midnight. Reservations are recommended for this but not required. Strike Zone also offers a snack shop, pool tables and an arcade area. Strike Zone is open Monday, Tuesday Wednesday and Thursday from noon to 10 PM, Friday and Saturday from noon to midnight and Sunday from 1 to 10 PM. Ask about their special deals.

Hiking

Island Creek Forest Walk
Croatan National Forest, 141 E. Fisher Ave., New Bern
(252) 638-5628

This half-mile trail is perfect for a morning or afternoon hike. As you traverse it, you will see a virgin-like stand of upland hardwoods, picturesque Island Creek with bottomland hardwoods and a managed stand of loblolly pines. Before setting out, stop at the district ranger's office on Fisher Avenue and pick up the Island Creek Forest Walk brochure. The brochure contains a self-guided tour that identifies trees and other trail features. It also gives a map and directions to the trail.

Neusiok Trail
Croatan National Forest, 141 E. Fisher Ave., New Bern
(252) 638-5628

This area is strictly for those who enjoy roughing it. No camping facilities exist along the trail, but you may primitive camp if you pack out your garbage. You'll need to bring along drinking water and wear boots to cross wet areas. The trailhead starts on the Neuse River at Pine Cliff

Recreation Area and ends at Oyster Point on the Newport River. It passes through a cypress-lined sandy beach, hardwood forests and thick pocosin with pond pines. The length of the trail is 21 miles, and it crosses several paved and unpaved roads. Except at Pine Cliff, camping is permitted anywhere along the trail. Hikers and campers need to bring their own drinking water and are advised to wear all-weather gear, waterproof boots and plenty of bug repellent. Because of summer's biting, stinging and zinging insects, fall, winter and early spring are better for camping and hiking. Catfish Lake and Great Lake also have additional primitive camping and earthen boat ramps. Boat ramps are available at Brices Creek, Cahooque Creek and Haywood Landing. Long Point, off N.C. Highway 58, has a ramp specifically for kayaks and canoes. Locals favor these spots for their natural beauty and handy access to water, but remember, insects can be prolific in the summer months. For directions, call or stop by the district ranger's office on Fisher Avenue.

Pine Cliff Recreation Area
Croatan National Forest, 141 E. Fisher Ave., New Bern
(252) 638-5628

Visitors can indulge in day-use activities such as picnicking, hiking and fishing at this Neuse River–based recreation area. Chemical toilets, well water and trailhead parking for the Neusiok Trail are also provided. Pine Cliff is open year round for day use only.

City Parks

New Bern has numerous parks that are great places to go for outdoor enjoyment. Below we describe many of the more popular parks with playgrounds, although the recreation department also maintains a number of smaller parks that for the most part serve only their surrounding communities. For more information about reserving shelters and/or parks at no cost for birthday parties, family reunions and other gatherings, call the New Bern Parks and Recreation Department at (252) 639-2901. We have indicated below which parks and shelters are available for reservations.

Fort Totten Park
New Bern Recreation & Parks,
Fort Totten Dr. & Trent Blvd., New Bern
(252) 639-2901

This 5.4-acre park has a lighted softball field and an impressive children's playground featuring swings, slides and climbing equipment, plus public restrooms and a picnic shelter with two grills and two picnic tables. This is a fantastic park that is always bustling with activity. The park and its picnic shelter can be reserved for parties and other celebrations.

Glenburnie Park
312 Glenburnie Dr., New Bern

In the Glenburnie Gardens residential area off Oaks Road, this 51-acre park is shaded by a grove of old pine trees and is considered one of New Bern's most scenic parks. It fronts the Neuse River and has a public boat ramp with paved parking, four picnic shelters with tables and grills, fishing piers, a playground, a disc golf course and public restrooms. Glenburnie Park and its shelters can be reserved.

Henderson Park
901 Chapman St., New Bern
(252) 639-2901

This 30-acre park offers a playground and two picnic shelters with grills and picnic tables. It can be reserved for private use. The surrounding grounds have two lighted regulation-sized basketball courts, two baseball fields, a half-mile walking trail, outdoor workout equipment and restroom facilities. The site adjoins the Stanley White Recreation Center.

Kidsville Playground
New Bern Recreation & Parks,
1225 Pine Tree Dr., New Bern
(252) 639-2912

Children are enchanted with this playground, and grown-ups find it special, too. Constructed by volunteers in just five days in 1994, this place is the wonderful gift to the City of New Bern from the community of New Bern. Even if you're not a child, don't miss it, especially if you still get a thrill from swinging on great swings. For more details, see our New Bern Kidstuff chapter.

Pierce Park
545 Neuse Ave., New Bern
(252) 639-2901

Pierce Park includes two lighted Little League fields with bleachers, a playground, public restrooms and a concession stand. The fields are used for baseball and tee-ball games and practices.

Public Docks - Lawson Creek Park
Downtown, New Bern
(252) 639-2900

Off Pembroke Road and fronting the Trent River, this 140-acre park has two boat landings and is a major attraction for water enthusiasts. Lawson Creek Park has something for everyone — two soccer fields, two fishing piers, a handicapped walkway and fishing pier, restroom facilities and a picnic area that includes a walkway with a gazebo, picnic tables and grills. The park and its picnic shelter are available for use by the public.

Seth West Parrott Park
1225 Pine Tree Dr., New Bern
(252) 639-2901

With 25 acres, Seth West Parrott Park is a major place for recreation and attractions for kids. The West New Bern Recreation Center is here as well as the Kidsville Playground. In addition, you'll find two lighted tennis courts, a lighted outdoor basketball court, two lighted baseball fields and the Heath and Cutler Babe Ruth fields, as well as restrooms and a picnic shelter. Both the park and Kidsville Playground are available for reservations.

Union Point Park Complex
E. Front St. and S. Front St., New Bern

This park is located downtown where the Trent River joins the Neuse. An old landfill site renovated in the early 1970s, Union Point Park is now a wonderful and scenic place to sit and watch the river traffic. For those who love being outdoors, Union Point Park offers two boat-launching ramps, a gazebo (used for weddings, festivals and special events), a fishing pier, picnic tables, grills, playground equipment and public restrooms. Park-goers who want to enjoy a walk downtown can use the walkway under the Trent River Bridge to avoid vehicular traffic on E.

Front Street. On the Fourth of July, Union Point Park is the perfect locale to watch the town's impressive display of fireworks (just be sure to bring your own chairs and mosquito repellent).

Other Parks

Creekside Park
Craven County, Old Airport Rd., New Bern
(252) 636-6606

Developed by the Craven County Parks and Recreation Department, Creekside Park is a 111-acre recreational complex located adjacent to Craven Regional Airport. The park features walking trails, a sand volleyball court, 12 athletic fields, playgrounds, restrooms and picnic shelters. The waterfront has a launch area for canoes and kayaks as well as a fishing dock, a gazebo and walkways to Brice's Creek. All of the facilities may be reserved for public use. There may be rental fees that apply for use of the picnic shelters, gazebo and athletic fields. Creekside Park is located in the James City community, across the bridge from downtown New Bern.

Extension Service Gardens
300 Industrial Dr., New Bern

The grounds of the Craven County Extension Service Building are dotted with a number of demonstration and community gardens, all open to the public free of charge. The Eastern North Carolina Rose Society maintains a community rose garden, with more than 70 varieties of roses ranging from climbers and shrubs to hybrid teas and miniatures. The Craven County Master Gardeners demonstrate various techniques and conduct classes utilizing their Demonstration Vegetable Garden. The food grown in the garden is donated to area programs for the needy. The Trent Woods Garden Club maintains a butterfly and bird garden. To visit the gardens, take U.S. 70 west from New Bern's Glenburnie exit about 5 miles to the Clarks exit. Take a right off the exit ramp. The immediate next right turn is Industrial Drive, and the Extension Service Building is the third building on the left.

 **CLOSE UP**

New Bern's Beloved Firemen's Museum

During the summer of 2002, city officials quietly decided during a budget crunch to close the Firemen's Museum, which was founded in 1955 to preserve the history of firefighting in New Bern. Little did they realize how beloved this museum on Hancock Street is to city residents and visitors alike. An uproar led city officials to reverse their decision and keep the museum open until a working committee of local business leaders and volunteers developed fund-raising plans to come up with the $52,000 needed annually to run the museum. (The committee also hopes to raise the additional funds needed to renovate the old New Bern fire station building on Broad Street as a new home for the museum.)

The museum documents New Bern's rich firefighting history, starting with the Atlantic Hook & Ladder Company, which was chartered on May 14, 1845. During the Civil War, when most of its members were away serving in the Confederate Army, the Atlantic Company was mostly inactive. Seeing a need for an active firefighting company, Union soldiers, many of whom stayed in New Bern after the war was over, formed the New Berne Steam Fire Engine Company No. 1 on January 1, 1865. This company was later nicknamed the Button Company for its 1884 Button fire engine.

The rivalry between the Atlantic and the Button stations was fierce, despite their consolidation into one fire department in 1867. This rivalry provided decades of entertainment during parades, fairs and tournaments, and local residents would gather at blazes in anticipation of seeing which company would arrive first. The rivalry continued until 1928, when both companies were housed in a central fire station on Broad Street.

Even though the technology is obsolete now, the Button Company still holds the world's records for producing standing steam (in 1 minute and 46 seconds) and for running quick steam (in 2 minutes and 12 seconds). However, the Atlantic Company won several competitions in its own right, including the state championship for reel racing several times. Prior to the arrival of the first motorized engines in 1914 for the Button Company and in 1925 for the Atlantic Company, fire engines were pulled by fire horses, several of which are honored in the museum with paintings and displays.

The first fire horses were "volunteers," owned by local merchants and loaned to the fire department as emergencies dictated. A painting honors the horse who pulled the hose wagon to a state championship in 1911, when members of the Button Company "laid 228 feet of fire hose, screwed on the fire nozzle and flowed water in 26 2/5 seconds," a world's record that still stands today. The mounted head of the Atlantic Company's fire horse, Fred, who pulled the fire wagon for more than 17 years and dropped dead while answering a false alarm in 1925, is on display, as are many of the early fire wagons, steam engines and fire trucks. Photographic exhibits document New Bern's greatest fires, including the 1922 blaze that consumed a 40-block area and left 3,000 people homeless.

The museum, located at 408 Hancock Street, is open Monday through Saturday from 10 AM to 4 PM. Admission is $5 for adults and $2.50 for children, and additional donations are greatly appreciated. For information call (252) 636-4087.

NEW BERN
GOLF

New Bern is renowned for its many excellent golf courses, and the area's year-round mild weather offers a perfect climate for this challenging game. Golf courses are abundant in and around the city, and many have won acclaim from professionals and amateurs alike.

Resident and visiting golfers are fortunate, as even the most popular courses are easily accessible, and, rest assured, there are courses perfect for for every level of player.

Local golf courses and organizations sponsor golf tournaments in every season except winter. The Craven County Convention and Visitors Bureau maintains a comprehensive calendar of annual events that includes many golf tournaments, and many events are publicized in *New Bern Magazine* and other local publications.

What follows is a list of semi-private courses in the immediate vicinity. The fees we quote here are for 18 holes of play, unless otherwise indicated, and membership is not required for play. For information about Carteret County golf courses, see our Crystal Coast Golf chapter, which details, among others, The Country Club of the Crystal Coast in Pine Knoll Shores; Star Hill Golf and Country Club in Cape Carteret; Brandywine Bay Golf Club near Morehead City; and Silver Creek Golf Club on N.C. Highway 58 near Cape Carteret.

Carolina Pines Golf and Country Club
390 Carolina Pines Blvd., Havelock
(252) 444-1000

On the scenic Neuse River just west of Havelock, this challenging 18-hole, par 72 course offers everything the golfer could want. The course features elevated greens, bermudagrass fairways, abundant sand traps and ample water that rewards the accurate shotmaker. Tim Dupre, the club pro, will arrange lessons for those who

are interested. Also available are a pool, a pro shop, a driving range, target greens and a clubhouse with a lounge and patio that overlooks freshwater lakes and the golf links. Fees are $30 weekdays and $33 weekends, including cart. Carolina Pines is directly off U.S. Highway 70 in Havelock; look for the signs.

The Emerald Golf Club
5000 Clubhouse Dr., New Bern
(252) 633-4440

Rees Jones designed The Emerald Golf Club, creating the 7,000-yard course to be a challenge for golfers of all skill levels. Jones used various grasses to give each hole a different feel and appearance and sculpted the 18-hole course to create variety. Most holes have four or five pin locations. The 4th tee, for example, features four locations that hit across the water and one high-land route. Golfers can take advantage of a fully stocked pro shop, a driving range and lessons from pros Jerry Briele and Catie Camacho. The fee for playing the course is $55 seven days a week year-round and includes the use of a cart. Only members are allowed to walk the course. Tee times should be reserved two weeks in advance for club members; one week for nonmembers. Anyone is eligible for membership in the club, which entitles you to the tennis, swimming pool and club facilities as well as golfing privileges.

Fairfield Harbour Golf Club
Harbour Pointe, 1105 Barkentine Dr.,
New Bern
(252) 638-5338

Fairfield Harbour Golf Club has just reopened one of its 18-hole championship courses. Harbour Pointe is planted with Tif Eagle bermudagrass greens and is open to the public seven days a week. Be sure to call ahead for the daily fees. To get there, cross the Neuse River Bridge on U.S. Highway 17. Turn right on N.C. Highway 55, continue about a half-mile to the traffic light and turn right onto Broad Creek Road. Signs will direct you from there.

Minnesott Golf and Country Club
806 Country Club Dr., Minnesott Beach
(252) 249-0813

This course, built more than 30 years ago, is an 18-hole, par 72. It offers several sand traps, eight holes with water, and a length of 6001 yards. Golfers can enjoy the large pines and oaks as they play the course's new championship bermudagrass fairways. To get there, cross the Neuse River Bridge on U.S. Highway 17 and turn right on N.C. Highway 55 and head toward Bayboro. Right before Bayboro, take a right on Highway 306 at the light and drive about 12 miles, following the road back toward the Neuse River and taking a right on Country Club Drive; at the end is the hidden treasure of Minnesott Golf and Country Club. Minnesott's greens fees are 18 holes for $36 and nine holes for $20 every day; afternoon golfers can play 18 holes for $30. All fees include a cart. There's a snack bar and pro shop on the premises, and PGA club pro Terry Bobbin is available for lessons.

Quaker Neck Country Club
241 Country Club Ln., Trenton
(252) 224-5736

Easily one of the area's best-kept secrets, Quaker Neck Country Club is located in neighboring Jones County, 12 miles south of New Bern just off U.S. Highway 17. This 18-hole championship golf course has a demanding layout and excellent greens that will challenge players of all skill levels. Greens fees vary according to season, so golfers are advised to call ahead for information. Quaker Neck County Club offers family and individual memberships, with amenities including an Olympic-size pool, two tennis courts, a driving range, a golf

shop and club repairs. Banquet facilities are available to the public for private parties and functions.

River Bend Golf and Country Club
94 Shoreline Dr., River Bend
(252) 638-2819

River Bend Golf and Country Club is a semiprivate, 18-hole, par 71 course that accepts public play with reservations up to seven days in advance. River Bend has always had one of the area's nicest golf course layouts, and the course itself was completely rebuilt in summer 2001 to include Tif Eagle bermudagrass greens, 15 new sand bunkers, significant mounding and re-sodded 419 bermuda fairways. Lights were added to the driving range and putting green so nighttime practice is possible.

Rates vary for members and non-members. Nonmembers can play 18 holes for $45 or nine holes for $28 any day of the week. Junior rates are 18 holes for $20 and nine holes for $15 seven days a week. Rates include the use of a cart; only members are allowed to walk the course. Keith Kelly, the club's PGA professional, offers lessons, clinics and club repair for all levels. River Bend also offers one of the most fully stocked golf shops in the area. One special event held every summer is the junior golf camp for ages 5 to 14. The camp culminates in a mini-tournament that allows participants to test the new skills they have learned. River Bend also has two tennis courts and the area's largest outdoor swimming pool available at no charge to members and guests of members. There is a grill and a catering facility that will accommodate up to 120 guests. The Grill Room is open to the public Monday through Saturday 7 AM to 7 PM for breakfast, lunch and dinner. Breakfast and lunch are served on Sundays, when the grill closes at 5 PM. Breakfast is available all day Sunday.

NEW BERN
REAL ESTATE AND  NEIGHBORHOODS

Craven County continues to grow as people from across the state and country decide to make their homes in New Bern and its environs. Many factors affect the area's growth, especially the tide of retirees flowing into the greater New Bern area and the demand for housing from nearby Cherry Point Marine Corps Air Station. New Bern's housing market has expanded substantially to meet the influx of new homeowners.

The city's vibrant community renaissance continues at a steady yet unhurried pace. In New Bern's four historic neighborhoods, you will still see some structures in need of repair among the beautifully restored buildings, but this is changing as Georgian, Federal and Victorian edifices are being returned to their former elegance, adding considerably to the city's charm.

Another big plus for the city is its proximity to water. Positioned where the waters of the Neuse and Trent rivers come together, New Bern is less than an hour's drive from the ocean. A moderate climate, nearby recreational waterways and challenging golf courses are added bonuses in making New Bern a popular vacation, relocation and retirement spot for people from all walks of life.

New Bern's expanding homes market offers newcomers a wide choice of neighborhoods and housing in styles and prices that are sure to appeal to any taste or income bracket. Choices include historic homes, contemporary structures, bungalows, ranch-style residences, riverfront condominiums, townhouses and building lots in ever-increasing new developments.

Because both waterfront and non-waterfront homes and lots are often within the same district, real estate values can vary widely within the same neighborhood. Prices for lots and houses quoted here are approximations and, of course, are subject to change. Our descriptions of neighborhoods will help orient you to the personality, price range and availability of New Bern housing.

If you are interested in New Bern neighborhoods, one of the most helpful guides is *HOMES* magazine, published by NCCoast Communications. This full-color publication contains descriptions and pictures of properties currently on the market. It's free, and you can get copies at restaurants, hotels, supermarkets, real estate firms as well as local businesses.

Neighborhoods and Developments

DOWNTOWN HISTORIC DISTRICT

New Bern's Downtown Historic District is a very attractive, 56-square-block area that for more than two centuries grew along the point of land jutting into the confluence of the Neuse and Trent rivers and extended west to Queen Street. The district was officially entered into the National Register of Historic Places in 1973. The neighborhood contains the town's oldest and most distinguished homes. Its buildings and landscape elements chronicle New Bern's growth — from its days as the Colonial capital of the Carolinas from 1766 until 1778, to its status as an important mercantile center in the mid-eighteenth and early nineteenth centuries, to its time of prosperity fueled by the lumber industry in the late nineteenth and early twentieth centuries.

The **New Bern Preservation Foundation** (NBPF), in the years since its organization in 1972, has bought, stabilized and sold more than 60 structures of historical or architectural significance in New Bern's historic downtown. People who purchase from the NBPF must abide by restrictive covenants that protect the architectural integrity of the house. Whenever possible, the foundation provides new owners with documentary evidence of the structure's original architecture and provenance, such as photos, floor plans and old insurance maps. Once a structure is sold, the preservation foundation serves as a source of expert advice to the owners who restore the dwellings. The foundation's work has provided the impetus for many other property owners to follow suit, resulting in the restoration of more than 150 residences. A few of these date from the mid-1700s, built shortly after New Bern was founded in 1710 by Swiss colonists under Baron Christoph von deGraffenried.

The focal point of historic downtown is **Tryon Palace Historic Sites & Gardens** on Pollock Street. The home of William Tryon, North Carolina's colonial royal governor, the palace's gardens and buildings have been beautifully reconstructed and restored. This state historic site draws thousands of visitors each year. (For information on Tryon Palace Historic Sites & Gardens, see our New Bern Attractions chapter.) Professional offices, businesses, and bed and breakfast inns occupy tastefully renovated old homes in the surrounding neighborhood. The city has an astonishing number of landmarks listed in the National Register of Historic Places, and most of these are found in the downtown district.

Facing the Neuse River are approximately a dozen square blocks of pedigreed houses dating from the eighteenth, nineteenth and twentieth centuries. Most of the elegantly restored homes have two or three stories. Fully restored historic houses are going for $250,000 and can run to more than $600,000. Smaller home restorations away from the river in this neighborhood are available starting in the $150,000 range. As you move farther away from the Neuse, blocks become more transitional and prices drop.

The cost of homes throughout the entire downtown district varies enormously, depending upon location and the degree of restoration. Sometimes homes along the fringes are offered in the $75,000 to $90,000 range, but you can bet they

require a tremendous amount of work and TLC. Preservation also has stimulated demand for smaller residential spaces in New Bern's historic downtown. Town homes and condominiums in this district range from $150,000 to $300,000.

RIVERSIDE HISTORIC DISTRICT

Riverside, also listed on the National Historic Register, consists of National Avenue and the section east of the avenue to the Neuse River. Development began in the late 1890s in response to the city's flourishing lumber industry. Riverside was originally a mixed-use community of residential buildings and commercial enterprises. People wanted to live where they worked. Regrettably, as lumber ceased to be economically important, Riverside fell into disrepair. The result is a neighborhood where beautifully refurbished homes and rundown buildings stand side by side. But fortunately for New Bernians, Riverside property owners are taking measures to restore this once-handsome community to its original function as home to businesses and private residences.

Many of Riverside's larger homes were built between 1896 and World War II, so there is a pleasant mix of architectural styles in the neighborhood. On National Avenue, high-peaked, two-story Victorian structures with wraparound porches and plenty of shade trees are situated well back from the road. On the cross streets perpendicular to National Avenue and the Neuse are rows of tidy bungalows. Homes along the River Drive waterfront are of an entirely different character. You will find pretty brick ranch dwellings on small lots with plenty of trees and meticulous landscaping. Real estate values vary widely, with some of the older bungalows offered in the $150,000 range, and some smaller dwellings starting at about $135,000.

GHENT HISTORIC DISTRICT

The Ghent neighborhood, which was added to the National Historic Register in 1988, contains private homes dating mostly from 1913 to World War II. The area encompasses Spencer, Rhem and sections of Park avenues. It began as a trolley-car suburb in the days when working folks wanted homes away from the hustle and bustle of downtown New Bern. Today,

Spencer Avenue is considered one of the prettiest streets in New Bern, with old-fashioned street lamps along a landscaped median separating two lanes of traffic. Large flowering fruit trees throughout the neighborhood are breathtakingly beautiful in April.

Ghent is an energetic, people-oriented neighborhood where residents take to the sidewalks whenever the weather permits, which is often in the mild New Bern climate. This neighborhood has become a highly desirable section for homeowners and has undergone a lot of sprucing up. Bungalows and cottage-style homes with neat lawns and open or screened porches make up a large part of the neighborhood.

The neighborhood is close to one of the area's nicest amenities, the Twin Rivers YMCA, which includes an outdoor swimming pool (covered with a "bubble" in the cooler months so the pool can used year-round), an indoor Junior Olympic-size swimming pool, a gymnasium, weight rooms and a racquetball court. The Y also offers day care and exercise classes. Ghent is also fortunate to be situated between Fort Totten Park, which has a playground, lighted baseball field, bleachers and rest-rooms, and the larger Lawson Creek Park, a popular fishing spot with nature trails, boat launches and picnic tables.

Homes in Ghent are larger than in many of the new housing developments surrounding New Bern, but many still require remodeling and renovation. Fully restored homes are in the $250,000 range and can run more than $600,000. Smaller homes away from the river are available for $150,000. As you move way from the river, prices drop. Newer homes in the neighborhood's Trolley Run area start at about $150,000.

DEGRAFFENRIED PARK

This distinguished neighborhood lies between Trent and Neuse boulevards directly north of the Ghent Historic District and has recently been granted on the National Register of Historic Places. Homes here are generally large and well-placed on spacious, beautifully landscaped lots. Sidewalks invite neighborhood strolls, and streets carry names such as Queen Anne Lane and Lucerne Way. Many of the neighborhood's more notable residences are stately, two-story Colonial Revival dwellings. Brick walls and wrought-iron fences embellish many of the houses in the district. You can expect to pay between $250,000 to $450,000 for these homes.

TRENT WOODS

This large, mature development lies between New Bern and the Trent River. It has been incorporated to give residents better control over their neighborhoods, and there is virtually no commercial development within its borders. Its winding lanes contain some of the most posh neighborhoods and dwellings in the area. New Bern Golf and Country Club is located in Trent Woods, and national best-selling author Nicholas Sparks is a resident of this upscale community.

Trent Woods is composed of several subdivisions, some of which are primarily waterfront property. Most of the residences tend toward conservative rather than contemporary architectural styles and are constructed of wood, brick or stucco. Homes are large, with two and three stories, and usually have attached or separate two-car garages. Lots are spacious, wooded and impeccably landscaped, often with Spanish moss draped in towering trees. If you take a drive through Trent Woods in the spring, you'll be greeted by a stunning display of flowering trees and shrubs.

In addition to the country club, the area boasts other amenities, such as the Eastern Carolina Yacht Club. The average price range for a non-waterfront home in Trent Woods is $150,000 to $800,000. Waterfront homes are quite pricey and can go up to $1.6 million.

OLDE TOWNE HARBOUR

This is one of the nicest subdivisions in New Bern, just east of Trent Woods and south of U.S. Highway 70. Though just

See this entire guide plus additional content online at insiderinfo.us

minutes from the downtown district and the shopping malls on U.S. Highway 17, Olde Towne Harbour offers quiet seclusion in a lovely, natural setting. Here, you can find some of the most lavish, custom-built contemporary homes and condominiums in New Bern. The largest of these sprawl along the shores of the Trent River and Olde Towne Lake (actually a river inlet). This is a strictly residential development. Homes range from $400,000 to $2 million.

TABERNA

Taberna (it means "place of hospitality"), about 5 miles east of downtown New Bern on U.S. Highway 70 East, combines the best of old-fashioned Southern hospitality with new-fangled charm. Residences at this 1,100-acre golfing community include single-family homes, patio homes and town houses. The focal point is the championship 18-hole golf course designed by Jim Lipe, a head architect for Jack Nicklaus. The community includes natural beauty such as rolling hills, dense foliage, lakes, streams and wetlands, along with man-made amenities like pedestrian

trails, a canoe dock and a canoe trail system, as well as a country club. Home prices in this lovely subdivision range from $250,000 to $800,000.

RIVER BEND

The 1,200-acre town of River Bend lies along a winding inlet on the north shore of the Trent River, about 5 miles east of New Bern. This location allows many of the homesites to have water frontage and private boat slips. The land was originally owned by the Odd Fellows, a fraternal group of black tenant farmers who raised tobacco. During the recession of 1914, they were forced to sell their land to the company store for supplies and debts. During the first half of the century, a wealthy family owned the land and continued to have it farmed for tobacco. In 1965, real estate speculator J. Frank Efird recognized the area's potential as a retirement development for people moving south from the Northeast. He organized The Efird Company to acquire and develop the old Odd Fellows farm.

True to Efird's vision, large numbers of retirees now live in River Bend, although

You'll pay a premium for water views, but it's worth it!

photo: Peter Doran

a number of young families live there too. The community has its own country club to service its 18-hole golf course. The club includes a well-stocked pro shop, a small sandwich shop, an outdoor swimming pool and four lighted tennis courts.

River Bend was incorporated in 1980 in order to maintain roads and provide other services. The municipal building, finished in 1986, has a 99-seat meeting hall and is adjacent to a small park with a children's play area, baseball field and small dock. The development consists mainly of single-family dwellings, all with attached or detached one- and two-car garages. In recent years, clusters of townhouses and duplexes have been added to the community. Prices begin at $90,000 and go way up.

FAIRFIELD HARBOUR

This well-known resort community is across the Neuse River off N.C. Highway 55 and 6 miles down Broad Creek Road. It is a 3,000-acre development that focuses on boating. The marinas offer unrestricted ocean access, 18 nautical miles from the Intracoastal Waterway, in sheltered waters.

Fairfield Harbour is a combination of mostly single-family homes, with some condominiums and townhouses. The development's large canal system gives many homes water access at their back doors. In general, you can expect homes to start in the $150,000 range to approximately $800,000. There are about 900 single-family homes and 120 condominiums.

Condominiums and townhouses at Fairfield Harbour are arranged around small artificial lakes. Winding paths and roads connect all locations, and the combination of layout and landscaping gives a feeling of privacy, even with neighbors only a few feet away. The condos were built at different times in different styles, and they have varying levels of modern amenities. Jacuzzis and Jenn-Aire ranges are common in most, as are balconies, decks and screened porches. Most have two or three bedrooms. Developers have shown careful respect for the trees that were on the lots first. It is not unusual to see decks cut to accommodate a tree.

The Harbour's combination of year-round residents and vacationers requires that a wide variety of activities be readily available. Established community activities are too numerous to list but include such interests as a chorus and clubs for quilting, weaving, garden, books, bridge, RV owners, tennis and yachting.

BRICES CREEK

The Brices Creek region lies southwest of New Bern and James City and south of the Trent River. A number of subdivisions exist in this area, including the Lake Clermont subdivision, Snug Harbor, Oakview, Deer Run, River Trace, Hunter's Ridge and The Homeplace. Many homes are on interior lots, but the more elegant residences face the waterfront and are set well away from the road on large, wooded lots. They tend to be brick or stucco in contemporary styles. Homes on the waterfront generally sell in the $400,000 range, depending on their water frontage. Houses away from the creek sell in the $215,000 to $400,000 range. The Craven County Airport is just east of Brices Creek.

GREENSPRINGS

Huge, contemporary dwellings on large, wooded lots grace the western banks of the Neuse River on Green Springs Road just off U.S. 70 E. between New Bern and Havelock. Waterfront homes start around $350,000, with lots in the $125,000 range. Farther east along Rivershore Drive, you can find older frame houses and large cottages tucked into the river bluffs. Prices vary greatly according to age, size and lot space. Many new neighborhoods have been developed in this area over the last few years. Prices of these homes start at about $100,000, but the value is increasing rapidly.

CAROLINA PINES

About 11 miles east of New Bern off U.S. 70 on Carolina Pines Boulevard, Carolina Pines is a large, well-established residential resort golf community along the Neuse River. It offers a blend of quiet countryside living combined with country-club flair and neighborhood charm. Housing varies and includes modest patio homes, ranch styles and elegant two-story showplaces. Houses in Carolina Pines often sell in the $100,000 to $160,000 range. Some of the neighborhood amenities include a challenging 18-hole golf course, a golf pro, a pro shop, tennis courts, a pool, a clubhouse with a restaurant and lounge and a patio overlooking freshwater lakes and the links. An added bonus is the adjacent Croatan National Forest, where residents can enjoy camping, hiking and horseback riding.

WEST NEW BERN

This area is bounded by Neuse Boulevard on the northeast, M. L. King Jr. Boulevard on the southeast, U.S. 70 on the southwest and Glenburnie Road on the northwest. Homes in this attractive neighborhood are large, brick, ranch houses and two-story dwellings on generous lots. This part of New Bern is wooded, and there is plenty of undeveloped pine forest bordering many lots. Most of the homes have numerous large trees in the yards. Prices here begin at about $90,000 and go up to $150,000. These homes are convenient to Kidsville and the West New Bern Recreation Center, which offers tennis courts, baseball fields, a basketball court and a supervised game room with pool tables.

GREENBRIER

Greenbrier is a distinguished 700-acre subdivision right in the middle of New Bern. It is off S. Glenburnie Road and is a neighborhood well-suited for families with young children and for retirees. Lots range from an eighth of an acre to more than a full acre, and excellent architectural planning has effectively blended a variety of home styles into a delightful community. Many homes are of contemporary brick designs. All utilities are underground. Homes on spacious lots range from $160,000 to $350,000.

The entire development surrounds an 18-hole championship golf course, The Emerald Golf Club, designed by Rees Jones. The clubhouse at The Emerald Golf Club is often the chosen location for major local charity events. It contains an Olympic-size, Z-shaped pool. Four lighted tennis courts are also available. Golf club members can sharpen their skills on one of the finest new practice complexes in the state. (For more information about the golf club, see our New Bern Golf chapter.)

From Greenbrier's front gate, you are within two minutes of major shopping, five minutes from the local schools and hospital, and adjacent to the campus of Craven Community College.

OUTSIDE NEW BERN

Cutter Bay
Oriental
(877) 633-0271

The planned, gated community of Cutter Bay is designed to bring together the architecture and landscape true to the water and the sailor. Featuring its own marina and harbor, Cutter Bay will honor the history and tradition of this area with many planned amenities throughout the property. Mother Nature provides the backdrop for many of the features destined to be found here, including open green spaces and parks, nature trails and tree-lined walking paths. These, combined with a beautiful clubhouse and swimming amenities, plus vintage architectural features in all common areas, a beautifully designed entrance and underground utilities, will make Cutter Bay one of the most welcoming communities on the coast.

Somerset
Little Washington
(252) 940-GROW

One of eastern North Carolina's newest and most exciting developments, Somerset, (252) 940-GROW (4769) broke ground in December 2005 and is nestled in the historic, waterfront town of Washington, among the spectacular waterways, forests and nearby beaches of eastern North Carolina. Offering a peaceful alternative to bustling city life, Somerset is conveniently located within easy driving distance of shopping and cultural meccas Greenville and Raleigh, as well as Raleigh-Durham International Airport, several regional airports and I-95. Prospective residents will enjoy the selection of spacious, open floor plans available in townhomes and single-family patio homes. With the community's unique maintenance-free living plan, homeowners can leave the mowing, edging and weeding to someone else, giving more time to explore eastern North Carolina's cultural heritage, enjoy their favorite hobbies, like boating,

golfing, hiking, traveling or simply taking a quiet stroll down the quaint streets of Little Washington, enjoying its celebrated Southern hospitality.

Real Estate Companies

Many reputable real estate agencies do business in New Bern. If you have questions about area real estate companies, consult the Neuse River Region Association of Realtors, (252) 636-5364. For questions about building contractors, contact the New Bern-Craven County Home Builders Association at (252) 636-3707. While many real estate companies in New Bern handle rental properties as well as sales, the New Bern Area Chamber of Commerce, (252) 637-3111, also offers a handy apartment directory.

Assist2Sell Buyers & Sellers Realty
1723 S. Glenburnie Dr., New Bern
(252) 636-5797, (800) 222-9714

"Full Service with $avings!" is Assist-2Sell's motto. Those in the market to sell their home will enjoy Assist2Sell's wide range of helpful options, while those in the market to buy will find friendly and informative assistance. Assist2Sell lists existing homes, new construction, land and lots in New Bern and surrounding communities. This company also offers a free buyers' hot sheet and a relocation package, sent upon request.

Century 21 Zaytoun Raines
312 S. Front St., New Bern
(252) 633-3069, (877) 639-2376

George Zaytoun began building homes in 1964, and Marvin Raines began a real estate career in 1971. In 1986 they combined their expertise to create what has become one of the area's most successful real estate companies. The firm has been awarded Century 21's most distinguished award, the Centurion Award, presented to only eight of Century 21's 176 offices throughout North and South Carolina. It's impossible to drive through New Bern and not see Zaytoun-Raines signs. Twenty full-time agents handle residential, commercial and investment properties, including those offered through the Century 21 Fine Homes & Estates program.

Coldwell Banker Willis-Smith Realty
115 Middle St., New Bern
(252) 638-3500, (800) 638-3500

This reliable firm's offices are downtown near the New Bern waterfront. The company operates as a seller's and buyer's agency, offering a full range of services that includes residential brokerage and development and referrals to and from its national network. Its well-trained and experienced agents are knowledgeable about housing in all of New Bern's long-established neighborhoods and new developments and subdivisions. Willis-Smith also handles rental properties in the New Bern area.

Nancy Hollows Real Estate
626 Hancock St., New Bern
(252) 636-3177, (800) 622-3177

Nancy Hollows likes working with people who are looking for a unique property, and New Bern has unique properties. Nancy established the agency in 1986 and has succeeded in helping satisfied buyers and sellers. Nancy's goal is to use her experience and knowledge to help the client make the most informed decisions possible in their real-estate transactions. The agency has vast experience in residential real estate, specializing in waterfront and historic properties. Nancy Hollows Real Estate is a licensed real estate auction firm in the state of North Carolina.

New Bern Real Estate
3601 Trent Rd. #5, New Bern
(252) 636-2200

New Bern Real Estate has experienced agents ready to serve you. They pride themselves on being local, low pressure and thoroughly familiar with the entire New Bern area. They have close working relationships with other agents in town and can help you no matter what your real estate need.

RE/MAX By the Water
242 Middle St., New Bern
(252) 633-9300

Daynette Orr added New Bern to the RE/MAX network when she took her real estate experience and opened her own office here in 2002. Daynette's knowledge of the local real estate market combined with her specialized marketing program allow her to provide complete customer satisfaction and positive results. Daynette specializes in properties in New Bern and throughout eastern North Carolina, and is a Certified Residential Specialist (CRS), a Graduate of the REALTORS ® Institute (GRI), and a Seniors Residential Specialist (SRES), as well as Broker/Owner of the New Bern office.

Trent River Realty
333 Middle St., New Bern
(252) 633-1442, (800) 663-3843

With two office locations, one in historic downtown New Bern and the other in River Bend, Trent River Realty's agents work with their customers and clients to make buying or selling a home as enjoyable as possible. Trent River Realty offers buyers and sellers not only exceptional real estate representation, but also the insight and expertise of the local real estate market that only comes with years of dedicated and outstanding customer service.

Tyson & Hooks Realty
2402 M. L. King Jr. Blvd., New Bern
(252) 633-5766

This firm has been serving Craven County and the New Bern area since 1972. Six agents provide general real estate services, including the sale of commercial and residential properties, while Tyson Management Company handles property management and rentals throughout the New Bern area.

The Tyson Group Real Estate/ Keller Williams Real Estate
2117 S. Glenburnie Rd., New Bern
(252) 675-9595

The Tyson Group are the top-selling Realtors in the New Bern and Havelock areas with sales and listings of more than $35 million in 2007–08. They look forward tp being your Realtor and can show you any property listing in the market, thanks to their membership in the Multiple Listing Service. Need information about New Bern, Havelock, Cherry Point and the surrounding area or about the process of buying or selling a home? The Tyson Group is at your service to help you achieve your dream. For more information contact Jana J. Tyson or Steve Tyson of The Tyson Group of Keller Williams Realty. The Tyson Group offers services for the mature buyer or seller and for those just starting out. The group is very experienced with retirees, relocation and military PCS. Call the Tyson Group today. They are the "Gold Standard in Real Estate."

Service Directory

TAX RATES

The Craven County property tax rate is 61¢ per $100 of assessed value (Craven County budget for 2008–09). City property is taxed at both the city and county rates. New Bern's tax rate is 50.5¢ per $100 valuation, with an additional 18¢ per $100 assessed valuation in the downtown municipal services district. These rates are subject to change each fiscal year.

OTHER UTILITY SERVICES

If your home has natural gas cooking and heating appliances, service in New Bern and Craven County is available through **Piedmont Natural Gas**, (800) 752-7504. Electrical service in the areas surrounding New Bern is provided by **Progress Energy Carolinas, Inc.** (formerly CP&L), (800) 452-2777. Water and sewer services outside of New Bern are provided by **Craven County Water and Sewer**, 2830 Neuse Boulevard, (252) 636-6615. A list of private companies providing garbage disposal services in Craven County is available from the **Craven County Solid Waste** office, (252) 636-6659. Requirements and deposits for establishing services vary, so be sure to call for more information.

City of New Bern Utlities
606 Fort Totten Dr., New Bern
(252) 639-2750

Electric, water, sewer and garbage disposal services within New Bern and Trent Woods are provided by the City of New Bern. You are required to appear in person to establish service and pay a deposit, and you must bring a picture ID card and your

rental lease or proof of property ownership. Deposits are based on the previous tenants' average usage, so this figure can vary. Deposits are refunded after a year if your bill has been paid in full and on time every month during your first year of service. Deposits can possibly be waived if you provide a letter of credit from your previous utility provider and pass a credit check, or if a current customer with a excellent credit rating agrees to co-sign for you. Office hours are Monday through Friday 8 AM to 5 PM. For same-day service, you must be in the office no later than 2 PM. The utility office is in the old Fort Totten branch of First Citizens Bank on the corner of Fort Totten Drive and Broad Street. There is a First Citizens ATM machine available on site.

EMBARQ
New Bern
(252) 633-9011

Phone service to the New Bern area is provided by EMBARQ. Based on your previous record, you may be asked to pay a deposit to establish phone service. This deposit is normally refunded after a year. Service connections can take up to four days. EMBARQ is also a provider of Internet, wireless and satellite television.

Apartments

Renting an apartment in New Bern can be an interesting adventure. As is the case in many towns, location is important. If you are interested in an apartment, Insiders advise that you drive through the neighborhood at different times of the day and night so you understand where you are moving. Rates can vary depending on the neighborhood — apartments in the historic district as well as newer apartment complexes will go for much higher than those on the outskirts of town. Most of the condominiums under development downtown are for sale rather than rent. Most apartment rentals in the area are handled by real estate firms or management companies. However, there are also a number of apartment complexes that Insiders feel comfortable recommending.

Carolina Club Apartments
1350 Trent Blvd., New Bern
(252) 633-3357

Carolina Club Apartments is located next to Fort Totten Park and very near to the historic Ghent and DeGraffenried neighborhoods. This well-maintained complex features one-bedroom and two-bedroom apartments. Each apartment includes central heat and air, a range and refrigerator and mini-blinds, and the monthly rental fee covers city water and sewer services. Residents have access to on-site laundry facilities. Up to two pets 25 pounds and under are permitted; however, a non-refundable pet deposit and an additional monthly rental fee are charged. A security deposit and a yearly lease are required.

Tryon Estates Apartments
307 Simmons St., New Bern
(252) 633-3357

Tryon Estates Apartments is one of New Bern's nicest apartment complexes. It features one-bedroom, one-bath units and two-bedroom, one-and-a-half bath townhouse garden and townhouse apartments in a beautifully landscaped area right off Simmons Street. The apartments feature either a private patio or balcony, and townhouses have private patios and outside storage areas. All have central air and heat and include a range, refrigerator with ice-maker, dishwasher and mini-blinds, and some townhouses are available with washer and dryer hook-ups. Other amenities include off-street parking, laundry facilities and a private swim-

ming pool. Tenants are required to pay a security deposit and sign a one-year lease. The monthly rent includes city water and sewer services, cable and 24-hour emergency maintenance. Up to two pets 25 pounds and smaller are permitted; however, a nonrefundable pet deposit and an additional monthly rental fee are charged. Insiders are glad to recommend Tryon Estates Apartments; it is within minutes of both downtown and the Dr. M. L. King Jr. Boulevard shopping corridor.

Woodland Crossing Apartments
2500 Woodland Ave., New Bern
(252) 633-5151

Located behind Berne Square Shopping Center, Woodland Crossing Apartments is located close to some of New Bern's finest shopping and restaurants. The complex offers a secluded setting that gives residents the quiet and privacy they expect. Floor plans feature one-bedroom, one-bath apartments and two and three-bedroom, two-bath apartments. Amenities include a tennis court, pool, business center, fitness center, playground, and garage and storage units. Ask about the discounts available for active military as well as a possible discount on your down payment for preferred employers. Woodland Crossing is pet-friendly; however, requirements include an interview, a partially refundable pet deposit and more; call for details. A Bark Park is available featuring a leash-free zone for games of catch and a dog run. The office is open Monday through Saturday.

NEW BERN
EDUCATION AND CHILD CARE

N ew Bern residents have excellent educational opportunities. Adults have access to a state-supported university, college-level classes and a first-rate community college. Parents have the option of sending their children to the Craven County public schools or one of the private schools in New Bern or in nearby towns. Several trustworthy child-care options are available for children who are too young for school.

Colleges and Universities

Those interested in furthering their education may choose from two-year associate's degrees, bachelor's degrees in partnership with East Carolina University, accelerated four-year degree programs,

plus vocational and continuing education classes.

Craven Community College
808 College Ct., New Bern
(252) 638-4131

Craven Community College offers two-year degrees and adult continuing education at its New Bern and Havelock campuses. Two-year associate's degree programs in the arts and sciences and more than 30 technical and vocational programs are available. Two feature programs cover aviation systems technology, information systems security and medical assisting. The college offers basic adult education programs, two-year technical and transfer programs, one-year vocational programs and extension programs in occupational, practical and vocational courses of study. Craven Community Col-

Nothing defines summer more than a barefoot stroll in the ocean.

photo: Carolyn Temple

lege is part of North Carolina's 58-campus community college system.

East Carolina University
Office of Undergraduate Admissions, Greenville
(252) 328-6640

A little more than an hour's drive from New Bern, East Carolina University in Greenville is a state-supported university that offers 104 bachelor's degree programs, 74 master's degree programs, four specialist degree programs, one first-professional MD program and 17 doctoral programs in professional colleges and schools. Two popular curriculum areas at this university are education and health sciences. Many working adults pursue degrees by commuting to the Greenville campus. Craven Regional Medical Center in New Bern is a clinical site for students enrolled in the ECU School of Nursing.

Mount Olive College at New Bern
2131 S. Glenburnie Rd., Ste. 6, New Bern
(252) 633-4464, (800) 868-8479

Mount Olive offers accelerated degree-completion programs in criminal justice and criminology, management and organizational development, healthcare management, religion and early childhood education. Adults who already have about two years of college credits can take advantage of a special time-condensed format that allows them to complete their degree while continuing to work full-time. For working adults who have little or no college credit, Mount Olive College in New Bern also offers a four-semester program, called the Heritage Plus Program, which leads to an associate's degree and also provides the core courses for admission to the bachelor's degree programs cited above. Also see our Higher Education and Child Care chapter.

Public Schools

Craven County Schools
3600 Trent Rd., New Bern
(252) 514-6346

The Craven County School System, which serves more than 14,616 city and county students, provides a free and ap-propriate public education to all students within its jurisdiction. The schools are fully accredited by the Southern Association of Colleges and Schools and the N.C. Department of Public Instruction. The system employs about 1,096 teaching professionals, 136 of whom are National Board Certified (and the number grows each year) and about 962 support personnel to staff the county's 15 elementary schools (kindergarten through fifth), five middle schools (sixth through eighth) and three high schools. Three of these schools operate on a year-round schedule, while the others follow the traditional August-to-May calendar.

The vision of the school system is that Craven County Schools will be the highest performing system of public education in North Carolina, and its mission statement reflects this — "Craven County Schools, united with families and communities, will continuously improve student learning and educational services through a focus on expectations and values which support performance excellence." The school system has adopted the Baldrige Approach for continuous improvement, not just on the students' parts but also the system and schools themselves, leading to performance excellence. The system's average teacher-student ratio is 1-to-26. The school system offers a comprehensive curriculum based on the North Carolina Standard Course of Study.

In addition to the traditional academic courses, the educational program includes music, foreign language, art, dance, theater, athletics, computer classes and advanced placement courses. Optimum Student Achievement is the major strategic direction for the school system.

Craven County students perform in the top 10 percent of school districts across the state. According to the most recent accountability report, nine schools in the system are Schools of Excellence, the highest awards given to schools in the state, and 10 schools are Schools of Distinction. Twenty of the 23 schools met or exceeded their school growth goals. Craven County Schools is also a leader in the state in efforts to close the achievement gap among all students.

Elementary education in Craven County encourages children to meet academic objectives through developmentally appropriate activities. Hands-on experiences and problem-solving strategies are designed to harmonize with the natural characteristics of children's developmental stages. Besides the core curriculum of communication skills, science, math and social studies, students and teachers are involved in enrichment programs such as art, physical education, computers, music and drama.

Middle schools emphasize educational experiences that bridge learning between elementary school and high school. All five middle schools operate on a team concept. Two to five teachers collaborate to develop plans and strategies to deal with the instructional, social and emotional needs and interests of students. Along with the core curriculum, students are exposed to critical thinking and problem solving, health and fitness, cooperative learning, and exploratory courses such as foreign languages, vocational education and visual arts.

The high schools focus on the creation of a positive school climate and the identification and prevention of problems that may lead to an unsuccessful high school career. All high schools are on block scheduling, which allows students to take four courses each semester in 90-minute class periods versus the traditional 55-minute classes. Instead of the maximum six courses per year, students are able to take as many as eight courses — four per semester. Among several advantages, block scheduling gives students the flexibility of enrolling in more electives without giving up required academic classes.

To prepare students for the workplace, the Craven County School System has implemented a developmental program that helps students entering high school to choose and focus on a career path. Students may select from four career pathways: engineering, industrial and manufacturing technology; business and marketing; health and human services; and liberal and fine arts. A student's choice of career path is aided by the develop-ment of a four-year educational plan and supplemented by career guidance that helps the student make a smooth transition into the work force, or into an associate or bachelor's degree program. ROTC programs also are offered in all three high schools.

The Craven County School System offers many support services: comprehensive testing, programs for exceptional and academically gifted students, dropout prevention and drug education programs, library/media skills programs and the services of school psychologists, social workers and nurses. In addition, numerous services are available for students with visual, hearing, speech, orthopedic and other health impairments as well as for the mentally handicapped, learning disabled and homebound. Contact Exceptional Children's Programs, (252) 514-6355, for more information.

School safety is a major consideration to the school community, as is facility improvement. Each school system operation has a threat condition process, a safe schools plan and a critical incident response plan. The Craven County Board of Education has a long-range facility plan. The construction of three elementary schools and two performing arts centers, major renovations to an existing middle school, plus new roofs for several schools have been completed within the past three years.

The Craven County School System has a free information portfolio that includes a county-wide activities calendar, descriptions of and directions to all 23 schools, a discussion of the system's educational curricula, and a central services directory with the names and phone numbers of all support staff. The school system encourages requests for information; write or call the Craven County Board of Education, Director of Public Relations, 3600 Trent Road, New Bern, NC 28562; (252) 514-6333.

Other Facilities

Some children fall behind in school and need a little help to catch up, while others need an accelerated program to offer them challenges. Private learning centers can provide such assistance. Other educational facilities in New Bern include a driving school to assist teens with earning their driving privileges.

The Driving School
2503-F Neuse Blvd., New Bern
(252) 637-0200

Teens who don't want to wait for their high school driver's education class can sign up for classes at The Driving School, located in Town Park Plaza on Neuse Boulevard. The driver's education class incorporates 30 classroom hours with six hours of driving time, where students learn defensive driving techniques, safe passing skills and how to avoid traffic hazards. The Driving School also offers adult refresher courses and driver improvement classes.

Sylvan Learning Center of New Bern
1314-B Commerce Dr., New Bern
(252) 633-6380

Sylvan Learning Center offers a variety of educational programs and services for students of all ages and specializes in helping students master basic learning skills, achieve potential and gain confidence. The New Bern center offers programs in reading, math, writing, study skills and Scholastic Aptitude Test (SAT) preparation.

Private Schools

New Bern offers several private schools and another school is about 40 miles west in Kinston. Additionally, many day-care and camp facilities offer private kindergartens for young children and summer programs for school children.

Arendell Parrott Academy
1901 Dobbs Farm Rd., Kinston
(252) 522-4222

Arendell Parrott Academy is a nonsectarian, college preparatory school offering co-educational instruction for students in transitional-kindergarten through 12th grade. Academy students in grades 7 through 12 participate in 31 team sports,

including field hockey and lacrosse. The fine arts program incorporates drama, chorus, orchestra, dance and visual art instruction for all grades. Arendell Parrott Academy offers transportation for out-of-town students, including those from the New Bern area.

Calvary Baptist Church School
1821 Rhem Ave., New Bern
(252) 633-5410

A ministry of Calvary Baptist Church, this private school serves approximately 95 students in kindergarten through grade 12. The school's uniforms consist of green shirts with the school logo, combined with khaki pants for boys and khaki skirts and jumpers for girls. There is an instrumental music program for the students as well as basketball, volleyball and cheerleading for middle and high school students.

Ruth's Chapel Christian School
2709 Oaks Rd., New Bern
(252) 638-1297

This school serves about 155 students in kindergarten through grade 12 and an additional 40 students in day-care and before- and after-school programs. Students are required to wear uniforms. A structured program is offered for 3- and 4-year-olds, while older children study the Abeka and Bob Jones University curricula. Volleyball, soccer, cheerleading and basketball programs are available for older students.

St. Paul's Education Center
3007 Country Club Rd., New Bern
(252) 633-0100

Serving about 200 students from pre-kindergarten (age 4) through 8th grade, this private school is affiliated with St. Paul's Catholic Church.

Child Care

As is the case across the nation, the need for quality day care continues to grow in New Bern. We have listed here, in alphabetical order, a few of the day-care

See this entire guide plus additional content online at insiderinfo.us

facilities in and around New Bern. Craven County and the State of North Carolina regulate day-care homes and centers through the issuance of registrations and licenses. Regulations call for all such facilities to meet health and safety standards. In the case of nonsectarian child-care institutions, standards for children's learning and play programs must be met. For a complete list of regulated day-care homes and licensed day-care centers, call the Craven County Child Care Resource and Referral at (252) 672-5921.

All About Children Day Care and Pre-School
2610 Neuse Blvd., New Bern
(252) 633-2505

This day-care center offers a variety of programs for infants, toddlers and school children. The day care accepts children ages 6 weeks to 5 years old and offers preschool classes for ages 2 and older in separated age groups. The After-School program offers before- and after-school care for children up to age 12. Transportation to all city schools is provided. Summer programs and swimming lessons are also available. The More at Four program with certified teachers is also available.

Childcare Network - Old Cherry Point Road
3705 Old Cherry Point Rd., New Bern
(252) 636-3791

Open Monday through Friday, Childcare Network offers day-care services and before- and after-school programs for children ages 6 weeks to 12 years (except for the Childcare Network facility at 301 Ninth Street in New Bern, which accepts children 12 months through 12 years). Star-licensed by the state of North Carolina, Childcare Network features such amenities as transportation to and from public schools, nutritious meals and snacks,

summer camp activities for older children, and computers for children. The Childcare Network staff prepares younger children for school by utilizing the Active Learning Series for infants and toddlers and the HighReach Curriculum for ages 2 to 5. Hours vary per location. Call ahead to confirm hours and availability.

First Steps Infant and Toddler Center
403 Ninth St., New Bern
(252) 638-3245

This full-service child-care facility — the only one in New Bern designed exclusively for infants and toddlers — accepts children ages 6 weeks through 36 months. With a staff trained in CPR, first aid and early childhood education, the center believes children learn best through play, so children not only gain valuable skills but have a delightful time doing so. First Steps is open Monday through Friday.

Kiddie Kollege Learning Center
704 Newman Rd., New Bern
(252) 633-1050

Open 6 AM until 6 PM Monday through Friday, this Christian faith–based school has an enrollment of approximately 150 children. It accepts 2- to 4-year olds for the pre-kindergarten program and offers after-school care for its students and for children enrolled in public schools.

Little Hands Day Nursery
2314 Elizabeth Ave., New Bern
(252) 638-1434

Preschool classes are available for toddlers age 2 and older, who also enjoy playing in Little Hands' large and shady playground. For students through age 12, Little Hands offers before- and after-school care, including transportation to and from local schools during the school year. They also offer summer camp from May to August.

NEW BERN
(H)HEALTHCARE

The availability of quality healthcare is a primary consideration for newcomers and residents of any area, and New Bern is particularly fortunate to have a wide range of top-notch professional healthcare services. The quality of life and the presence of an excellent medical center have attracted many physicians and specialized health professionals to the area.

With retirees continuously relocating to the New Bern area, additional health-care services, such as home-care professionals, cardiac rehabilitation services and geriatric care, are expanding in New Bern. These services are not often available in towns of similar size.

The Craven Regional Medical Center has an open-heart surgery unit that makes it the nearest hospital in North Carolina's central coastal region to offer the procedure. In addition, the medical center offers state-of-the-art diagnostic equipment and services at its New Bern Diagnostic Center, same-day surgery at New Bern Outpatient Surgery Center, a comprehensive medical rehabilitation center and a mental-health unit.

Alternative and complementary healthcare practitioners play an important role for many in the treatment of ailments and in the maintenance of good health. Holistic practitioners and massage therapists of varied philosophical orientations adjust mind and body. In this chapter

we offer a listing of alternative healthcare practitioners in the New Bern area.

Hospital

Craven Regional Medical Center
2000 Neuse Blvd., New Bern
(252) 633-8111

Craven Regional Medical Center is widely recognized as a leading medical facility serving eastern North Carolina and was the first in this part of the state to perform radiation therapy. Opened in 1962, the center is acutely attuned to quality medical care and implements a total quality management program. The 350-bed, full-service facility offers a comprehensive range of services not often found outside larger urban areas. At least partly because of that, it has been named a primary health provider for a number of area counties and, most recently, for Defense Department beneficiaries in eastern North Carolina.

An outstanding medical staff of more than 230-plus physicians, a dedicated professional and support staff of more than 1,800 and a progressive administration and board strive to combine the best of medical care with empathy for patients. In addition to the medical surgical areas, the medical center has dedicated units for neurosurgical, intensive and intermediate care, women's care, pediatric care and cancer care. Cardiac care is a focal point, with the area's most advanced services for diagnosing and treating heart disease, including interventional cardiology and cardiac surgery. This was the first eastern North Carolina hospital to offer cardiac rehabilitation on an outpatient basis. Its modern cardiac surgery suite includes surgical, recovery and intensive care rooms. Likewise, the medical center's oncology services lead the area in chemotherapy and radiation therapy on an inpatient or outpatient basis, including support services.

The medical center's outpatient services include the Craven Diagnostic Center, offering state-of-the-art diagnostic imaging radiography, Magnetic Resonance Imaging (MRI), CT scanning, digital mammography and bone densitometry in a comfortable private setting. PET scanning imaging provides cancer and Alzheimer's patients with the most sophisticated diagnostic and cancer staging capabilities. You can arrange same-day surgery at the Craven Surgery Center, which include procedures for cataracts, hernias and an ever-expanding list of surgical treatments. The Women's Center offers comprehensive gynecological care, including outpatient procedures and laser surgical techniques, and the Family Birth Place stresses family involvement in childbirth.

Specialty units include Crossroads, a 23-bed facility specializing in group-based care of adult mental-health disorders, and the Coastal Rehabilitation Center, a 20-bed unit designed to help victims of stroke, orthopedic and neurological disorders return to independent living and health as soon as possible. Extended patient support services of Craven Regional Medical Center include home-care and referral services, assuring that medical needs are met and services are provided.

Health Department

Craven County Health Department
2818 Neuse Blvd., New Bern
(252) 636-4963

Located in the Craven County Human Services Complex, the public heath department offers many adult health services, including chronic disease detection, family planning and maternal healthcare, adult immunizations and a sexually transmitted disease clinic. Child health services include well child care, illness and injury care, free immunizations and cardiac and neurology clinics through physician referrals. Other services provided by the health department include the Women, Infants and Children (WIC) Supplemental Foods Program for children age 5 and younger and pregnant women; nutritional counseling for special diets or weight loss; a mobile dental care unit that provides screenings, dental services and dental health education; and educational programs for the public. In addition, the Division of Environmental Health, (252)

636-4936, provides food, lodging and sanitation inspections, on-site wastewater inspections, lead poisoning investigations, indoor air quality and pediatric asthma management, rabies control and more.

Emergency and Important Numbers

Dial **911** from anywhere in the area for emergencies (police, sheriff, fire and rescue service).

Alcoholics Anonymous - New Bern, New Bern, (252) 633-3716

Alcoholics Anonymous/AL-ANON, (800) 344-2666

American Red Cross, (252) 637-3405, (866) 446-0979

Craven County Crisis Line, (252) 638-5995

Craven County Department of Social Services, New Bern, (252) 636-4900

Craven County Health Department, (252) 636-4920

Craven Regional Medical Center, (252) 633-8111

Craven-Pamlico Animal Services Center, New Bern, (252) 637-4606

Drug and Alcohol Dependency Problem Hotline, (252) 637-7000

Promise Place
(262) 633-3381, (800) 656-HOPE
Hotline for wellness, counseling, victim advocacy, rape and incest.

Urgent Care and Private Practices

Coastal Carolina Health Care
1020 Medical Park Ave., New Bern
(252) 514-2061
www.cchealthcare.com

Coastal Carolina Health Care
1020 Medical Park Ave., New Bern
(252) 514-2061

Atlantic Internal Medicine
730 Newman Rd., New Bern
(252) 634-9090

CCHC Endoscopy Center
975 Newman Rd., New Bern
(252) 514-6644

CCHC Hospitalists
2000 Neuse Blvd., New Bern
(252) 514-2061

CCHC Imaging Center
1030 Medical Park Ave., New Bern
(252) 637-5480

CCHC Sleep Lab
1020 Medical Park Ave., New Bern
(252) 634-2240

CCHC Urgent Care
1040 Medical Park Ave., New Bern
(252) 638-CARE (2273)

Coastal Internal Medicine and Cardiology
670 Cardinal Pl., New Bern
(252) 636-6222

New Bern Cancer Care
1010 Medical Park Ave., New Bern
(252) 636-5135

New Bern Family Practice
1040 Medical Park Ave., New Bern
(252) 633-1678

New Bern Internal Medicine and Cardiology
702 Newman Rd., New Bern
(252) 633-5333

Southern Gastroenterology Associates
3100 Wellons Blvd., New Bern
(252) 636-9000

310 Commerce Ave., Morehead City
(252) 726-7111

Twin Rivers Family Practice
3252 Wellons Blvd., New Bern
(252) 636-2664

Coastal Carolina Health Care (CCHC) is a multi-specialty medical group practice with 12 offices in New Bern and one in Morehead City. The physicians of CCHC specialize in general internal medicine, family practice, cardiology and pulmonary medicine, respiratory allergies, digestive disorders, hematology and oncology. CCHC also offers state-of-the-art diagnostic services, including mammography, bone densitometry, nuclear medicine, ultrasound, computerized tomography (CT), and the area's only open bore magnetic resonance imaging (MRI). The practice also has the area's largest group of hospitalists based 24 hours a day at Craven Regional Medical Center to provide timely and dedicated service to patients. The CCHC Endoscopy Center and CCHC Sleep Disorder Center are available to all patients with a referral. CCHC Urgent Care is located in the new medical complex at 1040 Medical Park Way. It is open Monday through Friday 8:30 AM to 8 PM, Saturday and all holidays except Thanksgiving and

Christmas from 9 AM to 4 PM and Sunday 2 to 6 PM. During normal business hours, no appointment is necessary for CCHC Urgent Care.

Coastal Children's Clinic
703 Newman Rd., New Bern
(252) 633-2900

Coastal Children's Clinic is proud to have offered the most comprehensive pediatric care in the area for more than 50 years. The practice specializes in pediatric medicine for children from birth through age 18. Coastal Children's Clinic is well known for providing excellence in pediatrics to the children of eastern North Carolina. The practice's 12 physicians, pediatric physician's assistant and pediatric nurse practitioner are committed to providing the highest quality pediatric care possible in an atmosphere that is both nurturing and friendly to children. They have had office hours seven days a week for more than 30 years, which is unique for this area. All three offices (New Bern, Maysville, Havelock) are open Monday to Friday 8 AM to 5 PM, and the New Bern office is open Saturday mornings 8 AM to noon and Sunday afternoons noon to 4 PM. A physician is always on call for emergencies

at (252) 633-2269 or by beeper at (252) 633-8817. Same-day appointments are available.

ECIM - Eastern Carolina Internal Medicine
100 Berne Sq., New Bern
(252) 638-4023

ECIM is a large medical group practice with offices in New Bern, Havelock and Pollocksville. A team of more than 41 physicians and medical providers specializes in internal medicine, family practice, pediatrics and emergency medicine. Subspecialists provide treatment in gastroenterology, hematology, neurology, nuclear medicine, infectious and pulmonary diseases, digestive disorders, arthritis, and cancer diagnosis and treatment. The practice offers full-time hospitalist service at Craven Regional Medical Center. Diagnostic services include radiology, nuclear medicine, laboratory work, CT scanning and ultrasound. The ECIM New Bern in Berne Square, (252) 638-4023, is a full-service medical office featuring laboratory services, X-ray capability (including mammography), and a state-of-the-art endoscopy suite. Relocated at the same site, but with a separate entrance, is ECIM Pediatrics, (252) 636-1919, which

The New Bern Fireman's Museum is perfect for a relaxing and informative afternoon.

serves children from birth through age 18. Another of ECIM's vast array of services is an Oncology Treatment Center at its Pollocksville location.

ECIM Urgent Medical Care
2117 S. Glenburnie Rd., New Bern
(252) 636-1001

This urgent-care center provides treatment for minor emergencies and family medical needs and offers "after office" and weekend hours. Hours of operation are Monday through Saturday 10 AM to 6 PM and Sunday 1 to 6 PM. No appointment is necessary. (ECIM Urgent Medical Care also has an office in Cape Carteret at 906 W. B. McLean Drive, (252) 393-9007, which is open Monday through Friday 8:30 AM to 5 PM.) Both centers have X-ray and laboratory services as well as emergency-trained physicians and physician extenders.

The Heart Center of Eastern Carolina
1001 Newman Rd., New Bern
(252) 635-6777

The Heart Center of Eastern Carolina is a full-service cardiology practice featur-

ing the most up-to-date services in the diagnosis, treatment and prevention of cardiac and vascular diseases. This medical practice of six board-certified cardiologists offers many kinds of non-invasive and invasive treatments: diagnostic catheterization, electrophysiology, balloon angioplasty, nuclear cardiology, peripheral vascular disease treatments, atherectomy, stent placement, pacemaker implant and follow-up echocardiology, hypertension treatment, ECP Therapy and lipid management. Patients are seen by referral and appointment. The Heart Center of Eastern Carolina, which is available 24 hours a day for emergency services for patients, also has offices in Morehead City and in Jacksonville.

New Bern Surgical Associates
701 Newman Rd., New Bern
(252) 633-2081, (800) 682-0276 x8419
www.newbernsurgical.com

The board-certified surgeons of New Bern Surgical Associates specialize in general, oncologic, vascular and advanced laparoscopic surgeries, as well as skin cancer diagnosis and treatment. Patients may call for an appointment or be referred by a primary physician. Office hours are 8 AM to 5 PM. For appointments, call (252) 633-2081. Patients with after-hours emergencies can call (252) 633-3557 or (800) 682-0276, ext. 8419.

Nova Pain Management
1815 S. Glenburnie Rd., New Bern
(252) 672-0095

Nova Pain Management, a multi-specialty rehabilitation facility, gives people in chronic pain a wide spectrum of the best combination of traditional and complementary medicine available. At Nova, the treatment plan is geared to the patient's special needs, and each practitioner is dedicated to making the patient feel better. Every patient is thoroughly examined to determine the source of the problem. If the problem concerns the neuro-musculo-skeletal systems, chiropractic care is available to help restore structural integrity and function. A Chinese acupuncturist is on staff to focus on pain reduction and other health issues. Physical rehabilitation is available and uniquely structured for the chronic pain patient. Nova is affordable and accepts most insurance plans, including Medicare, Medicaid, TriCare, BCBS, Cigna and Worker's Compensation. Office hours are Monday through Thursday 8 AM to 5 PM and Friday 8 AM to 1 PM. Nova also has offices in Alliance and Smithfield.

Southern Gastroenterology Associates
310 Commerce St., Morehead City
(252) 726-7111

Southern Gastroenterology Associates, part of Coastal Carolina Health Care, is located at 310 Commerce Street in Morehead City. If you have swallowing problems, colon polyps, ulcers, gas or bloating, liver disease, indigestion, gallstones or irritable bowel disease or if you need testing for colon cancer, call (252) 726-7111 and make an appointment with a board-certified gastroenterologist.

Home Healthcare

Many patient services provided by hospitals during long-term recoveries and illnesses are available at home with the assistance of home-health services. Home healthcare is an alternative to institutional or hospital care that fosters patient independence and family care. All services offer nursing, rehabilitation therapies, medical social work, in-home aides, medical equipment and supplies.

Craven Regional Medical Center Home Care Services
1300 Helen Ave., New Bern
(252) 633-8182

Craven Regional Medical Center provides continued recovery services at home for departing hospital patients as authorized by their physicians. Skilled nursing care is offered 24 hours a day, seven days a week. Other services include physical, speech and nutritional therapies and home-health aides. Home Care Services is certified for Medicare.

Home Health-Hospice Services of Craven County
2818 Neuse Blvd., New Bern
(252) 636-4930

The county health department provides home health and hospice services to homebound clients and those authorized for care by physicians. It provides in-home nursing services, 24-hour on-call care, home-health aid, nutritional counseling, and physical, occupational and speech therapy. It also offers hospice care for the terminally ill and their families.

Professional Nursing Service
1425 S. Glenburnie Rd., New Bern
(252) 636-2388

This service has licensed LPNs and RNs to assist with healthcare. It can provide sitter companions, certified nursing assistants, private-duty nurses and supplementary staffing.

Tarheel Home Healthcare
130 U.S. Hwy. 17 S, Pollocksville
(252) 224-1012, (800) 685-4539

Tarheel Home Healthcare is a private business that offers a full range of healthcare services for recoveries and care at home. Complete nursing services are offered in all infusion drug therapies, HIV/AIDS case management, and physical, occupational and speech therapy. Tarheel

Home Health also has a branch in nearby Washington, (252) 946-7145.

Acupuncture

Toni Rittenberg, Acupuncturist
Nova Pain Management,
1813 Glenburnie Rd., New Bern
(252) 672-0095

Licensed acupuncturist Toni Rittenberg began studying acupuncture at the age of 11 in her hometown of Beijing, China. After graduating from medical school in China, she moved the United States to complete her post-doctoral work at Harvard University. Toni served as Dean of Facility at an acupuncture school in Oakland, California, before moving to New Bern. She has been engaged in private practice in New Bern for more than a decade. She offers authentic Chinese acupuncture as a proven and effective way to treat many medical conditions. A full Chinese herbal pharmacy is also located on-site. Toni Rittenberg can be reached at Nova Pain Management at the number above.

Alternative Healthcare

The encouragement of wellness and methods of coping with recurrent pain and disease are taught and practiced in New Bern through various alternative therapies and philosophical approaches. Chiropractic services are available, as are massage therapy, acupressure, acupuncture and other approaches to pain management.

Flemming Chiropractic Health
& Wellness Center
Village Square, 3601 Trent Rd. #3, New Bern
(252) 638-6062

Dr. Lois Flemming and her staff vow to get you well and keep you well through chiropractic care, acupuncture, nutritional assistance, personalized exercise programs and more.

Healing To Your Body
1421 S. Glenburnie Rd., New Bern
(252) 635-3088

The vision of this online store is to provide clients with access to information and products to achieve optimum health and longevity. This alternative health outlet wants us all to be well and functioning at our best through alternative and anti-aging supplements and foods. They also sell Heavenly Scents — affordable fragrance lamp fuels, catalytic effusion lamps and wicks.

NEW BERN
RETIREMENT 🌴

New Bern's popularity as a delightful retirement location is evident in its relocation statistics. Nearly 2,000 retired people move to New Bern each year, an average of about six per day. It's too hard to pass up New Bern's combination of mild climate, relatively low cost of living, beautiful surroundings and friendly people. Active retired citizens enjoy fishing, golfing, sailing, hiking and boating within a stone's throw of anywhere in the river city. Gardeners appreciate the year-round growing season. The colonial setting of the city and the wide range of social, cultural and recreational activities make retirement in New Bern very attractive.

New residents find the city's regional hospital, doctors' offices, shopping centers, sports facilities, quality restaurants and numerous religious organizations important factors in making the decision to relocate for retirement. Those who decide to move to New Bern are seldom disappointed.

As more retirees settle in the area, a growing number of services and programs are created and tailored to meet their needs and interests. Several agencies and public service organizations offer an ever-expanding variety of services aimed at greeting, involving and assisting new and retired residents.

For retirees who need extra care in day-to-day living, retirement communities in New Bern are designed to create interesting, carefree and caring environments. The housing options available vary according to the needs of individuals and include assisted living, respite care, nursing and adult day-care services plus independent and assisted-living facilities and programs for memory-impaired residents. The Craven County Department of Social Services (see our listing in this chapter) is a clear-

inghouse for information on the various options in specialized-care facilities.

Services and Organizations

A number of service agencies and organizations in New Bern are equipped to deal with the needs or problems that may confront the older population.

Area Agency on Aging/ Eastern Carolina Council
233 Middle St., New Bern
(252) 638-3185

The State of North Carolina designated this agency to address the concerns and needs of the elder segment of the local population as mandated through the Older Americans Act. Local citizens make up the regional council policy board. The agency is responsible for direct contracting with local providers in a nine-county area for priority services such as transportation, nutrition, in-home care, case management, housing and home improvement, legal and other services. It also provides technical assistance involving training, grant preparation, community coordination efforts, needs assessments and resource inventories. It carries out regional ombudsman assistance to county-appointed nursing home and adult-care community advisory committees. The agency oversees development and implementation of aging programs, assists in the development of multipurpose senior centers and designates community focal-point facilities for delivering services to the older population. The Area Agency on Aging is also responsible for the Family Caregiver program that assists and supports caregivers with their day-to-day care-giving responsibilities. New programs are always in development; call for more information.

Craven County Department of Social Services
2818 Neuse Blvd., New Bern
(252) 636-4900

The Department of Social Services offers information and assistance to seniors concerning health, Medicare and rest-home and nursing-home facilities. The department operates an in-home aide program, a Medicare transportation program and an Adult Home Specialist Service that monitors nursing homes. It also refers clients to other agencies and organizations for help with special situations.

Craven County Senior Services
811 George St., New Bern
(252) 638-1790

Handling services geared toward senior citizens of Craven County, this agency offers a variety of programs and activities at its three senior centers for residents ages 60 and older. Popular center pastimes include quilting, crafts, exercise programs, yoga, line-dancing, self-help and supportive services, health screenings and various enrichment classes in cooperation with Craven Community College. Lunch is provided five days a week, except on designated holidays. The agency also operates the county's Meals on Wheels program.

Craven County Veterans Service Office
2818 Neuse Blvd., Ste. 15, New Bern
(252) 636-6611

The Veterans Service Office provides veterans and qualified dependents with information, assistance and problem-solving services regarding veterans' programs and benefits. The office also works to promote issues of relevance to veterans.

Gold Care - Craven Regional Medical Center
2000 Neuse Blvd., New Bern
(252) 633-8154

This wellness program, developed by Craven Regional Medical Center, is for adults ages 55 and older. Membership offers monthly education seminars, a physician-referral service, access to support groups, a quarterly newsletter, social opportunities and other activities. Annual

membership is $15 for a couple or $10 for singles.

Help-At-Home Senior Care
1202 S. Glenburnie Rd., New Bern
(252) 672-9300

Help-At-Home allows seniors in Craven, Pamlico, Carteret and Onslow counties who need just a little bit of help at home to stay in their homes and enjoy their independence. This service matches caregivers to senior clients and provides services such as meal planning and preparation, light housekeeping, medication reminders, bill-paying assistance, bathing safety monitoring, errand running and local transportation. Help-At-Home is available 24 hours a day, seven days a week.

Neuse River Senior Games and Silver Arts Competition
Craven County Recreation & Parks Department, New Bern
(252) 636-6606

Senior Games is an exciting health-promotion program for adults age 55 years and older. It includes events such as swimming, badminton, horseshoes, shuffleboard, cycling, shotput, discus, bowling, table tennis, basketball, race-walking and more, with gold, silver and bronze medals being awarded to the winners in each event. Medal winners also qualify for the North Carolina State Games in Raleigh. Silver Arts events include Heritage Arts, Literary Arts, Performing Arts and Visual Arts.

New Bern Parks and Recreation Department
248 Craven St., New Bern
(252) 639-2901

In addition to its regular programs (see our New Bern Parks and Recreation chapter for more information), the New Bern Parks & Recreation Department offers a number of special programs for seniors only, including dancing and exercise classes and a softball team. The department also hosts clubs devoted to special interests, such as model airplanes, miniatures, stamps and coins, needlepoint, ceramics and more.

In addition to clubs and classes, the department organizes special events for seniors only. Senior Activity Days are scheduled for Mondays and Fridays for adults age 55 and older at the West New Bern Recreation Center. Activities include table tennis, billiards, shuffleboard, basketball, badminton and more, while those who enjoy less-active pursuits can partake in chess, checkers or just walking around the gym. The department also sponsors the Golden Age Club for seniors age 55 and older. The club meets on the second and fourth Thursdays of each month at the West New Bern Recreation Center for fun and fellowship, with special trips planned throughout the year. For more information about Senior Activity Days or the Golden Age Club, call (252) 636-4061. The Henderson Park Senior Citizens Club, the oldest club of its kind in North Carolina, meets on the second and fourth Tuesdays of every month at the Stanley White Recreation Center; for information call (252) 636-4062.

Senior Pharmacy Program
502 Middle St., New Bern
(252) 638-3657

The Senior Pharmacy Program assists eligible seniors, ages 60 and older in Craven, Jones, Pamlico and Carteret counties, with costs for prescription medications. An outreach of Catholic Social Ministries, it helps pay for prescriptions that treat chronic diseases, such as cancer, high blood pressure, heart disease, diabetes, glaucoma, acid reflux, arthritis and clinical depression. Post-hospitalization medications may be covered on a limited basis. Sites for the monthly distribution of vouchers, to be used toward the prescription costs, are generally at area senior centers. Call ahead for an appointment. The program's mailing address is P.O. Box 826, New Bern, NC 28563.

Social Security Office
1420 McCarthy Blvd., New Bern
(252) 637-1703, (800) 772-1213

Administering the Social Security and Supplemental Security Income programs, this office is open weekdays to provide information concerning Social Security guidelines and requirements and to answer other related questions. Clients are seen on a walk-in, first-come, first-served

basis. Insiders recommend you either arrive early or come prepared for a wait.

Retirement Housing

The Courtyards at Berne Village
2701 Amhurst Blvd., New Bern
(252) 633-1779
www.courtyardsatbernevillage.com

The Courtyards at Berne Village, a 55-plus community in New Bern, is located in a residential neighborhood with shopping, entertainment and medical services just minutes away. Built in 1986 and renovated in 2004, the community provides a range of services that residents want and need to live as independently and actively as they would like. Residents enjoy a variety of social gatherings and planned activities. Meals are served daily in the private restaurant, and special diet plans are available if needed or requested. The Courtyards at Berne Village also offer scheduled transportation, housekeeping and 24-hour campus security and emergency-call system monitoring. Amenities include a private clubhouse for meetings and parties, a library, a chapel for meditation and religious services, a cafe with patio seating, a state-of-the-art fitness center, and a barber and beauty shop.

With more than 18 acres, the park-like campus provides plenty of space for outside recreational activities such as walking, gardening and bird-watching. On-site amenities include horseshoes, shuffleboard, a putting green, croquet and bocce ball. The Courtyards at Berne Village features one- and two-bedroom apartments with full-size kitchens, private baths and individual heat and air control, all on the ground floor.

For those who need more service or need help with the activities of daily living, assisted-living apartments are available in the main building. A Special Memory Care Program is designed for those with Alzheimer's or other memory impairments. Respite care and short-term rental accommodations are also available. The Courtyards at Berne Village offers a tour and complimentary lunch for prospective residents and clients.

Homeplace of New Bern
1309 McCarthy Blvd., New Bern
(252) 637-7133

Homeplace of New Bern can accommodate up to 40 residents, who can rent suites on a month-to-month basis with the security of 24-hour help on hand. Independence is encouraged, yet assistance is available for whatever the resident needs. Kitchenettes, private baths with walk-in showers to optimize safety, independent temperature controls and attractive furniture are some of the many amenities featured in individual suites. The healthcare coordinator, who also is a registered nurse, coordinates the care and services provided by certified nursing assistants around the clock. Three delicious meals are served daily, and laundry, housekeeping and transportation services are available. An enriching activities program and a caring staff give Homeplace a distinctive and friendly reputation. The activities are varied and unique, ranging from crafts, exercise and religious activities to musical performances and excursions out on the town.

An additional 20 residents can be accommodated in a special Alzheimer's and related dementia program. The special program for individuals with Alzheimer's and related dementias is designed to provide assistance to residents while maintaining a safe environment. Respite care and short-term stays are welcome. Prospective customers are encouraged to stop by to tour and experience the warmth and focus on customer service at Homeplace of New Bern.

The McCarthy Court Independent Living Apartments offers 85 luxurious apartments with all of the conveniences for senior adults to be comfortable while maintaining an active lifestyle. The one- and two-bedroom apartments range in size from 753 to 1,436 square feet and feature patios or balconies, washer/dryer hookups, computer hookups and full kitchens. Month-to-month rentals include all utilities except phone and cable, a full-service evening meal, weekly housekeeping, maintenance, scheduled transportation, recreational activities and access to common areas. The staff checks in daily with residents, who also have an emergency pull-cord to summon help if needed.

Two Rivers Neuse Campus and Trent Campus
1303 Health Dr., New Bern
(252) 634-2560

These two residential facilities, owned and operated by UHS Pruitt Corporation, are located on either side of Craven Regional Medical Center. Two Rivers Trent Campus offers 113 beds in its facility, which includes a large outdoor covered patio, an indoor sun room and a large rehabilitation room. Two Rivers Neuse Campus has 110 beds available in private and semi-private rooms, a safe outdoor courtyard and a comfortable living room space for visitations. Both facilities feature spacious and bright dining rooms, activity rooms, wide hallways that offer easy wheelchair access, and the Wander Guard Security System for keeping residents with a tendency to wander safe and secure. The centers provide skilled-nursing care, rehabilitative programs and a variety of therapies and recreational opportunities designed to keep residents healthy, alert and active. The centers also offer short-term care options for those unable to return home immediately after surgery or other treatments.

NEW BERN VOLUNTEER OPPORTUNITIES

M any of New Bern's public service agencies and nonprofit organizations rely on the services and talents of volunteers. Some simply could not operate without the assistance of their reliable volunteers. New Bern has a number of spare-time opportunities, and new ones are popping up all the time. While we've included several here, the New Bern Area Chamber of Commerce, 316 S. Front Street, (252) 637-3111, maintains a comprehensive list of contact names and phone numbers for nonprofit and civic organizations in the area. Volunteers often find that helping out with one organization often leads to developing interests in others. The organizations and agencies listed usually provide any necessary training for volunteers.

American Red Cross
Coastal Carolina Chapter
1916 S. Glenburnie Rd., Ste. 12, New Bern
(252) 637-3405, (888) 446-0979

Serving Carteret, Craven, Jones and Pamlico counties, this well-known nonprofit organization uses volunteers to assist with Bloodmobiles and to serve as instructors for classes in first aid, CPR, Learn to Swim, life-guarding, babysitting and more. It also needs volunteers to aid in local and national disaster situations. Volunteers are needed to represent the chapter at fairs, parades, public informational booths and fund-raising events; perform reception, data entry, clerical and organizational assistance in the office; and serve on committees involving special projects, fund-raising, grant-writing, budgeting, auditing and financial development.

Craven Arts Council
317 Middle St., New Bern
(252) 638-2577

Like any arts organization, the Craven County Arts Council relies on volunteers to keep its wheels moving. Council volunteers serve as hosts in the main gallery; help in the office; assist with mass mailings; conduct programs such as the popular Sunday Jazz Showcase in February and arts camps in summer; work on a variety of committees; and assist with city-wide arts projects, programs and fund-raising events throughout the year. If you have an affinity for art and organization, this is your place.

Craven County School System
3600 Trent Rd., New Bern
(252) 514-6333

The school system welcomes volunteers to aid teachers and students in a variety of ways and has an active community volunteer program in every school. Call the school of your choice directly or the central office at the number above if you are interested in volunteering in the schools. Perhaps most in demand is assistance for children having problems in particular subjects, such as reading, English or math. The school system also is looking for volunteer tutors who speak a foreign language. Volunteers are needed on school field trips and in school libraries. Parent-teacher organizations and volunteer coordinators at individual schools are pleased to have help with special programs and projects to benefit the schools and students.

Craven Literacy Council
202 S. Glenburnie Rd., Ste. 2B, New Bern
(252) 637-8079

The Craven Literacy Council trains volunteers to work as tutors with adult students who request services to improve reading skills or to learn English as a second language. Volunteer tutors are trained to work one-on-one with students, and together they decide on a convenient time to meet for reading sessions. Tutor training sessions are held several times a year; call for a schedule.

Craven Regional Medical Center
2000 Neuse Blvd., New Bern
(252) 633-8111

Officials here will tell you that the hospital would not run as well or as smoothly without its faithful volunteers. The center uses its nearly 500-strong volunteer corps for everything from delivering mail and running the gift shop to manning the Healthwatch personal emergency response system. There is a youth volunteer group especially for 14- to 18-year-olds and a volunteer chaplaincy program for ordained ministers. Volunteers also help in the library, newborn nursery, emergency department and critical-care waiting areas. They operate the book cart and humor cart in the hospital, work in offices and hand-craft comfort items for patients. The Gray Ladies and Gray Lads are perhaps the most active group, assisting with a variety of hospital-related duties. There's also an auxiliary group that coordinates activities in 25 different areas. If you have time and energy to spare, the center can put them to good use.

Habitat for Humanity of Greater New Bern
930 Pollock St., New Bern
(252) 633-9599

Through donations of money, materials and volunteer labor, Habitat for Humanity builds modest homes in partnership with qualified families who meet Habitat's selection criteria and who contribute 200 sweat-equity hours. Houses are sold to families on a no-profit, no-interest basis. To date, the New Bern affiliate has completed 43 houses toward its goal of eliminating poverty housing in the area. Construction work takes place each Tuesday, Thursday and Saturday morning starting at 8 AM. Volunteers, both groups and individuals, are always needed. Habitat also operates a "Resale" shop at the same address, (252) 633-5512. If you have expertise in building and would like to help build homes for the community or would like to help with merchandise pick-up and delivery, give Habitat a call.

Master Gardener Program
300 Industrial Dr., New Bern
(252) 633-1477

The Master Gardener Program is open to anyone who would like to learn more about gardening and at the same time assist the Cooperative Extension Service in its horticulture education efforts. Prospective Master Gardeners are provided with 40 hours of training in return for 40 hours of volunteer service during the first year; in subsequent years, volunteers donate 20 hours to stay active in the program. Activities include presentations of Saturday morning programs, speaking to garden clubs, answering phone calls from the gardening public, meeting walk-in visitors at the extension office, planting and maintaining demonstration gardens, working with schools, and assisting with a variety of one-time educational events. Numerous continuing educational opportunities are provided to make this an ongoing learning experience for the Master Gardeners.

New Bern Historical Society
512 Pollock St., New Bern
(252) 638-8558, (800) 849-7316

The historical society relies on volunteers for most of its vital functions. Volunteers make up the society's membership, education, marketing and program committees. They serve as tour guides, fundraiser staff and help produce the *Historical Society Journal*. They coordinate special projects and help maintain historical buildings and grounds. Volunteers are in great demand during the Spring Homes and Gardens Tour and the New Bern at Night Ghost Walk, the production of its popular historical dramas and to assist with the Battle of New Bern Preservation project. If you enjoy history and its preservation, you will find a niche here.

New Bern Police Department
601 George St., New Bern
(252) 672-4216

The local police department is always on the lookout for good volunteers. Volunteers work in many positions, such as clerical and court liaison positions and with programs such as the Explorers Program and the Pawn Shop Reporting Program. Volunteers get started by filling out a three-page application and undergoing a background screening and reference check. After the screening is completed, volunteers are matched to available positions that take into consideration the time constraints and interests of the volunteers. Monthly meetings also are scheduled to provide training and networking opportunities.

New Bern Preservation Foundation
510 Pollock St., New Bern
(252) 633-6448

Like the historical society, the preservation foundation counts on volunteers and uses their skills to operate its organization. Most volunteers are retirees, and the foundation could not function without them. Docents serve as hosts or hostesses for home tours; help in the office; work to produce the newsletter; help with the annual Antique Show and Sale in February and Homes Tour in the spring; cater meals; and assist with property cleanup and maintenance of historical buildings and grounds.

North Carolina Cooperative Extention
300 Industrial Dr., New Bern
(252) 633-1477

This group provides valuable services to the community through collaboration with agencies such as Craven Regional Medical Center, The River Club and Coastal Women's Shelter, to name a few. Its mission is to strengthen families through leadership development, volunteer work, educational opportunities and sharing research-based educational information generated from N.C. State and N.C. A&T universities. Membership is open to anyone who is a resident of Craven County. Residents of the county are invited to join an existing club or organize their own community club.

Public Radio East
800 College Ct., New Bern
(252) 638-3434

Volunteers interested in sharing their time with Public Radio East are welcome year-round to assist with clerical tasks and to answer telephones during fund drives. Training is provided when necessary.

Swiss Bear Downtown
Development Corp.
316-A S. Front St., New Bern
(252) 638-5781

Swiss Bear, Inc. is a nonprofit organization established in 1979 to coordinate the revitalization of the downtown area. It organizes and coordinates the annual three-day Mumfest, held the second full weekend in October. Volunteers are needed for a variety of duties during Mumfest and for New Bern's upcoming 300th Anniversary Celebration in 2010.

Tryon Palace Historic Sites & Gardens
610 Pollock St., New Bern
(252) 514-4900, (800) 767-1560

Tryon Palace Historic Sites & Garden's volunteer program offers a bounty of opportunities throughout the year. Assistance in the gardens at Tryon Palace is needed during every season but especially in the spring. Spring also brings about Young Sprouts, an elementary garden program for children; volunteers who enjoy working with children will welcome the opportunities available to lead that program. In addition, drama enthusiasts interested in portraying historical characters are needed, as are group leaders for school tours, guides for the New Bern Academy Museum, gate clickers and concert ushers. Prior to the holidays, hundreds of volunteers are needed to lend their talented hands with the holiday decorations for the entire site. If you have the time and interest in being a volunteer, contact the volunteer coordinator for an application.

Although New Bern's media scene is small, visitors and residents can find most of what they want to know from the news sources we describe here. The Raleigh-based *News & Observer*, which covers issues of statewide importance, also offers home delivery in this area. The New Bern *Sun Journal* is the local, seven-day-a-week newspaper. Suddenlink Communications offers the full panoply of cable channels.

Print

New Bern Magazine
201-3 N. 17th St., Morehead City
(252) 240-1811, (800) 525-1403

New Bern Magazine is published monthly and features information on events and attractions in Craven and Pamlico counties. It's distributed free at various locations, including the Craven County Convention and Visitors Bureau in the New Bern Riverfront Convention Center at the corner of East and South Front streets and at the New Bern Area Chamber of Commerce at 316 S. Front Street. *New Bern Magazine* also is available by mail subscription, 12 issues for $15 per year.

The Shopper/Community Newspapers
3200 Wellons Blvd., New Bern
(252) 635-5620

The Shopper, published weekly, features advertisements, specials and coupons offered by local businesses in New Bern and Havelock. *The Shopper* also prints special sections dedicated to home improvement, back-to-school, holiday gift giving and other topics, as well as annual medical and hospitality guides. This 36-year-plus publication is delivered free of charge on Wednesdays to more than 31,000 households in Craven County.

Classified ads may be placed by calling (888) 328-4802. *The Shopper* also publishes several monthly community newspapers, which are delivered free of charge to the residents they serve. These include the *Taberna Tribune*, *New Bern Herald*, *Greenbrier Gazette*, *The Fairfield Harbour Beacon*, *Trent Woods Times*, *River Bender*, *The Pines' Perspective* (Carolina Pines), *Sound Waves* (Brandywine Bay) and *The Shoreline* (Pine Knoll Shores).

Sun Journal
3200 Wellons Blvd., New Bern
(252) 638-8101

This daily morning newspaper, owned by California-based Freedom Communications, provides regional coverage of Craven, Pamlico, Jones, Onslow and Lenoir counties and reports on state and national events and sports. *Sun Journal* is available by home delivery or from vending machines.

Television Stations

Several television stations offer media coverage of the New Bern area, some based in New Bern and others based in nearby Washington, Greenville and Morehead City.

C-TV 10, Cox Communications Access, New Bern, (252) 638-3121

WCTI-TV 12 ABC, 225 Glenburnie Dr., New Bern, (252) 638-1212

WFXI-FOX 8/14, U.S. Hwy. 70, Morehead City, (252) 240-0888

WITN-TV 7 NBC, U.S. Hwy. 17 S, Washington, (252) 946-3131, 233 Middle St., New Bern, (252) 672-9486

WNCT - TV 9 CBS, 3221 S. Evans St., Greenville, (252) 355-8500

NEW BERN MEDIA

NEW BERN'S

ESPN

RADIO 1490 AM

www.1490espn.com

The very best of local and national sports including:

Kinston Indians Baseball
Cleveland Indians Baseball
Major League Baseball

NFL Football, Playoffs, & Super Bowl
College Football, Bowls, & BCS

ACC Men's Basketball Tournament
NCAA Men's Basketball Tournament

Carolina Hurricanes Hockey

New Bern High School Football
New Bern High School Baseball
New Bern High School Basketball

"Mike & Mike In The Morning"
"The Herd with Colin Cowherd"
"Pardon the Interruption"
"The Drive with Mark & Dave"

Cable Television

Suddenlink Communications
2907 Brunswick Ave., New Bern
(252) 638-3121

Suddenlink Communications is a provider of digital and high-definition cable service in the New Bern area. Featuring a variety of cable packages, Suddenlink Communications offers such popular channels as A&E, The History Channel, Turner Classic Movies, SciFi, Lifetime, The Discovery Channel, HBO, Cinemax, Showtime, Starz, pay-per-view movies, sports events and more. Suddenlink High Speed Internet features unlimited access, up to seven e-mail addresses and other benefits. Suddenlink now has home and business telephone services with one price for local and long distance phone calls.

Radio

Ten radio stations broadcast a variety of music, talk, sports and information in the New Bern area.

Public Radio East
800 College Ct., New Bern
(252) 638-3434

New Bern's public radio station broadcasts in the region on 89.3 FM, 90.3 FM, 91.5 FM, 88.1 FM and 88.5 FM.

WERO BOB 93.3 FM
1361 Colony Dr., New Bern
(252) 639-7900, (800) 260-0933

WERO plays Top 40.

WMGV V103.3 FM and KISS 101.9
207 Glenburnie Dr., New Bern
(252) 633-1500

These stations broadcast soft rock, R&B and contemporary music.

WNBB/WNBR The Bear 97.9/98.9 FM
233 Middle St., Ste. 107-B, New Bern
(252) 638-8500

The Bear stations play classic country.

WNCT Oldies 107.9 FM
207 Glenburnie Dr., New Bern
(252) 633-1599

This stations plays hits from the 1950s, 1960s and 1970s.

WNOS 1450 AM
116 S. Business Plaza, New Bern
(252) 638-8888
www.rfenc.com

WNOS, along with its sister station WWNB, is New Bern's talk and sports channel, broadcasting to Craven County and parts of Pamlico and Jones counties. Listen to the Phil Knight Show weekdays from 8 to 9 AM to catch up on local news and events and hear interviews with local residents. You'll also find Fox Sports Radio, The Dan Patrick Show and Dennis Miller, along with some local sports.

WRHT Hot 96.3 and 103.7 FM
1307 Glenburnie Rd., New Bern
(252) 672-5900, (800) 849-4688

These stations play contemporary and country music.

WSFL 106.5 FM
207 Glenburnie Dr., New Bern
(252) 633-1500

WSFL is the region's classic rock station.

WWNB 1490 AM
116 S. Business Plaza, New Bern
(252) 633-1490
www.1490espn.com

ESPN Radio 1490 is a sports-format radio station broadcasting to Craven, Jones and Pamlico counties. Programming includes syndicated sports talk shows from ESPN, local talk shows, and local and national game broadcasts. Listen here for the Kinston Indians games and New Bern high school sports. You can also catch the Carolina Hurricanes, NFL, college football, the Cleveland Indians games, the ACC Men's Basketball Tournament and the NCAA Basketball tournament.

WXNR 99.5 FM
207 Glenburnie Dr., New Bern
(252) 633-1500

WXNR plays modern rock.

NEW BERN
💼 COMMERCE AND INDUSTRY

Commerce and industry in New Bern are broad-based and receive strong support from the presence of **Marine Corps Air Station (MCAS) Cherry Point** and the **Fleet Readiness Center (FRC) East** in Havelock. FRC East, located aboard MCAS Cherry Point, is one of six aeronautical maintenance, engineering and logistics support facilities in the Navy and is one of the largest civilian employers in eastern North Carolina. Managed by Marine officers, the facility has a work force of about 3,700 employees, most of whom are civilian. FRC East refurbishes a variety of military aircraft and provides emergency repair and field modification teams to do repair work on aircraft unable to return to the center. For more information about FRC East, see our Havelock chapter.

Industries with large work forces in New Bern include Weyerhaeuser, Hatteras Yachts, BSH Home Appliances Corporation, Moen and Maola Milk and Ice Cream. **Weyerhaeuser** grows and harvests timber and processes it in a huge pulp mill just outside New Bern. The company employs up to 610 people and owns more than 500,000 acres in eastern North Carolina. **Hatteras Yachts** builds luxury watercraft in its New Bern plant and employs about 700 people. **BSH Home Appliances** has more than 1,200 workers in New Bern, manufacturing dishwashers, washers and dryers, cooktops, free-standing ranges and built-in ranges. A producer of plumbing fixtures, **Moen** has about 750 employees. **Maola Milk and Ice Cream** has about 240 workers.

Large non-industry employers in New Bern include **New Bern-Craven County Schools**, **Craven County** government, **Craven Regional Medical Center** and the **City of New Bern**.

Several groups are organized to encourage new businesses to locate in New Bern and to facilitate economic growth in the area.

The **New Bern Area Chamber of Commerce**, 316 S. Front Street, (252) 637-3111, represents the interests of the local business community in the regional, state and national government arenas. It also offers networking and professional opportunities, as well as numerous programs and events designed to promote the businesses of its members.

Swiss Bear Downtown Development Corp., 316 S. Front Street, (252) 638-5781, is a private, nonprofit group organized in 1979 to spearhead and coordinate the revitalization and redevelopment of downtown New Bern and its waterfront. An aggressive effort based in building public-private partnerships and developing creative fund-raising strategies and long-range plans has led to the investment of more than $70 million for the rehabilitation and construction of new commercial buildings and major public improvements, plus the creation of hundreds of jobs. As a result, tourism is now a major industry in New Bern.

The **Craven County Economic Development Commission** is responsible for encouraging manufacturing and development, especially to the county-owned, 519-acre **Craven County Industrial Park** that straddles U.S. Highway 70 about 5 miles west of New Bern. The park features an incubator facility that offers office and manufacturing space to new manufacturers. Industrial sites vary in acreage. The Economic Development Commission is always looking for existing businesses to expand or new businesses to move into the industrial park or into the county. Contact the Craven County Economic Development Commission, 100 Industrial Drive, New Bern, NC 28562, (252) 633-5300.

CLOSE UP

A Local Success Story: Hatteras Yachts

Hatteras Yachts, one of the best known names in the yachting world, is located in New Bern. Lauded the world over for its distinctive designs and high quality construction, Hatteras Yachts has sparked a revolution in boat design and elevated the expectations of boat owners worldwide since its inception in the 1950s.

The story of Hatteras Yachts started in 1959 when Willis Slane, unable to go fishing because of treacherous seas, decided to build a better boat. The result? The sleek, 41-foot Knit Wits, capable of taking on the fierce waters off Cape Hatteras. Knit Wits was one of the first boats of its size to be constructed from fiberglass. And the rest is, as they say, history.

Hatteras Yachts, which celebrated its 40th anniversary in 2000, was originally based in High Point, North Carolina. Its first manufacturing facility was located in an old Pontiac dealership on Wrenn Street. Building boats in High Point had its drawbacks — one of those being its location 200 miles from the ocean — and the decision was made to move the "launch and make ready" operations to New Bern in 1969. By 1997 the entire Hatteras Yachts manufacturing operation had relocated to New Bern.

Hatteras Yachts' 95-acre, state-of-the-art production and in-water facility is located on N. Glenburnie Drive on the banks of the Neuse River. The company's impact on the New Bern economy is immeasurable — Hatteras Yachts employs more than 700 local residents at an annual payroll approaching $30 million.

Best known for the innovation of fiberglass hulls, Hatteras Yachts produces 12 different models, ranging from 54-foot sport-fishing convertibles to cruising yachts in excess of 100 feet. Annual sales of watercraft made by Hatteras Yachts averages more than $78 million.

Tours of the Hatteras Yachts facilities can be arranged by calling (252) 634-4873.

The **Small Business Center at Craven Community College** offers workshops, seminars and group study sessions addressing the needs of small business owners. Also provided is one-on-one counseling and specialized employee training. Resource centers are available at both the New Bern and Havelock campuses and feature free computer and Internet access, specialized software, multimedia tools, books, magazines and other business-related materials. For more information, contact the Small Business Center Director, Craven Community College, 800 College Court, New Bern, NC 28562, (252) 638-7353.

Volunteers with the **Service Corps of Retired Executives (SCORE)** Down East Chapter 577 are available by calling (252) 633-6688. SCORE provides free counseling and low-cost workshops to promote the formation, growth and success of small businesses in Craven, Beaufort, Lenoir, Jones, Pamlico, Pitt and Greene counties.

NEW BERN
⊛WORSHIP

New Bern has a number of historic churches that are open to residents and visitors who would like to tour or attend services. In addition to the distinctive architectural styles seen in many of the downtown churches, several have features that stand out above the rest, such as the pipe organ at First Presbyterian Church on New Street; the stained-glass windows in Centenary United Methodist Church at Middle and New Streets; the gifts from King George II displayed at Christ Episcopal Church on Pollock Street; and the graceful white arches in First Baptist Church on Middle Street. All these churches are within three blocks of one another. New Bern's oldest churches are wonderful places to learn about the area's history, and you can explore most of them while walking in the downtown area. (See our New Bern Attractions chapter for more details.)

In New Bern, church-sponsored events attract community-wide interest. During the holidays, many churches conduct special concerts, plays and bazaars. Another staple of the town's holiday celebration is a full performance of Handel's *Messiah* by a community choir of hundreds of voices and soloists at Centenary United Methodist Church, usually around the time of Old Christmas in January. Musicians for the performance are members of the North Carolina Symphony.

All major Protestant religions as well as the Catholic and Jewish faiths have long-established churches in New Bern. Check the Yellow Pages or the church directory in the Saturday edition of the *Sun Journal* for a list of local options.

The parish of **Christ Episcopal Church**, which celebrated its 268th anniversary in 2008, is the oldest in New Bern and one of the oldest in North Carolina. The church, (252) 633-2109, is located at 320 Pollock Street. The current building was rebuilt in 1871–1885 after a fire gutted the c. 1821–1824 church. The church is noted not only for its Gothic Revival details but also its graveyard that still contains a number of eighteenth-century stone markers.

First organized as a congregation in 1772, the current **Centenary United Methodist Church**, (252) 637-4181, was designed by Herbert Woodley Simpson and completed in 1905. Standing at the corner of New and Middle streets, Centenary features rounded walls and turrets that give it an almost Moorish look.

The narrow Gothic Revival **First Baptist Church**, (252) 638-5691, was built in 1847, though its congregation was organized in 1809. The main entrance of the church is located at 239 Middle Street, next to the O. Marks building. The main sanctuary is strikingly simple and peaceful in its design. The Sunday service is televised by WCTI-TV 12.

The oldest continually used church building in New Bern, **First Presbyterian Church**, (252) 637-3270, was built in 1819–22 by local architect and builder Uriah Sandy. The congregation was established in 1817. Located at 412 New Street, the church is surrounded by a cast-iron fence that dates from 1903.

Although **St. Paul's Catholic Church**, (252) 638-1984, is the oldest Catholic parish in North Carolina, its current home on Country Club Road was constructed about 23 years ago. The church, which

See this entire guide plus additional content online at insiderinfo.us

was expanded in 2004, features strikingly modern architecture and is in a large, park-like setting. Sharing the land is St. Paul's Education Center, a private school. St. Paul's first church was built on Middle Street in 1840. That building is open to the public during daylight hours.

The stucco, neoclassical **Temple B'Nai Sholem Synagogue**, (252) 638-4545, is a beautiful, uncommon specimen of architecture in the area. A Herbert Woodley Simpson–designed structure, the synagogue was built on Middle Street in 1908 by the congregation, which was originally organized about 1824.

Six historic black churches in the New Bern area are listed on the National Register of Historic Places: **St. Peter's A.M.E. Zion**, **St. Cyprian's Episcopal Church**, **Ebenezer Presbyterian Church**, **Rue Chapel A.M.E. Church**, **St. John's Missionary Baptist Church** and **First Missionary Baptist Church**.

HAVELOCK

Welcome to the city of Havelock. Best known as the home to Marine Corps Air Station Cherry Point, the largest Marine Corps Air Station in the world, Havelock is a diverse city with much to offer visitors and residents. The city and the military base have a population of about 22,500, making Havelock the second-largest city in Craven County. This is a far cry from the 100 residents recorded in 1950. Admittedly, Havelock gained a few residents when the base was annexed, but it is still one of the fastest-growing urban areas in the state. More and more people are choosing to move here because of its proximity to the coast.

History

Havelock was named for Gen. Henry Havelock, a British general best remembered for his courageous rescue of hostages during a bloody uprising in India in the mid-1800s. A marble bust of Gen. Havelock stands in the Havelock City Hall.

First called Havelock Station, the community saw action during the Civil War when troops from the Rhode Island Heavy Artillery came ashore in 1862 near what is now the base Officer's Club. From that point, Union troops captured New Bern and Fort Macon on Bogue Banks.

Newcomers to Havelock should contact New Neighbors of Havelock by calling Linda Caccavaro at (252) 671-6987. Linda will arrange an in-home visit to provide information about local businesses, the community, schools and civic organizations.

At one time, the production of tar and turpentine had a large economic impact on Havelock, but once steam engines began replacing wooden ships as transporters of goods, the market for tar and turpentine waned. Because of its proximity to waters and forests, Havelock gained notoriety in the late 1800s and early 1930s for its fishing and hunting opportunities.

Area historians and artifact collectors value pictures of baseball great Babe Ruth, who often spent time in the area pursuing outdoor sports. Today's residents and visitors to the Havelock area can enjoy being outdoors in the Croatan National Forest. This 157,000-acre forest spreads in a triangle between Morehead City, Cape Carteret and New Bern, and it borders Havelock on three sides. The forest features many ecosystems, endangered animals, plant species and wildflowers. (You can find information about the Croatan National Forest in our Crystal Coast Attractions chapter.)

U.S. Highway 70 runs through the middle of Havelock. The growth of businesses along the highway — and the plethora of traffic lights that has resulted — has led to traffic delays and backups, particularly at rush hours and during the busy summer seasons. The Department of Transportation is planning to construct a bypass to guide traffic off the existing U.S. Highway 70 just west of Havelock to take that traffic south of Havelock and reconnect it to U.S. 70 at the Craven County-Carteret County line on the east side of Havelock. This bypass will be connected to the city in several areas as it loops the city. Funds for construction of the bypass have been diverted to another highway project; the start date at this point is 2015.

Havelock has a lot to offer, but don't just view the city from U.S. Highway 70. Take a turn here or there. Stop at a few businesses — you might be surprised at what you find.

In this chapter we offer a quick look at the city of Havelock. We have given some general information about Havelock businesses, events and services. You'll find listings for restaurants, accommodations, shopping, attractions, annual events, golf courses and real estate agencies. These sections are by no means comprehensive, but just a sampling of what you'll find in the city. Information about area industry and military services is at the end of the chapter.

Cherry Point

Havelock is often referred to as the "Gateway to Cherry Point." With more than 15,500 sailors, Marines and civilians working at the air station, Cherry Point is home to the Second Marine Aircraft Wing (2d MAW) and Fleet Readiness Center, which ranks as the number one single-site industrial employer east of Interstate 95.

The air station was first authorized by Congress in 1941. The arduous task of clearing the original 8,000 acres of swamp, farms and timberland began in August 1941, with actual construction beginning 17 days before the attack on Pearl Harbor. The air station was commissioned on May 20, 1942, as Cunningham Field, in honor of the Marine Corps' first aviator, Lt. Alfred A. Cunningham. In August 1942 the first troops arrived at the air station, and the 2d MAW officially made Cherry Point its home in April 1946.

Although stories abound on how the base took the name Cherry Point, it is believed to have been adopted from an old post office established in the area years before. The post office, used by the Blades Lumber workers, was closed in 1935. The original "Point" was just east of Hancock Creek, and "Cherry" came from the cherry trees that once grew there. The airfield itself, consisting of the runways and tower, is still technically named Cunningham Field.

From 1946 until the present day, the 2d MAW has been integral in training thousands of Marines for the Korean Conflict, the Vietnam War and the Persian Gulf War.

Now the Wing has elements permanently stationed at MCAS Cherry Point, MCAS New River, North Carolina, and MCAS Beaufort, South Carolina. It is equipped with helicopters, fighters, and attack and refueler/transport aircraft.

Over the years, Cherry Point has grown from a small airfield to one of the Marine Corps' most important air stations. The original 8,000-acre area has been expanded continuously and now encompasses over 13,000 acres with an additional 15,975 acres of auxiliary activities. Built in 1941 at a cost of $14.9 million, the value of the base is now more than $7.43 billion. Approximately 10,677 Marines and sailors stationed at Cherry Point earn an annual payroll of about $671 million. Combined with the station's nearly 5,575 civilian employees and 7,201 retired military personnel living in the area, more than $1.4 billion is pumped into the local economy every year from Cherry Point. These salaries, plus local expenditures for supplies and capital improvements, have an economic impact of more than $1.45 billion annually on the state of North Carolina.

Visitor Information

The City of Havelock's Tourist and Events Center is located next to Hampton Inn Havelock. The 17,000-square-foot facility includes an impressive aviation exhibit and is the site of many social and business meetings, weddings, receptions, military events and community events. For information call (252) 444-4348.

Restaurants

From fast food to family dining, Havelock eateries are sure to satisfy whatever craving you may experience. Our listings represent only a small portion of what is available. Ask locals for other recommendations.

PRICE CODE

The price code noted with the restaurant name will give you a general idea of the cost of dinner for two, excluding alcoholic beverages, tax and tip. Because

entrees generally come in a wide range of prices, the code reflects an average meal, not the most or least expensive items. Of course, lunch would cost less. The price code used is as follows:

$	Less than $20
$$	$20 to $35

Andy's Cheesesteaks and Cheeseburgers $
609 E. Main St., Havelock
(252) 444-0889

Looking for a quick and delicious lunch? Andy's is well-known throughout eastern North Carolina for its wonderful cheesesteaks, and the Havelock restaurant is no exception. Also try an Andy's cheeseburger or one of the other sandwich offerings. Andy's is open daily.

El Cerro Grande $$
Mexican Bar and Grill
498 W. Main St., Havelock
(252) 444-5777

Located in front of Westbrooke Shopping Center, El Cerro Grande offers Mexican food at its best and is a popular lunch and dinner spot. Appetizers include guacamole salad and dip, chili with cheese, and chicken nachos. Entrees vary from combination plates with a choice of chicken, cheese, beef, potato or spinach fillings to special dinner platters that offer tostadas, burritos, steak ranchero and fajitas. Desserts turn to such favorites as sopaipillas and fried ice cream. The restaurant, which is open daily for lunch and dinner, serves several Mexican beers, wine and mixed drinks, including fabulous margaritas.

Fontana Coffee Café $
600 Fontana Blvd., Havelock
(252) 444-5592

Those who love their cappuccinos and lattes need look no further than Fontana Coffee Café, Havelock's only coffee shop. Although items vary due to availability, Fontana Coffee Café serves hot and cold beverages, including coffees, teas, cocoa, fruit smoothies, Italian soda, Italian cream soda and more. If you're looking for something a little more substantial to go along with your beverage of choice, you can choose from muffins, bagels, pastries,

cinnamon rolls, scones and more, or enjoy one of the ham, turkey or veggie wraps.

Accommodations

Visitors to Havelock will be pleasantly surprised by the diverse accommodations available. For years, only two motels served the city, with the majority of their clientele limited to traveling members of the armed services. With the increased popularity of nearby beaches and a local effort to attract industry to the area, new accommodations establishments have sprung up in recent years. We have only described a few to give you an idea of what's available.

PRICE CODE

For the purpose of comparing prices, we have placed each accommodation in a price category based on the summer rate for a double occupancy room. Our code does not include taxes, which are 13 percent (Havelock has a 6 percent occupancy tax). Please note that amenities and rates are subject to change, so it is best to verify the information when making inquiries. The code is as follows:

$	Less than $50
$$	More than $50

Comfort Inn $$
1013 E. Main St., Havelock
(252) 444-8444, (800) 228-5150

Comfort Inn offers a total of 58 rooms in various configurations, including standard king and double-bed rooms and presidential and executive suites. All rooms offer a microwave, refrigerator, iron and ironing board, hairdryer and coffeemaker. Suites offer whirlpool tubs. Guests can enjoy an outdoor pool during the summer and an indoor exercise room year round. A free deluxe continental breakfast is served, and the inn is within walking distance of restaurants.

Days Inn $$
1220 E. Main St., Havelock
(252) 447-1122

Days Inn has 73 rooms that open to an interior hallway. The hotel offers the comfortable and clean rooms people have come to expect from the Days Inn chain. Each room is equipped with a microwave and refrigerator. The inn also has an outdoor swimming pool. Special rooms are available for those traveling with pets (an extra charge applies); smoking rooms are available.

Hampton Inn Havelock $$
105 Tourist Center Dr., Havelock
(252) 447-9400, (800) 426-7866

Hampton Inn Havelock features amenities such as in-room movies, a free newspaper, an exercise room and laundry services. An outside pool provides for relaxing fun during the warmer months. Meeting and banquet facilities, computer dataports in every room, and fax services also are available. A continental breakfast is available from 6 to 10 AM, and if you don't have time to eat, the staff will fix a bagged breakfast-to-go for you. Children younger than 18 stay free with their parents.

Holiday Inn $$
400 W. Main St., Havelock
(252) 444-1111, (800) 465-4329

This 102-room establishment's offerings range from a standard room to the executive suite, which features a small conference room and two adjacent bedrooms. A second executive suite with king bed, fireplace, living room, two full baths and king sleeper sofas is available. Royal Cup coffee is available free, 24 hours, in the lobby. All rooms include a microwave and refrigerator. Conference and banquet facilities for as many as 350 people are available. A restaurant and lounge are accessible from the inn's main lobby, and an outside pool is open during the summer months.

Journey's End Havelock $-$$
Inn and Suites
310 E. Main St., Havelock
(252) 444-1414

Journey's End has 31 rooms offering a selection of sleeping arrangements. From a standard double to the presidential and honeymoon suites, there is a size and style to fit any traveler. The inn offers rooms with televisions, kitchenettes and balconies. A restaurant, a lounge and an outdoor pool are on site.

Sherwood Motel $
318 W. Main St., Havelock
(252) 447-3184

The Sherwood Motel is well-established, having been in business for many years. Guests will find a clean, quiet motel offering 87 rooms complete with cable TV, HBO and all the expected comforts. Refrigerators and microwaves are available, and an outdoor swimming pool is open in the summer.

Shopping

While Havelock may not have any big shopping malls, it does have plenty of variety. Although many of the shops are service oriented — video outlets, hair-styling salons and laundry facilities — you'll also find a number of furniture stores, pawn shops and military surplus outlets. And, there is a new Wal-Mart store on U.S. Highway 70 E. In this section, we highlight a few of our favorite places.

Bike Depot
Century Plaza, 412 W. Main St., Havelock
(252) 447-0834

The Bike Depot offers Cannondale and Trek bicycles and makes repairs on all types. The store carries clothing, accessories, helmets and used bicycles. It's in the Century Plaza; turn into the shopping plaza when you see the big Rose Brothers Furniture sign. The Bike Depot is closed Sunday and Monday.

Bill's Pet Shop
491 U.S. Hwy. 70 W, Havelock
(252) 447-2750

Insiders love Bill's Pet Shop because it's a full-service store with everything you need to care for your pet — be it a dog, cat, bird, ferret, fish or reptile. They also have a knowledgeable staff that provides outstanding customer service. Bill's offers all types of pets for sale along with all the

---

The Havelock branch of the New Bern-Craven County Library is located at 301 Cunningham Boulevard. Call (252) 447-7509 for hours and other information.

supplies and products needed to care for them. Bill's also features a complete tropical and saltwater aquarium section and is willing to guide you in the proper set up and care of your tanks. There are sister stores in New Bern and Morehead City.

E. T. Military Surplus, Inc.
347 W. Main St., Havelock
(252) 444-1977

In business for more than 27 years, E. T.'s Military Surplus offers military wear, hats, leather and dog tags, boots, patches, medals, survival gear and more in its 6,000-square-foot showroom. E. T.'s is open daily.

Picture Perfect
600-C Fontana Blvd., Havelock
(252) 447-7654

Picture Perfect frames everything from military medals and diplomas to items such as golf clubs and christening gowns. Owners Don and Nancy Murdoch have been in business for nearly 22 years — Nancy does the custom design work and Don does the cutting and assembling on-site. Picture Perfect offers a variety of moldings, from the traditional wood to hand-finished, water-gilded gold. The shop, open Tuesday through Saturday,

also carries prints by local artists, including Alan Cheek and Philip Philbeck

Plaza Trade Center
Cherry Plaza, 1317 E. Main St., Havelock
(252) 447-0314

Plaza Trade Center used to be a flea market but now sells new furniture, appliances and household items. With many new items received on a regular basis, shoppers are sure to find something they both want and need for their homes. Plaza Trade Center is open nearly every day, year round (closing only for Thanksgiving and Christmas).

Swiss Chalet Bakery and Cafe
Westbrook Shopping Center,
492 W. Main St., Havelock
(252) 447-3980

Insiders from Carteret and Craven counties often stop at this bakery to pick up loaves of European-style breads made from scratch by owners Tom and Lisa Buehler. Mouth-watering pastries, pies and cakes are for sale too. Should you care to linger (and who wouldn't?), sit at one of the tables, munch a luscious pastry and drink a cup of freshly brewed coffee. The Buehlers make birthday cakes to order and provide catering service, including

Egrets snare prey by standing still and then attacking with their sharp bills.

photo: Peter Doran

box lunches and meat platters, for business meetings and other gatherings. The bakery is open Monday through Saturday year round. They are also open at the New Bern Farmers' Market in downtown New Bern on Saturdays from 7:30 AM until 1 PM.

Whiteman's Engraving
4 Jaycee St., Havelock
(252) 447-9793

Whiteman's Engraving, which has proudly served the award needs of MCAS Cherry Point for more than 30 years, has shipped its award plaques to more than 100 embassies throughout the world. But this business has so much more to offer, including custom engraving on plaques (including plaques featuring clocks, a perfect gift for a special birthday, anniversary or graduation), silver, crystal, glass, trophies and other items. Whiteman's prides itself on its flexibility and fast and courteous service, so step right up with any special requests. Whiteman's is open Monday through Friday 9 AM to 5:30 PM.

Annual Events

Havelock hosts a number of events that both residents and visitors look forward to each year. We have listed a few of the larger and most popular events.

MARCH-APRIL

Easter Egg Hunt
Havelock City Park, U.S. Hwy. 70 E,
Havelock
(252) 44-6429

All children younger than age 9 are invited to the park to hunt for eggs stuffed with gift certificates, money and toys. The hunt usually takes place the Saturday before Easter morning, but to confirm the date, be sure to call ahead. Children need to bring a basket.

JUNE

Cherry Point Air Show
MCAS Cherry Point, Havelock
(252) 466-4241

This is one of the largest events in the area, with more than 100,000 people attending when the air station opens its gates to the public. The free air show features a variety of aerial displays of military and civilian aircraft. The numerous static displays allow visitors to get a close look at many of the military's high-tech aircraft. Wear comfortable shoes, as you may have to walk a ways.

Flounder Jubilee Golf Tournament
Carolina Pines Blvd., Havelock
(252) 444-1000

This golf competition is sponsored by the Men's Golf Association of Carolina Pines each June. There is no deadline for entering, but early entrants are given first consideration. The event is a two-person Superball competition.

JULY

Old Fashioned Fourth of July
Walter B. Jones Park, U.S. Hwy. 70 E, Havelock
(252) 444-6429

As the name says, this is the city's Independence Day celebration. It is the prelude to a grand fireworks display in the evening. For years, crowds have enjoyed a variety of entertainment, including musical groups, clowns and games. Food is available.

SEPTEMBER

Havelock Four-Person Golf Tournament
Havelock area courses, Havelock
(252) 447-1101

The Four-Person Golf Tournament, sponsored by the Havelock Chamber of Commerce, draws a field of about 300 players. Held in September, tournament play takes place at Carolina Pines Golf & Country Club.

OCTOBER

Havelock Chili Festival
Walter B. Jones Park, U.S. Hwy. 70 E., Havelock
(252) 447-1101

Havelock hosts North Carolina's Chili Cook-Off Championship, and it really is a big deal. If you're a chili lover, Havelock is where you need to be on the third Saturday in October. You'll get a chance to sample some of the best chili there is. Premier chili chefs come from all over to vie for the title of state champion and the right to compete in the national cook-off contest later in the year. Contestants must follow the International Chili Society's rule: no beans of any kind. Chili without beans allows the judges to better detect the interplay of spices and assess the consistency of the chili. However, after submitting chili samples for judging, the forbidden beans are often added back to the pots, and festival-goers can pay a nominal amount at contestants' booths to taste the chili and cast a vote for the People's Choice Award. This is one event not to be missed, whether you like chili hot, mild or not at all. A salsa contest, music, crafts and other displays keep everyone happy. Many local charities benefit from the profits.

DECEMBER

Christmas in The Park
**Havelock City Park, U.S. Hwy. 70, Havelock
(252) 444-6429**

This is one of the area's favorite Christmas celebrations. It is usually held on a Thursday before Christmas. The event consists of a Christmas carol sing-along and a live nativity scene.

Christmas Parade
**U.S. Hwy. 70, Havelock
(252) 447-1101**

Havelock hosts a Christmas parade the second Saturday in December. Decorated floats and a visit from Santa Claus are part of the events. Holiday music is provided by the members of the Marine Corps 2nd Marine Air Wing Band as well as other area bands.

Attractions

Although there are few bona fide attractions in and around Havelock, other than Croatan National Forest, the ones listed here are must-sees for anyone traveling in the area.

AIRCRAFT VIEWING

The sound and sight of aircraft in flight is a regular occurrence for locals, and it is often the very thing a visitor wants to experience. Although there is no designated or best spot for prime viewing, a good vantage point is along N.C. 101 near the

main gate. Runway 5 ends here, and if the winds are right, it is often used by Harriers, Intruders and C-130 cargo planes. The sound can be deafening, so a few words of caution: Brace yourself, warn your children and protect infants' ears from the noise.

Croatan National Forest
**Ranger's Office, 141 E. Fisher Ave.,
New Bern
(252) 638-5628**

This 157,000-acre national forest borders Havelock on three sides and offers visitors and residents a wide range of activities. Outdoor recreational activities include camping, picnicking, boating, hiking, hunting and saltwater or freshwater fishing. For more information about the Croatan National Forest, see our Crystal Coast Attractions chapter.

Harrier Monument
**U.S. Hwy. 70 and Cunningham Blvd.,
Havelock**

An AV-8A Harrier jump jet looms at the intersection of U.S. 70 and Cunningham Boulevard. Mounted on a pedestal and encircled by flags, the AV-8A is a symbol of the past. Although Cherry Point is home to the largest number of Harriers in the world, the AV-8A jet was taken out of service during the mid-1980s and replaced by the new AV-8B. The most noticeable difference between the two jets is that the landing gear on the A was on the wing tips, while the B landing gear is closer to the center of the wings. This mounted jet was the second AV-8A military officials gave to civilians for display purposes (the first is on display at the Smithsonian in Washington, D.C.).

The Trader Store
Miller Blvd., Havelock

The Havelock Historical Preservation Society formed in late 1998, growing out of an ongoing effort to restore the landmark Trader Store on Miller Boulevard. The Trader Store, originally owned by Hugh and Elsie Trader and donated to the society by Ernest and Frances Trader, was once the center of commerce between New Bern and the coast, where families used the barter system to purchase everything from aspirin to plows. In the early 1900s, the store had the only telephone in the area. The restored store features early twentieth-century artifacts, including the store's original ledger. The Trader Store is open to the public Tuesdays and Saturdays from 10 AM to 5 PM.

Golf and Recreation

The two courses closest to Havelock are the Links at Plantation Harbour, a club on Adams Creek Road at the Carteret-Craven county line, and Carolina Pines Golf and Country Club, between Havelock and New Bern. Golfers staying in Havelock can catch the free Havelock-Minnesott ferry, cross the Neuse River and play golf at the Minnesott Golf and Country Club. You can find more information about these courses in our Crystal Coast Golf chapter and the New Bern Golf chapter.

Friends Billiards & Pub
571 U.S. Hwy. 70, Havelock
(252) 444-2076

Friends Billiards & Pub offers a casual atmosphere with cold drinks, pool, darts and video games. There is no cover charge to get in. From 9 AM until 8 PM, the under-21 crowd can enjoy soft drinks, video games and billiards. The pub is open until 2 AM. Those 21 and older can take advantage of drink specials. Friends also sponsors pool, dart and horseshoes tournaments where you can test your skills against the area's best.

Marinas

Those boaters with access to the air station also have access to a number of launching facilities. Two boat ramps will get you into either Slocum or Hancock creeks. Two other marinas, one on the Neuse River and the other on Slocum Creek, provide boat rentals and docking facilities. Without base access, your choices of marinas and ramps near Havelock are limited. Check the marina listings in the Crystal Coast Marinas chapter and New Bern On the Water chapter for nearby facilities. Below are a few of the closest choices.

Cahoogue Creek
Cahoogue Creek Rd., off N.C. Hwy. 101, Havelock

The National Forest Service offers a boat ramp at Cahoogue Creek, which allows boats to access Hancock Creek and the Neuse River. In addition to the ramp, the facility provides a grill, picnic table and small dock designed primarily to aid boarding. There are no restroom facilities. When driving on N.C. 101, there aren't really any landmarks to look for, so slow down and look for the road sign.

Matthews Point Marina
2645 Temples Point Rd., Havelock
(252) 444-1805

At the mouth of Clubfoot Creek, this membership marina often allows transient boaters to use an available wet slip overnight. A clearly marked entry channel is provided along with facilities to accommodate both sail and power boats up to 40 feet. The approach depth is 7 feet, with a dockside depth of 6.5 feet. Open year round, the marina has gas and diesel fuel, electricity, a pump-out station, laundry facilities, showers and ice. A clubhouse, cookout area and upper-deck lounge are available to boaters. Finding the marina by land is more difficult than by water. Land seekers should follow N.C. Highway 101 toward Beaufort. Just a few miles out of Havelock, a church marks the corner of the highway and Temples Point Road. The marina is at the very end of Temples Point Road. They now have seven premier RV sites available.

Real Estate

Residential housing is abundant in Havelock, with prices ranging from around $95,000 to $400,000. The majority of homes in Havelock and surrounding areas are less than 15 years old. Many planned communities have popped up in the neighboring areas and appeal to a wide range of individuals.

Lured by the mild climate, low tax rate and relatively low cost of living, many retirees, both military and civilian, are finding a home in the Havelock area. Some of today's primary growth areas are the

waterfront developments along the Neuse River and large creeks. To get a good overview of the properties in Havelock and the services offered by the town's real estate agents, pick up free copies of *Homes Magazine* and other real estate publications at the Havelock Chamber of Commerce.

Because of the number of military entering and exiting the Havelock area, renting is a lot easier than in most areas. Rentals are abundant and come in many forms, including houses, apartments or mobile homes. Rental prices vary according to the type of accommodation and could range from $450 to $1,250 per month. Many storage units are also available and vary in size.

1st in Flight Properties
249 U.S. Hwy. 70 W, Havelock
(252) 444-1904, (866) 515-1904

Let Broker/Owner Lana Cieszko put her more than 20 years of real estate experience to work for you. Serving all of Craven County, 1st in Flight handles residential and commercial sales, as well as offers property management services.

Century 21 Town & Country
406 W. Main St., Havelock
(252) 447-8188, (800) 334-0320

The oldest franchise real estate company in Havelock, Town & Country has been, for more than 33 years, a great place to start looking for a home in or around Havelock. An independently owned, full-service agency, Town & Country's agents handle sales of new and existing homes and investment properties. Also available are property management services and residential and commercial rentals.

Coldwell Banker First Realty
102 Roosevelt Blvd., Havelock
(252) 444-3333, (800) 396-7772

Owner-broker Gwen Schultz and her staff can show you excellent properties and lots available in Craven and Carteret counties. You can get assistance finding either commercial or residential property, including new construction. The staff members double as relocation specialists and are dedicated to making your next move a smooth one.

First Carolina Realtors
469-A U.S. Hwy. 70 W, Havelock
(252) 447-7900, (800) 336-5610

Located in the Westbrooke Shopping Center next door to the License Plate agency, First Carolina Realtors features listings for residential property, new construction, investment property, lots and land. Relocation services also are available.

John Vesco Real Estate
326 E. Main St., Havelock
(252) 444-3790

John Vesco Real Estate is highly recommended by Insiders who are impressed with the efficient and courteous service that retired Marine John Vesco and his staff of 15 agents offer. Working with buyers and sellers throughout eastern North Carolina, primarily in Carteret, Craven, Pamlico and Onslow counties, John Vesco features competitive rates for buyers and sellers.

Real Estate Management, Inc.
121 Roosevelt Blvd., Havelock
(252) 447-7368

This management company, located across from the main entrance to Cherry Point, offers property management and rental services in the Havelock community. Residential rentals are available with either six or 12-month leases, depending on the property owners' listed preferences.

Media

Havelock News
230 Stonebridge Sq., Havelock
(252) 444-1999

This newspaper is distributed every Wednesday, with a readership that includes both military and civilian readers. *Havelock News* covers city schools, government and other news of interest for Havelock residents

The Windsock
MCAS Cherry Point, Havelock
(252) 466-4241

The Windsock is published weekly and distributed on Marine Corps Air Station Cherry Point, to the Morehead City and New Bern Wal-Marts and other designated locations. The newspaper features messages from the Commanding General, Marine Corps News, Squadron spotlights and information from the Naval Air Depot (NADEP) Cherry Point. The paper also includes a sports section, recreation listings and classifieds. If you are interested in a subscription, call (252) 444-1999.

Commerce and Industry

The number of manufacturing companies in Havelock continues to grow. Through the years, several private firms have been established and are helping to diversify the economic base of the city. This growth is in part thanks to the efforts of the Craven County Economic Development Commission (EDC) and Craven County's Committee of 100. (See our New Bern Commerce and Industry chapter.) We have highlighted a few of the largest industrial and manufacturing influences on Havelock's economy. Although it is not a private company, we have listed first the Fleet Readiness Center (FRC) East because of its tremendous economic impact on the area. Wal-Mart has built a 184,000-square-foot Supercenter in Havelock, which employs about 400 people.

East Cherry Point
Fleet Readiness Center (FRC)
East Cherry Point, Havelock
(252) 464-7999

Fleet Readiness Center (FRC) East is one of six naval aviation maintenance operations that combine the skills and expertise of depot- and intermediate-level military and civilian maintainers to deliver cost-wise readiness to the U.S. warfighter. The FRC is North Carolina's largest industrial employer east of Interstate 95 and employs about 3,700 mostly civilian personnel.

Established in 1943 as the Assembly and Repair Department, the facility has gone through several name changes over the years as well as extensive modernization and expansion. Today it is one of the Navy's finest aeronautical maintenance, engineering and logistics support facilities. FRC East is known as the Navy's center

of excellence for vertical lift aircraft. The center refurbishes helicopters such as the H-46 Sea Knight, H-53 (Super Stallion/ Sea Dragon), AH-1 Cobra and UH-1 Huey. It is also the only depot-level repair point for the Marine Corps' unique vertical/short take-off and landing (V/STOL) AV-8B Harrier.

The center has extensive facilities to test and repair a number of different engine types, including the T58-400, which is used in the VH-3 presidential-executive helicopters. Fleet Readiness Center (FRC) East provides worldwide emergency repair and field modification teams to do repair work on aircraft unable to return to the center. At a moment's notice, these field teams can be sent to any location around the world during times of war and peace.

United Parcel Service
201 Belltown Rd., Havelock
(800) 742-5877

UPS offers express letter and parcel delivery, and the Havelock facility is a regional terminal. Opened in 1986, this facility currently employs about 50 people.

Military

The military plays a large part in the lives of Havelock residents. Nearly 15,050 Marines, sailors and civilians work at the air station, and many Havelock businesses count on the air station for patronage.

MILITARY ORGANIZATIONS

Marine Corps Air Station, Cherry Point includes more than 13,000 acres on the air station proper, with an additional 15,973 acres of auxiliary activities, including Marine Corps Auxiliary Landing Field Bogue, along Bogue Sound in Carteret County, and Marine Corps Outlying Landing Field Atlantic in "Down East" Carteret County.

The largest tenant command at Cherry Point is the Second Marine Aircraft Wing. Major commands in the wing include Marine Aircraft Group 14, Marine Wing Support Group 27 and Marine Air Control Group 28 located at Cherry Point. Other major commands within the 2d MAW include two helicopter groups at MCAS New River, N.C., and one Fighter/Attack aircraft group at MCAS Beaufort, South Carolina.

CLOSE UP

Trader Stories

Sitting alongside a quiet stretch of road in Havelock is a memorial to the past, to a time before large supermarket chains and a time when the roadside grocery/ filling station combination were mom-and-pop operations that also served as the center of the community. This was the Hugh Trader Store.

Restored by the Havelock Historical Preservation Foundation, the Hugh Trader Store on Miller Boulevard is open 10 AM to 5 PM Tuesdays and Saturdays for tours.

Dating back to the early 1900s, the store has retained many of its original features, including the wide-planked wooden floor and equipment, including the meat and cheese slicers, the sausage grinder and the safe and cash register. In its heyday, the store, operated by Hugh and his wife, Elsie, offered everything from aspirin to plows. Merchandise currently on display includes old-fashioned hats and shoes, pots and pans, a Mobile Oil can display rack, and soda and beer bottles. The preservation society is on the lookout for donations of other merchandise, particularly from the 1940s and 1950s, to add to the display. Photos hanging around the room depict the Trader Store at various times between the 1920s and the 1980s.

Outside, two old-fashioned gas pumps recall the heyday of the 1950s roadside station. The store, which was a stopping point not only for such famous customers as baseball legend Babe Ruth but also to thousands of Marines posted to Cherry Point during World War II. The marines arrived in Havelock at the old train station, just down the road from Trader Store. Hugh Trader died in 1961; the Trader Store, which often served as a gathering place for hosting oyster roasts and pig-pickings, closed its doors in 1977.

In order to fund its restoration projects, the Havelock Historical Preservation Society offers engraved bricks for sale along its Walk of Honor. Bricks can be engraved as a memorial to a loved one, in honor of a special birthday or anniversary, or as a show of support to the society's efforts to preserve Havelock's history. An on-going project has been the acquisition, relocation and restoration of the Havelock Railroad Station. For more information, call Harold Rawls at (252) 447-5616.

Locally, MAG-14's flying squadrons include four AV-8B Harrier squadrons, including the Marine Corps' only Harrier training squadron. There are also four EA-6B Prowler squadrons and one KC-130 Hercules transport and refueling squadron.

MWSG-27 provides logistical support for the wing with Marine Wing Support Squadron 274 at Cherry Point, and MWSS-271 at the auxiliary landing field in Bogue, N.C. MACG-28 employs some of the most advanced equipment for command of tactical air operations. The Marines who control the air war are defended by a battalion of Marines who employ the Stinger anti-aircraft missile system to control the skies overhead.

SERVICES

A number of services are available to the military and their dependents, ranging from housing to recreational facilities. Military family housing is now privatized and is available for all ranks. There are a number of ongoing construction and renovation projects underway as part of the Public-Private Venture (PPV) initiative. These projects are expected to enhance the quality of life for the military members and their families stationed at Cherry Point. More than 3,800 barracks rooms are available for single personnel.

Accredited by the Joint Commission of Accreditation of Health Care Organizations, the Halyburton Naval Clinic Cherry Point provides the primary medical needs for the local area's active duty and retired military community. The three-story facility was dedicated in memory of Pharmacist Mate Second Class William D. Halyburton, a North Carolina native, who was killed in May 1945, while rendering aid to a wounded Marine. Patients may be referred through the clinic for definitive care to other military treatment facilities or network civilian hospitals.

Other facilities on the base are designed to afford military personnel a wide variety of conveniences and recreation. The newly remodeled Marine Corps Exchange offers a department store, furniture store, grocery store, flower shop, liquor store and a number of small shops. There are also dry-cleaning and laundry facilities, a child-development center, a bank, a credit union and a service center with a convenience store, as well as a number of restaurants.

Recreational activities are geared to Marines and their dependents. These include a large gymnasium, fitness center, three pools, a bowling center, a number of marinas and the base stables.

The Sound of Freedom Golf Course has been opened to the public. Recently renovated, the 18-hole course is located directly on the picturesque Neuse River with great water views, a character unique to the area and completely natural setting with no homes or condos on the course. The course features a 24-hour driving range, chipping area, practice putting green, club rentals, a snack bar and a certified PGA teaching pro on staff.

Although the base offers many services for convenience and fun, the Marine Corps stresses the importance of improving one's education. The Jerry Marvel Training and Education Center provides a wide range of educational services. Offices are operated by Craven Community College, Distance Learning Center, Boston University and Park College. The center provides services such as admissions testing, independent-study course catalogs, counseling and a basic skills education

program. Civilian Career and Leadership Development (CCLD) is a series of programs designed to improve the knowledge skills and abilities of the civilian workforce of MCAS Cherry Point. Significant programs include leadership development, mentoring, academic degree completion, and certifications. The base has one of the most comprehensive libraries in the area with everything from reference materials to children's books. Many more services and facilities are on the base. MCAS Cherry Point is a community in itself. For more information, call Station Information, (252) 466-2811, or the Joint Public Affairs Office, (252) 466-4261.

Service Directory

TAX RATES

The Craven County and municipal tax rates are based per $100 valuation and are subject to change every fiscal year. For the 2006–07 fiscal year, Craven County's rate was 61 cents and Havelock's was 49 cents. There will be no change until 2010.

CABLE

**Time Warner Cable
(252) 447-7902**

Call (252) 447-7902 for service in Havelock. For service in Newport, call (252) 223-6400.

ELECTRIC

Carteret-Craven Electric Membership Cooperative, (252) 247-3107, (800) 682-2217

Progress Energy Carolinas, 1099 Gum Branch Rd., Jacksonville, (800) 452-2777

PHONE

Embarq Telephone, (252) 636-1514, (800) 362-2772

WATER

Havelock City Water and Sewer, (252) 444-6404

⚓ ORIENTAL AND PAMLICO COUNTY

O
n the banks of the Neuse River, Oriental is a tucked-away sort of place. Quiet, pretty and filled with genuinely friendly people, this small village is a haven for those needing a bit of tranquility in their lives. You can get to nearly every place in Oriental by foot or bicycle. But while not fast-paced, this riverside village is certainly far from boring. There's plenty to do — should you care to do anything at all.

ORIENTAL

Oriental is in Pamlico County, on the northern banks of the Neuse River across from Carteret County. The free Cherry Branch–Minnesott Beach Ferry leaves from outside Havelock (see our Getting Here, Getting Around chapter in the Central Coast section), crosses the Neuse River and docks in Minnesott Beach.

From there, Oriental is a short 10 miles away — just follow the road signs. The town is situated amid six creeks: Smith Creek, Camp Creek, Raccoon Creek, Green Creek, Whittaker Creek and Pierce Creek. A 10-foot channel connects Oriental with the Intracoastal Waterway. There are 875 residents here and 2,700 boats. Boat people are crazy about Oriental, which is known as the "Sailing Capital of North Carolina." Because it's on the Intracoastal Waterway, Oriental is a convenient and popular year-round port for sailing vessels. In winter, when yachts from the north are southbound, they stop in Oriental for a couple of days; in spring, headed back north again, they linger longer. An estimated 5,000 to 6,000 ICW travelers visit every year.

Unlike many other coastal communities that are experiencing newfound popularity and increased demands for housing

On the water – fishing or just looking – is where many citizens of the Central Coast prefer to be.

and services, Oriental is enjoying a relaxed time. In 1910 the town's population was 2,500. Today, year-round residents number about 875. In recent years, new neighborhoods and marinas have sprung up around the town, offering waterfront lots, boat ramps and recreational areas.

Oriental is named after the USS *Oriental*, a Yankee cargo ship that sank in stormy seas off the Outer Banks in 1862. Some years later, Rebecca Midyette, wife of the town's founder Louis Midyette, came across the ship's name board hanging on the wall of a private residence in Manteo, North Carolina. Mrs. Midyette liked the name, and after talking it over, the residents of Smith's Creek (the original name of the town) renamed their village Oriental. In 1899 Oriental was incorporated and the first post office was established with Louis Midyette as the first postmaster.

Oriental is a sailor's haven. That fact is apparent by the number of sail makers and chandleries offering marine supplies, equipment and repairs. In the last few years several art studios and crafts shops have opened. In our view, Oriental is the perfect getaway for relaxing, browsing, dining and enjoying the water.

It's a good idea to get an Oriental town map before you begin to explore the village. Free street maps and other information are available at most of the real estate companies in Oriental, and the helpful staff at Oriental Town Hall, 507 Church Street, (252) 249-0555, will also supply you with free information. (Town Hall's mailing address is P.O. Box 472, Oriental, NC 28571.) Oriental is also home to the Pamlico News, 406 Broad Street, (252) 249-1555, a weekly newspaper that comes out every Wednesday. The News is available by subscription or at stands throughout Pamlico County. The paper covers Pamlico, Hyde and East Beaufort counties as well as Aurora and Richland townships. Coverage of Pamlico County government and events is also provided by the daily *New Bern Sun-Journal*.

PAMLICO COUNTY

On your way to Oriental from New Bern traveling N.C. Highway 55, you'll pass through the towns of Grantsboro, Alliance and Bayboro. Bayboro is not only the county seat of Pamlico County, but also its oldest incorporated town (1881). In Grantsboro, you'll find the Pamlico County Heritage and Visitors Center, located just west of the county's only stoplight. The center, also the home of the Pamlico County Historical Association, is open Monday through Friday from 1 to 4 PM. Because it is staffed by volunteers whose availability sometimes varies, Insiders recommend you call first, (252) 745-3008, before stopping by.

N.C. Highway 55 is currently undergoing widening from two to five lanes from Craven County to the Pamlico County Courthouse in Bayboro. During the weekdays there are some construction delays.

Alliance

Alliance, a 2-square-mile town on either side of N.C. 55, is the middle municipality between Grantsboro and the Pamlico County seat of Bayboro. The town has a mile-long stretch of retail businesses, restaurants and shops lining either side of N.C. 55, which is being widened to five lanes. That project will be completed in the summer of 2009.

Incorporated in 1965, Alliance was named for the Farmers Alliance Movement. Several decades ago, it was the central site for most of the utilities in Pamlico County and as a result of a stockpile of funds from franchise taxes it received, the town does not have a property tax for its nearly 800 residents. The town provides residents with streetlights and maintains the roads in the town. Fire service is through the Triangle Voluntary Fire Department.

The town has a unique form of electing town leaders. Five board seats are open and the highest vote-getter in each elec-

 Handy tips and information for visitors are available at the Pamlico County Chamber of Commerce, (252) 745-3008, on N.C. Highway 55 in Grantsboro.

tion assumes the job of mayor, a position currently held by Ed Riggs.

A number of Pamlico County agencies are based in Alliance, including Senior Services, Social Services, the Cooperative Extension Service, Soil and Water Conservation and Farm Services.

According to the Pamlico County Historical Association, what is now the town of Alliance was once (1880s) two school districts – Oak Grove and Logger Head, which later became the community of Camperville. The postal service has operated in the community since 1890 when Albin B. Campen was appointed the first postmaster. Years later when farmers united and formed the Farmers Alliance, the people from the two school districts came together and named the community Alliance.

Though the town has a business district, farming has historically been the chief industry, and today, agricultural fields are still prevalent inside the town limits and on lands bordering Alliance.

Arapahoe

Arapahoe is one of several Pamlico County towns that are divided by a highway. The town's incorporated limits stretch several miles on either side of N.C. 306, one of two major roadways in the county. The road leads south to Minnesott Beach and the ferry, which makes daily trips to the Cherry Point side of the Neuse River. To the north, N.C. 306 goes to Grantsboro, where travelers can go east toward Bayboro and Oriental, or go west to New Bern, about 25 miles away.

Arapahoe has a limited number of businesses, although it is the home of Belangia's Super Market, one of just four full-service grocery stores within the 350 square miles of Pamlico County. The largest industry in Arapahoe and the area surrounding its borders is agriculture. Other businesses include Gary's Restaurant, a florist and entrepreneurs in seafood man-

agement, home improvement and various service industries.

The town, which has a population between 400 and 500 people, is expected to gain hundreds of new residents in the future with the building of several new developments. Chief among the new housing projects is Arlington Place on the south end of town. It could bring in as many as 1,200 new homes, along with boat docks. Other projects in or near the town include Shine Landing, with nearly 100 lots including some on the water; Shareheart Community, a development of small village condos along Dawson Creek and Cribbs Cove; and Dawson's Landing, with about 100 housing lots.

Arapahoe has long had a strong sense of community, and when consolidation closed the town's elementary school in the mid-1990s, residents came together to build the Arapahoe Charter School. The school has consistently ranked among the top charter schools in the state since its inception in 1997. The school has a student population for kindergarten through middle school of less than 400, with small-size classes. The school is in the public school system, although under state charter guidelines it is self-governed on the local level.

A large spring-to-fall enterprise in the Arapahoe area are four youth camps – YMCA–affiliated Camp Sea Gull for boys and Camp Seafarer for girls, along with Methodist Camp Don Lee and Christian Church Camp Caroline.

Legend has it Arapahoe was first known as "Cross Roads." There are versions of how it became Arapahoe. One is that it was named for Indians in the area, who traveled a trail south to the river that later became the footprint for N.C. 306. Another story is that the town was named for a racehorse owned by a prominent citizen. The town was settled early in the eighteenth century. A post office was established in 1886 and the town was incorporated in 1920.

See this entire guide plus additional content online at insiderinfo.us

Because N.C. 306 and the old Indian trail follow a sand ridge, Arapahoe and Grantsboro are among the highest points in the 350 square miles of Pamlico County, at 39 feet above sea level.

Bayboro

Bayboro is the county seat of rural Pamlico County, one of nine municipalities spread far and wide in a vast, 350-square-mile county of farmlands, forests, creeks and river shoreline. The town is centrally located in the middle of the county, compact within about 1.5 square miles that are bordered by a river and another town (Alliance), along with woods, farm fields and swampland. The town does not have a true commercial district and there are just a few businesses, although they are diverse — restaurants, convenience stores, farm supply stores, banks and a bookstore.

Among the longtime businesses is Charlie's Restaurant, located across from the high school. It has long been the breakfast, lunch and dinner gathering place for residents from around the county, as well as a popular mealtime gathering place for groups and organizations. Another is Forest Farm Supply, a key stopping place in an agriculturally oriented region. Because of its limitations to expand, land is precious, and most of the prime real estate is already taken — by non-taxable government entities.

The majority of Pamlico County's local government is headquartered in Bayboro, anchored by Courthouse Square at the intersection of N.C. highways 55 and 304. That complex includes the administration office, courthouse, health department, water department and a relatively new $8 million law enforcement center. The local Bay River Metropolitan Sewer District is also headquartered in Bayboro, as is the county's lone emergency response unit, Pamlico County Rescue Squad.

Three of the four schools in the county system — high school, elementary and primary schools — are located within the town. Pamlico Community College has a satellite cosmetology center built adjacent to the high school.

Most of the government buildings are located on the town's most valuable real

Oriental is close enough to the coast to make frequent daytrips to the beach.

photo: Carolyn Temple

419

estate, along N.C. 55, which is undergoing a major widening. Still, business and town leaders, such as Mayor Paige Ackiss and longtime commissioner and entrepreneur Joe Himbry, believe the town has potential to attract more than just drive-through traffic to waterfront destinations such as Oriental. The town has a revitalization plan to complement the N.C. 55 widening, along with hopes to enhance a town-owned park on the Bay River to attract water enthusiasts for canoe and kayak activities.

Grantsboro

While other municipalities in Pamlico County are sometimes called crossroads, Grantsboro truly is just that. Located 15 miles from Oriental to the east and New Bern to the west, the county's newest town is home of the county's only stop-light — at the intersection of Pamlico's two main highways, N.C. 55 and N.C. 306. The town is located on a sand ridge and along with Arapahoe, is the highest point in the county, at 39 feet above sea level.

According to the Pamlico County Historical Association, Grantsboro was named for William Grant, a New York bachelor who came to the area a peddler with his "pack upon his back." He built two store buildings and then the community of Grantsboro was on its way toward commercial development.

Today, no town in the county is expected to reap more commercial growth than Grantsboro from the $47 million N.C. 55 widening project (two to five lanes), which will be completed in the summer of 2009. The town already is home to two of the four full-service supermarkets in the large rural county — Food Lion and Piggly Wiggly. It has a fast-food restaurant, a convenience store and a variety of discount and food shops located within the shopping center anchored by the Food Lion.

A growing government and cultural complex greets visitors entering the county from the New Bern area. It includes the town post office, Grantsboro's new town hall and the developing Pamlico County Heritage and Visitors Center. The museum project has been the successful work of

the Pamlico County Historical Association, which has raised more than $800,000 through donations, grants and fund-raisers to build a 6,000-square foot museum to showcase the county's history of forestry, farming and fishing. In addition to the main structure, plans call for development of a Heritage Village, complete with a 1900s farmhouse and school house, along with a fish house and a fishing trawler.

The town was incorporated in 1998, in part as a response to rumored annexation plans by the adjacent town of Alliance. The town has had but one mayor in its short history, Clifton Stowe, who presides over a five-person town board for the population of nearly 800 people.

Accommodations

PRICE CODE

For the purpose of comparing prices, we have placed each accommodation in a price category based on the in-season rate for a double-occupancy room. Our code does not include taxes. As always, call ahead to verify information.

$	Less than $50
$$	$50 to $85
$$$	$85 to $199
$$$$	$200 or more

Boonedocks Guest House　　　　$$$
1108 Fork Point Rd., Oriental
(252) 249-0023

The Aft Cabin at Boonedocks Marina on Broad Creek, just minutes from Oriental, accommodates two adults gracefully with a separate bedroom featuring a queen-sized log bed. A built-in, over-sized window seat affords a cozy reading nook. Outdoors, guests enjoy the large screened-in porch with woodsy Adirondack chairs, bistro table and a view of Broad Creek, the well-tended gardens, surrounding forest and the marina. Indoors, this cedar-shingled "little cabin in the woods" boasts all the modern conveniences, including satellite TV, wireless Internet, heat/air, range, microwave and coffee maker. The innkeeper says guests should bring their sense of adventure and desire to relax but leave the cookware and linens at home, because the marina provides practically everything a guest needs, including cookware, dinnerware, bed and bath linens, board games, good books and even a DVD player. Paddlers will appreciate a handy put-in on Broad Creek, a wide, deep-water creek with miles of serene, flat-water paddling on the creek and up the guts. Paddle from the Boonedocks to River Dunes in less than 15 minutes. Two kayaks, a canoe and a Sunfish are available for very minimal fees of $10 to $25 per day. Bring your own boat and enjoy free dockage during your stay. The Aft Cabin is pet friendly, including a sheltered kennel. Prior approval and additional charges apply. Call for pricing and availability.

The Captains' Quarters Bed & Breakfast Inn $$-$$$
701 Broad St., Oriental
(252) 249-0002, (866) 946-0002

The Captains' Quarters Bed and Breakfast, located at the corner of Church and Broad streets in downtown Oriental, is the result of the restoration and renovation of a magnificent and gracious Victorian home built in 1897. This inn is a few minutes' walk to Oriental's port, marinas, restaurants and shops and it truly reflects Oriental's century-old tradition of friendly hospitality. There are four rooms and a suite available, and the owners say when the inn is full, breakfast is continental — muffins, quiches, juices and coffee. If it is less than full, you might get vouchers to the Harbor Deli, M&Ms or The Bean. Meet owners Annick, a native of Paris, and her husband, Roy, originally from Boston. Roy lived in Europe for 26 years where he was a CEO in the hospitality industry. The couple have brought their hospitality expertise to Oriental to create a pleasant, relaxed stay for guests from around the world. It makes for multi-lingual discourse and multi-national fun.

The Cartwright House $$-$$$
301 Freemason St., Oriental
(252) 249-1337, (888) 726-9384

Fireplaces adorn all the beautifully appointed rooms in Oriental's historic bed and breakfast, The Cartwright House. Conveniently located with a view of the Neuse

River and within strolling distance to all of the town, the inn hosts many weddings and local social events. On-site innkeepers Debbie and Durl Evans provide full breakfasts on the porch or in the dining room. If you have to stay connected, wireless Internet is available throughout the inn, but the kayaks and bikes might entice you to relax and enjoy "Oriental time." The Cartwright House is a member of the N.C. Bed and Breakfast Association.

Oriental Marina & Inn $$-$$$
103 Wall Street, Oriental
(252) 249-1818

Guests of this harbor inn are privy to beautiful views of Raccoon Creek and Old Town Harbor. The Oriental Inn features one, two and three-bedroom units with efficiency kitchens. All rooms have private balconies opening onto the courtyard, and each has a water view, a private bath and cable TV. A large deck and swimming pool complete with a tiki bar are in the courtyard. Guests also will enjoy the Toucan Grill & Fresh Bar, which is open for lunch and dinner. The marina offers 13 deep-water rental slips with 30- and 50-amp electrical hookups, a fuel dock, water and cable television hookups and complimentary wireless Internet throughout the complex. The inn, which is open year round, is handicapped accessible and accepts major credit cards. Children are welcome, and the inn is pet-friendly. Call and ask about the pet policy and seasonal rates.

River Neuse Suites $$-$$$
201 Mildred St., Oriental
(252) 249-1404

River Neuse Suites is Oriental's newest condotel, offering vacation rentals in the historic village of Oriental. All suites are available as daily and weekly rentals. Choose from first-floor efficiencies, a spacious wheelchair-accessible suite, two-level upstairs lofts, or the "Super Suite," featuring two bedrooms with king-sized beds and private baths, and a large sitting and dining area. All suites feature kitchenettes with marble counter tops, flat panel TVs and luxurious furnishings. Enjoy panoramic views of the four-mile-wide Neuse River. Adirondack chairs invite guests to linger and enjoy the peaceful vistas of the

Neuse River. If you're in Oriental to watch the sailing races, you'll have riverfront seats from here.

Stallings River House $$$$
500 South Ave., Oriental
(252) 249-1661, (252) 249-1662

One of Oriental's most popular places for the weekend, be it weddings, seminars, family reunions and retreats, this gracious home is located on the Neuse River in the historic section of town. Balconies and porches overlook large pecan trees and rolling lawns down to the water. Enjoy expansive views of the river and colorful sunsets or drop a line and catch a crab or fish for dinner. The home's interior transports you back to the early days of Oriental with the conveniences of today. Call ahead for availability and rates. Please note that our price code is high because this accommodation is the rental of an entire house for a weekend.

Restaurants

PRICE CODE

Our price code reflects the average price of a dinner for two that includes entrees and nonalcoholic beverages. Obviously, lunch would be less expensive.

 Construction is underway on widening a 14-mile stretch of N.C. Highway 55 in Craven and Pamlico counties from two to five lanes, with a center turn lane. The road will be widened between an area just past Bridgeton and the bridge exits, all the way to Bayboro. The first two segments of the project were scheduled to be completed by December 2008, with five lanes completed to just inside the Alliance town limits. The final leg of the project, to the Pamlico County Courthouse in Bayboro, is scheduled for completion in June 2009.

Prices are subject to change. Unless otherwise noted, all of these establishments accept credit cards.

$	Less than $20
$$	$20 to $35
$$$	$36 to $50
$$$$	More than $50

ORIENTAL

The Bean on the Harbor $
304 Hodges St., Oriental
(252) 249-4918

The Bean is a quaint coffee shop overlooking Oriental Harbor. It serves a full menu of coffee drinks, frozen drinks, ice cream, bagels, breakfast sandwiches, muffins, Danish and other home baked goods. Free Wi-Fi is available for customers. On Friday and Saturday nights and during special events, The Bean serves wine and ice cold beer. Owner Eric Kindle has also instituted bike rentals. Although closing time is optional (the store is open later in the spring, summer and fall), The Bean is open with hot coffee ready to go at 7 AM, seven days a week. Extended hours are offered to coincide with special events at The Old Theatre, Croakerfest, Spirit of Christmas and New Year's Eve. Check the website for events at The Bean.

Brantley's Village Restaurant $$
900 Broad Street, Oriental
(252) 249-3509

Brantley's Village Restaurant may be one of the most interesting stories in Oriental. The Normans owned this restaurant in 1978 and cooked delicious meals for folks for about 15 years. Now they're back — Brantley Jr., Brantley Sr. and Ms. Sil reopened the family-style restaurant about two years ago and are holding true to their motto: Good food, good price, good service. No alcoholic beverages — this is truly a family restaurant. Among the many reasons to love this restaurant are their special entree nights. On Tuesday night, try all-you-can-eat fried chicken with two vegetables for $7.95. On Friday nights, prepare for some good country cooking with slow-cooked roast beef and a choice of two other meats, which might include barbecue, fried chicken, baked chicken, ham or popcorn shrimp, four or five different vegetables, beets, coleslaw, potato salad, dessert and beverage for $9.95. On Saturday evening, enjoy an all-you-can-eat seafood buffet with shrimp, oysters, flounder, bay scallops, clam strips, deviled crabs and an array of vegetables with drink and dessert for $15.95. Other specials are offered nightly. Be sure to try the homemade soups, all made by Ms. Sil, the matriarch of the restaurant. Ms. Sil also bakes the chocolate, lemon and coconut meringue pies. The restaurant is open year round. Hours are Monday through Thursday 7 AM to 8:30 PM, Friday and Saturday 7 AM until 9 PM. Brantley's has a large banquet room for meetings, parties or family gatherings.

Broad Street Grill   **$$-$$$**
802 Broad St., Oriental
(252) 249-2707

Every town needs a place for great pizza, creative American regional cuisine and more. Broad Street Grill is Oriental's place. Owner Eric Stickrath provides delicious lunches and dinners, specialty pizzas and seasonal fresh-grilled seafood and steaks provide in an upscale yet casual dining atmosphere. Outdoor cafe tables and indoor seating provide comfortable options, and take-out is available. Broad Street Grill is open Friday and Saturday from 11 AM to 10 PM and on Sunday through Thursday from 11 AM to 9 PM. Beer and wine are available.

M & M's Cafe   **$**
205 S. Water St., Oriental
(252) 249-2000

Located near the water, M&M's Cafe offers outside dining. Owner Dave Sargent makes sure you leave sated and happy. M&M's is known for its seafood and steaks but there is a menu with something delicious for everyone. Pastas, rack of lamb, lobster and soft-shell crabs are some of the mouth-watering entrees available. M&M's has specials every night, including a sushi bar on Monday nights and different types of ethnic specials throughout the week. M&M's is open daily for lunch and dinner at 11:30 AM. Breakfast is available from 7 to 10 AM. The restaurant is closed on Tuesdays. Dave can book parties for 30 to 60 people. Call for information.

Oriental Harbor Deli & Bistro   **$-$$**
516-C Water St., Oriental
(242) 249-0550

Located in the Oriental Harbor Marina complex, the deli offers gorgeous outdoor dining under shady umbrellas overlooking the 120-slip marina. It's open seven days a week for breakfast, lunch and dinner. Fresh seafood, juicy steaks and lunch specials make this eatery a favorite of boaters and locals alike. Can't take time to eat? The deli will pack up its freshly cut meats, salads, muffins and meals to go. An inside seating area is perfect on those few inclement days. Wayne Lamm will also cater your party on the deck and arrange entertainment, including spectacular sunsets.

Oriental Steamer Restaurant   **$$-$$$**
and Tavern
401 Broad St., Oriental
(252) 249-3557

One of Oriental's long-time favorite chefs, Chef Jeff Tomczak continues to please his customers with interesting specials and old-time favorites. Many residents still remember the wood stove in the historic brick hardware store where the restaurant is located. The seafood couldn't be fresher. This restaurant is open for dinner nightly and lunch on Fridays, Saturdays and Sundays. We recommend the pasta dishes and the homemade desserts. A full-service bar and live entertainment in season keep the customers coming back. It's also available for large parties, monthly Rotary meetings and bridge club luncheons.

Toucan Grill & Fresh Bar   **$-$$**
Hodges St., Oriental
(252) 249-1818

Toucan Grill & Fresh Bar gives diners the option to eat indoors in the spacious and attractively decorated dining room or outside on the deck enjoying the breezes and views of the water. The menu is ap-

Many businesses in Oriental
close or shorten their hours
during the winter. If you
want information or plan to
visit in the winter, be sure to
call first.

propriate for a restaurant located in a fishing village. Seafood dishes offered as either appetizers or entrees include clam chowder, cold shrimp cocktail, crab cakes, fish & chips and fried shrimp. Try the steamed platter with cherrystone clams, mussels, shrimp and a crab claw or a Boatman's Stew, an old fisherman's tradition, cooked in a light broth with potatoes and a variety of fish of the day. The restaurant always serves locally caught shrimp. Those with a yearning for something other than seafood should consider the hot buffalo wings, Black Angus rib eye steaks cut to order, and full and half racks of barbecue ribs. There are specials every night. If you've got room after eating the restaurant's generous portions, consider the variety of homemade desserts, appropriate for the season. Toucan Grill & Fresh Bar has full ABC permits and features special nights, such as men's night (Monday) and ladies' night (Wednesday), with complimentary hors d'oeuvres. Toucan Grill is open daily; call for seasonal hours.

All boaters have to start somewhere.

photo: Molly Harrison

BAYBORO

The Bean $
301 Main St., Bayboro
(252) 745-4064

The Bean is a brand-new coffee shop that sits across from the Pamlico County Courthouse in Bayboro and a popular stop for teachers, students, lawyers, judges and law enforcement. It serves a full menu of coffee drinks, frozen drinks, ice cream, bagels, breakfast sandwiches, muffins, Danish and other home baked goods. Free Wi-Fi is available for customers. Although closing time is optional (the store may be open later in the spring, summer and fall), The Bean is open with hot coffee ready to go at 7 AM, Monday through Saturday. Check the website for information about local events and events at The Bean.

Shopping

Many businesses in Oriental close or shorten their hours during the winter. If you want information or plan to visit in the off season be sure to call first.

A Different Twist
509 Broad Street, Oriental
(252) 249-2498

Located in the heart of Oriental, A Different Twist offers a truly unique jewelry-shopping experience. Join the artists in a relaxing atmosphere and pick out an amazing piece of jewelry, handcrafted of beautiful semi-precious stones, crystal or glass beads, or precious metals. Other gift items include hand-crafted soaps, jewelry boxes and accessories. The jewelry artists are on-site and are happy to assist anyone looking for a one-of-a-kind gift. A Different Twist also offers jewelry repair. Look behind the store to see the Bottle House, built entirely of beer bottles. The store is open Tuesday through Friday 11 AM to 6 PM and Saturday from 11 AM to 4 PM.

Bay River Pottery
107 S. Water St., Bayboro
(252) 745-4749

Hidden away on the beautiful Bay River in Bayboro, Candace Young has been making one-of-a-kind stoneware and Raku pottery since 1981. Specializing in carved and pierced garden lanterns and lamps, Candace has designed clay tools to create exciting textures and shapes evocative of the natural environment of eastern North Carolina. Candace also has created a unique method of arranging flowers that anyone can use to make an free-form Ikebana arrangements and she gives free flower-arranging classes throughout the year. She also makes Raku pottery with a focus on "smoke painting" with feathers, horsehair and, upon request, pet hair for memorials. Smoke painting is a process that involves handling the pot at 1,800 degrees; the designs appear as the hair is smoked into the clay. The studio is always open and is accessible by car and boat. Visit the website or call for directions. Candace is always happy to demonstrate and give tours of the kilns and processes.

The Charlotte Garrett Gallery & Studio
502 Hodges St., Oriental
(252) 249-7244

The Charlotte Garrett Gallery features the watercolors of this North Carolina artist. Subjects include water birds, natural coastal scenes and commissioned works. Also displayed are prints of her work and photographs by her husband, Charlie. Custom framing is available on premises. Gallery hours are 10 AM to 4 PM Monday through Saturday and by appointment.

Circle 10 Art Gallery
1103 Broad St., Oriental
(252) 249-0298

Circle 10 Art Gallery is eastern North Carolina's oldest cooperative art gallery. In existence for 25 years, Circle 10 represents 18 award-winning artists offering original fine art, photography and contemporary fine craft. The artists work in pastels, watercolor, acrylic, charcoal, pencil, oils, original needlework and photography. There are two potters, two weavers, a Nantucket basket maker, two fine woodworkers, a stained-glass artist and a jeweler. Circle 10 serves the community by offering a monthly Visiting Artist exhibition, and it offers art classes and art trips as well as community outreach programs in the schools and prison. When you visit Circle 10, one of the artists will help you with your purchases. They are always happy to talk art as well. Hours are Wednesday through Saturday 10 AM to 5 PM, Sunday from 1 to 4 PM and on request at other times.

Inland Waterway Provision Company
305 Hodges St., Oriental
(252) 249-1797

Located by the harbor, Inland Waterway Provision Company offers discount pricing on everything you need for fishing, boating and outdoor activities. Beautiful nautical-themed treasures abound, ranging from brass lanterns and sextants to jewelry, wind chimes and flags. Inland Waterway features quality sportswear, footwear and foul-weather gear and offers a great selection of T-shirts for the whole family. Deck and casual shoes are always discounted 20 percent off the retail price. Inland Waterway is open seven days a week year round.

Marsha's Cottage
204 Wall St., Oriental
(252) 249-0334

Marsha's Cottage, located in a classic 1930s Sears-Roebuck bungalow, features distinctive, casually elegant clothing, gifts and accessories for all seasons. From backyard barbecue's to elegant, black-tie affairs, Marsha's Cottage has something special for each and every occasion. Marsha, Donna and Linda invite you to visit and enjoy an unhurried and memorable shopping experience. The store is open seven days a week.

Priscilla's Too/General Store
516 S. Water St., Oriental
(252) 249-3783

Priscilla's Too is located inside the General Store in the Oriental Harbor Village Center development. The General Store carries domestic and imported beer and snacks for those headed out on the water or elsewhere. Priscilla's Too, tucked away in a small alcove, features more than 100 labels of world-class wines. It's kept stocked by Priscilla Livingston, the owner of Priscilla's Crystal Coast Wine Store in Morehead City. She offers weekly specials

and discounts on cases. Both Priscilla's Too and the General Store are open daily.

Quarterdeck Marine Store
Whittaker Creek Yacht Harbor,
Whittaker Point Rd., Oriental
(252) 249-1020

This is a complete ship's store, offering all the marine hardware and supplies sailors and power boaters need. There are T-shirts, foul-weather gear, shoes and shorts for adults and children. Patrons will also find nautical books and charts, binoculars, sunglasses, and beer and wine. Quarterdeck offers discounts to BOAT/US card holders and is open seven days a week all year. Outboards, cruisers, sailboats and motor yachts are available for rent or charter, and marine services are available. Call for more information.

Rose Cottage
405 High St., Oriental
(252) 249-2431

Off the beaten path and not opened for long hours, Rose Cottage has developed a loyal following of persistent shoppers. Owner Virginia Mays fills her shop with wonderful decorative accessories, accent furniture and vintage Madame Alexander dolls. Just follow the signs along the river. You'll be glad you did. Call for days and hours of business.

The Shops at Croakertown
807 Broad St., Oriental
(252) 249-0990

The Shops at Croakertown are not your usual gift shops. With an extensive selection of cards and stationery, unique gifts and accessories, jewelry and original artwork by local artists and craftspersons and fiction and nonfiction books for all ages and interests, there is something for everyone — including gourmet goodies. Owner Lynn has 1,500 labels of domestic and imported wine, as well as cheese in Croakertown's new Oriental Wine and Cheese Shop. Another wonderful addition is the Southern Belle Gardens, a full-service florist and agent for Teleflora, FTD, Bloomnet and 1-800-Flowers, with the ability to ship anywhere. Choose your own design or let them create custom fresh flower arrangements or gift baskets for any occasion. Weddings are their specialty.

The Shops at Croakertown are open year-round, Monday through Saturday from 10 AM to 5 PM. The last Friday of every month is a wine-tasting, featuring new wines and a sampling of Croakertown's gourmet goodies for only $5 per person.

West Marine
1102 Broad St., Oriental
(252) 249-3200

The world's largest supplier of marine hardware and electronics is located on N.C. 55 coming into the town of Oriental. The knowledgeable staff can recommend the best foul-weather gear, boat accessories and appropriate replacement parts for your boat. This is also just a great place to browse for marine-related items. It's open seven days a week. Call for seasonal hours.

Things to Do and See in Oriental

SAILING CHARTERS AND SCHOOLS

For those who want the true Oriental experience, learning to sail or chartering a sailboat is the thing to do. **Oriental's School of Sailing**, located at 518 Water Street in the Oriental Harbor Village and Marina, (252) 249-0960, offers programs in sailing, powerboats and coastal navigation. Sailing school alumni can also sign up for advanced classes. Lessons begin the first week of March and go through November. Instructors emphasize safety and hands-on experience. The school's programs are designed to introduce the novice sailor to sailing theory in the classroom as well as the basics of chartering and boat ownership. Oriental's School of Sailing also is a U.S. Sailing Certified School offering certifications in Basic Keelboat.

Another option for learning how to sail is **Carolina Sailing Unlimited**, (252) 249-0850. Carolina Sailing offers chartered cruises. Or you can visit owner and captain Reginald Fidoe, who is from London by way of Detroit. He's at 502 Church Street. For the past 20 years, the school,

stressing safety above all, has tailored lessons to individual needs and interests. Capt. Reg offers personalized instruction aboard your own boat. Charter cruises for up to six passengers are offered aboard the 33-foot ketch, Puffin, for a half-day, a full day or evening sails.

If it's a captain's course you need, contact Captain Larry Walker at **World Wide Marine Training** in Oriental by calling (252) 249-2135 or (866) 249-2135. Coast Guard–approved **PT-1 Charters** in Oriental, (252) 249-1597, operated by Captain Roy Pittman, also gives the captain's course.

Bow To Stern Sailing School
310 Hodges St., Oriental
(252) 249-2424, (866) 396-5471
www.LearnSailing.com

Bow to Stern Sailing School is certified by the American Sailing Association. They

Enjoy the sights and sounds of Pamlico County's waterways by joining the annual Pamlico Paddle, which combines friends and fun on the water with explorations of local waterways by canoe and kayak. Paddlers of all experience levels are welcome to take part; call (252) 670-8465 for more information.

can teach all levels of sailing certification — Basic Keel Boat, Bareboat Certification through Offshore Passagemaking, Coastal Navigation and Cruising Catamaran. They will create custom classes for families, couples or groups. They also have a youth sailing program and are soon to initiate a sailing program in the Pamlico County School System.

Bow To Stern Yachts
310 Hodges St., Oriental
(252) 474-6000, (866) 395-5471
www.bowtosternyachts.com

Bow to Stern Yachts offers local and overnight charters (sunset, half day or full day). Enjoy these charters with or without instruction. Individualized vacation packages offer custom charters to Ocracoke, Cape Lookout or wherever you would like to venture, on a 52-foot Irwin with all the amenities, such as refrigerator/freezer, gas grill, washer/dryer, air conditioning and more. Corporate team-building programs are available for groups of up to 20 people. Sailing in Oriental is wonderful in spring, summer and fall with warm breezy weather, spectacular sunsets and abundant wildlife to admire.

Cape Lookout Yacht Sales & Charters
711 Broad St., Oriental
(252) 249-2111

When you charter a yacht from Cape Lookout Yacht Sales & Charters for your next vacation or weekend getaway you are setting yourself up for a truly memorable experience. Discover blue waters, quiet rivers, sparkling beaches, deserted islands and a wealth of interesting ports. For the price of a beach cottage weekend you can dine beneath a historic lighthouse or explore miles of beaches along the coast. Cape Lookout offers captained or bareboat charters. The website, www.capelookoutyachtsales, has information on yachts available for charter as well as smaller boats for rent.

Simple Boats
102 Starboard Ln., Oriental
(252) 617-1642

Don't have a boat of your own? Rent one from Simple Boats. They offer an array of sailboats and motorboats for your water adventures, whether you would like a quiet fishing trip, a sight-seeing expedition or a guided tour of the river and its views. Simple Boats has sailboats from 16 to 27 feet and motorboats from 18 to 26 feet. Rent a boat for a half day, all day or overnight trips. Simple Boats also rents fishing gear and coolers to make your time on the water as enjoyable as possible.

FISHING

If you want to go fishing or hunting on your Oriental vacation, the man to call is Captain George Beckwith at **Down East Guide Service**, (252) 249-3101. From the Roanoke River for bass fly-fishing to Cape Lookout or the Pamlico Sound for more migratory fishing, you're going to catch some fish. Ask him about his charters to Costa Rica.

Spec Fever is a shallow-water and near-coastal fishing guide service owned and operated by Captain Gary Dubiel. Join Captain Gary for some great fishing trips. In Oriental, you may fish the Pamlico Sound, Neuse River and its tributaries from March through January for redfish, speckled sea trout, flounder, striped bass, tarpon, giant red drum, black drum and weakfish. Fish from New Bern for redfish, stripers, sea trout, largemouth bass, shad and catfish. The cypress-lined shores of the Neuse and the Trent rivers can offer excellent fishing through much of the year. Charters are available in Morehead City, Beaufort and the Crystal Coast for summer cobia, dolphin, king and Spanish mackerel, bluefish, jacks, bonito and flounder, or try a fall trip for false albacore. Shallow-water redfish and family-oriented bottom-fishing and trolling trips are available as well. You can also fish out of Oregon Inlet each January for giant ocean stripers. Call (252) 249-1520.

For a half-day or full-day charter tailored to your specific needs and schedule, call Capt. Mark Hoff at **Sweet Water Charters**. Captain Mark offers morning, evening and night trips. He includes all bait, terminal tackle, lures and rod and reels in his price, although you may bring your own gear. Bring two coolers, one with drinks and snacks and one for your catch. Call (252) 249-2811.

PERFORMING AND CREATIVE ARTS

Pelican Players is the community's performance company. Organized in 1983, this nonprofit volunteer organization is affiliated with both the Pamlico and the North Carolina Arts Councils. The group stages several productions a year, with performances at the Old Theater at 609 Broad Street (across from the Town Hall). Dramas, Broadway hits and original productions make up their repertoire, along with an Annual Children's Workshop. Tickets are for sale at the theater door. For more information, call (252) 249-0477.

Also part of the Old Theater is **Pamlico Sounds**, an independent recording studio with a spring and fall series of concert presentations. Some of the previous acts have included George Winston, Loudon Wainwright III, Leon Redbone, Mike Cross and Livingston Taylor.

The **Pamlico Musical Society** presents eight to ten concerts a year by professional musicians performing everything from chamber music to down-home bluegrass. Season and individual concert tickets are available for sale at Croakertown in Oriental or on the web at www.pamlico-music.org. Most performances take place at the Old Theater. To join the society or to purchase season tickets, contact Patty Rosencrantz at (252) 249-3670.

At 1103 Broad Street is **Circle 10 Art Gallery**, operated by Oriental's artists' cooperative. Art lovers can admire and purchase original creations in a variety of media: acrylics, oils, watercolors, pastels, glass work, fiber art, jewelry and more. The gallery hosts a public reception on the first Sunday of each month to exhibit an individual member's new artwork. Workshops are offered throughout the year by local artists. Circle 10 is open 10 AM to 5 PM Wednesday through Saturday and 1 to 4:30 PM on Sunday. For more information about what's being scheduled, call (252) 249-0298.

Pamlico County Heritage Center
Grantsboro
(252) 745-2239

The Pamlico County Heritage Center in Grantsboro opened in 2008 and is a work in progress. The 6,200-square-foot museum is located behind the existing Pamlico County Visitors Center in Grantsboro. Work has begun on a heritage village on land behind the facility. The plans call for a working blacksmith shop, two grist mills, a pottery, a sugar-cane grinding facility, a one-room schoolhouse, a small country store and a small farmhouse. The 30,000 schoolchildren in the eight nearby counties will be able to visit this unique historical display.

EVENTS

In September don't miss the annual **Oriental Cup Regatta** — a good-time, three-day weekend party with a sailboat race in the middle. The race is geared to cruisers as well as racers, so all types of sailors, weekenders and competitors are encouraged to join the fun. Festivities start with a Friday night party with good food and live entertainment. Saturday, rain or shine, sailboats race a triangular course on the Neuse River, the silent auction tent remains open while the race is going on, and, after the race — guess what? — there's another party. Sunday finds folks at the last event, the awards brunch. All monies raised by the regatta and the silent auction go to the Bill Harris Memorial Scholarship Fund (scholarships are awarded annually to Pamlico County students who letter in at least one sport and are of good character). For registration forms and tickets, call Larry Summers at 757-508 0153.

Oriental's popularity soars on the Fourth of July weekend when thousands of visitors arrive for the annual **Croaker Festival**. The event honors the croaker, a very vocal, tasty fish found only in Southern waters. (If you've never heard a croaker's croak, you need to spend more time on the water.) The festival includes entertainment, the Croakette and Croaker Queen pageants, lots of good food, a baking contest, boat races, a street dance and more. But the more customary traditions of the Fourth are not neglected. The festival weekend concludes with a patriotic fireworks display that inevitably draws oohs and aahs from the holiday crowd. For information, call (252) 249-0555.

The **Annual Oriental Rotary Tarpon Tournament** is held every year around the last weekend in July. In case you didn't know, a tarpon is a big bony, silvery sport fish that averages 80 pounds and some 6 feet in length. (Tarpons have been known to weigh in at 200 pounds.) The fish winter in Florida's coastal waters and in the summer swim up the Atlantic, right into Pamlico Sound and the Neuse River. During July and August, tarpon abound in Oriental's waters. They are an excellent sporting fish, often fighting for 10 minutes to as long as an hour. The tournament, sponsored by the Oriental Rotary Club as a fund-raiser for the club's scholarship program, is a catch-and-release affair. Volunteer observers accompany the fishing boats to record official scores. The winning vessel is the one that catches and releases the most tarpon. Prizes are cash, and typically about 75 boats enter the tournament for a fee of $200. This three-day event includes a Saturday night barbecue and a Sunday afternoon awards ceremony. For information, call (252) 249-0555.

The Spirit of Christmas in Oriental is a holiday gift to the people of Oriental from the town's merchants, churches and civic groups. For well over a decade, on the second weekend in December (rain or shine), Oriental dresses up in resplendent holiday finery. Businesses and churches open their doors for fellowship and yuletide refreshments, and everyone is invited to stroll the candle-lit streets and enjoy the festivities, which start in the afternoon and continue throughout the evening. Townsfolk and visitors are entertained by local choral groups, musicians, Christmas puppets, decorated boats lining Oriental harbor, a Christmas parade and the ceremonious lighting of the Tree of Lights. This beautiful, free event is the work of nearly everyone in Oriental and is guaranteed to put you in a holiday mood. For information, call (252) 249-0555.

For more than 30 years, Oriental has commemorated New Year's Eve in its own special way. Every December 31, the community stages its annual **Running of the Dragon**. A huge golden Chinese dragon, with about 40 or 50 pairs of feet, appears twice during the evening beside the harbor. When it shows itself, New Year's

Eve revelers pursue the dragon as it winds in and out of the town's streets. How many feet propel the dragon body depends on how many folks don't mind running around in the dark under a blanket. Needless to say, Oriental's Dragon Run attracts lots of visitors. Kids can see the dragon at 8 PM, and grown-ups can stay up for the 11 PM run. For information, call (252) 249-0555.

The Aurora Fossil Museum
400 Main St., Aurora
(252) 322-4238

The Aurora Fossil Museum, founded in 1976, is a nonprofit fossil education resource center. The museum's mission is to increase knowledge of the geology and paleontology of the area by collecting and displaying fossils that come from coastal North Carolina. The fossil pile at the museum, dubbed the "Pit of the Pungo", is an unlimited source of Miocene-age fossils donated by the PCS Phosphate mining operation. In these fossil-rich soils, one may find the remains of ancient sharks, whales, bony fish, corals, shells and other invertebrates. The museum staff will willingly provide personal assistance and other resources to help you identify your finds. Bring a garden trowel or sifter and plastic bags, spend the day collecting and take home a piece of the past. There are many fossils on display here. The phosphate mine in Beaufort County has been called the most important source of Pliocene and Miocene fossils in the world.

School groups are welcome and the museum is happy to provide free fossil material and educational information for classroom use. Schedule your group of 10 or more in advance of a visit, and they will be better able to serve you. If your school is unable to make a trip to the museum, contact them and see if they can come to you. The presentation includes an exhibit of local fossils, free fossil material and educational resources suitable for grades 3 to 8.

The museum is open Monday through Saturday, 9 AM until 4:30 PM. In addition to regular hours, from March 1 through Labor Day, the museum is open on Sunday from 12:30 to 4:30 PM. The fossil Pit of the Pungo remains open for collecting from sun-up to sundown. Admission is free but donations are gladly accepted. A gift shop is open in the main building and offers fossils and souvenirs. Ample free parking is provided.

The town of more than 700 residents, named for the Bay River, was settled in the 1800s, and incorporated in 1881.

Real Estate

If you are interested in property or housing in Oriental, either to buy or rent, several firms can help you.

NEIGHBORHOODS

Pamlico County is in the midst of a growth spurt, and should you visit by car you may be quite aware of the 14-mile widening of N.C. Highway 55 from inside the Craven County line to the Pamlico County Courthouse at the intersection of N.C. Highway 304 in Bayboro. The road construction will be complete in mid-2009.

You may be visiting by boat from the Intracoastal Waterway, Pamlico Sound or Neuse River — possibly stopping at one or more of the pleasant small communities on the water. The towns of Vanmdemere, Bayboro, Oriental and Minnesott Beach are waterfront communities.

Pamlico County is a peninsula, bordered by water on three sides: Goose Creek and the Pamlico River on the north, Upper Broad Creek on the western boundary and the Neuse River to the south. Pamlico County was created out of part of Craven County in 1872 and parts of Beaufort County in 1874 and 1875.

The county historical association has built a museum – the Pamlico County Heritage and Visitors Center – in Grantsboro geared to Pamlico's heritage of fishing, farming and forestry. Visitors can stop by the museum, which also houses the offices of the Pamlico County Chamber of Commerce for maps and information.

There are many small businesses in Pamlico County and many of those are "multi-generational." Throughout history in Pamlico County, many residents became businessmen due to the needs of the community and handed those venues down

to family. New small businesses are being added to the mix as more residents and visitors come to the county.

Leading crops in Pamlico County consist mostly of corn, soybeans, white and sweet potatoes, wheat and cotton, mostly replacing the once prominent tobacco. Forestry is a prime industry with pines being planted, maintained and logged on a regular basis.

An estimated 10 percent of Pamlico County's total population is involved in the commercial fishing industry. Seafood commonly harvested in the waters of Pamlico County are flounder, grouper, king mackerel, sea bass, sea trout, Spanish mackerel, striped bass, croaker, blue fish, red drum, black drum, mullet, catfish, common eel, crabs, shrimp, oysters, sea scallops and squid. Much of the manufacturing output of Pamlico County has to do with seafood processing and boat building. Many small manufacturing operations are found throughout the county.

Construction and the building of new homes is another provider of jobs in Pamlico County. More than 20 percent of the employment in Pamlico County comes from government, education, social services and health jobs. Approximately 12 percent of residents are involved in retail.

Quiet rivers and creeks bring residents and tourists to fish, sail and relax by the water. The town of Oriental (874 residents in 2006) is known as the Sailing Capital of North Carolina. The number of sailboats to Oriental residents has been estimated at 3:1.

The towns of Pamlico County include the county seat of Bayboro, along with Oriental, Vandemere, Mesic, Stonewall, Alliance, Grantsboro, Arapahoe and Minnesott Beach. Well-known communities include Hobucken, Lowland, Merritt, Reelsboro, Florence, Whortonsville, Olympia and the Dawson Creek area.

Real estate in Pamlico County is as varied as a day in May. While there is no formal county-wide zoning outside of the nine municipalities, the county does have a subdivision ordinance and a group housing ordinance. Bayboro, Vandemere, Minnesott Beach and Oriental have regulations geared toward development. The average price range for new homes in Pamlico County is $214,000 to $246,000, although million-dollar homes have been built.

If you are interested in real estate in Pamlico County, pick up a copy of *HOMES Magazine* for Craven and Pamlico counties, published by NC Coast Communications. This full-color publication has pictures of properties currently on the market. It is free and can be found at restaurants, hotels, supermarkets, real estate firms and local businesses.

REAL ESTATE COMPANIES

Carol Wright, Buyer's Broker
502 Main St., Oriental
(252) 249-1700

An experienced boater and Realtor, Carol Wright can find that piece of waterfront property or an existing home overlooking one of the many beautiful creeks. Looking for a business and commercial property? Carol knows them all. As a buyer's broker, she works only for the buyer. Carol's hours are Monday through Friday 9 AM to 5 PM and Saturday by appointment.

Century 21 Sail Loft Realty Inc.
1000 Broad St., Oriental
(252) 249-1787, (800) 327-4189

Sail/Loft Realty is a family-owned company and the oldest real estate agency in Pamlico County. With that distinction comes a wealth of experience. Larry Gwaltney and his staff of knowledgeable brokers are leaders in today's real estate business. Century 21 is the industry leader in real estate training and marketing, with technology being the name of the game. The Brokers at Century 21 Sail/Loft Realty strive to be on top of their game in order to meet the needs of their clients. Select from an exquisite collection of luxury homes, wooded home sites, golf course and waterfront properties as well as commercial property, vacation and long-term rentals. Sail/Loft also offers property management services and rents storage for boats, RVs and household dry goods. Let the experienced Realtors at Century 21 Sail/Loft Realty introduce you to the

Boating and sailing are popular ways to tour the islands along the coast.

photo: Peter Doran

perfect property in the ideal location with the amenities to fit your lifestyle.

Coldwell Banker
Willis-Smith Realty - Oriental
401 Hodges St., Oriental
(252) 249-1000

Coldwell Banker Willis-Smith Realty is Pamlico County's largest full-service real estate brokerage firm. Located in the heart of the village of Oriental, North Carolina's Sailing Capital, this company serves Pamlico, Craven, Carteret and Beaufort counties with more than 40 real estate professionals in three convenient office locations. At Coldwell Banker Willis-Smith, their quality service is backed with nationally recognized excellence, comprehensive training and extensive advertising. The agency promises to listen closely to the needs and wants of its clients and will work with you to find the home that perfectly fits your lifestyle, or the homesite and builder to make your custom-built home a reality.

Mariner Realty Inc.
704 Broad St., Oriental
(252) 249-1014, (800) 800) 347-8246

Whether buying or selling residential, waterfront, commercial or development property, Mariner Realty's experienced team of broker-agents can assist you. Established more than 20 years ago, this family-owned business is well acquainted with the area. Whether your destiny is a retirement home, vacation retreat, investment property or just enjoying the casual coastal lifestyle in a vacation rental, their goal is making sure you are satisfied.

Oriental Harbor Real Estate Services
516 Water St., Oriental
(252) 249-3783

If you are interested in purchasing or renting land, cottages or condominiums, Oriental Harbor Real Estate Services is ready to work with you. Oriental Harbor provides a full-service real estate service that offers Oriental Harbor Place luxury condominiums for sale or rent. In addition, Oriental Harbor Real Estate Services has exclusive listings for lots and cottages throughout the village of Oriental. The brand-new Oriental Harbor condominium community offers unparalleled luxury

in this part of the North Carolina coast. These two- or three-bedroom residences, all with water views, are available for nightly, weekly and long-term rental. Call Steve Williams at (252) 617-2474, Mark Crowder at (252) 617-9692 or Jon Chesson at (252) 671-9275.

Tidewater Real Estate
22826 N.C. Hwy. 55, Oriental
(252) 249-9800, (866) 249-9800

Tidewater Real Estate handles listings for the Cabin Creek and Tidewater Ridge subdivisions and offers an extensive selection of land and lots plus residential golf course, waterfront, water-view and water-access properties. It also offers commercial properties. Tidewater handles residential and commercial rentals.

Village Realty
802 Broad St., Oriental
(252) 249-0509

Village Realty knows the Oriental market well. Established in 1988, this local independent firm and Broker Michelle Fodrey list and sell commercial and residential property, waterfront lots, boat slips and large tracts of land. Oriental is the home of approximately 900 people and three times as many sailboats, a distinction that has earned this small sailing, fishing and kayaking paradise the nickname of Sailing Capital of North Carolina. Oriental has been written up in *Sail Magazine* as one of the ten best sailing destinations in the United States. This is a great time to let Village Realty find you the perfect property and become a part of the village as it is still being discovered.

HOME SERVICES

D. Lamont Custom Cabinets
1105 Broad St., Oriental
(252) 249-2504

Doug Lamont has been building fine custom cabinets since 1976. He moved to Oriental in 1991 and began building cabinets in 1993 — kitchen cabinets, book cases, built-ins, entertainment centers and furniture. D. Lamont Custom Cabinets is also proud to announce the addition of Crystal Cabinets, a high-end custom factory line built like the finest furniture, complete with dove-tailed drawers and beautiful hand-rubbed finishes. Visit him at the showroom or check out his website and choose from 80 door styles as well as custom door styles, 25 stains, 15 paint colors and 12 standard wood species as well as exotic woods. Contact Doug for new construction as well as renovation. Doug works with people from design to installation and stands behind his company's work.

Marine Services

Inner Banks Sails and Canvas
112 Straight Road, Oriental
(252) 249-3001

Mark Weinheimer and LuAnn Parins believe that the quality and durability of their sails and canvas products at Inner Banks Sails and Canvas, combined with their years of racing, cruising, offshore and live-aboard experience, enable them to give the best value and service available. Mark has been a sailmaker all of his adult life and has worked with some of the great names of competition racing, including Peter Wormwood and Dennis Connor. LuAnn and Mark provide the finest in racing and cruising sails, full service on repairs, re-cuts, conversions and furlers as well as custom canvas products on-deck and below decks. They feature world-class Doyle Sails. Come and visit their new custom space just outside Oriental.

Marine Consignment Of Oriental
708 Broad St., Oriental
(252) 249-3222

Marine Consignment of Oriental (MCOO) offers great deals on thousands of new and quality used marine items. You'll find dinghies, davits, VHF radios, folding bikes, harkin blocks, seamaiden art and much more. Boaters will feel like a kid in a candy store. Hours are Monday,

 If you want to play golf while visiting Oriental, try the Minnesott Golf and Country Club, (252) 249-0813. The course is just a few miles away — near the Cherry Branch-Minnesott Ferry dock.

Thursday, Friday and Saturday 9 AM to 5 PM and Sunday 1 to 5 PM. Gift certificates are available. MCOO is in downtown Oriental, within walking distance of the marinas. Call for pick up and delivery.

Oriental Harbor Real Estate Services
516 Water St., Oriental
(252) 249-3783

Oriental Harbor provides a full-service real estate service that offers boat slips for sale and/or rent. At the heart of Oriental Harbor is the marina with 110 deep-water boat slips, serving both private and transient boat owners. Boat slips range in length from 30 to 100 feet and from 6 to 7 feet in depth. Slips are individually owned and deeded and are governed by a slip owners' association. Call Steve Williams at (252) 617-2474, Mark Crowder at (252) 617-9692 or Jon Chesson at (252) 671-9275.

Oriental Harbor Village Center & Marina
516 Water St., Oriental
(252) 249-3783

Oriental Harbor Village Center & Marina bills itself as the place "where the old and the new live quite comfortably side by side," and it's easy to see why recreational boaters will enjoy an opportunity to stop by one of Oriental's newest developments. Located at the mouth of the Neuse River, the complete marina includes 110 deep-water slips, serving both permanent and transient boaters. Transient slips are available for rent on a monthly or nightly basis. Amenities include power and water services, a pump-out station, shower and laundry facilities, concierge services and the use of bicycles, kayaks and small boats. The private Neuse River Club is open only to members and their guests. The historic old Oriental Train Station has been meticulously restored to house the development's General Store, where boaters will find a little bit of everything as well as the Oriental Harbor Deli & Bistro, Priscilla's Too's fine wines, Oriental's School of Sailing and the Red Rickshaw, featuring fine furnishings and interior design. The waterfront condominiums adjacent to the marina are finished and feature a pool, spa and elevators. Some are available for nightly rentals.

MARINAS

Boonedocks Guest House
1108 Fork Point Road, Oriental
(252) 249-0023

Boonedocks Marina has 10 slips on Broad Creek that are popular among boaters who want to get away from the city lights. With 6 feet of water at the end of the dock and 30 amp hookups, the slips can support boats with a beam up to 14 feet and 42 feet long. The 10 slips are all spoken for, but there are transient slips for those just passing through. The dock has shuttle service available so boaters can get into town for needed items. The dockmaster says the marina would be an ideal place to wait for a crew change as the marina comes complete with cabin. See Boonedocks Guest House listing in this chapter's Accommodations section. Internet is available on site and fuel is available nearby at River Dunes. The overnight charge is $30.

Oriental Harbor Village & Marina
518 Water St., Oriental
(252) 249-3783

Oriental Harbor Village Center & Marina bills itself as the place "where the old and the new live quite comfortably side by side" — and it's easy to see why recreational boaters will enjoy an opportunity to stop by one of Oriental's newest developments. Located at the mouth of the Neuse River, the complete marina includes 110 deep-water slips, serving both permanent and transient boaters. Slips are available for sale or rent on a monthly or nightly basis. Amenities include power and water services, a pump-out station, shower and laundry facilities, concierge services, use of bicycles, kayaks and small boats and more. The private Neuse River Club is open only to members and their guests. The historic Delmar Hardware building and old Oriental Train Station have been meticulously restored to house the development's General Store, where boaters will find a little bit of everything as well as Oriental Harbor Deli & Bistro, Priscilla's Too's fine wines, Oriental's School of Sailing and the Red Rickshaw, featuring fine furnishings and interior design. The waterfront condominiums adjacent to the

marina feature a pool, spa and elevators. Some are available for nightly rental.

Oriental Marina & Inn
103 Wall Street, Oriental
(252) 249-1818

This marina, just off the ICW, is open year round and serves sail and power vessels up to 80 feet long. It has 13 transient slips, an 8-foot entry channel, dockside depth of 6.5 feet, gas and diesel fuel, electrical hook-ups, cable TV, complimentary wireless Internet, ice, showers and laundry facilities. Marina guests may use the pool facilities. The Toucan Grill & Fresh Bar and the Oriental Inn are located adjacent to the marina.

Sea Harbour Yacht Club
Harbour Way, Oriental
(252) 249-0808

Sea Harbour Yacht Club is on Pierce Creek about a mile from town. It is open year round, has 90 slips, serves sail and power vessels up to 45 feet, and has gas and diesel fuel, a pump-out station, electricity, water hookups, a pool and restrooms.

Whittaker Creek Yacht Harbor
Whittaker Point Rd., Oriental
(252) 249-0666, (252) 249-1020

Whittaker Creek Yacht Harbor is open year round, has 160 slips including 20 transient slips, serves power and sailing vessels up to 120 feet and has a marked entry channel with 8 feet of water on approach and at dockside. Gas and diesel fuel are available, as are a pump-out station, electricity, free high-speed wireless

In his latest book, Living Waters, *Oriental resident and photographer Ben Casey tracks the Trent River from its beginning as a small stream in Lenoir County to where it empties into the Neuse River at New Bern. Casey's first book,* All in One River, *follows the Neuse River from Falls Dam to the Pamlico Sound. Both books are available at local bookstores and gift shops.*

Internet access, supplies, a ship's store, ice, laundry facilities and restrooms. The marina offers vessel repairs as well as sail and power charters.

YACHT SALES

Bow To Stern Yachts
310 Hodges Street, Oriental
(252) 474-6000, (866) 395-5471
www.LearnSailing.com
www.bowtosternyachts.com

Bow To Stern Yachts is a full-service yacht brokerage offering you the opportunity to fulfil your dream by helping you find that special boat, be it sail or power. Bow To Stern Yachts also offers charters and operates Bow To Stern Sailing School offering all levels of sailing certification (see our Sailing Schools and Charters section).

Cape Lookout Yacht Sales & Charters
711 Broad Street, Oriental
(252) 249-2111

Cape Lookout Yacht Sales & Charters is the exclusive Southeast dealer for the Mariner Yachts International line of trawlers, express and pilothouse yachts. Cape Lookout Yacht Sales also carries the Ca-

mano line of trawlers that can put you in a yacht designed by quality craftsmen — one that can become the investment of a lifetime. The website, www.capelookoutyachtsales.com, also has information on used boat brokerage.

Triton Yacht Sales
919 Midyette Street, Oriental
(252) 249-2210

Triton Yachts has been serving the boating world for more than two decades in Oriental. It is a complete marine business that includes yacht sales (new and pre-owned), boat transportation, boat service and storage.

Brokerage: Triton is staffed by experienced boaters — cruising sailors, racing sailors, sportfishing anglers and power boaters, who will work with you to find the right vessel. Whether you are listing a boat for sale or locating your perfect next boat, visit Triton Yacht Sales where they make it happen.

New Boat Dealer: Triton Yachts carries the Laser Performance line of sailboats, including Sunfish, Laser, Optimist, 420, Stratos and the indestructible Bahia and Vago. They stock a complete line of parts

Rowboats are nice vessels for exploring calm waterways.

photo: Carolyn Temple

and accessories for the Sunfish and Laser as well as Seitech launching dollies and custom boat covers.

Boat Transport: The experts at Triton are fully licensed and insured with 20 years of experience in moving sail and power vessels. Their custom hydraulic trailers provide a safe, smooth ride and offer the ability to wet launch as well as loading/offloading at remote locations.

Dry Storage and Repair: Triton has a 2.5-acre boatyard conveniently located in Oriental. Triton offers basic fiberglass repair, boat bottom painting and boat restoration. Their fenced, well lit, dry storage area offers the boater a do-it-yourself alternative. Contact Triton to discuss your individual needs.

Healthcare

Nova Urgent Care - Pamlico
13808 N.C. Hwy. 55, Alliance
(252) 745-7440

Nova Urgent Care provides quality medical care when you need it. Nova offers everything from physicals to minor emergency care for the people of Pamlico County. No appointment is necessary; you can walk right in. They specialize in Worker's Compensation injuries. The Urgent Care staff is highly qualified, consisting of a physician, board certified in family practice, a certified family nurse practitioner with ER experience, and a certified physician's assistant who served in the U. S. Air Force and has prior OR and urgent-care experience. The office is located in Alliance, next to Hardee's, and is open Monday through Friday from 8 AM to 8 PM and on Saturday from 10 AM to 3 PM.

Oriental Dental
403 Hodges St., Oriental
(252) 249-1551

This dentist's office is open Monday through Wednesday from 9 AM until 5 PM, Thursday from 9 AM until 1 PM and other hours by appointment.

Oriental Medical Center
901 Broad St., Oriental
(252) 249-2888

Oriental Medical Center specializes in family practice. The center is open Monday through Friday from 8:30 AM to 1 PM and from 2 to 5 PM.

DAYTRIPS

Daytrips are the ideal way to see and enjoy more of North Carolina's coast, so we've provided this quick guide to some of our favorite getaway spots. These places are close by and are Insiders' favorites for various reasons — the relaxed pace, scenic beauty, rich history, delicious restaurant fare or quiet evenings. After learning more about these places, you might want to plan a longer visit.

The North Carolina Travel and Tourism Division of the Department of Commerce, (919) 733-4171 or (800) VISIT-NC, offers information on sights throughout the state. Also check out other books in the Insiders' Guide® series, such as the *Insiders' Guide to North Carolina's Outer Banks* and *Insiders' Guide to North Carolina's Southern Coast and Wilmington*. To order books, call (800) 955-1860 or visit us online at www.insiders.com.

Ocracoke Island

They call it the Ocra-coma. It encompasses that vague rocking motion produced by the bed and breakfast's rocking chair and covers the inability to get off your towel on Ocracoke's pristine beaches. Folks in Ocracoke find it easy to forgive. There is just something about Ocracoke.

Perhaps it's the trip to the island — two and a half hours by ferry from Cedar Island, 40 minutes to the island by ferry from Hatteras Inlet, two and a half hours from Swan Quarter, a hop, skip and jump by air, a brief segue by private boat. At least the ferry trip there lets you experience how Blackbeard must have felt approaching this 16-mile long jewel of

an island wedged between the Atlantic Ocean and the Pamlico Sound.

Ocracoke was established as a port by the colony of North Carolina in 1715. Early maps refer to the settlement as Pilot Town, because it was home to the men who were responsible for piloting ships safely into the harbor. About that same time, Edward Teach, better known as Blackbeard, discovered the Outer Banks. The pirate and his crew robbed ships and terrorized island residents until 1718, when Lt. Robert Maynard of the Royal Navy and his crew ended Blackbeard's reign. Blackbeard was beheaded at a spot off Ocracoke now known as Teach's Hole. The pirate's head was mounted on the bowsprit of Maynard's ship, and Blackbeard's body was thrown overboard where, according to local legend, it swam around the ship seven times before it sank. (See our Closeup on Blackbeard's ship Queen Anne's Revenge in the Attractions chapter.)

The island's solid white lighthouse was built in 1823 to replace the 1798 lighthouse. **Ocracoke Lighthouse** is the oldest and shortest of the Outer Banks' lighthouses, measuring only 65 feet high, or 75 feet including the lantern. A keeper manned the light until 1929, when it was converted to electrical power. It is now operated by the Coast Guard. The lighthouse isn't open for tours or climbing, but sometimes volunteers offer historical talks and answer questions.

Ocracoke Village is nestled on the edge of Silver Lake on the southern end and the broadest part of the small island. There are docks for pleasure and commercial fishing boats, inns, gift shops, private homes, historic cemeteries, seafood

See this entire guide plus additional content online at insiderinfo.us

wholesale and retail businesses, restaurants and marshlands surrounding the water. Some homes date to the late 1800s. As more visitors discover the island hideaway and build more homes and lodgings, the face of the village is changing.

N.C. Highway 12, the island's main road, stretches the entire 16 miles of the island, from the Hatteras-Ocracoke ferry terminal on one end to the Cedar Island-Ocracoke ferry terminal at the other end. This is the southern tip of Cape Hatteras National Seashore, and it is the perfect spot for shelling, fishing, sunbathing and water sports. Ocracoke Island belongs to the Cape Hatteras National Seashore, with the exception of the village.

Bikes are available for rent, as are fishing supplies, sailboats and surfboards, beach umbrellas and chairs. Because of the town's small size, many of Ocracoke's businesses do double duty. Restaurants are also nightspots, inns feature restaurants, and restaurants offer gifts. Ocracoke has a surprising number of businesses. The more you explore the village, the more places you will find tucked away. There are all types of accommodation choices on the island, including inns, motels, bed and breakfasts, rental cottages and camping. While not all the places remain open year round, those that do offer some inviting winter rates.

Here is a small sampling of the shops, restaurants and accommodations you will find on Ocracoke. The village is dotted with arts, crafts, gift and apparel shops. **Harborside Motel & Shop**, (252) 928-3111, billed as a family tradition open daily, has long been known for quality gifts and clothing, including sportswear, batik dresses, jewelry, saltwater taffy, stuffed animals and more, in addition to offering lodgings. On School Road, visit a gift shop with books, handmade stoneware, island-made candles, children's gifts and toys, bath products and more for both home and garden at **Deep Water Pottery** and **Books to Be Red**, (252) 928-7472.

Those wishing for a unique dining experience have several excellent options available to them. **The Back Porch**, 1324 Back Road, (252) 928-6401, offers relaxed dining seven nights a week on its shaded

and sultry screened porch or in its air-conditioned dining room. The restaurant is an island favorite and is singularly a reason for a daytrip from the Crystal Coast, for its signature crab beignets, crab cakes, pastas, salads and creative seafood preparations, prime meats, house-secret sauces, and extensive wine list.

To book a room, try the **Island Inn**, N.C. 12, call (877) 456-3466 or (252) 928-4351. Guests are offered traditional rooms in the 1901 country inn or accommodations in the newly renovated villas fronting the island's only heated pool. **Bluff Shoal Motel**, N.C. 12, (252) 928-4301, features large, comfortable rooms with double beds, private baths, small refrigerators, cable TV and telephones. Open all year, Bluff Shoal Motel has a harbor-view deck that overlooks Silver Lake. **Anchorage Inn and Marina**, N.C. 12, (252) 928-1101, offers accommodations fronting Silver Lake Harbor and boasts of having the ultimate waterfront views. The five-story inn stands high above the traditional island structures, and its brick exterior is atypical of the local architecture. The inn features a pool, a full-service marina and dockside cafe, along with grills and picnic tables. Anchorage Inn can put together fishing packages, including the charter, lodging and food for four to six people on its boats from May to September. **Pony Island Motel & Restaurant**, N.C. 12, (252) 928-4411, offers rooms, efficiency units and cottages. This reasonably priced motel has offered accommodations for more than 25 years. Amenities include grills, a heated pool, bike rentals and more. The adjoining restaurant serves breakfast, lunch and dinner.

For more information about Ocracoke, stop by the **National Park Service's Ocracoke Visitors Center**, which is by the ferry terminal, (252) 928-4531, or visit the **Ocracoke Preservation Society Museum**, open April through November, (252) 928-7375. For information about Ocracoke, contact the **Greater Hyde County Chamber of Commerce**, (252) 926-9171 or (888) 493-3826.

If you venture a little farther north than Ocracoke, you will discover all of North Carolina's Outer Banks. Of course, once you leave Ocracoke on the Ocracoke-Hatteras Inlet Ferry, you really aren't

CLOSE UP

Saving the
Battleship *North Carolina*

By Martha L. Hall

Perhaps you didn't realize it, but the Battleship *North Carolina* belongs to me. In the 1960s, thousands of North Carolina school children, including me from Josephus Daniels Junior High School in Raleigh, saved our pennies, nickels and dimes and bought a battleship. I believe we had a little help from the United States Navy, Govs. Luther Hodges and Terry Sanford and Battleship Commission chairman Hugh Morton, but as far as my classmates and I were concerned, it was all due to our hard work, contributions and determination.

In 1961, because of the persistence of the people of North Carolina, the decommissioned battleship reached its berth on Eagle Island across the Cape Fear River from Wilmington. The ship was dedicated to the 10,000 members of all the armed services from North Carolina who gave their lives in World War II.

It took astute planning, a plethora of tug boats and a bit of luck to place a 728-foot vessel with a normal displacement of 35,000 tons in a 500-foot-wide slip, but history assures us, with the help of a land-based bulldozer, the attempt was successful.

The Battleship *North Carolina*, known as the "Showboat" because of its majestic appearance, was felt to be a lucky ship. The battleship survived a direct Japanese torpedo hit somewhere in the Eastern Solomon Islands in September 1942 — a hit that blew an 18-foot by 32-foot hole in her side. Despite the damage, the ship made some adjustments and resumed protection of her assigned carrier.

The *North Carolina* was the most decorated U.S. battleship of the war and was awarded 15 battle stars. She served in every major naval battle in the Pacific, from Guadalcanal to Tokyo Bay, earning a record of 24 enemy aircraft shot down, a merchantman sunk and the bombardment of nine Japanese-held areas. You can see these statistics painted on the ship. Tokyo Rose, infamous broadcaster of Japanese propaganda, declared the *North Carolina* sunk six times. She was wrong.

On the deck of the *North Carolina* rests a Vought Kingfisher floatplane, one of seven still in existence. The floatplanes allowed the battleships and cruisers the freedom to carry on necessary tasks without having to depend on the aircraft carriers. The Kingfisher did everything from scouting and bombing to towing aerial targets for gunnery practice. A Kingfisher from the North Carolina rescued 10 downed airmen in the Pacific by strategically draping the men over the wings and the floats.

The Battleship North Carolina *found a permanent home on the Cape Fear River in Wilmington.*

photo: Peter Doran

Below decks, visitors can see the engine rooms, the mess area and the crew's quarters, where 2,300 men worked, ate, showered, slept and dreamed about home and a world without war. Life aboard a battleship served almost the same amenities as home with its own newspaper, hospital, soda fountain, movie theater, post office, laundry and an ice cream shop where you could buy a sundae with a choice of topping for 10 cents.

The Battleship *North Carolina* in downtown Wilmington is open 365 days a year, from 8 AM until 8 PM in the summer and 8 AM until 5 PM in the winter. You should allow at least two hours to tour the ship. Only the main deck is handicapped accessible. Wear sensible shoes, as you will be climbing up and down ladders and they are steep. The self-guided tour includes portions of nine decks, the gun turrets, the bridge, crew's quarters, the sick bay, the engine room, the barbershop and recreation areas. It is a good idea to begin the tour in the Visitors Center with the orientation exhibit "Through Their Eyes: The Battleship Crew Remembers WWII." On summer evenings, try to make it to a "sight and sound" performance that recreates the battleship's WWII battles.

And, please remember that the Battleship is brought to you courtesy of 700,000 other children from across North Carolina who used their milk money to bring the battleship to Wilmington. I admit there were some other folks who helped raise the necessary $325,000 to keep the battleship off the scrap pile. Just remember how important saving that ship was to those North Carolina school children. We helped preserve an important piece of history.

There are no more battleships. The U.S. Navy does not build them anymore. But for a brief chapter, they were magnificent and powerful and helped the United States and their allies win the war. And we, those children of long ago, helped to keep intact that heritage for others to enjoy. No wonder we're a little possessive. Enjoy your visit!

daytripping anymore — you're traveling. The Hatteras Inlet Ferry, a 30-minute trip, puts passengers off at Hatteras Village. From there, N.C. 12 strings along the narrow islands all the way up to Corolla at the northern tip of North Carolina's Outer Banks.

Howard's Pub & Raw Bar
N.C. Hwy. 12, Ocracoke Island
(252) 928-4441

Howard's Pub is a fun, casual place enjoyed by both locals and visitors for excellent food and good times. The walls are filled with memorabilia from college banners and license plates to photos and patches. Enjoy local seafood, steaks, burgers, subs, salads, pizza, soup or any of the many menu choices and appetizers inside, on the large screened porch, or on the roof-top deck with its view from ocean to sound. In season, Howard's features live entertainment; other times, enjoy watching major sporting events on Howard's big-screen TVs. The Pub has more than 200 varieties of beer in addition to wine and cocktails. It is family friendly and suitable for all ages, from grandparents to babies. Kids' meals are served on a Frisbee. Howard's doesn't close for hurricanes

or holidays so you'll find the place open from 11 AM until late night every day.

Bath

The small, historic hamlet of Bath is North Carolina's oldest town. Located in Beaufort County, this coastal village is about two hours by car from the Crystal Coast. It can be reached by taking U.S. Highway 70 to New Bern to U.S. Highway 17, which will lead you to Washington, where you take N.C. Highway 264, then N.C. Highway 92 to Bath. Another option is to take the more leisurely and scenic ferry route. Board the Cherry Branch-Minnesott Beach Ferry outside Havelock (see our Getting Here, Getting Around chapter), which will take you to the north side of the Neuse River on N.C. Highway 306. Drive along N.C. 306 to the Aurora-Bayview Ferry, which will deposit you on the north side of the Pamlico River. You will soon reach N.C. 92, which you follow for a few short miles into Bath. If you time the trip so you don't have to wait for ferries it can be a half-hour shorter. However, given the Aurora-Bayview schedule, that's almost impossible. Only take the ferry if you're not in a hurry.

Incorporated in 1705, Bath remains almost entirely within the boundaries of the original town plan designed by John Lawson, surveyor general to the crown of England. Today's residents are proud of their heritage and the town's significant eighteenth- and early nineteenth-century restorations. Historical markers throughout the town denote many "firsts" — Christopher Gale, first Chief Justice of North Carolina, lived here, and the first public library and the first post road for mail delivery in the state were established here. Edward Teach, better known as Blackbeard, spent several months in Bath before his death, most likely living at Plum Point just across the creek from the colonial governor, Charles Eden. Blackbeard moved about the town quite freely and was probably the guest of many distinguished citizens. Local legend states that Blackbeard's 14th wife was a Bath girl.

The **Historic Bath Visitor Center**, located on Carteret Street (N.C. Hwy. 42), offers a map noting the sites of interest in the town. You can take a walking tour on your own, or tour one or both of the period-furnished houses with a guide. Guided tours of the homes are $1 for adults and 50 cents for children. At the Visitor Center, you also can watch a free 15-minute orientation film Bath: The First Town as background for your walking tour. For seasonal hours and other information, call the Visitor Center at (252) 923-3971.

Out the back door of the Visitor Center is an oyster-shell path leading to the **Van Der Veer House** (c. 1790), which serves as a small museum for the town. Also along the path is the **Palmer-Marsh House** (c. 1751), for which there is an excellent guided tour that points out, among other things, a large double chimney and basement kitchen. The building is an excellent example of a large house from the Colonial period, and its architecture and history were the basis for its designation as a National Historic Landmark.

Crossing Main Street to Harding's Landing you will find the **State Dock** offering free public docking as well as a picturesque view of the town shoreline. A few early twentieth century commercial structures remain on Main Street but there is no longer a business district. One of the largest buildings is **Swindell's Store**, built in 1905, which closed forever at the end of a business day in 1982, leaving merchandise on the shelves. Heading south on Main Street will take you by private homes, many of which date to the late nineteenth and early twentieth centuries. You may also notice ballast stone used for walls and building foundations of many of the town's structures — reminders of Bath's rich maritime heritage.

On the corner of Main and Craven Streets is the **Williams House**, often referred to as the Glebe House. Now owned by the Episcopal Diocese of East Carolina, this restored home is a private residence and not open to the public. Built around 1830, it has been the residence of several notable nineteenth-century Bath citizens. Behind the Williams House on Craven Street is probably the town's greatest landmark, the **St. Thomas Church**. The oldest church in North Carolina, the church was built in 1734 but not fully completed until 1762. The church still operates on a daily basis and is always open to the public for a self-guided tour. At the end of Main Street is the **Bonner House** (c. 1830). Built by Joseph Bonner, it was the home of the Bonner family, one of the distinguished families in Beaufort County history, for more than 100 years. It is an excellent example of North Carolina coastal architecture, characterized by large porches at the front and rear.

Belhaven

If you've ventured as far as Bath, you'll be doing yourself a great disservice if you don't drive the few extra miles to scenic Belhaven. The quaint village is located on the waterfront of Pantego Creek and has a population of about 2,246. Local waterways provide a variety of outdoor activities, such as swimming, sailing and water-skiing. Fishing for crab and a wide variety of fish is an important sport, as well as hunting of white-tailed deer, geese and ducks.

Located on the Intracoastal Waterway, the town is accessible by boat or car. From the Crystal Coast, you can get to Belhaven on four wheels by taking the Cherry Branch-Minnesott Beach Ferry and the Aurora-Bayview Ferry. By boat, simply follow the Intracoastal Waterway north.

The main industries in Belhaven are fishing, boat works, farming, phosphates and forestry. The county is the state's largest soybean and pulpwood producer and is one of the largest crab meat processing areas in the state. The Town of Belhaven offers shopping and services with small-town Southern flair. There are three beautiful bed and breakfast inns within walking distance of local shops. There are a variety of restaurants serving anything from cheeseburgers to seafood. Shopping opportunities include bookstores, jewelry shops, clothing, hardware, drug stores and car sales. Belhaven is fortunate to have excellent healthcare with the Pungo District Hospital located near the waterfront with a heli-pad and water access. Several local physicians provide primary care.

Pungo Wellness & Fitness Center is open seven days a week, located in one end of the John A. Wilkinson Center. The **John A. Wilkinson Center**, (252) 944-4JAW, serves the area by hosting community

concerts sponsored by the Beaufort County Arts Council and continuing education and G.E.D. classes sponsored by Beaufort County Community College. An art and music room is available to local artists who wish to hold workshops or classes, and the auditorium and other rooms are also available for rental to the public, businesses and local non-profits to hold events such as weddings, receptions, dinner/dances, meetings, company parties, holiday events and other gatherings.

Every year Belhaven hosts its **Independence Day Celebration** with craft and food vendors, a parade, military demonstrations, a fish fry, water-ski shows, art exhibitions, dances, pageants and concerts. The day of excitement ends with a fireworks display over Pantego Creek. This celebration has been occurring since the 1950s and attracts more than 20,000 people every year.

Belhaven's **Memorial Museum** is one of the 14 sites on the Historic Albemarle Tour. The City Hall, which houses the museum, is included in the National Register of Historic Places. The museum, open from 1 to 5 PM every day of the week except

An egret waits for an easy meal.

photo: Peter Doran

Wednesday, has a unique collection of items depicting the area's cultural and natural history. There is no charge for admission, but donations are welcome. Call (252) 943-3055 for information.

While the museum is open year-round, many visitors also enjoy Belhaven in mid-April when the **Dutch Festival** in nearby Terra Ceia celebrates the riot of color provided by fields of tulips and gladiolas grown there.

The **A-Bell Gallery** features the works of Ann Bell, folk artist, author and writer of her own line of limited-edition prints, note cards and books. A sharecropper's daughter, Ann uses her artistic talent to preserve the history of eastern North Carolina during the Great Depression. While the gallery is open free to the public, it is generally open by chance or by appointment only. For information, call (252) 943-2059.

For more information about Belhaven, contact the **Belhaven Community Chamber of Commerce**, P.O. Box 147, Belhaven, NC 27810, (252) 943-3770, or stop by the chamber office in the renovated railroad depot at 125 W. Main Street during its new office hours of Monday through Friday from 9 AM to 1 PM.

Lake Mattamuskeet National Wildlife Refuge

OK, so a trip to Lake Mattamuskeet might require a bit more than a day. We have included it in the Daytrips chapter because it seems like an appropriate side journey if you make the jaunt to Oriental, Bath or Belhaven. The expansive wildlife refuge is on U.S. Highway 264, and well-placed road signs make it easy to find.

Lake Mattamuskeet National Wildlife Refuge stretches from Englehard on the east to Swan Quarter on the west. The refuge's 50,180 acres of water, marsh, timber and croplands are managed by the U.S. Fish and Wildlife Service. This beautiful area lies in the middle of the Atlantic Flyway. From October to March, the shallow 40,000-acre lake, which is said to be no deeper than a swan's neck, is a winter refuge for many migrating birds.

Waterfowl populations are at their peak from December through February, and so are bird-watchers. According to refuge information, 35,000 tundra swans winter at Mattamuskeet, and more than 150,000 birds gather at the lake between October and March. Thousands of snow and Canada geese and 22 species of ducks are seasonal inhabitants. The refuge provides habitat for osprey, red-tailed hawks, coots, blue herons, green-winged teals, black and ruddy ducks, cormorants, widgeons, mergansers, loons and many other birds. The refuge is also home to otters, bobcats, deer and black bears. Several endangered bird species, such as the peregrine falcon and the bald eagle, seek refuge around the lake. The refuge provides public hunting of swans, ducks and coots in season. For information on hunting, contact the refuge manager at (252) 926-4021.

The 18-mile-long and 5- to 6-mile-wide lake is the state's largest natural lake, making it and its adjacent canals a popular spot for boating and sport fishing. Largemouth bass, striped bass, catfish, bream and other species can be taken from March 1 to November 1. Fishing is excellent in the canals and along the lake shore in spring and fall.

Catching blue crabs is a very popular sport enjoyed by all ages and is permitted year round from the water control structures. All fishing activities must be conducted in accordance with state regulations. Bow-fishing for carp and other rough fish is permitted during the fishing season.

Prohibited activities in the refuge include herring dipping, camping, littering, swimming, molesting wildlife and collecting plants, flowers, nuts or berries. Fires and firearms are also prohibited without special authorization. The speed limit on

An estimated 35,000 tundra swans winter at Lake Mattamuskeet National Wildlife Refuge. Their arrival is celebrated with Swan Days, an annual December weekend festival.

refuge roads is 25 miles per hour, and no vehicles, such as overland vehicles or trail bikes, are allowed outside regularly used roads and trails. Boats may not be left on the refuge overnight without a special-use permit.

The **Lake Mattamuskeet Lodge** is the former pumping plant constructed in the early 1900s in an investment effort to convert the lake bottom to agricultural land and model community patterned after similar projects in Holland. The bankruptcy of one company after another in this effort led to its eventual abandonment, and the land was acquired by the U.S. Government in 1934 for the establishment of a waterfowl sanctuary. The pumping station was converted to a lodge for visitors and hunters and operated until 1974. It is now a National Historic Site of architectural and historic interest.

Plans to renovate the lodge as an environmental education center are in motion as a coordinated effort of several nonprofit organizations. The building is currently closed due to structural problems from extensive corrosion. Funding has been appropriated by Congress to correct these problems, and the U.S. Fish and Wildlife Service is currently stabilizing the building.

During the fall migration, a couple of weekend events make Lake Mattamuskeet an exciting destination. In early November, an annual **Mattamuskeet Fun Ride** is organized by the Hyde County Chamber of Commerce. Bicyclists may choose to take a 35-, 45- or 70-mile course around and across the lake. The courses begin and end at the lodge and offer lots of waterfowl viewing opportunities. The first weekend of December, **Swan Days** celebrate the annual return of tundra swan and other waterfowl for the winter. At the refuge, visitors may enjoy the exhibition and sale of native crafts, decoys and local food, and participate in educational programs and tours of the refuge.

For information about **Mattamuskeet National Wildlife Refuge**, contact the refuge headquarters, 38 Mattamuskeet Road, Swan Quarter, NC 27885, (252) 926-4021. Nearby accommodations can be found in Engelhard, Fairfield, Swan Quarter and Belhaven. For additional information about area accommodations, restaurants and events, write or call **Greater Hyde County Chamber of Commerce**, P.O. Box 178, Swan Quarter, NC 27885, (252) 926-9171, (888) 493-3826.

Kinston

Although not normally considered a tourism destination, Kinston has a number of features that make a daytrip there a pleasant outing. Located on U.S. Highway 70 about two hours east of the Crystal Coast, Kinston has a year-round population of around 25,227.

Incorporated in 1826, Kinston is home to the **CSS Neuse State Historic Site and Gov. Richard Caswell Memorial**, located at 2612 W. Vernon Avenue (U.S. 70 Business). This historic site is designated as an official project of Save America's Treasures. The CSS Neuse is only one of three Civil War ironclad gunboats that have been recovered and the only commissioned Confederate ironclad on display in the world. In addition, the site celebrates the life of Gov. Richard Caswell, the first governor of the independent state of North Carolina. The site is open year-round, Tuesday through Saturday. For hours and more information, call (252) 522-2091.

Built in 1772, **Harmony Hall**, located at 109 E. King Street, was the home of Richard Caswell, North Carolina's first constitutional governor. Open for tours, it has been tastefully restored with eighteenth-century furnishings. For hours and tour information, call (252) 522-0421.

The **Community Council for the Arts**, 400 N. Queen Street, is housed in a three-story, 30,000-square-foot historical building that features six galleries with changing exhibits. There are five galleries in the basement that are rented out. The center is also home to a large permanent model train exhibit. Numerous classes and workshops are available for adults and children at a nominal charge. The gift shop offers many unique handcrafted items for sale. Admission is free; for more information call (252) 527-2517.

The **Caswell No. 1 Fire Station Museum**, 118 S. Queen Street, showcases the world of the late 1800s firefighter. This station was built in 1895 after a disastrous fire destroyed much of downtown Kinston. A 1922 American LaFrance Pumper is the focus of the museum, along with a collection of helmets, nozzles, ladders, fire extinguishers and other memorabilia that span a 100-year period. Admission is free; call (252) 522-4676 for seasonal hours.

And, of course, what summertime trip to Kinston would be complete without seeing a **Kinston Indians** baseball game? A North Carolina minor league baseball team affiliated with the Cleveland Indians, the K-tribe plays at historic Grainger Stadium from April through September. Reserved seats cost $6 while general admission is $5 for adults, $4 for senior citizens, military and students, and free for children age five and younger. Concessions and souvenirs are available. Discounted rates apply for groups of 15 or more. For more information call (252) 527-9111 or (800) 334-5467, write P.O. Box 3542, Kinston, N.C. 28502, or stop by 400 E. Grainger Avenue in Kinston.

Race fans will enjoy watching IHRA–sanctioned racing at its finest every weekend at the **Kinston Drag Strip**, N.C. Highway 11 South. Call (252) 527-4337 or (252) 522-5403 for a schedule and admission fees.

For information about attractions, accommodations, restaurants and more, contact the **Kinston Convention & Visitors Bureau** at (252) 523-2500 or (800) 869-0032, or stop by the Visitors Bureau offices at 301 N. Queen Street.

Washington

Washington, called the Heart of the Inner Banks, has forever been known as "Little Washington." The town was named for the nation's first president in 1776. Washington remains an area of natural beauty up the Pamlico River from the Intracoastal Waterway, an area with recreational, cultural and educational activities that will make a trip well worth your time.

Visit the **North Carolina Estuarium**, (252) 948-0000, with its more than 200 exhibits, interactive presentations and guided river tours. Kayak, hike, become a birder and explore **Goose Creek State Park**,

(252) 923-2191. Learn about the geological history of the area at the **Aurora Fossil Museum**, (252) 322-4238.

Washington is known for its historic waterfront district where you can enjoy fine dining or take a historic walking tour; call (800) 546-0162 for tours. There are 30 one-of-a-kind structures dating from 1780; the entire waterfront district is listed on the National Register of Historic Places. If art is your thing, check out some of the galleries in the waterfront district. You can sip native wines at the **Bennett Vineyards** or buy a bottle and go sailing. There are chartered sailing vessels available for a weekend on the water. There is something for everyone in Washington.

Washington is proud of its seasonal events — in February, the East Carolina Wildlife Arts Festival; in May, the Aurora Fossil Festival; in June, the Washington Summer Festival, and in October, Smoke on the Water and the Fine Arts Show. You can go online at www.visitwashingtonnc. com to see a listing of events.

Wilmington

A visit to Wilmington will probably require more than a day if you want to do more than drive into town, walk the waterfront and return to the Crystal Coast. This upscale but laid-back river city is about 45 miles south of Jacksonville on U.S. Highway 17, about a two-hour drive from the Crystal Coast area. It's a good jumping-off point to explore several nearby beaches and attractions.

There is much to discover about this delightful city and its nearby attractions. For a complete guide to accommodations, restaurants, shopping, sightseeing and beaches, pick up a copy of the Insiders' Guide® to North Carolina's Southern Coast and Wilmington, or call (800) 955-1860 to order a copy.

There are two plantations that make interesting side trips while in the Wilmington area. Former peanut plantation, **Poplar Grove Historic Plantation**, (910) 686-9518, is an estate at Scotts Hill, 9 miles north of Wilmington at the Pender County line on U.S. 17. The 16-acre plantation is open to the public until mid-December and opens again in February, but call ahead for seasonal hours. Admission to the grounds and outbuildings is $7; tickets for the guided house tours are $10 for adults, $9 for seniors and military, $5 for students age 6 to 15, and free for children age 5 and younger. Poplar Grove also hosts special programs and events throughout the year, such as the Classy Chasis Car Show and Country Flea Market in July, Herb and Garden Fair, the Christmas Open House and the most popular — the Halloween Festival the last two weekends in October. Poplar Grove also hosts a farmer's market Wednesday mornings 8 AM-1 PM from April 8-December 16. Poplar Grove Plantation is listed on the National Register of Historic Places.

Orton Plantation Gardens, just south of the city and a few miles off U.S. 17, is halfway between Wilmington and Southport on NC Hwy. 33. The gardens feature brilliant azaleas, Luola's Chapel (built in 1915) and an exterior view of Orton House, built in 1725. The house is one of the region's oldest historically significant residences in continuous use. The plantation gardens are open March through November. Admission is $9 adults, $8 for ages 60 and older, $3 ages 6 to 16, and free for children younger than 6. For information, call (910) 371-6851.

Several beaches and attractions are a few minutes drive from downtown Wilm-ington. Fifteen minutes from the town hub lies **Wrightsville Beach**, which is primarily a family beach and small island community that features a number of quality hotels, motels, apartments, cottages, condominium developments and many marvelous seafood restaurants.

Down U.S. Highway 421 is **Carolina Beach**, best known for its wide, uncrowded shore, swimming, surfing, pier fishing and deep-water charter-boat fishing. Its shops, water slides and boardwalk offer something for everyone. **Carolina Beach State Park**, on the Intracoastal Waterway at Carolina Beach, is known for its collection of diverse plants, including the endangered Venus flytrap. The state park has 761 acres with picnicking spots, hiking trails and a camping area. Call (910) 458-8206 for general information.

Continuing down U.S. 421 is **Kure Beach**, a site convenient to several attractions. It is adjacent to **Historic Fort Fisher** and is less than 2 miles from the **N.C. Aquarium at Fort Fisher**. The **Fort Fisher State Historic Site** on U.S. 421, (910) 458-5538, is near the mouth of the Cape Fear River and includes the remains of the old fort, a visitors center and gift shop, a museum with items salvaged from blockade runners and a reconstructed gun battery. It's a must-see for the Civil War and history buffs of the family. Nearby, N.C. Aquarium at Fort Fisher highlights

Downtown Wilmington has a lovely and lively waterfront area.

photo: Peter Doran

the theme "Waters of the Cape Fear." Features include a half-acre conservatory, the Coquina Outcrop touch pool and a 250,000-gallon ocean aquarium, with two-story, multi-level views of sharks, stingrays, eels and more. The aquarium offers a complete schedule of educational programs, including two daily dive presentations. Call (910) 458-8257 for more information about topics and schedules.

Back to the river city of Wilmington. This historic town is home to one of North Carolina's two deep-water ports. During the Revolutionary War, Wilmington gained importance as a point of entry, and its port was the last one on the Atlantic coast open to blockade runners during the Civil War. Continuous restoration and preservation make the town a history-buff's delight. Its fast-growing population includes many students who attend the state university, UNC-Wilmington.

Serving southeastern North Carolina since 1962, the **Cameron Art Museum** has assembled an important collection of North Carolina art and become a showcase for national and international exhibits. This 42,000-square-foot facility is located at the intersection of Independence Boulevard and 17th Street Extension, (910) 395-5999. Designed by architect Charles Gwathmey, the museum offers galleries complete with paintings, ceramics and sculptures ranging from the eighteenth century to the present. Cameron Art Museum also offers a number of cultural programs and has become a center of learning for both adults and children in the area. After touring the expansive permanent collections and intriguing featured exhibitions, stop by the Museum Shop for a keepsake and then have lunch at The Forks restaurant. Museum admission is $8 for adults, $5 for students with a valid ID, $3 for ages 2 to 12, and free for children younger than 2. Museum members get in for free. The museum is open Tuesday through Sunday; call for hours.

The **Bellamy Mansion Museum of History & Design Arts**, 503 Market Street, (910) 251-3700, is a classic Victorian example of Greek Revival and Italianate architecture. The mansion, a stewardship property of Preservation North Carolina, currently houses a museum of the design arts, embracing regional architecture, landscape architecture, preservation and decorative arts. It is open Tuesday through Saturday from 10 AM to 5 PM and Sunday from 1 to 5 PM. Admission is $10 for adults and $4 for children ages 5 to 12. The last tour of the day starts at 4 PM.

Cape Fear Museum of History and Science, 814 Market Street, (910) 798-4350, is a must for history buffs. The long-term exhibition "Waves and Currents: The Lower Cape Fear Story" follows the progress of the Lower Cape Fear from settlement to the twentieth century and presents an expansive picture of southeastern North Carolina's heritage. Scenes come alive with life-size figures and miniature re-creations of Wilmington's waterfront c. 1863, and the Fort Fisher Battle paints a picture of antebellum and Civil War times. Interactive children's activities, videos, changing exhibitions and special events add vitality to this learning experience. Personal items belonging to retired basketball great Michael Jordan are on display in the Michael Jordan Discovery Gallery, which also features an interactive natural history exhibit for the entire family. Special science programs for the entire family also are scheduled throughout the year. Admission is $6 for adults, $5 for seniors, students and military with ID and $3 for children ages 3 to 17.

Built in 1855-1858, the **Thalian Hall Center for the Performing Arts**, (910) 343-3660 or (800) 523-2820, is the only surviving theater designed by John Montague Trimble, one of America's foremost nineteenth-century theatre architects. Located at 310 Chestnut Street, the City Hall/ Thalian Hall building has had the unusual distinction of serving as both the area's political and cultural center. Listed with the National Register for Historic Places and with the North Carolina Division of Archives and History, historic Thalian Hall has, since its 1990 renovation, become the centerpiece of the city's thriving civic and arts community. The renovated and expanded complex, housing both the restored opera house theater and City Hall, provides three excellent performance spaces: the Main Stage Theatre, with reserved seating for

575 and additional gallery seating for 100; the 225-seat Council Chambers Ballroom and the versatile 100-seat Studio Theatre. The lobby and technical support areas combine state-of-the-art technical facilities within the beauty and grandeur of an exceptional historic theater. Each year, Thalian Hall hosts over 475 performances and events, with more than one of the three facilities frequently in use simultaneously.

For shopping, Wilmington's downtown streets are lined with unique stores and restaurants. Be sure to check out **The Cotton Exchange**, 321 N. Front Street, (910) 343-9896. Housed in eight restored nineteenth-century buildings on the waterfront, it features distinctive shops and several good restaurants. Also worth noting are the **Chandler's Wharf Shops** at 2 Ann Street and 225 S. Water Street, which feature garden ornaments, jewelry, candles, gifts and more. **Independence Mall** at Oleander Drive and Independence Boulevard, (910) 392-1776, is home to more than 150 stores and boasts a 400-seat food court.

For an overnight stay, Wilmington has a number of fine chain hotels, and delightful bed and breakfasts are bountiful in the downtown historic district. A few noteworthy examples are the **Graystone Inn**, www.graystoneinn.com, 100 S. Third Street, (910) 763-2000, (888) 763-4773; **C. W. Worth House**, www.worthhouse.com, 412 S. Third Street, (910) 762-8562, (800) 340-8559; **Rosehill Inn Bed and Breakfast**, 114 S. Third Street, (910) 815-0250, (800) 815-0250; and **Hoge-Wood House Bed and Breakfast**, 407 S. Third Street, (910) 762-5299.

The river city abounds with fine restaurants offering delectable food. Some that come highly recommended are **Elijah's**, www.elijahs.com, in Chandler's Wharf, (910) 343-1448 and **The Pilot House**, overlooking the river at Chandler's Wharf, (910) 343-0200. But these are only two of the many wonderful eateries available.

In early April, Wilmington's annual **Azalea Festival** draws visitors from miles around. Hundreds of lovely, old Southern homes are surrounded by blooming azaleas and huge trees draped with Spanish moss. The entire community gets in on the act, with home tours, parades, contests and citywide celebrations.

When you're downtown, stop at the **Cape Fear Coast Convention & Visitors Bureau**, 24 N. Third Street, (910) 341-4030 or (800) 222-4757, for answers to specific questions while you're in the Cape Fear area. Complete area information is available at www.insiders.com/wilmington.

Battleship NORTH CAROLINA
1 Battleship Rd., Wilmington
(910) 251-5797
www.battleshipnc.com

Almost everyone who visits Wilmington includes a tour of the Battleship *North Carolina*, located on the Cape Fear waterfront across from historic downtown Wilmington. Commissioned in 1941, the 44,800-ton, 728-foot warship wielded nine 16-inch turreted guns among its arsenal and carries nickel steel hull armor 16 to 18 inches thick. It was this platform that helped her survive at least one direct torpedo hit in 1942. The battleship, which came to its present home across the river from the downtown area in 1961, stands as a reminder of history and of the more than 10,000 North Carolinians who lost their lives in World War II. The battleship is open for tours 365 days a year. From Memorial Day weekend through Labor Day, it's open from 8 AM to 8 PM; from Labor Day through Memorial Day it's open 8 AM to 5 PM. The self-guided tour begins with a 10-minute orientation film. The entire experience will give you a true feel for what life was like aboard this vessel. You can visit the bridge, the Admiral's cabin, the crew's quarters, the galley and sick bay, the engine room and the radio central area. Tours cost $12 for adults and children age 12 and older, $10 for seniors and active and retired military, and $6 for children ages 6 to 11. Children 5 and younger get in free. Ticket sales end one hour prior to closing. Keep a lookout for old Charlie, the alligator who makes his home beside the ship in the marsh. The Visitors Center has exhibits of the crew's recollections and WWII artifacts as well as a great gift shop.

INDEX

I

J

K

L

O